238 – 281

MARVIN LASER, Ph.D. Northwestern University, is Professor of English and Chairman of the Division of Language Arts at Los Angeles State College. He taught previously at the Wilson Branch of the Chicago City Junior College and at Chicago Teachers College. He is a member of the Board of Directors of the College English Association.

ROBERT S. CATHCART, Ph.D. Northwestern University, is Professor of Speech at Los Angeles State College. He formerly taught at the University of Maryland, the United States Naval Instructor Training School, and Purdue University.

FRED H. MARCUS, Ph.D. New York University, is Professor of English at Los Angeles State College, Vice-President of the California Association of Teachers of English, and a member of the Board of Reviewers for the "Professional Publications" section of *The English Journal*. He taught previously at the State University of New York College at Oneonta and New York University.

Ideas and Issues

READINGS FOR
ANALYSIS AND EVALUATION

Edited by

MARVIN LASER

ROBERT S. CATHCART

FRED H. MARCUS

Los Angeles State College

THE RONALD PRESS COMPANY • NEW YORK

Library of Congress Catalog Card Number: 63–9255
PRINTED IN THE UNITED STATES OF AMERICA

PREFACE

This book has grown out of both our convictions and our practices in the teaching of college courses in composition, speech, and communication skills. We are convinced that effective communication develops from an inductive approach rather than a theoretical one. In our own classes we have learned that a student most readily develops ability in reading, writing, speaking, and thinking by starting with close analysis and evaluation of the actual practices that human beings engage in as they go about their tasks of informing, explaining, advocating, and debating the substance of issues which concern them deeply. A problem-solving approach, we have found, becomes most provocative of meaningful writing and speaking when the problems themselves are meaningful and relevant to the real world in which we all have our existence—a world not confined to the boundaries of the campus nor the limits of our times—and when the students themselves become involved emotionally and intellectually.

In Part I of this book we present a collection of eleven topics, each one a problem which is both contemporary in immediate interest and perennial in terms of its underlying implications. The problems themselves are samplings from many different areas of human knowledge. What is more, each topic involves a genuine controversy which in the presentation here has not been simplified, tidied up, or sanitized out of an undue regard for conventional notions about students' minds.

In each of the sections we have also confronted the student with a diversity of viewpoints from a multiplicity of sources. The viewpoints do not fall simply and neatly into categories of pro and con but, as in life itself, open up many alternative, conflicting choices reflecting the complexities inherent in problems that superficially may look easy. Our focus rejects the oversimplified, blandly devised formulas of "looking at both sides of the question," of reducing every problem to the level of "true or false" solutions. If life is not the big, buzzing confusion which William James described, neither is it the homogenized decoction so often served up in the pages of some of the popular journals. The student may even discover that some of the problems admit of no final resolution. As for the sources we have drawn from, there are represented here pamphlets, chapters from popular and technical books, articles from general magazines and from scholarly journals, advertisements, newspaper columns, a television script, an excerpt from the *Congressional Record*, selections from the catalog of an art exhibition, and pieces from many other kinds of communications media, both mass and specialized.

In our introductory essays, exercises, and assignments we have attempted to guide the student toward a heightened understanding not only of what is explicitly said in each selection but of basic attitudes, purposes, value systems, assumptions, inferences, and strategies of exposition and argument.

In Part II we bring together sixteen essays which deal with observation, language, thought, and the processes of human communication. This section provides the student with a set of basic concepts and techniques which he will find helpful at appropriate times in analyzing and evaluating the selections in Part I. Some teachers may elect to begin the course with the materials of Part II, but most, we believe, will prefer an inductive approach, working with the "ideas in conflict" themselves and using the essays of Part II as supplemental. For while it is possible to learn about principles and methods of communication in the abstract, we reiterate our conviction—borne out by our own experiences in using the materials in this book in our classes—that most students best learn the skills of critical thinking, reading, writing, and speaking by working with these processes as they actually function in specific problems.

M. L.
R. S. C.
F. H. M.

Los Angeles, California
January, 1963

CONTENTS

v

Part II
READINGS IN LANGUAGE, THOUGHT,
AND COMMUNICATION

PART I

SOURCE MATERIALS FOR CRITICAL THINKING AND COMMUNICATION

1. LITERARY HISTORY
The Authorship of Shakespeare's Plays

No one has been able to account for the unflagging interest that is still displayed by large numbers of people in the dispute about who wrote Shakespeare's plays. As a by-product of your assignments in this project, you may wish to consider possible explanations for the long life of this controversy. Is it the amateur's delight in hoping to prove the "experts" wrong? Is it a wish for a demonstration of the triumph of common sense over the dreary accumulation of scholarly "facts"? Is it a healthy manifestation of the rejection of rigid orthodoxies? Is it a sublimated desire to challenge the overassertiveness of generations of English teachers? Whatever the explanations may be, it is curious that almost no other topic in literary history has exerted such fascination for so many people and for so long a time.

The sheer mass of publications bearing on the controversy makes any brief selection quite obviously an arbitrary one. In the selections that follow it has not been possible to represent all the candidates named at various times as the author of Shakespeare's plays, nor to provide illustrations of all the many kinds of evidence used to support arguments. Nevertheless, the six pieces we have chosen will at least introduce you to a number of the problems involved.

The essay by Mark Twain totally rejects the orthodox view of Shakespeare of Stratford as author of the plays; but you will want to analyze Mark Twain's skepticism carefully, rather than letting yourself get carried away with his exuberant humor. The case for the Earl of Oxford as author of the plays is represented here through an essay by William McFee; however, you will note that McFee's essay is an introduction to a book and not a summary of the arguments advanced in the book.

Bergen Evans's article is a non-technical discussion by a college professor who does not present himself as a Shakespeare expert. Evans is also the author of the amusingly skeptical books *The Natural History of Nonsense* and *The Spoor of Spooks*, both of which you may someday want to dip into. In the essay given here, however, Evans's skepticism is directed not against the traditional view but against those who have challenged it.

Calvin Hoffman's essay advances the case for Christopher Marlowe as the man who wrote the plays of Shakespeare. If you go on to read Mr. Hoffman's book, *The Murder of the Man Who Was 'Shakespeare'* (to which his essay is prefatory), you will discover that he shirks none of the problems raised by advancing Marlowe as his candidate—including the crucial one that Marlowe is thought by most scholars to have died in 1593, *before* the publication of the bulk of Shakespeare's plays. Finally, Hallett Smith's article places the controversy about authorship in the larger context of twentieth-century Shakespeare studies.

You may conclude this project with your present convictions either strengthened or weakened. But in the process of making a critical analysis of the pieces that follow you will certainly discover what complexities are involved in making judgments.

From IS SHAKESPEARE DEAD?*

Mark Twain

[1] Am I trying to convince anybody that Shakespeare did not write Shakespeare's Works? Ah, now, what do you take me for? Would I be so soft as that, after having known the human race familiarly for nearly seventy-four years? It would grieve me to know that any one could think so injuriously of me, so uncomplimentarily, so unadmiringly of me. No-no, I am aware that when even the brightest mind in our world has been trained up from childhood in a superstition of any kind, it will never be possible for that mind, in its maturity, to examine sincerely, dispassionately, and conscientiously any evidence or any circumstance which shall seem to cast a doubt upon the validity of that superstition. I doubt if I could do it myself. We always get at second hand our notions about systems of government; and high-tariff and low-tariff; and prohibition and anti-prohibition; and the holiness of peace and the glories of war; and codes of honor and codes of morals; and approval of the duel and disapproval of it; and our beliefs concerning the nature of cats; and our ideas as to whether the murder of helpless wild animals is base or is heroic; and our preferences in the matter of religious and political parties; and our acceptance or rejection of the Shakespeares and the Arthur Ortons and the Mrs. Eddys. We get them all at second-

hand, we reason none of them out for ourselves. It is the way we are made. It is the way we are all made, and we can't help it, we can't change it. And whenever we have been furnished a fetish, and have been taught to believe in it, and love it and worship it, and refrain from examining it, there is no evidence, howsoever clear and strong, that can persuade us to withdraw from it our loyalty and our devotion. In morals, conduct, and beliefs we take the color of our environment and associations, and it is a color that can safely be warranted to wash. Whenever we have been furnished with a tar baby ostensibly stuffed with jewels, and warned that it will be dishonorable and irreverent to disembowel it and test the jewels, we keep our sacrilegious hands off it. We submit, not reluctantly, but rather gladly, for we are privately afraid we should find, upon examination, that the jewels are of the sort that are manufactured at North Adams, Mass.

[2] I haven't any idea that Shakespeare will have to vacate his pedestal this side of the year 2209. Disbelief in him cannot come swiftly, disbelief in a healthy and deeply-loved tar baby has never been known to disintegrate swiftly, it is a very slow process. It took several thousand years to convince our fine race—including every splendid intellect in it —that there is no such thing as a witch; it has taken several thousand years to convince that same fine race—including every splendid intellect in it—that there is no such person as Satan; it has taken several centuries to remove perdition from the Protestant Church's program of postmortem entertainments; it has taken a weary long time to persuade American Presbyterians to give up infant damnation and try to bear it the best they can; and it looks as if their Scotch brethren will still be burning babies in the everlasting fires when Shakespeare comes down from his perch.

[3] We are The Reasoning Race. We can't prove it by the above examples, and we can't prove it by the miraculous "histories" built by those Stratfordolaters out of a hatful of rags and a barrel of sawdust, but there is a plenty of other things we can prove it by, if I could think of them. We are The Reasoning Race, and when we find a vague file of chipmunk-tracks stringing through the dust of Stratford village, we know by our reasoning powers that Hercules has been along there. I feel that our fetish is safe for three centuries yet. The bust, too—there in the Stratford Church. The precious bust, the priceless bust, the calm bust, the serene bust, the emotionless bust, with the dandy moustache, and the putty face, unseamed of care—that face which has looked passionlessly down upon the awed pilgrim for a hundred and fifty years and will still look down upon the awed pilgrim three hundred more, with the deep, deep, deep, subtle, subtle, subtle, expression of a bladder.

Questions

1. What is the tone of Mark Twain's opening sentences? Would you describe it as serious, frivolous, sarcastic, playful—or what? How does this tone relate to his apparent strategy?
2. Mark Twain says, "We get them [notions, codes, beliefs, preferences] all at second-hand, we reason none of them out for ourselves." Do you accept this assertion? Why or why not? What does the statement have to do with the question of who wrote Shakespeare's works?
3. What is Twain's purpose in introducing the tar baby (end of paragraph 1)?
4. What does Twain mean by the phrase "every splendid intellect" (paragraph 2) and how does he use it? What does he mean by "The Reasoning Race" (paragraph 3) and how does he use this phrase?
5. Examine paragraph 3. Account for such phrases as "a hatful of rags and a barrel of sawdust," "chipmunk-tracks," and "expression of a bladder."
6. Twain relies on the method of argument by analogy. Do you see any weaknesses in his use of this method?

THE MASTER MYSTERY*

William McFee

[1] Some ten years ago two London journalists published a lively book, "This Shakespeare Industry," which revealed to an astonished public the extent to which Stratford-on-Avon had become big business, drawing many thousands of tourists annually from all over the world. There was "The Birthplace." Awed Americans could gaze upon the very spot where the creator of Hamlet came into the world. There was the church where he was buried, adorned with the famous monument. There was the weird doggerel which he was supposed to have written, or dictated, warning the profane, under penalty of his curse, from disturbing his bones. There was Anne Hathaway's cottage, another shrine, and Mary Arden's lovely home at Wilmcote, very carefully and lovingly restored. There was, in short, something for the tourist on every hand. . . .

[2] "Shakespeare" . . . has long since ceased to be a "writer" in the ordinary sense for the British. It would not be an exaggeration to say that at present he occupies, in the conventional Englishman's mind, a position midway between a tutelary deity and a solar myth. To question the Bard's work, or to cast doubt on his credentials is bad form, akin to

* From J. Thomas Looney, "Shakespeare" Identified in Edward de Vere, the Seventeenth Earl of Oxford. Copyright 1949 by Elizabeth Looney. Reprinted by permission of Duell, Sloan & Pearce, Inc., an affiliate of Meredith Press.

eating peas with a knife or wearing brown shoes with a morning coat. It isn't done. It is not necessary to read "Shakespeare." It is obligatory to revere him. And Stratford-on-Avon has the same sanctity for the English as Lourdes for the faithful. It is a national shrine. The correct attitude toward a shrine is not criticism but faith.

[3] All heavy industries, however, suffer from competition. The conventional legend of the poor Stratford boy, faring up to London, like Dick Whittington, to make his fortune, starting at the bottom and working up in the theatrical business until he had written the greatest dramas of all time, and then retiring modestly to his native town, where he bought the largest house, dying, as the Thane of Cawdor lived, a prosperous gentleman—this pretty story did not appeal to certain skeptical minds. There was too little known about the Stratford lad. There were too many holes in the narrative, holes which had to be filled with "doubtless," "perhaps," "probably," "it is assumed that . . ." and such unsatisfying subjunctive phrases. Why was this? Why had the world's greatest dramatist left no records at all? Why had he apparently been unable to write a letter, or even to sign a paper without appearing to be utterly unused to holding a pen?

[4] Unfortunately what should have been a scientific inquiry fell into the hands of undisciplined and emotional lunatics. They were known generically as Baconians. Numerous sects burgeoned in the new group of nonconformists, but they all subscribed to the extraordinary notion that the plays were written in code by Lord Bacon. Sometimes the revelation took the form of religious ecstasy. Delia Bacon, an American girl of good family but no relation to the author of "Novum Organon," obtained permission from the vicar of Stratford to spend the night in the sacred edifice where the playwright's bones were buried. The result of her hallucinations was the notion that the plays were written by Lord Bacon and several other Elizabethans. The curious will find a fascinating picture of this excellent but unbalanced lady in Nathaniel Hawthorne's essay in "Our Old Home," which he calls "Recollections of a Gifted Woman." The author of "The Scarlet Letter" and the campaign biography of Franklin Pierce even wrote an introduction to Miss Bacon's book, although he evidently did not accept her theory. It did not occur to him that if he did not believe in her theory he should have had nothing to do with her book.

[5] Ignatius Donnelly, Orville Owen, and Mrs. Elizabeth Gallup, Americans all, offered their "Cryptogram Theory." Mr. Donnelly, finding, for example, that the word "bay" occurred in one line of a poem and the word "can" in the next line, instantly divined that the author's name was Bay-can or Bacon. Donnelly's "Biliteral Cypher" was even

more confounding to anyone who by profession was a writer of books.

[6] There is no doubt that the antics of the Baconians caused the general public to shy away violently from any infidelity to the Stratford tradition. If *that* were what happened when you doubted the truth of the legend, then they would grapple that legend to their bosoms with hoops of steel. Stratford-on-Avon became bigger and better. Anyone who expressed skepticism of its pretensions was classed with flat-earth fanatics and the Germans who called the Bard "Unser Shakespeare," claiming him as German property by right of appreciation.

[7] In 1920, however, there was published in London, very quietly, a book which attacked the problem of the authorship of the plays from a new angle. Instead of spending nights in the church where the Stratford man was buried, J. Thomas Looney, a north-country schoolmaster, spent days, weeks, and months in libraries where he thought the "Shakespeare" secret was buried. He had been working on the mystery for a long time when the First World War intervened. As a schoolmaster he had been familiar with the plays in general and with "The Merchant of Venice" in particular. He had been unable to satisfy himself that the illiterate, untraveled countryman, as "Will Shaksper, Gent." undoubtedly was, could have written that play. Doubts arose in the schoolmaster's mind. He set out on a quest. "Here, then," he says in his own introduction to this book " 'Shakespeare' Identified," "were the greatest literary treasures of England, ranked by universal consent the highest literary achievements of mankind, to all intents and purposes of unknown origin."

[8] It was not a problem, he felt, for a literary critic, which he did not pretend to be, but for a detective; in Dr. Gilbert Slater's pungent phrase, "for the man from Scotland Yard." " 'Shakespeare' Identified" is the sober, careful, conservative record of what he found. On the surface it is as deceptively undramatic as the evidence of a policeman in court who is reporting that he has found the murderer. . . .

[9] It may be believed that in 1920, when J. Thomas Looney issued the book now here re-published, very little notice was taken of it by the intrenched interests whom we call the Bardolators. There is nothing sensational in Looney's methods of presentation, nothing smacking of the Sunday supplement. It resembles in its general tenor "The Origin of Species." In my own opinion, after several readings, " 'Shakespeare' Identified" is destined to occupy, in modern Shakespearean controversy, the place Darwin's great work occupies in evolutionary theory. It may be superseded, but all modern discussion of the authorship of the plays and poems stems from it, and owes the author an inestimable debt.

[10] It was the quietness of treatment, the cool, scientific approach, which made Looney's book appear less important than it really was. It made no appeal to fanaticism. The Stratfordians could ignore it and the Baconians could forget it. It was only later that the Looney method, of a detective methodically and relentlessly closing in on the author, not of a crime but of a mystery, caused uneasiness. His book is a combination of a detective thriller, a mystery story, and a historical narrative built solely from authentic historical data. At the present writing the convictions of those who have followed the arguments of the book are expressed in the words of the authors quoted at the head of this introduction.[1] It would be difficult to select two writers more diverse in temperament, background, and achievement than Henry James and Sigmund Freud. Each was a master in his own realm of authorship. Both were convinced that, whoever did write the works known as Shakespeare's, the Stratford man did not. And Freud, who was never celebrated for jumping hastily to a conclusion, declared himself "almost convinced" that Edward de Vere, Earl of Oxford, was the real author. In fact he called himself, later, one of Looney's followers.

[11] There is a subtle reason, not before mentioned, I think, for the reluctance of modern British and American readers to accept the claims of a man like Oxford. The nineteenth and twentieth centuries have tended inexorably toward what we nowadays call the era of the common man. Democracy, in politics and sociology, is in the saddle. The tradition has gained favor, and has almost achieved the status of a doctrine, that the true hero is he who starts as a poor, barefoot boy, and, by his own transcendent efforts, rises to the highest position. "From Log Cabin to White House," and from humble shepherd's cottage to Downing Street, embody a dream our modern world holds passionately if subconsciously. This dream the legend of the butcher boy of Stratford, who went to London, wrote immortal plays and became wealthy, has fulfilled so neatly, so satisfyingly, that those who have grown up believing it, refuse to abandon it.

[12] Particularly are they loath to abandon it in favor of an aristocrat, seventeenth of his line in unbroken descent. Edward de Vere's ancestors did "come over with the Conqueror." One of the earls watched King John sign Magna Carta, another fought at Agincourt, another at Barnet, when the Kingmaker fell, and another at Bosworth when the Tudors entered into their kingdom. He himself fought in Flanders and against the Spanish Armada. Compared with Edward de Vere, Queen Elizabeth was an upstart, and her first minister, Lord Burleigh, one of

---

[1] The introductory quotations from James, Freud, etc., are omitted [Eds.].

the groundlings. To suggest that such a magnifico as Oxford was also a supreme poetic genius is too much for the non-thinking, democratic, twentieth-century citizen. It runs counter to his political philosophy, which teaches him that aristocrats are, ipso facto, degenerates, incompetents, and nonentities.

[13] Equally powerful support for the traditional Stratfordian legend is to be found in the intellectual indolence of the average man. It is so much easier for him to go on muzzily believing in the immense, empty façade of Stratfordiana than to make an effort to examine the evidence. His attitude is that of the burgesses of Stratford when P. T. Barnum offered to buy Shakespeare's birthplace, take it down, and ship it to his exhibition in America. Where then was the birthplace? Nobody knew, but "the most likely spot" was hastily selected, and the house renovated by Elizabethan experts. The town, however, refused to allow the sacred relic to be moved. It was too valuable where it was.

[14] The intellectual integrity of the Stratfordian priesthood, the professors, pedagogues, and curators who refuse to discuss the possibility of error, will be dealt with by more competent pens than mine. Like all hierarchies they tend to disparage heretics.

[15] We who believe that J. Thomas Looney was on the right track face the same opposition as those who suggested that the sun did not really go around the earth, and those who questioned the literal story of Creation in Genesis. It is to be hoped that the issue of " 'Shakespeare' Identified" in this new edition will arouse fresh interest in one of the most absorbing of historical mysteries.

Questions

1. How does McFee initially attack the Stratfordians?
2. Examine in paragraph 2 these words and phrases: "tutelary deity," "revere," "sanctity," "national shrine," "faith." What is McFee's basic metaphor here and why does he use it?
3. In paragraph 3 McFee cites "doubtless," "perhaps," "probably," "it is assumed that . . ." as instances of lack of evidence. What other explanations might be advanced for the use of such terms?
4. In paragraph 4 McFee refers to "undisciplined and emotional lunatics." Who are these people? What basic assumptions is McFee making about them? What inferences does he want the reader to draw?
5. What contrasts does McFee draw between the methods of J. Thomas Looney and the methods of earlier non-Stratfordians? Why?
6. In paragraph 9 McFee compares Looney's book to Darwin's *The Origin of Species*. Why? Comment on the assumptions underlying the last sentence of this paragraph.
7. In paragraph 10 McFee refers to James and Freud as supporters of Looney's thesis. Does the evidence McFee provides establish his case?

8. What new arguments for his position does McFee advance in paragraphs 11–13? Analyze the appropriateness and validity of these arguments.
9. What is the strategy of McFee's final paragraph? Whose support is he trying to enlist?

GOOD FREND FOR IESVS SAKE FORBEARE: WAS SHAKESPEARE REALLY SHAKESPEARE?*

Bergen Evans

[1] Dissertations on the subject of who wrote the plays commonly ascribed to William Shakespeare of Stratford-on-Avon now exceed what could be read in a lifetime. More than 4,000 separate books and articles, in six languages (according to a bibliography prepared by the late Professor Joseph S. Galland), support and dispute the claims presented for seventeen possible alternate authors. *The Saturday Review* has recently published a number of letters excitedly for or against the various proposed pretenders. Of them, Bacon leads the field (if we overlook Shakespeare) with Edward de Vere, the seventeenth Earl of Oxford, a strong runner-up and gaining rapidly. Hard at their heels come the Earls of Rutland and Derby and scattered down the track are Sir Edward Dyer, Robert Burton, Sir Walter Raleigh, Christopher Marlowe, and bringing up the rear amid the plaudits of the feminists, Anne Hathaway! . . .

[2] To the faint extent that the backers of the various entries feel any compulsion to be reasonable, their chief argument is a negative one. How, they ask, could an uneducated provincial have ever acquired the universal knowledge manifested in the plays?

[3] Ironically, this question is founded on the hysterical claims of omniscience for their idol by the bardolators (such as Schlegel's pronouncement that Shakespeare had mastered "all the things and relations of this world"), claims which have been steadfastly refuted by informed critics from Ben Jonson on but which seem to have an irresistible appeal to the unscholarly. And to support their assumption the various theorists have labored mightily to present the Stratford man as an illiterate oaf and his home town as a benighted spot through whose mired alleys trudged as low a group of cretins as ever gibbered in the suburbs of Dogpatch.

[4] Actually, however, sixteenth-century Stratford was a pretty civilized place. It is true that one John Shakespeare, probably the poet's father, was fined for leaving refuse in the street, but the significance of this is surely not that refuse littered the streets but that householders were fined if it did—an indication of a civic pride considerably in advance of that of twentieth-century Chicago. The town had a grammar school and a fine church and several other buildings more substantial than one would find in most American communities of the same size today, and was probably more self-sufficient in cultural matters. All intellectual activity had not yet been sucked into the metropolis; culture was not then mass-produced in one spot and piped back into the country towns as wobbling shadows and syndicated banalities.

[5] As for the man himself, it cannot be denied that his report cards have not been preserved, but surely the writing of the plays ought to render them unnecessary as proof of his literacy. Lincoln had practically no schooling, but the author of the Gettysburg Address and the Second Inaugural can hardly be considered uneducated. Indeed, if the Stratford man were half the ignorant boor his denigrators insist he was, it reflects very little subtlety in the true author to have selected him as a front. J. Thomas Looney, the one-eyed monarch of these blind guides, perceived this pitfall and attempted to prevent his ardent followers from making a gadarene plunge into it by begging them to remember that Shakespeare, though of low extraction and mean capacities and reduced, through Mr. Looney's researches, to a "somewhat ignominious" position, was, after all, Lord Oxford's stooge and as such entitled to at least courtesy.

[6] As for the great Shakespeare "mystery," it consists, in brief, of our not knowing as much about the man as we wish we did. But, even so, we know more about him than we do about any of the other claimants except Bacon. He was, apparently, one of the best-known citizens of his day. Plays attributed to him were published as by him over a period of thirty years and not only was their authorship never challenged but more than a score of contemporary men of letters, at various times, mentioned him, praised him, and estimated his genius about as we do now. There are periods in his life about which we know nothing, but so are there in the lives of almost all of those who are advanced to supplant him, and when we consider the difference between his social position and that of some of them we can consider ourselves fortunate for knowing so much.

[7] The first of all the challengers, in point of time, bulk of literature and noise, number and ingenuity of supporters, is Francis Bacon, whose

claim, first advanced in 1785, rests fundamentally on the assumptions that the author of the plays was omniscient and that Bacon not only knew everything but had practically a monopoly on information.

[8] Both assumptions are false. The plays abound with errors: Bohemia is endowed with a seacoast; characters board ship at Verona for passage to Milan; Cleopatra, laced in a corset, plays billiards; Hector quotes Aristotle and Hamlet attends an as-yet-not-founded university; there are clocks in ancient Rome and cannon in the time of King John; Edgar, though a contemporary of the pre-Roman Lear, is familiar with Bedlam, and there is a king of France at a time when All Gaul was still divided into three parts. The list of such blunders could be extended through many pages. The entire subject received its definitive treatment thirty years ago in "Shakespeare's England," a symposium by a score of authorities that canvassed Shakespeare's knowledge in a dozen fields and concluded that he had no such immense and specialized information as some of his admirers had given him credit for. His vast knowledge of law, for instance, a pillar of the whole Baconian structure, proved upon examination by an expert in Elizabethan law, Arthur Underhill, to have been "neither profound nor accurate."

[9] Bacon's omniscience has stood scrutiny no better. It is true that he boasted to have taken all knowledge for his province, but the opinion of the best scouts for several centuries now has been that he failed to occupy the entire province. His book learning is considerably greater than that of the author of the plays, to be sure, but it still falls short of the claims made for him.

[10] There is no disgrace in that, however, for much has been claimed. He has been hailed as the author of the entire Elizabethan drama, with "The Faerie Queene" and "The Anatomy of Melancholy" thrown in. Less rational enthusiasts (for, incredible as it may seem, the distinction is possible) have also credited him with Montaigne's "Essais," "Pilgrim's Progress," the "Tale of a Tub," and "Robinson Crusoe." The first of these may have been, as claimed, a youthful exercise in French, but the last three present a biographical problem since they were published from fifty-two to ninety-three years after a body presumably his was buried at St. Albans. One explanation is that he left them in manuscript. Another is that he merely feigned death and found someone else willing (for the sake of the sarcophagus, possibly) to take his place in the tomb in order that he might be free from interruption, a convenience necessary for so voluminous an output. And a third is that he dictated them from the spirit world, as he did the particular cipher that he communicated to Mrs. F. C. A. Windle of San Francisco.

[11] Unfortunately, Bacon is a peculiarly *un*likely candidate. The extent of his known duties and the bulk of his acknowledged works would make the production of thirty-six such plays in addition and in secret, in or out of cipher, more incredible than their being written by the most unlettered hind in the land. Then it would be difficult to find two men whose styles vary more widely. Bacon is stately, grave, and condensed; Shakespeare is impetuous, sparkling, and extravagant. Jonson, who knew both men, tells us that Bacon's speech was so concise that if his listener coughed or turned aside he missed the meaning, whereas Shakespeare's volubility overflowed the bounds of decorum and stood constantly in need of restraint. Spedding, one of the greatest students of Bacon, doubted whether one could find as many as five lines together in any of Bacon's works that could be mistaken for Shakespeare's by anyone familiar with their styles. . . .

[12] Those who oppose the commonly-accepted authorship grant that no one point they can advance suffices to prove their argument but insist that the cumulative effect of their many points (what Mr. Halle calls "the vast accumulation of little facts") is irresistible. But their own logic works as much against as for them; for the difference between a fact and a possibility is a measure of uncertainty, and the residual doubt which attends each of their surmises is also cumulative. The "bigoted venitent" who is unable to accept their initial postulates is likely to conclude his investigation with more doubt of the doubters than of the facts they impugn.

[13] He will, indeed, be a man of exceptional patience if he does not break off the whole investigation with disgust and indignation. The delusions of honest zeal can be excused the first few times, but after one has strained his eyes for the invisible spoor of a dozen of these nebulous chimeras he feels that he has been sent on a very tedious fool's errand.

[14] Take the much-publicized assertion that X-ray and infra-red photographs have revealed a portrait of Oxford underlying the "Ashbourne" portrait of Shakespeare. If it could be proved that the Ashbourne picture is a contemporary portrait of Shakespeare; if it could be shown that there is another portrait under it, and if it could be shown that this portrait is a portrait of the Earl of Oxford, it would be, to say the least, curious.

[15] But not one of these suppositions can be established as a fact—particularly, and most strikingly, the second, upon which, of course, the third is wholly dependent. One would certainly have assumed, after all the brouhaha, that there was *some* portrait underlying the Ashbourne picture. But let any dispassionate seeker after the truth turn to the

photographs of these "findings" (he may see them in *Scientific American*, January 1940, pages 4–8) and compare them with a genuine disclosure by X-rays of one portrait underlying another (such as the "Portrait of a Lady," supposedly by Franz Pourbos the Younger, reproduced in its various stages of detection and restoration on Plate I, opposite page 64F, Vol. 17 of the 14th Britannica) and ask himself if there is the slightest indication of anything except a few preliminary strokes and minor alterations underlying the surface portrait in question. Nor is the "discovery" of "Oxford's Crest" on the signet ring worn by the subject of the portrait any more convincing. Only the eye of faith could have detected the resemblance and only the effrontery of fanaticism drawn it in crudely with white paint and solemnly presented it as evidence.

[16] Next to abuse of those who disagree with them, no term is more common in the writings of the anti-Stratfordians than "it is impossible to doubt" or "it cannot be questioned." But men who have espoused one of the most startling doubts ever conceived cannot be permitted the use of such phrases. If we are not going to doubt, then the Stratford man must be left in possession. And if we are, we can hardly accept anyone who has yet been advanced to displace him.

Questions

1. The term *ethical proof* is used to describe a method by which a speaker or writer attempts to establish his own character in such a way as to win support for his arguments. What character is Evans attempting to present himself in throughout the essay? Cite examples.

2. What statements about Shakespeare's life and learning does Evans want us to accept as fact? What inferences does he then draw from these statements? How does he use these inferences to support his position and to attack that of the anti-Stratfordians?

3. In paragraph 5 Evans describes Looney as "the one-eyed monarch of these blind guides." Comment on the connotations of this description. Find other instances of similar use of language. What is Evans's purpose in using language in this way?

4. What arguments does Evans use to refute the Baconians? Evaluate these arguments.

5. What conclusions does Evans come to in paragraphs 12–13? What assumptions are they based on? Why then does Evans cite still another case in paragraphs 14–15?

6. To what extent, throughout his essay, does Evans rely on fact and the language of report, and to what extent does he rely on judgment and the language of opinion? (See Hayakawa's essay, pp. 618–626.) Do you think Evans has presented his case in the most effective way? Why or why not?

THE OXFORD PRIMER*

Gelett Burgess

Since not a single one of my traditional opponents has shown any knowledge of the recently discovered historical facts indicating the Oxford authorship of the Shakespeare plays, let me state briefly the basic reasons for the Oxford cause that they may know what we are talking about. Space prevents documents, but the Shakespeare Fellowship can show proof of the truth of every one of these statements. I call them "The Oxford Primer."

1. It is unimaginable that the author of the immortal plays was not known for his literary genius by his contemporaries. Webbe, the anonymous author of "The Arte of English Poesie," Peacham, Day, and many others praised Edward de Vere, Seventeenth Earl of Oxford, for his creative "doings" in superlatives and accounted him a poet and dramatist of the highest order. He was an acknowledged leader in the literary life of the Shakespearean age. Many other veiled allusions to his genius, in the symbolic diction affected at the time, have been found in which Oxford is easily identified, notably in a contemporary description of the author of "Venus and Adonis" by Thos. Edwards in his "Narcissus" (1593).

2. The plays give *prima facie* evidence that the author was an aristocrat with a feudal point of view. Oxford was the premier Earl of the Realm, the head of one of the oldest families, the most loyal supporter of the Crown.

3. The author must have been familiar with the theatre. Oxford was supervising patron of several companies of actors performing Shakespearean plays. He was a lessee of Blackfriars' Theatre. He frequently acted himself in court masques and revels, and had a lifelong interest in the stage.

4. The author must have been well educated and had read widely. Oxford received degrees from both Oxford and Cambridge universities. He was a well-known patron of the arts. Golding was his uncle and Lyly his secretary. Of the "source books" which Shakespearean critics agree that the author must have read, Oxford is known to have owned at least a dozen. Several of these were dedicated to him, and records have been found of his purchase of the others. He is known to have read

* From the Letters to the Editor section, *Saturday Review*, June 4, 1949. Reprinted by permission of the Estate of Gelett Burgess.

Latin easily and to have had considerable knowledge of French and Italian.

5. The author must have been well acquainted with court life and manners. Oxford, when twelve, became a Royal Ward, was brought up in the home of Lord Treasurer Burghley, and was for some years a favorite of Queen Elizabeth.

6. The author must have had a thorough knowledge of the law. Critics have found his technical phraseology accurate; and a great many of his figures of speech have reference to legal practice. Oxford studied some years at Gray's Inn and was familiar with the intricacies of the jurisprudence of the time.

7. The author must have had a personal knowledge of Italy, its topography and customs. Oxford traveled for over a year on the Continent, and spent several months in Italy.

8. The author must have been an expert sportsman, familiar with its slang, with a knowledge of music and botany. Oxford from his youth was experienced in falconry, and was the winning champion in at least two tournaments. He was a composer of music of professional skill. His home, while with Burghley, had the most complete botanical garden in Britain.

9. Oxford was known to his intimates as "Gentle Master William." He had a favorite estate in Warwickshire on the river Avon. His crest as Lord Bulbec was a lion shaking a broken spear.

10. The author must have had personal knowledge of war and of navigation. Oxford fought for some time in the Low Countries and, with Sussex, on the Scottish border. At his own expense he equipped a ship and fought it against the Spanish Armada.

11. The First Folio Shakespeare is dedicated to the Earls of Montgomery and of Pembroke. One became Oxford's son-in-law, and the other was at one time engaged to his other daughter. The Earl of Southampton, to whom "Venus and Adonis" was dedicated, had been strongly urged to marry Elizabeth Vere by Lord Burghley and others. "A Midsummer Night's Dream" was given at Greenwich Palace in January 1595 in celebration of the marriage of Oxford's daughter Elizabeth to the Earl of Derby.

12. It was the custom of Elizabethan writers of noble birth to publish their works anonymously; but some, even clerics, used stooges whose names were put as authors on the title pages of the true authors' works. "And he that cannot write true English without the help of Clerkes of Parish Churches will need make himself the father of interludes." So says Greene in his "Farewell to Follie."

But Oxford had special personal reasons for desiring anonymity. He fell into disgrace through his love affair with Anne Vavasor; he dissipated an immense estate in bad investments and his maintenance of his theatrical companies, and became almost bankrupt; and he earned an unsavory reputation by preferring the companionship of writers and players to the artificiality of court life. He could not afford, while seeking a remunerative official position from Elizabeth, to acknowledge publicly that he was the author of plays revealing so many autobiographical secrets and ridiculing so many prominent personages.

13. Lastly, Charles Wisner Barrell has proved that three famous portraits of "Shakespeare," the Ashbourne and Janssen in the Folger Library at Washington and the Hampton Court portrait owned by the King of England, are all overpainted portraits of Edward De Vere, X-ray and infra-red photographs showing that the original head and ruff have been redone and identifying details changed or obliterated.

14. An intimate connection has been definitely traced between members of Oxford's family surviving him and the accepted contemporary authority on "Shakespeare," Ben Jonson.

If we compare these facts with the complete lack of any similar contemporary certification of the Stratford Shakespeare's association with any literary activity, the logical conclusion is evident, *i.e.*, that Oxford used the name "Shakespeare" as a pseudonym. Not only did Shakespeare possess *none* of these qualifications for authorship, but Oxford was the *only* Elizabethan writer who possessed them all. One of the happiest results of the scholarship and research that have been given to Oxford's life is the fact that a new and authentic chronology of the plays has proved that the so-called "crude" plays which Shakespeare has been supposed to rewrite and improve were actually pirated publications of memory versions of his own works, which rescues the author's name from the traditional charge of plagiarism.

Thus, in bringing to light the life, environment, and activities of Edward De Vere, a consummate genius who, though neglected and maligned heretofore by history, was the true leader of the British Renaissance, there has been revealed the man who, by all scientific standards, is the most logical and believable candidate for the authorship of the Shakespeare plays and sonnets.

Questions

1. Analyze Burgess' opening sentence. What is his approach to the controversy? Do you find his approach convincing? Why or why not?
2. Why do you think Burgess uses the procedure of numbering the basic reasons for the Oxford cause? How effective is this device?

3. Examine the logical structure of the numbered paragraphs 3–8 and 10. What similarities in structure do you find? Comment on the validity of these arguments.
4. Analyze Burgess' twelfth basic reason (both paragraphs). What kind of argument does he use? Is it valid?
5. Why does Burgess give special emphasis to the argument in numbered paragraph 13? How is the evidence cited here different from the kind of evidence given in his other arguments? What other conclusion might one draw?
6. In the next to last paragraph Burgess states: "If we compare these facts . . . " What is Burgess' intended referent for the term *these facts*? Would you agree in calling the referents *facts*?
7. In the last two paragraphs Burgess uses such phrases as "logical conclusion," "has proved," "by all scientific standards." What other such phrases do you find? What effect is Burgess striving for? Are these phrases justified?

THE REAL AUTHOR OF SHAKESPEARE'S PLAYS*
Calvin Hoffman

[1] When I first began my researches—more than nineteen years ago —into the problem of Shakespeare authorship, I had no wish to add my contribution to a literary recreation which, over the years, had acquired a slightly bar-sinister cast. For many, many years theories on whether or not Shakespeare wrote the plays that bear his name have issued thick and fast from the brains of diverse literary authorities, each of whom brought forth his own special candidate. However, all were united in their disunity by a certain conviction that *something* was wrong with the premise that William Shakespeare was the author of the Works attributed to him.

[2] Before I began my investigation, which finally led to the publication of this book, I was convinced—like most other people—that William Shakespeare was the author of the most magnificent English dramatic prose ever written, and certainly the most magnificent poetry.

[3] Nineteen years later my feelings toward the qualities of this writing have not changed; they are magnificent.

[4] Only, William Shakespeare of Stratford on Avon never wrote the plays and poems.

[5] For almost two decades I pursued a literary will-o'-the-wisp that gave me no rest. My investigations took me to England, France, Den-

mark, and Germany. I roamed through graveyards, I crawled into dusty tombs, I shivered in the dampness of veritable archives, and in the musty atmosphere of libraries whose book-lined shelves had remained undisturbed for centuries. Across my mind's eye there still unreels the endless procession of ancient houses, decaying churches, and old universities which I patiently investigated as an unofficial detective in a murder mystery that rivals any Sir Arthur Conan Doyle ever wrote. I uncovered a real-life literary "thriller," complete with murder, brawls, duels, and normal and abnormal sexuality. A violent, crimson-colored pattern unfolded itself, with England as the background and the splendidly barbaric Elizabethan era as the setting.

[6] As the clues came thick and fast, I found the load of my inquiry often too heavy to bear. I earnestly prayed that sufficient reason might be found to abandon my search, since it gradually consumed most of my thinking hours, to the sacrifice of more worldly rewards.

[7] The deeper I entangled myself in the evidence at hand, the more carefully I examined the few facts, the welter of conjecture that moldily surrounded the life of William Shakespeare, the more I became convinced, almost against my will, that my search could never be dismissed or ignored as just another unorthodox theory.

[8] Finally, there grew to dominate my days and dreams an imposture unbelievable in magnitude. History had rarely recorded its like. Here was a masquerade that created heartbreak, doomed its protagonist to eternal anonymity, while strait-jacketing him into everlasting silence.

[9] That the life of the man responsible for the greatest poetry and the greatest dramatic prose and verse in the history of the English language should have been deliberately shrouded in anonymity during the most creative years of his life, that he might have been fated so to remain forever is nightmarish to contemplate.

[10] Certainly no character the author envisioned on paper ever matched the depth of his own tragedy. If ever a hell was created for a writer, it was this. Here was a man of surpassing genius, rich with words and overflowing with creative fervor, doomed to live his life watching another gain the plaudits, the rewards, and the fame that rightfully belonged to him. And all he could do was to continue to write and to suffer in silence.

[11] Stifled by a suffocating gag, his soul galled with disappointment, he must have departed life an embittered, lacerated man.

[12] And yet, while living under this weight of spiritual and mental hell, he never ceased to write. A torrent of exquisite poetry, sublime plays, and unmatched ideas endlessly poured from his pen. . . .

[13] The first dissenters favored Francis Bacon as the author of the Shakespeare plays and poems. Following the Baconians, other candidates were brought forth. The Earls of Oxford, Rutland, Southampton, and Derby were among the perennials. The contention was that only those born into the nobility or associated with it could have written the noble thoughts and described the aristocratic characters in the plays.

[14] Though the choices offered are symptomatic of an ability to renounce Shakespeare in general rather than a thoughtful selection of the right candidate, I applaud these "doubters" nevertheless. They have managed to unshackle themselves from the handcuffs of a declining tradition. They form part of the crusade to win for the rightful author his merited due.

[15] But the brave and articulate individuals who have in books or pamphlets championed other men as author of the plays and poems are not alone in rejecting William Shakespeare as author. An impressive array of unbelievers—none of whom has necessarily written a book on the subject or presented a candidate for the authorship—have made known their sentiments. All meet in the belief that Shakespeare just cannot be accepted as the author of the works credited to him.

[16] Such men as Nathaniel Hawthorne, Lord Palmerston, Walt Whitman, Sir George Greenwood, Mark Twain, Prince Bismarck, Oliver Wendell Holmes, Sigmund Freud, John Bright, Henry James, Lord Broughton, Ralph Waldo Emerson, Lord Penzance, John Greenleaf Whittier, Dr. W. H. Furness; and Charles Dickens, who declared: "The life of William Shakespeare is a fine mystery, and I tremble every day lest something should turn up."

[17] What is the significance of these doubts? The stature of the members of the Shakespeare revolutionaries speaks for itself. They cannot be dismissed as "clowns" or "cranks" or "crackpots." Scholars, students, critics, and commentators have contributed to the Shakespeare study—and are numbered among the unbelievers. Even though their theories as to *who* wrote Shakespeare's plays appear untenable, yet their unified disavowal of Shakespeare's authorship—the major premise behind all their conclusions—cannot be lightly disregarded. These men are not irresponsible eccentrics. But, then, who did write the plays, and the poems?

[18] To begin with, a successful candidate must fulfill certain conditions. Before superimposing on Shakespeare's image the image of another—a nameless one—and then identifying that superimposition, certain qualities must be found, examined, and proved. The supporters of the faceless candidate must be able to produce reasons relentless and

inevitable, or else join the ranks of Francis Bacon, Oxfordites, and other contenders. Until such a nominee is presented, capable of passing the most stringent critical tests known to logic and literature, denial of Shakespeare's authorship, while intriguing, stimulating, and often conclusive, does not deserve acceptance. A god cannot fall unless another god arises.

[19] In the following pages I present for your consideration a poet-dramatist whose genius, education, known literary output, and accomplishments prove to my mind that it was impossible for anyone else to have written the works attributed to William Shakespeare.

[20] For one of the first times the name of this poet-dramatist is put forth in the pages of a book as the author of Shakespeare's works. Seventeen years of effort and research have buttressed, and made secure, this writer's claim to title. I present the name confidently. For, once the pieces of the literary puzzle have been put together and the complete picture studied with critical eye, it is almost with a sense of anti-climax that Christopher Marlowe, duelist, scapegrace, genius, and poet, stands gloriously accused.

[21] In the winter of 1936 I traveled to the south shore of eastern Long Island, where, in the quiet, I hoped to finish some writing. At first everything went well. For two weeks I wrote confidently, and without cease. Then one morning I awoke feeling that the spell had been broken. I couldn't get on with my work. There is nothing on earth more unhappy than a writer who cannot write. . . .

[22] After three days of this mocking misery I finally went to the local library, where I borrowed books of most Elizabethan dramatists available. I carried home with me the works of Kyd, Greene, Lyly, Marlowe, and Jonson. I concluded that if I couldn't write I might as well read.

[23] For more than a month I did little else. And of all the Elizabethan plays, I came to know and like those of Christopher Marlowe the best. At all times there seemed to hang over his works an atmosphere of déjà-vu—a nagging, compelling memory that disturbed me as I re-read *Tamburlaine, Dr. Faustus,* and *The Jew of Malta.*

[24] I began to jot down phrases, expressions, and lines from Marlowe, and similar phrases, expressions, and lines I recalled from Shakespeare. Placed side by side, these quotes formed the first clue to what was to develop into a gigantic literary jigsaw puzzle, which would occupy me for many years to come.

[25] Later I checked my memory of Shakespeare's quotations with the text of his plays. I found they squared with those of Marlowe's. An example:

Marlowe's *Tamburlaine:*

> Holla, ye pampered Jades of Asia.
> What, can ye draw but twenty miles a day. . . .

Shakespeare's *Henry IV* (Part II):

> And hollow pampered jades of Asia,
> Which cannot go but thirty miles a day.

Marlowe's *Dr. Faustus* (conjuring Helen of Troy):

> Was this the face that launched a thousand ships?

Shakespeare's *Troilus and Cressida* (referring to Helen of Troy):

> . . . She is a pearl,
> Whose price hath launched above a thousand ships.

[26] After a while I realized that what I had done was to extract stylistic similarities, known as parallelisms, from the works of the two authors. The number of these parallelisms grew, and my interest grew along with them. I reread most of the Shakespeare plays. With renewed vigor I found myself startled by the astonishing affinity that Shakespeare had for Marlowe, and Marlowe for Shakespeare. Not only was this affinity one of style, but every facet, every nuance of the dramatic and creative mechanisms in their works seemed incredibly harmonious. Both dramatists created the same emotional, intellectual situations for their characters; more often than not, they were psychologically identical.

[27] It seemed as though versification, vocabulary, imagery, and allusion stemmed from the same psychic root.

[28] Of course, the two poets were contemporaries. Perhaps, I thought, I was overeager; and what I had begun to read between the lines of my Oxford Shakespeare was the result of my own imagination. I reread Kyd, Greene, and Peele, scrupulously setting their lines against Shakespeare's as I had previously done with Marlowe. Quite unconsciously, I was performing a literary "control" experiment.

[29] The results were unexpected. Shakespeare's whole style and treatment differed radically from that of these other playwrights; so did Marlowe's. I found that Marlowe and Shakespeare stylistically agreed with each other in the same inverse proportion as they disagreed with their dramatic contemporaries.

[30] I reread the works of both dramatists. Marlowe's *Edward II, Hero and Leander, Dido, Queen of Carthage,* and Shakespeare's *Timon of Athens, Two Gentlemen of Verona,* and *Cymbeline* engaged me. Thematically, the works were poles apart. Yet the medley disclosed further evidence of a literary relationship between Marlowe and Shake-

speare so close, so united that it seemed to me to be almost a blood relationship.

[31] I began to draw parallelisms again. After a while I had collected an enormous number. And it was time for me to leave Long Island.

[32] During all this time my knowledge of the lives of Shakespeare and Marlowe amounted to no more, and no less, than that of the average, reasonably informed person. I accepted the usual academic and textual pronouncements literally.

[33] William Shakespeare died a respectable Stratford on Avon death at the age of 52.

[34] Christopher Marlowe, by contrast, died in a tavern brawl at Deptford at the age of 29—when he was stabbed, murdered in a quarrel over either a wench or an ale bill.

[35] These were statements found in books. I had never questioned them in any way.

[36] The last night before my departure I spent tossing restlessly from side to side. It was one of those euphemistically named "white" nights, which are, in reality, black as pitch; a foretaste of hell, for any tense or nervous person who is liable to brood progressively about loss of rest. Instead of black sheep, I counted parallelisms. And around three o'clock in the morning, with the waves of the ocean moaning outside my window, I began to brood over Marlowe's death. And sometime during that quiet period I asked myself a question: "Was the report of Marlowe's assassination true?"

[37] I don't know quite why, but I felt intuitively that somehow it was not. A small doubt persisted. It was to grow with boom-food rapidity during the months and the years to follow. I determined to seek confirmation of Marlowe's murder; solid, incontrovertible evidence that he had truly died as reported.

[38] That was the beginning of a nineteen-year search for the needle of truth in a haystack of literary conjecture that had been piling up for centuries. And at the end of that time I was ready to prove, beyond any reasonable doubt, that every single play and poem we have been led to believe was written by William Shakespeare had been written by Christopher Marlowe—a poet-dramatist who had outlived his own death, in a most "strange and marvellous fashion."

[39] Let me emphasize here that it was *not* by first denying Shakespeare that my theory came into being. It was the growing conviction that no one *but* Christopher Marlowe could have written the works of Shakespeare.

[40] In spite of doubts, in spite of feeling that I was tilting at the windmills of established authority, I could not help but think that the poet who had written:

> I . . . hold there is no sin but ignorance.
> (*The Jew of Malta*)

had written:

> I say there is no darkness but ignorance.
> (*Twelfth Night*)

[41] That the poet who wrote:

> Weep not for Mortimer
> That scorns the world, and, as a traveller
> Goes to discover countries yet unknown.
> (*Edward II*)

had also written:

> The undiscovered country from whose bourn
> No traveller returns.
>
> (*Hamlet*)

[42] These were but two of a multitude of similar parallelisms. There were other reasons, too. One of them came from Sir Edmund Kerchever Chambers, a knowledgeable Shakespeare authority. Thus, Sir Edmund, in his biography of William Shakespeare:

The percipience of style is a very real quality. It had its origin in the same natural feeling for the value of words and the rise and fall of rhythm, which is the starting point of literary expression itself; it may be trained, half unconsciously, through reading and reflection and comparison, into a valuable instrument of criticism. A quasi-intuitive sense is developed.

[43] And further:

A writer forms his own rhetorical habits in the building of lines and the linking of line to line, in the use of exclamation, antithesis, iteration and cumulation; in the balance of noun against noun and verb against verb. A writer has his own small mannerisms of locution, his recurrent catch-phrases. . . . These are the most characteristic because they become unconscious and are often, at first sight, unnoticeable. . . . Naturally each writer has his individual range of thought, of dramatic situations, of imagery, of allusion, or vocabulary.

[44] Sir Edmund confirmed the value of my work—the weeding out of parallelisms between the works of Marlowe and Shakespeare on the basis of "the starting point of literary expression itself."

[45] But no matter how I might be cheered by this helping hand (unconscious or otherwise) of authority, there were other factors to consider. Marlowe's homicide at the age of 29—a matter of historical

record—had cut him off at an age when he could not possibly have written the bulk of the Shakespeare Canon.

[46] And yet—and yet—it must be Marlowe!

Questions

1. Hoffman's opening sentence begins: "When I first began my researches—more than nineteen years ago . . ." What is he trying to establish?
2. What sort of character does Hoffman attempt to establish for himself in this selection? Cite details to support your response. What connection is there between his procedure and his arguments?
3. How would you explain the picturesque details in paragraph 5? What assumptions has he made about his anticipated audience?
4. Examine the language and the logic of paragraphs 13–16. (See Thouless, pp. 667–676, and Davis, pp. 608–617.) What are Hoffman's intentions? What specific purpose does he have in citing the names in paragraph 16?
5. Analyze the strategy and the style of paragraph 18. What is Hoffman's apparent purpose? Does he achieve it?
6. Most of the remainder of Hoffman's essay is devoted to asserting the parallelisms between Marlowe and Shakespeare. What basic assumption is Hoffman making? What different assumptions might be made?
7. Sir Edmund Chambers, who is quoted in Hoffman's conclusion, is generally acknowledged as one of the most eminent Shakespeare scholars of the twentieth century. What use does Hoffman make of the quotations from Chambers? Do these quotations actually "confirm the value of my work," as Hoffman puts it?

IN SEARCH OF THE REAL SHAKESPEARE*

Hallett Smith

[1] Some years ago two English critics, Ivor Brown and George Fearon, surveyed the fuss the modern world makes about Shakespeare in a book they called "The Amazing Monument." With a proper sense of wonder and detachment they contemplated the results of an idolatry which began in the eighteenth century and has continued down to the present time. Despite such occasional outbursts as Margaret Halsey's "I'm a big girl now and I don't believe in Shakespeare," the mid-twentieth century is as fascinated by the great mystery as the mid-nineteenth century was. The avenues of approach have changed, but the destination is still the same. What kind of person was it who wrote the plays and the poems? Can we form any picture of him which we would all recognize? Is it anyone we know?

* From *The Yale Review*, Vol. 40, March, 1951. Copyright by Yale University Press. Reprinted by permission.

[2] According to Freud, God is a projection of the father-image, and so is the devil. This principle perhaps accounts for the wide variety to be found in the projections of Shakespeare. For the accounts of Shakespeare the man, whether given by respectable orthodox academic authorities or by the extravagant and erring spirits who support Bacon, Oxford, Derby, or Dyer, are all projections. Shakespeare is not only fantastical himself, but the cause that fantasy is in other men. . . .

[3] Bernard Shaw, whose vision of the world was strongly conditioned, according to H. N. Brailsford, by the destruction of an ideal father-image by his own drunkard father, projected a notorious picture of Shakespeare. How much of Shaw's "Shakespear" is merely a comic device for self-dramatization in the Prefaces is of course a problem for the critic of Shaw, but the picture of the poet himself concerns us. He is, according to Shaw, a snapper-up of unconsidered trifles, a literary jackdaw, a man who could show much but teach little. As the projection of a father-image, this is interesting, and we observe that when Shaw can, he eagerly falls back upon conformity with the Bard, as when he says, in the epistle dedicatory to "Man and Superman," that Shakespeare had no conscience, and neither has he.

[4] The general tendencies in Shakespeare projection have, however, changed somewhat in recent years. Before the first World War the great concern was to draw a picture of the man who could have written the plays, and either to reconcile this picture with the known facts in the life of William Shakespeare of Stratford, actor and sharer in the company of players known as the Chamberlain's, and later the King's Men; or else to show that the two did not fit, and find some other candidate for the authorship. The latter course appealed to a large number of zealous men and women, beginning with Hawthorne's friend Delia Bacon of New Haven and coming down to the members of societies in England and America which still publish obscure journals devoted to the cause of Bacon or Oxford as the author of the plays. These people have been almost all amateurs in literary scholarship, though some have been distinguished in other fields. This makes them vulnerable to such dry remarks as that of Pearsall Smith: "I do not wish, however, to speak with any disrespect" (he has just compared the Baconians to the Gadarene swine) "of that view of the authorship of Shakespeare's plays which is so firmly held by officers in the Navy and the Army, by one of His Majesty's judges, and the manager of more than one large drapery establishment, and is corroborated by the authority of Mark Twain, Mrs. Henry Pott, Prince Bismarck, John Bright, the late Mr. Crump, K.C., and several thoughtful baronets."

[5] Such a reply, for all its wit, is mere snobbery, of course. The Baconians, and the Oxfordians, can be refuted; they have been refuted, over and over, but they never recognize the refutation. In fact, it is one of their constant complaints that their arguments are ignored by the professional academic authorities. A decade ago Professor O. J. Campbell, of Columbia University, met directly and demolished the Oxfordian thesis, but the editors of undergraduate newspapers still get letters asking them to demand from their English teachers an explanation of why they do not discuss with their students the proofs of Oxford's authorship. Several offers have been made to American universities to endow a chair for the teaching of one or another of the Shakespeare heresies. When these offers are refused, the professors are commonly charged with a conspiracy to keep the truth from light. So the temptation to reply by wit and snobbery is very great.

[6] The adherents of Bacon, Oxford, or Derby, though perhaps as numerous since 1920 as before, are somehow less prominent today. One is more likely to encounter Mrs. Henry Pott than Mark Twain. And since the issue has quieted down somewhat for the time being, it might be instructive to look at the heretics and see what we can learn from them.

[7] The most powerful argument to win converts to the heresy is of course the argument from education. Shakespeare's plays were thought, in the nineteenth century, to show a mastery of law, of seamanship, of history, of politics, of society, of natural science, and of philosophy and the arts which a rude untutored boor from the market town of Stratford could not possibly possess. The modern refutation of this argument has been twofold. In the first place, Shakespeare's plays show no very unusual amount of learning, if they are judged by Elizabethan standards; the works of Ben Jonson, the stepson of a bricklayer, show a great deal more. In fact, there are contemporary references to show that in his own time Shakespeare was considered remarkable for his freedom from learning:

> Here I would let slip,
> If I had any in me, scholarship,
> And from all learning keep these lines as clear,
> As Shakespeare's best are, which our heirs shall hear
> Preachers apt to their auditors to show
> How far sometimes a mortal man may go
> By the dim light of Nature.

So writes Francis Beaumont about 1615.

[8] The other refutation of the argument from education is complementary. It is an examination of the curriculum of the Elizabethan

grammar school to show that if Shakespeare went to the school at Stratford he could have accumulated a knowledge of classical rhetoric, poetic, and philosophy which would put to shame a classics major in a modern American college. Professor Baldwin, of the University of Illinois, has recently published three volumes, amounting to some 1700 pages, describing Shakespeare's education. The reader may well wonder, when he finishes, how the poet ever happened to be described as warbling his native woodnotes wild. If he was exposed to all this, no wonder he speaks of the whining schoolboy, with his satchel and shining morning face, creeping like a snail unwillingly to school.

[9] So the heretical claim that the plays show much learning and William Shakespeare of Stratford little has been devastatingly refuted, perhaps over-refuted. It need trouble us no more. But before we leave the point, it is worth notice how many of the heretics were also self-made men. What they doubted it was possible for Shakespeare to do was merely an enlargement of what they had themselves done. Mark Twain could not credit the rustic from Stratford, though when he looked in the mirror he saw a boy from the Mississippi River boats who charmed and entertained the world. Ignatius Donnelly was himself the great orator of backwoods Minnesota but could not believe in the great dramatist from remote Warwickshire. Senator Albert J. Beveridge, himself an example of a gifted American provincial, thought it required a man of the cosmopolitan experience of Sir Walter Raleigh to write the plays. So the projection of Shakespeare which any man makes is often enough that of his opposite, not of himself. And this seems to hold true for some of the orthodox Shakespearians as well. Sir Sidney Lee was for long the standard authority on Shakespeare's life. His image of Shakespeare has been described as that of "a typical English manufacturer who happened to deal in *Twelfth Nights* and *Lears* instead of brass tacks." Now, says Dover Wilson, who made this summary of Lee, "Lee himself was not in the least like this. Where then did his image come from?" Where, indeed? Where do all the images come from? . . .

[10] Sir Edmund Chambers, our generation's standard authority, has summed it up. He realizes that for most readers it would be intolerable to suppose these plays anonymous, or the work of a ghost as elusive as the one in his own drama which legend says William Shakespeare played. It is better, we feel, to have an implausible author than an intangible one. But Chambers is concerned with "Facts and Problems," and he is scrupulous about allowing the facts no heavier burden than they are able to bear. "We are entitled to assume," he says, "a roving and apperceptive mind, conversant in some way with many men and manners, and gifted with that felicity in the selection and application

of varied knowledge, which is one of the secrets of genius. What has perhaps puzzled readers most is the courtesy of Shakespeare; his easy movement in the give and take of social intercourse among persons of good breeding. We have not, indeed, to think of the well-to-do inhabitants of Stratford as boors; but the courtesy of a provincial town is not quite the courtesy of a Portia. Probably the true explanation is that, once more, it is a matter of apperceptiveness, of a temper alive, not only to facts, but to human values."

[11] Since this summary of twenty years ago, the pursuit of Shakespeare the man has taken a somewhat different direction. It has been argued with some plausibility, by Miss Spurgeon especially, that the way to track Shakespeare is to watch him when he is intent upon something else—at such times he may reveal himself unconsciously. When he was writing a play, his conscious mind was concerned with problems of dramatic technique—exposition, characterization, emotional contrasts, exits and entrances, soliloquies and asides. But he wrote in verse; the speeches are poetry, and they are full of images, most significantly metaphors. These images, thrown off in the speed of composition, may show us something about the man himself.

[12] Chambers, writing in 1944, finds this technique useful in reinforcing our belief that the author of the plays was an actor, a man who simply could not help reverting to images from the theater: "That Shakespeare's mind was permeated by the atmosphere of the stage, in which he lived and moved and had his being, seems to me indisputable." But this is hardly revolutionary, or new. Anyone who contributes 36 or 38 plays to the stage is obviously interested in it, whether he be an actor or an aristocrat. His nature is subdued to what it works in, like the dyer's hand. . . .

[13] The most ambitious successor of Miss Spurgeon, Mr. E. A. Armstrong, has discovered other image-clusters and has tried to explain the whole thing on a psychological basis. And the most he can give us, aside from the image-clusters, is a warning: we must recognize that there are various ways in which motifs come to be associated. "Some," he says, "are there because of their emotional significance and others are conjoined by reason of some similarity of sound or sense, or even because of mere contiguity in the past." Punning and rhyming, we recall, are both modes of association by sound, and a man so accustomed to both these kinds of linkage must have often found his mind or imagination guided by them. Such associations would not account for the fawning-candy image, but Mr. Armstrong points out that the last of the three quoted passages is followed immediately by another metaphor:

and this *pine* is *bark'd*
That overtopp'd them all.

The sudden jump from the dinner table to the stripped forest tree is really only a step, we are told, because "the thought of the spaniel aroused a memory of the dog's bark and 'bark' suggested the stripped pine metaphor."

[14] Linkages of words, sounds, and images provide material for the psychologist, of course, and we may expect further and more adventurous essays by the adherents of the various schools. Freud's work on Leonardo led to Dr. Ernest Jones's explanation of "Hamlet" in terms of the Oedipus complex, but it remained for the late Miss Ella Sharpe to find in "King Lear" evidence of early trauma induced in William Shakespeare the child by his mother's pregnancies in 1566 and 1568–9. One is dazzled by such revelations, and somewhat alarmed, for instead of knowing too little about Shakespeare the man it seems possible that we may soon know too much. What kind of curse would the Stratford gentleman have ordered for his tomb if he had foreseen distinterment by psychoanalysts as well as by sextons? (*Good friend, for Jesus' sake forbear!*)

[15] The direction of the most recent approach to Shakespeare, then, is interesting because it is a more literary or verbal one. This is, I suppose, just what we should expect, since in recent years literary criticism in general has concerned itself more closely with words and their functions. Whether this approach, with its auxiliary of psychology, will tell us any more about the mystery of the man remains to be seen. There will always be people who say the peculiarities of the man do not matter: what is valuable is the works. But they will probably always be a minority, for the instinct of curiosity about personality will not be stilled, even when the means of finding an answer seem to be exhausted by repeated trials.

[16] We can console ourselves, however. The projectors of Shakespeare make a fine show of their creations, if we are in the proper mood. Theseus, in "A Midsummer Night's Dream," has some difficulty in persuading Hippolyta, that tough and serious Amazon, to enjoy herself watching the efforts of Bottom, Snug, and the rest of the rude mechanicals to produce a play. To her, the desperate devices of the Athenian laborers, caught between the demands of symbol and realism, are only "the silliest stuff that ever I heard." This may be the feeling of many in the mid-twentieth century about the efforts to visualize William Shakespeare the man. But Hippolyta is answered, as perhaps the impatient

skeptics should be answered now: "The best in this kind are but shadows; and the worst are no worse, if imagination amend them."

Questions

1. What major thesis is Smith advancing? Where do you find it stated?
2. What are some of the varying projections of Shakespeare, according to Smith? What method does he use to establish his case?
3. At the end of paragraph 4 Pearsall Smith is quoted. What point is made here with which Hallett Smith agrees?
4. In the first sentence of paragraph 9 Smith says that the argument from education has been "devastatingly refuted." Do you accept this conclusion? Why or why not? What is the purpose of the remainder of paragraph 9? Why does Smith cite so many cases?
5. In paragraphs 10–14 Smith cites the views of Chambers, Spurgeon, Armstrong, and Ella Sharpe. Where does all of this leave the reader? What position does Smith himself take?
6. In paragraph 14 Smith says, "One is dazzled by such revelations, and somewhat alarmed, for instead of knowing too little about Shakespeare the man it seems possible that we may soon know too much." What are the implications of the sentence? What does it tell you about Smith's attitude?
7. What, in brief, is Smith saying in his final paragraph? Can you restate it in a sentence of your own?

ASSIGNMENTS

1. A recent anthology of English literature contains this statement: "In all probability, the boy [Shakespeare] attended the grammar school in the village. So far as is known, he had no further formal education, although there is a tradition that he was for a time a schoolmaster in the country." Consult in your library a biography of Shakespeare (such as E. K. Chambers') or the book *The Facts About Shakespeare* by Neilson and Thorndike. Prepare a report in which you cite the established facts about Shakespeare's education. Do these facts substantiate the views quoted above?
2. Write a paper in which you summarize—from the selections in this project —the main arguments (*a*) for the case that William Shakespeare of Stratford on Avon is the author of the plays, or (*b*) for the case that he could not have been the author of the plays.
3. Interview one or more of the members of the English department of your college to inquire about their beliefs concerning the authorship of Shakespeare's plays, and their reasons. Report your findings to the class.
4. Reread the selection by Calvin Hoffman. Rewrite his chapter in the language of report.
5. Select one or more paragraphs from the essay by Bergen Evans which you think illustrate slanted language, distortion, or other emotional appeals. Rewrite these paragraphs in the language of report.
6. If your library has William Friedman's *The Shakespeare Ciphers Ex-*

amined, read one or more of his chapters. Prepare a report on Friedman's conclusions about ciphers which attempt to prove that Bacon wrote Shakespeare's plays.

7. Prepare to participate in an informal debate on the topic of the authorship of Shakespeare's plays. You will, of course, need to supplement the information furnished in this project by further investigation. The members of the class who do not participate in the debate should be prepared to conduct a cross-examination of the debaters.

8. Prepare a report in which you summarize and evaluate the qualifications of the authors of the selections in this project. Do not limit yourself to explorations in *Who's Who.*

2. PUBLIC HEALTH
The Fluoridation Controversy

In this project you will discover that even so apparently simple a matter as the composition of drinking water arouses conflicting opinions. This specific controversy is one that may actually have been debated in your own community. But whether it has or not, you have probably read or heard references to fluoridation of drinking water.

In the following pages you are presented with a variety of information and opinions from a great variety of sources—for example: an official government publication, an article by a medical doctor, a report by two medical scientists, a magazine advertisement, an editorial from a public health journal.

Each of these states a point of view concerning fluoridation. In some instances the writers are presented—or present themselves—as experts; in other cases it is not known who wrote or prepared the item. Moreover, one of your problems is to determine the expertness of each writer or source and to what degree his remarks on the subject are valid.

A problem of even greater magnitude has to do with the fact that much conflicting evidence is presented. Different sets of facts or purported facts about the same point are set forth and the reader is asked to accept these as a basis for the writer's conclusions. Which selections contain the "real" facts or the most facts or the pertinent facts is something that you will have to decide before you can begin to draw your own conclusions.

Besides examining the items presented, you will want to look further into this controversy by reading other sources not contained here. At once you will discover that only a very small sample of the ceaseless barrage of material on the subject is presented here. Obviously, six or seven articles on fluoridation do not reveal the whole story. Nor is the story finished, for you can expect to find the controversy continuing in literally thousands of articles and an endless number of public and private meetings.

Finally, when you read the excerpt from Anatole France's story at the end of this project, you will begin to realize that no controversial issue is really simple but that it is usually part of a larger issue—in this case, the great issue of how much freedom the individual should have and how much power or control the government should have. In drawing any individual conclusions about fluoridation of the water supply, ultimately you will want to consider how they relate to your beliefs and feelings about the larger issue of individual freedom and social control.

DENTAL PROTECTION IN YOUR DRINKING WATER

Department of Public Health, State of California

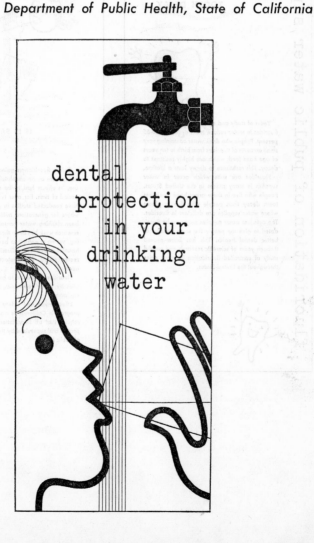

fluoridation of public water supplies

FLUORIDATION LESSENS TOOTH DECAY

Years of study and research have shown that fluorides in water reduce tooth decay by 50-65 percent. People who drink water containing very small amounts of fluorides from birth to ten years of age have teeth which are highly resistant to decay. This resistance to decay lasts a lifetime.

Fluorides are salts which occur in water supplies in many places in the United States. People who live in these areas have much less tooth decay than people who live in places where water supplies are deficient in fluorides. The deficient water supplies may now be fluoridated to give the people the same benefits of better dental health. This has been proved through years of scientific research and careful study of controlled fluoridation in many cities throughout the United States.

IT IS SAFE

Before fluoridation gained general scientific acceptance as an absolutely safe health measure, its effects had to be studied over a long period of time. For over twenty years scientists have conducted studies in parts of the country where for generations millions of people have been drinking water containing fluorides. This research work has been thorough and painstaking, yet no scientist has been able to find any harmful effects from fluorides in the amount recommended for protection against tooth decay.

Fluorides are added to community water supplies by water companies, using safe, modern equipment.

Effectiveness and safety of the fluoridation program in California is assured by laws which require that all fluoridation programs be approved and supervised by the State Department of Public Health.

THE COST IS LOW

The money spent for a pair of shoes can buy the benefits of fluoridation for a lifetime.

The cost of fluoridation varies in different communities. The average cost based on the experience of hundreds of communities has been about 5 to 15 cents per person per year.

The big saving to families in their dental bills is many, many times the few cents paid for fluoridation.

OTHER THINGS ABOUT FLUORIDES

Fluorides do not affect taste, odor, color, or hardness of water. Fluorides present no problems for domestic, industrial, or agricultural users of water.

GET AUTHENTIC INFORMATION FROM THE PEOPLE WHO KNOW—

Your Dental Society

Your Medical Society

Your Health Department

These are the people who protect your health. They have all the authentic information or can tell you where you can get it.

DON'T BE MISINFORMED!

fluoridation of
water supplies has
been endorsed by:

PHYSICIANS

American Medical Association
California Medical Association
Local Medical Societies

DENTISTS

American Dental Association
California State Dental Associations
Local Dental Societies

PUBLIC HEALTH EXPERTS

American Association of Public Health Dentists
American Public Health Association
Association of State and Territorial Health Officers
California Conference of Local Health Officers
California State Board of Public Health
State and Territorial Dental Health Directors
United States Public Health Service

AND ASSOCIATED GROUPS

American Association for the Advancement of
    Science—Subsection on Dentistry
Inter-Association Committee on Health (of the
    six major national health and welfare groups in the U. S.)
National Research Council

**DOES YOUR COMMUNITY
HAVE THE PROTECTION
OF FLUORIDATED WATER?**

Your local health department can tell you
if water supplies in your community need to be
fluoridated and how this can be accomplished.
Find out what is being done in your community
and help put this sound program into effect.

Women's clubs, parent-teacher associations, civic and business groups, labor unions and other organizations are interested in bringing this protection to your community. You, as an individual and as a member of an organized group, can help.

Fluorides in drinking water can reduce tooth decay by one-half to two-thirds.

Fluorides in water now give this protection to thousands of Californians and to millions of people all over the United States.

Fluoridation of public water supplies has been widely endorsed by medical, dental, and public health authorities, and by many other organizations interested in health.

Fluoridation of water supplies means a great savings in family dental bills. The cost of fluoridation is small.

Fluoridated water is safe, economical, and beneficial to health. All water supplies deficient in fluorides should be fluoridated.

You can help your community obtain the benefits of fluoridation. Work with your health department, medical and dental societies, and other local organizations in their efforts to achieve fluoridation for your community.

Prepared by
State of California
DEPARTMENT OF PUBLIC HEALTH
2151 Berkeley Way
Berkeley 4

printed in CALIFORNIA STATE PRINTING OFFICE

Questions

1. What do you think is the purpose of this pamphlet? For whom is it intended? Who wrote it? Why is the pamphlet form used? Explain your answers.
2. Here are two statements made on the last page of the pamphlet: "Fluorides in drinking water can reduce tooth decay by one-half to two-thirds" and "Fluoridated water is safe, economical, and beneficial to health. All water supplies deficient in fluorides should be fluoridated." Does the pamphlet supply factual information to support these conclusions? Explain your answer.
3. Examine the artwork. Why do you suppose it is included?
4. Examine the list of organizations endorsing fluoridation of water supplies. What kinds of organizations are they? What is the purpose in listing them?

POISON IN YOUR WATER*

Leo Spira, M.D.

[1] The proposal to add fluorine to the public water supplies to make up a concentration of 1.2 parts per million (p.p.m.) for the purpose of allegedly reducing the incidence of dental decay in children is a subject of heated controversy all over the country. It is strongly opposed by an ever-growing section of the nation on several grounds: constitutional, legal, medical, religious, moral and ethical, amongst others. In numerous cities and towns, citizens have organized themselves for the purpose of opposing the wanton addition of the poison to their drinking water, which would have to be ingested by everybody irrespective of age and state of health, and without taking into consideration whether it is wanted or not.

[2] Thus, the controversy between the fluoridators, on the one hand, and their opponents, on the other, has entered the realm of several professions and industries, each of which has taken part in the dispute according to their special spheres of knowledge and interest. The apprehensiveness about the project centers to a great extent around the accumulating knowledge of the harmful effects caused by the long-continued ingestion of even small quantities of the chemical substance.

[3] Fluorine is the most potent protoplasmic poison known to toxicology. It affects the enzymes, material essential for the proper utilization of food and for the maintenance of the organic functions of the body. It has a special affinity for the nervous system, on whose enzyme cholinesterase it exerts a suppressing effect. Being a cumulative poison, its deleterious action is bound to increase with advancing age.

[4] Damage to the nervous system, namely, the brain and spinal cord, the peripheral nerves supplying the voluntary muscles of the body, and the vegetative nerve bundles which supply the involuntary muscles as well as the inner organs, including the endocrine glands, will be manifested by an abnormal function of the respective organs supplied by the damaged constituent part. Since, however, fluorine does not necessarily attack the entire nervous system in any one person at the same time, its manifestations will vary according to the particular part affected. . . .

[5] The harmful effect of fluorine will depend, amongst other factors, on the susceptibility of the person ingesting it, on the quantity

* From *The American Mercury Magazine*, August, 1957. Copyright 1957 by *The American Mercury Magazine*. Reprinted by permission.

ingested, and on the length of time during which it has been ingested. It is thus clear that it is not the concentration of fluorine in any one article of food or drink which determines its toxic effect, but the sum total ingested in the course of the day. The margin between the tolerated quantity of the poison ingested and the quantity producing signs and symptoms of chronic fluorine poisoning is very narrow. The risk of transgressing the threshold of fluorine tolerance in the older generations, as well as in those chronically ill, suffering, for example, from kidney disease and unable sufficiently to excrete the poison, is a very real one.

[6] Signs and symptoms of chronic fluorine poisoning having been shown to be capable of being produced by appreciable amounts of fluorine contaminating the average diet, it is undeniable that any addition, however slight, of the poison to the drinking water is bound to increase the risk and gravity of the disease.

[7] To ascertain that the clinical findings obtained on man were in fact due to nothing but the action of fluorine, I carried out animal experiments at the Department of Physiology, Middlesex Hospital Medical School, London, England. Sodium fluoride, the substance proposed by the fluoridators to be added to the drinking water of this nation, was added to the drinking water of experimental rats. It was observed that, whereas in man the ingestion of a drinking water with a concentration as low as 1 p.p.m. is sufficient to produce mottling of the teeth, in my rats mottling was produced by the ingestion of a water with a concentration of not less than between 60 and 100 p.p.m. of the poison. This means that man is between 60 and 100 times more sensitive to fluorine than rats are.

[8] In the course of the experiments on rats several signs of poisoning developed which were identical with those clinically observed on man. The earliest amongst them was intense scratching, without any visible cause. Later on, deep sores developed on the skin in various parts of the body, accompanied by loss of hair. On the scalp a baldness occurred which was very similar in its distribution to the baldness seen in man. On replacing the fluoridated water by distilled water, which is free from fluorine, and on addition of calcium to the food, the sores healed promptly and there was a complete regrowth of hair over the denuded areas.

[9] X-ray examination showed a diminished scrotal shadow, and the testicles degenerated to such a degree that they could be regarded as having to all intents and purposes disappeared altogether.

[10] At autopsy, the thyroid gland was found to have undergone profound changes; it was enlarged and histological examination re-

vealed a lesion similar to that observed in toxic goitre in man.

[11] The kidneys were the organ showing advanced damage; under the microscope they could not be distinguished from those seen in nephrosis in children.

[12] Several investigators reported the development of gastric and duodenal ulcers in their experimental animals. I could find none in my rats, probably owing to the fact that I increased the concentration of fluorine in their drinking water slowly.

[13] The results obtained from the clini·al examination on man and from the animal experiments were significant enough for me to try to find out whether they could be utilized in a practical manner for application in certain diseases of a hitherto obscure origin.

[14] A man suffering from chronic inflammation of the kidneys (Bright's disease) in its terminal stage was submitted to treatment directed against chronic fluorine poisoning, after every other kind of treatment had failed. After four weeks' treatment he was restored to a useful life. . . .

[15] Of two patients suffering from mental illness, which was complicated by the presence of pronounced brown discoloration of the skin characteristic of chronic fluorine poisoning, one was discharged from the mental hospital as completely cured from both the mental illness and the pigmentation of the skin after not more than 3 months' treatment directed against chronic fluorine poisoning; the other was considerably improved.

[16] Moreover, in the course of my recent investigation of the effect produced by the long-continued ingestion of fluorine on the urinary system, chemical analysis of stones removed by operation from kidneys of patients living in New York City, whose drinking water is now practically fluorine-free, revealed the presence of variably large amounts of the poison up to 1790 p.p.m. derived from normal every-day diet.

[17] These being the true facts emanating from a careful investigation, both clinical and experimental, their importance seems to warrant an equally careful checking and re-checking, so as either to confirm or to deny them. Nothing of the sort has, however, been done by the advocates of compulsory fluoridation, who claim that they have only altruistic motives at heart, aiming at the elimination of dental decay. Instead, advocates persistently deny any knowledge of reports on harmful effects of increasing the sum total of fluorine ingested with numerous articles of daily food and drink by adding the poison to the drinking water. Some of them shun continued investigation by stating that "further experiments (on fluorine) are unnecessary."

[18] In this connection, it would seem that their great haste to have communities approve fluoridation is certainly most remarkable.

[19] While discrediting the work, both clinical and experimental, carried out by the opponents of fluoridation, they rely on their own admittedly deficient examination of children in a fluoridated area. In spite of warnings against such unreliable investigation, they adduce negative laboratory findings obtained on children as proof of the harmlessness of their project, oblivious of the fact that serious consequences of fluoridation will not, in all likelihood, become evident before the poison has been ingested over a period of some 25-30 years, too late to undo the harm. The increased occurrence of "mottled nails" amongst children in an experimentally fluoridated area, in comparison with a control area in which no fluorine was added to the drinking water, indicates that, like "mottled teeth," they are the result of the absorption of increased amounts of fluorine into the general blood circulation; although this fact is admitted by those in control of the experiment at the top level, it is being hushed up by those at the lower levels and omitted from their talks and writings for popular consumption. It must, therefore, be concluded that their statements concerning the greatly reduced incidence of "mottled teeth" following fluoridation of the drinking water must be taken with "a grain of salt." Findings obtained by dental investigators opposing fluoridation on the ground the fluorine does not prevent, but only delays, the onset of dental decay by a few years and that the incidence becomes equalized after the calcification of the permanent teeth is completed at the age of 8 years, are simply ignored.

[20] The fluoridators close their eyes and stop their ears to the grave objection that, in view of the widely varying quantities of water drunk individually at any time of the year at any one locality, and, more especially, in hot climates, the risk of transgressing the threshold of fluorine tolerance is a very real one. Nor will they recognize the risk arising from the fact that the amount of fluorine does not diminish when water is boiled, with the result that a concentration of 1 p.p.m. of the poison turns into a much higher concentration.

[21] Since fluorine is already present in our average normal food in quantities sufficient to produce chronic illness, it is obvious that any increase in the fluorine content is certain to be extremely dangerous.

[22] An enlightened public opinion will have nothing whatsoever to do with, and will resist by all lawful means at its disposal, any attempt to force the nation to take a medicine which is neither desired nor required. Nor will the freedom-loving American citizen submit to an endeavor to have any kind of drug, however useful, deliberately added

to the drinking water administered to him by those who are advocating compulsory mass medication, such as fluoridation undoubtedly represents. He rejects arguments put forward by those who have given him abundant reason for mistrust concerning the safeguarding of dental health. He does not forget that state dental directors and public health officers, the agents upon whose shoulders the administration of fluoridation rests, have accepted, without a single word of protest, instructions on how to persuade the nation into the false belief that fluoridation is completely safe and on how to advocate it with the professed altruistic aim of eliminating dental decay in children. Obviously, the fluoridators have something to hide, when at the expense of the taxpayer, they employ every kind of propaganda, through which they uncritically endorse each other's opinion but silence or discredit valid findings obtained by the hard work of their opponents.

[23] Apart from these constitutional and legal aspects of the matter, it is objected by some groups that fluoridation is a violation of their right to free exercise of religion, when they are forced to take any kind of medicine added to the drinking water or through any other medium.

[24] Others consider the heavy expenditure involved as a burden imposed on public funds, when it is proposed that the entire public water supply should be fluoridated for the alleged prevention of dental decay in children, although only one per cent of the water is used for drinking purposes, the remaining 99 per cent being used for industrial and other requirements.

[25] Without conceding any merit whatever to fluoridation while the permanent teeth are forming up to 8 or 10 years of age, one naturally inquires as to what medical theory justifies this medication for 90 per cent of the population over 10 years of age. Of course, there are the moral and legal objections as to compulsory medication even if beneficial. As to adults, many sick, infirm, with permanent teeth or having false teeth, it is not supportable on any theory.

[26] It would, for all these reasons, appear more logical to give children up to the age of 8 years, whose parents so desired, the amount of fluorine claimed to prevent dental decay in media other than through the drinking water, on a prescription from, and under the supervision of, their attending physician or dentist. The advantage of this method of application seems to be so obvious that its rejection suggests the influence of vested interests.

[27] In this connection, it is pertinent to point out that in the process of manufacture of the metal aluminum fluorides derived from the cryolite unavoidably employed emerge as a waste product, which up to a

few years ago was not wanted by anybody, even if given away for nothing. It used to be thrown into the sea and into rivers, with the result that the fish died. The discovery that traces of fluorine were capable of delaying by a few years (though not preventing) the onset of dental decay in children pointed out to the aluminum and chemical industries a lucrative way of making use of the waste product. This is rather like an invitation to mankind to dig its own grave and pay for the privilege.

Questions

1. Why does Spira call fluorine a poison? Why does he do this in the first paragraph?
2. Is it a fact that fluorine is always poisonous to human beings?
3. In paragraphs 7–11 Spira reports the results of his experiments in administering fluorine to rats. What do these results prove about the effects of fluorine on humans?
4. Precisely what degree of concentration of fluorine did Spira add to the drinking water of rats in the various stages of his experiments? What relationship does this have to the 1.2 p.p.m. in paragraph 1 and to the "even small quantities" in paragraph 2?
5. Spira uses the following phrases: "freedom-loving American citizen" (paragraph 22), "compulsory mass medication" (paragraph 22), "violation of their right to free exercise of religion" (paragraph 23), "the influence of vested interests" (paragraph 26). What is his purpose? Can you find other examples of this kind of language in the article?
6. What kinds of groups is Spira appealing to in paragraphs 23–25?
7. What purpose is served in the last paragraph by making reference to the "manufacture of the metal aluminum"?

SOME PUBLIC HEALTH ASPECTS OF WATER FLUORIDATION[*]

Harold C. Hodge and
Frank A. Smith[1]

The important clinical effects of fluoride may be grouped in four categories; three of these are toxic effects, the fourth is the use of fluorides in preventive dentistry.

[*] From *Science*. Copyright 1954 by the American Association for the Advancement of Science. Reprinted by permission.
[1] This paper is based on work performed under contract with the U.S. Atomic Energy Commission at the University of Rochester Atomic Energy Project, Rochester, New York.

Special emphasis should be given the importance of time in any consideration of fluoride effects.

1. *Acute Poisoning*. The rapidity of death following the ingestion of a large dose of fluoride is characteristic.

2. *Chronic High-Grade Poisoning*. The extended period of years during which relatively large daily doses must be absorbed before crippling fluorosis develops is of prime importance. Fluoride exposure of this magnitude always should be detected and since the quantitative analysis of the fluoride content in the urine permits a reliable estimation of the hazard, crippling fluorosis may be classed as a preventable disorder that should never be seen in a modern industrialized community.

3. *Chronic Low-Grade Poisoning*. Mottled enamel as an endemic dental health problem has been thoroughly studied by Dean and colleagues since the classical description by Black and McKay. The period of childhood during which enamel is being formed is the only period when this unesthetic toxic effect can originate. Very mild or mild dental fluorosis probably is the only toxic effect of fluoride that will be seen in communities that fluoridate their water supplies. (This problem is discussed in some detail later.)

4. *Preventive Dentistry*. The effectiveness of water fluoridation on the one hand and topical applications of concentrated fluoride solutions on the other are being reviewed elsewhere in this volume. Having fluoride available during the years that the enamel is calcifying probably confers maximal caries resistance; the available evidence also indicates that fluoride in drinking water must have some topical effect because children who move into fluoride areas after teeth have erupted exhibit some reduction in caries incidence. Suffice it to say that a rapidly growing body of evidence confers something like certainty of fluoride's beneficial effects.

Whenever a proposal is made to fluoridate the water supply of a community, a critical question—*Is it safe?*—is always raised. At the outset our opinion can be given: All the available evidence indicates that there is no danger in water fluoridation. To present the basis for this opinion is the task of this report; our knowledge of the toxic effects of fluorides has been brought together in such a way as to permit an estimation of the factors of safety between the amounts of fluoride evoking toxic responses and the amounts ingested by those who drink water containing 1 ppm F. Although numerous toxic effects of fluorides have been described, only a few effects have been studied in sufficient detail to serve as a basis for reliable, *quantitative* comparisons. Four such well-established toxic effects are the subject of the first part of this review: (*a*) acute lethal poisoning (the first listed clinical effect, above); (*b*) growth retardation (observed in experimental animals); (*c*) various structural changes in bone (characteristic of crippling fluorosis); and (*d*) mottled dental enamel (the third listed clinical effect). It is not necessary to describe these effects in detail or to discuss possible mechanisms. The important thing is to search for the range of dose responsible in various species for each effect and relate these ranges to water fluoridation. Although little is known of the fate (distribution, excretion, storage) of fluorides in the body, the aspects bearing on water fluoridation are discussed in such detail as is justified by current knowledge.

In the second part of this report is a résumé of the information available on the health of human populations drinking F-containing water.

Toxic Effects of Fluorides and the Safety of Water Fluoridation

1. *Acute Lethal Dose; Factor of Safety in Water Fluoridation.* Sixty reported cases of acute human poisonings from inorganic fluorides were reviewed by Roholm in 1935. From the literature since 1935, Smith *et al.* have recently compiled a total of 77 deaths attributed to fluorides. For a number of reasons it is difficult to make a reliable estimation of the minimum amount of fluoride that will certainly cause death in a human adult. Nevertheless it may be stated with a high degree of probability that a retained dose of 5 to 10 g. of sodium fluoride will be lethal. When this figure is compared with the 1 mg ingested daily by an adult who drinks a quart of fluoridated water (1 ppm), an acute lethal effect is clearly seen to be impossible. A factor of safety of 2,500- to 5,000-fold is established. In a child, the safety factor may be estimated at 250- to 500-fold.

Occasionally the question is raised whether an accident in a water treatment plant (for example, dumping a day's supply of fluoride into the water in an instant) might produce dangerously high concentrations. A little arithmetic will provide a reassuring answer. If a day's supply were delivered over a period of an hour, the water would contain only 24 ppm; this amount might be taken daily for 10 years without serious difficulty. Furthermore, for a city like Rochester, New York, to add to the water supply a sufficient amount to be acutely toxic, i.e., deadly, a total of 400 tons of fluoride would have to be added to the volume of water distributed daily to the city. The machine in Rochester that adds fluoride to the water has a hopper that contains 1,000 lb; an acute poisoning is mechanically impossible.

2. *Doses Producing Growth Retardation; Factor of Safety in Water Fluoridation.* There are no known cases of growth retardation in children as the result of fluoride exposure. Several species of animals, however, have been observed for variable periods up to about four years, during which fluoride in one form or another was added to the ration over a wide range of amounts, viz., from 10 to 6,500 ppm; when sufficient fluoride was ingested, effects on growth have been noted. The species included the mouse, rat, rabbit, guinea pig, chicken, dog, swine, sheep, goat, cattle and monkey. Despite the large differences in size and in lifespan, the dietary level above which growth retardation is noted is surprisingly alike from species to species. With only a few exceptions, rations containing less than 100 ppm consumed for periods of a year or less were reported to have no deleterious effect on growth. This dietary level may also fail to produce a significant effect on the body weight of adult animals even for extended periods of time. An exception was found, however, when cattle went through repeated periods of gestation and lactation; under this stress body weight was lost when the ration contained as much as 50 ppm of fluoride.

There may well be considerable differences in susceptibility from species to species. Rabbits were found to grow normally on a ration containing 200 ppm, swine at 300 ppm. In contrast, dogs, calves, chicks, sheep, and monkeys all exhibited growth retardation when given rations containing 100 to 125 ppm F or more. On the basis of the amount of fluoride required to reduce growth, the factor of safety for water fluoridation is 50- to 100-fold.

3. *Doses Producing Skeletal Changes; Safety Factor of Water Fluoridation.* Among the prominent toxic effects observed after long-continued exposures to large amounts of fluoride (20 to 80 mg per day or more) are abnormalities of the skeleton. Sufficiently large doses produce osteosclerosis, sometimes simultaneously with "moth-eaten" areas of osteoporosis, and frequently with exostoses of the long bones and of the vertebra, pelvis, jaw bone, and other flat bones. With lower doses, characteristic minor alterations in bone architecture, e.g., thickening of trabeculae, have been described. The frequency of occurrence of these bony changes in human populations is largely unknown; the total number of patients that have been examined in this country is less than 300. To add to the uncertainty, several of the investigators who have carried out radiographic bone studies have been unable to fix precisely the fluoride exposure of their patients. There is nevertheless a suggestion of uniformity in the relation between the quantity of fluoride ingested (in most cases water-borne fluoride) and the incidence of osteosclerotic

changes in the skeleton disclosed by x-ray examination. None of approximately 140 residents of communities in which the drinking water contained 2 or 3 ppm F or less had any detectable skeletal changes. In a survey of 114 residents of Bartlett, Texas, where the drinking water contained 8 ppm F, 13 persons were described as showing some osteosclerosis, this water concentration therefore may be taken as a plus or minus level of effect. X-ray changes were found in 21 of 178 residents of the Pampas whose drinking water was reported to contain about 16 ppm. A still higher incidence of osteosclerosis, but in only a few patients, has been found when the daily intake was probably 25 to 60 or more milligrams. Between the amount of fluoride that will produce osteosclerosis in humans and the amount obtained by drinking fluoridated water (1 ppm F), there is a safety factor of 8- to 20-fold. . . .

From the animal studies, it appears that the factor of safety between amounts producing skeletal changes and amounts probably taken in when the drinking water contains 1 ppm is about 50-fold. The lower factor of safety estimated from the observations on human subjects is really an expression of the importance of the time of exposure; none of the animal studies extended for periods longer than five years; in contrast, many of the human exposures were known to have gone on for 10 to 20 years or longer.

4. *Doses Producing Enamel Hypoplasia; Factor of Safety in Water Fluoridation.* Detectable enamel hypoplasia in the human is endemic in areas in which the drinking water contains 2 to 5 ppm F or more. In these populations there is no other known toxic effect of fluorides; enamel hypoplasia (mottled enamel) is therefore the most delicate index of fluorosis.

It should be emphasized that the hypoplastic effects of fluorides on the developing tooth enamel can only be produced during the years that the enamel organ is functioning. Once the ameloblasts have completed their task, no mottling can ever appear regardless of amounts of fluorides taken into the body. Once teeth have erupted into the mouth, enamel mottling cannot occur. The histogenesis of mottled enamel and the epidemiological studies that have fixed the relation between ppm F in the drinking water and severity of mottling have been fully presented and discussed in previous AAAS monographs on the dental effects of fluorides. Attention is directed to the extraordinarily precise relation between the community indices (severity of dental fluorosis) and the logarithm of the ppm F in the drinking water. The intersection of the index of fluorosis line with the DMF (caries incidence) line at 1 ppm F gives this concentration the significance of maximal tooth health with minimal hazard. On the basis of the available evidence from human studies, a 2-fold factor of safety exists between levels of fluoride producing enamel hypoplasia and the level of 1 ppm. . . .

A number of investigators in various parts of the world have noted the appearance of endemic mottled enamel in domestic animals. Repeated references have been made to the brittleness of hypoplastic teeth, e.g., the sheep in Iceland that ingest fluoride-containing volcanic dust along with foliage develop a tooth fragility that leaves sharp points on the teeth, known in Iceland as "gaddur" or "spike" tooth. There is a sizable number of experimental studies in which observations of enamel hypoplasia have been recorded. Some of these studies have covered experimental periods of two to four years and a variety of species have been examined: data are available on rats, sheep, pigs, rabbits, cattle, dogs, and monkeys. There is little doubt that amounts less than 10 ppm F in the ration or drinking water will interfere with the activity of enamel-forming cells to the extent of producing easily detectable changes in the tooth surface. Specifically, in periods of 7 to 11 months, dogs (puppies) given about 4 ppm F show enamel changes, and cows given 4 ppm F over periods of 2 to 4.5 years exhibit alterations in the tooth surfaces. There are no studies in which the fluoride dosage is related to mottling, i.e., there are no animal data to compare with the well-established S shaped curve published by Dean and colleagues for human children aged 12 to 14 years. There is no indication as to what experimental animal is best suited for this kind of study, nor whether there is an experimental animal that will respond quantitatively like the human. Once the proper experimental animal is located, an intensive program to discover what factors are important in producing enamel hypoplasia can be undertaken under controlled conditions. . . .

The possibility of acute fatal poisoning is nil. Children drinking fluoridated water will grow normally. No detectable alterations will occur in bone structure: such changes have been found in a small fraction of a population taking 8 times the recommended 1 ppm but there is no evidence that the alterations were harmful. Only a 2-fold factor of safety exists in the case of mottled enamel—yet this response in large groups of children has been so mathematically related to dosage that the prediction can be made with confidence that unesthetic mottling will not be seen. . . .

The Health of Adults. In areas of the country where drinking waters are naturally fluoridated, large population groups have been exposed for generations with no readily evident ill effects (save mottling of the enamel when more than 2 ppm of fluoride are present). Careful epidemiological studies are needed to prove statistically this impression. The growth of men in these areas appears to be normal. McClure found that the average height and body weight of boys and young men in fluoride areas compare favorably with accepted standards. He also recorded the bone fracture experience of about 4,000 young men and found no differences related to how much fluoride had been in the drinking water.

More information is needed on the incidence and severity of diseases such as arthritis that might conceivably have some component of skeletal change involved. More information is needed on the occurrence of anemia, of thyroid disease, of kidney disease, as well as of oral disease. To be valuable, these epidemiological investigations must be conducted with the greatest care. Such studies are expensive. Funds should be made available immediately to carry out these surveys and to back up conclusively the apparent freedom from injury. Let it be emphasized that no one anticipates the uncovering of unsuspected illness that will damn the water fluoridation program; if injuries of such magnitude were present they would have been long since recognized. Almost certainly only minor and insignificant, if any, effects of fluoride will be found; we need the scientific evidence to confirm or confute this opinion. . . .

The best evaluation of the effect on the general health of populations of small amounts of fluoride in the drinking water has been given recently by the Department of Public Health of the State of Illinois. Their conclusions may be quoted: "Mortality statistics show that there is no significant difference in the general death rates between areas where fluoride is present and those where it is absent. Similarly there is no significant difference in the risk of death from specific diseases such as heart, cancer, nephritis and diabetes. . . .

Summary

The four most carefully studied toxic effects of fluorides have been presented in considerable detail. Certain conclusions may be drawn from this mass of evidence.

Adequate factors of safety are unquestionably present so that lethal poisoning will never occur, nor will the growth of children be retarded, nor will bone changes be produced in children or in adults drinking water containing 1 ppm F.

In the case of mottled enamel, the factor of safety is not large, but it is sufficiently great to permit a confident prediction that severe mottling in the form of stained teeth with grooved and pitted surfaces will not be seen. Although the margin of safety for mild mottling is only twofold, this safety factor is established firmly. The mathematical relationship between the severity of mottling and the level of fluoride in the drinking water gives an exceptional reliability to this prediction.

Considerations of the metabolism of fluorides in the body increase our conviction of the safety of water fluoridation. The body possesses two potent detoxification mechanisms: (1) rapid excretion in the urine and (2) rapid storage in the skeleton. Deposition in bone mineral, although it increases the content of fluoride in the body, is harmless per se and is not permanent; mobilization and excretion continuously remove fluoride. Even if all the fluoride ingested in the drinking water (1 ppm) in a lifetime were stored in the skeleton, no injury would thereby accrue.

The ultimate proof of the safety of water fluoridation is the good health of populations drinking fluoride-containing water. At present the most extensive information comes from the Newburgh-Kingston study. Based on the exceptionally detailed pediatric study in which more than 500 children in each city have been examined annually in a program that up to the spring of 1953 had been in existence nearly eight years, it has been concluded that no deleterious systemic effects have occurred. The relatively few observations from fluoride and non-fluoride areas by which it is possible to compare height, body weight, bone fracture experience and death rates from heart disease, cancer, nephritis consistently show no ill effects (save mottling of the enamel from excessive amounts of fluoride).

Conclusion. When all the available evidence is considered, it is our opinion that the health hazards do not justify postponing water fluoridation.

Questions

1. What purpose do Hodge and Smith have in this article and for whom is it intended? Cite evidence to support your statements.
2. The Hodge and Smith article is a fairly typical example of scientific or technical writing. Aside from the use of medical terms (e.g., hypoplasia) what other characteristics of scientific or technical writing do you find?
3. Scientific writing presents difficulties for the lay audience. What are some of these difficulties as you see them in this article? Why then do scientists persist in this style of writing?
4. Can you find any instances where Hodge and Smith have drawn conclusions or presented opinions which are not supported with data?
5. Hodge and Smith use the words *osteoporosis, exostosis, hypoplasia,* and *fluorosis.* Do you know the meaning of these words? Look them up in a

dictionary (along with any others you are not sure of) and find the meanings as used here. Why do you think the authors use such words?

3. Hodge and Smith make several references to a "safety factor." What do they mean by this term and how is it arrived at? What evidence is presented to establish the safety factor?

OUR DRINKING WATER*

Clare E. Hoffman

Mr. HOFFMAN of Michigan. Mr. Speaker, if we assume that fluoridation of our drinking water will prevent decay of our teeth, does it follow that citizens should be deprived of their right to drink unadulterated water if that be their desire?

If the advocates of fluoridation are to have their way, are others who think or who can prove that certain types of food are more nutritious than others, that certain types of clothing are more healthful than other kinds of clothing; that those who can show that certain types of houses are more beneficial to health than other types, follow in the footsteps of the advocates of fluoridation and, by law, force all of the people to either wear what a certain group can show is beneficial to the human race, to live in the kind of a home that is most healthful?

In brief, just how far are we to be forced to accept what might be called "standardization" of our daily lives?

That some are vigorously opposed to fluoridation is evident by the statement carried in a letter from the Dickinson County Anti-Fluoridation Council of Iron Mountain, Mich., under date of May 27, and which reads as follows:

DICKINSON COUNTY
ANTI-FLUORIDATION COUNCIL
Iron Mountain, Mich., May 27, 1954.

HON. CLARE E. HOFFMAN,
Chairman, House Committee on Government Operations,
Washington, D. C.

DEAR SIR: Your letter of May 20, 1954, has been received and contents noted.

* Extension of remarks by Clare E. Hoffman of Michigan in the House of Representatives, Wednesday, May 26, 1954. Reprinted from *The Congressional Record*.

In reply you ask for evidence as to the Communist influence in the Unite
States Public Health Service and here is the outside appearance of it:

1. The utter brutality of the United States Public Health Service in pract
cally demanding that all communities fluoridate, a polite name for poisonir
their public water supplies.

2. This is a must, otherwise the Chief Surgeon General will withhold a
Federal funds and aid to any State or local health units that do not subscrib
to the infallible pronouncements of the United States Public Health Servic

3. The denial of the right to vote by local communities by agents of th
United States Public Health Service operating through local health depar
ments, is a Communist influence.

4. The slow mass poisoning of the entire population of the United Stat
is the main objective of communism.

5. The bulldozing, browbeating, and pressure attempts on all citizens wh
oppose this poisoning of our public water supply is other evidence.

6. Consult the United States Public Health Service payroll for the nam
of the Russian-born and Iron Curtain doctors and dentists and other en
ployees.

7. There is unlimited power conferred on the United States Public Heal
Service under the bill H. R. 7397.

8. Enclosed find brief analysis of the bill H. R. 7397, which we understa
was passed by the House April 28 without any amendments. No wonder v
folks back home wonder why Congress gives the bureaucrats more and mo
power, especially with our health. These so-called doctors in the Publ
Health Service are nothing, in the public opinion, but a bunch of bureaucra
seeking vast political powers and which they do not hesitate to use.

9. The people of this Nation are entitled to protection by Congress agair
the encroachments of their rights as guaranteed to them under the Unite
States and State constitutions against all bureaucrats.

10. For instance, here in Michigan, to illustrate the pressure from t
United States Public Health Service, a Dr. Jay, professor of dentistry at A
Arbor, Mich., and chief propaganda agent of the profluoridation group,
against the people voting on fluoridation and so stated at a public meeting
the Iron Mountain City Hall in the presence of at least 30 people on Septe
ber 26, 1952.

11. At this same meeting, Dr. Wertheimer, of the Michigan State Board
Health, was designated by Dr. Jay as his fighting man, when the writer spo
against fluoridation without the people having permission to vote on t
question.

12. When we questioned the Michigan State Board of Health what w
meant by the statement that "Dr. Wertheimer was their fighting man," the
was no answer.

13. In Des Moines, Iowa, a Dr. Abraham Gelperin, Russian born, a
former United States Public Health Service employee, became their hea
officer. He forced fluoridation on the people of that city, not by popular vo
but through a five-man city commission.

14. There are more Dr. Gilperins scattered throughout the local and St
health boards under the direction of the United States Public Health Servi

15. See the payroll of the United States Public Health Service for more

ltration of Iron Curtain employees and so-called doctors and dentists, who
ame over in the last Roosevelt emigration deluge.

16. Evidence of subversive action by the Communist influence in the
United States Public Health Service is the concentrated effort to fluoridate all
United States military establishments and all areas furnishing either raw
materials or manufactured for the national defense.

17. Further evidence is the secretiveness with which fluoridation is
sneaked in wherever possible without the vote of the people.

18. The vicious attempts to keep the people from voting on socialized
medicine and against a Federal health dictatorship is characteristic of communism.

19. We object to the use of Federal funds to poison the water supplies
throughout the United States and the use of said funds to promote the sales
of poisonous sodium fluoride.

20. Once the damage to public health is done, there is no cure.

21. Enclosed find articles on Grand Rapids, Mich., showing the deplorable
dental situation there.

22. The expenditures of the United States tax funds by the United States
Public Health Service for propaganda advertising the makers of sodium
fluoride poison and dispensing machinery should be prohibited.

23. The outrageous dictatorship of public health by the United States
Public Health Service at Washington, D. C., should be looked into.

24. The United States Public Health Service does not want to know anything about the dangerous poison sodium fluoride or its effects upon the
health of the people. They do not even know the rudiments of chemistry as
pertains to sodium fluoride; still they advocate the use of it. Why? Because
some Communists in the service advocate it.

25. Taken all in all, their propaganda methods are typical of Iron Curtain
tactics, and all their profluoridation actions undermine public health.

Thanking you for your courtesy in this matter, we remain,

Respectfully yours,

DICKINSON COUNTY ANTI-FLUORIDATION COUNCIL,
W. A. HENZE, *Chairman.*

Mr. Speaker, for myself, in my judgment, if we are to have freedom
here in America, people should be permitted to eat, drink, wear, and
live where they may wish—in the type of home they wish—so long as the
practice of their desires does not injuriously affect others.

Just because I have no objections to you putting whatever chemical
you may desire in your drinking water, does not, in my judgment, give
you a right to put whatever you may choose in my drinking water.

Why not let each individual decide for himself what he will do and
how he will live; yes, and how he will think, if he does not harm the rest
of us?

So far as I have been able to learn, decay of the teeth is neither contagious nor infectious, not unless one swaps teeth.

Questions

1. What is the *Congressional Record*? Is it an official government document? How does material get into it? Who reads it?
2. The beginning note has the phrase "Extension of Remarks." What do you think this means?
3. Why is Congressman Hoffman raising the question of fluoridation of the water supply in the U.S. House of Representatives? Is there anything in the first three paragraphs which indicates the congressman's position on fluoridation?
4. What do you think is Hoffman's purpose in reading W. A. Henze's letter into the record? Who is Mr. Henze? Why did he write this letter to Congressman Hoffman?
5. In his opening statement Henze implies that there is evidence of "Communist influence in the United States Public Health Service." Go through the 25 paragraphs of the quoted letter and list all the factual evidence that Henze cites.
6. In paragraphs 6 and 15 Henze refers to "Russian born and Iron Curtain" doctors and dentists and other employees "in the Public Health Service." What connection is he trying to make between these persons and "Communist influence"? Do you find any fallacy in his reasoning? (See Davis, "Logical Fallacies," pp. 608–617.)
7. In paragraph 25 Henze refers to "their propaganda methods." To what is he referring? How would you describe Henze's own methods?
8. Does Congressman Hoffman accept Henze's statement as being true? On what do you base your answer?

FLUORINE AND DENTAL CARIES: An Editorial*

American Public Health Association

[1] It was nearly thirty years ago that Black and McKay demonstrated the relation of an excess of fluorine in drinking water to mottled enamel; and later researches showed that the presence of over 1. p.p.m. of fluorine in a public water supply was definitely associated with the presence of this particular dental condition.

[2] In 1938, Dean, of the U. S. Public Health Service, noted that

* From *American Journal of Public Health*, May, 1954. Copyright 1954 by the American Public Health Association. Reprinted by permission.

among school children, in areas supplied with drinking water of high fluorine content and in which mottled enamel was endemic, incidence of dental caries was noticeably low. The relationship thus suggested was confirmed by chemical studies of the fluorine content of carious and non-carious teeth and by animal experimentation. It seems clear that we have, in this case, an intriguing example of the desirability of maintaining in the human body an optimal concentration of a particular chemical element—a value below this optimum tending to favor one diseased condition and a value above this optimum to cause another disease of a different type. It is possible that data with regard to fluorine content of water and food may explain in part the remarkable freedom from dental caries of certain primitive peoples and the alleged differences in this disease in first and second generation immigrants in this country.

[3] In view of the extensive incidence of dental caries and of the baffling obscurity which has shrouded its causation, these discoveries are of primary importance; and the symposium presented on this subject was one of the highlights of the last A.P.H.A. meeting.

[4] The possibility of controlling the development of dental caries by increasing the fluorine-content of public water supplies deficient in this element is obviously suggested; and Faust and other engineers have pointed out the practicability and economy of such a procedure. It would appear from the extensive studies of the U. S. Public Health Service that a 50 per cent reduction in the incidence of dental caries could be anticipated.

[5] The addition of fluorine to water supplies would, however, chiefly affect the population of the future, since the process is fully effective only on individuals supplied with fluorine during the first eight years of life; and it could obviously influence only those persons served by public water supplies. Bibby and Cheyne in 1942 suggested the direct topical application of fluorides to the permanent teeth of older children. Recent studies have been made by Knutson and Armstrong of the U. S. Public Health Service group, in which the teeth in one quadrant were treated and future development of caries noted and compared with an untreated quadrant as a control. These studies have indicated an approximate 40 per cent reduction in newly developed dental caries as a result of this procedure. The treatment is not effective in checking extension of caries on an individual tooth already attacked. Bibby has recently been a strong advocate of the topical application of fluoride for prevention of caries.

[6] If both the treatment of water supplies and the topical applica
tion of fluorine to the teeth were employed, there would be ample need
for all the conventional facilities in the form of dental service which we
can hope to provide. Gruebbel points out that in one Missouri county
the adequate treatment of carious teeth in children between 6 and 14
years of age would require four-fifths of the time of all the dentists in
the county. The studies of the Committee on the Costs of Medical Care
showed that in 1929—at the peak of peacetime prosperity—the individ
ual in the lower half of the population from an economic standpoint had
on the average one-tenth of a visit to a dentist per year.

[7] If the new knowledge in regard to dental caries can be prac
tically applied it will make a contribution to the health of the people of
the first magnitude. In all new developments of science there arise un
suspected obstacles, and we should always be on guard against any
attempt to exploit them permaturely. The evidence seems, however
sufficiently clear to warrant carefully controlled experiments on "fluo
rinization" of water in communities where the fluorine content of water
is low (which must obviously be continued over a period of years); and
the accumulation by dentists of more extensive evidence as to the effec
tiveness of topical treatment.

Questions

1. This is an editorial. What distinguishes an editorial from other types of
   writing?
2. This editorial appears in the official journal of the American Public Health
   Association. What action is the organization advocating? What weight do
   you attach to its stand? Why?
3. How is this editorial organized? In the light of your answer, how do you
   explain the presence of paragraph 6?
4. Examine the opinions and conclusions presented which begin with these
   statements: "It would appear from extensive studies . . ."; "If the new
   knowledge can be practically applied . . ."; etc. How would you explain
   this cautious wording? What does this tell you about the writer and the
   intended readers?
5. What is the meaning of "topical application" of fluorides? Why does the
   A.P.H.A. recommend both topical application and fluoridation of water
   supplies?

"LOOK, MOM—NO CAVITIES!"*

The Procter & Gamble Co.

"Look, Mom—no cavities!"

Riverside Professional Building

Room 712

Miss Hotchkiss
Ben's teeth are in fine
condition. Not one new cavity

D.D.S.

Norman Rockwell

Simply by switching to Crest with fluoride, you can cut your family's cavity rate almost in half.

Nothing you could do for your family is so simple . . . yet so rewarding . . . as switching them to Crest Toothpaste. Just by making Crest your family toothpaste, you can cut their cavity rate almost in *half*.

We know this—because it's worked this way with thousands of people in tests. The reason is *fluoride*.

You see, Crest has a fluoride formula (called Fluoristan) with the same fluoride dentists put on teeth to prevent cavities. It works the same way. Every Crest brushing puts fluoride right on your teeth. Regular use of Crest means lasting fluoride protection for you and your family—*from toddlers on up.*

Why not switch to Crest today?

Regular use of Crest is advised for every member of the family—including children of all ages.

THE FLUORIDE TOOTHPASTE   Crest TOOTH PASTE—fluoristan

Fluoristan is a trademark for Procter & Gamble's exclusive tooth decay fighter. ©1958, The Procter & Gamble Co.

Questions

Look at the artwork. Who is Norman Rockwell? Can you think of reasons why he might have been hired to illustrate the advertisement?

Notice the card "Ben" is holding. What is it intended to suggest?

What questions would you raise about the statements made in this ad?

* Reprinted by permission.

From THE PROCURATOR OF JUDAEA*

Anatole France

"I also," said Pontius, with a sigh, "I also wished to set afoot public works of great utility. When, for my sins, I was appointed Governor of Judaea, I conceived the idea of furnishing Jerusalem with an abundant supply of pure water by means of an aqueduct. The elevation of the levels, the proportionate capacity of the various parts, the gradient for the brazen reservoirs to which the distribution pipes were to be fixed—I had gone into every detail, and decided everything for myself with the assistance of mechanical experts. I had drawn up regulations for the superintendents so as to prevent individuals from making unauthorized depredations. The architects and the workmen had their instructions. I gave orders for the commencement of operations. But far from viewing with satisfaction the construction of that conduit, which was intended to carry to their town upon its massive arches not only water but health the inhabitants of Jerusalem gave vent to lamentable outcries. They gathered tumultuously together, exclaiming against the sacrilege and impiousness, and, hurling themselves upon the workmen, scattered the foundation stones. Can you picture to yourself, Lamia, a filthier set of barbarians? Nevertheless, Vitellius decided in their favour, and I received orders to put a stop to the work."

"It is a knotty point," said Lamia, "how far one is justified in devising things for the commonweal against the will of the populace."

ASSIGNMENTS

1. In the essay "The Language of Reports" by S. I. Hayakawa (pp. 618–627), the following terms are used: language of report, language of opinion, fact, judgment, "snarl words," "purr words," and slanting. Select any one of the pieces in this project and write a short paper in which you cite examples of each of the above.
2. Read "The Method of Scientific Investigation" by Thomas Henry Huxley (pp. 572–579). Evaluate the Spira and the Hodge and Smith essays point out how closely they do or do not conform to the methods described by Huxley.
3. Consider the statement made by Lamia at the conclusion of the excerpt from "The Procurator of Judaea." What implications does this statement

* From Anatole France, "The Procurator of Judaea," in *Mother of Pearl*. Translated by F. Chapman, 1902.

have for the fluoridation controversy? Be prepared to state your own position and to justify it.

4. Review all the selections in this project. Be prepared to participate in a small discussion group (five to eight students) in which you identify the key problems in the fluoridation issue, evaluate the evidence, and draw whatever conclusions the group can substantiate.

5. Review Dr. Spira's charges that the advocates of fluoridation have failed to check the possible harmful effects. What evidence can you find to confirm or deny his charges? Report your findings to the class.

6. Find out if your community water supply is fluoridated. If so, write a paper in which you give an account of when and how fluoridation was begun and what the results have been. If not, interview at least one public official and one dentist to find out why the water is not fluoridated and write a paper in which you report your findings.

7. Rewrite the paragraph beginning "Occasionally the question is raised" (p. 47) of the Hodge and Smith article for a non-technical audience.

8. The editorial in the *American Journal of Public Health* was written in 1954. Assume you are the editor of the magazine today. Rewrite the editorial in the light of more recent findings.

3. HISTORY

Davy Crockett — Man and Myth

As Irwin Shapiro observes in his preface to *Yankee Thunder*, the "biographer of Davy Crockett is immediately confronted with a problem: which Davy Crockett shall he write about? For if ever there was a man of multiple identity, that man was Davy Crockett."

In his article, "Six Davy Crocketts," Walter Blair makes essentially the same point. He writes: "One who studies what historians say about David Crockett (1786–1836), hunter in the Tennessee canebrakes, Congressman, and hero of the Alamo, will find many contradictions in their interpretations. Some call him a rascal, some call him a hero, and some claim that—in alternate periods—he was each. Outside the history books, a great deal has been written about a mythical Davy Crockett, a legendary giant who . . . accomplishes superhuman feats."

In this project you encounter one kind of problem faced by historians and biographers. What are the facts? Where facts are limited or unavailable, how may inferences be arrived at? Finally, given conflicting evidence, which reconstructions are most valid? Even when there is agreement about the facts, the motives of earlier writers must be assessed. Which evidence has been used by what writers for what purposes? Have selected omissions occurred in the data reported? Why?

The complexities of analyzing Crockett increase when one discovers that statements of fact overlap reports that are a mixture of evidence and political myth-making. Even Crockett's autobiographical writings must be viewed cautiously, for their political overtones also contribute to the mythical Davy. Indeed, a still unresolved literary-historical controversy concerns the extent to which ghost-writers assisted in Crockett's autobiography.

The materials of this project fall into several classifications. The Davy Crockett designed primarily for children emerges from "The Ballad of Davy Crockett," a Walt Disney–created hero who re-achieved renown in 1955 via national television and recordings. The selections by Constance Rourke, folklorist and biographer of Davy Crockett, and

Irwin Shapiro, a writer and collector of legends for children, are from their biographies of Davy Crockett, written for juvenile readers.

Contrasting with the Crockett for juveniles are analyses by scholars. Vernon L. Parrington devotes a brief section of *Main Currents in American Thought*, a three-volume literary and intellectual history of the United States, to David Crockett as man and symbol. Walter Blair, a professor of American literature, describes one historical Crockett, a man who was successively pro- and anti-Andrew Jackson—with all the political ramifications these shifts produced. Finally, James A. Shackford, a Crockett scholar, turns to holographs, court records, public documents, and state archives to produce "the man himself."

Subsequent to Crockett's re-emergence in 1955, popular writers produced articles and books in great numbers. Three of these articles are included here. Kenneth S. Davis' "Coonskin Superman" appeared in *The New York Times Magazine;* John Fischer's statements appeared in *Harper's Magazine;* John Haverstick's "The Two Davy Crocketts" was published in the *Saturday Review*.

Crockett's autobiography is represented by two short excerpts. A commentary on the language used by Crockett is contained in an excerpt from Richard M. Dorson's *American Folklore*.

In working with this project, then, you are in the position of the historian-biographer. To what extent have early and contemporary historians and biographers accurately portrayed the man, David Crockett? To what extent has myth encroached upon reality?

THE BALLAD OF DAVY CROCKETT*

Tom Blackburn

[Stanza 1]
Born on a mountain-top in Tennessee,
Greenest state in the land of the Free,
Raised in the woods so's he knew ev'ry tree,
Kilt him a b'ar when he was only three.

Davy—Davy Crockett,
King of the wild frontier!

[Stanza 6]

Fought single-handed through the Injun War
Till the Creeks was whipped an' peace was in store,
An' while he was handlin' this risky chore,
Made hisself a legend for evermore.
Davy—Davy Crockett,
King of the wild frontier!

[Stanza 8]

Home fer the winter with his family,
Happy as squirrels in the ol' gum tree,
Bein' the father he wanted to be,
Close to his boys as the pod an' the pea.
Davy—Davy Crockett,
Holdin' his young 'uns dear!

[Stanza 15]

He went off to Congress an' served a spell,
Fixin' up the Gover'ment an' laws as well,
Took over Washington so we heerd tell
An' patched up the crack in the Liberty Bell.
Davy—Davy Crockett,
Seein' his duty clear!

[Stanza 18]

When he come home his politickin' done,
The western march had just begun,
So he packed his gear an' his trusty gun,
An' lit out grinnin' to follow the sun.
Davy—Davy Crockett,
Leadin' the pioneer!

[Stanza 19]

He heard of Houston an' Austin an' so,
To the Texas plains he jest had to go,
Where Freedom was fightin' another foe,
An' they needed him at the Alamo.
Davy—Davy Crockett,
The man who don't know fear!

[Stanza 20]

His land is biggest an' his land is best,
From grassy plains to the mountain crest,

He's ahead of us all meetin' the test,
Followin' his legend into the West.
Davy—Davy Crockett,
King of the wild frontier!

Questions

1. Stanza 6 mentions Davy Crockett as a "legend." Do the lyrics of this song encourage the listener to think of Davy Crockett as a legend? If so, how?
2. What purpose might be served by stanza 8 of this song?
3. What implications concerning political philosophy do you find in stanza 15?
4. Would the opening line of stanza 18 produce a different effect if you knew that Davy Crockett's coming home followed a defeat for re-election to Congress? Explain.
5. What reasons are implied in stanza 19 for Crockett's trip to Texas? Why might Blackburn have suggested these motives? Is the tone consistent with the other stanzas of *The Ballad of Davy Crockett*? Explain.

COONSKIN SUPERMAN*

Kenneth S. Davis

As everyone now knows—thanks to Walt Disney's TV series, movie and song about David Crockett—the "king of the wild frontier" was born in Tennessee, "kilt him a b'ar when he was only 3," fought valiantly in the Creek "Injun" War, "patched up the crack in the Liberty Bell" while a Congressman, and died the greatest fighter of all at the Alamo.

The most remarkable thing about this now vastly commercialized legend is that it accords well with the known facts of Davy's life and character.

Born the son of an Irish immigrant in Hawkins County, Tennessee, Aug. 17, 1786, Davy grew to be more than six feet tall, had black hair and a magnificent physique, became a fabulous woodsman and marksman with his long-barreled "Betsy," and had a genius for story telling (the b'ar killing at 3 is typical).

He married a fair-haired, blue-eyed girl named Polly Findlay, kept moving westward with her and his two boys as the country filled up behind him, performed heroically as a scout for Andrew Jackson's army during the Creek War of 1813, was virtually drafted into Tennessee's Legislature, and served three terms as a Democrat in Congress.

* From *The New York Times Magazine*, August 24, 1955. Copyright © 1955 by The New York Times Co. Reprinted by permission.

In Washington he displayed remarkable good sense and such rare moral courage as to make him an authentic spiritual as well as physical American hero.

During his first two terms as a "coonskin" Congressman (1826–1830), two of his slogans became part of the American language. "Be sure you're right," said he, in a phrase of small help to Hamlet types, "then go ahead." He also swore and proved in action that he would "wear no man's collar," not even that of Andy Jackson, whose nefarious Indian Bill—a brutal violation of Indian treaties—he fought tooth and toenail. He also fought Jackson on the public land question, introducing an Administration-opposed bill to protect actual settlers against speculators, who acquired legal but unjust land titles.

Davy was licked on both bills and, opposed by the Jackson men, was narrowly defeated when he ran for re-election in 1830. Two years later, against the same opposition, he won, but was defeated a second time in 1834, whereupon, as some have it, he left Tennessee "in disgust." A more probable motive was his desire for adventure down Texas way, where he joined the company of James Bowie (of Bowie knife fame) and William Travis at the Alamo.

It has been claimed that Davy was one of five survivors who surrendered at the Alamo and were executed by the Mexicans. But a Mrs. Dickenson, who was hidden at the Alamo during the siege and spared by Santa Anna, insisted she saw Crockett lying dead where the last fight had been thickest, his coonskin cap beside him, on March 6, 1836.

Though he boasted he was so ugly he could bring a coon down from a tree with a grin (he once grinned the bark off a knot he'd mistaken for a coon), the evidence is that Crockett was as attractive in appearance as he was magnetic in personality. And if he deliberately promoted his own legend in two autobiographical works he wrote (or dictated, for he was barely literate), the legend, to those who knew him best, seemed consistent with the reality.

Seemingly authentic, for instance, is the story of how Davy, lacking money or credit, managed to stand treat to his thirsty constituents at a "stump-speakin'" when running for his second Congressional term. He traded a coonskin for a quart of rum, then filched the skin from beneath the bar and traded it again, finally obtaining twelve quarts from the Yankee Trader for the same skin—a joke which helped win him the election.

Some forty "Crockett Almanacs" published between 1835 and 1836 contributed to Davy's stature as a backwoods superman, a figure of American mythology like Mike Fink or Paul Bunyan. But Crockett remained a good-natured superman—salty, humorous, even modest in a reverse-English sort of way—and his present revival may be taken as a healthy sign by those who have deplored the vogue of comic-book supermen.

Questions

1. What does Davis mean by describing Crockett's phrase "Be sure you're right, then go ahead" as being of "small help to Hamlet types"?
2. How does Davis describe Jackson's Indian Bill? Why?
3. Why does Davis reject the idea that Crockett left Tennessee in 1834 "in disgust"? Does his alternative suggestion make any difference in assessing Crockett? Explain.
4. Davis uses the verb *filched* to describe Crockett's trick on the Yankee trader. Would other verbs like *stole* or *sneaked* make any appreciable difference in describing the incident? Explain.
5. Davis describes Crockett as standing "treat to his thirsty constituents . . . when running for his second Congressional term." What is the tone of this statement? What was Crockett's purpose in standing treat? How else might this sentence be phrased to produce a different inference?

THE EMBARRASSING TRUTH ABOUT
DAVY CROCKETT*

John Fischer

Admittedly the Chinese are pretty good at retail brainwashing. Given enough time, they apparently can chivvy a few dozen forlorn prisoners into believing almost anything. When it comes to a wholesale operation, however, they still have plenty to learn from the United States.

A bare six months ago, for example, practically all American boys from five to eight were loyal Space Cadets, wholly devoted to blasting each other out of galactic apple trees with their atomic disintegrators. (A few backward types were still in the Hopalong, or chrysalis, stage; but they were merely waiting for their space helmets to arrive from the breakfast-food company.)

Then, almost overnight, two million clean, patriotic youngsters were seduced into switching allegiance. Forgetting all about their sworn duty to defend the planet against swarming Martians, they turned—

* From *Harper's Magazine*, July, 1955. Copyright 1955 by Harper & Row, Publishers. Reprinted by permission.

within the course of a single television program—into Davy Crocketts. Crowned with coonskin, they now infest the trash-can forests and parking-lot prairies from coast to coast, brandishing their Old Betsies in an endless war for the kingship of The Wild Frontier.

Moreover, these infant brain-washees have been bedazzled into worshipping a Crockett who never was—a myth as phony as the Russian legend about Kind Papa Stalin. The historic truth is that Davy Crockett was a juvenile delinquent who ran away from home at the age of thirteen, to dodge a well-deserved licking by his father, a country saloon keeper. For three years he bummed around Baltimore, scratching a living in various ways he never cared to talk about. At eighteen he went to school for six months, while making a pass at a girl who preferred a boy friend who could read, but he gave it up as soon as he found that even the ABCs wouldn't get him to first base. (Later he married a less intellectual woman, whom he deserted after she had produced a small herd of children.) He proved himself—according to accepted historical authority—"a poor farmer, indolent and shiftless." He also was an unenthusiastic soldier: during the Creek War he weaseled his way out of the army by hiring a substitute to fill out his term of service.

Since work was distasteful to Davy, he became, in turn, a backwoods justice of the peace who boasted about his ignorance of law; an unsuccessful politician; a hack writer, heavily dependent on some unidentified ghost; and—hear this, Junior—a violinist. Whenever a steady job threatened, he took to the woods. He never was king of anything, except maybe the Tennessee Tall Tales and Bourbon Samplers' Association. When he claimed that he had shot 105 bear in nine months, his fellow tipplers refused to believe a word of it, on the sensible grounds that Davy couldn't count that high. . . .

Questions

1. What thinking prompted Fischer's use of the title "The Embarrassing Truth about Davy Crockett"?
2. What is Fischer's purpose when he describes "two million clean, patriotic youngsters" as "seduced into switching allegiance"?
3. What effect is intended by the clause "they now infest the trash-can forests"?
4. What are the connotations of "a small herd of children" and "weaseled his way out of the army"?
5. Why does Fischer refer to Crockett as a "violinist" in this article?
6. What is the tone of the two closing sentences? How do they fit into the context of the article?
7. Fischer purports to give the "real facts" about Davy Crockett. What attitude does he expect the reader to take toward his presentation? Discuss.

From DAVY CROCKETT* *Pro*

Constance Rourke
admirer

[1] . . . At the end of the summer Crockett stood again for election. But he had failed to measure the depth of envy and dislike that he had created. Sectional prejudices were rife. His journey to New England was used against him. The concerted force of the Jacksonian party in Tennessee was brought into opposition. Many small schemers were at work; and whatever his faults, Crockett had no aptitude for scheming. It was a savage campaign. Crockett's opponent was Adam Huntsman, whom he had met before in the political field. Huntsman had a wooden leg. Crockett called him Old Timbertoes, and accomplished a few explosive practical jokes at his expense. Huntsman's tactics were on much the same level. The issues at stake for the small farmers, for the struggling frontiersmen, went down in a welter of jokes and personalities, and Crockett was defeated by a narrow margin.

[2] He was by no means friendless; soon after the election a public dinner was given in his honor at the Planter's Hotel in LaGrange, and later testimony shows that he commanded the confidence of men of substantial character in Tennessee. But he had decided to abandon politics. "I have announced through the newspapers that I never expect to offer my name again to the public for any office," he wrote in accepting the invitation to the dinner. "I hope to spend the evening in a social manner, leaving politics out of the question."

[3] Crockett had reached a turning point. In the six or seven years just past his entire course had been changed; he could now hardly return to hunting and farming in the Shakes. All his life he had been on the move, and he had repeatedly gone on from one frontier to another. He made a quick decision. "I'm going to Texas," he said. . . .

Questions

1. Rourke describes a Crockett defeat at the polls. What inference can you draw from sentences 2 through 6 in paragraph 1 about her attitude toward Davy Crockett? Explain.
2. Discuss the connotations in the last three sentences of paragraph 1.

* From Constance Rourke, *Davy Crockett*. Copyright 1934 by Harcourt, Brace & World, Inc.; renewed 1962 by Alice D. Fore. Reprinted by permission of the publishers.

3. In the second paragraph Rourke quotes Crockett as saying, "I never expect to offer my name again to the public for any office." How does she
use this quotation to characterize Davy Crockett? How might a less sympathetic biographer use this quotation to establish an entirely different
impression?
4. Rourke describes Davy Crockett as a man who "had repeatedly gone on
from one frontier to another." In what different senses might she be using
the word *frontier*? What motive might have prompted this statement in
its context?

THE TWO DAVY CROCKETTS* anti

John Haverstick

[1] . . . We might as well say right off that [there] are two different
versions of Davy Crockett and that, although we can't be sure where
Mr. Disney got his, we do know where we got ours. Ours is the Vernon
L. Parrington-Dictionary of American Biography-Standard Encyclopedia version. Perhaps Mr. Disney got his Davy from an erudite article
by Walter Blair in *The Southern Review*[1] of July 1940.

[2] In that article Mr. Blair points out that there were actually six
different Davy Crocketts, one real and the rest built on top of that one
by Davy's political backers and by his political opponents—some of
whom praised and some of whom damned the original Davy during his
lifetime. For the Disney Davy is a pretty big fellow right from the beginning. He was born on a mountain-top and he killed a bear at the age
of three. Before too long he is fighting the Creek Indian War single-
handed, fixing up the Government almost single-handedly as a Congressman, and, though not quite single-handedly this time, dying a
hero's death at the Alamo.

[3] Our Davy Crockett was born in Limestone—or else in Rogers-
ville or perhaps in Hawkins County or Greene County, since encyclo-
pedias differ—all in Tennessee, in 1786, and did none of these things
precisely as Mr. Disney describes them. He never finished the Creek
Indian War; he was a downright bumbler as a Congressman, and he
only managed to get to the Alamo because he was something of a sore-
head. "Strip away the shoddy romance that has covered up the real

* From *Saturday Review*, July 9, 1955. Copyright © 1955 by Saturday Review,
Inc. Reprinted by permission.
[1] Mr. Haverstick is in error. The journal in question is the *Southwest Review*
[Eds.].

man," says Mr. Parrington in his "Main Currents of [sic] American Thought," "and the figure that emerges is one familiar to every backwoods gathering, an assertive, opinionated, likable fellow, ready to fight, drink, dance, shoot, or brag, the biggest frog in a very small puddle, first among the Smart Alecks of the canebrakes." Then Mr. Parrington adds, "Davy was a good deal of a wag, and the best joke he ever played is the one he played upon posterity that has swallowed the myth whole and persists in setting a romantic halo on his coonskin cap."

[4] We were somewhat disconcerted by this information, so we turned quickly to the Dictionary of American Biography. "In the Creek War of 1813–1814," William J. Ghent tells us there, "he served with distinction as a scout but retired before the end of the campaign, hiring a substitute to fill out his term of enlistment." We turned immediately to one of Davy's most ardent admirers, Miss Constance Rourke. But she was not much help. "The next movements of Crockett make a small riddle," admits Miss Rourke. "His horse had been crippled by this last hard ride against the Creeks, but the wish to save a valued animal can hardly account for his journey to Tennessee after this battle. The six months of service which Jackson had demanded had not yet passed, nor even the sixty days which Crockett and some others had promised."

[5] Not wanting to shatter our illusions completely, we turned next to a children's reference book, Compton's Pictorial Encyclopedia. But even here it was easy to see that Congressman Crockett was a political buffoon. "Crockett's fight against Jackson [over Indian rights]," it says, "made him a favorite of the Whig party. The Whigs saw in him a chance to create an opponent to Jackson with the same backwoods appeal as Jackson . . . Crockett did not realize he was being used in this fashion and he went along, believing all that the shrewd Whigs told him." So we turned back to Parrington. "When Davy first went to Congress," Mr. Parrington says, "he was anti-tariff and had won his seat on that issue; but he was invited to Lowell (Mass.), shown an idyllic picture of contented and prosperous millhands, dined, given a prepared table of statistics proving how industrialism is calculated not only to give individual happiness and prosperity, but to add to our national wealth and prosperity, and bidden Godspeed in the work of spreading the true gospel among the honest, simple-minded, and patriotic frontiersmen. After having been presented by Mr. Lawrence with a fine suit of domestic broadcloth Davy would have been an ingrate not to vote for a protective tariff." Then, dispelling all Disney illusions, Mr. Parrington adds, "But alas! the opportunity [to vote for a protective tariff] never came. A backwoods constituency that had never been dined

by Lowell capitalists and had little use for fine broadcloth, a constituency that persisted in throwing up coonskin caps for Old Hickory in spite of Lowell statistics, resented his apostasy from the Democratic faith and at the next election invited him to stay in the canebrakes. . . . In a fit of anger he quitted his family and the state of Tennessee, went off on the mad chase to Texas, and in March of the next year fell at the Alamo. Vain, ignorant Davy Crockett!"

[6] We must confess that we had liked Mr. Disney's Davy so much that we felt completely flattened by Mr. Parrington's. But we slept on it and now feel much better. We have even decided that we have grown rather fond of Mr. Parrington's Davy. Less impressive, perhaps. But more human.

[7] We see no reason why our Davy couldn't shoot bears, kill Indians with the butt of his rifle, and still be a failure as a soldier and a Congressman. In fact, we rather prefer him that way. . . .

Questions

1. Haverstick compares his sources on the subject of Davy Crockett with a possible source used by Walt Disney. Which does he prefer? Why? How do you know?
2. What source does Haverstick obviously accept as most useful and accurate? Does he cite supporting evidence for any of the judgments he accepts? Explain.
3. Why does Haverstick begin paragraph 5 with the statement "Not wanting to shatter our illusions completely . . ."?
4. Why does Haverstick say he has "grown rather fond of Mr. Parrington's Davy"?

DAVY CROCKETT*

Richard M. Dorson

[1] Curiously the boom that first catapulted Davy Crockett to national fame in the 1830's repeated itself in 1955. The Tennessee bearhunter originally captured national attention through a cascade of manufactured publicity. From the stimulus provided by the television and cinema films of Walt Disney, Crockett again became known to millions of Americans. A juvenile audience relishes the motheaten conception of the frontier hero who fights Indians, kills b'ar, and dies

* From Richard M. Dorson, *American Folklore*. Copyright © 1959 by The University of Chicago Press. Reprinted by permission.

gloriously. But that image of Davy bears only a small and skimpy resemblance to his fabulous nineteenth-century portrait.

[2] The process of legend-building began with the election of the backwoodsman to Congress in 1827. Already in the 1820's journalists and travelers had noticed a new kind of American, an "original" cradled and nurtured in the trans-Appalachian clearings, half a horse and half an alligator, with an added touch of snapping turtle. Now this b'ar-hunter had marched head on into the nation's capital as duly elected representative of the people. The press found delicious copy in reporting his alleged quips and gaucheries. When Crockett broke with Andrew Jackson, his fellow westerner, for opposing the Bank of the United States, the Whig party eagerly embraced this potential vote-getter from the newly enfranchised West. Publicists went to work to exalt further the salty personality of their recruit, whose backwoods wisdom was turned towards praise of Whig policies and abuse of the Democrats. This ferment culminated in popular books that crystallized further the image of Crockett.

[3] The *Sketches and Eccentricities of Colonel David Crockett of West Tennessee* (1833) brought together in patchwork fashion ephemeral anecdotes that had circulated in the papers and by word of mouth. . . . Throughout the book Davy crows and brags in the western tradition. He boasts how his powerful grin could bring a coon down from a tree, although on one occasion he mistook a knothole for a coon's eye and grinned all the bark off. A rumor spread that the President had authorized Davy to wring the tail off a comet.

[4] Presumably to counteract the misrepresentations of the anonymous author in the *Sketches,* Crockett next year took up pen himself to set the record straight in an *Autobiography.* Thomas Chilton, Congressman from Kentucky, collaborated with him on this new work, which contributed further to the burgeoning legend and would eventually win a permanent place in American literature. A connected narrative and a taut style replace the loose and scrappy composition of the *Sketches,* although some of the same expressions and anecdotes remain. Davy continues to brag western fashion and to despise skinflint Yankees. What especially gives sauce and tang to the *Autobiography* is a wealth of homespun proverbial expression. Crockett customarily speaks and thinks in vivid metaphor: as dry as a powder horn; as cool as Presbyterian charity; as thick as Kentuck land titles; as sharp as a steel trap, and as bright as a pewter button; as little use as pumping for thunder in dry weather. To make his point he invokes old saws and adages: salting the cow to catch the calf; a fool for luck, and a poor

man for children; a new country where every skin hangs by its own
tail; a short horse is soon curried. He indulges in far-fetched hyperbole:
"we would give him a little of the hurricane tipp'd with thunder";
"lean, lank, labbersided pups, that are so poor they have to prop up
again a post-and-rail fence, 'fore they can raise a bark"; "a chap just
about as rough hewn as if he had been cut out of a gum log with a
broad-ax"; "had brass enough in his face to make a wash kettle." Davy's
sayings express the personality coming to focus in the two books, a
self-reared woodsman, courageous physically and morally, "determined
to stand up to my lick-log, salt or no salt." . . .

[5] In the almanacs the heroic and the comic aspects of Davy are
sharply drawn. The tales concentrated on his prowess as a hunter
and fighter, his hostility to Yankees and sharpers, his salty and extravagant speech. Eventually the characterization reached the point of caricature; the language dissolves into absurd misspellings, the adventures
move to faroff lands and fantastic climaxes. . . ."

[6] For all their disjointed and uneven quality, the almanacs display consistent themes and attitudes. The Crockett they create speaks
with the brash and strident voice of Jacksonian America. Davy represents frontier crudity, violence, anti-intellectualism, chauvinism, and
racism. He butchers the varmints of the forest, sneers at book learning
and educated Easterners, despises niggers, Injuns, and Mexicans, and
arrogantly trumpets the supremacy of Uncle Sam in foreign lands. Confronted by the Emperor of Haiti, whose black subjects were all abjectly
kneeling, Davy announced, "I am Col. Davy Crockett, one of the sovereign people of Uncle Sam, that never kneels to any individual this
side of sunshine." Then when the Emperor ordered his field hands
against the stranger, he demolished the whole army with two sun-dried
sugarcanes. In the name of freedom and patriotism, Davy rants and
kills. Those characteristics which Frederick Jackson Turner associated
with frontier society emerge in garish colors in the almanacs; Crockett
is self-reliant and individualistic, scornful of cultural institutions, intensely confident and braggart, and a thorough nationalist.

Questions

1. How does Dorson explain the early nineteenth-century reputation of Davy
   Crockett? Does Dorson see any similarities in Davy's twentieth-century
   fame?
2. Why does Dorson begin his fourth paragraph with the word *presumably*?
   Would deletion of the word modify the impact of that sentence?
3. Dorson describes Crockett as taking "up pen himself to set the record
   straight in an *Autobiography*." He then adds, "Thomas Chilton, Congress-

man from Kentucky, collaborated with him . . ." Does this juxtaposition
of sentences seem unusual to you?
4. What is Dorson's major judgment about Crockett's use of language? Does
he support his judgment to your satisfaction? Explain.

THE DAVY CROCKETT MYTH*

anti

foundation

Vernon L. Parrington

[1] *The Narrative of the Life of David Crockett of the State of Tennessee* was woven from the same stuff that Longstreet made use of, but
the fabric is of far better texture. It is the great classic of the southern
frontier, far more significant than *Georgia Scenes*, far more human and
vital. Realistic in method, it is romantic in spirit. In its backwoods
vernacular it purveys the authentic atmosphere of the cabin and the
canebrake; it exhibits the honesty, the wit, the resourcefulness, the
manly independence of a coonskin hero; it reveals, in short, under
the rough exterior of a shiftless squatter and bear-hunter, qualities that
are sterling in every society where manhood is held in repute. It is an
extraordinary document, done so skillfully from life that homespun becomes a noble fabric and the crudest materials achieve the dignity of
an epic. . . .

[2] Romantic America found a new hero and Davy Crockett reaped
a surprising reward. He had the good fortune to preëmpt the romance
of the backwoods, to file on an unsurveyed tract of western life, and
when the lines were run it was found that his claim embraced all that
was native and picturesque along the Mississippi frontier. Popular imagination seized upon him and endowed the mighty hunter of the canebrakes with the fugitive romance that had been gathering for years.
He was erected into a mythical figure that drew to itself the unappropri-
ated picturesque that sprang spontaneously from the crude western life.
How this astonishing result came about, how good fortune came to
single out Davy Crockett for her smiles, offers a somewhat amusing
commentary on the ways of an unsophisticated generation.

[3] That in its later development, if not in the beginning, the Davy
Crockett myth was a deliberate fabrication scarcely admits of doubt,
nor that its immediate purpose was frankly partisan. It did not spring

---

from the soil of the Tennessee canebrakes; it was created at Washington. It was not the spontaneous product of popular imagination; it was the clever work of politicians. The successive stages through which it passed in its triumphant progress can be traced fairly accurately with the aid of a little historical imagination. Roughly they were three; the exploitation of Davy's canebrake waggery, the exploitation of his anti-Jackson spleen, and the exploitation of his dramatic death at the Alamo. . . .

[4] It was the politicians who contributed most to the success of the myth. They exploited Davy as a convenient weapon against Jackson, saw their work prosper beyond all expectation, get out of their hands, enlarge itself to a cento of backwoods romance and pass into folklore. It was an unforeseen outcome that must have been vastly amusing to those who set the thing going.

[5] The early thirties, it will be remembered, were robustious times when broadcloth in politics had suddenly gone out of style and homespun had come in. The new coonskin democracy had descended upon Washington, and picturesque figures provided with ample plugs of tobacco were making themselves free with Congressional perquisites. Nothing like it had been seen before in the city of dignified politicians, and the spectacle must have delighted the wags of the capital. But to the members of the overthrown dynasty the Jacksonian votes which these picturesque backwoodsmen represented were very far from amusing. The loss of desirable offices was a hard lesson that taught them the need of catering to this new element of the great American democracy. In their remunerative occupation as representatives of the prosperous and genteel constituencies of the East, the old-school politicians had too long overlooked the power of the plain voter which the progress of manhood suffrage was daily increasing. Hence began a desperate campaign to counteract the Jacksonian appeal. The coonskin vote could no longer be ignored and shrewd plans were laid to capture the backwoods for the new Whig party. The program of internal improvements was well enough in its way, and the old Revolutionary cry of the sword and the purse might prove useful, but the party needed a picturesque figure to draw the coonskin democracy to its standard. Men rather than principles appealed to the West, self-made men, speaking the western vernacular, imbibing western views with their whisky, uncorrupted by broadcloth. This explains the tremendous Whig hurrah over log cabins and hard cider that marked a later campaign; and this explains likewise the singular fate that overtook Davy Crockett, the bear-hunter from the canebrakes.

[6] Davy had first come to Washington during Adam's administration, and in four years' loafing and boasting at the Congressional bar had achieved some distinction as a picturesque original with the tongue of a wag. He spoke rarely in the House and the few records in the *Congressional Debates* are sadly commonplace. Until after he broke with Jackson his political influence at Washington was negligible. But that fortunate break was the beginning of his fame. He had unwittingly made himself. He had become a valuable asset to the Whig party. To find a native Tennessean, a real coonskin democrat, one who had served under Jackson and been sent to Congress as a Jacksonian, as authentic a Westerner as the General himself, at bitter personal odds with Old Hickory, ready to talk out in meeting and eager to repudiate the latter's attack upon the Bank, was a find indeed to the hard-pressed Whigs; and they would have been no politicians if they had not used what God sent. In consequence Davy soon found himself talked about. His picturesque eccentricities began to be exploited. His rugged western honesty was applauded; his shrewd backwoods intelligence was praised; his frontier humor was skillfully touched up; his characteristic motto, "go ahead," was seized upon as an expression of the progressive spirit of the lusty young Whig party. In short he was speedily turned into a myth by ways not unknown in our time, and sent forth as useful campaign material in the fight for political righteousness. Davy was vastly surprised at his sudden rise to fame. He had never realized how great a man he was; but he accepted it as an agreeable fact and went ahead. . . .

[7] He began to take himself seriously and set about the business of propagating the myth. . . .

[8] . . . The loquacious Davy joined heartily with his managers to cash in on his reputation. His egotism was played upon at every turn and he was quite unconscious that he had become a mere cat's paw to pull Whig chestnuts out of the coals. He was paraded at meetings with Daniel Webster, given great dinners, applauded for his rustic wit and homespun honesty, presented with a fine rifle; and he seems never to have realized how grossly he was being exploited. His self-esteem was proof against disillusionment and he accepted the applause greedily. Wherever he went he was taken in charge by the young Whigs. Everything was carefully arranged beforehand. News was sent forward that he was coming; crowds were gathered to greet him; publicity was attended to; morning, noon, and night he was invited to speak, and the speeches were carefully reprinted—not the authentic speeches, prob-

ably, but good campaign material nevertheless. It was a gratifying experience and Davy swelled up like a turkey cock.

[9] As a result of his tour he was immensely strengthened in his new political faith and became a staunch nationalist. When he first went to Congress he was anti-tariff and had won his seat on that issue; but he was invited to Lowell, shown an idyllic picture of contented and prosperous mill-hands, dined, given a prepared table of statistics proving how industrialism "is calculated not only to give individual happiness and prosperity, but to add to our national wealth and prosperity," and bidden Godspeed in the work of spreading the true gospel among the honest, simple-minded and patriotic frontiersmen. After having been presented by Mr. Lawrence with a fine suit of domestic broadcloth, Davy would have been an ingrate not to vote for a protective tariff. But alas! the opportunity never came. A backwoods constituency that had never been dined by Lowell capitalists and had little use for fine broadcloth, a constituency that persisted in throwing up coonskin caps for Old Hickory in spite of Lowell statistics, resented his apostasy from the Democratic faith and at the next election invited him to stay in the canebrakes. The gorgeous bubble was pricked. Davy had expanded under prosperity and could not now endure adversity. In a fit of anger he quitted his family and the state of Tennessee, went off on the mad chase to Texas and in March of the next year fell at the Alamo. Vain, ignorant Davy Crockett! A simple-minded frontiersman, he went down to Jericho and fell among thieves, and when they were done with him they left him despoiled politically but invested with a fame that has grown to this day. After his death other hands took up the work, wove around his name the humor and romance of the frontier, and made of him a legendary figure. It would have pleased Davy to know how the myth had prospered. . . .

[10] The real Davy was very far from romantic. An honest picture of the Tennessee democracy in its native habitat would reveal few idyllic features. It was a slovenly world and Davy was pretty much of a sloven. Crude and unlovely in its familiar details, with its primitive courtships and shiftless removals, its brutal Indian campaign and fierce hunting sprees, its rough equality, its unscrupulous politics, its elections carried by sheer impudence and whisky, the autobiography reveals the backwoods Anglo-Irishman as an uncivilized animal, responding to simple stimuli, yet with a certain rough vigor of character. Wastefulness was in the frontier blood, and Davy was a true frontier wastrel. In the course of successive removals he traversed the length of Tennessee, drinking, hunting, talking, speculating, begetting children, scratching

a few acres of land to "make his crap," yet living for the most part off the country; and his last squatting place on the Obion River, seven miles from the nearest neighbor, was as primitive as the first. Willing to endure almost incredible hardships to obtain a keg of gunpowder to celebrate Christmas, risking his skin to kill a bear with a butcher knife, he was never much given to mending fences or enlarging his plow lands. He was a hunter rather than a farmer, and the lust of killing was in his blood. With his pack of hounds he slaughtered with amazing efficiency. A later generation would call him a game-hog. His family must have had Gargantuan appetites to have consumed one-tenth of the meat that fell before his beloved Betsy; the rest went to the dogs and hogs and buzzards. His hundred and five bears in a single season, his six deer shot in one day while pursuing other game—two of which were left hanging in the woods—serve to explain why the rich hunting grounds of the Indians were swept so quickly bare of game by the white invaders. Davy was but one of thousands who were wasting the resources of the Inland Empire, destroying forests, skinning the land, slaughtering the deer and bear, the swarms of pigeons and turkey, the vast buffalo herds. Davy the politician is a huge western joke, but Davy the wastrel was a hard, unlovely fact.

[11] Strip away the shoddy romance that has covered up the real man and the figure that emerges is one familiar to every backwoods gathering, an assertive, opinionated, likable fellow, ready to fight, drink, dance, shoot or brag, the biggest frog in a very small puddle, first among the Smart Alecks of the canebrakes. Davy was a good deal of a wag, and the best joke he ever played he played upon posterity that has swallowed the myth whole and persists in setting a romantic halo on his coonskin cap. . . .

Questions

1. How does Parrington account for Davy Crockett's early reputation? Is this account complimentary to Crockett?
2. According to Parrington, Davy's political influence stemmed from his break with popular Andrew Jackson. Explain Parrington's reasoning.
3. Parrington writes: "Davy was vastly surprised at his sudden rise to fame. He had never realized how great a man he was; but he accepted it as an agreeable fact . . ." Describe Parrington's tone here. What is he trying to communicate? Illustrate other examples of similar tone in this essay.
4. In the eighth paragraph Parrington uses the word "loquacious" and the phrase "to cash in." What effect are they designed to produce? Are there similar uses of such language in the rest of the paragraph? Explain.
5. Why does Parrington report the detail about Crockett being presented "with a fine suit of domestic broadcloth" (paragraph 9)?

6. Does Parrington support the closing words of the tenth paragraph: "Davy the wastrel was a hard, unlovely fact"?
7. What does Parrington mean in his closing sentence? Explain fully.

SIX DAVY CROCKETTS*

Walter Blair

[1] One who studies what historians say about David Crockett (1786 to 1836), hunter in the Tennessee canebrakes, Congressman, and hero of the Alamo, will find many contradictions in their interpretations. Some call him a rascal, some call him a hero, and some claim that—in alternate periods—he was each. Outside the history books, a great deal has been written about a mythical Davy Crockett, a legendary giant who still lives and accomplishes superhuman feats. It has seemed worth while to examine the documents about this man to find out the reason for these contradictory versions.

[2] The basic fact that emerges from such a study is that one source of information about a man active in politics in the 1830's—the newspaper—in this instance may easily confuse the scholar. The reason, probably, is that in journals of the day Crockett was unmercifully exploited for political purposes. Journalists use him thus, I think, because he happened to offer very good material for a type of political argument which was being discovered in his heyday—the argument based on the great respect in America for mother wit. Most of what was written about the man, in other words, was definitely shaped to appeal to the national love for gumption.

[3] The image the name of Crockett conjures up today is, it appears, anything but that of a person tied up with a virtue so unimaginative as horse sense. The Tennessean, as he is now recalled, is a backwoods demigod, a fabulous hunter and fighter wafted to immortality in the rifle smoke of the Alamo. And the frontier yarnspinners created an even more fantastic figure than people now recall. In the 1830's and 1840's, a series of almanac stories, some of them written by Crockett's one-time neighbors, set forth details of a biography which claimed that even when he was born, Davy was the biggest infant that ever was and a little the smartest that ever will be; that, watered with buffalo milk and

weaned on whiskey, he grew so fast that soon his Aunt Keziah was saying it was as good as a meal's vittles to look at him. . . .

[4] But there was a quirk of Crockett's character, in real life, which made frontier folk elect him and re-elect him to the state legislature and to the United States House of Representatives. That he was poor, that he was uneducated, made no difference to them: they thought he could get along because they guessed he had good horse sense. This fact suggests the paradox of Crockett's renown. He won fame and office because he had horse sense; he remained famous because of the nonsense associated with his memory. How this came about is an interesting story.

[5] The pre-eminent rôle of horse sense in Crockett's rise to fame is made clear in the account of his first activity in government, which appeared in the book purporting to be his autobiography. This book shows that he reached manhood in a sparsely settled part of Tennessee after suffering only four days of schooling; then, as a man, he went to school perhaps a hundred days. "In that time," he says, "I learned to read a little in my primer, to write my own name, and to cypher some in the three first rules in figures. And this is all the schooling I ever had in my life. . . ."

[6] This untaught man was living with his second wife and their children in a clearing on Shoal Creek when, about 1818, the people of the district decided they had to have a temporary government. So, he says,

. . . we met and made what we called a corporation, and I reckon we called it wrong. . . . we lived in the backwoods, and didn't profess to know much, and no doubt used many wrong words. But we met, and appointed magistrates and constables to keep order. We didn't fix any laws for them, tho'; for we supposed they would know law enough, whoever they might be; and so we left it to themselves to fix the laws.

Appointed one of the magistrates, Colonel Crockett carried on his work in a way which would have made any lawyer shiver with horror, but which seemed to him sensible enough. When he wanted to judge a man, he would say to his constable, "Catch that fellow, and bring him up for trial." This seemed a proper way to do things, he says, "for we considered this a good warrant, even if it was only in verbal writings."

[7] In time, the legislature gave the district a more formal government, and Crockett, now a squire, had the task of writing out warrants and recording proceedings, a chore which was, he said, "at least a huckleberry over my persimmon." Helped by his constable, though, the squire eventually learned to put everything in writing. His procedure

was still a bit irregular, but this irregularity troubled the officer not a whit. The account of his squireship ends with a smug summary:

My judgments were never appealed from, and if they had been they would have stuck like wax, as I gave my decisions on the principles of common justice and honesty between man and man, and relied on natural born sense, and not on law learning to guide me; for I had never read a page in a law book in all my life.

[8] From that time the Colonel moved onward and upward, running for elective offices and winning campaigns which would have ended in dismal beatings anywhere except in a section where book learning was thought less of than mother wit. When, for instance, in 1821, he offered for the legislature, he had read no newspapers, had never seen a public document, could not make a speech about governmental affairs. But this tall hunter in buckskin could knock down plenty of squirrels at a neighborhood hunt and, between horns of chain-lightning whiskey, he could tell good stories; so he more than doubled the vote of his rival. After another session in the state legislature, in 1827 he offered for the United States Congress, told more jokes, passed around horns of the creature to possible supporters, "not to get elected of course," he said righteously, "for that would be against the law; but just . . . to make themselves and their friends feel their keeping a little." . . .

[9] . . . It is hardly necessary to say that the first Crockett, the flesh and blood being who was born in Tennessee, who married, had children, and went to Congress, was no figment of the imagination. People who saw him—a man more than six feet tall, broad-shouldered, red-cheeked, black-haired, dressed in buckskin—had no feeling that he was an impalpable spirit. An old gaffer who had heard him speak in the Big Hatchie district in the late 'twenties had no doubts, two score years later, about having heard a speech which was "plain and sensible . . . with now and then a dry, witty allusion to his educated opponents, which would bring thunders of applause."

[10] But though Crockett the First offered no difficulty to people who saw and heard the man, keen Americans of the time who learned of Davy only through the newspapers may have had trouble believing that the backwoodsman was any more real, say, than a character in a joke book story. The reason was that, shortly after the Tennessean started to Congress, newspaper wags began to print tales about him which were more fictional than factual. . . .

[11] By contrast with Crockett the First, presumably created by God, Crockett the Second and Crockett the Third were created, then, by anti-Jackson papers and pro-Jackson papers, respectively. Crockett the

Second was a Westernized version of a fool character like the one Benjamin Franklin had used to advocate, in such a futile fashion, the hateful policies of the British; Crockett the Third was a Westernized version of Poor Richard, uneducated but rich in common sense gained by experience. These propagandistic versions of the frontiersman were just getting established when the real Davy did something which caused the two sets of political journalists to bring out clean canvases and start new pictures of him.

[12] He changed sides—joined the anti-Jackson forces. And that, eventually, meant the creation of a Crockett the Fourth and a Crockett the Fifth.

[13] The pro-Jackson papers, in this second period (from January, 1829, when the Colonel switched allegiance, until his death in 1836), turned the picture of Crockett the Third—of a bumptious but canny frontiersman—to the wall. In its place they hung a picture of Crockett the Fourth. The new portrait drew some details from the earlier anti-Jackson portraits; it showed "the coon killer, the Jim Crow of Congressmen, the buffoon of the House of Representatives . . . the authorized Whig jester." These were the titles bestowed on Crockett by the New York *Times,* in one vituperative editorial. The Washington *Globe* emphasized the man's alleged grossness by ironically calling him "Dainty Davy."

[14] But the Jacksonians added new touches which made the backwoodsman not only stupid and clownish but also vicious. James K. Polk, for example, prepared for Tennessee newspapers five articles, signed "Several Voters" and so written that they seemed to come from Davy's constituents. They claimed that Crockett had often missed House meetings, that he had done "literally nothing" for the poor in his district. And they stressed a detail constantly emphasized in the new portrait in various papers—that the Congressman had been bought out and used as a tool. Similarly, the Washington *Globe,* the official Jackson organ, made much of the enlistment by the opposition of "mercenaries," with Crockett as the "first recruit." Frequent mention of "David Crockett & Co." suggested organization on a commercial basis. Jackson, now President, stormed at his enemies and "Crockett their tool," and often spoke of "Crockett & Co."

[15] The anti-Jacksonites in turn set up their picture of Crockett the Fifth, akin to Crockett the Third, but greatly added to the earlier suggestion of their subject's shrewdness. He now became a homespun oracle, outraged by the horrible carryings-on of the party in power and capable of attacking them with telling digs because he was so abun-

dantly blessed with unerring horse sense. Aphorisms headed "Crockett's Latest"—shrewd witticisms hurled at the Jackson crowd—came out in the newspapers. . . .

[16] Late in 1833, the Congressman from Tennessee sent to the newspapers an announcement that he was very angry about the way he had been misrepresented, particularly in a book which retold many newspaper stories about him. He was therefore going to write an autobiography, to "strive to represent myself, as I really am, a *plain, blunt, Western man,* relying on honesty and the woods, and not on learning and the law, for a living." In February, 1834, he had his preface ready, and it too was sent to the papers. It repeated the charge that people had been so misled by portrayals of him that they had "expressed the most profound astonishment at finding me in human shape, and with the *countenance, appearance,* and *common feelings* of a human being. It is to correct all these false notions . . . that I have written." When the book, titled *A Narrative of the Life of David Crockett,* appeared, the Boston *Transcript* said of it that it was the "Simon Pure edition," published to correct lies about Crockett cooked up by "the roguish wags of the Capitol."

[17] The newspaper notice makes it clear that the *Narrative* was part of the campaign of the anti-Jackson forces to show Davy as a normal being, worthy of much respect. This "plain, homespun account," as its author called it, was, in other words, a full-length portrait of the Crockett the Fifth sketched in friendly newspapers. The same politically useful character appeared also in *An Account of Col. Crockett's Tour to the North and Down East* (1835). Here is a blunt, honest man, pathetically misrepresented—a man so chockful of mother wit and humor, however, that he can laughably state the obvious case against his rivals. . . .

[18] Crockett's partisans urged readers to believe that the Crockett the Fifth of these two books was the real article—Crockett the First. "Veracity," said one newspaper firmly, "is stamped on every page." But the matter is open to doubt. The public figure of the man is so well fitted to political appeals that one suspects the character is at least partly assumed. In fact, anyone looking for a beginner of the tradition of the "just folks" politician in America will do well to study the case of the coonskin Congressman.

[19] And all the credit, in the end, will not go to Davy, since both books clearly were touched up by collaborators (both of whom have been identified) eager to give the writings partisan usefulness. A result is that almost anywhere you look for Crockett the First you are baffled. In the Congressional records you will find speeches which obviously

vere doctored up before they were printed. Authentic letters in the Colonel's own hand show, first, that they support the guess that his other writings have been thoroughly edited, and second, that they do not offer a sure basis for guessing at his character.

[20] Hence, as has been suggested, historians have trouble dealing with the details about this man's life; they study the documents and announce findings which vary a great deal. "Restless, assertive, unsocial . . obsessed with the faith that better land lay farther west, cultivating a bumptious wit . . ." says one, "he was only an improvident child who fled instinctively from civilization." He was "the incipient poor white," says another, with "the elements of decay in him." Another finds that he was a valiant hunter, an efficient farmer, a farseeing legislator, and a heroic warrior. Still another cannot explain him except as a split personality. The one thing that is sure is that a clean-cut image of him was fogged up by the factional portraits all labeled with his name. . . .

[21] . . . Crockett the Sixth, the mythical demigod whose fantastic life history was unfolded in the almanacs . . . had little or no political value, and the happenings in his comic career leaped from the green earth into a backwoods fairlyland. . . .

[22] The folk mind, in short, refusing to be misled by the political propaganda associated with Crockett the First, the Second, the Third, the Fourth and the Fifth, in time made known the People's Choice for immortality—the only consistent character it could find in a mess of contradictory portraits, Crockett the Sixth. And today, if you get far enough away from paved roads and roadside pop stands in Tennessee and Kentucky and sit by the fire with backwoods yarnspinners, you will learn that this Crockett, somewhere or other, is still carrying out his boasts in superhuman ways.

Questions

. What major generalization does Blair suggest in the opening two paragraphs? Why does he caution anyone studying David Crockett?

. Blair plays with the terms *horse sense* and *nonsense* at the end of the fourth paragraph. What is he suggesting? Does he make a persuasive case for his beliefs? Explain.

. Colonel Crockett is described as passing "around horns" (of whiskey) and quoted as saying that this action was "not to get elected of course . . . but just . . . to make themselves and their friends feel their keeping a little." What are Blair's reasons for this quotation?

. According to Blair, why were Crockett the Fourth and Fifth created? How much credence does Blair give to these portraits of Crockett? Why?

. What does Blair's attitude seem to be toward Crockett the Sixth? Why?

. Would you be surprised to learn that Walter Blair wrote a biography of Davy Crockett for children? Explain.

From DAVID CROCKETT: THE MAN AND THE LEGEND[*]

James A. Shackford

The purpose of this work is to present an authentic biography of David Crockett against the background of his times, a new and creative period of American history, so that the reader may see him as an individual, as a type, and as an exponent of a type—a true pioneer not only of advancing geographical frontiers but also of the frontiers of a new democratic spirit. Crockett's life and writings can shed a needed light upon the issues of our era. Incidentally, by presenting the real Crockett, this study aims at correcting the time-honored fictional versions of his life which seem first to have taken root in the legend and literature of backwoods America more than a hundred years ago. It also aims at counteracting the new emphases, and the unfortunate consequences thereof, which scholars have given those incorrect fictional versions within the last twenty years. So shrouded in fiction and myth and error has Crockett become that only the most careful and painstaking research into all available sources can hope to recapture the man himself. This will make necessary the introduction of much of the evidence into the body of this work; for only so can the true man now be reclaimed as authentic in the mind of the reader.

A popular notion initiated by recent students of American literature is that the historical David Crockett is unknowable, a notion which has resulted in an unsalutary neglect of the historical man and of his authentic *Autobiography*. Writing in an otherwise fine article which he called "Six Davy Crocketts," Professor Walter Blair too readily wrote off as unrecapturable "the Crockett God made," the historical Crockett of this biography, and turned his attention to the other five Crocketts, all various combinations of newspaper creations and folklore. If one had to depend merely on secondary sources and on all of the political, journalistic, and "literary" capital which has been made of David for a good deal more than a hundred years, as Mr. Blair did, and had his assumption been sound that few authentic records of David existed inasmuch as few had been published, his conclusion would have been correct. The assumption was in error. Though none of the Crockett writers has ever gone to many of the original sources for their work, such sources did exist: holographs, court records of the counties where he lived, locuments of the Creek Indian War in which he fought, archives of the tate where he dwelt for most of his life, legislative and Congressional ecords, authentic reminiscences about him by those who had known him during the various periods of his life. Nevertheless, the erroneous ssumption was made, and the historical Crockett was dismissed as being forever lost.

. . . .

On January 1, 1821, David resigned his position of Commissioner of Lawrenceburg, having offered his name as legislator for Lawrence and Hickman counties. The *Autobiography* gives us an account of a curiously nonchalant campaign opening. He announced his candidacy in February. Then, "about the first of March," he "started . . . with a drove of horses to the lower part of the state of North Carolina. This was in the year 1821, and I was gone upwards of three months." This would have brought him back about June first. The elections were scheduled for the following August, and for the next two months David went electioneering through Hickman and Lawrence counties. Thus David was launched into a political career that would ultimately lead him to his bitter end.

Crockett was new at campaigning and unfamiliar with the intricacies of state and national politics. However, he was not nearly so ignorant of procedure as he would lead us to believe, and he was relatively no worse off than many of his fellow legislators. Going first into Hickman County, he was soon in hot water with two rival parties over the question of moving the Hickman county seat from Vernon to a point nearer the county center or retaining it at Vernon. David pretends that he had not the slightest idea what they meant by "moving a town." He kept silent and sided with neither. From the success of his campaign, we suspect that he sided with both.

About this time a great squirrel hunt was projected, to be held on Duck River. Politicking in the canebrakes was an occasion for partying and fun. The hunt was to last two days, and the hunters divided into two parties to compete in the kill. At the end of the hunt, all were to meet and count squirrel scalps. The party having the fewest scalps was bound to foot the bill for the big public barbecue and country frolic to follow.

David joined one of the parties, and, according to his own account, his superior marksmanship enabled his group to outscalp their opponents. Then came the politicking as a prelude to the dancing. When David was called on for a political speech, he tried to beg off with the excuse that in the polished forensic arts he was no match for his opponent. Nevertheless, since he was forced to speak, he adopted the canny tactics he was to follow throughout his political career—tactics based upon a shrewd recognition that what these backwoods people really wanted to relieve their sense of isolation amid the hardships of frontier life and to satisfy their hunger for social companionship and fun, was not enlightenment, but entertainment. David had a peculiar gift for entertaining. He told them numerous jokes, including one hilariously appropriate to his own predicament. He compared his present situation to that of a man he had heard of not long before who, found beating on the head of an empty barrel and asked what he thought he was doing, replied that there *had* been cider in that barrel a few days before, and he was determined to get some of it out. There had been a little speech in himself a little while ago, David explained, but it seemed that something had happened, for he didn't believe he would have much success now in getting it out, beat about as he might.

When he saw that he had the crowd "in a first-rate way," he concluded with a remark that he was as dry as a powder horn and he thought it time for all parched throats "to wet a whistle." Whereupon he got down and led the way to the liquor stand, leaving few customers indeed for his opponent's wares. Throughout his opponent's speech he remained at the liquor stand telling good yarns to a delighted audience. This incident probably occurred at Centerville in Hickman County.

On another electioneering occasion, a barbecue was held in Vernon, on a Saturday before court convened on the following Monday, a real occasion for a big week-end gathering. The candidates for Congress, for Governor, and for the legislature all attended, and in this company Crockett was understandably uneasy. But he analyzed the situation with good sense:

. . . as good luck would have it, these big candidates spoke nearly all day, and when they quit, the people were worn out with fatigue, which afforded me a good apology for not discussing the government. But I listened mighty close to them, and was learning pretty fast about political matters. When they were all done, I got up and told some laughable story, and quit. I found I was safe in those parts, and so I went home, and didn't go back again till after the election was over. But to cut this matter short, I was elected, doubling my competitor, and nine votes over.

In this manner Crockett won his first seat in the Tennessee State Legislature.

Thereafter he recounts a public meeting in Pulaski between himself and James K. Polk, who was to be Clerk of the State Senate during David's first term in the legislature, 1821–22, and who in 1823–24 was himself to become a representative in that legislature. (In 1825 Polk was elected to the first of seven consecutive terms to the national Congress, so that for the whole of Crockett's legislative and Congressional careers he served in the company of James K. Polk.) In the presence of a large gathering, Polk said to Crockett, "Well, colonel, I suppose we shall have a radical change of the judiciary at the next session of the Legislature." David replied, "Very likely sir," and, as he avers, "put out" from there as fast as he decently could, for he had no idea that there was such a thing as a "judiciary" in all of nature. Again we get that pose of pretended ignorance which so pleased his constituents then and so pleases his readers today. Even scholars, Parrington among them, have apparently been deceived by this pose into overemphasizing his ignorance. The reader can judge for himself whether or not a man who had been around the judiciary for four years as a justice of the peace, court referee, and town commissioner, being daily in the courts and signing official records, having been elected to several political positions of military rank and now to the state legislature, would be unfamiliar with the word "judiciary" in the summer of 1821, at thirty-five years of age.

Questions

1. What major assumption does Shackford make about scholars of the past twenty years?
2. What is Shackford's attitude toward Professor Walter Blair? Why does he describe "Six Davy Crocketts" as "an otherwise fine article"?
3. Does Shackford's charge about Blair's "assumption" seem valid to you? Explain.
4. What is Shackford's attitude toward David Crockett's early political strategies? How do you know?
5. Shackford refers to Crockett's "pose of pretended ignorance." Does he support his assertion that this was merely a pose? Explain.

From YANKEE THUNDER*

Irwin Shapiro

[1] The biographer of Davy Crockett is immediately confronted with a problem: which Davy Crockett shall he write about? For if there ever was a man of multiple identity, that man was Davy Crockett.

[2] First of all there was—or at least there exists some fairly reliable evidence to that effect—the flesh-and-blood Crockett, the frontiersman

and hunter of early Tennessee. There was the historical Crockett, with his heroic exploits at the Alamo duly recorded in history. There was the political Crockett, a figure alternately built up and deflated by the Jacksonites and anti-Jacksonites, according to the exigencies of the moment. And then there was the mythical Crockett, the Crockett of legend and folksay, of the tall tales and fireside yarns and almanac stories—the veritable yaller blossom of the forest, half horse, half alligator, with a little touch of snapping turtle, the ring-tailed roarer who could bring a coon out of a tree, ride a streak of lightning, wade the Mississippi, and come down off the Peak o' Day with a piece of sunrise in his pocket.

[3] It was to this last Crockett, in the grand American tradition of Paul Bunyan, John Henry, Old Stormalong, and Pecos Bill, that I turned as being obviously the most credible, authentic, significant, and true.

[4] Having made the obvious choice, I went to the Crockett almanacs. This series of anonymous pamphlets, published for a period of about fifty years beginning in 1836, justified the title of almanac by carrying a page or so of information on the phases of the moon and similar subjects. The almanacs' real reason for existence was their main text, a collection of tales, anecdotes, and plain and fancy whoppers that had grown up around the name of Davy Crockett. I found them so outrageous, so fantastic, so far-fetched and contrary to the laws of nature, that I knew I was on the trail of the real Crockett.

[5] The trouble was that the tales were too fragmentary for my purpose. Some were coarse, even brutal, and not consonant with the larger outlines of Davy's character. There were glaring discrepancies. We are told, for instance, that as a child Davy was as big as a mountain and weighed over three hundred pounds. But in later life his size is given as no larger than an ordinary man's. There were innumerable omissions, innumerable questions unanswered. How did Davy meet his wife, Sally Ann Thunder Ann Whirlwind? How did he acquire his famous pets, the bear Death Hug and the buffalo Mississip? How did he get to the South Seas and back again? As Constance Rourke has said, "No effort is made to create a consistent mythology in the almanacs."

[6] Faced with a problem within a problem, I had to read between the lines. I reconstructed, filled in, elaborated. I jumped to some conclusions, I guessed, reckoned, surmised, fabricated, concocted, and wound up with some whoppers of my own. I gathered a little information from books written about Davy and those purportedly written by him. And finally—I confess it with shame—I had to fall back on history. . . .

[7]   Well, then, I took what I could from history, from the almanacs, from the books. In the end I had to more or less shift for myself, with nothing to guide me but Davy's own motto: *Be sure you're right, then GO AHEAD!* I sat down and put my yarn on paper, writing it for younger readers because I felt they would be less biased against the true and the wonderful, the absurd and sublime story of the real Crockett. . . .

Questions

1. Shapiro describes Crockett as being "in the grand American tradition of Paul Bunyan, John Henry, . . . and Pecos Bill." How do you interpret this statement? Does it reflect Shapiro's values?
2. In paragraph 4 Shapiro describes how he knew he "was on the trail of the real Crockett." Why does he make this statement? What is the tone of the entire paragraph?
3. Shapiro implies that he rejected some Crockett materials as "not consonant with the larger outlines of Davy's character." What inferences do you draw from this statement? Do you assume that Shapiro was seeking "realistic" details? Explain.
4. Shapiro states that he "had to fall back on history." Why does he make this statement?
5. *Yankee Thunder* is a legendary biography written for "younger readers" who would be "less biased." Why does Shapiro say that younger readers would be "less biased"?
6. From this preface to *Yankee Thunder*, what would you assume to be the style and content of this biography? Explain.

TARGET SHOOTING*

David Crockett

[1]   As there was considerable time to be killed, or got rid of in some way, before the dinner could be cooked, it was proposed that we should go beyond the village [of Little Rock], and shoot at a mark, for they had heard I was a first-rate shot, and they wanted to see for themselves, whether fame had not blown her trumpet a little too strong in my favor; for since she had represented "the Government" as being a first-rate statesman, and Colonel Benton as a first-rate orator, they could not receive such reports without proper allowance, as Congress thought of the Post Office report.

[2]   Well, I shouldered my Betsey, and she is just about as beautiful a piece as ever came out of Philadelphia, and I went out to the shooting

* From *A Narrative of the Life of David Crockett—Written by Himself* (1834).

ground, followed by all the leading men in Little Rock, and that was a clear majority of the town, for it is remarkable, that there are always more leading men in small villages than there are followers.

[3] I was in prime order. My eye was as keen as a lizard, and my nerves were as steady and unshaken as the political course of Henry Clay; so at it we went, the distance, one hundred yards. The principal marksmen, and such as had never been beat, led the way, and there was some pretty fair shooting, I tell you. At length it came to my turn. I squared myself, raised my beautiful Betsey to my shoulder, took deliberate aim, and smack I sent the bullet right into the centre of the bull's eye. "There's no mistake in Betsey," said I, in a sort of careless way, as they were all looking at the target, sort of amazed, and not at all over pleased.

[4] "That's a chance shot, Colonel," said one who had the reputation of being the best marksman in those parts.

[5] "Not as much chance as there was," said I, "when Dick Johnson took his darkie for better for worse. I can do it five times out of six any day in the week." This I said in as confident a tone as "the Government" did, when he protested that he forgave Colonel Benton for shooting him, and he was now the best friend he had in the world. I knew it was not altogether as correct as it might be, but when a man sets about going the big figure, halfway measures won't answer no how; and "the greatest and the best" had set me the example, that swaggering will answer a good purpose at times.

[6] They now proposed that we should have a second trial; but knowing that I had nothing to gain and everything to lose, I was for backing out and fighting shy; but there was no let-off, for the cock of the village, though whipped, determined not to stay whipped; so to it again we went. They were now put upon their mettle, and they fired much better than the first time; and it was what might be called pretty sharp shooting. When it came to my turn, I squared myself, and turning to the prime shot, I gave him a knowing nod, by way of showing my confidence; and says I, "Look out for the bull's eye, stranger." I blazed away, and I wish I may be shot if I didn't miss the target. They examined it all over, and could find neither hair nor hide of my bullet, and pronounced it a dead miss; when says I, "Stand aside and let me look, and I warrant you I get on the right trail of the critter." They stood aside, and I examined the bull's eye pretty particular, and at length cried out, "Here it is; there is no snakes if it ha'n't followed the very track of the other." They said it was utterly impossible, but I insisted on their searching the hole, and I agreed to be stuck up as a mark my-

self, if they did not find two bullets there. They searched for my satisfaction, and sure enough it all come out just as I had told them; for I had picked up a bullet that had been fired, and stuck it deep into the hole, without any one perceiving it. They were all perfectly satisfied, that fame had not made too great a flourish of trumpets when speaking of me as a marksman; and they all said they had enough of shooting for that day, and they moved, that we adjourn to the tavern and liquor.

Questions

1. Does Crockett's closing remark in the second paragraph that "there are always more leading men in small villages than there are followers" affect your attitude toward him?
2. How well does Crockett seem to understand the men of Little Rock? Illustrate your response.
3. Crockett makes a number of comparisons: "as steady and unshaken as the political course of Henry Clay"; "as confident a tone as 'the Government' did"; and "eye was as keen as a lizard." What is your impression of Crockett based on the literary style of the writing? Explain.
4. Crockett does considerable swaggering in this situation. Is he justified in doing so?

RULES FOR THE GUIDANCE OF POLITICIANS*

David Crockett

"Attend all public meetings," says I, "and get some friends to move that you take the chair; if you fail in this attempt, make a push to be appointed secretary; the proceedings of course will be published, and your name is introduced to the public. But should you fail in both undertakings, get two or three acquaintances, over a bottle of whiskey, to pass some resolutions, no matter on what subject; publish them even if you pay the printer—it will answer the purpose of breaking the ice, which is the main point in these matters. Intrigue until you are elected an officer of the militia; this is the second step towards promotion, and can be accomplished with ease, as I know an instance of an election being advertised, and no one attending, the innkeeper at whose house it was to be held, having a military turn, elected himself colonel of his regiment." Says I, "You may not accomplish your ends with as little difficulty, but do not be discouraged—Rome wasn't built in a day.

"If your ambition or circumstances compel you to serve your country, and earn three dollars a day, by becoming a member of the legislature,

* From *A Narrative of the Life of David Crockett—Written by Himself* (1834).

you must first publicly avow that the constitution of the state is a shackle upon free and liberal legislation; and is, therefore, of as little use in the present enlightened age, as an old almanac of the year in which the instrument was framed. There is policy in this measure, for by making the constitution a mere dead letter, your headlong proceedings will be attributed to a bold and unshackled mind, whereas, it might otherwise be thought they arose from sheer mulish ignorance. 'The Government' has set the example in his attack upon the constitution of the United States, and who should fear to follow where 'the Government' leads?

"When the day of election approaches, visit your constituents far and wide. Treat liberally, and drink freely, in order to rise in their estimation, though you fall in your own. True, you may be called a drunken dog by some of the clean shirt and silk stocking gentry, but the real rough necks will style you a jovial fellow, their votes are certain, and frequently count double. Do all you can to appear to advantage in the eyes of the women. That's easily done—you have but to kiss and slabber their children, wipe their noses, and pat them on the head; this cannot fail to please their mothers, and you may rely on your business being done in that quarter.

"Promise all that is asked," said I, "and more if you can think of anything. Offer to build a bridge or a church, to divide a county, create a batch of new offices, make a turnpike, or anything they like. Promises cost nothing, therefore deny nobody who has a vote or sufficient influence to obtain one.

"Get up on all occasions, and sometimes on no occasion at all, and make long-winded speeches, though composed of nothing else than wind—talk of your devotion to your country, your modesty and disinterestedness, or on any such fanciful subject. Rail against taxes of all kinds, officeholders, and bad harvest weather; and wind up with a flourish about the heroes who fought and bled for our liberties in the times that tried men's souls. To be sure you run the risk of being considered a bladder of wind, or an empty barrel, but never mind that, you will find enough of the same fraternity to keep you in countenance.

"If any charity be going forward, be at the top of it, provided it is to be advertised publicly; if not, it isn't worth your while. None but a fool would place his candle under a bushel on such an occasion.

"These few directions," said I, "if properly attended to, will do your business; and when once elected, why a fig for the dirty children, the promises, the bridges, the churches, the taxes, the offices, and the subscriptions, for it is absolutely necessary to forget all these before you can become a thorough-going politician, and a patriot of the first water."

Questions

1. How would you assess the practicality of Crockett's opening paragraph? What is the tone of his writing?
2. What basic assumption about means and ends do you find in these "Rules"?
3. Since these "Rules" are intended for the "Guidance of Politicians," would you assume that Crockett perceived himself as a politician?
4. What familiar clichés does Crockett mention? Why?
5. What is the tone of the concluding sentence?
6. On the basis of this excerpt, what is your impression of David Crockett?

ASSIGNMENTS

1. Study *The Ballad of Davy Crockett*, "Coonskin Superman," *Davy Crockett* by Constance Rourke, "The Two Davy Crocketts," and "The Davy Crockett Myth" and compare their descriptions of Davy's motives for going to Texas. Write a paper in which you assess the language used in these pieces to describe this moment in Crockett's life.
2. Davy Crockett served as a scout for Andrew Jackson's army during the Creek War of 1813. Compare the handling of this historical episode in *The Ballad of Davy Crockett*, "Coonskin Superman," "The Embarrassing Truth About Davy Crockett," and "The Two Davy Crocketts."
3. Write a paper analyzing the language used by John Fischer in his article "The Embarrassing Truth About Davy Crockett."
4. Prepare a talk in which you evaluate Haverstick's assessment of Davy Crockett. Be prepared to comment on Mr. Haverstick's use of authoritative evidence.
5. Note Richard Dorson's description of Davy's language; then read the two excerpts by Crockett. Prepare a paper in which you analyze Mr. Dorson's judgments in the light of the excerpts.
6. Write a paper indicating the major areas of agreement and disagreement among Parrington, Blair, and Shackford. Document your statements with concrete references to these scholars' statements. Be prepared to report which interpretations you are prone to accept and why.
7. Read Crockett's "Rules." Write a paper in which you evaluate David on the basis of this one piece. Support any judgments you make with references to the "Rules."
8. In the light of Crockett's two pieces, report on the merit of Shackford's major judgment about David's pretended "ignorance."

4. ART
Abstract Painting

Conventional wisdom (or folk wisdom) has supplied a number of familiar statements about art which embody explicit judgments. One such statement you certainly know, and perhaps have used, is this: "I don't know anything about art but I know what I like." Another goes back to classical Latin, *de gustibus non disputandum* ("there's no use disputing taste" or, more colloquially put, "one man's meat is another man's poison"). Still others: "It may be art but I don't see anything in it." "These modern artists are frauds and fakes—real artists are painters like Rembrandt or Michelangelo or Leonardo." And undoubtedly you can add other examples to these. Yet naïve though these judgments may appear to be, they do reflect the fact that paintings invariably evoke some kind of response from the people who look at them.

As a matter of fact, these judgments actually reflect one or another of various aesthetic positions of long standing. Those who utter them are assuming (even though unconsciously) certain standards as necessary to art, and even the most casual of these remarks is akin to a more elaborate and sophisticated formulation which has appeared at one time or another in the long history of aesthetics. Indeed, most discussions of art (including art criticism) are part of a never ending controversy about such questions as form vs. content, means and ends, convention and revolt, the artist and society, expression vs. communication, art and nature, the image vs. reality, representation vs. interpretation, and a long list of other dichotomous terms.

Among the continuing controversies about art one of the liveliest in this century has been that concerning "modern" art in general and abstract art in particular. The term *abstract* itself has been defined in several different ways; in one sense at least, as Frederick Gore points out in one of the following essays, all painting is abstract to some degree. Furthermore, although the passage of time and the wide diffusion of paintings or their reproductions has gradually resulted in acceptance and admiration of "modernist" works that were once violently attacked (consider, for example, the present status of the paintings of Cézanne,

Monet, Whistler, van Gogh, or Toulouse-Lautrec), there are always in each generation the avant-garde painters to affront anew the tastes and sensibilities of the public.

In the following selections we have tried to exhibit some of the conflicting viewpoints of recent writers on abstract art. The first selection, "The Origins of Abstract Art," by Frederick Gore, an English art critic, is the opening chapter of a brief book written to explain abstract art to the layman. In the essay "Non-Communicative Art," Max Eastman, poet, critic, and editor, attacks both abstract artists and their defenders. Another attack forms the substance of a speech delivered in Congress by former Representative George A. Dondero of Michigan. The title of his speech, "Modern Art Shackled to Communism," is a forthright indication of the basis of his approach.

One particular variety of abstract painting has come to be known as "abstract expressionism" or "action painting." Harold Rosenberg, who coined the latter phrase, is a poet and critic; his article "Extremist Art: Community Criticism" was originally published in *ARTnews,* one of the leading art journals to espouse the cause of this kind of painting. Cleve Gray is a contemporary American painter who is not an abstract expressionist; his essay, "Narcissus in Chaos: Contemporary American Art," is a reassertion of what he calls the artist's "aesthetic responsibility" and hence may be read as a rebuttal of Rosenberg's position.

The Museum of Modern Art in New York is perhaps the nation's leading showcase for paintings of the past hundred years. In addition to organizing exhibitions for the Museum itself and for tours of other cities, members of its staff have published numerous books, catalogues, and articles. In 1959 the Museum organized a now famous show of American abstract expressionist paintings for a European tour. For the catalogue of the exhibit Alfred H. Barr, Jr., of the Museum staff wrote an introduction; we have reprinted both Mr. Barr's essay and the statements furnished by some of the artists represented in the exhibit, including Jackson Pollock, Willem de Kooning, William Baziotes, and others.

As a closing episode in our presentation of the controversy we have chosen two letters to *The New York Times,* whose art critic, John Canaday, has long admired and praised "modern art" and "abstract art" but who draws the line at abstract expressionism. These letters are partly about Mr. Canaday's own views, but mostly they are about the motives attributed to artists, critics, and collectors who applaud or attack American abstract painting.

We have also included reproductions of some of the abstract and abstract expressionist paintings which are discussed, but you will certainly not want to form judgments based solely on these black and white reproductions, all greatly reduced in size. If your college art department has color slides of these paintings, you would find it helpful to see the reproductions projected in color. But best of all, a visit to the art galleries may provide you with a firsthand acquaintance with these or other examples of abstract art.

THE ORIGINS OF ABSTRACT ART[*]

Frederick Gore

> What I am saying is not directly obvious. I must try to make it clear. I will try to speak of the beauty of shapes, and I do not mean, as most people would think, the shapes of living figures, or their imitations in painting; I mean straight lines and curves and the shapes made from them, flat or solid by the lathe, ruler and square, if you see what I mean. These are not beautiful for any particular reason or purpose, as other things are, but are always by their very nature beautiful and give pleasure of their own, quite free from the itch of desire, and colours of this kind are beautiful too and give a similar pleasure.
>
> PLATO: *Philebus*

[1] The appearance in this century of abstract painting still seems astonishing. It began among the movements which appeared in the heroic period of experiment between 1900 and 1914. In every country painters, aware of a great awakening, toiled and argued, banding themselves into groups and issuing manifestoes, inspired by an intense desire to play their part in the creation of a new age—by inventing a new means of expression and not least by destroying all that seemed sterile and worthless in the past.

[2] First came the stage of Fauve, Expressionist and Neo-Impressionist experiments inspired by Gauguin, Van Gogh and Seurat. Objects painted became subservient to handling and colour, the mood of the artist and the needs of the picture as a whole. Then came the dominant influence of Cézanne and the excitement over Negro carving together with a realization that the boundaries of human experience were being

[*] From Frederick Gore, *Abstract Art*. Copyright © 1956 by Methuen & Co. Ltd. Reprinted by permission of Crown Publishers, Inc.

vastly extended by new knowledge and new techniques. From 1909 those movements appeared which were dedicated to the utter destruction of all accepted images—Cubism, Futurism and Abstraction, under various names. The painters who belonged to these movements were all equally determined to abolish the sovereignty of appearances, some to banish altogether the natural world or any recognisable objects from it.

[3] There has always been some form of two-dimensional abstract art, but such art in the past was intended to ornament buildings, clothing or household goods rather than to communicate ideas and feelings, or, as in the case of the printed page, to set out in a way which was visually effective ingredients whose meaning was wholly symbolic. In tile or mosaic, on jewellery, textile or pottery, repeating patterns or symmetrical designs were used decoratively and symbolically as part of larger artistic or purely utilitarian purposes. Among familiar things only certain Persian carpets and woven rugs give a close parallel to abstract painting, suddenly delighting with qualities which transcend good craftsmanship and pleasing decoration. No doubt in Islam, where human likeness was forbidden, the shape and colour of abstract symbols acquired a greater sensuality, achieving a richness and variety parallel to natural forms.

[4] Although abstract painters have accepted ideas from decorative and folk art, yet the origins of contemporary abstraction are to be found in the development of European painting itself. The Christian story had inevitably to be illustrated by human and natural forms. But mistrust of the world and the flesh, or faith in certainties beyond, gave to both Byzantine and Western Mediæval art a symbolic rather than an imitative attitude towards nature, encouraging craftsmen to explore the expressive possibilities of wood, stained glass, tapestry or ivory, and to make a direct appeal to the senses by form and colour. In Northern Europe growing curiosity towards the natural world went hand in hand with a delight in pure design. From the later illuminators through the Flemish primitives to the masterpieces of Brueghel, increasing humanity and realism are contained within abstract conventions which are appropriate and moving. Similarly throughout Italian painting we certainly see the elaboration of naturalistic techniques, but within the framework of systems of picture-making which are profoundly intellectual, architectural and abstract—Raphael and Tintoretto as much as Giotto or Uccello assert the abstract and plastic nature of pictorial invention. Finally, those painters who seem most concerned to find the truth by faithfully realising appearance—Rembrandt, Vermeer, or Char-

din—are found to have just as intense a preoccupation with the mathematics of design.

[5] Only in the nineteenth century did popular taste demand that the surface imitation of natural objects should become the sole criterion of skill.

[6] Throughout history we see the dual nature of the artist's activity: at the same time as he represents the objective world, he is busy making a composition in which dark and light, warm and cold, colour, mass and line submit to a rule which is wholly aesthetic. It now seems inevitable that the two functions, already (at least since Poussin) separated in the mind, should finally have been separated in fact; just as it seems inevitable after the event, that landscape painting should have emerged from the background of the grand figure composition or the tiny window behind the virgin's head. But if abstract painting has lain dormant within realistic painting waiting for release, that does not mean that in every realistic painting there is some sort of underlying abstract skeleton which can be regarded separately. Formal and representational means have been inextricably mingled in the unifying act of creation.

[7] Abstraction is, paradoxically, an extension of subject matter: the selection jury and the gallery-goers accept an "abstract" as they accept a "landscape" or a "portrait." But it is also a reversal of tradition. It was natural that the painters and sculptors, of the early Renaissance starting with what the eye could see and hand reach, should begin that exploration of the material world which later became the province of science, asking what lay beneath and beyond. Through them the whole course of European painting was turned toward naturalism.

[8] Naturalism was first the enquiry into the nature of things, later the conventional pursuit of likeness. If events in the physical universe were to be accounted for as the consequence of physical cause and effect (and not the result of spiritual forces), then the physical universe must be self-sufficient and therefore finite. The painters who began to observe and examine the structure of physical events asserted instinctively the finite nature of the universe, making each painting a complete world in itself—a microcosm in which space and solid are represented by a series of continuous relationships and the composition contained within the frame. These conventions became a part of the common language of realism and the core of tradition. Handed on by the schools, the pursuit of naturalism and the architectural unity of Italian composition finally degenerated into the vapid illusionism and monumental pomposity of nineteenth century salon art.

[9] The Impressionists rejected the tired formulae for composition, reviving art by a direct approach to visual experience, accepting contemporary life and scientific development. As Post-Impressionists, they rediscovered the creative act of composition and began the revolution. Finally abstract painting, admitting no compromise with naturalism, has become the core of a new anti-naturalistic tradition. For Impressionism, Expressionism, Fauvism, Cubism, Futurism must interpret or transpose natural objects where abstract painting can abolish them altogether.

[10] The development of abstract painting is bound up with the lives of two great painters—Wassily Kandinsky, the Russian, and Piet Mondrian, the Dutchman. Before the First World War Russian artists were in the forefront of the modern movement, painters such as Kandinsky, Malevitch, Annenkov, Tatlin and Chagall as well as the great professional designers who gave to Diaghilev's ballet an authority which influenced popular and intelligent taste. . . .

[11] But it is Wassily Kandinsky whom we must honour as the first consistently abstract painter. By 1912 he was painting a series of pictures which were completely non-figurative without even the flavour of recognisable objects from the natural world and even without suggestion of natural space. Loose areas of rich positive colour and black coloured lines move across each other or a lighter variegated ground without uniting together to form any sort of real or imagined object, but orchestrated in a way similar to music. Kandinsky himself pursued this analogy; for in music he saw a parallel to the "pure" painting which he sought. Both Gauguin and Van Gogh had talked of a purer form of painting in which colour would have a musical significance. Later on Kandinsky and Beothy tried together to transpose works by Beethoven and Bach into forms and colours. Kandinsky's early paintings also resemble the involuntary coloured shapes which seem to move across a field of vision when our eyes are closed. . . .

[12] Kandinsky arrived at abstraction by natural stages: first he was intrigued by passages in the work of Gauguin where the meaning seemed independent of what was represented, and attracted by the patterns of Russian folk art; he painted Fauve landscapes in which the subject matter was dominated by the brilliant colour which his feelings suggested, and the rhythms which he discovered in handling paint; the painting became more important than the things painted. Then he painted "improvisations" in which forms and colours extracted from the subject were put down for their own sake: from them he built up a new image, orchestrating his first simple themes, which he called his

"composition." In 1911 he declared that he painted the first abstract picture. He also made use of the world revealed by the microscope, not only because it is easier to paint in a new way something that has never been painted before and because micro-organisms, transparent and dyed in bright colours, provided an enchanting new world, but because this world existed as a thin film on a glass slide: it was a two-dimensional world without any depth at all. Only colour could give the sensation that one form was suspended in front of another. . . .

[13] He returned to Russia during the 1914 war and may there have been influenced by Malevitch, who was developing his "suprematist compositions"—paintings composed from flat rectangles, rhomboids or triangles in positive red or black on a light ground. After his return to Munich in 1912 Kandinsky began to use curves, straight lines or serpentine lines, circles, squares and triangles—definite shapes which could be organised in a less emotional and dynamic spirit. This is the start of his "cool" period, which is parallel to the work of Mondrian and the other abstract painters at this time. His work became relatively calm and architectural as he developed the grammar of abstract art, and corresponds to the period when he taught (with Paul Klee) at the Bauhaus at Weimar. The last ten years of his life were spent in Paris where he produced large and impressive paintings in which both flowing and precise forms play their part. Kandinsky also wrote two books— "The Art of Spiritual Harmony" and "On the Problem of Form"; and throughout his life he made the attempt to develop a systematic theory partly practical and logical, partly mystical.

[14] It was his belief that the artist has absolute freedom limited by an inner necessity—a necessity which depends on something in the artist which demands to be expressed (personality), the spirit of his age (style), and the service of art itself. The question of composition becomes of relative importance: there are no general academic rules, since each work will have its own laws. He also declares the objective nature of the language used—"Every formal element has its own absolute psychic effect."

[15] While Kandinsky's pure painting had its start in Fauvism, that of Mondrian stems from the Cubists. Parallel with the experiments of Kandinsky, Picasso and Braque were breaking down recognisable objects, in almost monochromatic painting by the use of flat planes which intersect across the surface of the picture, contradicting the boundaries of space and solid. Depth is limited and arbitrary, controlled not by the requirements of nature but of design. Although these paintings retain the semblance of visual experience, only a few hints are there to remind

us of the orginal guitar or clarinet player. Mondrian, arriving in Paris when he was thirty-eight, saw such early Cubist work and was filled with admiration. By 1914 he is producing his own version—compositions in which a regular mosaic of short intersecting lines appear as the boundaries of little rectangular planes. These are very like the experiments of Braque and Picasso, but have already a different intention. Picasso and Braque are only out to show the objects in their painting who is master. But with Mondrian it is all or nothing: the apple tree or the waves of the sea, his initial starting point, must finally be transformed and forgotten in a pattern of plus and minus signs. By 1917 he is no longer abstracting from nature, but building up his design from within, experimenting with the simplest possible pictorial means—one kind of geometrical shape and three primary colours. But as with Kandinsky, these abstract signs become endowed with a vigorous life of their own—the little black tabs in relation to the coloured rectangles become the embodiment of a certain sort of movement—a prelude to the link which we see between abstract and Surrealist painting in Klee or Miró.

[16] During the 1914 war, back in Holland, he was one of the group of young Dutch architects and painters who formed the group and published the magazine called "De Stijl" (Style). Van Doesberg, poet, novelist, art critic, architect, painter and sculptor, is their brilliant apologist; Mondrian the most influential artist. They preached the amalgamation of painting, sculpture and architecture into a universal language; individual personality would be limited in the serving of a general principle. Today we must recognise the success of their crusade. Abstract art, providing such a basic language of design, has had profound influence on architecture and every kind of industrial art. . . . The impersonal forms used by such artists as Mondrian, Ben Nicholson, Moholy-Nagy or Arp, can be translated into any medium and have become the common property of engineers, builders, interior decorators, furniture designers or advertising men. . . .

[17] After the war Mondrian returned to Paris and took his place as the leader of abstraction at its most geometric. For him the Cubists had not followed out to the end the conclusions implicit in their own experiments. They had only used abstraction to achieve an attitude of freedom towards natural objects so that they could distort them according to the demands of emotion, the logic of composition, or an arbitrary whim. For him the only conclusion was a pure painting liberated from the tyranny of appearances and entirely independent of particular objects. This platonic programme he pursued with an almost religious

devotion and a moral, as much as aesthetic, preoccupation with principles. As if the geometric signs which he is using have already become images which are too particular, he moves on to a still more austere stage. He composes with large rectangles of pale tone and occasional rectangles of primary colour, separated from each other by a grid of thick black lines, as if to preclude any possible suggestion of relationships in space. At the same time he denies himself all personal qualities in the handling of pigment. All that matters is to establish a dynamic equilibrium; the proportions of each area, the weight of colour, the thickness of line, should all add up to a critical balance of opposed and contrasting elements. It is this search for critical proportions which so closely and inevitably links abstract art to architecture and all the applied arts: it is a test of Mondrian's greatness that we can hardly enter a flat or a shop, move in the street or the underground, without meeting forms which by accident or influence come from Mondrian's ideal world. He succeeded in producing the art of the machine age where Futurism failed: it is appropriate that his final triumph came in New York where he spent his last four years painting the series called Boogie-Woogie. The grids of bright coloured lines broken by little other-coloured squares, the larger rectangles between of red, yellow, blue, containing smaller white rectangles, combine to suggest perforated music rolls and celluloid sound tracks in movement, traffic which moves past city blocks, or trains on elevated railways (in between, juke boxes playing, movie screens, sky-scrapers in plan) the syncopated beat of modern folk music, the boogie-woogie movement of city life and lights. For abstract art has this power to provoke simultaneous images while itself representing nothing. . . . [See Fig. 5, p. 112.]

[18] It is often said that the camera has forced painters to eliminate description from their work. The causes of the revolution lie deeper: it is against that mechanistic view of the universe and that faith in material things which is the background of the camera and of popular demand for an art which is wholly imitative. The artist must seek reality beneath the surface. His function becomes prophetic. For when philosopher and physicist, psychologist and sociologist, each withdraws onto his own small rock of specialised certainties, only the painter and the poet may explore the unknown areas between. Only they can speak as individual men to individual men and from man's whole personality. We find the abstract painter equally absorbed by what he has to say and the semantic problem of how to say it, attempting to purify the language but also searching for the meaning of his existence in the prophetic caves below the threshold of consciousness.

[19] Action Painters, who have been prominent since 1946, . . . are rtists who are pioneering on the frontiers of aesthetic experience—not nowing where it may lead, but conscious of the immediate importance f a new experience. Squeezing paint from the tube, pouring it from teapot, splashing and slapping it on, makes it possible to retain a eneral improvised control, while the painting develops, out of the ction of painting, automatically: what seems to arrive most acciden- illy may be truest to the deeper levels of personality. The American ackson Pollock and others who use the unconscious in this way, unlike 1irò or Klee, adhere to the strict principles of pure abstraction; nothing emotely like an object is permitted to appear.

[20] Because an abstract painting represents nothing, and contains o objects, it is felt that it must take on an objective existence of its wn. In doing this it achieves something which all modern art seems ɔ attempt and also fulfils a destiny implied in tradition. The magical elationship between object and image in Byzantine art, the way in vhich the early Italian naturalists established a painting as a micro- osm complete in itself and the idea of an objet d'art as something vhich exists for aesthetic reasons alone, have been reinforced by a new ympathy for the culture of primitive peoples, who endow a stone or tree with magical power, and similarly give to their created images an stounding inner life.

[21] During the last decade painters have branched in different di- ections in the attempt to give the work of art its own reality. Strangely nough these differing points of view seem to fall loosely into the tra- itional categories of classical, romantic and realist. Those seem most lassical who have inherited the tradition of the pure painting of "De tijl" and the Bauhaus. Of these some have inevitably been led by heir search for pure forms to construct three-dimensional objects (in ingland Victor Passmore and Kenneth Martin). The romantics, who re in the majority, are those who rely on making painting the embodi- 1ent of a strong psychic force using a personal mixture of Surrealist nd Expressionist means, deriving their forms from nature (poetic ainters like Talcoat, Santomaso, Manessier, Afro, or more Expression- t painters such as Bazaine, da Silva, Winter, Dova, de Kooning, Wer- er). The realists impress on us the physical existence of the object vhich they have made from paint (de Stäel, Riopelle).

[22] These new tendencies are a reaction against past abstract paint- 1g and to life in the present. To younger men in the decade after the 939–45 war the platonic programme of the early idealistic abstract ainters seemed most unsatisfactory: painting also should be existen-

tial. Philosophically Mondrian or Nicholson represented idealism. Their painting contained squares and circles but these were representative squares and circles. Since the war there has been a swing to painterly qualities, to personal handwriting or richness of texture, which make each painting a unique event which cannot be repeated. . . .

[23] Libraries, telephones, wireless, telescopes, aeroplanes, psycho-analysis, relativity, atomic theory—all offer the new dimensions of space in which we live. As a result abstract painters have been intensely concerned to realise new kinds of pictorial space—space which includes memory or organic growth, the space that is round us and within us rather than the space in front of our eyes; the Renaissance convention of a view in perspective through a window is contradicted. Also the search is not necessarily now for absolute relationships, but for relative values which may be read in different ways. Especially in America there is opposition to the tradition that a painting is an ordered microcosm; there is curiosity toward the chaos prior to creation—that exuberant and incalculable flux which is the other aspect of nature.

[24] It seems appropriate that since it is the essential art form of the 20th century much of the success of abstract painting has depended on American support, and many American painters were pioneers of abstraction. Gradually abstract art of every kind has become the most recognised and enduring form of modern art in America, ranging from geometric abstraction (Fritz Glarner, Pereira) to more recent abstract expressionism (Gorky, Mark Tobey, Franz Klein, Robert Motherwell) and even abstract impressionism (Mark Rothko, Philip Guston). In France and England it is since the war that abstraction has had most influence among painters and most public success.

[25] People of simple tastes need not be baffled by abstract art. Abstract painters speak to us by means as simple as the mediaeval craftsmen spoke to folk who thronged the churches; they ask only a frank response to form and colour. Abstraction is only difficult because the meaning is contained in a direct and personal message between man and man; we cannot use as a bridge between ourselves and the artist our interest in the familiar objects painted, mistaking our admiration for the skill with which he represents a cloud, a leaf, or a girl's throat for the understanding of the whole work. But all works of art must speak in riddles, for, like life itself, they are best understood when we do not demand a meaning.

[26] Representational painting gives us time to make up our minds tempting us with naturalistic bait to take the first mouthful. An abstract

work seems to call on us to make an immediate aesthetic judgement, and that needs honesty—and courage. So with abstract painting it is all the more necessary to see a number of paintings and know something of the painter's development. Almost everyone seems to accept abstraction when it is applied, in the theatre, on posters or textiles. Paintings in a public gallery or in Bond Street are in an unnatural situation. A painting should also be applied to a purpose; it takes on its true meaning in a chosen setting, as part of a room and part of the life and taste of the owner. One of the rewards of studying abstract art is paradoxical; instead of the painter showing us the patterns which he has found in nature, he shows us how patterns are made and sends us back to nature to find them for ourselves: abstract art offers to teach every man the pleasure of seeing as a painter sees. To the painter it offers freedom to design to the limit of the materials he is using and new powers of evocation.

[27] Abstraction is not a temporary phase or fashionable fad, but an essential part of the new tradition and the new culture which we are creating. Abstraction is not a "Movement" opposed to realism or expressionism, for these are complementary attitudes. It is not "escapist": on the contrary, art which does not mirror contemporary life but alters and reshapes it must in some sense be the most creative and realistic of all. For the living art of every age is a part of our endeavour to dominate or transcend circumstances.

Questions

1. You might describe Gore's chapter as a kind of history of the development of abstract art. However, his selection of facts and his points of emphasis suggest (as is usually true of histories) that his history has a point of view as well as a purpose. What is his point of view? What is his purpose?
2. What is the motive of paragraphs 3 through 5? What attitude toward abstraction is Gore subscribing to?
3. Paragraph 7 suggests an important distinction between the way in which an informed and an uninformed person "sees" a painting. Do you accept this distinction? Why or why not?
4. What does Gore suggest as Kandinsky's chief departure from the painting of his predecessors? Why does Gore suggest that it is Kandinsky "whom we must honour as the first consistently abstract painter" (paragraph 11)? What does Gore's use of the word *honour* imply?
5. How important does Gore think Mondrian's contribution is? What evidence can you cite to support your answer?
6. What is Gore's attitude toward American "Action Painters"? Explain.
7. Consider the rhetoric of Gore's final paragraph. Is it appropriate to his overall purpose? Do you find the paragraph convincing?

Fig. 1. Wassily Kandinsky, *Composition* (3) (1914). Oil on canvas, 64″ × 36¼″. (Collection, The Museum of Modern Art, New York; Mrs. Simon Guggenheim Fund)

Fig. 2. Pablo Picasso, *Girl Before a Mirror* (March, 1932). Oil on canvas, 63¾″ × 51¼″. (Collection, Museum of Modern Art, New York; Gift of Mrs. Simon Guggenheim)

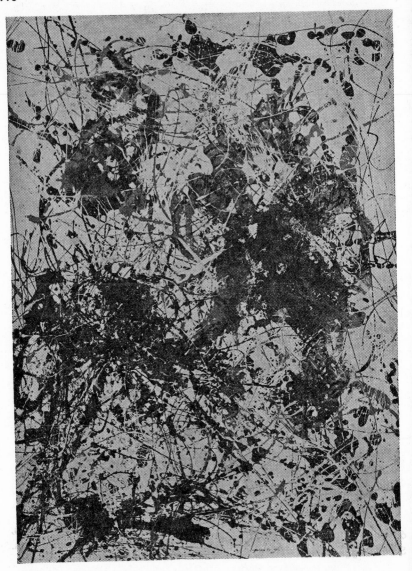

Fig. 3. Jackson Pollock, *Number 12* (1949). Oil on paper mounted on composition board, 31″ × 22½″. (Collection, The Museum of Modern Art, New York; Gift of Edgar Kaufmann, Jr.)

Fig. 4. Willem de Kooning, *Woman, I.* (1950–52). Oil on canvas, 75⅞" ×
58". (Collection, Museum of Modern Art, New York; Purchase)

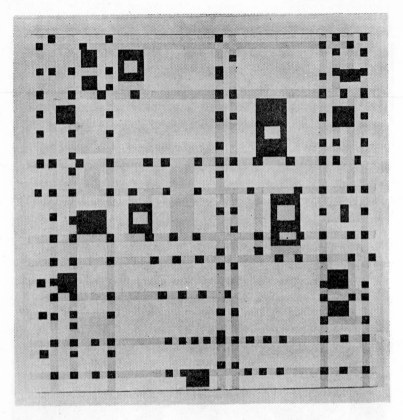

Fig. 5. Piet Mondrian, *Broadway Boogie-Woogie* (1942–43). Oil on canvas, 50″ × 50″. (Collection, Museum of Modern Art, New York)

NON-COMMUNICATIVE ART*

Max Eastman

My friend Bernard Berenson, prince of art critics, has written an astute little book called "Seeing and Knowing" in which he reviews the history of artistic conventions as a series of compromises between conceptual knowledge and visual experience. He does not conceal his low opinion of the present convention culminating in what is called "abstract art." He feels sure, he says, that the "confusion, struttings, blustering, solemn puerilities that are now practiced, taught, admired, and proclaimed," will not last forever. But he does not say why he feels sure of this.

To my mind these manifestations in the world of art associate themselves with what is happening in the political world, and I feel evangelical about it. Although I admire Berenson profoundly, I never could quite imitate the serene detachment with which he dwells among ideas —and among pictures, and books innumerable, and a beautiful garden and a too beautiful sky—in his shrinelike villa on a hill overlooking Florence. I feel we have to descend into the plain and raise an army and go to war for civilized values in art as well as politics and economics.

So far as poetry is concerned, I did go to war for these values twenty-five years ago in an essay called "The Cult of Unintelligibility." I was defeated, and very soon disappeared under a flood of extremely erudite and awfully overwhelming language which goes by the name of the New Criticism, but none of my arguments were answered.

I am not going to trundle out all the old cannon I employed in that purely literary engagement, but I do want to recall one maneuver which has especial relevance to modern art.

I was talking about Gertrude Stein as the Founder and high priestess of the Cult, and I adduced this example of the Gertrudian prose:

"I was looking at you, the sweet boy that does not want sweet soap. Neatness of feet do not win feet, but feet win the neatness of men. Run does not run west but west runs east. I like west strawberries best."

One can hardly deny, I remarked, a beauty of ingenuity to those lines. They have a fluency on the tongue, a logical intricacy that is intriguing. And no doubt anyone who dwells with idle energy on their plausible music will find thoughts and impulses from his own life rising

* From *The Freeman*, May 3, 1954. Reprinted by permission.

to employ them as a symbol or pattern for a moment of thought or imaginative realization. But the impulses that rise to those lines from the reader's life will never by one chance in a million be the same as those that dictated them in the life of the author. Communication is here reduced to a minimum. It is a private art, just as private as the emotional life of the insane. In fact the passage I quoted was not from Gertrude Stein, but from the stenographic report of the ravings of a maniac cited by Kraepelin in his Clinical Psychiatry. Here is a passage that *is* from Gertrude Stein:

> Any space is not quiet it is so likely to be shiny. Darkness very darkness is sectional. There is a way to see in onion and surely very surely rhubarb and a tomato, surely very surely there is that seeding.

It is just the same thing, you see, only perpetrated voluntarily—and, in my opinion, not quite so well.

It seems to me that exactly the same maneuvers might be executed, and with a like success, against present tendencies in the plastic arts. The essential thing that has been disappearing from both fields is intelligible communication. The artist mulls around with patterns, diagrams, and symbolic entities that contain both thought and emotion for him, and then leaves it to the beholder to invest them, if he can, with other thoughts and emotions that belong to *him*. Once more it is private art—and once more just as private as the emotional life of the insane.

In the spring of 1950 the University of Vienna put on an exhibition of thirty paintings, half of them by well-known surrealist or abstract painters, the other half by patients from a mental hospital. (Among the well-known were Picasso, Miro, Enrico Donati, Max Ernst, and the American, Yves Tanguy.) An audience of presumably normal persons, 158 of them, were unable to say which was which. Their answers, that is, were fifty per cent wrong and fifty per cent right, as pure chance would predict.

Functional insanity, in its most general form, as everybody knows, is an extreme withdrawal into a world of private values and meanings. However, I am not saying, and neither did the Viennese experimenters, that the artists in question are insane. My thesis is that they might just as well be, so far as the social or communicative values of their work are concerned.

This does not fully apply, of course, to the values of what is called pattern or design. Here the difference between literary and artistic talking-to-oneself is considerable. It is impossible to put paint on canvas, or lines on paper, or mold a figure in clay, without creating a pattern. Whether good or bad, the pattern is objective, it is accessible to all beholders. But no one would have the hardihood to call these modern artists "designers." Designers make linoleum, tablecloths, dress goods, wallpaper, paper for Christmas packages. To identify abstract art with their craft would deflate and destroy the whole revolution. It would deprive the artist of the excited thoughts and emotions he experiences while creating his work. It would deprive the beholder of the thoughts and emotions he experiences while contemplating it. Neither of these experiences is necessarily insincere. That is not my implication, but merely that, apart from the perception of design, these experiences are not, by a million chances to one, the same. They are not, by a million chances to one, in any important respect, similar.

The insincerity lies in the pretense on the part of the critics, patrons, guardians of our culture, and provincial, half-educated, half-alive aspirants to a reputation for expert familiarity with it, that any part of this experience is conveyed by the artist to the beholder. In so far as the most renowned "abstractions" are anything more than the art of the designer, this pretense is false; it is phony. It has filled the world of culture with poses, lies, hypocrisies, false claims to eminence, and fatuous bombast posing as esoteric knowledge inaccessible to the simple mind. It has enthroned mountebanks and bunk-shooters where men of the highest mind and most refined perceptions used to sit. . . .

We must, of course, be tolerant of the aberrations of creative genius in any field. As Plato observed of the poets, they have to be a little crazy in order to escape from the nearsighted practicality that life forces on us all. At least they have to be childlike. They have to play seriously. They have to experiment. They have to fool around with all sorts of ideas and nonideas a good deal of the time. But this is not true of the critics, the estheticians, the directors of galleries, the art dealers, the editors of art magazines, the writers of books about art. The professional art critic is a breed of being that the world got along without well into the nineteenth century. We could get along without him again if he fails to defend the unquestionable and enduring values against commercial fads and frauds and fashionable fake-evidences of superior culture. The artists, I believe, would soon get back on the path of good sense and dignity and social communion and *hard work*, if the critics held the standards firm.

To prove that, with hardly an exception besides Berenson himself they are not holding standards firm, let us recall a costly and convincing experiment. In 1948 Life Magazine assembled a group of sixteen eminent art critics and connoisseurs from all over the world to debate the question "Whether modern art as a whole is a good or a bad development." So far as Life's eighteen-page report of the debate reveals, not one word was said on this question by any of them. They disagreed about all the pictures presented to them, not only about whether they were good or bad, but about what they were and what they had to do with.

The one thing upon which they did unanimously agree—with a single half-hearted exception—was the magnificence of the painting by Pablo Picasso entitled *Girl Before A Mirror*. [See Fig. 2, p. 109.] It is "accepted on every hand as a great modern classic," according to Life's editors. "However," they add, "it is not an extreme example of 'modernism.' . . . The form of the girl is still recognizable; hence the layman can see the physical distortions to which the artist has subjected it, and thereby learn much about what the artist was trying to do."

That allusion to the layman, I must pause to remark, is of the essence of the trick by which this cult of non-communication is propagated. The pretense that an experienced critic and connoisseur can tell the difference between the work of a schizophrenic or a dabbling schoolboy, and that of a Master of Modernism, has been refuted above. But it was still better refuted in this same experiment conducted by Life. That not one of these learned connoisseurs assembled at vast expense from all over the world had the slightest idea what Picasso had in mind with his *Girl Before A Mirror* was frankly acknowledged by all of them in the very same conference in which it was hailed as a "great modern classic." Remember this when tempted to say, "I don't understand modern art." Say instead: "I like art which can be understood."

Let us consider briefly what happened in this conference of supersensitized estheticians when Picasso's picture was placed before them. To begin with, Meyer Schapiro, professor of fine arts at Columbia University, burst forth with an excited exposition of what this picture meant *to him*, an exposition which according to Life's reporter, "held the conference spellbound." As everything was taken down by a stenographer, we are privileged to know just what it was that held them spellbound.

Schapiro began by saying that there are two images of the human body: one as it is seen from the outside, the anatomical image, and another, the image we form of it from the inside. As imaged from the inside, it is "full of distortions and strange relationships," owing to the way we feel about it. "For instance, when you have a toothache, one ide of your face feels bigger than the other. . . . In a similar way, in antasy, our conception of the bodies of others is affected by our feelngs. It is this kind of personal, internal image that Picasso is portraying here."

Now it does not happen to be true, at least in my case, that when you have a toothache one side of your face feels bigger than the other—not unless the dentist puts novocaine in the gum, which of course alters the purely sensory experience. It is certainly not true, in general, that an emotional interest in some part of a body, whether your own or another's, entails an enlargement or distortion of the image of that part. No such correspondence between emotional interest and imaginary shape and size has ever been established, or, so far as I know, even proposed as an hypothesis by any psychologist. It is just one of those irresponsible remarks that professional talkers about art feel free to make. However, it gave Meyer Schapiro a good start, and from that point on he read things into this picture that I am sure nobody else would ever think of in a million years.

Picasso, he averred, has "discovered for art the internality of the body, just as the impressionists discovered blue shadows, which were at first a scandal." And more scandalous still, in this picture the girl's body is seen from the inside and the outside both at once! The girl is in "a state of tension which is highly sensual in character," and Picasso also, it seems, is amorously excited about the girl. And that accounts for all these various loops, lobes, and protuberances inhering in her body in the similitude of a toothache as seen from the inside looking out.

I am not meaning to ridicule what Schapiro said about the picture, although I cannot conceal the fact that I think it was old-maidish, academical, purely cerebral, and unrelated to any real facts. No live man feeling adolescent about a girl's body would want it to protruberate like that in various places. I cannot imagine anything that would kill passionate feeling more quickly. Picasso, I'm sure, would jump out of the bedroom window if a girl developed any of these manifestations, whether inside or out. However, all I meant to prove is that Schapiro's interpretation is too ingeniously complicated to have occurred to any other human being on examining the same picture.

For that purpose, let us have a little more of it.

"Thus the body is represented both from outside and within, and in the mirror is still another image of the body." Schapiro did not say whether this other image is an outside or an inside one, and I for the life of me cannot tell. But at any rate it is a different image, and Schapiro thinks it is a "wonderful magical, poetic idea, to show the human body which is ordinarily represented in one way . . . as belonging to three different modes of experience within one picture."

"I don't know of another painting in all history which does that," he exclaims.

And I must say that I don't either. Nor do I think this painting does it, or any painting could possibly do it. He seemed unaware that he was harking back to "representative art" to explain a phenomenon that rose out of a revolt against it.

"The shapes," he continued, "are forcibly contrasted and tied together. The repeated form of the breasts, and what we may take to be the womb . . ." (A layman, of course, might want to know whether it *is* a womb before drawing any important conclusions about it, but not so the connoisseur.) "The breasts . . . and what we may take to be the womb, and the form at the elbow—the green circle—are all clearly related." How related he does not say.

"The roundness of the face belongs with these circles." What "belongs with" means he does not explain. "But in the face is also a moon crescent which occurs elsewhere on the body and there is a large contrast like that of the sun and moon in the relation of the real body and the mirrored body and indeed the moon has a reflected light." And he concludes: "Whether the symbolism is deliberate, unconscious or accidental, I would not dare to say. . . ." In any case "These contrasts and repetitions . . . have a manifest purposiveness which to me is grand."

That was what held the experts spellbound—an elaborate invention on the part of Mr. Schapiro, and one characterized by what to his mind was a grand purposiveness. But he quite frankly acknowledged that he did not know whether the purposes in question existed, even unconsciously, in the mind of the artist or not. The whole thing may have been purely accidental. That is, it may have been made up by Meyer Schapiro, as in my opinion it undoubtedly was.

Indeed when the question was raised explicitly whether, as a matter of fact, Picasso had intended to express any of these notions with which Schapiro had held them spellbound, those experts agreed that the question was "of course unanswerable," and that it was also "irrelevant to the enjoyment of the picture."

Thus we have reached a phase in the development of the plastic art where it does not make any difference to the high-up critics and connoisseurs what, if anything, the artist was trying to convey. They have no criteria by which they can decide whether he was, in fact, an artist or a lunatic. They can be hoaxed into reading "advanced" values into a painting composed by a six-year-old boy with the help of his cat's tail

nd a saucer of paint accidentally stepped on while the cat was at work.
They write glowing tributes to a piece of old cardboard on which
painters have wiped their brushes. We need no further proof, it seems
to me, that the essential thing which has disappeared from the field
of art as well as poetry is intelligible communication. And I need hardly
add that when art is unintelligible and people go right on forming
judgments about it, the basic thing that is disappearing is intelligence.
In art and poetry, alike, the net result is a consecration of the mental
blur, a benediction upon the vice of cloudy and confused thinking.

The relation of this to what is happening in the political world seems
fairly obvious. That so many highly placed critics have accepted a return to mumbo-jumbo, and even helped to put it over on the public
in the name of intellectual culture, is to me but a part of that general
surrender of mental and moral integrity to crude primitive and un-
illumined states of passion which threatens our whole Graeco-Christian
civilization with ruin. I think this will seem quite obvious to future
historians if history survives.

Questions

. Who was Bernard Berenson? When you have learned something about
  him, explain why you think Eastman makes reference to Berenson in the
  beginning of the essay.

. What is Eastman's objection to modern poetry? How is it related to his
  objections to modern art?

. What does Eastman mean by the "social or communicative values" of
  works of art? What does he mean by the "cult of non-communication"?

. What is the purpose of Eastman's lengthy discussion of the symposium
  devoted to Picasso's *Girl Before a Mirror?*

. Why is Eastman's argument with Schapiro unlikely to result in a change
  in either's opinion?

. Discuss Eastman's concluding paragraph. Why do you think he relates
  his discussion of art to happenings in the political world?

. Do you agree with Eastman's basic premise that art must communicate
  intelligibly? Why or why not? What does the word *communicate* mean in
  this context?

MODERN ART SHACKLED TO COMMUNISM*

George A. Dondero

[1] Mr. Speaker, quite a few individuals in art, who are sincere in
purpose, honest in intent, but with only a superficial knowledge of the

* From a speech delivered in the House of Representatives, August 16, 1949.
Reprinted from *The Congressional Record.*

complicated influences that surge in the art world of today, have written me—or otherwise expressed their opinions—that so-called modern or contemporary art cannot be Communist because art in Russia today is realistic and objective.

[2] The left-wing art magazines advance the same unsound premises of reasoning, asserting in editorial spasms that modern art is real American art. They plead for tolerance, but in turn tolerate nothing except their own subversive "isms."

[3] The human art termites, disciples of multiple "isms" that compose so-called modern art, boring industriously to destroy the high standards and priceless traditions of academic art, find comfort and satisfaction in the wide dissemination of this spurious reasoning and wickedly false declaration, and its casual acceptance by the unwary.

[4] This glib disavowal of any relationship between communism and so-called modern art is so pat and so spontaneous a reply by advocates of the "isms" in art, from deep, Red Stalinist to pale pink publicist as to identify it readily to the observant as the same old party-line practice. It is the party line of the left wingers, who are now in the big money, and who want above all to remain in the big money, voiced to confuse the legitimate artist, to disarm the arousing academician, and to fool the public.

[5] As I have previously stated, art is considered a weapon of communism, and the Communist doctrinaire names the artist as a soldier of the revolution. It is a weapon in the hands of a soldier in the revolution against our form of government, and against any government or system other than communism.

[6] From 1914 to 1920 art was used as a weapon of the Russian Revolution to destroy the Czarist Government, but when this destruction was accomplished, art ceased to be a weapon and became a medium of propaganda, picturing and extolling the imaginary wonders, benefits and happiness of existence under the socialized state.

[7] Let me trace for you a main artery from the black heart of the isms of the Russian Revolution to the very heart of art in America.

[8] In 1914 Kandinsky, a Russian-born Expressionist and nonobjective painter, who found it safer to live in Germany, returned to Russia and 3 years later came the revolution. He is the man who preached that art must abandon the logical and adopt the illogical. He dominated a group of black knights of the isms, who murdered the art of the Russian academies. They were Cubists, Futurists, Expressionists, Constructionists, Suprematists, Abstractionists, and the rest of the same ilk. Kandinsky was a friend of Trotsky, and after the revolution founded the

Moscow Institute of Art Culture. He was Communist leader in Red art —the commissar of the isms. [See Fig. 1, p. 108.]

[9] Kandinsky remained in Russia until 1921, when the art of the isms began to feel the iron grip of the new art control, the art for the sake of propaganda, the art of social realism. Kandinsky went back to Germany.

[10] The Communist art that has infiltrated our cultural front is not the Communist art in Russia today—one is the weapon of destruction, and the other is the medium of controlled propaganda. Communist art outside Russia is to destroy the enemy, and we are the enemy of communism. Communist art in Russia is to delude the Russian workers.

[11] The art of the isms, the weapon of the Russian Revolution, is the art which has been transplanted to America, and today, having infiltrated and saturated many of our art centers, threatens to overawe, override and overpower the fine art of our tradition and inheritance. So-called modern or contemporary art in our own beloved country contains all the isms of depravity, decadence, and destruction.

[12] What are these isms that are the very foundation of so-called modern art? They are the same old lot of the Russian Revolution, some with transparent disguises, and others added from time to time as new convulsions find a new designation. I call the roll of infamy without claim that my list is all-inclusive: dadaism, futurism, constructionism, suprematism, cubism, expressionism, surrealism, and abstractionism. All these isms are of foreign origin, and truly should have no place in American art. While not all are media of social or political protest, all are instruments and weapons of destruction. To trace the origin, development and history of all these isms is a task too lengthy for the time available to me here, and also beyond the scope of my intention. But I do tag them specifically, as well as generally, as instruments of destruction.

[13] Cubism aims to destroy by designed disorder.

[14] Futurism aims to destroy by the machine myth. The futurist leader, Marinetti, said: "Man has no more significance than a stone."

[15] Dadaism aims to destroy by ridicule.

[16] Expressionism aims to destroy by aping the primitive and insane. Klee, one of its three founders, went to the insane asylums for his inspiration.

[17] Abstractionism aims to destroy by the creation of brainstorms.

[18] Surrealism aims to destroy by the denial of reason.

[19] Let me touch briefly on some of the "isms": The four leaders of the Cubist group were Picasso, Braque, Leger, and Duchamp, but

what these reds are today is another matter. The artists of the "isms" change their designations as often and as readily as the Communist front organizations. Picasso, who is also a dadaist, an abstractionist, or a surrealist, as unstable fancy dictates, is the hero of all the crackpots in so-called modern art. The left-wing critics call him the "gage" by which American modernists may measure their own radical worth, and a dozen years ago it was arranged that he address his disciples in the Red American Artists Congress by international telephone hook-up. But no matter what others call Picasso, he has said of himself: "I am a Communist and my painting is Communist painting."

[20] Concerning the other three, Braque, Leger, and Duchamp, there is variation only in degree of unbalance. Leger and Duchamp are now in the United States to aid in the destruction of our standards and traditions. The former has been a contributor to the Communist cause in America; the latter is now fancied by the neurotics as a surrealist.

[21] The founding of surrealism is attributed to one Andre Breton. Samuel Putnam, former Red art critic for the Communist publication New Masses, says: "The surrealists are avowed Communists."

[22] In his book, the Politics of the Unpolitical, Herbert Read, English author advocate of surrealism, says surrealism "is actually Communist, though generally anti-Stalinist. They are performing a very important revolutionary function. The particular method they adopt is to so mingle fact and fancy that the normal concept of reality no longer has existence."

[23] There is a book titled "Out of This Century," written by one Peggy Guggenheim, formerly owner of Modern Art Galleries in London and New York, and financial sponsor of Herbert Read. This book is vile, and its further sale has been stopped. In its pages are many truths, carelessly revealed, concerning persons now notorious in modern art. Max Ernst, a surrealist, was formerly married to the author.

[24] According to the printed statement of Peggy Guggenheim, the Museum of Modern Art in New York arranged the flight passage of Max Ernst to the United States, and paid a deposit to hold a reservation for him at Lisbon. This is the same Max Ernst who directed the 1920 Dadaist exhibition in Cologne, where the only entrance was through a public urinal. The approach was but a nonprophylactic dose of the main exhibit. Baargeld, the artist leader of the Dadaists in Cologne, was also leader of the Communist Party in the same district.

.   .   .   .

[25] Another surrealist leader in this same disreputable group is Aragon—the Frenchman. He is a well-known Red, in fact, along with Maxim Gorky and Whitaker Chambers, self-confessed Communist, he

has been an editor of the publication International Literature, organ of the Soviet International Union of Revolutionary Writers—Citations. Concerning Aragon, the voluble Peggy Guggenheim says:

> One day Rigid Edgwell invited me for dinner and asked me if I would render a great service to the Communist Party. They wanted to borrow my flat for Aragon and a whole convention of Communist writers who were coming to London.

[26] I do not know why Aragon has not been brought to the United States. But if Aragon has been overlooked, such is not the case with Kurt Seligman, the Swiss surrealist, who has been brought over to help pollute American art. He is another intimate of Max Ernst and of Marcel-Duchamp, and it is in Seligman's residence that surrealists have gathered in New York City. He has been named as one of three artist judges by the Hallmark Christmas Card Co., of Kansas City, to determine the winner in their $30,000 contest now in progress. This man, must I remind you, is a leader of surrealism, which holds our cultural heritage of religion is an obstacle to be overcome.

[27] A second of the three artist judges is Yasuo Kuniyoshi, presumably a Buddhist, but unquestionably a Red Fronter. These two are a majority of the three artist judges who are going to select the pictures that will be on the Christmas cards of a Christian people for the greatest of all religious holidays.

[28] Others of this surrealist group are Miro of Spain, Masson of France, and Henry Moore of England, the last named being invariably lauded by New York City Communists, The New Masses and International Literature—Communist publications.

[29] Salvador Dali, another Spanish surrealist, is now in the United States. He is reported to carry with him at all times a picture of Lenin.

[30] English surrealists are Barbara Hepworth and Stanley Hayter, the latter now resident in the United States and a member of the American contingent on the Panel of Visual Art of UNESCO.

[31] Add to this group of subversives the following American satellites, and the number swells to a rabble: Motherwell, Pollock, Baziotes, David Hare, and Marc Chagall. The last named is lauded by Communist publications and is a sponsor of the School of Jewish Studies, cited by Attorney General Tom Clark "as an adjunct in New York City of the Communist Party." At this school Chagall is associated with some of the old gang, including Minna Harkavy, Louis Lozowick, William Gropper, Phillip Evergood, Raphael Soyer, and Lena Gurr.

[32] Abstractivism, or nonobjectivity, in so-called modern art was spawned as a simon pure, Russian Communist product. Sidney Janis says:

It was in Russia that this latter absolute form of expression came into being, and its creators were Kandinsky and Malevich.

[33] That you may see clearly the definite, positive link between the Communist art of the "isms" and the so-called modern art of America, let me state that Kandinsky was elected vice president in 1923 of the Société Anonyme, which was established in New York in 1920 by Katherine Dreier, as an international association for the promotion of the study in America of the progressive in art. Nor was the election of Kandinsky a passing fancy or a light gesture. This Communist of the Russian Revolution, ex-teacher of the Moscow Museum of Pictorial Culture and ex-founder of the Russian Academy of Artistic Sciences, served as vice president of this New York organization for many years.

[34] The Société Anonyme, according to the American Art Annual, was first organized as Museum of Modern Art. Katherine Dreier, its president, is an aging but active left-winger, born in Brooklyn, pal of Kandinsky in Germany, a sponsor of Henry Wallace, and an author of several books published by the Société Anonyme, among them one on Burliuk, that Communist patron and teacher of Mayakowsky, the revolutionary poet of Russia, and one on Kandinsky, the commissar of the "isms."

.   .   .   .

[35] It makes little difference where one studies the record, whether of surrealism, dadaism, abstractionism, cubism, expressionism, or futurism. The evidence of evil design is everywhere, only the roll call of the art contortionists is different. The question is, what have we, the plain American people, done to deserve this sore affliction that has been visited upon us so direly; who has brought down this curse upon us; who has let into our homeland this horde of germ-carrying art vermin?

[36] Last year, in 1948, the Museum of Modern Art brought Herbert Read here from England to address the sixth annual conference of the committee on art education, a committee of 1,000 American art educators and teachers, offering their bared breasts for free injections of the evil virus of the "isms," anti-Christian, antisanity, antimorality, and anti-American. This is the same Read who lauds surrealism and abstractionism, both Communist, and avowed instruments to destroy our traditional culture. Read has boasted:

We in England have announced our adherence to this movement. What I wish to stress now is that surrealism is an application of the same logical method (dialectical materialism) to the realm of art. By the dialectical method we can explain the development of art in the past and justify a revolutionary art at the present time.

[37] What is the relationship between Read's benefactor, this Museum of Modern Art, stated to have been organized in 1929, and the Museum of Modern Art, organized in 1920, alias the Société Anonyme, which bestowed honor and made obeisance to Kandinsky, the commissar of isms, in 1923?

[38] Daniel C. Rich in his article in the Atlantic Monthly has this to say:

> The Museum of Modern Art, opening in 1929, included all types of twentieth century expression and crystallized a number of earlier efforts, of which the Société Anonyme, founded in 1920 by K. S. Dreier and the artists Marcel Duchamp and Man Ray, was probably the most notable.

[39] There you have the record. The Museum of Modern Art, founded in 1920, officered in 1923, and for years thereafter, by Kandinsky, Russian commissar of "isms," becomes crystallized in 1929 as the present Museum of Modern Art. As an enduring link between the two, Alfred H. Barr, Jr., member of the board of directors of the Société Anonyme, is the director of the present Museum of Modern Art.

[40] The Museum of Modern Art has published a pamphlet by this Herbert Read, titled "Culture and Education in World Order." By so doing it would seem to give approval to Read's expressed conviction, that "our vested interests of great antiquity and power," as represented by our kindergartens, schools, academies, colleges, universities, institutes, and laboratories, "must be left to die a natural death."

. . . .

[41] How did we ever let this horde of art distortionists, these international art thugs descend upon us? Daniel Catton Rich, director of fine arts, Art Institute of Chicago, explains:

> The arrival of a boatload of famous European modernists, just before the war, also vastly stimulated the nonrepresentational ° ° ° the present group of refugees met and influenced American painters ° ° °. Other modernists ° ° ° had already landed in American universities and art schools, where they set to work busily teaching the precepts of advanced European expression.

[42] In the world of so-called modern art this Daniel Catton Rich pulls a heavy oar. He is director of fine arts, Art Institute of Chicago, and a pupil of Paul J. Sachs, head of the Fogg Museum of Harvard University. Rich sits as chairman on the panel of visual art of UNESCO along with three specimens from the Museum of Modern Art, and Ben Shahn, Sam Lewishon, and William Zorach, which last three have an aggregate of 21 references against them in the reports of the Committee on Un-American Activities.

[43] The maestro of this Rich, Paul J. Sachs, head of the Fogg Museum at Harvard, is an honorary trustee of the Museum of Modern Art, at 11 West Fifty-third Street, New York City.

[44] Thomas Craven, foremost art critic in the United States, refers to the Fogg Museum as "the rendezvous of an effeminate and provincial tribe." Under the administration of Paul J. Sachs it has accepted, nurtured, and exalted the whole school of so-called modern and contemporary art, but more catastrophic than that, the Fogg Museum has trained many of its effeminate elect to be directors of museums throughout our land. These individuals have gone forth predisposed to promote the art of the "isms," and they to a large degree have been responsible for the acquisition at inflated fictitious prices of so-called master works of this hog-scrapple of art that the public does not like, does not understand, and does not want to buy. They blanket our museums of art from Maine to California—and on to Hawaii. Not only do they persist in jamming this art trash down the throats of the public, but they have effectively aided in excluding the works of our real American artists from exhibitions and competitions, by loading the juries against the academic artists—in innumerable instances the committees on invitations are so fixed that the traditional artist is no longer invited to send his paintings. Most of the finest artists that our Nation numbers no longer exhibit at all.

[45] We are now face to face with the intolerable situation, where public schools, colleges, and universities, art and technical schools, invaded by a horde of foreign art manglers, are selling to our young men and women a subversive doctrine of "isms," Communist-inspired and Communist-connected, which have one common, boasted goal—the destruction of our cultural tradition and priceless heritage. Many of our museum repositories of art treasures are now under the guidance of judgments that have been warped, and eyes that are blinded, seeing not the inevitable destruction that awaits if this Marxist trail is not abandoned.

[46] All, or nearly all, of these cultural centers have an upper level of conservatism, substance, extreme respectability and unchallenged Americanism, but these tolerant complacents cover a very active lower stratum of pink busybodies, who squander institutional funds in an orgy of spending to hasten the destruction of the art of our great inheritance.

[47] In my previous addresses on this subject, I have used the word infiltration in describing the present Red element in American art. This is an understatement. Communist art, aided and abetted by misguided Americans, is stabbing our glorious American art in the back with murderous intent.

[48] Among the artists themselves I see two distinct divisions in Communist influence. There are some very able artists, who paint excellently in our established and revered tradition, but who are radical, or Communist, or Communist in sympathy in their ideology. When these individuals are presented for consideration as members of our highest art organizations, many members say, in effect: "I will not vote against a good artist because of his politics." This is evidence of very shallow thinking. In the first place, communism or any near approach to it is not politics. Communism, regardless of the limitations of our present laws, is treason. Why should our highest art organizations have any different standard of membership than our bar associations? The fact that a man knows law is only a bare essential requirement of admission to a bar association. A candidate must pass the strict requirements of the character committee, and it seems to me clearly indicated that in these troubled times, no man shall be admitted to an organization of honor unless he be a man of honor, of good character, and of unshaken allegiance to his Government.

[49] These Marxists of talent, who paint in the academic tradition, are the door openers for the polyglot rabble of subversives who detest and scorn all academic traditions and culture.

. . . .

[50] From every section of this Republic I have received letters from artists, thanking me for the truths I have spoken to them. Among the hundreds are communications from persons whose names are the most distinguished in real American art. Generally, they have implored me to help them in the battle that finds them now so sorely tried. To them I say, that the things I have revealed here are the truths they have told me, and I stand ever ready to help defend the heritage of the land that has given us all so much; but, ultimately, whether we triumph for American ideals of culture depends upon their willingness to protect what providence and freedom has given them. In their readiness to smite an organized, subversive minority, no matter how deeply entrenched, depends their future and America's welfare.

Questions

1. How does Dondero support his thesis that modern art is a weapon of communism? What proofs does he furnish?
2. Consider Dondero's catalogue of art movements (paragraph 12) and his statement: "All these isms are of foreign origin, and truly should have no place in American art." What other art movements can you trace back to foreign origins?
3. What is Dondero's basic objection to Picasso, Braque, Leger, and Duchamp? Is his objection political or aesthetic?

4. "In 1914 Kandinsky . . . returned to Russia, and 3 years later came the revolution" (paragraph 8). Comment on the implied relationship between these two events.
5. Summarize the genesis of the Museum of Modern Art as Dondero states it. Are his statements factually correct?
6. What does Dondero mean by characterizing alumni of the Fogg Museum at Harvard as "effeminate elect" (paragraph 44)? What do you suppose is his purpose in this accusation?
7. What kinds of art does Dondero admire? How does he describe such works?
8. Do you find Dondero's speech generally convincing? Why or why not?

EXTREMIST ART: COMMUNITY CRITICISM[*]

Harold Rosenberg

> MOSCOW, Nov. 14. The official view was still that the Impressionist school was a setback for French art because it was formalistic and divorced from realism.
>
> *The New York Times*, Nov. 15, 1955

[1] It is lugubrious to relate that the New American Conservatism (sometimes styling itself "humanism," though nothing could be more remote from the spirit of Rabelais and Montaigne) having inspired a few drab volumes and labored essays in literature and social polemics, has begun turning its melancholy and aggressive attentions in the direction of painting.

[2] To analyze separately the position of these latest foes of Cézanne, Cubism, Mondrian, European Expressionism and American Action Painting would be a waste of time. Despite their pose of last-ditch resistance to the radical and de-individualizing tendencies of our age, their arguments and terminology are the old ones of the Communists and other social disciplinarians. About this homogeneity there is no great mystery. Whether coming from the right or the left, the attack on modern extremist art, especially at the moment when it is still extreme, always is launched from the standpoint of The Community. Each ideology has, of course, its own definition of what The Community is; but all agree that its voice is not heard in the representative painters of our time and that art itself in our century has not done right by it—apart, perhaps, from a contribution to linoleum patterns.

[3] The gist of Community Criticism is to be found in the quotation at the head of this page, the dateline of which could just as well have

been Washington, the Vatican or The Art of the Ages. The key is the word "formalistic," which in the pseudo-esthetic jargon of the anti-modern front is an indictment that includes automatically "lacking in significant content," "alien to the real world," "pathologically self-isolated and private," "insensitive to the tragedies and hopes of our epoch," "snobbish refusal to communicate with the people," etc.

[4] It is characteristic of the babel of Community denunciation of the mental and moral dwarfishness of this century's creations that it projects itself above the heads of artists, art critics and intellectuals interested in art, in order to exhort the "layman," who for this occasion has been outfitted free of charge with suitable tastes and emotions. The Common Man has thrust upon him by the anti-formalist cults a powerful natural admiration for Rembrandt, El Greco, Goya, even Giotto or Cimabue, that is to say of any painter of "pictures," since all one needs to "get" these painters is an eye, with perhaps a hint here and there from the Community Critic of profundities concerning Dutch life or Spanish death.

[5] This same simple citizen art lover, the fable goes, was of yore happily stimulated, refined, enlightened and uplifted by art into being a still better citizen; but having arrived at the epoch of Cézanne and Picasso he feels frustrated, irritable and led by the nose; inhuman formalism has stiff-armed him out of the reach of art; he would protest against these inane exercises and underground insults forced upon him by The Modern Art Hoax except that he is intimidated by its organized promoters. "Don't let them bully you," cries courageously the humanist, dismounting from his chariot. "An art that does not appeal to your deepest feelings is no art at all. The task of painting is to depict the Great Common Experiences of Man."

[6] Naturally, the Great Common Experiences, to stage which on canvas painting has received an historical retainer, inevitably turn out to be situations which exemplify the values of the humanist, Communist, nationalist, etc., i.e., dramas of high ethical purport, episodes of class struggle and defense of the Revolutionary Homeland, patriotic and homey scenes, the folk and its heroes (Fascist), miracle and martyrdom (religious). The "experience" which they discover in the paintings of the past as their grand Content is never the experienced experience of an individual artist—like the experience of Leonardo as discovered by formalist Valéry—but an antiqued contemporary ready-made, suitable for packaged distribution.

[7] If there is anything the humanist resents more than the content-less art of our epoch, it is statements about this art which explicate its content. If Mondrian or Miro or some informed commentator describes

the motives, origins and references in experience of an extremist style
or work, the tactic is to remain silent about this reflection—how grant
that a formalist has even wanted to communicate?—or to attack it as
humanistically, or mass-intellectually, speaking even more obnoxiously
empty and mystifying than the paintings themselves. The thought of
painters (as distinguished from gossip about them) only adds verbal
insult to retinal injury, and the less the humanist sees in a canvas the
stronger is its evidence to him of conspiracy to drive everybody mad.

[8] The humanist's reflex to writings about extremist art demon-
strates that his argument of Content versus Formalism has nothing to
do with the actual meaning or obscurity of paintings but is, primarily,
a *political* argument. It is designed to shark up a militant solidarity of
Plain Men in behalf of an ideology seeking social power and to "integrate" the artist into a *polis* ruled by this ideology.

[9] A book like Selden Rodman's *The Eye of Man* (Devin-Adair),
while full of shotgun judgments of paintings and artists in many periods
and especially in our own, is political and nothing else—not because it
pushes for some definite party or movement but because it creeps up
on painting with an order of concepts based on whether or not the artists have shown signs of being "detached from the community." To
Rodman, as to *Novy Mir*, the Pope or Harry Truman, "formalistic" work
smells of society's outsiders and is without substance, except the artist's
private pathology (e.g., Soutine); in painting following the tradition of
Cézanne, Rodman finds, Content has, as never before, "suffered a total
eclipse."

[10] As art criticism, it is pretty plain that this contention doesn't
mean anything. As politics, however, its connotations are exceedingly
specific: a society that does not allow outsiders, or which condemns
their thought as *ipso facto* void, is a special kind of community. Rodman wants to lay on his yardstick somewhat differently from Hunting-
ton Hartford or the buffoons of city censorship councils—he, for instance, finds a religious message in Rouault's fat whores who are just
ugly to Hartford, and instead of attacking de Kooning expresses the
hope that the Venus that has risen out of his waves of paint will get
married and settle down. But Rodman's disagreements with the civic
commandos is a family quarrel. A book "addressed to laymen" in order
to arouse them with appeals to exalted values against the vacuous and
deranged art of their day, without giving those laymen a hint of their
own abstractness and inner isolation nor of the motives and disciplines
of extremist styles, cannot be considered as pertinent outside its own
circle of agitation, either to art or popular education.

[11] That in this century when all the sciences operate under the

regimen of mathematical symbolisms or methodological jargons, so that the physical and social universe appears as separate capsules of incomprehensibles, while, on the other hand, mass-injected superstitions represent the essences of politics, domestic life, virtue, the past, as a trayload of variously colored powders—that in such a situation works of art should function as precisely the exclusive language of the concrete human event, but by this very fact sever themselves from general intelligibility and, especially, easy definition in proportion to their authenticity, this rudimentary historical datum seems to have eluded the esthetic traditionalists of all society-renovating Fronts. In practical effect the organized opposition to abstraction in art by non-artists is simply a clamor for a still larger number of abstract responses by the populace to favored themes. (To forestall the possibility of prematurely rising temperatures, may I note that I am *not* taking sides here in the question of Abstract vs. Realist art, and that this pseudo-antithesis will be dealt with later?)

[12] Reality . . . by all means more of it and not only in painting! The Common Man himself could use a bit—and above all the Conservative critic. As for painting, one can admire new images and still be bored to death, apart from agitators and school teachers, by artists who likewise believe that the contribution of the past fifty years has been to redefine painting as an arrangement of colored shapes.

[13] What kind and how much reality or experience a work of art can "contain" at any given moment, and to what extent "content" has vanished from the pictures and poems of the past through the hollowing out of the esthetic language, is known only through efforts in which artists are the chief specialists. Ezra Pound, incomparable teacher of the art of poetry to Americans, derided John Milton because for Pound poetry existed only in the tension of the verbal surface. Yet compared with the huge shadow figures and cosmic chaos and dark night of *Paradise Lost*, Pound's translated elegancies, inside stuff about personae and chop chop at our "dying civilization" seem picayune. Does this make Pound a "formalist" who wilfully shrank the content of poetry through a mistaken emphasis on its means? Nonsense. Poe had testified a century earlier that *Paradise Lost* had collapsed into a pile of isolated passages and individual lines whose effect changed each time one read a few pages. The grand outlines of the work could be seen but it was no longer possible to get near it as poetry. But if Milton's esthetic content had evaporated the problem was not how to re-bottle it. Pound's judgment of Milton was wrong but he was right about what poetry needed; in the long run this would make him a help also to Milton.

[14] In the art of the past the artist can only choose between what is art for him and what has become non-art; to keep the art he may have to throw away most of it. Nor in his own work will the scale of its meaning be for him to decide. For an artist today not to feel that painting has lost a great deal since Rubens only makes it more difficult for him to realize that Rubens is not an issue. Admiring inherited masterpieces in order to saddle contemporaries with the responsibility to equal them is a trick of totalitarians and busybodies. The various currents of Community Criticism converge in misleading the public into believing that an artist has a free choice as to what the true content of his painting shall be and that his failure to concern himself with social ideals and problems is evidence of malice. Once this myth has been established, "Significant Content" can be introduced with the aid of Sanitation Committees and the police.

[15] For American painters the question of willed content was settled for a generation by the frustrating adventure into 1930s politics, as well as by individual sorties into commercial and commissioned work. Artists who discovered their social will under the stimulation of the Left Front tried to reason out a conclusion concerning History's demand on art—after all, you couldn't have a more important boss. Some wasted years before the intuition dawned on them that *any* decision both as to form and subject matter might be deadly if it happened to be incompatible with the psychology of the creative process, over which no artist has final control. Only when the collapse of the arts in the USSR, Germany and Italy demonstrated beyond doubt the irreconcilability of art and ideological utility, and that to be told what to paint was inevitably to be told how to paint, did artists in America shake off the nightmare of "Responsibility."

[16] Following the debacle of class-conscious art, regional-scene painting, Americana, WPA history and other "communicating" modes, Reality, left, center and right wing, was for a time unnaturally quiescent, perhaps because the corpse left by assignments, resolutions, artist congresses, seemed unlikely to disconcert anyone by making a fresh move. During the War and for some time thereafter, painting was obviously not the arena in which to stage a popular rally in behalf of either social protest or order.

[17] When, however, I reported a few years ago that American painting, having revived from its mortification by Values high and low in a cave happily devoid of pioneer and proletarian totems or the reflection of middle-class faces, sheep or street corners, essayed to evoke through the gesticulations of a limb ending in paint-clotted bristles an image on the underside of which the artist could, like Odysseus, be

carried out of the reach of the howling Polyphemus of Responsible Art to the open sea of an act of dramatic self-identification—no sooner had I recounted this simple tale than it became obvious that the Thirty Years War of leaflet sowers had recovered its normal frenzy, although it was already the most open of secrets that the slogans of both Realism and Abstraction now clumsily disguised the defense of vested interests in certain obsolete techniques. That American Action Painting had been demonstrated to be exclusively content of a particular order prevented no one from whooping for or against its total preoccupation with Form. Of all the humanists who have since attacked this painting, not one, to my knowledge, has gone farther in the way of discussing its human and metaphysical testimony than to affix to it some phrases turned into their opposites by removal from their context, in order to support charges of formalistic emptiness, irrationality and anti-social withdrawal which had become platitudes decades before these canvases were conceived.

[18] If a veteran New York painter, finding himself in art's dugout at the beginning of the '40s, had the ingenuity, inspired by years of submarine existence, to fill it to the top with water and reproduce in Kodachrome the hues generated on different levels by the light falling through his fishpond, is his image less a "communication" of experience than, say, Jack Levine's reminder on canvas that in a big city there are gangsters? I had heard about these gangsters before Levine commented on them and so had other people, including the gangsters. But before this painter, to the humanist a mere geometer, I knew much less about being a fish, although there had been a few passionate outcries about this condition—for example, in Eliot's *Wasteland* [sic] and some German novels. The "Formalist" communicated a significant content through paint, while Levine, or Blume, organizing in color everybody's Reality, are the true formalists. In fact, Levine's flickering monochrome funeral parlor, with its sun-falling-through-leaves quality of a last-century Continental lawn, augmenting with its anachronistic gentility the quiet pleasure aroused by the way the fat politician holds his head on a side, is to such an extent an absorption of big-city unexperienced newspaper Reality into art history that it could serve as a model of Formalism. Except that—there is no such thing. Because, as the Hindus say, Realism is one of the fifty-seven (or some other number) varieties of decoration.

Questions

1. What is the "New American Conservatism" (paragraph 1)? Does Rosenberg ever define this term as he uses it?

2. What is meant by the "Great Common Experiences of Man" (paragraphs 5 and 6) as the humanist presumably defines the term? How does Rosenberg use this term? Why?
3. Rosenberg finds much similarity in the motives of humanists, Communists, and nationalists when they state their conceptions of the purposes of art. What does he accuse them of? What is his own position?
4. What are "Community Critics"?
5. "Admiring inherited masterpieces in order to saddle contemporaries with the responsibility to equal them is a trick of totalitarians and busybodies" (paragraph 14). What do you think Rosenberg means by this statement? How is his argument relevant to abstract paintings?
6. What charges does Rosenberg find have been leveled against American action painting? How does he refute these charges?
7. How does Rosenberg deal with the *form vs. content* argument?
8. Comment, with examples, on Rosenberg's style in this essay. What assumptions is he apparently making about his readers?

NARCISSUS IN CHAOS: CONTEMPORARY AMERICAN ART*

Cleve Gray

[1] The modern revolt against academicism is more than a century old, yet we are still flailing the horse that has long died. The new and the shocking in all arts are still so eagerly received that they are scarcely questioned so long as they are not academic. Branded as conservative and reactionary are any suggestions that order is intrinsic to art, that an artist has an obligation of aesthetic responsibility, that individuality should be disciplined. But if these standards are no longer reputable, what has replaced them?

[2] The director of the most influential contemporary art museum in this country and his staff are making a collection of art that sets the standard of public taste. He has often been asked, on behalf of the public, how he makes his choices. To paraphrase his various answers, he tells us that he picks the work of artists who significantly reflect the age they live in, work which he believes will stand the test of time as unique and intensely imaginative expressions of individuality. One cannot argue with this aim, although it is one that presupposes vast knowledge. It presupposes, for one thing, a profound understanding of the relation of present-day American culture to Western civilization;

* From *The American Scholar*, Vol. 28, No. 4, 1959. Copyright © 1959 by United Chapters of Phi Beta Kappa. Reprinted by permission.

and, even more, it requires ability to project into the future with a perspective developed only by time. On a lower plane, it also demands ability to distinguish between works of art that will have lasting meaning from those that are simply curious and irresponsible.

[3] Undoubtedly the most respected art critics and museums in the United States have bet their chips heavily on a group called "avant-garde," a group composed of "abstract expressionists" and "action painters" in particular, and of non-objective artists in general. Leading painters in the group are Pollock, De Kooning, Motherwell, Still, Kline and Sam Francis, along with the older and influential teachers, Hans Hofmann and Stuart Davis. Paintings by members of this group were gathered together to represent United States art at the Brussels Fair. These painters have declared over and over, both in words and in paint, that they were not painting the visual world but rather their inner responses, that they were dealing with pure forms of vision and re-creating a new world, that they had replaced old types of art with the new art of their own unique symbols.

[4] Stuart Davis typifies these thoughts in describing one of his own paintings: "Instead of the usual illusionist method, the emotions and ideas were equated in terms of a quantitatively coherent dimensional color-space system." The art critic Herbert Read gives further details about these intentions: "Modern man . . . will seek his ideal in some abstract harmony or in some symbol rising unaided from the depths of his unconscious."

[5] This is a presumptuous program for an artist. It is presumptuous because it deliberately states that the visual declaration the artist makes is not about his conception of the visual world, but is only about his own individuality. The artist assumes that his own ego and unconscious are worth contemplating, are more worthy of contemplation than the objective world. Yet he will admit to you in the very moment he sets his unique individuality before you that he is saying nothing more than, "Here I am!" To quote Hans Hofmann: "Everyone should be as different as possible. There is nothing that is common to all of us except our creative urge. It just means one thing to me, to discover myself as well as I can."

[6] What is the origin of this egotism? One is tempted, at first sight, to find it in nineteenth-century Romanticism, but this association is false. The Romanticists of the nineteenth century looked into themselves in order to discover what men really felt, after a period in which feeling had been desiccated and sophisticated. The Romanticists were not only ready to abandon any introspection that was not borne out by

common experience, but they used nature and history as touchstones by which to sort out the genuine from the fanciful. The Romanticists were, in a sense, conducting a new survey of human experience under conditions akin to scientific observation. But it is a far cry from their open and tentative results, couched in intelligible forms that all could criticize, to the esoteric pronouncements that modern artists seek to impose by fiat. As Clement Greenberg, critic and champion of the avant-garde, has said: "The image or object can be put back into art only by pastiche or parody."

[7] The modern egotist is saying that, except for its parody, the object *must* be eliminated, that *we dare not* put the object back into the painting. This modern singularism-by-decree is something very different from the Romanticist's imaginative interpretation of self and nature seeking to communicate truth.

[8] Most of us have a conception of the difference between an ordered and a disordered life; but few of us stop to consider what is meant by order and disorder in art. The word "order" has taken on many special and honorific connotations; but what it comes down to is methodical and harmonious relationships. Whether or not one is speaking of the church, of law, of the military, of grammar, or simply saying, "My refrigerator is out of order" or "My bank account is in good order," one means the same thing. Order is the working principles of organization and intrinsic authority. With reference to art, the meaning is the same; it can be emphasized by the relation of the words "art" and "articulate." Both words derive from *ars*, "to join." To articulate means to make clear and to function; it often refers to joints that operate or to speech that is distinct. Just so does the word art refer to the problem of expressing the burden of a new creation with clarity. This is accomplished by a working relation of parts, and in the visual arts by an articulation of all the components that can be used for expression. The more imaginative and inclusive use of these components is, the greater is the significant value of the work.

[9] An artist has two different kinds of elements or components to articulate: the explicit parts, which are his lines, brushwork, color, form and the like; and the implicit parts, which are the various connotations and meanings implied and contained in the visual work. A painting or sculpture that consists simply of a vertical line has almost entirely eliminated the possibilities of implicit significance that enrich a work of art. A painting or sculpture that is mechanically realistic has eliminated most of the possibilities of significance inherent in the explicit parts. Actually, no work of art can make exclusive use of either of these two kinds of components without some reference to the other

ind; but the character of the references and the degree of penetration into the relations between explicit and implicit expression determine he ultimate value of the work of art.

[10] A sense of responsibility in life denotes respect for the obligation to act according to one's best intentions and powers. The artist's responsibility is no different. His obligation is to use the rich possibilities of his chosen art. We say a man is irresponsible if his actions are unrelated to standards of order. An irresponsible artist likewise holds himself not accountable to standards of visual reference. We judge whether the artist achieves responsible expression when we see how he uses visual references.

[11] Academic art destroys the significance of individual expression by making unchangeable rules for the use of the explicit and implicit elements. But the reaction against academicism is no more worthy if it ignores or reduces possibilities of expression to insignificance. The more significant the expression, the greater the work of art. One may justly destroy old standards of order only if new standards replace them. The act of destruction by itself is not a creative act; it is irresponsible unless it prepares the ground for creation. Old standards give way to new ones only if the newer standards are more expressive and constructive.

[12] The character of subject matter in painting bears directly upon the significance of the work of art because it helps determine the implicit component. Distinguishing his ideas from the classic idea that subject matter is real and belongs to the artist, the American avant-garde sculptor and painter will frequently describe how necessary it is before beginning work to spend a period of time in contemplation; and, if he has subject matter at all, this subject matter will be forced to disappear and to become his own reactions. Elaine de Kooning, painter, critic, wife of Willem de Kooning, writes: "The main difference, then, between abstract and nonabstract art is that the abstract artist does not have to choose a subject. But whether or not he chooses, he always ends up with one." Creative will must apparently abdicate in favor of the creative accident. Subjective contemplation preceding work has long been characteristic of Oriental rather than Occidental art, developing from the philosophy of a world in disorder rather than an ordered universe. But, what is to the point, the Oriental artist always depicted reality. He never professed to give us a non-objective world. He invariably stated in his work that through the contemplation of visual reality he had passed to the high plane of spiritual unity, and that *his work showed this passage*. Indeed, that was its purpose.

[13] It is related of Wu Tao-tzu, the Giotto of China, that one day he

disappeared into his own painting of a landscape and was never seen again. In the contemporary American abstract expressionist action painting, it is the landscape that disappears into the artist. The unhappy spectator stares at an unintelligible vacuum.

[14] It is a widespread cliché that in the twentieth century standards of order no longer exist, although Western civilization has always conceived of an orderly universe. Man in the Far East, perhaps because of a more brutal environment, has seen mainly the disorder of his personal life. As an artist he sought and found an escape in metaphysics; as a philosopher, possibly defending himself against a world in disorder, he dissolved his individual identity in the infinite oneness of the universe; whereas Western man, in a kinder, more submissive environment, attempts to dominate nature, forming it in his own image. Western man's identity is part of, even necessary to, all his metaphysical systems.

[15] In twentieth-century America, the emphasis on the precious identity of the individual has been more intense than ever before. We place a priceless worth on the existence of every person. We feel a tremendous necessity to cultivate his physical and spiritual demands. We value a man's creations *according to the very degree of their individuality.*

[16] Western civilization has from time to time turned to Greece as a period in which an ideal balance of creative individuality and individual responsibility was achieved. It is a telling fact that the Greek word for "idiot" ($ἰδιώτηζ$) has also the meaning "his own" or "private person." In other words, the individual becomes idiotic at the point where his experience is unrelated to a responsible conception of reality, the communal reality, and becomes entirely "his own." One may legitimately ask what is the relation to communal reality of the avant-garde artist. Harold Rosenberg, one of the first champions of action painting, describes its process: "He [the artist] gesticulated upon the canvas and watched for what each novelty would declare him and his art to be."

[17] It is, indeed, unnecessary for an artist to engage in communal activity outside his work. His communal activity is his work. His sense of communal responsibility ought to be present in the work itself, in the character of the aesthetic ideas communicated. Heaven forbid that the American artist should ever be required to communicate political ideas. But he should of his own accord feel the desire to use his freedom positively and constructively.

[18] The painting of Jackson Pollock is today widely accepted in a

great part of the world as being an important and highly individual contribution to art. Since his violent death, it has attained great monetary value, so that both aesthetic and financial judgment sustain it. It is extremely decorative and strong, and it possesses a degree of monumentality. Above all, it makes a kind of statement about the unlicensed freedom of an artist. But let us look further into the character of these attributes. After a long period of "classical" restraint surviving into the first half of the nineteenth century, the creative artists of Western Europe broke away from conventions of vision and technique, and they successfully established the artist's right to re-create visual reality according to conceptions that transcended ordinary visual experience. The assertion of the creative individual reached a Himalayan peak from 1900 to 1915. About 1915 destructive dangers, which are inherent in all revolutionary extremes, began to assert themselves. These were, perhaps, best typified by the Dadaists. The Dadaists clearly saw the result of the increased emphasis upon the individual's right to destroy his subject without re-creating a substitute. They saw that it led to a denial both of the validity of the subject and the necessity of the artist to create anything at all. Followed to its logical conclusion, this aesthetic declares that non-art is superior to art, that Marcel Duchamp should indeed abandon painting and devote his life to playing chess, and that, in the end, the most appropriate museum for modern art would be an empty building.

[19] Since the first years of this century, therefore, little work of truly unique style has been achieved. There have been simply different exaggerations of different aspects of the already liberated imagination. *Most men who have worked in paint have not used the liberated language of their individuality to make constructive assertions.* They have climbed a familiar peak only to hear their own voices echo back, "I made it!"

[20] It is ironical that the school of American art that calls itself the avant-garde, far from being ahead of its time, is rather drifting in a backwater of ideas significant half a century ago. The initial shock value that gave the group a purpose has worn off. In fact, the so-called avant-garde is now a phase of the academicism it abhors. It works by unimaginative conformity with set rules. It is also ironical that this group is promoted as the reflection of the spirit of American individualism and action; for by neglecting the responsibility inherent in a communicative individualism, and by failing to recognize laws of order and expression, it has lost the only individuality it could claim for itself.

[21] What I am saying is that although the best work of the con-

temporary non-objective painters, such as Pollock's, may be agreeably decorative, it is nothing more. Whether one displays oneself in dripped lines, in rectangular voids, in misty circles or in regulated squares is not important, because it expresses no defensible or disputable assertion. The artist who is so attracted to himself that he is content with his private shorthand, and the group that enjoys the contemplation of his narcissism will, one hopes, be replaced by artists who have learned the importance of human relations. And at this point I simply recall that Western civilization has developed because of its belief in ordered existence.

[22] In relating contemporary American painting to the Western conception of the individual, it is informative to ask what kind of order, if any, Western philosophy finds in life today. It has been stylish to blame science for upsetting our conventional faith, leaving us without a standard of order. But the Western scientist is continuously remarking upon the order of the universe and constantly searching for its grand design. The design of the scientist, who is increasingly dominating our mode of thinking, gives emphasis to his conviction that the order imposed upon life may not be imposed entirely by metaphysics, as we have believed, but is rather the spontaneous process of nature; in fact, it is the *necessary* process for the maintainance of the natural development of life. Without this natural order, life would cease. Biologists, biochemists and astronomers agree that systems of life that lose their process of order give way to systems that can maintain themselves through their own innate order. Life exists because it is ordered; it is not ordered because it exists. Science is constructing still more reasons for the belief in an ordered universe.

[23] To return to Pollock as an example of the best of the avant-garde group, it is helpful to review an aspect of his work which is often praised: its dancelike character. His work is praised for having been painted with bodily participation in the movement his canvases display. It is explained that he entered his creations physically in a new way. This achievement, action painting, is thus described by one of its first champions, Harold Rosenberg: "The painter no longer approached his easel with an image in his mind; he went up to it with material in his hand to do something to that other piece of material in front of him. The image would be the result of this encounter. . . . the painter gets away from Art through his act of painting. . . . This work, the act, translates the psychologically given into the intentional, into a 'world' —and thus transcends it." Well, Michelangelo painted the Sistine Chapel painfully on his back, Renoir's last work was done in a wheel

chair, and some Chinese painters of the "wild men" school used fingers instead of brushes; but this, I submit, should have not the slightest influence on our judgment of their value as works of art.

[24] I doubt, moreover, if the word "rhythmic" is properly used in describing the movement in Pollock's or other abstract expressionists' works. Rhythm is, in essence, regulated by inherent law; rhythmic harmony represents an organized conception of proportions. The conscious use of disharmony only serves to accent measurement. Without bounds upon it, rhythm becomes mere flux—the word that better describes the type of movement abstract-expressionist action painting creates. For flux is unrestrained and unregulated. It may be compared to a stream of consciousness, possessing the materials of expression but for lack of precision not *artfully* expressive. This flux has gained its present prominence because of a mistaken belief that it is "justified" by psychiatry. But the unrestrained freedom necessary to psychiatric investigation has never been intended as an end in itself; it is rather a method used to achieve order out of chaos. Proust and Joyce kept order in their free associations and dealt with ideas which humanity shares, their work being, in consequence, neither narcissistic nor chaotic.

[25] Similar considerations arise in discussing the emphasis placed upon the calligraphy of Pollock and others of the avant-garde. "Much has been said of the parallels between contemporary abstraction and Oriental esthetic, and Kline's bold strokes are among those having the nearest affinity to Eastern calligraphy," states the *Magazine of Art* in May of 1953. The word "calligraphy" is in this context improperly used. Oriental calligraphy refers to linear movement with inherent meaning. The civilization of the Orient has for centuries judged great calligraphy to be among the highest art forms. Painting technique in the Far East was founded on calligraphic movement. It should be obvious enough that a great difference exists between a calligraphy with implicit meaning behind every stroke and a would-be calligraphy without this inherent order. Tobey has also been hailed as an artist who has interpreted in Western terms the calligraphic character of Oriental art. He himself discusses this, saying: "I have just had my first lesson in Chinese brush from my friend and artist Teng Kwei. The tree is no more a solid in the earth, breaking into lesser solids bathed in chiaroscuro. There is pressure and release. Each movement, like tracks in the snow, is recorded and loved for itself." This suggests a child's first attempts to imitate his parent's writing. Movement of this tentative kind and "loved for itself" is linear meandering.

[26] It is poetic justice that the contemporary museum director, caught in the web of his own making, is all but required to exhibit the work of talented children because of its close relation to some contemporary painting. The work of children is praised, as it should be, for a quality of imaginative directness, but its exhibition in a museum is an inexpensive way of hedging one's bets. The museum director has so confused himself that he is no longer sure either of what to exhibit or what really constitutes a work of art.

[27] I do not know whether it is truly possible for Occidental art to express itself in Oriental terms. Before attempting this, it would be advisable for the avant-garde to gain more than a superficial knowledge of what Oriental art really is. Principles of Chinese art are often quoted. The intelligent critic and painter William Seitz has written: "Thanks to the analogous concern of both the modern and the Oriental artist for life rhythm and dynamic resolution of antithesis, we have gained for the first time a sympathy with the attitude of the Chinese toward reality." Sensing that the first principle of Hsieh Ho, properly translated as "spirit's breath and life movement," a prime requisite of Chinese painting, is somehow different from our Western concept of rhythm and must not be translated as "rhythm," most contemporary Western abstract expressionist action painters have interpreted this principle of vitality essential to Oriental art as license to give way in their own work to violent caprice and eccentricity.

[28] The fact that the breath of spirit and the movement of life must be present in a work of art means that the Far Eastern artist insists on a specific quality of life that makes the subject significant: its life. Indeed, objects that a Westerner calls inanimate, such as rocks, water, trees, have for the Oriental this quality of breath of spirit and life movement. All of disordered existence is pervaded with this vital force, yet it is not an ordering force; the Chinese artist does not search for an underlying structural order in the Western sense, but rather for nature's pervasive vitality. By losing himself in the magnitude of this vital force, the Chinese re-creates through his brush a visual representation of the appearance of this force as it manifests itself in objective reality. Nor is Oriental painting composed in the same manner as Western painting. A non-Western conception of dynamic unity comes into play that is neither abstract expressionist flux nor Western geometric composition. But, above all, the purpose of great Oriental art is to bring about the passage of the human soul from actuality and its disorder to the unity of an all-pervading spirit beyond life.

[29] We may, therefore, conclude that the object of all great art

Oriental or Occidental, is to elevate the spirit. Masterpieces of Western art achieve this end by an insistence on underlying structure, that is, order. Its source is metaphysical or, as science tells us, the fundamental requisite of life. Either way it is the order of life itself that exalts the Western soul. The painter's job is to find his way of interpreting this positive philosophy in visual terms. Many young American artists are working toward this goal, but they are not members either of the conservative realist or surrealist groups, nor are they part of the publicized avant-garde. In its honest effort to understand modern art, let us hope that the American public will soon be shown more of the constructive and less of the capricious.

Questions

1. Comment on Gray's title. What is the myth about Narcissus to which his title alludes? Is the allusion appropriate here?
2. What are the standards for art to which Gray subscribes (paragraph 1)? Where in his essay does he supply arguments in support of these standards?
3. Why does Gray describe the program of abstract expressionists as egotism (paragraphs 5–7)? Exactly what does he object to?
4. What is Gray's objection to academic art? When is a revolt against academicism justifiable? When not?
5. Gray dismisses the paintings of Jackson Pollock as "agreeably decorative . . . nothing more." What does Gray mean by this criticism? What *more*, according to him, should a painting be?
6. What is Gray's attitude toward the attempts of some abstract expressionists to borrow from Oriental art? Why does he think these attempts must fail? Do you agree with his judgment?
7. Examine Gray's concluding paragraph. Does he justify the fundamental assertion in it?

PICTURES FOR AN EXHIBITION: THE NEW AMERICAN PAINTING*

EDITORS' NOTE: An art show "devoted specifically to Abstract Expressionism in America" was organized by The Museum of Modern Art (New York) for exhibition in eight European countries during 1958–59. For this exhibition there was prepared a catalogue from which we have extracted the introduction and a few of the statements made by the artists themselves. Several of the reproductions of the paintings are included on pages 108–12 of this book.

* From *The New American Painting as Shown in Eight European Countries, 1958–59.* Copyright © 1959 by The Museum of Modern Art (New York). Reprinted by permission.

INTRODUCTION

Alfred H. Barr, Jr.

We are now committed to an unqualified act, not illustrating outworn myths or contemporary alibis. One must accept total responsibility for what he executes.

CLYFFORD STILL 1952

Voyaging into the night, one knows not where, on an unknown vessel an absolute struggle with the elements of the real.

ROBERT MOTHERWELL

There is no more forthright a declaration, and no shorter a path to man's richness, nakedness and poverty than the painting he does. Nothing can be hidden on its surface—the least private as well as the most personal of worlds.

JAMES BROOKS 1956

Art never seems to make me peaceful or pure . . . I do not think . . of art as a situation of comfort.

WILLEM DE KOONING 1951

The need is for felt experience—intense, immoderate, direct, subtle, uni fied, warm, vivid, rhythmic.

ROBERT MOTHERWELL 1951

Subject is crucial and only that subject matter is crucial which is tragic and timeless.

MARK ROTHKO

What happens on the canvas is unpredictable and surprising to me . . As I work, or when the painting is finished, the subject reveals itself.

WILLIAM BAZIOTES 1952

Usually I am on a work for a long stretch, until a moment arrives when the air of the arbitrary vanishes and the paint falls into positions that feel destined . . . To paint is a possessing rather than a picturing.

PHILIP GUSTON 1956

The function of the artist is to make actual the spiritual so that it is there to be possessed.

ROBERT MOTHERWELL

[1] Of the seventeen painters in this exhibition, none speaks for the others any more than he paints for the others. In principle their individ ualism is as uncompromising as that of the religion of Kierkegaard whom they honour. For them, John Donne to the contrary, each man is an island.

[2] Though a painter's words about his art are not always to be taken at face value, the quotations preceding this preface—like the statements printed further on—suggest that these artists share certain strong convictions. Many feel that their painting is a stubborn, difficult, even desperate effort to discover the "self" or "reality," an effort to which the whole personality should be recklessly committed: *I paint, therefore I am.* Confronting a blank canvas they attempt "to grasp authentic being by action, decision, a leap of faith," to use Karl Jaspers' Existentialist phrase.

[3] Indeed one often hears Existentialist echoes in their words, but their "anxiety," their "commitment," their "dreadful freedom" concern their work primarily. They defiantly reject the conventional values of the society which surrounds them, but they are not politically *engagés* even though their paintings have been praised and condemned as symbolic demonstrations of freedom in a world in which freedom connotes a political attitude.

[4] In recent years, some of the painters have been impressed by the Japanese Zen philosophy with its transcendental humour and its exploration of the self through intuition. Yet, though Existentialism and Zen have afforded some encouragement and sanction to the artists, their art itself has been affected only sporadically by these philosophies (by contrast with that of the older painter, Mark Tobey, whose abstract painting has been deeply and directly influenced by Tao and Zen).

[5] Surrealism, both philosophically and technically, had a more direct effect upon the painting of the group. Particularly in the early days of the movement, during the war, several painters were influenced by André Breton's programme of "pure psychic automatism . . . in the absence of all control exercised by reason and outside of all aesthetic and moral preoccupation." Automatism was, and still is, widely used as a technique but rarely without some control or subsequent revision. And from the first Breton's dependence upon Freudian and Marxian sanctions seemed less relevant than Jung's concern with myth and archaic symbol.

[6] The artists in the exhibition comprise the central core as well as the major marginal talent in the movement now generally called "Abstract Expressionism" or, less commonly, "Action Painting." Both terms were considered as titles for this exhibition.

[7] Abstract Expressionism, a phrase used ephemerally in Berlin in 1919, was re-invented (by the writer) about 1929 to designate Kandinsky's early abstractions that in certain ways do anticipate the American movement—to which the term was first applied in 1946. However, al-

most to a man, the painters in this show deny that their work is "abstract," at least in any pure, programmatic sense; and they rightly reject any significant association with German Expressionism, a movement recently much exhibited in America.

[8] Action Painting, a phrase proposed in preference to Abstract Expressionism by the poet-critic, Harold Rosenberg, in an important article published in 1952, now seems to overemphasize the physical act of painting.[1] Anyway, these artists dislike labels and shun the words "movement" and "school."

[9] The briefest glance around the exhibition reveals a striking variety among the paintings. How could canvases differ more in form than do Kline's broad, slashing blacks from Rothko's dissonant mists, or Pollock's Dionysiac *perpetuum mobile* from Newman's single, obsessive, vertical line? What then unites these paintings?

[10] First, their size. Painted at arm's length, with large gestures, they challenge both the painter and the observer. They envelop the eye, they seem immanent. They are often as big as mural paintings, but their scale as well as their lack of illusionistic depth are only coincidentally related to architectural decoration. Their flatness is, rather, a consequence of the artist's concern with the actual painting process as his prime instrument of expression, a concern which also tends to eliminate imitative suggestion of the forms, textures, colours and spaces of the real world, since these might compete with the primary reality of paint on canvas.

[11] As a consequence, rather than by intent, most of the paintings seem abstract. Yet they are never formalistic or non-objective in spirit. Nor is there (in theory) any preoccupation with the traditional aesthetics of "plastic values," composition, quality of line, beauty of surface, harmony of colour. When these occur in the paintings—and they often do—it is the result of a struggle for order almost as intuitive as the initial chaos with which the paintings begin.

[12] Despite the high degree of abstraction, the painters insist that they are deeply involved with subject matter or content. The content, however, is never explicit or obvious even when recognizable forms emerge, as in certain paintings by de Kooning, Baziotes, and Gottlieb. Rarely do any conscious associations explain the emotions of fear, gaiety, anger, violence, or tranquillity which these paintings transmit or suggest.

[13] In short these painters, as a matter of principle, do nothing deliberately in their work to make "communication" easy. Yet in spite of

[1] Harold Rosenberg, "American Action Painters," *Art News*, Vol. 51, December 1952.

their intransigence, their following increases, largely because the paintings themselves have a sensuous, emotional, aestheic and at times almost mystical power which works and can be overwhelming.

[14] The movement began some fifteen years ago in wartime New York. American painting in the early 1940's was bewilderingly varied and without dominant direction. The "old masters" such as John Marin, Edward Hopper, Max Weber, Stuart Davis, were more than holding their own. The bumptious Mid-Western regionalism of the 1930's, though still noisy, was dying along with its political analogue, "America First" isolationism. Most of the artists who during the decade of the Great Depression had been naïvely attracted by Communism had grown disillusioned both with the machinations of the party and with Socialist Realism. There were romantic realists who looked back nostalgically to the early nineteenth century, and "magic realists" and painters of the social scene such as the admirable Ben Shahn. The young Boston expressionists Hyman Bloom and Jack Levine had considerable success in New York, while from the Pacific coast came the visionary art of Mark Tobey and Morris Graves, reflecting Oriental influence in spirit and technique. There was also a lively interest in modern primitives, but no one discovered an American *douanier* Rousseau.

[15] Late in the artistically reactionary 1930's, the American Abstract Artists group had stood firm along with their allies, *Abstraction-Création* in Paris and Unit One in England. Working principally in rather dry cubist or non-objective styles, they did not seem much affected by the arrival in the United States of Léger, Mondrian and several Bauhaus masters. Quite other young painters, not yet identified as a group, were however strongly influenced by the surrealist refugees from the war, notably Max Ernst, André Masson, Marcel Duchamp (who had been the leader of New York Dadaism during World War I), the poet André Breton, and the young Chilean-Parisian painter Matta Echaurren. Equally important was the influence of the former surrealist associates, Picasso, Miró and Arp, who had stayed in Europe.

[16] Chief among the supporters of the surrealist group in New York was Peggy Guggenheim whose gallery, "Art of This Century," opened in the autumn of 1942 and served as the principal centre of the *avant-garde* in American painting until the founder returned to Europe in 1947. Her brilliant pioneering was then carried on by the new galleries of Betty Parsons, Charles Egan and Sam Kootz. "Art of This Century" gave one-man shows to Motherwell, Baziotes, Rothko and Still, and no less than four to Jackson Pollock. Arshile Gorky, the most important early master of the movement, showed at another (and prior) surrealist centre, the Julien Levy Gallery, with the poetic blessing of Breton.

[17] The work of certain older American painters, notably Ryder, Marin and Dove, interested some of the artists, and for a time Rothko, Pollock, Gottlieb and Still were influenced by the symbolic imagery of primitive art, especially of the American northwest coast. All during this early period and afterwards, Hans Hofmann, a Parisian-trained German of Picasso's generation, taught the young inspiringly and became their *doyen* colleague, though with little obvious effect on the leaders.

[18] Before 1950 most of the artists in this show had hit their stride. And they had won general, though usually reluctant, recognition as the flourishing vanguard of American painting, thanks to the courageous dealers just mentioned, enthusiastic critics such as Clement Greenberg, a handful of editors, teachers, collectors, and museum officials, and above all to their own extraordinary energy, talent, and fortitude.

[19] They were not, however, a compact phalanx. Gorky had been a quite well-known but rather derivative painter for fifteen years before he found himself about 1943. Pollock and Baziotes, both born in 1912, worked in obscurity until 1942–3, when they emerged along with the youthful and articulate Motherwell. Pollock exhibited his first highly abstract pictures about 1945 and invented his "drip" technique in 1947. [Exhibitions early in 1959 confirmed that Pollock had painted abstract expressionist paintings as early as 1937; and that Hofmann was using a drip technique as early as 1940.] By 1947, Rothko and Still, working some of the time in California, were developing their characteristic styles, Gottlieb was turning away from his "pictographic" forms, and Stamos, twenty years younger than they, had had his first show. In 1948, de Kooning, then forty-four, publicly entered the movement and quickly became a major figure; Tomlin was nearly fifty. Kline, Newman, Brooks and Guston, all mature painters, also transformed their art, Guston after having relinquished a brilliant success in a more realistic style. Since 1950, hundreds upon hundreds of American artists have turned to "abstract expressionism," some of them, like Tworkov, in mid-career, others like Hartigan and Francis while they were still students. Sam Francis is unique as the only expatriate in the show and the only painter whose reputation was made without benefit of New York, having moved directly to Paris from San Francisco where Still and Rothko had been honoured and influential teachers. . . .

[20] The movement, after several tentative early years, has flourished in its maturity since about 1948, roughly the starting point of this show. Naturally, because of its dominance, it has aroused much resistance in the United States among other artists and the public, but it has excited widespread interest and even influenced the painting of some of its

most stubborn adversaries. Others are staunchly resisting what has inevitably become fashionable. There will be reactions and counter-revolutions—and some are already evident. Fortunately, the undogmatic variety and flexibility inherent in the movement permits divergence even among the leaders; a few years ago, for instance, both Pollock and de Kooning painted a number of pictures with recognizable figures, to the dismay of some of their followers who had been inclined to make an orthodoxy of abstraction.

[21] For over a dozen years now, works by some of these artists have been shown abroad, first in Europe, then in Latin America and the Orient. They have met with controversy but also with enthusiasm, thanks in part to artists working along similar lines, and to other champions.

[22] To have written a few words of introduction to this exhibition is an honour for an American who has watched with deep excitement and pride the development of the artists here represented, their long struggle—with themselves even more than with the public—and their present triumph.

AS THE ARTISTS SPEAK FOR THEMSELVES*

I. Jackson Pollock[1]

My painting does not come from the easel. I hardly ever stretch my canvas before painting. I prefer to tack the unstretched canvas to the hard wall or the floor. I need the resistance of a hard surface. On the floor I am more at ease. I feel nearer, more a part of the painting, since this way I can walk around it, work from the four sides, and literally be *in* the painting. This is akin to the method of the Indian sand painters of the West . . .

When I am *in* my painting, I'm not aware of what I'm doing. It is only after a sort of "get acquainted" period that I see what I have been about. I have no fears about making changes, destroying the image, etc., because the painting has a life of its own. I try to let it come through. It is only when I lose contact with the painting that the result is a mess. Otherwise there is pure harmony, an easy give and take, and the painting comes out well. [See Fig. 3, p. 110.]

* From *The New American Painting as Shown in Eight European Countries, 1958–59.* Copyright © 1959 by The Museum of Modern Art (New York). Reprinted by permission.
[1] From a statement by the artist in *Possibilities,* I, Winter 1947–48 ("Problems of Contemporary Art," No. 4). Copyright by Wittenborn, Inc.

II. William Baziotes[2]

I cannot evolve any concrete theory about painting. What happens on the canvas is unpredictable and surprising to me. But I am able to speak of certain things that have occurred up to now in the course of my painting.

Today it's possible to paint one canvas with the calmness of an ancient Greek, and the next with the anxiety of a Van Gogh. Either of these emotions, and any in between, is valid to me.

There is no particular system I follow when I begin painting. Each painting has its own way of evolving. One may start with a few color areas on the canvas; another with a myriad of lines; and perhaps another with a profusion of colors.

Each beginning suggests something. Once I sense the suggestion, I begin to paint intuitively. The suggestion then becomes a phantom that must be caught and made real. As I work, or when the painting is finished, the subject reveals itself.

As for the subject matter in my painting, when I am observing something that may be the theme for a painting, it is very often an incidental thing in the background, elusive and unclear, that really stirred me, rather than the thing before me.

I work on many canvases at once. In the morning I line them up against the wall of my studio. Some speak; some do not. They are my mirrors. They tell me what I am like at the moment.

III. Willem de Kooning[3]

Art never seems to make me peaceful or pure. I always seem to be wrapped in the melodrama of vulgarity. I do not think of inside or outside—or of art in general—as a situation of comfort. I know there is a terrific idea there somewhere, but whenever I want to get into it, I get a feeling of apathy and want to lie down and go to sleep. Some painters, including myself, do not care what chair they are sitting on. It does not even have to be a comfortable one. They are too nervous to find out where they ought to sit. They do not want to "sit in style." Rather, they have found that painting—any kind of painting, any style of painting—to be painting at all, in fact—is a way of living today, a style of living, so to speak. That is where the form of it lies. It is exactly in its uselessness that it is free. Those artists do not want to conform. They only

2 *Ibid.*
3 From a statement by the artist in "What Abstract Art Means to Me," *Bulletin* Vol. XVIII, Spring, 1951. Copyright by The Museum of Modern Art.

want to be inspired . . .

That space of science—the space of the physicists—I am truly bored with by now. Their lenses are so thick that seen through them, the space gets more and more melancholy. There seems to be no end to the misery of the scientists' space. All that it contains is billions and billions of hunks of matter, hot or cold, floating around in darkness according to a great design of aimlessness.

The stars I think about, if I could fly, I could reach in a few old-fashioned days. But physicists' stars I use as buttons, buttoning up curtains of emptiness. If I stretch my arms next to the rest of myself and wonder where my fingers are—that is all the space I need as a painter. See Fig. 4, p. 111.]

IV. Adolph Gottlieb[4]

I am . . . concerned with the problem of projecting intangible and elusive images that seem to me to have meaning in terms of feeling. The important thing is to transfer the image to the canvas as it appears to me, without distortion. To modify the image would be to falsify it, therefore I must accept it as it is. My criterion is the integrity of the projection.

I frequently hear the question, "What do these images mean?" This is simply the wrong question. Visual images do not have to conform to either verbal thinking or optical facts. A better question would be, "Do these images convey any emotional truth?"

This, of course, indicates my belief that art should communicate. However, I have no desire to communicate with everyone, only with those whose thoughts and feelings are related to my own. That is why, even to some pundits, my paintings seem cryptic. Thus when we are solemnly advised to consolidate our gains, to be humanists or to go back to nature, who listens seriously to this whistling in the dark?

Painting values are not just black and white—I prefer innocent impurity to doctrinaire purism, but I prefer the no-content of purism to the shoddy content of social realism. Paint quality is meaningless if it does not express quality of feeling. The idea that a painting is merely an arrangement of lines, colours and forms is boring. Subjective images do not have to have rational association, but the act of painting must be rational, objective, and consciously disciplined. I consider myself a traditionalist, but I believe in the spirit of tradition, not in the restatement of restatements. I love all paintings that look the way I feel.

[4] From a statement by the artist in *The New Decade: 35 American Painters and Sculptors*. Whitney Museum of American Art, New York, 1955.

V. Jack Tworkov[5]

My hope is to confront the picture without a ready technique or a prepared attitude—a condition which is nevertheless never completely attainable; to have no programme and, necessarily then, no preconceived style. To paint no Tworkovs. It does not mean I can face the canvas with an empty head and an empty heart. In such an event I go to sleep. Does one not need to put limits around oneself to keep from being overwhelmed by the stream of art? The fashioned person is already limited enough—the hope is to be fashioned by the work. The task of painting is to discover and squeeze out, from all the forces streaming through it, all that is not necessary. Such impurities as remain are finally present to lend coherence to the process.

I am against the negativism which intellectuals foster that every advance, even where that is not simply an illusion, takes place in an atmosphere of quarrel with the past, and dissidence from the present. But I abhor the adulators, the masochistic art-victims on their knees to "great masters." Their chief passion is to put everything in chains.

I offer to thoughtful artists this quotation: "The man who reduces [the] encounter between the cosmos of history and its eternally new chaos, between Zeus and Dionysus, to the formula of the 'antagonism between fathers and sons,' has never beheld it in his spirit. Zeus the Father does not stand for a generation but for a world, for the Olympic, the formed world; the world of history faces a particular generation, which is the world of nature renewed again and again, always without history."[6]

Questions

1. What do you suppose is the purpose of the brief quotations at the opening of Barr's article? Who are the people quoted? What do the quotations have in common?
2. Why does Barr introduce allusions to Existentialism and Zen (paragraphs 3 and 4)? What are these movements? What possible relationships do they have to abstract painting?
3. What common elements does Barr find in the pictures in the exhibition? How does he account for them?
4. What does Barr have to say about the political backgrounds of the action painters? Why does he discuss this topic?
5. How, in general, would you describe Barr's attitude toward the paintings? What aesthetic qualities does he find in them?

[5] From a statement by the artist for the catalogue of an exhibition of his paintings Stable Gallery, New York, 1957.
[6] Martin Buber, *Between Man and Man* (London, The Macmillan Company 1947).

6. Comment on the separate statements made by Pollock, Baziotes, de Kooning, Gottlieb, and Tworkov. Do these statements communicate? What do the statements tell you about the artists, their methods, their purposes?
7. How well do Barr's introduction and the statements by the artists clarify the techniques and the values of abstract painting? What problems are not discussed?

A LETTER TO *THE NEW YORK TIMES**

To The New York Times:

Reading Mr. John Canaday's columns[1] on contemporary art, we regard as offensive his consistent practice of going beyond discussion of exhibitions in order to impute to living artists en masse, as well as to critics, collectors and scholars of present-day American art, dishonorable motives, those of cheats, greedy lackeys or senseless dupes.

Here are some instances:

Sept. 20, 1959: "* * * a situation built on fraud at worst and gullibility at best has produced a school of such prolix mediocrity * * *."

July 24, 1960: "The chaotic, haphazard and bizarre nature of modern art is easily explained: The painter finally settles for whatever satisfaction may be involved in working not as an independent member of a society that needs him, but as a retainer for a small group of people who as a profession or as a hobby are interested in the game of comparing one mutation with another."

Sept. 6, 1959: "But as for the freaks, the charlatans and the misled who surround this handful of serious and talented artists, let us admit at least that the nature of abstract expressionism allows exceptional tolerance for incompetence and deception."

"In the meanwhile, critics and educators have been hoist with their own petard, sold down the river. We have been had."

Sept. 11, 1960: "* * * for a decade the bulk of abstract art in America has followed that course of least resistance and quickest profit."

"There is not a dealer in town, nor a collector, nor a painter hoping to hang in the Museum of Modern Art who doesn't study each of Mr. Barr's syllables in an effort to deduce what he should offer for sale, what he should buy, or what he should paint * * *."

Oct. 23, 1960: "* * * brainwashing * * * goes on in universities and museums."

* From *The New York Times*, February 26, 1961. Reprinted by permission.
[1] John Canaday is art critic of *The New York Times* [Eds.].

Mr. Canaday is entitled, of course, to the freedom of his opinions regarding works of art. We submit, however, that his terminology of insults is scarcely adequate to describe emerging art works and tendencies, and we scorn this waging of a polemical campaign under the guise of topical reporting.

If Mr. Canaday has a political or social or esthetic "position" or philosophy, let him state what it is and openly promote his aims. Every style and movement in art history contains examples of work by imitative or uninteresting artists. To keep referring to these in order to impugn the whole, instead of attempting to deal seriously with the work of the movement, is the activity not of a critic but of an agitator.

JAMES S. ACKERMAN, Professor of Fine Arts, Harvard.
WILLIAM BARRETT, Professor of Philosophy, N. Y. U.
DONALD BLINKEN, Collector.
WALTER BAREISS, Collector.
BERNARD BRODSKY, M. D., Collector.
JAMES BROOKS, Painter.
JOHN CAGE, Composer.
BERNARD CHAET, Chairman, Dept. of Art & Architecture, Yale.
HOWARD CONANT, Chairman, Dept. of Art Education, N. Y. U.
STUART DAVIS, Painter.
EDWIN DENBY, Writer.
HENRY EPSTEIN, Collector.
JOHN FERREN, Painter.
ALFRED FRANKFURTER, Editor & President, "Art News."
PERCIVAL GOODMAN, Architect, F. A. I. A.
ADOLPH GOTTLIEB, Painter.
JACK M. GREENBAUM, Collector.
MR. & MRS. I. HAROLD GROSSMAN, Collectors.
DAVID HARE, Sculptor.
BEN HELLER, Collector.
THOMAS B. HESS, Executive Editor, "Art News."
HANS HOFMANN, Painter.
SAM HUNTER, Director, Rose Art Museum, Brandeis.
KENNETH KOCH, Writer.
WILLEM DE KOONING, Painter.
STANLEY KUNITZ, Poet.
KERMIT LANSNER, Writer.
BORIS LEAVITT, Collector.
ERLE LORAN, Painter and Teacher.

ARNOLD H. MAREMONT, Collector, Chicago.
ROBERT MOTHERWELL, Painter.
E. A. NAVARETTA, Poet and Critic.
ALBERT H. NEWMAN, Collector.
BARNETT NEWMAN, Painter.
RAYMOND PARKER, Painter.
PHILLIP PAVIA, Sculptor, Editor, "It Is."
GIFFORD PHILLIPS, Collector, Publisher, Frontier Magazine.
WILLIAM PHILLIPS, Editor, "Partisan Review."
FAIRFIELD PORTER, Art Critic, "The Nation."
DAVID A. PRAGER, Collector.
ROBERT ROSENBLUM, Assistant Professor, Dept. of Art & Archaeology,
    Princeton.
BARNEY ROSSETT, Publisher, Grove Press.
IRVING SANDLER, Writer and Critic.
KENNETH B. SAWYER, Art Critic, Baltimore Sun.
DAVID SMITH, Sculptor.
WHITNEY S. STODDARD, Director, Lawrence Art Museum, Williams.
MEYER SCHAPIRO, Professor of Art, Columbia.
PAUL WEISS, Professor of Philosophy, Yale.

EDITORS' POSTSCRIPT: On March 5 and 12, 1961, *The New York Times* printed a number of other letters supporting or attacking Mr. Canaday. Calling a halt to further publication, the *Times* on March 12, 1961, also printed this note:

At the time of going to press 367 letters have been received, of which 311 were in defense of Mr. Canaday and 56 aligned with his critics. In these columns there appear excerpts from letters received in the course of the past week.

With this symposium, the debate is concluded—for the moment at least—in these pages.

LETTER ON A DILEMMA*

Lester D. Longman

To the Art Editor:

I think it is important to point out just now that in addition to those who say so openly, there are many artists, museum men, professors, teachers of art and art critics who now privately question the views they have held supporting abstract expressionism, action painting and neo-

* From *The New York Times*, April 30, 1961. Reprinted by permission.

dadaism in art. The trouble is that many who had been enthusiastic about these forms of modern art (until, like myself, they began dropping off the bandwagon in increasing numbers during the decline of the Nineteen Fifties) still cannot afford to express openly their true opinions.

Some of these men have told me so, after exacting a pledge of secrecy. Others would tell only their best friends or no one at all. The dilemma is that so many have so much to lose by re-examining their fundamental premises in evaluating art. The loss is primarily in terms of self-esteem and professional reputation, but often in financial investment as well.

Non-art

The producers of art with a built-in non-art value have a lifetime investment in the *Zeitgeist* theories that support the movement, and their livelihood depends upon preventing damaging criticism of it. Almost as serious is the case of the collectors, museum directors, and trustees who have purchased at high prices and exhibited and defended such works of art. Can they now suddenly say they made a costly, but an honest mistake?

Then there are the professors and artist-teachers who have sincerely taught a generation of students to esteem radical eccentricities and to be ultratolerant of experimental work because it is "contemporaneous in spirit." Their students have learned to do nothing else, so that even though they may harbor doubts they have not the technical and conceptual resources to undertake anything more demanding. They must go on imitating those abstract artists who are successfully promoted, must continue teaching academic "self-expression" to another generation of high school and college students.

It is quite true that "we have been had." But it would be hard to say that anyone is at fault. We all did it to ourselves, usually with the utmost sincerity, by convincing ourselves that we were being original and contemporaneous and that this is all that really counts.

Precedent

In the late nineteenth century, the major artists and critics nearly all made similar fundamental errors of judgment, and much of the work that was then highly esteemed and bought is now in the basements of museums or otherwise disposed of. Very likely, a generation hence, the art now enjoying highest prestige will suffer the same fate. But there is too much at stake among the participants for this re-evaluation to occur quickly. We will know the corner has been turned when the press no longer considers it news to publish the latest neo-dada prank in its art columns.

We may hope this time will come soon, since we seem to be reaching a turning point in history. The new mood in the United States to re-define our ultimate purposes, and to take more constructive steps to control our destiny, leaves little time to dissipate our spiritual resources in self-expression as an end in itself, or escapism through trivial abstractions, or action painting, rubbish constructions, and other anti-art gestures.

Obligation

Obviously, we have the competence to distinguish between the better artists now in vogue by accepting the premises of the theory of art that supports them. But the time has come for the most serious artists, professors, museum authorities and critics to call in question the whole movement. Its superficial radicalism yields increasingly minimal returns, and has become the true conservatism of our day. The truly radical critic today must be the one who goes to the roots of the question of value, who is in advance of his time and consequently misunderstood. Our problem now is to locate artists who are equally advanced and give them due recognition.

LESTER D. LONGMAN.

(Dr. Longman is chairman of the Department of Art, University of California at Los Angeles.)

Questions

1. What is the apparent purpose in having the first letter bear the signatures of so many people? Do you judge this to be effective strategy?
2. Who are the signers? How many names do you recognize?
3. According to the first letter, what is Mr. Canaday accused of? What is the purpose of citing dated quotations from his articles?
4. What argument is advanced in the last two paragraphs of the letter? Is it valid?
5. If you were the editor of *The New York Times*, what would you do about the letter? Why?
6. What is the purpose of Professor Longman's letter? Why do you suppose he sent it to *The New York Times?*
7. What kinds of proof does Longman advance for his argument?
8. Why does Longman believe it is time for reorientation of directions in art? What "new mood in the United States" do you think he has in mind?

ASSIGNMENTS

1. Write a paper in which you contrast the views of Eastman and Rosenberg. Discuss the value each critic attaches to the concept of "communication" in art and explain how each defines the term.
2. Contrast the account of the political background of the American action painters as related by Dondero and by Barr. Write a paper in which you show to what extent they agree about any factual matters and how they vary in their interpretation of these facts.
3. Locate two or three different critical analyses of a painting by Picasso or Kandinsky or de Kooning. Bring a reproduction of the painting to class. Give a talk in which you summarize the various critical views and illustrate by pointing to specific details in the reproduction.
4. Frederick Gore says that abstract art has had a profound influence on architecture and every kind of industrial art. Collect illustrations which show the influence of abstraction in architecture, furniture design, advertising, etc. Prepare a talk in which you display your collection and provide a commentary.
5. Look up an account of the exhibition of American painting at the Brussels World's Fair. Write a paper in which you summarize various critical reactions to the exhibition and relate these reactions to the position taken by any of the authors of the essays in this section.
6. What is the status of action painting in your own community at the present time? Visit art galleries, examine the art commentary in local newspapers, talk to art teachers. Prepare a talk in which you report your findings.
7. During the 1930s the Mexican mural painter Diego Rivera, during the 1940s the singer Kirsten Flagstad and the conductor Wilhelm Furtwängler, during the 1950s several movie actors and script-writers, and during the 1960s other artists have become involved in controversies because of political affiliations or beliefs. Make a study of one of these controversies and write a report of your findings.
8. Who are some of the representational artists ("non-abstractionists") of major status at the present time? Prepare an informative talk in which you discuss some of these artists and their work.
9. Make a detailed study of the work of one action painter. Give an account of his background, his major work, critical reception. Try to demonstrate particularly whether his art shows change and development from painting to painting or whether he tends to repeat himself.
10. Prepare to participate in a panel discussion in which the topic is stated in these terms: Is abstract art a serious and lasting development in the history of painting or is it likely to disappear as an eccentricity of the twentieth century?
11. In a letter to the editors of this book, Professor Ackerman of Harvard made this comment with reference to the letter which he and many others addressed to *The New York Times* (see pp. 153–155): "I hope that you may find a way to demonstrate that the controversy for and

against abstract expressionism that followed this letter is not relevant to the purpose of the signatories. What we said was that a critic should not accuse those who disagree with him of fraud. I believe it is ridiculous to be for or against abstract or figurative art. It's like being for or against the English language—the controversy degenerated into foolish expressions of taste for one vocabulary or another."

Prepare to participate in a group discussion in which you consider Professor Ackerman's statements in relationship to several of the articles in this issue.

5. PSYCHOLOGY
Freudian Psychoanalysis as a Science

The name of Sigmund Freud and the term *psychoanalysis,* which he invented, have become part of the common currency of everyday language in our century. Indeed, allusions to Freudianism are easily recognizable in comic strips, in the dialog of TV entertainments, in musical comedy songs, in advertising, in college "bull sessions," and in conversations at the family dining table.

Yet throughout Freud's career (he was born in 1856 and died in 1939) acrid controversies raged among physicians, psychologists, and psychiatrists concerning the validity of his theories. Nor were these controversies confined to medical and scientific experts. Pronouncements on Freud and his "scandalous" influence were also issued by newspaper columnists, literary men, clergymen of various faiths, teachers, counselors, congressmen, and almost anyone else who represented himself as concerned about mental and emotional health or about sex (which some took to be the sole substance of Freud's interest).

In recent years much of the controversy has centered about the validity of psychoanalysis, particularly its claim to be recognized as a science. In the selections that follow, this topic is represented by a considerable range of opinion from both experts and laymen.

We begin, as seems appropriate, with a brief extract from Freud himself, who had no doubts at all about the propriety of viewing his work as scientific. This is followed by a lengthier essay by Dr. Gregory Zilboorg, who was a practicing analyst and an orthodox Freudian. (You may wish some day to read Zilboorg's sympathetic book-length study of Freud, from which our selection has been taken.)

Erich Fromm provides an evaluation from the viewpoint of what may be called a Freudian "revisionist"—that is, a psychoanalyst who has departed from orthodox Freudian doctrine and moved in other directions. His essay (also excerpted from a book-length study) provides an illuminating contrast with Zilboorg's.

Two widely read syndicated newspaper columnists provide sharp attacks on psychoanalysis. One, Dr. Walter C. Alvarez, was for many

years on the staff of the Mayo Clinic at Rochester, Minnesota. The
other, Rudolf Flesch, achieved fame several years ago as the author
of *Why Johnny Can't Read* and of several other books on the skills
of communication.

H. J. Eysenck is a British psychologist who has been especially concerned with scientific design in psychological experimentation and who
finds psychoanalysis quite lacking in scientific rigor. Sidney Hook, a
philosopher on the faculty of New York University, is also critical of
what he regards as the unscientific procedures of psychoanalysts. Finally, Dr. Leopold Bellak, who is a practicing analyst, furnishes a brief
statement originally prepared as an introduction to a scientific symposium.

Taken together, these eight selections provide only an initial exploration of the issue of psychoanalysis as a science. But many of the key
questions are raised about the characteristics of scientific method and
about the extent to which psychoanalysis conforms to the demands of
science.

ON PSYCHOANALYSIS[*]

Sigmund Freud

[1] There is no more urgent need in psychology than for a securely
founded theory of the instincts on which it might then be possible to
build further. Nothing of the sort exists, however, and psychoanalysis
is driven to making tentative efforts towards some such theory. It began
by drawing a contrast between the ego-instincts (the instinct of self-
preservation, hunger) and the libidinal instincts (love), but later replaced it by a new contrast between narcissistic and object-libido. This
was clearly not the last word on the subject; biological considerations
seemed to make it impossible to remain content with assuming the
existence of only a single class of instincts.

[2] In the work of my later years (*Beyond the Pleasure Principle,
Group Psychology and the Analysis of the Ego,* and *The Ego and the
Id*), I have given free rein to the inclination which I kept down for so
long to speculation and I have also taken stock of a new solution of the
problem of the instincts. I have combined the instincts for self-preservation and for the preservation of the species under the concept of *Eros*

and have contrasted with it an instinct of death or destruction which works in silence. Instinct in general is regarded as a kind of elasticity of living things, an impulsion towards the restoration of a situation which once existed but was brought to an end by some external disturbance. This essentially conservative character of instincts is exemplified by the phenomena of the *compulsion to repeat*. The picture which life presents to us is the result of the working of Eros and the death-instinct together and against each other.

[3] It remains to be seen whether this construction will turn out to be serviceable. Although it arose from a desire to fix some of the most important theoretical ideas of psychoanalysis, it goes far beyond psychoanalysis. I have repeatedly heard it said contemptuously that it is impossible to take a science seriously whose most general concepts are as lacking in precision as those of libido and of instinct in psychoanalysis. But this reproach is based upon a complete misconception of the facts. Clear fundamental concepts and sharply drawn definitions are only possible in the mental sciences in so far as the latter seek to fit a department of facts into the frame of a logical system. In the natural sciences, of which psychology is one, such clear-cut general concepts are superfluous and indeed impossible. Zoology and Botany did not start from correct and adequate definitions of an animal and a plant; to this very day biology has been unable to give any certain meaning to the concept of life. Physics itself, indeed, would never have made any advance if it had had to wait until its concepts of matter, force, gravitation, and so on, had reached the desirable degree of clarity and precision. The fundamental concepts or most general ideas in any of the disciplines of science are always left indeterminate at first and are only explained to begin with by reference to the realm of phenomena from which they were derived; it is only by means of a progressive analysis of the material of observation that they can be made clear and can find a significant and consistent meaning. I have always felt it as a gross injustice that people always refused to treat psychoanalysis like any other science. This refusal found an expression in the raising of the most obstinate objections. Psychoanalysis was constantly reproached for its incompletenesses and insufficiencies; though it is plain that a science based upon observation has no alternative but to work out its findings piecemeal and to solve its problems step by step. Again, when I endeavoured to obtain for the sexual function the recognition which had so long been withheld from it, psychoanalytic theory was branded as "pansexualism." And when I laid stress upon the hitherto neglected importance of the part played by the accidental impressions of early

youth, I was told that psychoanalysis was denying constitutional and hereditary factors—a thing which I had never dreamt of doing. It was a case of contradiction at any price and by any methods.

[4] I had already made attempts at earlier stages of my work to arrive at some more general points of view, starting from the observations of psychoanalysis. In a short essay, "Formulations regarding the Two Principles of Mental Functioning," published in 1911, I drew attention (and there was, of course, nothing original in this) to the domination of the *pleasure-pain principle* in mental life and to its displacement by the so-called *reality principle*. Later on (1915–17) I made an attempt to produce a "Metapsychology." By this I meant a method of approach according to which every mental process is considered in relation to three co-ordinates, which I described as *dynamic, topographical,* and *economic* respectively; and this seemed to me to represent the furthest goal that psychology could attain. The attempt remained no more than a torso; after writing two or three papers— "Instincts and their Vicissitudes," "Repression," "The Unconscious," "Mourning and Melancholia," etc.—I broke off, wisely perhaps, since the time for theoretical predications of this kind had not yet come. In my latest speculative works I have set about the task of dissecting our mental apparatus on the basis of the analytic view of pathological facts and have divided it into an *ego,* an *id,* and a *super-ego.*[1] The super-ego is the heir of the Oedipus complex and represents the ethical standards of mankind.

[5] I should not like to create an impression that during this last period of my work I have turned my back upon patient observation and have abandoned myself entirely to speculation. I have on the contrary always remained in the closest touch with the analytic material and have never ceased working at detailed points of clinical or technical importance. Even when I have moved away from observation, I have carefully avoided any contact with philosophy proper. This avoidance has been greatly facilitated by constitutional incapacity. I was always open to the ideas of G. T. Fechner and have followed that thinker upon many important points. The large extent to which psychoanalysis coincides with the philosophy of Schopenhauer—not only did he assert the dominance of the emotions and the supreme importance of sexuality but he was even aware of the mechanism of repression—is not to be traced to my acquaintance with his teaching. I read Schopenhauer very late in my life. Nietzsche, another philosopher whose guesses and intuitions often agree in the most astonishing way with the laborious find-

[1] *The Ego and the Id.*

ings of psychoanalysis, was for a long time avoided by me on that very account; I was less concerned with the question of priority than with keeping my mind unembarrassed.

[6] The neuroses were the first subject of analysis, and for a long time they were the only one. No analyst could doubt that medical practice was wrong in separating those disorders from the psychoses and in attaching them to the organic nervous diseases. The theory of the neuroses belongs to psychiatry and is indispensable as an introduction to it. It would seem, however, that the analytical study of the psychoses is impracticable owing to its lack of therapeutic results. Mental patients are as a rule without the capacity for forming a positive transference, so that the principle instrument of analytic technique is inapplicable to them. There are nevertheless a number of methods of approach to be found. Transference is often not so completely absent but that it can be used to a certain extent; and analysis has achieved undoubted successes with cyclical depressions, light paranoic modifications, and partial schizophrenias. It has at least been a benefit to science that in many cases the diagnosis can oscillate for quite a long time between assuming the presence of a psycho-neurosis or of a dementia praecox; for therapeutic attempts initiated in such cases have resulted in valuable discoveries before they have had to be broken off. But the chief consideration in this connection is that so many things that in the neuroses have to be laboriously fetched up from the depths are found in the psychoses upon the surface, visible to every eye. So that the best subjects for the demonstration of many of the assertions of analysis are provided by the psychiatric clinic. It was thus bound to happen before long that analysis would find its way to the objects of psychiatric observation. At a very early date (1896) I was able to establish in a case of paranoid dementia the presence of the same aetiological factors and the same emotional complexes as in the neuroses. Jung explained some most puzzling stereotypies in dements by bringing them into relation with the patients' life-histories; Bleuler demonstrated the existence in various psychoses of mechanisms like those which analysis had discovered in neurotics. Since then analysts have never relaxed their efforts to come to an understanding of the psychoses. Especially since it has been possible to work with the concept of narcissism, they have managed, now in this place and now in that, to get a glimpse beyond the wall Most of all, no doubt, was achieved by Abraham in his elucidation of melancholia. It is true that in this sphere all our knowledge is not yet converted into therapeutic power; but the mere theoretical gain is not to be despised, and we may be content to wait for its practical application. In the long run even the psychiatrists have been unable to resist

the convincing force of their own clinical material. At the present time German psychiatry is undergoing a kind of "peaceful penetration" by analytic views. While they continually declare that they will never be psychoanalysts, that they do not belong to the "orthodox" school or agree with its exaggerations, and in particular that they do not believe in the predominance of the sexual factor, nevertheless the majority of the younger workers take over one piece or another of analytical theory and apply it in their own fashion to the material. All the signs point to the proximity of further developments in the same direction.

Questions

1. What is the purpose of the third paragraph? Why does Freud introduce zoology, botany, and physics into his discussion?
2. Why does Freud call psychoanalysis a science based on observation?
3. How do you account for Freud's "careful avoidance of contact with philosophy proper"? Why did he avoid reading Schopenhauer and Nietzsche until late in life?
4. What uses does Freud find for the observation of psychotic patients since analysis, he says, does not achieve therapy of psychotics?
5. What is the purpose of the last paragraph? What differences is Freud pointing to between psychoanalysts and psychiatrists?
6. Vocabulary: What meanings does Freud attach to these terms: *ego, libido, id, super-ego, Oedipus complex, Eros, neurosis, psychosis?* Does your desk dictionary furnish adequate definitions?

THE ACHIEVEMENT OF SIGMUND FREUD*

Gregory Zilboorg

[1] Sigmund Freud died at midnight on September 23, 1939. His *Interpretation of Dreams,* which has become the most famous classic of Freudian psychoanalysis, was first published in 1900. Freud might, therefore, be considered an integral part of our twentieth century, since forty of his approximately fifty years of independent scientific work fell in this century.

[2] Freud was a doctor, a neurologist who strayed away from pure neurology very early in his career and soon found himself isolated yet famous, a founder of a new type of medical psychology which was almost exclusively the product of his own creative intuition. . . .

[3] In his manner of living and thinking, in his almost devotional attitude to work and to the ideals this work was promoting, Freud re-

* Reprinted with the permission of Charles Scribner's Sons from Chapter I of *Sigmund Freud* by Gregory Zilboorg. Copyright 1951 by Charles Scribner's Sons.

minds one of the sixteenth-century humanists. With this difference, however: Freud's ideal, his god, was not religious charity and human perfection in this faith and charity, but science, knowledge, enlightened reason. This was his "illusion," he was willing to admit; it was his "mythology" as he himself once stated; the names of his faith were *Logos* and *Eros*. . . .

[4] Freud . . . did not hesitate from the very outset to take himself as an object of observation whenever the scientific study of the deeper layers of human psychology required. He exposed some of his own unconscious impulses and propensities with utmost candor whenever he wanted to give a particularly poignant illustration of the workings of the unconscious in the formation and the structure of dreams. In this respect he represented the best tradition in the history of medicine. Doctors, whether pure clinicians or research workers, have always been ready to make experimental self-observations as to the effect of this or that drug, or this or that condition of the atmosphere, or even this or that germ, on our bodily functions.

[5] How the young Freud started as a research worker in brain pathology, from which work he learned nothing about human psychology; how he went to Paris to study with Charcot; how he studied hypnotism, in which Liébault and Bernheim were excelling at the time; how Freud worked with Dr. Josef Breuer, a general practitioner in Vienna, on their first cases of hysteria; how Freud's first psychological hypotheses as to the role of sexuality and of childhood in the development of neuroses were formulated; how he first conceived of the nature of the unconscious—all this has been told many times by Freud himself, and by his pupils and friends and enemies. These interesting and fundamental yet so simple events need not be reiterated here.

[6] We are dealing now not so much with the question of how psychoanalysis came into being—but of how psychoanalysis expanded its influence and grew, in the very atmosphere of negation and hostility in which it first began to function, and what it has become. More than that: we are concerned with the problem of the essence and the strength of psychoanalysis, the influence of which is now felt in science and literature, in religious discussions, and even in the clinical work of the internist and the surgeon. What is the secret of this new psychology, and how new is it?

[7] The expansion of psychoanalysis may be judged from a few simple illustrations. By 1927 John Rickman, the English psychoanalyst, had compiled a complete psychoanalytic bibliography. This bibliography lists 4739 titles, published in many languages and in many lands. Of these nearly five thousand titles, 427 are by Freud. (This includes

translations of some of his articles into various languages.) The first ten volumes of Freud's *Gesammelte Schriften* appeared by 1924. His complete works first appeared—paradoxically enough—in Spain, in a good translation into Spanish, in 1922. During the twenty-three years which have followed the publication of Rickman's *Index Psychoanalyticus,* almost another five thousand, if not more, separate articles and books on psychoanalysis and closely related subjects have been published. Special psychoanalytic journals began to be published in America, England, France, India, Japan, Argentina. Institutes for psychoanalytic training have dotted the map of many a country. Berlin, Vienna, Paris, London, New York, Chicago, Boston, San Francisco, Buenos Aires, are only a few of the many which have been or still are functioning in the Old and the New World.

[8] A psychoanalyst is no longer some kind of neurologist or psychiatrist or especially trained layman who specializes in the treatment of neuroses. There are now psychoanalysts who do not treat sick people but who are research workers in the fields of art, anthropology, sociology and social psychology. There are psychiatrists who are avowedly not psychoanalysts but whose work is psychoanalytically oriented. There are ministers of the gospel who study psychoanalysis in order to use it in their practice of pastoral psychology and pastoral counseling. And this is not all. Child guidance and educational psychology have been deeply affected by Freud's psychoanalytic hypotheses and principles. In many schools and colleges today there are attending psychologists and psychiatrists whose orientation is deeply influenced by Freudian thought.

[9] The field of criminology has been brought into the main stream of psychoanalytic influence. The Second International Congress of Criminology, held in Paris in September, 1950, had a special section on psychoanalysis. More and more, juvenile and regular courts of justice find it necessary to listen to opinions which are based essentially on psychoanalytic principles. The old English tradition which culminated in the famous McNaghten rule as a test of insanity has been deeply undermined by the newer psychological understanding of the criminal mind and the criminal act. In England, and particularly in the United States, an immense volume of research in the field of forensic psychiatry has been done, and expert testimony in the courts has been correspondingly affected. In many medical schools, psychoanalysis is taught either under its own name or as a part of general psychopathology and clinical psychiatry.

[10] This immense influence, in extension as well as in depth, in all its ramifications, has as its source the work of Freud himself. He origi-

nated child analysis when he reported the famous case of "Little Hans." He originated the newer trends in criminology when he described people whose antisocial behavior or psychological symptoms are caused by an unconscious sense of guilt. He originated psychoanalytic anthropology when he published his *Totem and Taboo*. He originated the newer trends in social psychology and psychoanalytic sociology when he published his study of *Group Psychology* and *Civilization and Its Discontents*. He originated the psychoanalytic investigation of literature when he published his study on *Delusion and Dreams in Jensen's* [novel] *"Gradiva."* His study of Michelangelo's Moses revealed the methodological approach toward research in the psychology of art or the artist. Ultimately, his *The Future of an Illusion* and *Moses and Monotheism* opened one of the most passionate and revealing and instructive debates on the problem of religious faith and the psychology and psychopathology of certain religious trends.

[11] You will notice the words "originated" or "opened" have been used here repeatedly. For, despite many thoughtful and fruitful contributions by many followers of Freud, and many gifted, eclectic students of the psychoanalytic method as applied to many fields of human endeavor, the problems mentioned are more repeatedly stated than solved. Many are inclined to see in this fact a decline in the influence of psychoanalysis, or the recognition of its fundamental inefficacy as a method. Whether this is true or not, only history will answer. What is undoubtedly true is that fifty years is for a science what childhood is for a human being. Not enough time has elapsed for the student (and even less for the casual observer) to be able to form a definite opinion as to the permanence of the contributions made by psychoanalysis. Its vitality and power remain amply demonstrated in the fact that psychoanalysis has been a potent factor in determining many a direction of our thought (scientific and artistic) during the past half-century.

[12] There is another reason why psychoanalysis has displayed so much vitality in so short a period and at the same time, despite its almost protean influence, appears to have solved so few problems. This reason is the curious fact that psychoanalysis is not easily defined. The term is very popular, but it has become also very vague. It has come to mean many different things to many people. Among the more or less intelligent but uninitiated one hears not infrequently: "He went to a doctor the other day and had himself psychoanalyzed." Here, to be analyzed obviously means to be diagnosed (as regards one's psychological troubles). There is also a rather familiar expression that has acquired almost an idiomatic character: "Don't psychoanalyze me, but

let us talk it over." Here, psychoanalysis obviously means probing into one's motives, or questioning one's sincerity.

[13] The semantic confusion which has developed around the term "psychoanalysis" is enhanced by many inferential concepts which are only vaguely related to psychoanalysis itself. To some psychoanalysis means sexual freedom, scientifically and benevolently bestowed upon one by a respectable science. To others psychoanalysis also means cold faithlessness to one's family and to God, as if it were devilishly contrived and mechanically engrafted upon innocent people by some sort of pseudoscientific, medico-psychological imperialism which wants to conquer the family, the school, the Church, the State, medicine itself, and society in the broadest sense of the word. Somewhere between these exaggerated misconceptions, people talk very seriously about psychoanalysis. But even those who are earnestly initiated and professionally skilled are hard put to give a comprehensive definition of psychoanalysis. The point is that such a definition is really impossible without a number of qualifications, parenthetic insertions, and cross references. The reason for this state of affairs is that psychoanalysis is not one thing. It is many things. Freud himself sensed this fact very early, and seems later to have become convinced of it.

[14] From the very beginning, Freud the physician, the doctor whose early job seemed to be to treat sick people, found little intellectual companionship among physicians. His friendship with Wilhelm Fliess during the very beginning of his career was fruitful. For some fifteen years after he returned from the Charcot Clinic in Paris (1886), Freud kept in close touch with Fliess and confided in him his preoccupation with the newer problems of human psychology as he saw them arise out of his study of the content of dreams and infantile sexual trends. In due course this friendship resolved itself from the purely scientific point of view, as did his collaboration with Breuer when the latter failed to follow Freud in his conclusion as to the unconscious sexual motivations of the neuroses—which Breuer and Freud had observed and studied together in full harmony for a while. The unconscious Breuer could accept; the unconscious *sexual* motivations he could not.

[15] For a while Freud stood quite alone. Then scientific friends and collaborators began to gather around him; many of them were laymen. Freud began to be inclined to think that to become an analyst medical education was not entirely, if at all, necessary. Some saw in this attitude of Freud's an expression of resentment against the way the conservative medical profession had treated him, driving him into scientific and professional isolation. I doubt whether Freud felt piqued by his medical

colleagues any more than by society as a whole—educators, philosophers, clergymen, intellectuals, and various and sundry volunteer moralists who rejected him from the very outset. Apparently, having found himself in involuntary solitude, Freud gradually found it necessary to look around for kindred minds, or let in those who first came to him and sought a place at the table at which he sat studying.

[16] Among the many nonmedical men who came, we find Hanns Sachs, who later emigrated to take an honorable and respected place in Boston and at Harvard. Sachs was by education a lawyer; he became a psychoanalyst-teacher and one of the most profound psychoanalytical students of Shakespeare and of medieval painting. We find among them also Theodor Reik, who before his digressive, post-emigration development was one of the best psychoanalytic students of the Bible, of Anatole France, and of literature in general. Later on there came Otto Rank, whose studies of myths and mythological traditions were well-nigh revolutionary, and inspired in their depth of insight. Still later there was Géza Róheim, the psychoanalytic anthropologist par excellence.

[17] Freud seems to have arrived ultimately at the unshakable conclusion that psychoanalysis is not exclusively a branch of medicine, and that it is a special field by itself requiring special training and aptitude. He never fully defined this field. I would assume without much risk of being in error that, if pressed for a definition of the field of psychoanalysis, Freud would have preferred the laconic answer: Man. Even today, it is difficult to define more specifically the field of psychoanalysis.

[18] Is it a curative art? The answer is yes. It was born out of medicine despite medicine's own initial repudiation of psychoanalysis. It was born as a system of technical procedures for the treatment of those more or less mild but widespread and stubborn afflictions generally called neuroses. As a curative art, psychoanalysis deals with sick people, learns from them, and tries to cure them. In other words, psychoanalysis is a part of medical discipline.

[19] But, is psychoanalysis only a curative art? The answer is no. For psychoanalysis seeks to penetrate into the deeper layers of human motivations and seeks to formulate general laws which govern the unconscious and its expression in or influence on man's manifest behavior. In other words, psychoanalysis is, or legitimately strives to become, a system of individual psychology. What is striking in this connection is this: the material obtained for the formulation of such a system is obtained from the analyses of neurotic children and adults—in other words from

"handling" pathological conditions of men by analyzing them—that is, by treating people afflicted with these conditions.

[20] It would seem then, as it did seem to Freud, that the non-medical, general psychologist who does psychoanalytic research cannot pursue this research without *treating* people and trying to cure them. This is exactly what happened in psychoanalysis. Freud established and recognized a specialty called psychoanalysis, in which research and curative endeavor are intimately connected (they are indivisible, as a matter of fact). For some time the question of *lay analysis* was discussed with detachment as well as with passionate professional subjectivity by the medical and nonmedical members of the International Psychoanalytic Association. It is a question that has not yet been solved. The psychoanalytic societies in the United States have more or less adopted the principle that in so far as psychoanalysis is a curative procedure, whatever else it may be only a doctor of medicine may be accepted for psychoanalytic training. But this principle is not strictly followed even in the United States. For there is need for social scientists, philosophers, anthropologists, psychologists, and religious leaders whose contributions to psychoanalysis are as essential as those of the medical analyst. A medical psychoanalyst cannot at one and the same time be all of these things—although it might theoretically be most desirable that he be a true encyclopedic, civilized man.

[21] As a result of these contingencies and needs, psychoanalysis has become a separate field in which anthropology, psychology, sociology, moral philosophy, criminology, and psychiatry are all brought together in the search for a special scientific synthesis. It is this circumstance that makes psychoanalysis so confusing and so complex. It is not one thing yet. It is every one of those branches of human knowledge mentioned above, and yet it is not each one of those things separately. Like man himself, it is all those things together which only in theory could be considered separately. Its only meaning is within the broad frame of reference mentioned above, without which it has no existence—and that frame of reference, be it said again, is man, man in his life totality.

[22] Since man is the only frame of reference (and social mass behavior is also man in a special guise), it is from dealing with man that psychoanalysis learns. And the source of learning is always the same: it is the sick individual, the neurotic, the deviant, the criminal—in short, the pathological. Whatever the social scientist or anthropologist observes in undeveloped, commonly but mistakenly called "primitive" people, he cannot fully understand unless he also studies pathological individuals in our society, who either still seem to be socially tolerable

and are ambulatory sick people, or who are already so compromised that they are to be found only in hospitals for the mentally ill and in penal institutions. In other words, the "material" must come from direct observations of living people whose innermost mainsprings of behavior cannot be brought to the surface for the observer to see and the student to study and the research worker to find and the scientist to comprehend—without psychoanalytic investigation. The psychoanalyst thus deals with all manner of abnormalties in order to find the "normal," just as the clinical pathologist deals with abnormal tissues cut out of human bodies, or with dead bodies carefully studied at the autopsy table and mutilated for study in the laboratory. The pathologist who is constantly so busy with dead tissues and dead bodies, is so occupied not because he enjoys contemplating the frailty and the rottenness of human flesh, but because he is interested in the secrets of the vigor and liveliness of the human body, because he seeks the secret for restoration to health and prolongation of healthy human life. He must descend into the very depth of the stench of death, and do so without undue anxiety, in order to learn how to eliminate as much of it as possible from among the living and bring out the full flavor of healthy, vigorous life.

[23] The psychoanalyst is in a situation similar to, yet quite different from, that of the clinical pathologist. His situation is different because it is denied to him to study the *silent* end-products of life. Dead people have no psychology; you can study the human mind only in the living. The psychoanalyst cannot cut out a piece of a man's mind and send it to the laboratory for examination. In mental sickness and in health man remains one and indivisible, and the psychoanalyst must study him in his totality, in his indivisibility. However, the position of the psychoanalyst has this in common with the pathologist: he must descend into the lowermost strata of man's life—into the abnormal, the perverted, the criminal—in order to learn what man is as a normal, nonperverted, non criminal individual. The psychoanalyst is no more immoral or criminal or perverted because of the special subject of his studies than the pathologist is a lover of death, or the student of the best conditions of the soil is a lover of worms and manure.

[24] Freud's descent into the unconscious of the individual patient aroused so much suspicion and disgust among the conventional and sensitively prudish formalistic scientists of his day, just because he so simply and so serenely described the inner hatreds, the criminal drives the sexual deviations, the so many other unsavory features which are stored up within us. He found them there and described what he found, and his startled, unheeding contemporary colleagues mistook all for Freud's predilection for human perversity.

[25] This attitude, not uncommon in the history of science whenever a new discovery about man and his world is made, has done a great deal to confuse the issues and to cause the fact to be overlooked that during the short span of a mere quarter of a century, or at most thirty years, psychoanalysis became a new and separate discipline, albeit one not yet easily definable. Its medical aspect is a part in itself, and perhaps (Freud himself was at times inclined to think so) not the most important part of psychoanalysis. Just as chemistry and physics and biology are used by medicine and produce chemotherapy and physical therapy and bio-therapy, so psychoanalysis is used by medicine, by medical psychology or clinical psychiatry, and a special technique has been developed called psychoanalytic therapy.

[26] At first even the therapeutic aspect of psychoanalysis (although it was for a time the only one psychoanalysis possessed) was rather restricted. Even as late as the close of the 'twenties psychoanalysts, particularly the European psychoanalysts who were closer to Freud, were inclined to think that they should limit their therapeutic work to cases of more or less mild neuroses. The severer forms of mental illness did every now and then come within the purview of the psychoanalyst, but only in isolated cases. The severe chronic mental illnesses were shied away from, and institutionalized cases on the whole were not considered as proper subjects for psychoanalytic treatment.

[27] There were the beginnings of psychoanalytic psychiatry of course, here and there. Simmel (later of Los Angeles, where he died) opened in Berlin a psychiatric sanatorium toward the close of the 'twenties, where psychoanalysis was used. Viktor Tausk wrote on some aspects of schizophrenia. Nunberg wrote on catatonia. Ruth Mack Brunswick worked psychoanalytically with a chronic case; it was an old schizophrenic whom Freud had described some years previously; Freud saw the patient when the latter was still very young, and he became known in the psychoanalytic literature as the "Wolfman." Freud also gave his own detailed psychoanalytic views of the case of Schreber (1911). He did not know the case personally, but he studied carefully the description of this case given in detail by the patient himself, the demented German judge who suffered from what is called today a paranoid schizophrenia, a form of what used to be called—and some laymen still call—"persecutory insanity."

[28] However, psychiatry, the field of the severer forms of mental illness, was never a strong point of Freud's own education or of his studies and fundamental formulations. One might say that Freud, and with him European psychoanalysis, stood aloof from psychiatry. It was in America that psychoanalytic psychiatry developed its own roots dur-

ing the decade or so preceding World War II. During that War a num
ber of psychoanalysts served in the armed forces and did a great dea
toward establishing a psychoanalytic understanding of psychiatric wa
casualties. Military psychiatry in America is to a great extent influence
by psychoanalytic psychopathology. During the War the chief of psy
chiatry in the United States Army was himself a trained psychoanalyst

[29] While it is taken here for granted that the reader is familia
with the fact that Freud dealt with the unconscious, with infantil
sexuality and other obscure, instinctual drives of man, and while it i
not the writer's intention to dwell in detail on how these discoverie
were made, a word or two about some special aspects of these discov
eries is definitely in order. However, before we can go into the sub
stance of these findings, it would be well to mention the general skepti
cism and opposition with which Freud's first statements were met.

[30] There were specific reasons, of course, why psychoanalysi
should have been met with considerable opposition, but it would be a
mistake and an overestimation of the meaning of this opposition if we
were not to bear in mind that everything new, *even* in science and
medicine, is always met with suspicion and even arrogant opposition
The bearers and keepers of "established scientific truths" are humar
beings, and as such they do not particularly like anything new. A new
idea, a new finding in science—like a new shoe—must fit very well but
must feel "comfortably old" in order to be accepted. That feeling of
being comfortably old is seldom aroused by anything new unless it is
something that could be at once capitalized upon and used, unless it
offers immediate tangible returns. Freud was right when he met the
"convinced" opposition by saying: "No one has a right to conviction
[on these matters] who has not worked at this subject for many years,
as I have, and has not himself experienced the same new and astonishing discoveries."[1] And Dalbièz, a nonanalyst and respectful opponent
of many aspects of psychoanalysis, states: "Many neuropsychiatrists,
some of whom are very distinguished scholars in their own fields but
who have had no *personal* experience with psychoanalysis, express some
very trenchant judgments against it. It is necessary to remind them that
even when dealing with the subject of psychoanalysis one must earn
the right to have an opinion."[2] . . .

---

[1] *Introductory Lectures on Psychoanalysis.* London, George Allen & Unwin, Ltd.,
& International Psycho-Analytical Institute, 1933, p. 207.

[2] Dalbièz, *La Méthode psychanalytique et la doctrine Freudienne,* Desclée de
Brouwer & Cie., 1936. t. II, p. 239.

Questions

1. What is Zilboorg's attitude toward Freud? Point to specific details in the essay in which his attitude is revealed.
2. Why does Zilboorg emphasize the "semantic confusion" which has developed around the term *psychoanalysis?* What are the sources of the confusion? What does Zilboorg mean by saying (paragraph 13) that "psychoanalysis is not one thing. It is many things"?
3. What connections does Zilboorg try to establish between psychoanalysis and medicine? Why does he also see a need for psychoanalysts who are not doctors of medicine?
4. What point is Zilboorg trying to make when he says that "fifty years is for a science what childhood is for a human being" (paragraph 11)? Do you find this convincing?
5. What is the meaning of the statement that the frame of reference for psychoanalysis is "man, man in his life totality" (paragraph 21)? What is Zilboorg's strategy in making so all-inclusive a statement? Do you find this strategy effective?
6. According to Zilboorg, why does the psychoanalyst study the "abnormal, the perverted, the criminal"? What analogies does Zilboorg draw with other scientists? Are these analogies valid?
7. How does Zilboorg account for the opposition and general skepticism which greeted Freud's findings? What kind of argument does he use? What rejoinder might be made by an anti-Freudian?
8. What sort of reader do you think Zilboorg is addressing himself to? What evidence can you give to support your answer?

From SIGMUND FREUD'S MISSION*

Erich Fromm

The foregoing analysis [the preceding chapters] has tried to show that Freud's aim was to found a movement for the ethical liberation of man, a new secular and scientific religion for an elite which was to guide mankind. . . .

But the new religion shared the fate of most religious movements. The original enthusiasm, freshness and spontaneity soon weaken; a hierarchy takes over, which gets its prestige from the "correct" interpretation of the dogma, and the power to judge who is and who is not a faithful adherent of the religion. Eventually, dogma, ritual and idolization of the leader replace creativity and spontaneity.

The tremendous role of the *dogma* in orthodox psychoanalysis hardly needs any proof. In fifty years, there has been relatively little theoretical development beyond Freud's own theoretical innovation.[1] Mainly, one has applied Freud's theories to clinical material, always with the tendency to prove that Freud was right, and with little thought for other theoretical possibilities. Even the most independent development, the new emphasis on the Ego, seems to be to a large extent a rephrasing of many well-known insights in terms of the Freudian theory, without leading to many new vistas. But aside from the relative sterility of the "official" psychoanalytic thought, its dogmatism is manifested in its reaction to any deviation. One of the most drastic examples, I have already given—Freud's reaction to Ferenczi's idea that the patient needed love as a condition for his cure. This only emphasized what was and is going on everywhere in the movement. Analysts who criticize Freud's ideas explicitly, frankly and publicly are considered as outside the fold, even when they have no intention of founding "schools" of their own, but only set forth the result of their thinking and observation based on those of Freud.

The *ritualistic* element in orthodox psychoanalysis is equally obvious. The couch with the chair behind it, the four or five sessions every week, the analyst's silence, except when he gives an "interpretation"—all these factors have been transformed from what once were useful means to an end, into a sacred ritual, without which orthodox psychoanalysis is unthinkable. The most striking example of this is, perhaps, the couch. Freud chose it because he "did not want to be stared at for eight hours a day." Then, other reasons were added: that the patient should not recognize the analyst's reaction to what he is telling—and, thus, that it is better if the analyst sits behind him; or, that the patient feels freer and more relaxed if he does not have to look at the analyst; or, and this has been emphasized lately, that the "couch-situation" creates artificially an infantile situation which should exist for the better development of the transference. Whatever the merits of these arguments are—I personally believe that they are not valid—in any "normal" discussion on therapeutic technique, they could be freely argued. In psychoanalytic orthodoxy failure to use the couch is already evidence of digression and considered *prima facie* evidence for not being an "analyst."

Many of the patients are attracted by this very ritualism; they feel themselves to be part of the movement, experience a sense of solidarity

---

[1] The one great creative revision in psychoanalytic thought, the concept of the life and death instinct, was made by Freud himself and was never fully accepted by all orthodox psychoanalysts nor further developed. Freud himself never undertook the drastic revision of his older mechanistic concepts which the new theory, in my opinion, would have made necessary. For these reasons and in view of the limited space of this study I have throughout referred only to what is the bulk of Freud's theory, the stage before the discussion of the death instinct.

with all others who are analyzed, and a sense of superiority over those who are not. Often, they are much less concerned with being cured than with the exhilarating sensation of having found a spiritual home.

Eventually, the *idolization of Freud's personality* completes the picture of the quasi-political character of the Movement. I can be short here and refer to Jones's idolatric picture of Freud, his denial of Freud's intense concern for public recognition, his authoritarianism and any kind of human foible. Another well-known symptom of the same complex is the habit of orthodox Freudian writers to begin, end and intersperse their scientific papers with "as Freud has already said" remarks, even when such frequent citations are quite unnecessary in the context of the paper.

I have tried to show that psychoanalysis was conceived as, and developed further into, a quasi-religious movement based on psychological theory and implemented by a psycho-therapy. This in itself is perfectly legitimate. The criticism, expressed in these pages, is directed against the inherent errors and limitations in the way psychoanalysis developed. First of all, it suffered from the very defect it aims at curing: repression. Neither Freud nor his followers admitted to others or to themselves that they aimed at more than scientific and therapeutic achievements. They repressed their ambition to conquer the world with a messianic ideal of salvation, and thus were caught in ambiguities and dishonesties, which are bound to follow from such repression. The second defect of the movement was its authoritarian and fanatical character, which prevented the fruitful development of the theory of man, and led to the establishment of an entrenched bureaucracy which inherited Freud's mantle, without possessing his creativity, nor the radicalism of his original conception.

But more important still than the points mentioned so far is the *content* of the idea. Indeed, Freud's great discovery, that of a new dimension of human reality, the unconscious, is *one element* in a movement aiming at human reform. But this very discovery bogged down in a fatal way. It was applied to a small sector of reality, man's libidinal strivings and their repression, but little or not at all to the wider reality of human existence and to social and political phenomena. Most psychoanalysts, and this holds true even for Freud, are not less blind to the realities of human existence and to unconscious social phenomena than are the other members of their own social class. In a sense, they are more blind because they believe they have found *the* answer to life in the formula of libidinal repression. But one cannot see in certain sectors of human reality and remain blind in others. This is especially true since the whole phenomenon of repression is a social phenomenon. The individual in any given society represses the awareness of those feelings and phantasies which are incompatible with the thought patterns of his society. The force effecting this repression is the fear of being isolated and of becoming an outcast through having thoughts and feelings which nobody would share. (In the extreme form the fear of complete isolation is no other than the fear of insanity.) Considering this, it is imperative for the psychoanalyst to transcend the thought patterns of his society, to look at them critically, and to understand the realities which produce these patterns. *The understanding of the unconscious of the individual presupposes and necessitates the critical analysis of his society.* The very fact that Freudian psychoanalysis hardly ever transcended a liberal middle-class attitude toward society constitutes one reason for its narrowness and for the eventual stagnation in its proper field of the understanding of the individual unconscious. . . .

What, then, is our conclusion with regard to the role which Freudian psychoanalysis has played since the beginning of the century?

First of all, it must be noted that in the beginning, from 1900 to the twenties, psychoanalysis was much more radical than it became after it had gained its great popularity. For the middle class brought up in the Victorian age, Freud's statements about infantile sexuality, the pathological effects of sexual repression, etc., were radical violations of their taboos, and it took courage and independence to violate these taboos. But thirty years later, when the twenties had brought with them a wave of sexual libertinism and a widespread abandonment of Victorian standards, the very same theories were no longer shocking or challenging. Thus, psychoanalytic theory gained popular acclaim in all those sectors of society which were averse to genuine radicalism, that is, to going "to the roots," and yet which were eager to criticize and to transgress the conservative mores of the nineteenth century. In these circles—that is to say, among the liberals—psychoanalysis expressed the desirable middle-of-the-road attitude between humanist radicalism and Victorian conservatism. Psychoanalysis became a substitute satisfaction for a deep human yearning, that of finding a meaning to life, of being in genuine touch with reality, of doing away with the distortions and projections which put a veil between reality and ourselves. Psychoanalysis became a surrogate for religion for the urban middle and upper-middle classes, which did not want to make a more radical and comprehensive effort. Here, in the Movement, they found everything— a dogma, a ritual, a leader, a hierarchy, the feeling of possessing the truth, of being superior to the uninitiated; yet without great effort, without deeper comprehension of the problems of human existence, without insight into and criticism of their own society and its crippling effects on man, without having to change one's character in those aspects which matter, namely to get rid of one's greed, anger and folly. All one tried to get rid of were certain libidinous fixations and their transference, and while this may sometimes be significant, it is not sufficient for the achievement of that characterological change which is necessary to be in full touch with reality. From a forward-moving and courageous idea, psychoanalysis became transformed into the safe credo of those frightened and isolated members of the middle class who did not find a haven in the more conventional religious and social movements of the time. The decay of liberalism is expressed in the decay of psychoanalysis. . . .

Questions

1. Why does Fromm characterize Freud's movement as "a new religion"? What specific details does he supply in drawing the analogy?
2. How does Fromm develop the concepts of dogma, ritual, and idolization of the leader? Would you accept these three concepts as a necessary part of religion?
3. How does Fromm treat the psychoanalyst's couch? What is his purpose?
4. What defects does Fromm point to in the development of psychoanalysis? How do these defects relate to his basic argument?
5. What is Fromm's purpose in emphasizing the "narrow" social viewpoint of Freudian psychoanalysis? How does this relate to his original argument by analogy with religion?
6. What is the purpose of Fromm's final paragraph? Does he indicate different attitudes toward (a) Freud, (b) the Freudian movement, (c) Freud's followers? Illustrate by specific examples.
7. Fromm rarely refers to any scientific aspects of psychoanalysis. Why not?

ABOUT PSYCHOANALYSIS*

Walter C. Alvarez, M.D.

One of the most moving experiences of my medical career came a few weeks ago at the annual convention of the Student American Medical Assn.

As one of their guests, I listened to a brief talk by a remarkably fine psychiatrist—Dr. Corbett Thigpen, the man who recently wrote up the case of the woman in "The Three Faces of Eve."

Time and again, when he would say perhaps that many of the ideas of modern psychiatry are just theories for which no one can adduce any

* From Dr. Alvarez' column, July 8, 1959. Copyright © 1959 by The Register and Tribune Syndicate. Reprinted by permission.

scientific proof, the audience—much stirred—applauded. At those moments, I wished all dynamically inclined psychiatrists could have been present just to sense the relief that seemed to come over these students when told that if they were reluctant to swallow a lot of weird theories, they were perfectly justified.

Modern Psychiatry Lacks All the Answers

Dr. Thigpen emphasized that he was not attacking anyone. All he wanted was to find ways to cure his patients. After years of experience, he knows—to his sorrow—that modern psychiatry does not give all the answers; in fact, in many cases of mental aberration, even good psychotherapy does not help.

Dr. Thigpen told me that he and his eminent chief, Dr. Hervey Cleckley, had started in practice with analytic indoctrination, but later had turned away from it. In their practice, they have come to behave like any good scientific physician does who will use any form of treatment that he finds useful—psychotherapy, rest, tranquilizers, brain stimulators, electro-shocks, or hypnosis.

Dr. Thigpen was sorry to have to admit that, for the last 30 years or more, under the dominating influence of theories of early sex trauma, psychiatry has largely stagnated, so that there has been little advance in it.

Return to Scientific Research Hoped For

Many psychiatrists have cultivated the habit of writing in such an almost unintelligible jargon that few people can guess what they are trying to say. They have fooled themselves—and some of their readers—into thinking they know something.

As Dr. Thigpen, Dr. Freyhan, and others have pointed out, much of psychiatry has changed from a science into a religion with Freud as its prophet.

Dr. Thigpen said he prays that psychiatry may soon come out of the doldrums to become again a field for scientific research. Perhaps the change-over is now being effected by the brain physiologists, pharmacologists, surgeons and geneticists who are getting interested in the problems of mental disease. We will hope so.

Naturally, there is little hope of changing the mental processes of the older psychiatrists; they are too firmly set in their way. Our hope must be in the young men of the present generation. If they will accept only ideas for which there is scientific proof, we will get somewhere.

Dr. Thigpen told of the similar talk he gave at a recent meeting of a great psychiatric association. There, also, he pleaded for scientific honesty. After the talk, a physician came to the podium and asked, "Would you have us give up our practice and starve?"

Dr. Thigpen said, "I have no desire to rob anybody of his livelihood, but I feel that if patients are paying us for our services, they deserve to receive scientific knowledge—not beliefs."

Questions

1. Why does Dr. Alvarez applaud the views expressed by Dr. Thigpen?
2. What is Dr. Alvarez' attitude toward psychoanalytic psychiatry? Where is his attitude revealed?
3. What do you think Dr. Alvarez and Dr. Thigpen are alluding to in the phrase about "early sex trauma"? Is this an adequate characterization of psychoanalytic techniques?
4. Dr. Alvarez objects to the "almost unintelligible jargon" in which psychiatrists write. What kind of argument is this? How valid is it?
5. What do you think Dr. Alvarez means by "scientific proof"? What evidence can you supply to support your statement?
6. Comment on the language of the quotation in the last paragraph. Why do you think Dr. Alvarez concludes with this quotation?
7. What rejoinder do you think a psychoanalyst might make to this article?

PSYCHOANALYSIS—A MONSTROUS FRAUD*

Rudolf Flesch

"What's wrong with psychoanalysis?"

This is one of the chapter titles in a little 85-cent paperback I picked up the other day, "Uses and Abuses of Psychology" by Dr. H. J. Eysenck (Penguin).

Dr. Eysenck, who is a distinguished British psychologist, has a simple answer to his question. Everything, he says, is wrong with psychoanalysis.

Having said so—in much more polite terms, of course—Dr. Eysenck proceeds to take psychoanalysis apart until there isn't a shred of it left. It is "nonscientific"; it is "to be judged in terms of belief and faith"; it is like Christian Science; it resembles the practices of the Jesuits; it has been disproved by experiments time and time again. In short, "psycho-

* From Rudolf Flesch's column, July 5, 1959. Copyright © 1959 by The Register and Tribune Syndicate. Reprinted by permission.

analysis as a system claiming to afford a scientific view of human nature is dead."

But, you say, what about the hundreds and thousands of expensive analysts people go to? What about the famous cures, the rescues of hopeless neurotics, the glamorous, life-restoring 30-dollar sessions on the couch?

Nonsense, says Dr. Eysenck. He answers all that with a stunning set of figures and facts.

According to the psychoanalysts themselves, their patients recover at the rate of about 50%. Add to that those who walk out on their analysts in the middle of the treatment and you may say that two out of three patients get well—giving the analysts the benefit of doubt.

Now, says Dr. Eysenck, compare this with a large-scale study of neurotic patients in American state mental hospitals who didn't get any psychotherapy at all—just custodial care. How many of those patients got well again? Precisely two out of three—just as many as the well-to-do alumni of the analysts' couches.

Another similar study dealt with 500 neurotics who were treated by their family doctors. The treatment consisted of sedatives, tonics, suggestion and reassurance, and no psychotherapy whatever. How many of those patients recovered? Yes, you guessed it—exactly two out of three.

"It is difficult," says Dr. Eysenck in his precise academic fashion, "to interpret these results as supporting in any way the hypothesis that psychotherapy has a beneficial effect."

Which means, in plain English, that the whole business of psychoanalysis is a monstrous fraud.

Questions

1. Flesch's article was written as a syndicated newspaper column. What specific details do you notice in style, tone, and vocabulary which perhaps point to Flesch's assumptions about his audience?
2. Apart from the use of the phrase "a distinguished British psychologist," what evidence does Flesch provide to establish the authority of H. J. Eysenck? What evidence would you want?
3. Look up H. J. Eysenck in the British *Who's Who*. Is he a doctor of medicine? What impression do you gain from Flesch's article? Why?
4. How many separate arguments does Flesch cite from Eysenck's book? Evaluate each one.
5. How does Flesch attempt to characterize Eysenck through such phrases as "in much more polite terms, of course," and "in his precise academic fashion"? Why does Flesch do so?
6. Consider Flesch's final sentence. Is it justified by the evidence he has cited? Why or why not?

WHAT IS WRONG WITH PSYCHOANALYSIS?*

H. J. Eysenck

[1] So far we have criticized analytic procedures on general grounds; it may be useful to particularize and state a few of the objections which psychologists have brought forward against various features of contemporary psychoanalysis. In the first place, then, *psychoanalytic conclusions are based on unreliable data.* Its data are introspections (of the analyst) and verbalized statements (of the analysand). Data of this kind are essentially subjective, and therefore present special difficulties to the scientist. These difficulties are not insuperable; verbatim recordings can be made of the analytic session, and Roger and other non-analytic workers have shown how useful and indeed invaluable such recordings can be in tracing the course of therapy, in validating hypotheses advanced by the therapist, and in checking the accuracy of the extremely fallible memory of the therapist. In relying on his memory alone, the therapist easily becomes selective, and what is recorded by him in the case history tends to be what fits in with his preconceived ideas. Thus what is reported by the analyst in articles and books is seldom the whole evidence; it is a highly selected part of the evidence, usually taken from a few highly selected cases. No general conclusions can be drawn from such data, particularly as the analyst seldom attempts the essential cross-check of going through his data to find evidence against his preconceived notions, and in favour of a hypothesis different to the one suggested by Freudian theory.

[2] This would not be so dangerous if the data presented by the analyst were at least direct records, however selected, of what occurred in the analytic session. But usually *psychoanalytic data prejudge the issue* by mixing inextricably raw data and analytic interpretation. The reader who is familiar with Freud's own writings, or with those of any of his followers, will be able to check for himself the ratio of fact and interpretation in the cases there reported. As Wittels admits in his biography of Freud, "Freud's specific method of investigation . . . was not suitable for setting up boundaries and strict definitions. Through insight into himself, he came to understand a psychological phenomenon, and from the beginning his discoveries carried a strong inner conviction of certitude." As Ellis comments on this passage, "while an inner con-

* From H. J. Eysenck, *Uses and Abuses of Psychology.* (A Pelican Book.) Published by Penguin Books Ltd., 1953. Reprinted by permission.

viction of certitude is indubitably a fine trait for a prophet to possess, its liabilities for the scientist should be sufficiently obvious to warrant no further comment." It is this inner conviction of certitude which presumably makes the analytic writers eager to convince by argument, rather than to prove by fact, and which leads to this inextricable combination of verbal report and interpretation.

[3] *Psychoanalysts overgeneralize their conclusions.* Freud based his imposing edifice on the verbal statements of a few hundred middle-class Viennese neurotics. Instead of confining his conclusions to the population of which this was a sample—as would have been the proper scientific procedure—he extended them to all human beings, at all times, everywhere. In other words, he thought to have divined universal truth from an extremely unrepresentative sample of human beings. What is true of his neurotic patients (assuming for the moment that his observations were accurate, and his hypotheses correct) is obviously not necessarily true of non-neurotic Trobriand Islanders; indeed, Malinowsky has shown with a wealth of detailed illustrations that Freudian theories are very strongly culture-bound, and have to undergo considerable modification if they are to be applied in any way to other groups. What is true of middle-class people is not necessarily true of working-class people; in another chapter I have discussed the facts supporting this statement at some length, and will therefore not deal with them again here. Nor does the fault lie with Freud alone. Most of his followers have emulated his example, and there are several cases where what has been alleged to have been found true in one case has been generalized to the whole of humanity! Overgeneralization of this kind puts psychoanalysis outside the pale of science; before findings are extended beyond the group on which they were originally established, there must be acceptable proof that each extension is warranted.

[4] *Psychoanalysts apply their putative principles to general social phenomena without proof of their applicability.* Even if Freud's theories and hypotheses were strictly applicable to human beings as individuals, it would not follow that we could account for social phenomena such as war, industrial unrest, or artistic production by their means. Many analysts, however, have extended these theories to deal with almost all the social problems which beset us, always from a theoretical point of view, i.e. without any reference to fact, and usually without the humility of the scientist presenting a hypothesis. These dubious speculations are presented as facts, and society is urged to take action accordingly. . . . I have seen it suggested in a serious document intended for official consumption that part of the unrest in the coalfields was due to the unconscious conflicts aroused in the miner by having to use his

ick-axe (a phallic male symbol) on "mother earth" (a mother symbol).
o the layman, who finds difficulties in distinguishing between psy-
nology, psychoanalysis, and psychiatry, such far-fetched ideas are
kely to bring all three into disrepute, although there is probably no
erious psychologist who would subscribe to views of this type. Freud
imself has issued a warning against "indiscriminate psychoanalyzing"
f all and sundry; it is unfortunate that his followers have not always
ollowed this sober advice.

[5] *Where Freudian hypothses are used to guide research, this re-
earch is often illustrative of preconceptions, rather than a crucial test
f the hypothesis.* Thus the hypothesis that broken homes produce
eurosis may lead to a demonstration that neurotics frequently come
om broken homes. This fact, of course, is not crucial unless it can also
e shown that people who do not suffer from neurosis tend to come
om broken homes in a significantly smaller number of cases. But this
econd part of the experiment is hardly ever performed by Freudians.
igures published by the American Army showed that a large proporon of neurotics did indeed come from broken homes; they also show,
owever, that normal and especially well-adapted soldiers also came
om broken homes in almost equally large proportion. These figures
idicate that the broken home had only a vanishingly small part, if any,
) play in the genesis of neurosis.

[6] This neglect of control groups to provide the negative part of
ne inductive argument is a very characteristic part of Freudian ex-
erimentation. Again and again a causal sequence is asserted because
ertain events are found to occur frequently in the early years of the
ves of neurotics; hardly ever is there any attempt to show that these
vents occur less frequently, or not at all, in the lives of non-neurotics.
he analyst may retort that we are all neurotic, after all, unless psycho-
nalyzed according to the dictates of Freud (of Jung, or Stekel, or
dler, or whoever may be the father-figure of the analyst who is talk-
ng), and that therefore these events would be expected to occur uni-
ersally. But this argument clearly proves too much; we may all be
eurotic, but some of us are more neurotic than others, and it is the
auses of these individual differences which we wish to know about. If
he causes adduced by Freudians are universal, then by that token they
annot help us in accounting for the fact that one person has a nervous
reakdown, while another overcomes his difficulties in less neurotic
vays.

[7] *Psychoanalytic arguments from facts beg the question.* Let us
urn to the preceding argument that broken homes cause neurosis, and
et us assume that it had been established beyond doubt that broken

homes were more frequent in the histories of neurotics than in the histories of non-neurotics. To argue from this that the broken homes were in any way responsible for the subsequent neurosis would be a clear example of an ancient logical fallacy, namely, that of the *post hoc, ergo propter hoc* argument. To the statisticians, this fallacy is known as "arguing from correlations to causes." All that could be regarded as established would be that broken homes and neurosis are correlated; this correlation tells us nothing whatsoever about the causal sequences involved. The Freudian interpretation is an environmentalistic one; it would be just as reasonable to invoke a hereditary one, somewhat along these lines. Predisposition to neurosis is inherited—neurotic parents, neurotic children. But neurotic parents are likely to have their marriages fail, so that their children will grow up with the background of a broken home. Consequently, we shall find that neurotics will tend to come with disturbing frequency from broken homes—not because the broken home causes the neurosis, but because the parents' neurosis causes both the broken home and (through heredity) the child's neurosis. I do not claim that this second hypothesis, along hereditarian lines, is more likely to be true than the Freudian (although there is considerable evidence for the view that neurotic predisposition and emotional instability are to a considerable extent inherited traits); I am concerned with the calm disregard by psychoanalysts of non-Freudian hypotheses which might explain the alleged facts equally well. Science advances by eliminating counter-hypotheses through carefully controlled experiments; it does not advance by begging the question. When it is realized that the alleged facts themselves are of very doubtful standing, and often merely the projections of the analyst's own wishes and desires, it will be realized why scientists are chary of accepting the analytic account of human nature as anything but brilliant speculation.

[8] Protests against these methods of conducting research and of advancing arguments and proofs are not confined to psychologists; many orthodox psychiatrists are equally severe in their censure. Elliot Slater sums the matter up extremely well when he says: "There has . . . been an increasing tendency among clinicians to minimize the effects attributable to genetical causes, and to teach a psychiatry in which they receive little or no mention. This tendency has been marked in Britain, but it has assumed formidable strength in the U.S.A. Instead of a harmonious development, in which the psychoses and neuroses, constitution and environment, psychogenesis and physiogenesis receive their due share of attention, interest among practical workers has been devoted more and more exclusively towards psychotherapy, psycho-

nalysis, social psychiatry, personnel selection, group therapy, and pre-
ccupations with anthropology, sociology, and political theory. In its
ne-sidedness, this development is not healthy.

[9] "It would not perhaps be putting it too high to say that we are
witnessing the manifestation of an anti-scientific tendency which is
winning an increasing number of supporters. The customary canons of
cientific reasoning are ignored by these schools. Uncomfortable facts
re left unconsidered. Hypotheses are multiplied regardless of the
rinciple of economy. Explanations which may be valid for certain
members of a class of phenomena are regarded as true for the class
s a whole. Interpretations which conform with theory, and which
might be true, are regarded as established. Possible alternatives are not
onsidered, and no attempt is made to seek for evidence of critical
alue which shall decide between them. Criticisms from outside are
gnored, and only the initiate may be heard. Utterance is dogmatic and
acks scientific humility and caution. These are the mental mechanisms
which we associated with the growth of a religious orthodoxy, and not
with the progress of science."

[10] If this chapter has been critical, it has been so because I am
oncerned about the future of psychology. However much psychologists
may show their desire not to be held responsible for the views advanced
by psychoanalysts, society often fails to mark the distinction between
cientific statement, based on fact and rigorous logical and statistical
easoning, and the kind of *obiter dicta* discussed in this chapter, based
on assumptions and loose and wishful thinking. If the latter are in due
ourse discredited, this discredit will almost certainly attach to the
whole of psychology and psychiatry, instead of only to the group re-
ponsible.

[11] I would not like to be understood as condemning psychoanaly-
is hook, line, and sinker. Like most psychologists, I appreciate the
breath of fresh air which Freud introduced into the musty dry-as-dust
atmosphere of nineteenth-century academic psychology. The brilliance
of his mind has opened doors which no one now would wish to close
again, and his keen insight has given us a store-house of theories and
hypotheses which will keep researchers busy for many years to come.
All this one can appreciate without accepting the totality of his views
as revelations from a higher authority, and without losing one's critical
ense. There is much that is supremely important in Freud's contribu-
ion to psychology, but there is also much that is bad. To eliminate the
atter, without losing the former, must be the task of a scientifically-
orientated psychology. The answer to the question which forms the title

of this chapter—What is wrong with psychoanalysis?—is simple: Psycho-analysis is unscientific. It is only by bringing to bear the traditional methods of scientific inference and experimentation that we can hope to reap all the benefit of its founder's genius.

Questions

1. Eysenck's main arguments are indicated by the italicized statements in his separate paragraphs. Are these arguments of the same kind or of different kinds?
2. Note that the objections to the methods of psychoanalysis are attributed to psychologists. Why does Eysenck classify psychologists as scientists?
3. To what extent does Eysenck distinguish between the work of Freud and that of his followers? How do you account for the distinctions made?
4. In paragraph 6 Eysenck objects to the "neglect of control groups to pro-vide the negative part of the inductive argument." What does this lan-guage mean? On what is Eysenck's objection based?
5. In paragraph 8 Eysenck cites the objections of Elliot Slater, who is not a psychologist but an "orthodox psychiatrist." Why does Eysenck place Slater's statement at this point? What effect do you think Eysenck is aim-ing at?
6. In paragraph 10 Eysenck contrasts scientific statement "based on fact and rigorous logical and statistical reasoning" with the arguments of psycho-analysts "based on assumptions and loose and wishful thinking." Is this a legitimate distinction? Why?
7. Eysenck thinks it necessary to preserve the reputation of psychology by dissociating its research methods from those of psychoanalysis. What kind of strategy does he employ?
8. What estimate of Freud himself does Eysenck offer in his final paragraph? Why do you think he does this?
9. Would you say that Eysenck's language is mostly report or opinion? Sup-port your response by specific illustrations from his essay.

SCIENCE AND MYTHOLOGY IN PSYCHOANALYSIS[*]

Sidney Hook

[1] Logically, the question concerning the scientific status of psycho-analysis depends upon an answer to a prior question, viz., What makes any subject scientific? . . . Is psychoanalysis more like meteorology, medicine, or agronomy, to which only a purist would deny the adjective "scientific," or is it more like phrenology, chiropractice or Christian

[*] From *Psychoanalysis, Scientific Method, and Philosophy, A Symposium.* Edited by Sidney Hook. Published 1959 by New York University Press. Copyright © 1959 by New York University. Reprinted by permission.

Science? So far as I know nobody has ever denied scientific status to psychoanalysis on the ground that it is not like physics. For we would then have to rule out the whole of biology as a science, which would be absurd.

[2] A subject is usually regarded as unscientific if in principle no observable state of affairs could falsify its claims, so that by *ad hoc* modifications its assertions can be made compatible with any state of affairs whatsoever. It was in order to pinpoint the discussion on the possibility of falsifying one of the central doctrines of psychoanalysis that I asked the psychoanalysts present to describe what kind of evidence they were prepared to accept which would lead them to declare in any specific case that a child did not have an Oedipus complex.

[3] This question has a history. I have asked it innumerable times since I read Freud in 1919. The history of the answers I have received would make interesting reading. Three responses stand out in my memory. The first was from Dr. Ernst Kris, who, after some thought, replied that a child lacking an Oedipus complex would be one who acted like an idiot. This was hardly satisfactory because it was not clear whether the possession of the Oedipus complex was being taken as a criterion of normality or whether it was associated with its presence. At any rate there are different degrees and types of subnormal children, and what differentiates them from normal children seems much more general than the behavior frequently interpreted as part of the oedipal behavior pattern. The second response was made by Dr. Sandor Rado, who at first questioned the validity of the question but who after discussion manifested a genuine perplexity quite rare in the circumstances. The third memorable response, at a meeting of the Conference on Methods in Science and Philosophy at the New School in New York was made by a leading practioner whom I will identify only by an initial—call him Dr. Z. It consisted in the charge that I was quite clearly a misogynist and in a histrionic denunciation of troublemakers who lure psychoanalysts into traveling long distances to meetings and then needle them with sophistical questions. Making up his facts as he went along, he asserted that psychoanalysts no longer used the term "complex" (this was in the early fifties), and therefore the question was meaningless. Although an extreme illustration, until recently this typified, I am sorry to say, the most frequent generic response to my question.

[4] In asking this question I was *not* assuming that an Oedipus complex can be seen or touched or directly observed any more than intelligence can be seen or touched or directly observed. I was not even assuming that it was an observable. All I was asking for was the evi-

dence on the basis of which one could legitimately deny its presence. This is not a tricky question but one often asked to specify the meaning of terms, the statements that contain them, and the conditions under which the statements are warranted. For example, we hear that someone is "intelligent" or "friendly." Many types of behavior can be cited as evidence for the presence of "intelligence" or "friendliness." But unless we are also told what we would have to observe to conclude that an individual is not intelligent or not friendly, the terms could be applied to anyone in all situations.

[5] In asking this question I was making no assumption that its answer would be the citation of an atomic simple or an isolated feature independently of a gestalt, context, or systematic connection. The situation may be as complex as one in which we attribute to an individual the absence or presence of moral courage. A specific trait is rarely if ever decisive when we are describing a pattern. None the less, no one particular trait, in and of itself, can count as evidence for *both* the presence and absence of a particular pattern.

[6] Finally, in asking the question I was not demanding that someone describe a crucial experimental test that would decisively confirm or refute the hypothesis that any particular individual had an Oedipus complex. This may be as unfeasible as a crucial experimental test of whether an individual is a true friend. Some tests, however, are more significant and reliable than others; and unless one can describe what would count as unfriendly behavior, even if he never lives to see it, one does not really understand the meaning of friendly behavior.

[7] The Second Annual Meeting of the New York University Institute of Philosophy will always remain memorable to me because after waiting forty years I received something of an intelligible answer to my question. In the discussion Dr. Charles Brenner undertook to describe the behavior of a child who would show no signs of the presence of an Oedipus complex. And Dr. Arlow . . . develops this reply a little more explicitly, making a distinction, unessential for our purposes, between "oedipal phase" and "oedipal complex," using the former expression to designate what is usually intended by the latter. Dr. Arlow's reply will repay close study. I content myself with just a few observations. He writes:

Phenomenologically, the little boy who does not achieve the oedipal phase of development would express no tender or romantic feelings or fantasies regarding his mother. He would not express any wish to grow up and marry her, nor try to oust his father as the rival from the marriage bed. Manifestations of a wish to exhibit his penis to the mother, to press his penis against her, to have her admire and fondle his penis would not appear. . . . Such a child would hardly regard the other individuals in his environment as distinct entities or personalities. They would be important to him only in so far as they could grant immediate satisfaction of his bodily wants or needs. He would hardly refer to them, conjure up few images or memories concerning them. . . . Consideration of masculinity or femininity would be minimal. . . . We would anticipate in such a child impulsive emotionality and very meager identification with the standards, the ideals and behavior of his human environment. These are only a few features of the picture of a child who does not develop an oedipal phase, but sufficient features have been mentioned to indicate that the concept of an oedipal phase is not a procrustean bed into which analysts wish to force all the data of observation. The existence of an oedipal phase in the development of the young child is based upon definite, observable patterns of behavior, upon a concrete set of interpersonal relations and upon a host of other mental phenomena.

[8] In this passage it is noteworthy that Dr. Arlow leaves it unclear whether the evidence of any one of these traits is sufficient to justify the inference that the oedipal phase of development has not been achieved, or whether all of these traits must be observed to warrant the inference. The reference to "a host of other mental phenomena" leaves open the possibility that even if all the traits enumerated above have been observed, which point to the absence of the oedipal phase, it may still be manifested if some of the "host of other mental phenomena" are present.

[9] Secondly, Dr. Arlow seems to be explicating Dr. Kris's statement that a child without an Oedipus complex would be an idiot. Yet some children classified as idiotic exhibit some of the traits whose presence Dr. Arlow may regard as sufficient to indicate the achievement of the oedipal phase, for example genital play.

[10] Thirdly, if one takes Dr. Arlow's description at its face value, I believe that an unprejudiced observation of the behavior of children who are not judged idiotic by reference to psychoanalytic criteria alone, will show that the oedipal phase is far from being universal. Many normal children do not manifest it. This would seriously invalidate one of Freud's central hypotheses. It would tend to indicate that the absence of the oedipal phase as well as variations in the extent, intensity, and mode of its expression are determined by social and cultural institutions. It suggests that the *significance* of the child's unlearned behavior depends upon the responsive reaction of adults and the institutional framework within which it is interpreted and channeled.

[11] Fourthly, if we follow the lead of this last point, acute doubt arises as to whether Dr. Arlow's reading of infantile behavior is not already determined by his theoretical prepossessions. He is *not* giving a phenomenological description of children's behavior, properly brack-

eted off from causal imputation, but presupposes that the child's expression of "tender or romantic feelings" towards its mother contains a predominantly sexual component. There is a profound difference in the elements enumerated as evidence of the oedipal phase, between saying of the child that (a) he expresses tender and romantic feelings, (b) he expresses a wish to grow up and marry his mother, etc., and (c) he manifests a wish to exhibit his sexual organ, etc. At most (c) is a clear expression of a libidinal impulse; (b) may be a highly questionable reading of the child's language or a misinterpretation of attention-getting behavior when a habit pattern set up by the mother (or anyone in the same role) is disrupted; (a) may be a perfectly "innocent" imitative reaction to the behavior of the parent. Whatever significance may be found in a mother's caress, it is the sheerest dogmatism to read the same or similar significance in the returning caress of the child. As well argue from the almost reflex-smile with which the infant responds to a beaming countenance that it is committed to a principle of cosmic benevolence.

[12] Fifthly, the same question-begging assumptions seem to me to be involved in the inferences Dr. Arlow makes concerning behavior which is allied to the absence of the oedipal phase of development. Why does it follow that a child who has not achieved the oedipal phase "would hardly regard the other individuals in his environment as distinct entities or personalities"? Because such a child is an idiot? This is much too broad a base for the inference; even objects may not be clearly distinguished by such a child, and persons are sometimes better distinguished than objects. Or is it the case that Dr. Arlow assumes that the differentiation in the child's environment is based primarily upon different sexual responses? But this is precisely what is in question.

[13] As grateful as I am to Dr. Arlow for his patient attempt to reply to my query, I must confess that I still am not satisfied that I understand from his account in what circumstances the behavior of a non-idiotic child would be necessary and sufficient evidence that he had not achieved the oedipal phase of development. A further specification of the behavior pattern of such a child would go a long way towards resolving our methodological perplexities on this key point.

[14] Since psychoanalysis does claim to function as a therapy, its clinical successes and failures seem to me to be highly relevant in evaluating the truth of its theories. If it has no clinical successes and if it is not confirmed by experimental findings, then it has no more scientific standing than any other consistent mythology. Since the experimental findings are unclear, it seems to me of the first importance, as difficult

as it may be, to assess the clinical experiences of psychoanalysts. I am sorely puzzled that some psychoanalysts seem inclined to dismiss the question of therapeutic efficacy as an irrelevant intrusion into the evaluation of its truth claims. . . .

[15] Unless psychoanalysis has better clinical or experimental successes than alternative theories, it can hardly aspire to scientific status. The difficulty is that even if it has these successes, this is not sufficient evidence for its validity. It must find ways of eliminating other hypotheses compatible with the same results. If, as a priest of some Mithraic cult, I give an ailing penitent mouldy bread and say a prayer over him, he may recover. If the recovery takes place several times when penitents are treated in this fashion, I am justified in continuing to use this technique. But the success of the treatment is not decisive with respect to the validity of the theory that prayer is efficacious unless I can deduce from my theoretical assumptions something specific not otherwise known, and not explicable by any other supposition.

[16] That the clinical successes of psychoanalysis, however modest, may be explicable without assuming the validity of psychoanalytic theory is a point made with increasing frequency by students of scientific methodology today. This criticism was made long ago and sometimes by psychoanalysts themselves. After sixteen years of psychoanalytic practice, Dr. Trigant Burrow wrote:

I have come to feel that what we have called analysis in the sense of our present personalistic system is just another application of the method of suggestion, and that with us analysts, as with others, the method involves a situation in which we are as truly the unconscious dupes of the suggestive process we employ as are the unconscious subjects upon whom we employ it.[1]

[17] It is not surprising that Dr. Burrow holds this position in view of his contention that "the attitude of the psychoanalyst and the attitude of the authoritarian are inseparable."[2] I am not endorsing this judgment but merely reporting it as an illustration of the fact that therapeutic successes by an analyst may be accounted for in theoretical terms other than those of psychoanalysis. . . .

Questions

1. Examine the second sentence of paragraph 1, beginning with "Is psychoanalysis more like meteorology . . .?" Analyze Hook's strategy in this sentence.
2. What does the discussion of the Oedipus complex have to do with Hook's

[1] *The Social Basis of Consciousness* (New York, 1927), p. 3.
[2] *Ibid.*, p. xvii.

argument? What is his purpose in reviewing the "history" of his question about the Oedipus complex?

3. What evidence does Hook supply to refute Dr. Arlow's explanation of the probable behavior of a child who does not achieve the oedipal phase of development? What is the basis of Arlow's statements? What is the basis of Hook's refutation?

4. What does Hook mean by "question-begging assumptions" (paragraph 12)?

5. In his last four paragraphs Hook turns to an evaluation of psychoanalysis as *therapy*. What aspect of psychoanalysis does he deal with in the preceding portions of the essay?

6. Why does Hook think it likely that the therapeutic successes claimed by an analyst might be due to other causes than psychoanalytic treatment?

7. How in general would you describe Hook's attitude toward psychoanalysis?

THE SCIENCE OF PSYCHOANALYSIS*

Leopold Bellak

[1] Each field of science probably passes through more or less well-defined phases of development. In psychoanalysis the great pioneering has been done by Freud and the early generations of students. Now, this one genius and his collaborators having laid the foundations, an era of methodological refinement should follow. It is necessary to redefine the hypotheses, test limits, validate, reformulate, and by such methods again to extend the clinical and theoretical horizon.

[2] Freud himself was aware that concepts are nothing but approximations of the truth and that a gradual and continued development of hypotheses is necessary. In 1915, in the opening paragraphs of his paper *Instincts and Their Vicissitudes*,[1] he discusses the formulation of models of thought very lucidly: "It is only after more searching investigation of the field in question that we are able to formulate with increasing clarity the scientific concepts underlying it and progressively so modify these concepts that they become widely applicable and, at the same time, consistent logically. Then, indeed, it may be time to immure them in definition."

[3] Now, more than forty years after these words were written, psychoanalysis has as yet spent little time considering its concepts in the

* From Leopold Bellak, "Introduction: The Frame of Reference of the Monograph," publications of a conference on "Conceptual and Methodological Problems in Psychoanalysis," *Annals of The New York Academy of Sciences*, Vol. 76, Art. 4, January 23, 1959. Copyright © 1959 by The New York Academy of Sciences. Reprinted by permission.

orderly, systematic, and experimental way of science. Unfortunately, such an approach has not infrequently, been quite strongly, unnecessarily, and incorrectly considered antithetical to psychoanalysis and barred from its forum.

[4] Of course, one could wait longer before attempting to put the house in order, but clinical and theoretical psychoanalysis seem to have advanced to a point where an orderly statement of hypotheses as well as some attempt to arrive at an increasingly better definition of our concepts (and, wherever possible, experimental exploration of constructs and of the process of psychoanalysis) are mandatory. Too many round-table discussions terminate in frustration because semantic confusion does not even enable the participants to agree precisely on what they are discussing. Furthermore, clinical psychoanalysis is still taught with little reference to general principles, and preceptorship still takes the place of systematic teaching.

[5] One of the reasons for this difficulty is doubtless the fact that psychoanalysts are predominantly applied scientists, professionals, or therapists and, as such, sometimes ambivalent in their attitudes toward theory. Also, neither medical-school training nor postgraduate training in psychiatry or psychoanalysis provides any schooling in scientific method, concept formation, or other rigors of thought taught to graduate students of other sciences. On the other hand, clinicians generally, and psychoanalysts particularly, have good reason to be wary, at times, of the academic approach. Among theoreticians there are those ambitious ones who prefer to be so far removed from life that they choose to study problems with a telescope; there are also those so very precise that they consider any exploration coarse if not restricted to the confines of an ultramicroscope.

[6] I recommend the type of theoretical approach that uses a "magnifying glass": interested primarily in problems but one step removed from what one can see with the naked clinical eye; the approach, of course, being in keeping with and in steady interchange with daily experience.

[7] The relationship between the clinician and the academic theoretician can best be illustrated by the story of the two people who decide to learn how to swim: the first jumps into deep water and, almost drowning, flails about desperately, trying to stay afloat. The other takes lessons on land from the best of teachers and perfects details of his technique for years, but never gets into the water at all.

[8] Psychoanalysts are also justifiably wary of innovators. Too often an entire structure is discarded by people who have indeed a valuable brick or two to offer but mistake it for a whole housing project. I be-

lieve it only parsimonious never to discard a theory until it has been thoroughly tested and all its possibilities exhausted.

[9]. It seems to me that Freudian psychoanalytic theory, to date, still supplies the most internally consistent and most comprehensive theory of personality and has predicated upon it the most effective therapy. The hypotheses of psychoanalysis are poorly defined and poorly integrated, but they are probably largely verifiable, and they are useful in their ability to help understand, predict, and control behavior, therapeutically and otherwise.

[10] In short, the application of the scientific method of inquiry to psychoanalysis is possible and necessary. It is evident that such a method is but a vantage point, not an ideology, and neither a cure-all nor an end in itself. A steady interchange of data from clinical, empirical work with theoretical, methodologically refined viewpoints is necessary in any science.

[11] It is my hope that the papers arrayed for this monograph and for the conference upon which it is based will help examine critically some of the basic concepts of psychoanalysis and, wherever necessary, recast them in a form that will make them still more useful for practice and theory. . . .

Reference

1. FREUD, S. 1915. Instincts and Their Vicissitudes. Collected Papers of Sigmund Freud. 4: 60–83. Hogarth Press. London, England.

Questions

1. What characteristics of a scientific field does Bellak find psychoanalysis possesses?
2. What phase of scientific development does he think psychoanalysis is now in?
3. What is Bellak's purpose (paragraph 5) in calling psychoanalysts "predominantly applied scientists, professionals, or therapists"? Is he indicating a strength, a weakness, or something else?
4. In paragraph 9 Bellak takes a specific stand on Freudian psychoanalytic theory. What value does he find? What shortcomings does he point to?
5. How would you describe the style and tone of Bellak's paper? Do you consider these qualities appropriate to the occasion? Why or why not?

ASSIGNMENTS

1. Write a paper in which you contrast the views of Eysenck and Hook with those of Bellak. Discuss specifically the alleged shortcomings of psychoanalysis as a science and the way in which Bellak does or does not refute the allegations.

2. Read Weaver's essay "Science and Complexity" (pp. 579–583). Prepare a report in which you show as specifically as you can what requirements of scientific method are referred to in the Eysenck and Hook essays.

3. Write an expanded definition of the terms *psychology, psychiatry, psychoanalysis*. In addition to the sources available in this project, consult such a reference work as Harriman's *Encyclopedia of Psychology* or *New Dictionary of Psychology*.

4. Interview one or more faculty members in your college's department of psychology to obtain their opinions about the scientific standing of psychoanalysis and some of the reasons for their views. Report your findings in oral or written form.

5. Sidney Hook is the editor of a volume entitled *Psychoanalysis, Scientific Method, and Philosophy, A Symposium* (1959). If your library has this book, read two or three of the essays. Prepare a written report in which you summarize and evaluate the essays you have read.

6. Both Flesch and Eysenck deal with the question, "What's wrong with psychoanalysis?" Compare Flesch's statement of Eysenck's answer to this question (see paragraph 3 of Flesch's article) with Eysenck's own answer (last paragraph of Eysenck article). Write a paper in which you indicate the various implications you find in the two statements.

7. Ernest Jones is the author of a three-volume biography of Sigmund Freud, a work which Freudians in general think of as definitive. Look up Jones's account of the scientific status of psychoanalysis. Write a report in which you contrast Jones's viewpoint with Eysenck's.

8. To what extent do you find Dr. Alvarez' views about psychoanalysis typical of the medical profession. As a possible source of an oral or written report, consult the index to the *Journal of the American Medical Association* to discover editorials which may have been published in the *Journal* on this subject during the past ten years.

9. Read "Seeds," a short story by Sherwood Anderson. Prepare a report in which you indicate Anderson's attitude toward psychoanalysis. Cite specific details in the story to support your beliefs.

6. PHYSICAL SCIENCE
Evolutionary or Steady-State Universe?

The physical sciences are not usually thought of by the layman as very likely to generate "purely scientific" controversies. While everyone knows that atomic scientists, for example, have argued about the wisdom of using atomic weapons in warfare or about continuing nuclear tests in the atmosphere, such controversies are generally viewed as belonging to the spheres of morals, politics, or military strategy rather than to the sphere of "pure" science. A viewpoint to which even many scientists themselves subscribe is that the methods of science, the rigors of scientific demonstration, and the objectivity required for verification of findings seem to preclude the kinds of controversy represented by other issues in this book. Hence scientific "truths"—unlike the "truths" of literature, art, philosophy, or politics—are thought of as being uncontaminated by taste, prejudice, opinion, or differing value judgments.

Actually, controversies about purely scientific topics do arise in the physical sciences, but when one impinges on the awareness of the layman, he is likely to feel both incompetent, in an attempt to grasp the issues involved, and unconcerned. The highly technical subject matter of the physical sciences, the manipulation of difficult mathematical equations, and the use of special signs and symbols all combine to elude his grasp. The layman's lack of concern is perhaps attributable to what C. P. Snow in his book *The Two Cultures* has described as the deplorable split between humanistic and scientific emphases in our education and our civilization. Snow, who is himself both a distinguished scientist and a novelist, suggests, for example, that a typical layman educated in the humanistic tradition takes it for granted that only an ignoramus could be unfamiliar with *Hamlet* but would see no particular reason why he, himself, might be expected to be familiar with the Second Law of Thermodynamics.

Fortunately, quite a number of scientists have thought themselves responsible for carrying on communication about their work not only with specialists like themselves but with the lay public as well. The authors of all the selections in this issue have made important contributions to their field in technical publications addressed to specialists, but they have also presented their theories and their findings in nontechnical terms for the enlightenment of the lay reader.

The issue in this section—an evolutionary or a steady-state universe—is a topic that has recently emerged in cosmology (Greek *kosmos*, universe, + *logos*, discourse), a special branch of astronomy and astrophysics concerned with questions of the structure and origin—if it had one—of the universe. Since the discoveries announced by Edwin P. Hubble, an American astronomer, in 1929 of the so-called "red shift," which indicates that all the galaxies are rapidly moving away from each other, astronomers have been in agreement that we live in an expanding rather than a static universe. Controversy now centers on rival theories: did the universe begin at some given moment, is it now evolving, and will it ultimately cease to exist (the evolutionary theory); or is matter continually being created so that the universe cannot be said to have either beginning or ending (the steady-state theory)? The four selections that follow are devoted to an examination of these questions.

The first selection, "The Origin of the Universe," is from a series of lectures broadcast over the BBC by A. C. B. Lovell. He is professor of radio astronomy at the University of Manchester and is also director of the Jodrell Bank Experimental Station in Cheshire, England, the site of one of the world's major radio telescopes. Lovell's lecture examines both the background of the issue and the implications of some of the divergent views.

An advocate of the evolutionary theory, the concept that all matter, time, and space originated billions of years ago in a "primeval atom" and that the universe exploded into being with a "big bang," is George Gamow, a physicist at the University of Colorado. His article "The Evolutionary Universe" is one of many publications in which he has discussed cosmology, astrophysics, relativity, radioactivity, and other scientific topics in popular terms.

The theory of the steady-state universe was first advanced by a group of astronomers at Cambridge University during the 1950s (the so-called Bondi-Gold-Hoyle group) and has been further developed and popularized particularly by Fred Hoyle. The article printed here, "The Steady-State Universe," is a brief statement of Hoyle's position; fuller treatment is contained in his book *The Frontiers of Astronomy* (1955).

The last selection, "Peculiar Galaxies," is an article by Margaret and Geoffrey Burbidge, a husband-wife team on the staff of the Yerkes Observatory of The University of Chicago at Williams Bay, Wisconsin.

Mrs. Burbidge is an astronomer, Mr. Burbidge an astrophysicist. Their article is an account of recent astronomical observations they have made and of the extent to which their findings can be accommodated within the rival cosmological theories.

Because of the very nature of their subject matter, astronomers and cosmologists must rely largely on observation, extrapolation, deduction, and the theoretical devising of models. Unlike other physical scientists such as chemists or physicists, they cannot set up experiments in which they can control their actual materials of study. A chemist can manipulate substances in a retort; a physicist can bring about nuclear fission in an atomic pile. But a cosmologist cannot manipulate galaxies; he cannot visit Alpha Centauri; he cannot personally scrutinize a single galaxy for light-years of time; he cannot, indeed, escape from the space-time continuum itself. Nevertheless, the controversy between the proponents of the evolutionary and the steady-state theories may one day come nearer resolution. Perhaps some clues will be gained through the actual development of the "unified field theory," toward which Albert Einstein had been working until the time of his death. Or perhaps the establishment of astronomical observatories in outer space, unimpeded by the interference of earth's atmosphere and equipped with as yet undevised optical and radio instruments, may yield conclusive data.

One final note. As you study the selections that follow, you will quickly become aware that the materials are unlike those of most of the other issues in this volume. You will realize that these writers *describe* but do not actually present the raw data with which they work; you will observe that details of their calculations are omitted; and you will immediately conclude, in all likelihood, that you cannot independently verify or challenge the accuracy of their reports of investigations and observations. However, their statements are not all purely informative; you will discover lines of arguments, strategies in the marshalling of evidence, and processes of reasoning. And here, of course, you can apply the methods of critical analysis just as you do in the other issues.

THE ORIGIN OF THE UNIVERSE[*]

A. C. B. Lovell

[1] In this lecture . . . I want to talk to you about the problem of the origin of the universe. I suppose it would hardly be an exaggeration to say that this is the greatest challenge to the intellect which faces man, and I cannot pretend that I have any new solution to offer you. However . . . today the air is alive with a new hope and expectancy, because our new instruments may be reaching out so far into space that we may soon be able to speak with more confidence. I am going to set out the problem as I see it, and I hope you will get an idea of these vast cosmological issues and of the implications of the alternative solutions which lie ahead. At the end I shall tell you what I think about it all as an ordinary human being.

[2] We have seen that observational astronomy tells us about the universe as it exists out to distances of about two thousand million[1] light years. At that distance we are seeing the universe as it existed two thousand million years ago. Within this vast area of space and time we can study the innumerable stars and galaxies, and from these observations we can attempt to infer the probable nature and extent of the cosmos beyond the range of observations.

[3] I think there are three stages in which we might consider this problem. The first stage is to inquire whether the observations are likely to be extended in the future to even greater distances and thereby penetrate even farther into past history than the present two thousand million years. The second stage is an appeal to cosmological theory, an inquiry as to the extent to which the present observations agree with any particular cosmology and the nature of the past and future as predicted by these theories. Finally, we shall reach a stage where theories based on our present conceptions of physical laws have nothing further to say. At this point we pass from physics to metaphysics, from astronomy to theology, where the corporate views of science merge into the beliefs of the individual.

---

[*] From A. C. B. Lovell, *The Individual and the Universe* (The BBC Reith Lectures 1958). Copyright © 1958, 1959 by A. C. B. Lovell. Reprinted by permission of Harper & Bros.

[1] In British usage the word *billion* means one million million; hence, Professor Lovell writes two thousand million where an American writer would say two billion [Eds.].

[4] The vast region of space and time enclosed by the present observations includes several hundred million galaxies of stars. As far as we can see, the overall large-scale structure of the universe within these limits has a high degree of uniformity. When we look at these distant regions we find that the light is reddened, indicating that the galaxies are receding from us. As far as we can see, the red shift of the most distant nebulae is still increasing linearly with distance. There is no indication that we are seeing anything but a small part of the total universe. However, in the second stage of our inquiry we shall see that an observational test between rival cosmological theories demands a still further penetration, and an extension of the present observational limit is a matter of some urgency in cosmology. Unfortunately there are fundamental difficulties introduced by the recession of the galaxies which no device of man will ever surmount. At the present observable limit of the large optical telescopes the galaxies are receding with a speed of about one-fifth of the velocity of light. From this aspect alone we face a limit to future progress. Even if no other effects intervened we could never obtain information about those farther regions of space where the velocities of recession of the galaxies reach the speed of light. The light from the more distant galaxies will never reach us. In Eddington's phrase "Light is like a runner on an expanding track with the winning post receding faster than he can run."

[5] There are, moreover, further difficulties which will hinder the approach to this fundamental limit. If the remote galaxies were stationary, then all the light emitted, say, in one second would reach our telescopes. But the galaxies are moving away with speeds which are an appreciable fraction of the velocity of light, and as the speed increases less and less of the light actually emitted by the galaxies in one second reaches our instruments. This degradation of the intensity of the light coupled with the accompanying shift in wave-length to the red end of the spectrum worsens still further the technical difficulties of these observations.

[6] The radio telescopes may well be in a stronger position with respect to these hindrances. To begin with, the collisions of galaxies . . . generate very powerful radio emissions, and the shifts in wavelength which accompany the recession do not present the same observational difficulties as in the optical case. In fact, the present belief is that many of the objects already studied by their radio emissions lie at distances which exceed considerably the present two thousand million light years' limit of the optical telescopes. Therefore, we can, I think, answer the first stage of our inquiry with some degree of certainty in the following

way. The present observable horizon of the universe will be pushed back by a limited amount in the near future, perhaps to a few thousand million light years. Then we must be content. No further strivings or inventions of man will enable us to probe the conditions which existed in epochs of history beyond these few thousand million years. They are gone for ever beyond the fundamental limits of observability.

[7] At this point we reach the second stage of our inquiry, where we appeal to cosmological theory. The question is this. Can we formulate a theory in terms of known physical laws whose predictions agree so well with the present observable universe that we can predict the past and future?

[8] Indeed, when we turn to the cosmological theories which are today seriously considered by astronomers we find a most absorbing state of affairs. Not one, but several theories can explain from acceptable postulates the present observable state of the universe. These predictions bring us face to face with the ultimate problem of the origin of the universe in ways which are startlingly different. But the new techniques in astronomy may be on the verge of producing observational data which may be decisively in favour of one or other of these cosmologies. . . .

[9] First of all, though, I want to discuss the cosmological theories which are generally classed as the evolutionary models of the universe. I think it would be correct to say that these theories, which are a consequence of Einstein's general theory of relativity, are regarded with the most favour by the majority of contemporary astronomers. In passing, perhaps I should add that in the light of our present knowledge it does not seem worth while discussing for our present purpose any of the cosmological theories which preceded the introduction of the theory of general relativity in 1915. . . .

[10] The possible types of non-static universes fall into three main families determined by the various possible combinations of the sign of the cosmical constant and the space curvature. These are a universe which starts from a point origin at a finite time in the past and expands continuously to become infinitely large after an infinite time, a universe whose radius has a certain finite value at the initial moment of time, and thence expands to become infinite after an infinite time, and lastly a universe which expands from zero radius to a certain maximum and then collapses to zero again, this process of oscillation being capable of indefinite repetition. Within each of these three main categories a large number of possible models can be constructed differing in various points of detail. For the past thirty years cosmologists have sought for

arguments based on the observed characteristics of the universe which would identify the actual universe with one of the theoretical models.

[11] All that I propose to do here is to give some examples of these evolutionary models, one of which is today believed by many cosmologists to describe the past history with some degree of certainty. The first example is a solution discovered by the Abbé Lemaître in 1927 and developed by Eddington. I have already said that by introducing the cosmical constant Einstein was able to specify a static condition of the universe in which the Newtonian attraction and cosmical repulsion are in exact balance. However, this equilibrium is unstable. If something upsets the balance so that the attraction is weakened, then cosmical repulsion has the upper hand and an expansion begins. As the material of the universe separates, the distance between the bodies becomes greater, the attraction still further weakens, the cosmical repulsion ever increases, and the expansion becomes faster. On the other hand, if the equilibrium was upset in the other way so that the forces of attraction became superior, then the reverse would occur and the system would contract continuously. Eddington's view was that in the initial stage the universe consisted of a uniform distribution of protons and electrons, by our standards very diffuse. This proton-electron gas comprised the entire primeval universe, which would have had a radius of about a thousand million light years. At some stage an event or series of events must have occurred in this diffuse gas which determined that the universe was launched on a career of expansion and not contraction. There were many views as to how this might have happened. Eddington held that the accumulation of irregularities in the gas started the evolutionary tendency. Soon, condensations formed in the gas and those ultimately became the galaxies of stars. On these views the present radius of the universe must be about five times that of the initial static primeval universe.

[12] In the light of modern knowledge this theory receives little support. The time scale of its evolution is too short, and one cannot find a compelling reason why the primeval gas should have been disturbed in such a way as to determine that the universe was launched on a career of expansion rather than contraction. The initial condition is a special case, ephemeral and fortuitous. As far as the laws of physics are concerned, one can only say that by chance the initial disturbances were such as to determine the history of the universe. One cannot feel very happy that such a chance occurrence some thousands of millions of years ago should have determined the fundamental features of the universe. Moreover, although originally the theory as expounded by

Jeans and Eddington undoubtedly had attractive features for some theologians, I feel now that this might well have been enhanced by feelings of relief that the vastness, uniformity, and organization of the universe which had just been revealed still remained outside the conceivable laws of physics in its initial state. Indeed, when considering these initial conditions Jeans spoke in terms of "the finger of God agitating the ether," implying a divine intervention at a predictable time in past history after which the laws of physics became applicable. This degree of familiarity with divine processes is, I think, undesirable theologically, and for science it evades the problem by obscuring the ultimate cosmological issue.

[13] Moreover, there is another problem which must be faced. The event which we have considered in the unstable static assemblage of primeval gas predetermined the subsequent history of the universe. One must still inquire how long the gas existed in this condition of unstable equilibrium and how the primeval gas originated. Science has nothing to say on this issue. Indeed, it seems that the theory requires the exercise of yet another divine act at some indeterminate time before the occurrence which set off the gas on its career of condensation and expansion. . . .

[14] I have already mentioned the Abbé Lemaître. His original work in 1927, published in a little-known journal, was discovered by Eddington. Although Eddington remained faithful to this idea that the universe evolved from the static but unstable Einstein universe, the conception was soon abandoned by Lemaître himself. For the past twenty-five years Lemaître's name has been associated with another model whose origin recedes even farther back in time than the static Einstein state. Of all cosmologies, it is, perhaps, by far the most thoroughly studied. We shall see later that during the last few years a tremendous clash has occurred with other opinions, but at the present time there are no known features of the observable universe which are incompatible with Lemaître's evolutionary cosmology. Lemaître's model is typical of one of the groups of theories inherent in general relativity, according to which the universe originated at a finite time in the past and expands to an infinite size at an infinite future time.

[15] Perhaps we can most easily visualize this conception by taking the universe as we see it now and inquiring quite simply what might have been the situation long ago. The observations of the distant galaxies show that their light and radio emission is shifted in wavelength so that as received on the earth the light is redder and the radio waves longer in wavelength than those which are actually emitted. The in-

terpretation of this shift is that we are separating from the galaxies at a very high speed, and that the speed of recession increases as we move out into space. At the limits of present-day observation the speed of recession is about thirty-seven thousand miles per second, which is a fifth of the velocity of light. The observation which gives us this figure is of a cluster of galaxies in Hydra photographed in the two-hundred-inch telescope. The so-called cosmological principle which is inherent in Lemaître's theory implies that if human beings equipped with similar instruments existed on a planet in this Hydra cluster of galaxies, then they would see the cluster of galaxies to which we belong at the limit of their powers of observation, and the velocity of recession would also be thirty-seven thousand miles per second. It is important to rid ourselves of any idea that because all around us we find galaxies in recession, then we are the centre of the recessional movement. This is not the case. It is an impression which we obtain because we can see only a small part of the total universe.

[16] To return to this cluster of galaxies in Hydra. We are now seeing it as it was two thousand million years ago moving away at a rate of thirty-seven thousand miles a second. What is the likely past history of this and all other similar galaxies? Up to a point this question is not too difficult to answer. For example, a minute ago we were two million miles closer to this cluster than we are now. A year ago we were over a billion miles closer. If we recede back into history in this manner we realize that the galaxies such as Hydra which are now almost beyond our view must have been very much closer to us in the remote past. In fact, if we proceed in this way, then we reach a time of about eight or nine thousand million years ago when all the galaxies must have been very close together indeed. Of course, the galaxies themselves have evolved during this time, but the primeval material from which they were formed must have existed in a space which is very small compared with the universe today.

[17] With important reservations which I shall deal with now, this in essence is the fundamental concept of Lemaître's theory, namely, that the universe originated from a dense and small conglomerate which Lemaître calls the primeval atom. I shall return in a moment to the conditions which might have existed at the beginning, and to the possible events which might have initiated the disruption and expansion of the primeval atom. It is in fact necessary to emphasize that the theory does not demand the formation of the galaxies in the first phase of the expansion. The primeval atom contained the entire material of the universe, and its density must have been inconceivably high—at

least a hundred million tons per cubic centimetre. The initial momentum of the expansion dispersed this material, and after thousands of millions of years the conditions applicable to the so-called Einstein universe would have been reached. Then the size of the universe was about a thousand million light years and the density would have been comparable to that with which we are familiar on earth. According to Lemaître, at this stage the initial impetus of the expansion was nearly exhausted and the universe began to settle down into the nearly static condition which we have previously considered, where the forces of gravitational attraction and cosmical repulsion were in balance. The mathematical treatment indicates that the universe must have stayed for a long time in this condition. It is during this phase that the great clusters of galaxies began to form from the primeval material. Then the conditions of near equilibrium were again upset, the forces of cosmical repulsion began to win over those of gravitational attraction, and the universe was launched on the career of expansion which after nine thousand million years brought it to the state which we witness today.

[18] The time scale determined by tracing back the past history of the galaxies brings us not to the beginning of time and space, but merely to a condition which existed a few thousand million years ago when the universe was probably about one-tenth of its present size and consisted of the original gaseous clouds from which the clusters of galaxies began to form. The processes of the formation and evolution of the galaxies from this early stage are the subject of very detailed mathematical treatment. There is, at present, every reason to believe that a satisfactory explanation of the evolution of the universe from that condition can be given in terms of the known laws of physics. But when we pass on to consider the even earlier stages, difficulties and uncertainties appear. How much farther do we have to go back in time to the condition of the primeval atom? The theory does not determine this with any precision, because the delay which the universe suffered during the equilibrium phase when the gaseous clouds were forming into galaxies cannot be specified. One can, however, say this—that the explosion or disintegration of the primeval atom must have occurred between twenty thousand million and sixty thousand million years ago. In other words the period of about nine thousand million years ago, when the galaxies began to form and the present period of expansion began, represents a comparatively recent phase in the history of the universe. . . .

[19] An alternative picture of the condition of the primeval atom has been given by Gamov, who believes that it consisted entirely of

high-temperature thermal radiation. Five minutes after the expansion began the temperature of the universe was a thousand million degrees, after a day it had fallen to forty million degrees—say, nearly to the temperature of the centre of the sun; after ten million years it had fallen to an average temperature, which we call room temperature. On this theory of Gamov all the chemical elements which we deal with today must have been formed within the first thirty minutes of the life of the universe.

[20] Gamov differs from Lemaître in other important respects. In Lemaître's theory the force of the initial disintegration was exhausted after a few thousand million years, and the expansion which we witness today came into play only as a result of the forces of cosmical repulsion which developed when the galaxies began to form. In Gamov's theory the force of the initial explosion was so great that the expansion of the universe is attained without invoking the force of cosmical repulsion. In other words, the beginning in the Gamov theory is close to the nine thousand million years which we deduce by tracing back the history of the galaxies, and there is no protracted period in the state of diffuse gas with all the major forces balanced as in Lemaître's theory.

[21] The most distinguished living exponent of the evolutionary theory or the origin of the universe is himself in Holy Orders. For him and for all who associate their universe with God, the creation of the primeval atom was a divine act outside the limits of scientific knowledge and indeed of scientific investigation. The probable condition of intense radiation in the primeval atom is entirely consistent with the divine command "Let there be light." It would, of course, be wrong of me to suggest that this view of the origin of the universe demands necessarily the possibility of creation of matter by a divine act. On the contrary, those who reject God adopt a strictly materialistic attitude to the problem of the creation of the primeval atom. They would argue that the creation of the primeval material had no explanation within the framework of contemporary scientific knowledge, but would escape from the dilemma by reserving the possibility that science would, if given the opportunity of studying these initial conditions, find a satisfactory solution. Or they would evade the problem of a beginning altogether by following a further line of thought due to Gamov that the primeval atom was not the beginning, but merely a state of maximum contraction of a universe which had previously existed for an eternity of time. I think, however, that for theology, there is one important observation to make. If the universe was created and evolved in the manner just

described, then the conception that the creation of the primeval material was a divine act can never be attacked by scientific investigation.
A set of conditions which existed over twenty thousand million years
ago, and which can never return again, is for ever beyond investigation.

[22] The theory which we have discussed envisages a once for all
creation in the remote past followed by a steady evolution to the present conditions. The alternative to this theory is that the creation of matter is taking place continuously and that although stars and galaxies
evolve from this basic material, the universe, when considered as a large-
scale structure, is in a steady state. We can illustrate this view by considering the future history of the galaxies which are now near the limit
of observation. We are receding at great speed from these galaxies. In
a billion years' time the galaxies will have passed for ever from our field
of view and other galaxies which are now closer to us will have moved
out to our observable horizon. So much is common ground on both the
evolutionary and steady-state theories. The sharp distinction arises
when we compare the picture of the universe within the observable
horizon now and in a billion years' time. On the evolutionary theory
more and more galaxies move out of our field of view, and the number
of galaxies which we can see with our instruments will for ever decrease. In other words, the average spatial density of the universe is
decreasing. On the steady-state theory this is not the case. Although
individual galaxies recede beyond the observable horizon, others are
always being created to take their place. In a billion years' time the
universe will look to us very much as it does now. The individual galaxies will have changed, but their average spatial density remains the
same, because matter is always in creation throughout all of space. The
cosmological principle of the evolutionary theory in which the universe
would appear to be the same to any observer, wherever he was situated
in space, has become the perfect cosmological principle according to
which the universe is the same throughout all space and time.

[23] The implications of this point of view are, of course, profound.
For example, there cannot have been a beginning in any scale of time
at all. If we trace back in time the history of the galaxies, they dissolve
into gas and then into uncreated matter as they move in towards us,
whereas others come into view from beyond the observable horizon. At
a time of twenty thousand million years ago the evolutionary models
picture the universe as a concentrated conglomerate of gas, whereas the
steady-state universe would have appeared as it does today. Indeed,
however far we go back in time, there is no stage at which we can say

that the universe, as a whole, had a beginning. In the only language at our command we can say that the history of the universe on the steady-state theory extends to an infinite time in the past.

[24] Whereas there is hope that we can put our inferences about the past to an experimental test, we can discuss the future only in terms of the predictions of cosmological theory. Here again there are great differences between the evolutionary and steady-state models. The predictions of the steady-state theory are quite clear. The universe has an infinite extent in space and an infinite future in time. There is, of course, a limit to the observable universe from any one place in it determined by the speed of expansion. But if an intelligent being exists at our observable limit he would find himself surrounded by a similar universe of galaxies and so on without end. Neither does the theory of continuous creation place any limitation on the future extent in time. In the same way that a billion years ago the universe would look the same as it does now, so in a billion years of future existence the overall large-scale picture will be unchanged.

[25] The future on the evolutionary models is quite different. The total content of matter was fixed once and for all at the time of creation. The expansion is thinning out the galaxies, and in a billion years our view of space would indeed be vastly different from what it is today. In some variations of the evolutionary theory the process of expansion is expected to reverse when the spatial density has fallen to a certain value, and then the contraction of space would bring the ageing galaxies into view again. But even in such variations of the evolutionary models the ultimate death of the universe seems inescapable, because the energy with which the universe was imbued at its creation is relentlessly becoming less available. . . .

[26] I think it is true to say that during the last few years the cosmological issue has crystallized into a conflict between these evolutionary and steady-state theories of the origin of the universe. The variations in detail within these two broad principles are numerous. Many of these differences are highly abstract, but in so far as the stream of human thought is concerned these internal variations are of small consequence compared with the major issue as to whether creation is occurring now and throughout all time in the past and in the future, or whether the fundamental material of the universe was created in its entirety some billions of years ago.

[27] It seems possible that we may be on the verge of settling by experimental observation which of these two principles is correct. In fact, the group of young cosmologists who have promulgated the the-

ories of continuous creation have always emphasized that, as distinct from the theoretical arguments which have surrounded the variations of evolutionary cosmology in the last thirty years, the new theories should be capable of direct experimental test. For example, if with our telescopes we could penetrate so far into space that we could see a cluster of galaxies from which the light had taken nine thousand million years to reach us, then it would be possible to reach a clear decision. For at that time in the past on the evolutionary theory the clusters of galaxies were only just beginning to form from the primeval gas. Well, of course, such a straightforward observation is impossible because of the limited range of our telescopes. I said earlier that the most distant object yet identified in the telescopes is the cluster of galaxies in Hydra at about two thousand million light years. Although the light from this cluster has been travelling through space for two thousand million years, it is too close to us in time and space to be of use in distinguishing between the two theories.

[28] It is, however, on the verge of the regions of space and time where the universe would be expected to be significantly different if creation was still in progress compared with the conditions in an evolutionary universe. If time and space had a beginning, then when the universe was only a few thousand million years old it would be much more compact than it is today. The galaxies would be in existence, but they would be packed closer together compared with their spatial density today. The spatial density today—by which I mean the number of galaxies within, say, fifty or a hundred million light years of the Milky Way —can be determined by the large telescopes. If we could count the number in a similar volume of space at a distance of several thousand million light years we should in effect be making a count of the galaxies as they existed several thousand million years ago. If creation is still taking place, then on the steady-state theories this number should be the same as today. If the evolutionary model is correct, then the spatial density at this distance in time and space will be much greater.

[29] The possibility of carrying out this decisive observational test excites the imagination. Unfortunately it seems likely that the hindrances introduced by the atmosphere of the earth will prevent the great optical telescopes from penetrating to the required regions of space. It may well be that only when optical telescopes can be carried in earth satellites or erected on the moon will it be possible to look back into the past to this extent. Before the advent of such futuristic enterprises it seems likely that the great radio telescopes will give us the answer we require. . . . In a previous talk I referred to the collisions of galaxies

which, for reasons not yet understood, generate radio waves which can easily be picked up in the radio telescopes, although the light from these galaxies is so faint that they are near the limit of the normally observable universe. We can already study galaxies in collision at such distances that they must be far beyond the range of the optical telescopes. We believe that these investigations are already taking us so far out in space and so far back in time that the radio waves have been on their journey for a few thousand million years. The circumstantial evidence for this belief in the origin of many of the unidentified radio sources is very strong, and if this is confirmed we have the tools with which human beings can bring the cosmological issues to a decisive test.

[30] The concept of continuous creation also presents us with another opportunity to make an even more direct and decisive test. If the theory is correct, then the hydrogen gas which forms the primeval material of the galaxies must be in creation at a considerable rate. The theory demands the appearance of hydrogen at the rate of several billion trillion tons per second in the observable universe. Although this figure is vast, in fact, by ordinary human concepts of terrestrial space the rate is exceedingly slow. It represents the creation of only a few atoms of hydrogen per cubic mile of space per year. The presence of this hydrogen in intergalactic space may well be detectable in the near future by the radio telescopes.

[31] As individuals we must therefore face the possibility that within the next few years astronomers may be able to speak with unanimity about the ultimate cosmological problem. Only the materialist can turn aside unmoved by this prospect. For others, a settlement of this cosmological issue might mean an affirmation or rejection of deeply embedded philosophical and theological beliefs.

[32] So far I have tried to present the contemporary background without prejudice, but no doubt before I finish you will expect me to say a word about my own personal views. At the moment our outlook in astronomy is optimistic. A new epoch has been opened by the development of radio telescopes, and we are perhaps within a generation of an even more astonishing one because of the inherent possibilities of astronomical observations from earth satellites or the moon. We can only guess as to the nature of the remote regions which might be photographed by telescopes removed from their earth-bound environment. In the case of radio telescopes this development is still very young. Three hundred years elapsed between Galileo's small telescope and the inauguration of the 200-inch telescope on Palomar Mountain. In the development of radio telescopes we have not covered a tenth of that time-

pan. I think therefore that our present optimism may well be of the ind which comes from the initial deployment of great new instruments nd techniques. I have no doubt that within a few years these instruents will enable us to resolve the conflict which I have described between the evolutionary and steady-state models. In this process new ifficulties will certainly appear, and these might make my present escription of the universe as out of date as the static egocentric description which was in vogue in the first twenty years of this century. Vhen we are dealing with time-spans of thousands of millions of years would be sheer impudence to suggest that the views of the cosmos hich have evolved from the techniques developed in our age possess ny degree of finality. My present attitude to the scientific aspects of he problem is therefore neutral in the sense that I do not believe that here yet exist any observational data which are decisively in favour of ny particular contemporary cosmology. The optimism with which I elieve that we are on the verge of producing the necessary observaonal data is tempered with a deep apprehension, born of bitter expeience, that the decisive experiment nearly always extends one's horizon to regions of new doubts and difficulties.

[33] On the question of the creation of the primeval material of the niverse it seems to me unlikely that there can ever be a scientific description, whether in terms of the evolutionary or steady-state theories. f the idea of continuous creation is substantiated, then science will ave penetrated very far indeed into the ultimate processes of the universe. It might then appear that a completely materialistic framework ould have been established, but it does not seem to me that this is the ase. If one imagines a scientific device which is so perfect that it could ecord the appearance of a single hydrogen atom as demanded by the ontinuous creation theory, then the scientific description of the process ould still be imperfect. The same basic and quite fundamental difficulty would appear, as I have described in the case of the primeval tom, in the further effort to obtain information about the nature of the nergy input which gave rise to the created atom.

[34] If I were pressed on this problem of creation I would say, therefore, that any cosmology must eventually move over into metaphysics or reasons which are inherent in modern scientific theory. The epoch f this transfer may be now and at all future time, or it may have been wenty thousand million years ago. In respect of creation the most that ve can hope from our future scientific observations is a precise determination of this epoch. I must emphasize that this is a personal view. The attitudes of my professional colleagues to this problem would be

varied. Some would no doubt approve of this or a similar line of meta-physical thought. Others would not be willing to face even this funda-mental limit to scientific knowledge, although, as I have said, an analo-gous limitation occurs in modern scientific theory which describes the well-known processes of atomic behaviour. Some, I am afraid, will be aghast at my temerity in discussing the issues at all. As far as this group is concerned, all that I say is that I sometimes envy their ability to evade by neglect such a problem which can tear the individual's mind asunder.

[35] On the question of the validity of combining a metaphysical and physical process as a description of creation, this, as I said earlier, is the individual's problem. In my own case, I have lived my days as a scien-tist, but science has never claimed the whole of my existence. Some, at least, of the influence of my upbringing and environment has survived the conflict, so that I find no difficulty in accepting this conclusion. I am certainly not competent to discuss this problem of knowledge outside that acquired by my scientific tools, and my outlook is essentially a sim-ple one. Simple in the sense that I am no more surprised or distressed at the limitation of science when faced with this great problem of crea-tion than I am at the limitation of the spectroscope in describing the radiance of a sunset or at the theory of counterpoint in describing the beauty of a fugue. . . .

Questions

1. How has Lovell adapted his material for radio presentation? Cite some specifics in your answer.
2. What does he mean by the statement at the end of paragraph 1: "I shall tell you what I think about it all as an ordinary human being"? How does a scientist differ from "an ordinary human being"? Find examples in which Lovell speaks as "an ordinary human being."
3. Can you see any particular justification for the organization of the lecture which Lovell announces in paragraph 3? Does he actually follow this or-ganization?
4. Why does Lovell think it necessary after one stage of the discussion to appeal to cosmological theory? Does the shift weaken the value of what follows?
5. "For the past thirty years cosmologists have sought for arguments based on the observed characteristics of the universe which would identify the actual universe with one of the theoretical models" (paragraph 10). Com-ment on the assumptions underlying this statement. Comment on the im-plications.
6. Why does Lovell say that the theories of both Lemaître and Gamow (or Gamov), after a certain point, are "outside the limits of scientific knowl-edge and indeed of scientific investigation"? What assumption is Lovell making about the limitations of science? Do you accept this assumption?

7. What weaknesses does Lovell find in both the evolutionary and the steady-state theories? What further evidence does he require? Why?
8. How does Lovell define the term *materialist?* Why does he think a materialist might find the steady-state theory attractive?
9. What point does Lovell make in his two concluding paragraphs? Why does he emphasize that it is a personal view?

THE EVOLUTIONARY UNIVERSE*

George Gamow

[1] . . . In the year 1922 a major turning point came in the cosmogical problem. A Russian mathematician, Alexander A. Friedman from whom the author of this chapter learned his relativity), discovered an error in Einstein's proof for a static universe. In carrying out is proof Einstein had divided both sides of an equation by a quantity vhich, Friedman found, could become zero under certain circumstances. Since division by zero is not permitted in algebraic computaions, the possibility of a nonstatic universe could not be excluded under he circumstances in question. Friedman showed that two nonstatic nodels were possible. One pictured the universe as expanding with ime; the other, contracting.

[2] Einstein quickly recognized the importance of this discovery. In he last edition of his book *The Meaning of Relativity* he wrote: "The nathematician Friedman found a way out of this dilemma. He showed hat it is possible, according to the field equations, to have a finite denity in the whole (three-dimensional) space, without enlarging these eld equations ad hoc." Einstein remarked to me many years ago that ne cosmic repulsion idea was the biggest blunder he had made in his ntire life.

[3] Almost at the very moment that Friedman was discovering the ossibility of an expanding universe by mathematical reasoning, Edwin . Hubble at the Mount Wilson Observatory on the other side of the vorld found the first evidence of actual physical expansion through his elescope. He made a compilation of the distances of a number of far alaxies, whose light was shifted toward the red end of the spectrum, nd it was soon found that the extent of the shift was in direct proporon to a galaxy's distance from us, as estimated by its faintness. Hubble nd others interpreted the red shift as the Doppler effect—the well-

* From *The Universe—A Scientific American Book.* Copyright © 1956, 1957 by cientific American, Inc. Published by Simon & Schuster. Reprinted by permission.

known phenomenon of lengthening of wave lengths from any radiating source that is moving rapidly away (a train whistle, a source of light or whatever). To date there has been no other reasonable explanation of the galaxies' red shift. If the explanation is correct, it means that the galaxies are all moving away from one another with increasing velocity as they move farther apart.

[4] Thus Friedman and Hubble laid the foundation for the theory of the expanding universe. The theory was soon developed further by a Belgian theoretical astronomer, Georges Lemaître. He proposed that our universe started from a highly compressed and extremely hot state which he called the "primeval atom." (Modern physicists would prefer the term "primeval nucleus.") As this matter expanded, it gradually thinned out, cooled down and reaggregated in stars and galaxies, giving rise to the highly complex structure of the universe as we know it today.

[5] Until a few years ago the theory of the expanding universe lay under the cloud of a very serious contradiction. The measurements of the speed of flight of the galaxies and their distances from us indicated that the expansion had started about 1.8 billion years ago. On the other hand, measurements of the age of ancient rocks in the earth by the clock of radioactivity (i.e., the decay of uranium to lead) showed that some of the rocks were at least three billion years old; more recent estimates based on other radioactive elements raise the age of the earth's crust to almost five billion years. Clearly a universe 1.8 billion years old could not contain five-billion-year-old rocks! Happily the contradiction has now been disposed of by Walter Baade's recent discovery that the distance yardstick (based on the periods of variable stars) was faulty and that the distances between galaxies are more than twice as great as they were thought to be. This change in distances raises the age of the universe to five billion years or more.

[6] Friedman's solution of Einstein's cosmological equation, as mentioned, permits two kinds of universe. We can call one the "pulsating" universe. This model says that when the universe has reached a certain maximum permissible expansion it will begin to contract; that it will shrink until its matter has been compressed to a certain maximum density, possibly that of atomic nuclear material, which is a hundred million million times denser than water; that it will then begin to expand again—and so on through the cycle ad infinitum. The other model is a "hyperbolic" one: it suggests that from an infinitely thin state a eternity ago the universe contracted until it reached the maximum density, from which it rebounded to an unlimited expansion which will go on indefinitely in the future.

[7] The question whether our universe is actually "pulsating" or
hyperbolic" should be decidable from the present rate of its expansion.
he situation is analogous to the case of a rocket shot from the surface
f the earth. If the velocity of the rocket is less than seven miles per
econd—the "escape velocity"—the rocket will climb only to a certain
eight and then fall back to the earth. (If it were completely elastic, it
ould bounce up again, etc., etc.) On the other hand, a rocket shot
ith a velocity of more than seven miles per second will escape from
he earth's gravitational field and disappear in space. The case of the
eceding system of galaxies is very similar to that of an escape rocket,
xcept that instead of just two interacting bodies (the rocket and the
arth) we have an unlimited number of them escaping from one an-
ther. We find that the galaxies are fleeing from one another at seven
mes the velocity necessary for mutual escape.

[8] Thus we may conclude that our universe corresponds to the
hyperbolic" model, so that its present expansion will never stop. We
ust make one reservation. The estimate of the necessary escape veloc-
y is based on the assumption that practically all the mass of the uni-
erse is concentrated in galaxies. If intergalactic space contained matter
hose total mass was more than seven times that in the galaxies, we
ould have to reverse our conclusion and decide that the universe is
ulsating. There has been no indication so far, however, that any matter
xists in intergalactic space, and it could have escaped detection only if
were in the form of pure hydrogen gas, without other gases or dust.

[9] Is the universe finite or infinite? This resolves itself into the
uestion: Is the curvature of space positive or negative—closed like that
f a sphere, or open like that of a saddle? We can look for the answer by
udying the geometrical properties of its three-dimensional space, just
we examined the properties of figures on two-dimensional surfaces.
he most convenient property to investigate astronomically is the rela-
on between the volume of a sphere and its radius.

[10] We saw that, in the two-dimensional case, the area of a circle
creases with increasing radius at a faster rate on a negatively curved
urface than on a Euclidean or flat surface; and that on a positively
urved surface the relative rate of increase is slower. Similarly the in-
ease of volume is faster in negatively curved space, slower in posi-
vely curved space. In Euclidean space the volume of a sphere would
crease in proportion to the cube, or third power of the increase in
dius. In negatively curved space the volume would increase faster
an this; in positively curved space, slower. Thus if we look into space
d find that the volume of successively larger spheres, as measured by

a count of the galaxies within them, increases faster than the cube of
the distance to the limit of the sphere (the radius), we can conclude
that the space of our universe has negative curvature, and therefore
open and infinite. By the same token, if the number of galaxies increases
at a rate slower than the cube of the distance, we live in a universe of
positive curvature—closed and finite.

[11] Following this idea, Hubble undertook to study the increase in
number of galaxies with distance. He estimated the distances of the
remote galaxies by their relative faintness: galaxies vary considerably in
intrinsic brightness, but over a very large number of galaxies these
variations are expected to average out. Hubble's calculations produced
the conclusion that the universe is a closed system—a small universe
only a few billion light-years in radius!

[12] We know now that the scale he was using was wrong: with the
new yardstick the universe would be more than twice as large as he
calculated. But there is a more fundamental doubt about his result. The
whole method is based on the assumption that the intrinsic brightness
of a galaxy remains constant. What if it changes with time? We are
seeing the light of the distant galaxies as it was emitted at widely different times in the past—500 million, a billion, two billion years ago.
the stars in the galaxies are burning out, the galaxies must dim as they
grow older. A galaxy two billion light-years away cannot be put on the
same distance scale with a galaxy 500 million light-years away unless we
take into account the fact that we are seeing the nearer galaxy at an
older, and less bright, age. The remote galaxy is farther away than a
mere comparison of the luminosity of the two would suggest.

[13] When a correction is made for the assumed decline in brightness with age, the more distant galaxies are spread out to farther distances than Hubble assumed. In fact, the calculations of volume are
changed so drastically that we may have to reverse the conclusion about
the curvature of space. We are not sure, because we do not yet know
enough about the evolution of galaxies. But if we find that galaxies
wane in intrinsic brightness by only a few per cent in a billion years,
we shall have to conclude that space is curved negatively and the universe is infinite.

[14] Actually there is another line of reasoning which supports the
side of infinity. Our universe seems to be hyperbolic and ever-expanding. Mathematical solutions of fundamental cosmological equations
indicate that such a universe is open and infinite.

[15] We have reviewed the questions that dominated the thinking
of cosmologists during the first half of this century: the conception of a
four-dimensional space-time continuum, of curved space, of an expand-

ng universe and of a cosmos which is either finite or infinite. Now we must consider the major present issue in cosmology: Is the universe in truth evolving, or is it in a steady state of equilibrium which has always existed and will go on through eternity? Most cosmologists take the evolutionary view. But in 1951 a group at the University of Cambridge, whose chief spokesman has been Fred Hoyle, advanced the steady-state idea. Essentially their theory is that the universe is infinite in space and time, that it has neither a beginning nor an end, that the density of its matter remains constant, that new matter is steadily being created in space at a rate which exactly compensates for the thinning of matter by expansion, that as a consequence new galaxies are continually being born, and that the galaxies of the universe therefore range in age from mere youngsters to veterans of 5, 10, 20 and more billions of years. In my opinion this theory must be considered very questionable because of the simple fact (apart from other reasons) that the galaxies in our neighborhood all seem to be of the same age as our own Milky Way. But the issue is many-sided and fundamental, and can be settled only by extended study of the universe as far as we can observe it. Hoyle presents the steady-state view in the following chapter.[1] Here I shall summarize the evolutionary theory.

[16] We assume that the universe started from a very dense state of matter. In the early stages of its expansion, radiant energy was dominant over the mass of matter. We can measure energy and matter on a common scale by means of the well-known equation $E = mc^2$, which says that the energy equivalent of matter is the mass of the matter multiplied by the square of the velocity of light. Energy can be translated into mass, conversely, by dividing the energy quantity by c^2. Thus we can speak of the "mass density" of energy. Now, at the beginning the mass density of the radiant energy was incomparably greater than the density of the matter in the universe. But in an expanding system the density of radiant energy decreases faster than does the density of matter. The former thins out as the fourth power of the distance of expansion: as the radius of the system doubles, the density of radiant energy drops to one sixteenth. The density of matter declines as the third power; a doubling of the radius means an eightfold increase in volume, or eightfold decrease in density.

[17] Assuming that the universe at the beginning was under absolute rule by radiant energy, we can calculate that the temperature of the universe was 250 million degrees when it was one hour old, dropped to 6,000 degrees (the present temperature of our sun's surface) when it was 200,000 years old and had fallen to about 100 degrees below the

[1] See the following article by Fred Hoyle [Eds.].

freezing point of water when the universe reached its 250-millionth birthday.

[18] This particular birthday was a crucial one in the life of the universe. It was the point at which the density of ordinary matter became greater than the mass density of radiant energy, because of the more rapid fall of the latter. The switch from the reign of radiation to the reign of matter profoundly changed matter's behavior. During the eons of its subjugation to the will of radiant energy (i.e., light), it must have been spread uniformly through space in the form of thin gas. But as soon as matter became gravitationally more important than the radiant energy, it began to acquire a more interesting character. James Jeans, in his classic studies of the physics of such a situation, proved half a century ago that a gravitating gas filling a very large volume is bound to break up into individual "gas balls," the size of which is determined by the density and the temperature of the gas. Thus in the year 250,000,000 A.B.E. (after the beginning of expansion), when matter was freed from the dictatorship of radiant energy, the gas broke up into giant gas clouds, slowly drifting apart as the universe continued to expand. Applying Jeans's mathematical formula for the process to the gas filling the universe at that time, I have found that these primordial balls of gas would have had just about the mass that the galaxies of stars possess today. They were then only "proto-galaxies"—cold, dark and chaotic. But their gas soon condensed into stars and formed the galaxies as we see them now.

[19] A central question in this picture of the evolutionary universe is the problem of accounting for the formation of the varied kinds of matter composing it—i.e., the chemical elements. . . . My belief is that at the start matter was composed simply of protons, neutrons and electrons. After five minutes the universe must have cooled enough to permit the aggregation of protons and neutrons into larger units, from deuterons (one neutron and one proton) up to the heaviest elements. This process must have ended after about 30 minutes, for by that time the temperature of the expanding universe must have dropped below the threshold of thermonuclear reactions among light elements, and the neutrons must have been used up in element-building or been converted to protons.

[20] To many a reader the statement that the present chemical constitution of our universe was decided in half an hour five billion years ago will sound nonsensical. But consider a spot of ground on the atomic proving ground in Nevada where an atomic bomb was exploded in 1953. Within one microsecond the nuclear reactions generated by the bomb produced a variety of fission products. In 1956, 100 million million

microseconds later, the site was still "hot" with the surviving fission products. The ratio of one microsecond to three years is the same as the ratio of half an hour to five billion years! If we can accept a time ratio of this order in the one case, why not in the other?

[21] The late Enrico Fermi and Anthony L. Turkevich at the Institute for Nuclear Studies of the University of Chicago undertook a detailed study of thermonuclear reactions such as must have taken place during the first half hour of the universe's expansion. They concluded that the reactions would have produced about equal amounts of hydrogen and helium, making up 99 per cent of the total material, and about 1 per cent of deuterium. We know that hydrogen and helium do in fact make up about 99 per cent of the matter of the universe. This leaves us with the problem of building the heavier elements. I hold to the opinion that some of them were built by capture of neutrons. However, since the absence of any stable nucleus of atomic weight 5 makes it improbable that the heavier elements could have been produced in the first half hour in the abundances now observed, I would agree that the lion's share of the heavy elements may well have been formed later in the hot interiors of stars.

[22] All the theories—of the origin, age, extent, composition and nature of the universe—are becoming more and more subject to test by new instruments and new techniques. . . . Allan Sandage reports a tentative finding that the expansion of the universe may be slowing down. If this is confirmed, it may indicate that we live in a pulsating universe. But we must not forget that the estimate of distances of the galaxies is still founded on the debatable assumption that the brightness of galaxies does not change with time. If galaxies actually diminish in brightness as they age, the calculations cannot be depended upon. Thus the question whether evolution is or is not taking place in the galaxies is of crucial importance at the present stage of our outlook on the universe.

Questions

1. What does Gamow accomplish by describing the work of Friedman and Hubble? Is his purpose to furnish information? To advance a line of argument? To do something else?
2. Does Gamow accept the explanation of the red shift as the Doppler effect (paragraph 3)? Why does he use the wording, "If the explanation is correct"?
3. Examine Gamow's analysis of the "pulsating" and "hyperbolic" models of the universe (paragraphs 6 and 7). What is the function of the rocket analogy?
4. Why does Gamow conclude that the universe is "open and infinite" rather

than "closed and finite"? Does he provide evidence to support this conclusion?
5. Gamow describes the steady-state theory in paragraph 15. Comment on
his strategy in the organization and development of the paragraph. What
effect is produced?
6. Who is "we" in paragraph 16?
7. What assumptions does Gamow make in paragraphs 16–17? Are they
capable of being verified?
8. In accounting for the formation of varied chemical elements, Gamow uses
such phrases as "my belief," "in my opinion," "I hold to the opinion," and
so forth. What different kinds of data does he supply to substantiate these
opinions?
9. What attitude toward the evolutionary theory does Gamow reveal in his
concluding paragraph?

THE STEADY-STATE UNIVERSE*

Fred Hoyle

[1] The theory of a steady-state universe leads to many startling conclusions: that the universe had no beginning and will have no end, that
space as well as time is infinite, that matter is continually being created
throughout space—to mention a few. Human nature being what it is,
there has been a tendency to become involved in emotional attitudes
toward these concepts, instead of confining the discussion to purely
scientific criteria. If the writer, along with critics, has transgressed in
this respect, he promises to give some redress in this article.

[2] The steady-state theory holds that the large-scale features of the
universe do not change with time. Only the galaxies and clusters of
galaxies change; if we "smear out" their material uniformly through
space and consider the general properties of the cosmos, it is unchanging. The expansion of the universe is a basic feature of the theory. The
question arises: If the galaxies are moving apart from each other, why
does space not become more and more empty? The answer of the theory
is that new galaxies and clusters of galaxies are constantly being
formed, their rate of formation just compensating for the separating
effect of the expansion. So a stable situation is preserved.

[3] Before we go on to consider the reasoning, predictions and tests
of steady-state cosmology, the writer should point out that his own
approach to the theory, and also that of William H. McCrea of the

University of London, differs rather markedly from the approach of Hermann Bondi and Thomas Gold. The writer's approach is a mathematical one developed in the framework of the theory of relativity. Bondi's and Gold's is founded on an intuitive but powerful physical principle. To understand their outlook we must look into the nature of this postulate, which is called the "cosmological principle."

[4] Cosmology differs from all other branches of physical science in a very important respect. Whereas other physical scientists deal always with isolated systems, whose "boundary conditions" can be defined, a cosmologist has to deal with a nonisolated system. To cope with this unhappy situation he is forced to adopt a "symmetry" postulate, which says that, local fluctuations apart, the universe will look the same from wherever one views it. That is to say, it assumes that observers attached to different galaxies anywhere in the cosmos would all obtain exactly the same large-scale picture of the universe. But if the universe changes with time, this implies that the different observers compare their pictures at the same time, which of course requires us to have a definition of what we mean by "at the same time." In order to make a definition of simultaneity possible, the mathematician Hermann Weyl advanced the additional postulate that the motions of the galaxies follow a regular type of pattern, whose exact nature need not be described here.

[5] Instead of this additional postulate Bondi and Gold proposed a single all-embracing "cosmological principle": namely, that the large-scale features of the universe are the same not only from every point of view in space but also from every point of view in time. This symmetry hypothesis leads immediately to the conclusion that the universe is in a steady state. It is then immaterial whether the observers compare their pictures "at the same time" or not.

[6] The outlook of Bondi and Gold has a compelling simplicity. Moreover, symmetry postulate have repeatedly demonstrated their power in theories of physics during the present century (e.g., the positive and negative particles of nuclear physics). But to my own taste it is preferable to start with a mathematical definition of the continuous creation of matter within the framework of the relativity theory and then to derive the steady-state solution as a consequence of field equations.

[7] At first sight the creation of matter may seem a queer concept to be invading scientific thought. But . . . the origin of matter must enter all cosmologies. Nowadays we are coming more and more to realize that hydrogen is the original material—the material out of which

the other elements have been produced by nuclear reactions inside star
This transmutation of hydrogen is going on all the time.

[8] Why is there any hydrogen remaining in the universe? Why wa
it not all used up in the production of heavy elements eons ago? If w
assumed that the hydrogen of the universe has existed for an infinit
time, there would be two conceivable answers. We might suppose tha
the hydrogen has not had sufficient time to become transmuted int
other elements because the stars were born only recently, that is, withi
the last five billion years or so. But it would follow from this that th
hydrogen remained stable for eons of time and then suddenly fiv
billion years ago began to condense into stars and galaxies. This seem
less than plausible. The other possibility, assuming the hydrogen i
infinitely old, is that we still find it on hand because the higher element
formed from it break down to hydrogen again. The chief objection t
this idea is the difficulty of explaining how the energy necessary fo
the breakdown would be supplied. Decomposition of the heavier ele
ments into hydrogen requires absorption of energy—the reverse of th
release of energy that occurs when hydrogen nuclei combine. To pro
vide an amount of energy adequate to account for a sufficiently large
scale reconversion of the heavier elements, nothing less than an im
plosion of the whole universe (as opposed to an explosion) apparentl
would suffice.

[9] We are thus led to the conclusion that the hydrogen we observ
is not infinitely old: it has originated within some finite time and ha
not yet been converted to heavier elements. Both the evolutionary an
the steady-state theories of the universe agree on this point. But ther
the similarity between them ends. The evolutionary theory argues tha
all the hydrogen was created in an explosive beginning some five an
a half billion years ago (see the preceding chapter).[1] The steady-stat
hypothesis holds that hydrogen has been created at a steady rat
throughout infinite time and is still being created at the same rate today

[10] If hydrogen has been present for an infinity of time, and ha
steadily been converted to heavier elements in stars, why don't we se
galaxies made of very old matter? Why do we see only comparativel
young galaxies, composed almost entirely of hydrogen? The answer o
the steady-state theory is that the expansion of the universe spread
galaxies apart as they age, and the old material is rapidly diluted, i
terms of its mean density in the universe as a whole. Meanwhile nev
hydrogen, and new galaxies, are just as rapidly being created. Accord
ing to the mathematics of the theory, the expansion of the universe and
the creation of new material go on at rates such that the mean densit

[1] See the preceding article by George Gamow [Eds.].

of 200-billion-year-old material, for example, is less than that of recently formed material by a factor of 10^{43} (1 followed by 43 zeros). It must be emphasized that this figure is a mean averaged over the universe as a whole: it does not apply to individual galaxies or clusters of galaxies. Expansion takes place in space *between* galactic systems: the individual galaxies and clusters do not themselves expand. The very old material of the universe is concentrated in very old galaxies. By virtue of the universal expansion these are now extremely far apart. Possibly there are some moderately old galaxies within the range of our telescopes. If a method could be worked out to identify distant galaxies composed of comparatively old matter, it would provide a test of the steady-state theory.

[11] Approaching the steady-state theory from the mathematical point of view, our first step evidently must be to construct a mathematical law representing the origin of matter. We wish to formulate this law within the logical framework of the theory of relativity: like the evolutionary theory, steady-state cosmology makes use of the powerful equations devised by Albert Einstein to describe the four-dimensional space-time continuum. We can indicate briefly here some of the main principles involved, though the equations themselves are too complex to examine in detail.

[12] The theory of relativity begins by generalizing the ordinary laws of motion in three-dimensional space to describe the properties and the non-Euclidean geometry of the four-dimensional space-time field. These laws can be set down in four equations: one equation for the law of conservation of energy and three for the conservation of momentum. Our problem is to frame the law of origin of matter in such a way that it can be introduced into these four conservation equations.

[13] As a first step we must define energy and momentum, for the theory of relativity does not itself define them. It is most reasonable to choose definitions which will yield equations as closely analogous as possible to the ordinary equations describing the laws of conservation in our familiar (Euclidean) world. The evolutionary cosmologists seem at first sight to have done this, but it turns out that their conservation equations do not contain any generalized analogue of certain terms, known as "fluid stresses," which play a part in the ordinary equations. Now when we define energy and momentum in a way that yields such a generalization, the outcome of the equations is a steady-state universe, not an evolutionary one.

[14] The equations, so generalized, imply a "feedback" relation between the expansion of the universe and the origin of matter. If the expansion rises above a certain critical rate (related to the rate of origin

of matter), the feedback slows the expansion. If the universe's expansion slows down to less than the critical rate, the feedback speeds it up. Thus the interaction between the expansion and the creation of matter maintains a steady state in which the mean density of matter in the universe remains constant.

[15] To many people the notion of continuous creation of new matter in space seems an outright violation of the conservation of energy. But this indicates a confusion between a closed system and the very different situation in an open system. The theory of relativity says that in an open, infinitely expanding universe, local concentrations of energy are related to the energy of expansion of the whole universe. The energy of expansion can take a form leading to a continuous creation of local matter.

[16] The same question that is asked about the creation of matter might be asked about the red shift of light from distant galaxies. The reddened light is weaker than when it started on its journey. Where does the lost radiant energy go to? It goes into a slight increase in the rate of expansion of the whole universe. The point is that for a total reckoning of the conservation of energy and matter in the cosmos we must take the expansion of the universe into account. We cannot balance the energy books strictly and completely within the confines of any locality, because no locality in the universe is entirely closed.

[17] Before we drop this issue it is perhaps worth noting that we can consider the conservation question in purely operational rather than theoretical terms and come out with the same result. Suppose observers on the earth measured the energy content of a given portion of the universe, say that within the reach of the 200-inch telescope, and suppose this was done on several occasions at widely separated times. If the conservation of energy is to hold, the measured energy content must remain unchanged from one occasion to another. This would be true in a steady-state universe, but not in an evolving one. Furthermore, in a steady-state universe conservation in this operational sense holds good for an observer in any galaxy.

[18] The two features of the steady-state theory that seem to cause the greatest general surprise are (1) that the theory possesses a clear-cut mathematical basis, and (2) that the theory is highly susceptible to test by observation. How can it be tested? Obviously we cannot test it in the laboratory—unless we were to find some way to speed up the creation of matter artificially—for the rate of creation, according to the theory, is negligible in terrestrial terms: in the space of the average physics laboratory one new hydrogen atom would materialize in about 1,000 years. But on the cosmological scale there are many possible tests.

[19] First, at the farthest range of our telescopes we are seeing galactic systems as they were a billion or more years ago. Hence information can be obtained about how things used to be in the past, and this information can be compared with the cosmic scene close by us in space and time. Since the steady-state theory requires that there be no difference in large-scale properties between the past and the present, the theory is clearly exposed to check by this comparison. Large-scale properties can be estimated from many different clues: the density of the populations of galaxies, the magnitude and color of their light, the radio emissions signaling collisions and other significant events, the relation between the red shift and distance of galaxies, and so forth.

[20] Second, there are tests which can be made without looking so far away from home. We can think of the formation of new galaxies as equivalent to birth in the biological sense, and of their separation by expansion as equivalent to death. In terms of this analogy a new generation of galaxies is born, not every 30 years as in the case of human beings, but every few billion years. Now, just as an animal population becomes extinct if it fails to reproduce its numbers from generation to generation, so large-scale properties of the systems of galaxies fail to survive unless they reproduce themselves in the same sense. If the universe is infinitely old, as the steady-state theory says, we should expect to see surviving only properties which have stabilized themselves so that they are reproduced at precisely the same level from generation to generation. In other words, according to the steady-state theory the galaxies are not a product of random fluctuations and condensations, as in the evolutionary theory, but represent a very strictly controlled system obeying a kind of cosmic ecology, with the origin of matter playing a critical role. This crucial difference between the two theories can form the basis of stringent tests. The tests can be applied to such properties as the density of galaxies in space and the distribution of sizes in masses of galaxies. That is, we can check whether the distribution follows a regular frequency curve or shows no regular pattern.

[21] During the past five years it has twice been claimed that observations disproved the steady-state theory, but it now appears that in both cases the observations are open to serious doubt. The United States astronomers Joel Stebbins and A. E. Whitford thought that certain distant galaxies showed more reddening than could be attributed to the usual red shift, and this was construed to support the evolutionary theory. But Whitford later found that certain data they had made use of were incorrect. Recently Martin Ryle in England reported a count of radio sources which indicated that the density of galaxies in

space increases with distance from us—again an apparent support for the evolutionary hypothesis. However, Ryle's findings have been questioned by the radio astronomer B. Y. Mills in Australia.

[22] In my view the most serious potential contradiction of the steady-state theory lies in the recent red-shift studies by the astronomers in California, which are reported . . . by Allan Sandage. . . . As Sandage points out, however, the findings so far are highly uncertain.

[23] George Gamow has offered against the steady-state theory the objection that elliptical galaxies (which are thought to consist only of old stars) apparently do not show the age variations that the theory predicts. In defense of the theory it can be said that the measurements cited (studies of the color of the galaxies, in two colors) are not a very sensitive index of the galaxies' ages. In the color test a galaxy six billion years old should look much like one three billion years old. More sensitive measurements are required.

[24] The steady-state theory gains support, on the other hand, from recent studies indicating that the elements beyond hydrogen are formed in stars. These studies . . . make it appear more likely that the elements are constantly being "cooked" in the stars, as the steady-state cosmology suggests, than that they were created in a primeval explosion, as Gamow has urged.

[25] Radio astronomy offers the exciting possibility of something close to a direct test of the creation of matter in space. The total amount of matter in the galaxies we can observe is estimated to come to about 10^{-30} of a gram per cubic centimeter if it were spread evenly all through space. The steady-state theory predicts that the average density of matter should be 10 or more times greater than this. The difference, according to the theory, is accounted for by hydrogen spread through intergalactic space. Up to now it has not been possible to detect intergalactic matter. But in the next few years new radio telescopes, tuned to the one-note "song of hydrogen," may be able to test whether such quantities of hydrogen do or do not exist in space.

Questions

1. Examine the second sentence in paragraph 1. Why do you suppose "there has been a tendency to become involved in emotional attitudes toward these concepts"? What does Hoyle mean by "purely scientific criteria"?
2. Why does Hoyle reject the "cosmological principle" of Bondi and Gold? What is the meaning of "taste" in his statement, "to my own taste it is preferable to start with a mathematical definition" (paragraph 6)?
3. "At first sight the creation of matter may seem a queer concept to be invading scientific thought" (paragraph 7). Why does Hoyle make this

statement? Does the subsequent line of reasoning convince you of the relevance of the statement? What possible negative arguments does he omit?

4. "We are thus led to the conclusion that the hydrogen we observe is not infinitely old" (paragraph 9). How does Hoyle come to this conclusion? Exactly what methods of argument does he use? Is the argument valid?

5. Why would identifying distant galaxies of "comparatively old matter" provide a test of the steady-state theory?

6. Examine the distinction between "operational" and "theoretical" terms discussed in paragraph 17. Why is the distinction important? What is involved in each of these approaches? Can you say that one is more valid than the other? (You may find it useful to consult the essay "What Do You Mean?" by Anatol Rapoport, pp. 648–655.)

7. Why does Hoyle stress the fact that the steady-state theory is "highly susceptible to test by observation"? What is he implying about the evolutionary theory?

8. How does Hoyle dispose of the claims that tended to disprove the steady-state theory?

9. Why is the test for hydrogen in intergalactic space crucial for Hoyle's theory? Why hasn't this test been carried out?

PECULIAR GALAXIES[*]

Margaret and Geoffrey Burbidge

[1] The observable matter in the universe appears to aggregate in units that can be arranged in a hierarchy of sizes. Stars, taken as the fundamental unit, typically have diameters of 10^{11} centimeters (a million kilometers). One next observes clusters of stars with diameters of 10^{20} centimeters (100 light-years). Stellar clusters are a prominent feature of spiral galaxies such as our own, which have dimensions of the order of 10^{23} centimeters (100,000 light-years). The galaxies themselves are gathered in clusters that may contain a few galaxies or many thousands and measure up to 10^{25} centimeters (10 million light-years) across. Whether there are clusters of clusters remains uncertain at this time. The ultimate hierarchical unit is of course the universe, the radius of which is 10^{28} centimeters, or 10 billion light-years.

[2] To explain how these aggregations came to be is the task of the astronomer and cosmologist. Stars are formed out of interstellar gas and dust. Although there is much evidence that this is still going on in regions of our own galaxy such as the Great Nebula in Orion, theories

[*] From *Scientific American*, February, 1961. Copyright © 1961 by Scientific American, Inc. Reprinted by permission.

about how it takes place are still rudimentary. Once a star has become hot enough for thermonuclear reactions to occur within it, its evolution can be predicted quite well, at least up to the point where the star becomes a red giant.

[3] Presumably star clusters form in the condensation of large interstellar clouds. It is postulated that by an analogous process the galaxies and clusters of galaxies condensed—and may now be condensing—from matter diffusely spread throughout the universe. But when it comes to these larger units in the cosmic hierarchy, the data are uncertain and cosmologists are divided.

[4] Of all the possible cosmologies only two broad types have been worked out in any detail, and at present theories about the formation of galaxies must stay within these two frameworks. For one category of cosmological models the universe can be thought of as originating in a gigantic explosion at the instant of creation. These are called evolutionary cosmologies, because they assume a universe that has changed radically since the time of its origin. In such a universe all the galaxies would have been formed at an early stage. Against this view is opposed the steady-state cosmology, which holds that the universe has always had a constant density—its expansion is balanced by the genesis of new matter and the new matter continues to condense into new clusters of new galaxies.

[5] To the meager body of available astronomical evidence there has recently been added a set of observations that supports the idea that galaxies and clusters of galaxies are now being formed. The Soviet astronomer B. A. Vorontsov-Velyaminov, in a systematic search of the sky-survey plates made with the 48-inch Schmidt telescope on Palomar Mountain, has assembled a catalogue of "irregular," multiple and otherwise peculiar galaxies visible from the Northern Hemisphere. His catalogue lists several hundred of them.

[6] For the past two years the authors have been using the 82-inch reflecting telescope of the W. J. McDonald Observatory at the University of Texas to study some of these galaxies. Our investigations suggest that many peculiar galaxies are galaxies in the earliest stage of evolution and so perhaps still in the process of formation. Analysis of clusters in which such galaxies occur indicates that the clusters too are much younger than the universe. These observations are few and preliminary and even further studies giving the same result would not of themselves provide a basis for choice between an evolutionary and a steady-state cosmological model. The observations, in fact, raise difficulties for both schools.

[7] In the first place, it is difficult to explain how galaxies can condense out of intergalactic matter if it is thinly diffused throughout space. (The matter may, for example, be condensed into cold lumps that are invisible from the earth.) Thinly diffused intergalactic material may be very hot or very cold. If it is cold, it will consist of un-ionized atoms and molecules and perhaps some dust, in which case it might absorb or scatter light and show some observable effects. If it is hot, then it must be ionized; that is, the atoms must be dissociated into their component nuclei and electrons. In this case it would have a negligible absorbing or scattering effect upon light from distant parts of space. In either case it is so thin that it has so far escaped observation. Apart from the bridges of luminous material that join a few pairs of galaxies, there is only indirect evidence for the existence of intergalactic matter. This is based upon computation of the mean density of matter in the universe, and the computation in turn depends upon the distance scale of the universe and the cosmological model used. Present ideas suggest that this density is of the order of one atom per 100,000 cubic centimeters of space. For the universe as a whole, however, this represents a mass of material so great that no more than 1 per cent of it has ever formed into galaxies.

[8] Such a low density in the intergalactic gas raises no difficulties for evolutionary cosmology. In the first epochs after the explosive moment of creation the average density of the universe would have been far higher than it is today. Under these conditions density presents no problem in explaining the origin of galaxies. But a corollary of such an explanation must be that the galaxies are nearly as old as the universe and that the clusters have sufficient inherent stability to have endured for a corresponding length of time. Until recently neither assumption has been questioned. Actually the evolutionary cosmology has had to withstand a quite different test. Recent observations and calculations have suggested that stars in our own galaxy and some of the chemical elements are older than the age of the universe as estimated from the expansion rate. For example, calculations of stellar evolution made by Fred Hoyle of the University of Cambridge indicate that the rich star cluster Messier 67 has an age of about nine billion years, and a class of old stars, typified by Delta Eridani (a star quite near the sun), was found to have an age of 15 billion years. Similarly, calculations by Hoyle, William A. Fowler of the California Institute of Technology and ourselves originally found an age of eight billion years for the elements, based upon the observed abundances and decay rates of the isotopes thorium 232, uranium 235 and uranium 238. A revised calculation has

increased this age to about 15 billion years with an uncertainty of several billion years.

[9] How does this compare with the expansion age of the universe? The expansion age can be calculated from the present-day rate of expansion and the correct cosmological model. Most models will give an age that is less than $1/H$, where H is the Hubble constant, or expansion rate. Allan R. Sandage of the Mount Wilson and Palomar Observatories has currently estimated $1/H$ to be about 13 billion years, giving an expansion age of eight billion years with the cosmological model that he uses. Though this may be modified by future work, at present all indications point to an age of the order of 10 billion years. Thus current arguments suggest that all of these ages are comparable, although if taken at their face value the ages of some objects in our galaxy may be significantly greater than the expansion age. However, the expansion age is only a very approximate value for the age of the universe, and it depends on the cosmological model.

[10] The steady-state cosmology, propounded by Hoyle, Hermann Bondi of King's College in London and Thomas Gold (now at Cornell University), postulates no upper limit for the age of the universe. But the average age of an observable sample should be a fraction of the time scale given by the expansion rate of the observable universe. In a steady-state universe, in other words, it is expected and indeed demanded that the hierarchical units should show a considerable disparity of ages, with young galaxies and young clusters of galaxies to be seen still in formation along with galaxies and clusters in late phases of evolution.

[11] If time-scale discrepancies eventually discredit evolutionary models, and other arguments rule out the steady-state model, we may have to abandon the so-called cosmological principle. This principle states that, except for local irregularities, the universe looks the same from every point in it. The consequences of abandoning the principle have not as yet been seriously considered. So it seems that theoretical considerations alone cannot settle the question of whether the condensation of galaxies took place in the distant past or whether formation is going on at an appreciable rate today. More to the point is the evidence offered by direct observation.

[12] Of the billion or more galaxies detectable by modern instruments, several thousand are close enough to permit detailed inspection. Some of them are spiral in structure—great pin wheels consisting of a central core of stars with more or less wide-flung, spiral arms described by lanes of bright stars and bearing much dust and gas. In some gal-

axies, known as barred spirals, the arms trail out from a bar across the center. Many of the galaxies are "elliptical," consisting of a single dense globular or ellipsoidal mass of smoothly distributed stars, with hardly any gas and no dust between them. A still smaller class of galaxies is labeled SO. They are flat, like spirals, and in outline look somewhat like spirals that have lost their arms. They contain almost no gas and little or no dust. Finally, there are the irregular galaxies, which contain conspicuously large amounts of dust and gas and exhibit no particular structure.

[13] Now if one were looking for a galaxy that is young in the evolutionary sense, one would expect to find in it a number of huge stars in process of formation. The larger protostars contract far more rapidly than do smaller ones. Stars that have the mass of the sun take 50 million years to contract; stars 50 times more massive need only a few hundred thousand years. Therefore if a number of protostars of a wide range of masses all begin to contract at the same time, those of greater mass will become stars and will go through their whole evolutionary sequence, turning into dying white-dwarf stars long before stars of solar mass have even begun to radiate. On this basis a young galaxy would be an irregular system full of highly luminous, hot, massive stars embedded in a large amount of dust and gas.

[14] Several of the irregular galaxies appear to be just such objects. One of the most remarkable is known as NGC 2444–45. The designation NGC means that it was noted in the New General Catalogue of the Danish astronomer John L. E. Dreyer in 1888. Vorontsov-Velyaminov first pointed out the unusual character of this galaxy and brought it to our attention.

[15] As its label indicates, NGC 2444–45 is really two different objects. One is apparently a normal elliptical galaxy; such galaxies are thought to be old in the evolutionary sense because all their dust and gas have condensed into stars. The second object consists of a number of bright knots, which are gigantic regions of hot gas—mainly ionized hydrogen—each several thousand light-years in diameter, embedded in a more tenuous, luminous haze, which may contain stars and cooler gas.

[16] From the spectra of each of these knots we have measured the Doppler effect (the shift in the lines of the spectrum due to motion) and have calculated the velocity with which the system appears to be receding from us. Both the knots and the elliptical galaxy are receding at about 4,000 kilometers per second. Both lie about 150 million light-years away. Since both objects are the same distance from us, it can be

assumed that they form a physical group. The energy that makes the large knots glow must come from many high-luminosity stars embedded in them. These gigantic regions of ionized hydrogen can only be rather short-lived features, characteristic of the early stages of the formation of a galaxy. Thus NGC 2444–45 is an old galaxy alongside what may be a new one. It is tempting to conclude that the young system started to form with the help of the older one.

[17] We have studied two other rather similar systems. In each case a normal elliptical galaxy is seen near what appears to be an agglomeration of hot gas and luminous stars. Here we do not as yet have observations proving that the objects in the pairs are actually together in space. The irregular galaxy might be in front of or behind the other as seen from the earth.

[18] Another irregular galaxy that is hardly likely to remain stable in its present form is NGC 4676. It is one of a number of objects that are characterized by long tails or plumes, which are possibly fans of matter seen edge-on. NGC 4676 has two nuclei, one with a long tail and the other with a faint, curving plume extending in the opposite direction. Spectra show that the galaxy is receding at 6,500 kilometers a second. It lies in the outer part of the cluster of galaxies in the constellation Coma Berenices, one of the richest clusters known. The average recession velocity of the cluster is 6,900 kilometers per second. NGC 4676 therefore belongs to the cluster, which is made up mostly of old elliptical and SO galaxies.

[19] Spectral analysis of the two nuclei of NGC 4676 shows stars of high luminosity and much ionized gas. Furthermore, both nuclei are rotating rapidly. Since we cannot determine the direction of the axes of rotation we cannot calculate the total amount of rotation. However, the outer part of each nucleus is moving in the line of sight at a velocity of 200 kilometers per second with respect to the center. The tail stretches across at least two minutes of arc, which means that it is approximately 150,000 light-years long. This does not seem to be a very stable structure on the time scale associated with galaxies. It follows that the object may be evolving rapidly and may even have arisen "recently" from gas left over after the majority of the Coma Berenices galaxies were formed.

.   .   .   .

[20] Still another type of peculiar object consists of pairs of galaxies linked by streams of matter. In the past it has been supposed that pairs that are bound together by gravity have been formed by collisions between previously separate systems. However, the Soviet astronomer Victor A. Ambartsumyan has argued that double and multiple systems

are too common to have been formed in this way. He has proposed that galaxies often actually arise in pairs or groups analogous to the many stars that originate as members of multiple-star systems. For protostars this appears to be a feasible way of redistributing the colossal amount of angular momentum (energy of rotation) in the system so that the system can become stable as it contracts. Perhaps galaxies form multiple systems for the same reason. . . .

[21] . . . At present it seems likely that the spiral and the elliptical galaxies have followed their own course of evolutionary development starting from different conditions in the protogalaxies that gave rise to them. On the other hand, there are indications of an evolutionary trend from irregulars to spirals. Irregular and spiral galaxies have an important feature in common: they are on the average less massive than elliptical galaxies, though the mass ranges of all three types overlap. Some irregulars may very well evolve into spirals. This would occur because an irregular mass of gas and dust that possesses some angular momentum will revolve faster as it contracts, and in a few revolutions such a mass will tend to acquire a more orderly and symmetrical structure. Gas and dust clouds with little or no angular momentum may never go through this progression.

[22] Before much progress can be made in understanding any evolutionary sequence, several problems associated with spiral galaxies must be solved. For example, it is not known why the spiral arms persist. A few rotations should wind them up and distort them beyond recognition. Furthermore, the arms are made up of giant hot young stars and the gas that such stars illuminate. Since stars of this kind have a short lifetime, they will evolve and fade before the galaxy has made one revolution. Spiral arms must somehow be continually renewed.

[23] It is not understood either how the bar across the center of barred spirals is formed or how long it will last. Bars made up mainly of stars have presumably lasted a long time by evolutionary standards and are fairly stable; those with a large supply of gas and dust may have shorter lifetimes. There may even be a tendency for barred spirals of a certain sort to change into normal spirals.

[24] The new evidence for the presence of young galaxies in the universe fits well into the increasingly persuasive picture of galaxies as unstable and continuously evolving systems. It may apparently be concluded that the galaxies are by no means all the same age and that a significant number of them are younger than the universe. . . .

[25] A growing body of circumstantial evidence therefore indicates that galaxies and clusters of galaxies are still forming today. The conclusion agrees well with the steady-state theory of cosmology. It can be

accommodated, however, within the terms of evolutionary cosmology. The argument can be made, for example, that a protogalaxy might have formed 10 billion years ago and not have condensed into stars, remaining dark and invisible until conditions were right for the condensation of stars. A strong magnetic field in such a gigantic cloud of gas might prevent star formation for a very long period. If the stars had formed in the last 100 million years, the ancient protogalaxy would now appear as a very young galaxy.

[26] To sum up, we believe there are galaxies and clusters of galaxies that seem to be young because they evidently cannot last long in their present form, and because the natural forces acting in a rotating mass of gas always tend to produce order from disorder—symmetry from dissymmetry. That young galaxies exist implies that galaxies may be forming even today. Yet although the steady-state cosmology predicts the continuous formation of galaxies, we still cannot go further and choose one cosmological model over another.

Questions

1. Is there any significance in the inclusion of the word *observable* in the first sentence? Explain. Do you also assume this word is meant to apply to the statement that the radius of the universe is 10 billion light-years?
2. Why do the authors use the phrase "can be arranged in a hierarchy of sizes" (sentence 1) rather than "*are* arranged"? Is paragraph 1 predominantly factual or theoretical?
3. Why do the Burbidges believe that theories about the formation of galaxies must be viewed in the framework of only two cosmological models (paragraph 4)? Is this an argument that one of the two must finally be the correct one?
4. Is the statement in paragraph 5 about "the meager body of available astronomical evidence" damaging to the cosmological models? What other sort of evidence might be used? Why is evidence from observations not necessarily more conclusive?
5. In relating the findings of their two years of study with the 82-inch telescope in Texas, do the authors give you factual reports, interpretations, arguments, or a combination of these? Discuss.
6. The discussion beginning with comments on galaxy NGC 2444–45 (paragraph 14) is different in several ways from the preceding part of the article. What differences can you cite? What is the function of this discussion?
7. Does the final sentence follow logically as a conclusion to the discussion? Is it in conflict with any other statements in the article?

ASSIGNMENTS

1. Write a paper in which you compare and contrast Gamow's and Hoyle's articles.
2. Read a fuller treatment of Gamow's or Hoyle's position, for example

Gamow's book *The Creation of the Universe* (revised, 1961) or Hoyle's *The Frontiers of Astronomy* (1955). Prepare a report in which you discuss additional evidence cited by the author to support some major aspect of his theory.

3. Is further light thrown on the controversy by very recent studies? Locate current articles in journals such as *Science* or *Scientific American* and prepare a report of your findings.

4. Various developments in the controversy about cosmological theory have been reported in news magazines such as *Time* or *Newsweek*. By consulting appropriate indexes, locate and read several such articles. Prepare a report in which you discuss the treatment given to the topic in such articles.

5. In an elementary textbook in physical science or astronomy currently used in your college, read the discussion on the origins of the universe. Present a report of your findings with specific attention to (*a*) the extent to which the topic is covered, (*b*) whether or not conflicting views are represented, (*c*) the position taken by the author of the text.

6. Prepare for participation in a panel discussion on the topic "The Limitations of Science." Do not rely solely on Lovell's article, but consult several sources.

7. Write a paper in which you compare and contrast the methods of Gamow or Hoyle in this issue with those of writers on a non-scientific issue, such as James A. Shackford on Davy Crockett or Hallett Smith on the authorship of Shakespeare's plays. Discuss specifically such topics as the use of evidence, distinctions made between fact and opinion, introduction or exclusion of emotional appeals.

8. Read an account of the development of radio telescopy. Write a paper in which you explain the relationships between the findings of radio telescope studies and the limitations of optical telescopes.

9. Interview at least two instructors in physical science at your college concerning their views on the steady-state vs. the evolutionary cosmologies. Report your findings.

7. LITERATURE
J. D. Salinger's *The Catcher in the Rye*

Writing in the *Saturday Review* several years ago, the literary critic Granville Hicks remarked, "There are, I am convinced, millions of young Americans who feel closer to Salinger than to any other writer." In this assertion Mr. Hicks is assuredly on safe ground, for rare indeed is the literate college student who has not read and reread *The Catcher in the Rye, Nine Stories,* or *Franny and Zooey.*

But an interest in the fiction of J. D. Salinger—and in the writer himself—is by no means confined to young people. Literary critics and journalists have been giving him serious attention ever since the publication of *The Catcher in the Rye* in 1951. Magazines as diverse as *Western Humanities Review, College English, Mademoiselle,* and *Life* have all published lengthy studies of the man or his work. (The *Life* article, a twelve-page essay by Ernest Havemann garnished with photographs, is a gossipy account largely concerned with Salinger's disinclination to be interviewed by *Life* or anyone else.) And a rapid sellout is almost inevitable for an issue of *The New Yorker* (circulation over 400,000) when, from time to time, it prints a new episode in the life of the Glass family, Salinger's current fictional interest.

That critics of *The Catcher in the Rye* do not always agree should surprise no one. Literary criticism is at least as ancient as Aristotle's *Poetics* (fourth century B.C.), and approaches to criticism vary enormously. Putting it simply, perhaps too simply, the major critical positions may be classified under these headings: (1) concentrating on the literary work itself; (2) relating the work to the author—his life, his mind, his experiences; (3) relating the work to the world—the times or the social milieu it is thought to reflect; (4) analyzing the effects of the work on its audience; (5) relating the work to a literary tradition or perhaps locating its position in some kind of timeless hierarchy. Even critics who work within one of these positions will not necessarily come to agreement, for within any single critical position there are also variations in the terms and processes used and in the value judgments adopted. And there are also what may be called eclectic critics who may range across a combination of several critical modes.

Not all discussions of a book, incidentally, can accurately be called literary criticism. Many journalistic reviews attempt nothing more than to treat a book as news. Reports of sales, publicity releases, interviews with writers as celebrities, and many other kinds of comment—interesting though they may be—perform a function which is quite different from that of criticism.

Although all the essays that follow are concerned with *The Catcher in the Rye,* not all are essays in criticism. Robert Gutwillig's article, reprinted from a special supplement of *The New York Times* entirely concerned with paperback books, provides a printing history of the novel and a résumé of its reception. The language of the novel, to which some readers have objected, is analyzed by Donald P. Costello, an instructor in speech, for the scholarly journal *American Speech.* Edward P. J. Corbett is a professor of English at Creighton University; his article is a defense of *The Catcher in the Rye* against attacks arising from its alleged immorality.

One of the earliest extended critical analyses of the book was written by Arthur Heiserman and James E. Miller, Jr., both professors of English. Their essay, "J. D. Salinger: Some Crazy Cliff," sees the novel as belonging to the narrative tradition of the quest. Two critics who specialize in American fiction are Maxwell Geismar and John W. Aldridge; both examine *The Catcher in the Rye* from a social perspective, but they find quite different things to say.

Dan Wakefield's "Salinger and the Search for Love" concentrates upon what Wakefield considers a central theme both in *The Catcher in the Rye* and in other stories by Salinger. Mr. Wakefield is a free-lance writer who has published articles in *Harper's, The Nation,* and *Commentary.* George Steiner has taught in several colleges and has written criticism for *Kenyon Review, The Nation,* and other journals; "The Salinger Industry" is about both *The Catcher in the Rye* and about possible reasons for the continuing critical interest in Salinger.

Aside from discussions by critics and journalists, *The Catcher in the Rye* has also been the subject of occasional controversy among school boards, legislatures, and other official bodies. One example was reported in *Harper's Magazine:*

. . . A prominent Houston lawyer and member of the Port Commission announced he was withdrawing his daughter from the University of Texas at the end of the semester when he learned she was required to read *Catcher in the Rye* in an English class. The aggrieved father sent copies to the governor, the chancellor of the university, and a number of state officials. The state senator from Houston threatened to read passages from the book on the senate floor to show the sort of thing they teach in Austin. The lawyer-father said Salinger used language "no sane person would use" and accused the university of "corrupting the moral fibers of our youth." He added that the novel "is not a hard-core Communist-type book, but it encourages a lessening of spiritual values which in turn leads to communism."[1]

It would be interesting to speculate about J. D. Salinger's (or Holden Caulfield's) possible rejoinder to these statements.

EVERYBODY'S CAUGHT *THE CATCHER IN THE RYE**

Robert Gutwillig

Many an observer of the manners and mores of American youth contends that a first novel published ten years ago occupies much the same place in the affection of today's college generation as F. Scott Fitzgerald's "This Side of Paradise" did for their parents in the Nineteen Twenties.

The novel is "The Catcher in the Rye," by J. D. Salinger, which since its publication on July 16, 1951, has sold a total of 1,500,000 copies in the United States alone—1,250,000 of them, significantly enough, in paperbound form. This year, for the second successive year, so many bookstores, especially those in college communities, reported it among their most-wanted paperbacks that it has won a place on this Review's paperback bestseller list.

Of the 250,000 paperback copies sold this year, a goodly number went to students of Yale, Northern Baptist Theological Seminary and 275 other colleges and universities across the country who have adopted the book for required or supplementary reading in English, psychology and other courses. The appeal of "The Catcher in the Rye" extends also to the younger brothers and sisters of the college crowd. Thousands of secondary school students find themselves academically involved with Holden Caulfield and the week-end of his flight from Pencey Prep, although Holden's actions, thoughts and language have occasioned moral tremors in the past among parents and school officials in Tulsa, Miami

[1] Willie Morris, "Houston's Superpatriots," *Harper's Magazine,* October, 1961, p. 50.

* From *The New York Times Book Review Paperback Section,* January 15, 1961. Copyright © 1961 by The New York Times Co. Reprinted by permission.

and Louisville. There is currently a similar convulsion in Marin County, Calif.

"The Catcher in the Rye" is available in four editions, three in hard cover and the best-selling paperback. Little, Brown, Holden's original publisher, reports that its edition sold better last year than in the preceding several years. Grosset and Dunlap reprinted the book in 1952. New American Library, which offers the novel in its paperback Signet series at 50 cents, reports it as one of its steadiest sellers since it became available in March, 1953. Modern Library issued the novel in 1958 and has had a most satisfactory sale, again largely to college and university bookstores.

One of the more obvious tests of a book's quality, appeal and endurance, is the sale of translation rights for publication in foreign countries. There never has been a more "American" novel than "The Catcher in the Rye"; that is, a novel that in the publishing trade's opinion is so colloquial it will not translate easily or well and whose surface, values, interpretations and meanings are so right, unique and hidden that foreigners will find the book ultimately inscrutable. Imagine, for instance, what would happen to the rhythms of Holden's opening salvo if translated into Finnish.

> If you really want to hear about it, the first thing you'll probably want to know is where I was born, and what my lousy childhood was like, and how my parents were occupied and all before they had me, and all that David Copperfield kind of crap, but I don't feel like going into it, if you want to know the truth.

And yet the novel has been published with great commercial and critical success in about a dozen countries, including Finland, Germany, France, Italy, Poland, Israel and Great Britain. In 1959, everywhere I went, England, France, Germany, Poland, Czechoslovakia, I was asked if I knew Salinger and did I know what his new book was about and when it was coming out. "The Catcher in the Rye" will shortly be published in Russia, and perhaps a mark of even greater distinction is that it was banned on moral grounds for short periods in Australia and South Africa.

Critically, ten years after publication, Salinger, his novel, and his previous and subsequent work are not only the subjects of numerous articles in Time, Newsweek, Harper's Magazine, Saturday Review, The Nation, New Republic and The Commonweal, but also are soberly and not so soberly evaluated in master theses, "little" magazines and literary quarterlies such as the Chicago Review, the Western Humanities Review, College English and American Quarterly. Currently, a mild critical reversal is in progress. Mr. Salinger, we are told, is a minor writer, a *brilliant* minor writer, to be sure, but still one who has published just one short (277-page) novel and a dozen or so serious short stories. But Salinger and Caulfield continue to move and amuse the current school and college generation, and the quarterly critics, most of whom are college teachers, know it. One of them wrote recently in some exasperation: "Mr. Jerome David Salinger is neither Molière nor Chekhov. He is not yet Mark Twain (and by a long shot)."

Clearly, "The Catcher in the Rye," its critical and commercial success past and present, are literary phenomena of the first order and, therefore, it might prove illuminating to look back and see how and why it all happened. On July 16, 1951, J. D. Salinger was 32 years old, but he was not an unknown young writer. He had been publishing short stories for ten years in the Saturday Evening Post, Collier's and elsewhere but most importantly, of course, in the New Yorker. In fact, seven of his 1953 collection, "Nine Stories" appeared between 1948 and 1951. Curiously, almost no one remembered that two chapters of "The Catcher" had already appeared in somewhat different form as short stories: "I'm Crazy," in Collier's in 1945, and "Slight Rebellion off Madison" in the New Yorker in 1946.

There's nothing quite like the Book-of-the-Month Club to give a publisher confidence, and when the club made the novel its mid-summer selection there must have been joy as well as shock at Little, Brown in Boston. Clifton Fadiman wrote the board's report, concluding: "That rare miracle of fiction has again come to pass: a human being has been created out of ink, paper and the imagination." William Maxwell of the New Yorker wrote a brief profile of Salinger for the club news. It has been quoted and plagiarized for ten years now, chiefly, one suspects, because more literary and personal information about the author has not been forthcoming.

The book was reprinted five times that July, three times in August and twice in September. Two weeks after publication it was fourteenth on The New York Times best-seller list; three weeks later it was fourth. And that was the summer "The Caine Mutiny" and "From Here to Eternity" shared the top two spots. Looking back over the contemporary reviews of "The Catcher in the Rye" one is immediately struck by two things: how many of them there were and how poor they were, too. Almost two hundred newspapers and magazines reviewed or commented upon the book; no more than twenty (if that many) were perceptive, let alone intelligent. A good many were inaccurate: Holden was misnamed Homer, his age was variously given as 15, 16 and 17

he is 16), and the novel's action was said to have taken place over
three, four or five days (three is correct). Mr. Salinger may have been
pleased, bored or annoyed by these pieces; he could not have learned
very much, nor could the readers.

Most of the reviews were wildly or mildly favorable. Time, Newsweek, Saturday Review liked it very much. Charles Poore wrote in
Harper's: "* * * Probably the most distinguished first novel, the most
truly new novel in style and accent of the year." The reviewers for both
the daily and Sunday Times thought the book good. The critique in this
review was written entirely in Holdenese, something to which a number of other reviewers partially succumbed (and it's still happening.
John Wain gave it a go in his review of the Penguin edition of the novel
in the Observer in 1959). William Poster in The Commonweal remarked unhappily and accurately that Salinger's idiom and style were
"a tour de force the American fiction writer will probably find himself
increasingly doomed to attempt * * *." Not only American, it's turned
out.

"The Catcher in the Rye" was favorably compared to "The Adventures of Huckleberry Finn," "Seventeen" and "The Lost Weekend" (of
all books), and Salinger also reminded people of Ring Lardner. But not
everyone was so taken. Some reviewers, like The New York Herald
Tribune's, simply did not like the novel: "* * * an irritated and irritating bore * * * the book just about killed me, it really did." Some
felt the novel, which originally had been a ninety-page novelette, was
attenuated, thin and merely a character sketch. Finally, a small but
vocal minority felt "The Catcher in the Rye" was a dirty book. "* * *
not fit for children * * * Many adults as well will not wish to condition themselves to Holden's language. Indeed, one finds it hard to
believe that a true lover of children could father this tale," said the
Christian Science Monitor.

What was it about the novel that struck Americans so squarely ten
years ago and continues to hit the mark still? Primarily it was, I think,
the shock and thrill of recognition. Many of my friends and this writer
himself identified completely with Holden. I went to a school much like
Pencey Prep. One of my friends had a younger brother like Allie, who
had died, another an older brother like D. B., still another a younger
sister like Phoebe. After reading the novel, several of us went out and
bought ourselves red caps with earflaps, and we all took to calling each
other "Ace" and "Prince."

Salinger has, to quote Arthur Mizener, "his own special insight into
the meaning of experience," an insight and a method of expressing it

that set him apart from other contemporary writers and seem to push him closer than anyone else to his characters and his readers. "The Catcher in the Rye" has become a crucial American novel without the help or hindrance of television, movies, or dramatization, for Salinger has always refused to permit any kind of adaptation of the book, possibly as the result of a film, "My Foolish Heart," starring Susan Hayward and Dana Andrews, based, as the saying goes, on "Uncle Wiggly in Connecticut."

The book has not only been bought, it has been read. I believe that, despite its flaws, it will continue to be read. As others have noted, toward the end of the book Holden fulfills his ambition to become a catcher in the rye when he refuses to let Phoebe run away with him. "What I have to do," Holden says, "I have to catch everybody if they start to go over the cliff." So there is hope and, more important, there is moving, communicated urgency. Holden takes Phoebe to the carousel. He stands in the rain, watching her "going around and around in her blue coat and all." "God," he says, "I wish you could have been there." We are there.

Questions

1. Why might *The Catcher in the Rye* be required reading in psychology courses or other courses than English?
2. What does Gutwillig mean by the "moral tremors" occasioned by the book?
3. What does *colloquial* mean? Why might the colloquial quality of the book cause problems in translation?
4. Can you offer an explanation of why the novel has been so widely read in foreign countries?
5. Several times Gutwillig talks about personal experiences and observations. What do these have to do with the book? Why does he use this procedure?
6. What does he mean by calling it "a crucial American novel"? Does he furnish evidence for this judgment?
7. What thought or feeling is conveyed in the last few sentences? What critical judgment is implied in the final sentence?
8. Does the article have a structure? How many main topics does it treat? Is there a connection between them?
9. What does Gutwillig mean by "the shock and thrill of recognition" to which he attributes much of the success of the novel?
10. Would you call the article chiefly informative, argumentative, appreciative? Why?

SALINGER AND THE SEARCH FOR LOVE*

Dan Wakefield

> Fathers and teachers, I ponder "What is Hell?" I maintain
> that it is the suffering of being unable to love.
>
> DOSTOEVSKI

Late one night in a New York apartment a boy who has just been
kicked out of his third prep school is trying to explain his troubles to a
former teacher, and the teacher is struggling to give the boy some hope
and advice:

> Among other things, you'll find that you're not the first person who was
> ever confused and frightened and sickened by human behavior. You're by no
> means alone on that score, you'll be excited and *stimulated* to know. Many,
> many men have been just as troubled morally and spiritually as you are right
> now. Happily, some of them kept records of their troubles. You'll learn some-
> thing from them—if you want to. It's a beautiful reciprocal arrangement. And
> it isn't education. It's history. It's poetry.

The boy is Holden Caulfield, the teacher is Mr. Antolini, and the author
of the novel they live in, *The Catcher in the Rye,* is J. D. Salinger. The
jacket of the novel tells us that Salinger was born in New York City,
attended public schools, a military academy, and three colleges, and
the reader perhaps may imagine that Salinger himself was kicked out of
school once and given such advice as Mr. Antolini gave Holden Caulfield. Whatever our speculations may be, we know for certain that
J. D. Salinger has "kept a record of his troubles"—a record it is possible
to think of not as education but as history and poetry.

The record is essentially the record of a search, and some of the seeds
of its later development can be found in the stories that Salinger began
to write and publish at the age of fifteen. But the real beginning of the
search was marked by the publication of Salinger's first and as yet his
only novel and has continued through a series of stories, most of which
have appeared in *The New Yorker* magazine. The search begins with
the troubled odyssey of sixteen-year-old Holden Caulfield in *The
Catcher in the Rye,* and has, through that one novel and a dozen stories,
moved from the mere revulsion from "phoniness" to a concept of love
so large that it enables Franny Glass and her brother Zooey (in the

* Copyright © 1958 by Dan Wakefield. Reprinted by permission of the author
and James Brown Associates. Inc. First published in *New World Writing No. 14.*

latest Salinger story, "Zooey") to turn from the desire of withdrawa from the world to an entry, through love, into the midst of life.

Salinger's search has been followed by a great many people, for Th Catcher in the Rye was acclaimed by book reviewers all across th country on its publication in 1951, made a Book of the Month Clu selection, and, since then, along with his book of Nine Stories, bee selling steadily and well. The three latest stories, published in The Nev Yorker, were awaited with great anticipation and received as event of the first order by the growing group of Salinger's admirers. It ha only been in the past few years, however, that professional literar critics have taken Salinger under their microscopes for examination Even this belated inspection has been not so much out of interest i his search as it has in him as a species held in high regard by "Th Young Generation." Surely this is of interest, but to make it the mos important thing in considering Salinger is to distort the meaning of hi work.

Out of my own personal experience, which is that of a student o Columbia College in the early fifties who has spent the last severa years in New York, I know that Salinger is indeed regarded highly b many young people. I have heard his work discussed among my friend: and acquaintances more than any other contemporary author, and have heard enough speculation about Salinger himself to feel tha there is indeed a "Salinger Myth," as there was in the twenties, thougl in a different way, a "Fitzgerald Myth." Certainly any myth alive in ou fact-smothered era is of interest, and this one perhaps especially sinc its nature is so extremely different from the twenties myth. The Fitz gerald myth had its hero in Gatsby-like parties and dunkings in the fountain at Union Square; the Salinger myth has its hero living in a cabin in the woods or going to Japan to study Zen. But in both cases the work of the man is of far more importance than the myth. Limiting Salinger's work to its interest as some kind of "document" that appeals only to people of a certain age and social background is as sensible and rewarding as considering The Great Gatsby as a sociological mono-graph once enjoyed by a now extinct species known as "Flaming Youth.'

And yet it seems to follow in the eyes of some older observers that if Salinger is indeed a myth and mentor of many young people, interest in his work is restricted to young people and that this is symptomatic of the fact that it is really childish, sentimental, adolescent, and irrelevant

Significantly enough, the only critical writer to speak at all in real understanding and appreciation of Salinger's search was one of the group in England labeled "The Angry Young Men"—a group of writers who feel the need for such a search themselves, and who are most inflamed by what they feel is the moral decay of their country. In the Angry Young Men's" *Declaration,* London drama critic Kenneth Tynan asks:

Do I speak for you when I ask for a society where people care more for what you have learned than for where you have learned it; where people who think and people who work can share the common idiom; where art connects itself instead of separating people; where people feel, as in the new Salinger story, that every fat woman on earth is Jesus Christ . . . ?

He speaks, surely, for all who have not lost hope—or even if they have lost hope, have not lost interest—in the search for love and morality in the present-day world. There is the need for such a search in any time, and certainly in our time. The need has not changed—and, if anything, has become more acute—since the young writers of the twenties discovered that they were "lost" in a time when, as Fitzgerald put it, all wars were fought, all gods were dead. More wars have been fought, but they have become increasingly depersonalized wars, and the next one that threatens offers the ultimate depersonalization. There have been no new gods, and the old ones have sunk continually deeper in their graves. The inheritors of the "lost" tradition have only produced variations on the theme of being lost, and in attitudes described by the adjectives "beat" and "silent" they have sunk deeper into that state, losing interest even in the possibilities of a search to be "found." The anger expressed by the young English writers is the first sign of interest in revival of such a search, and we have to go back to the time of the simply "lost" to hear a similar desire expressed. It was expressed by a young French writer named Marcel Arland in 1924 when he wrote a piece for the *Nouvelle Revue Française* which better than anything I have read can serve to describe the search going on in the writing of Salinger:

Morality will be our first concern. I cannot conceive of literature without an ethic. No doctrine can satisfy us, but the total absence of doctrine is a torment to us. . . . Between miracle and suicide, and before one reaches resignation, there is room for an extremely individual literature, dangerous, to be sure, and sometimes lyric and abnormal. . . .

It is not men and women who happen to be past the age of thirty-five who are automatically uninterested in such a concern, but men and women who have, at whatever age, reached resignation. A doctor who spoke at a recent convention of the National Geriatrics Society said that "Age is physiological—not chronological." If we can alter his judg-

ment to read that "Age is moral—not chronological," I think we ca
better understand the nature of the "youthful" appeal of Salinger'
work.

Moral senility can come at any age, or need not come at all, and w
have recently borne painful witness through the Howls of the writer
of the "Beat Generation" that moral senility can afflict quite young me
and women. This group dismisses the search of Salinger on the ground
that he is "slick" (he writes for *The New Yorker,* and as any sensitive
person can tell, it is printed on a slick type of paper). But now that th
roar from the motorcycles of Jack Kerouac's imagination has begun t
subside, we find that the highly advertised search of the Beat ha
ended, at least literarily, not with love but with heroin. The appropriate
nature of the symbol can be seen in the fact that the physiological ex
perience of heroin is one of negation (it is the ultimate tranquilizer)
releasing the user during the duration of his "high" from the drive fo
sex, for love, and for answers. Fortunately for the rest of us, the char
acters in Salinger's fiction have found no such simple formula as
"fix" for relief from their troubles.

Sixteen-year-old Holden Caulfield was (just like Jack Kerouac) sick
ened by the material values and the inhumanity of the world around
him. That sickness, however, marked the beginning and not the end o
the search of Salinger's characters to find an order of morality and
possibility of love within the world. The things that Holden finds s
deeply repulsive are things he calls "phony"—and the "phoniness" i
every instance is the absence of love, and, often, the substitution of pre
tense for love. Holden's revulsion is a meaningful one, for he does not
like the "Beat" thinkers, simply equate material values with some ab
stract social evil embodied by "Madison Avenue." Holden is repulse
because material values draw on what little store of love there is in th
world and expend it on "things" instead of people.

> "Take most people. They're crazy about cars. They worry if they get a littl
> scratch on them, and they're always talking about how many miles they ge
> to a gallon, and if they get a brand-new car already they start thinking abou
> trading it in for one that's even newer. I don't even like *old* cars. I mean the
> don't even interest me. I'd rather have a goddam horse. A horse is at leas
> human, for God's sake. . . ."

Holden, through the course of his search, is repulsed and frightened
not by what people do to him (he feels sorry for the teacher who flunk
him in history, and when accused of knowing nothing about the course
says, "I know that, sir. Boy, I know it. You couldn't help it.") but rathe
by what people do to each other. and to themselves.

There is only pretense, and therefore lack of love, and therefore human injury, in the actions of the headmaster of one of his former boys' schools who charmed all the "best" parents on Sunday visits, but ". . . if a boy's mother was sort of fat or corny-looking, and if somebody's father was one of those guys that wear those suits with very big shoulders and corny black and white shoes," then "old Haas" the headmaster paid no attention to them.

There is only the pretense of love in the rich alumnus undertaker who comes back to Pennsey [sic] Prep to give a chapel speech and tells the boys that they shouldn't be afraid to pray to God:

"He told us we ought to think of Jesus as our buddy and all. He said *he* talked to Jesus all the time. Even when he was driving his car. That killed me. I can just see the big phony bastard shifting into first gear and asking Jesus to send him a few more stiffs. . . ."

When Holden flunks out of school and goes to New York he tries to explain to a girl friend he meets for a date why he thinks all boys' schools are "full of phonies," and what he explains is the cruelty of pretense and of the separation that walls off the possibilities of love:

". . . all you do is study so that you can learn enough to be smart enough to buy a goddam Cadillac someday, and you have to keep making believe you give a damn if the football team loses, and all you do is talk about girls and liquor and sex all day, and everybody sticks together in these dirty little goddam cliques. The guys that are on the basketball team stick together, the goddam intellectuals stick together. Even the guys that belong to the goddam Book of the Month Club stick together. . . ."

In the course of his wanderings around New York, Holden is constantly running into walls that separate people—from each other and from themselves—and shut out love. He goes to Radio City Music Hall for the Christmas Pageant, and there, as in so many other places, pretense has become institutionalized and emotion therefore paralyzed:

"It's supposed to be religious as hell, I know, and very pretty and all, but I can't see anything religious or pretty, for God's sake, about a bunch of actors carrying crucifixes all over the stage. When they were all finished and started going out the boxes again, you could tell they could hardly wait to get a cigarette or something. . . ."

Holden can only find genuine love in children, who have not yet learned the deadening rituals of pretense. The only person he really can talk to is his ten-year-old sister, Phoebe, and when she listens to his troubles and says that he doesn't like anything, the only thing he can think of that he really likes is the memory of his dead brother Allie and sitting there talking to Phoebe. As for something he'd like to *be*—there

is no job in the world he can think of that fulfills his rigorous requirements of genuine love, and all he can do is create such a job in his
imagination:

". . . I keep picturing all these little kids playing some game in this big field
of rye and all. Thousands of little kids, and nobody's around—nobody big, I
mean—except me. And I'm standing on the edge of some crazy cliff. What I
have to do, I have to catch everybody if they start to go over the cliff—I mean
if they're running and they don't look where they're going I have to come out
from somewhere and *catch* them. That's all I'd do all day. I'd just be the
catcher in the rye and all. I know it's crazy, but that's the only thing I'd really
like to be. I know it's crazy."

Later on, Holden imagines escaping to a cabin in the woods where
"I'd have this rule that nobody could do anything phony when they
visited me. If anybody tries to do anything phony they couldn't stay."
But the cabin in the woods and the field of rye—those unspoiled places
of love and refuge—are not to be found in the real world. Holden can
find the world of love only within his imagination, and, finally breaking
down from his strenuous search, ends the recitation of his story in a
hospital where he is getting psychiatric care. It is not, however, the end
of his search—or of Salinger's. It is the end of one leg of the journey, for
Holden and for Salinger, and as far as the future is concerned, Holden
perhaps was speaking for Salinger as well as himself, when the psychiatrist asked him if he was going to apply himself when he went back
to school in the fall and Holden said:

"It's such a stupid question, in my opinion. I mean how do you know what
you're going to do till you do it? The answer is, you don't." . . .

Questions

1. Is the quotation from Dostoevski appropriate? Is it relevant that Salinger
   has also used this quotation as an epigraph for one of his stories?
2. What does Wakefield mean by a "Salinger Myth"? By a "Fitzgerald
   Myth"?
3. Who is Jack Kerouac? What are the "Beat" thinkers? What is the relevance
   of Kerouac and the Beats to the discussion of Holden Caulfield?
4. Why does Wakefield include several direct quotations from the novel?
   Why does he discuss certain incidents? Do you see any principle that
   might have governed his selection?
5. What connections does Wakefield attempt to establish between Holden
   Caulfield and J. D. Salinger? Comment on the validity of this procedure.
6. What is Wakefield's own attitude toward *The Catcher in the Rye*? Where
   and how is it revealed?
7. The excerpt printed is about half of Wakefield's article. Can you guess
   what the remainder probably deals with? What clues can you point to in
   support of your guess?

J. D. SALINGER: SOME CRAZY CLIFF*

Arthur Heiserman and
James E. Miller, Jr.

[1] It is clear that J. D. Salinger's *The Catcher in the Rye* belongs to an ancient and honorable narrative tradition, perhaps the most profound in western fiction. The tradition is the central pattern of the epic and has been enriched by every tongue; for not only is it in itself exciting but also it provides the artist a framework upon which he may hang almost any fabric of events and characters.

[2] It is, of course, the tradition of the Quest. We use the medieval term because it signifies a seeking after what is tremendous, greater than the love of a woman. The love of woman may be part of the seeking, part even of the object sought, for we have been told that the Grail has gender and Penelope did wait in Ithaca. But if the love of woman is essential to the seeking or to the object sought, we must call the search a romance. These two terms (quest and romance) distinguish thematic patterns, and have nothing to do with tragic or comic effects. Furthermore, the same plots, characters, and idioms might be employed inside either pattern. But somewhere upon the arc of the Quest, the love of woman must be eschewed or absorbed: the hero must bind himself to the mast, or must seek his Ducalinda because she is Virtue, not because she is Female.

[3] There are at least two sorts of quests, depending upon the object sought. Stephen Dedalus sought a reality uncontaminated by home, country, church; for like Eugene Gant and Natty Bumppo he knew that social institutions tend to force what is ingenious in a man into their own channels. He sought the opposite of security, for security was a cataract of the eye. Bloom, on the other hand, was already an outcast and sought acceptance by an Ithaca and a Penelope which despised him. And, tragically enough, he also sought an Icarian son who had fled the very maze which he, Bloom, desired to enter. So the two kinds of quests, the one seeking acceptance and stability, the other precisely the opposite, differ significantly, and can cross only briefly to the drunken wonder of both heroes. Bloom, the protagonist of *The Waste Land,* the Joads, Alyosha Karamazov, Aeneas, Ulysses, Gatsby—these heroes seek acceptance, stability, a life embosomed upon what is known

* From *The Western Humanities Review*, Spring 1956. Copyright © 1956 by the University of Utah. Reprinted by permission.

and can be trusted. Dedalus, Huck Finn, Ishmael, Hans Castorp, Huxley's heroes, Dostoevski's Idiot—these protagonists place themselves outside the bounds of what is known and seek not stability but a Truth which is unwarped by stability.

[4] (American literature seems fascinated with the outcast, the person who defies traditions in order to arrive at some pristine knowledge, some personal integrity) Natty Bumppo maintains his integrity out-of-doors only, for upon the frontier a man must be a man or perish. For Huck Finn both sides of the Mississippi are lined with fraud and hatred; and because the great brown river acts as a kind of sewer, you're liable to find murderers and thieves afloat on it—even the father whom you fled might turn up dead in it, as though the river were a dream. But in the middle of the great natural river, when you're naked of civilization and in company with an outcast more untarnished and childlike than yourself—*there* is peace. And in northern Mississippi, in the ante-Snopes era, frontiersmen conquer the wilderness using only their courage and their fury; and they behave, even when civilization has almost extinguished them, with the kind of insane honor that drives Quentin Compson outside of society and into suicide. And the hunter, as he tracks the great mythic bear or the incredible whale, must leave behind whatever is unnatural or convenient. Similarly, when the bull charges, you are faced with the same compulsion for integrity as is required by the wilderness, the whale, the bear, the river; and very often, the world so botches things that you must "make a separate peace" in order to maintain your moral entity intact.

[5] All the virtues of these American heroes are personal ones: they most often, as a matter of fact, are in conflict with home, family, church. The typical American hero must flee these institutions, become a tramp in the earth, cut himself off from Chicago, Winesburg, Hannibal, Cooperstown, New York, Asheville, Minneapolis. For only by flight can he find knowledge of what is real. And if he does not flee, he at least defies.

[6] The protagonist of *The Catcher in the Rye*, Holden Caulfield, is one of these American heroes, but with a significant difference. He seems to be engaged in both sorts of quests at once; he needs to go home and he needs to leave it. Unlike the other American knight errants, [*sic*] Holden seeks Virtue second to Love. He wants to be good. When the little children are playing in the rye-field on the clifftop, Holden wants to be the one who catches them before they fall off the cliff. He is not driven toward honor or courage. He is not driven toward love of woman. Holden is driven toward love of his fellow-man, charity—

virtues which were perhaps not quite virile enough for Natty Bumppo, Ishmael, Huck Finn, or Nick Adams. Holden is actually frightened by a frontier code of masculinity—a code which sometimes requires its adherents to behave in sentimental and bumptious fashions. But like these American heroes, Holden is a wanderer, for in order to be good he has to be more of a bad boy than the puritanical Huck could have imagined. Holden has had enough of both Hannibal, Missouri, *and* the Mississippi; and his tragedy is that when he starts back up the river, he has no place to go—save, of course, a California psychiatrist's couch.

[7] So Salinger translates the old tradition into contemporary terms. The phoniness of society forces Holden Caulfield to leave it, but he is seeking nothing less than stability and love. He would like nothing better than a home, a life embosomed upon what is known and can be trusted; he is a very wise sheep forced into lone wolf's clothing; he is Stephen Dedalus and Leopold Bloom rolled into one crazy kid. And here is the point; for poor Holden, there is no Ithaca. Ithaca has not merely been defiled by a horde of suitors: it has sunk beneath waves of phoniness. He does, of course, have a Penelope who is still intact. She is his little sister Phoebe whom he must protect at all costs from the phantoms of lust, hypocrisy, conceit and fear—all of the attributes which Holden sees in society and which Huck Finn saw on the banks of the Mississippi and Dedalus saw in Dublin. So at the end, like the hero of *Antic Hay*, Holden delights in circles—a comforting, bounded figure which yet connotes hopelessness. He breaks down as he watches his beloved little Phoebe going round and round on a carousel; she is so *damned* happy. From that lunatic delight in a circle, he is shipped off to the psychiatrist. For Holden loves the world more than the world can bear.

[8] Holden's Quest takes him outside society; yet the grail he seeks is the world and the grail is full of love. To be a catcher in the rye in this world is possible only at the price of leaving it. To be good is to be a "case," a "bad boy" who confounds the society of men. So Holden seeks the one role which would allow him to be a catcher, and that role is the role of the child. As a child, he would be condoned, for a child is a sort of savage and a pariah because he is innocent and good. But it is Holden's tragedy that he is sixteen, and like Wordsworth he can never be less. In childhood he had what he is now seeking—non-phoniness, truth, innocence. He can find it now only in Phoebe and in his dead brother Allie's baseball mitt, in a red hunting cap and the tender little nuns. Still, unlike all of us, Holden refuses to compromise with adulthood and its necessary adulteries; and his heroism drives him berserk.

Huck Finn had the Mississippi and at the end of the Mississippi he had the wild west beyond Arkansas. The hero of *The Waste Land* had Shantih, the peace which passes human understanding. Bloom had Molly and his own ignorance; Dedalus had Paris and Zurich. But for Holden, there is no place to go.

. . . .

[9] The flight out of the world, out of the ordinary, and into an Eden of innocence or childhood is a common flight indeed, and it is one which Salinger's heroes are constantly attempting. But Salinger's childism is consubstantial with his concern for love and neurosis. Adultism is precisely "the suffering of being unable to love," and it is that which produces neurosis. Everyone able to love in Salinger's stories is either a child or a man influenced by a child. All the adults not informed by love and innocence are by definition phonies and prostitutes. "You take adults, they always look lousy when they're asleep with their mouths open, but kids don't . . . They look all right." Kids like Phoebe shut up when they haven't anything to say. They even say "thank you" when you tighten their skates, and they don't go behind a post to button their pants. The nuns expect no swanky lunches after standing on a corner to collect money. Young James Castle would not go back on his word even though he had to jump from a window to keep it.

[10] Holden is the kind of person who feels sorry for the teachers who have to flunk him. He fears for the ducks when the lagoon freezes over, for he is a duck himself with no place to go. He must enter his own home like a crook, lying to elevator boys and tip-toeing past bedrooms. His dad "will kill" him and his mother will weep for his incorrigible "laziness." He wants only to pretend he is a deaf-mute and live as a hermit filling-station operator in Colorado, but he winds up where the frontier ends, California, in an institution for sick rich kids. And we can see, on the final note of irony in the book, that that frontier west which represented escape from "sivilization" for Huck Finn has ended by becoming the symbol for depravity and phoniness in our national shrine at Hollywood.

. . . .

[11] It is . . . poignance which characterizes all of Salinger's humor, this catch in the throat that accompanies all of the laughs. Holden Caulfield is no clown nor is he a tragic hero; he is a sixteen-year-old lad whose vivid encounter with everyday life is tragically humorous—or humorously tragic. At the end of the novel, as we leave Holden in the psychiatric ward of the California hospital, we come to the realization that the abundant and richly varied humor of the novel has reenforced

the serious intensity of Holden's frantic flight from Adultism and his frenzied search for the genuine in a terrifyingly phony world.

[12] Holden Caulfield, like Huckleberry Finn, tells his own story and it is in the language of the telling in both books that a great part of the humor lies. In the nineteenth century, Huck began, "You don't know about me without you have read a book by the name of *The Adventures of Tom Sawyer:* but that ain't no matter." The English of Huck's twentieth century counterpart, Holden Caulfield, is perhaps more correct but none-the-less distinctive: "If you really want to hear about it, the first thing you'll probably want to know is where I was born, and what my lousy childhood was like, and how my parents were occupied and all before they had me, and all that David Copperfield kind of crap, but I don't feel like going into it, if you want to know the truth."

[13] The skepticism inherent in that casual phrase, "if you want to know the truth," suggesting that as a matter of fact in the world of Holden Caulfield very few people do, characterizes this sixteen-year-old "crazy mixed up kid" more sharply and vividly than pages of character "analysis" possibly could. In a similar manner Huck's "that ain't no matter" speaks volumes for his relationship to the alien adult world in which he finds himself a sojourner. But if these two boys lay their souls bare by their own voices, in doing so they provoke smiles at their mishandling and sometimes downright mangling of the English language.

[14] Huck's spelling of *sivilization* gives the word a look which makes what it stands for understandably distasteful. Holden's incorrectness frequently appears to be a straining after correctness ("She'd give Allie or I a push. . . .") which suggests a subconscious will to nonconformity. But the similarities of language of Huck and Holden are balanced by marked differences. Both boys are fugitives from education, but Holden has suffered more of the evil than Huck. Holden's best subject in the several schools he has tolerated briefly is English. And, too, Holden is a child of the twentieth century. Mark Twain himself would probably be startled not at the frankness of Holden's language but at the daring of J. D. Salinger in copying it so faithfully.

[15] But of course neither J. D. Salinger nor Mark Twain really "copied" anything. Their books would be unreadable had they merely recorded intact the language of a real-life Huck and a real-life Holden. Their genius lies in their mastery of the technique of first person narration which, through meticulous selection, creates vividly the illusion of life: gradually and subtly their narrators emerge and stand revealed, stripped to their innermost beings. It is a mark of their creators' mastery that Huck and Holden appear to reveal themselves.

[16] It is not the least surprising aspect of *The Catcher in the Rye* that trite expressions and metaphors with which we are all familiar and even bored turn out, when emerging from the mouth of a sixteen-year-old, to be funny. The unimaginative repetition of identical expressions in countless situations intensifies the humor. The things in Holden's world are always jumping up and down or bouncing or scattering "like madmen." Holden always lets us know when he has insight into the absurdity of the endless absurd situations which make up the life of a sixteen-year-old by exclaiming, "It killed me." In a phony world Holden feels compelled to reenforce his sincerity and truthfulness constantly with, "It really is" or "It really did." Incongruously the adjective "old" serves as a term of endearment, from "old" Thomas Hardy to "old" Phoebe. And many of the things Holden does, he does, ambiguously, "like a bastard."

[17] Holden is a master of the ludicrous irrelevancy. Indeed, a large part of *The Catcher in the Rye* consists of the relevantly irrelevant. On the opening page, Holden says, "I'm not going to tell you my whole goddam autobiography or anything. I'll just tell you about this madman stuff that happened to me around last Christmas. . . ." By the time we have finished *Catcher* we feel that we know Holden as thoroughly as any biography could reveal him, and one of the reasons is that he has not hesitated to follow in his tale wherever whim and fancy lead him. For example, in the early part of the novel, Holden goes at some length into the history of the Ossenburger Memorial Wing of the new dorms, his place of residence. Ossenburger, we are told, was the Pencey alumnus who made a "pot of dough" in the undertaking business, and who, after giving money to Pencey, gave a speech in chapel "that lasted about ten hours." "He told us we should always pray to God—talk to Him and all—wherever we were. He told us we ought to think of Jesus as our buddy and all. He said *he* talked to Jesus all of the time. Even when he was driving his car. That killed me. I can just see the big phony bastard shifting into first gear and asking Jesus to send him a few more stiffs." Ossenburger, of course, has nothing to do, directly, with the "madman stuff" that happened to Holden around Christmas; but Holden's value judgment of the phony Ossenburger is certainly relevant to Salinger's purpose, the revelation of Holden's character.

[18] When Holden refuses to express aggressive dislike of the repulsive Ackley, the pimply boy whose teeth "looked mossy and awful," he is not being facetious nor is he lying. He is simply expressing an innocence incapable of genuine hatred. Holden does not suffer from the inability to love, but he does despair of finding a place to bestow his

love. The depth of Holden's capacity for love is revealed in his final words, as he sits in the psychiatric ward musing over his nightmarish adventures: "If you want to know the truth, I don't *know* what I think about it. I'm sorry I told so many people about it. About all I know is, I sort of miss everybody I told about. Even old Stradlater and Ackley, for instance. I think I even miss that goddam Maurice. It's funny. Don't ever tell anybody anything. If you do, you start missing everybody." We agree with Holden that it is funny, but it is funny in a pathetic kind of way. As we leave Holden alone in his room in the psychiatric ward, we are aware of the book's last ironic incongruity. It is not Holden who should be examined for a sickness of the mind, but the world in which he has sojourned and found himself an alien. To "cure" Holden, he must be given the contagious, almost universal disease of phony adultism; he must be pushed over that "crazy cliff."

Questions

1. What is the effect of the opening paragraphs? What purpose is served by relating *The Catcher in the Rye* to the tradition of the epic quest?
2. Can you identify these literary allusions: Stephen Dedalus, Eugene Gant, Natty Bumppo, Leopold Bloom, the Joads, Ishmael, Hans Castorp, Quentin Compson, Nick Adams? What assumptions have Heiserman and Miller made about their readers?
3. "So Salinger translates the old tradition into contemporary terms" (paragraph 7). Is this statement made in praise or in blame? What assumptions lie behind it?
4. Why is Holden Caulfield called an American hero (paragraph 6)? Later in the essay (paragraph 11) we are told he is "no clown nor is he a tragic hero." Is there a contradiction here?
5. What is meant by the phrase "phony adultism"?
6. How do the writers account for the language and style of *The Catcher in the Rye*? Discuss.
7. Do the writers accept Holden's evaluation of the world of adults? What evidence can you cite to support your response?

J. D. SALINGER: THE WISE CHILD AND THE NEW YORKER SCHOOL OF FICTION*

Maxwell Geismar

[1] He worked on *The Catcher in the Rye* for about ten years, J. D. Salinger told us, and when it appeared in 1951, it evoked both critical

* From *American Moderns: From Rebellion to Conformity* by Maxwell Geismar. Copyright © 1958 by Maxwell Geismar. Reprinted by permission of Hill and Wang, Inc.

and popular acclaim. Here was a fresh voice, said Clifton Fadiman in the Book-of-the-Month Club *News*. "One can actually hear it speaking, and what it has to say is uncannily true, perceptive and compassionate." The novel was brilliant, funny, meaningful, said S. N. Behrman. It was probably the most distinguished first novel of the year, said Charles Poore in *Harper's* magazine. The real catch in the *Catcher*, said *Time*, was novelist Salinger himself, who could understand the adolescent mind without displaying one.

[2] Salinger's short stories in the *New Yorker* had already created a stir. In undergraduate circles, and particularly in the women's colleges, this fresh voice, which plainly showed its debt to Ring Lardner, but had its own idiom and message, began to sound prophetic. Salinger was the spokesman of the Ivy League Rebellion during the early Fifties. He had come to express, apparently, the values and aspirations of college youth in a way that nobody since Scott Fitzgerald (the other major influence in his work) had done as well. He is interesting to read for this reason, and because he is a leading light in the *New Yorker* school of writing. (He is probably their *ultimate* artist.) And besides, Salinger's talent is interesting for its own sake.

[3] But just what is the time spirit that he expresses? The *Catcher's* hero has been expelled from Pencey Prep as the climax of a long adolescent protest. The history teacher who tries to get at the causes of Holden Caulfield's discontent emerges as a moralistic pedagogue, who picks his nose. ("He was really getting the old thumb right in there.") During his farewell lecture, Holden is restless, bored—"I moved my ass a little bit on the bed"—and then suddenly uneasy. "I felt sorry as hell for him all of a sudden. But I just couldn't hang around there any longer." This refrain echoes through the narrative; and the rebellious young hero ends up by being "sorry" for all the jerks, morons, and queers who seem to populate the fashionable and rich preparatory school world.

[4] He is also scornful of all the established conventions as "very big deal." (Another standard refrain in the story.) He seems to be the only truly creative personage in this world, and, though he has failed all his courses except English, he has his own high, almost absolute, standards of literature, at least.

[5] "They gave me *Out of Africa* by Isak Dinesen. I thought it was going to stink, but it didn't. It was a very good book. I'm quite illiterate, but I read a lot." By comparison, *A Farewell to Arms* is really a phony book, so we are told. As in Saul Bellow's work, the very human hero of *The Catcher*, who is a physical weakling, who knows that he is at least

half "yellow," is also a symbol of protest against the compulsive virility of the Hemingway school of fiction.

[6] The action of the novel is in fact centered around the athlete Stradlater, who is "a very sexy bastard," and who has borrowed Holden Caulfield's jacket and his girl. Stradlater is "unscrupulous" with girls; he has a very *sincere* voice which he uses to snow them with, while he gives them the time, usually in the back seat of the car. Thinking about all this, Holden gets nervous ("I damn near puked"). In his room, he puts on his pajamas, and the old hunting hat which is his talisman of true rebellion and creativity, and starts out to write the English theme (which Stradlater will use as his own) about his dead brother Allie's baseball mitt. Yet when the athlete returns from his date, full of complacency about Holden's girl and of contempt for Holden's essay, this weakling-hero provokes him into a fight. "Get your dirty stinking moron knees off my chest," says Caulfield to Stradlater. "If I letcha up," says Strad, "willya keep your mouth shut?" "You're a dirty stupid sonuvabitch of a moron," says Holden Caulfield.

[7] Later, nursing a bloody nose as the price of his defiant tongue, he wanders in to old Ackley's room for companionship. "You could also hear old Ackley snoring. Right through the goddam shower curtains you could hear him. He had sinus trouble and he couldn't breathe too hot when he was asleep. That guy had just about everything. Sinus trouble, pimples, lousy teeth, halitosis, crumby fingernails. You had to feel a little sorry for the crazy sonuvabitch." But he can find no comfort or solace in the room which stinks of dirty socks. Ackley is even more stupid than Stradlater. "Stradlater was a goddam genius next to Ackley." A familiar mood of loneliness and despair descends upon him. "I felt so lonesome, all of a sudden, I almost wished I was dead. . . . Boy, did I feel rotten. I felt so damn lonesome." He counts his dough ("I was pretty loaded. My grandmother'd just sent me a wad about a week before.") and says good-by:

When I was all set to go, when I had my bags and all, I stood for a while next to the stairs and took a last look down the goddam corridor. I was sort of crying. I don't know why. I put my red hunting hat on, and turned the peak around to the back, the way I liked it, and then I yelled at the top of my goddam voice, "*Sleep tight, ya morons!*" I'll bet I woke up every bastard on the whole floor. Then I got the hell out. Some stupid guy had thrown peanut shells all over the stairs, and I damn near broke my crazy neck.

[8] These are handsome prose passages, and *The Catcher in the Rye* is eminently readable and quotable in its tragicomic narrative of pre-adolescent revolt. Compact, taut, and colorful, the first half of the novel

presents in brief compass all the petty horrors, the banalities, the final mediocrity of the typical American prep school. Very fine—and not sustained or fulfilled, as fiction. For the later sections of the narrative are simply an episodic account of Holden Caulfield's "lost week end" in New York City which manages to sustain our interest but hardly deepens our understanding.

[9] There are very ambiguous elements, moreover, in the portrait of this sad little screwed-up hero. His urban background is curiously shadowy, like the parents who never quite appear in the story, like the one pure adolescent love affair which is now "ruined" in his memory. The locale of the New York sections is obviously that of a comfortable middle-class urban Jewish society where, however, all the leading figures have become beautifully Anglicized. Holden and Phoebe Caulfield: what perfect American social register names which are presented to us in both a social and a psychological void! Just as the hero's interest in the ancient Egyptians extends only to the fact that they created mummies, so Salinger's own view of his hero's environment omits any reference to its real nature and dynamics.

[10] Though the book is dedicated to Salinger's mother, the fictional mother in the narrative appears only as a voice through the wall. The touching note of affection between the brother and sister is partly a substitute for the missing child-parent relationships (which might indeed clarify the nature of the neurotic hero), and perhaps even a sentimental evasion of the true emotions in a sibling love. The only real creation (or half-creation) in this world is Holden Caulfield himself. And that "compassion," so much praised in the story, and always expressed in the key phrase, "You had to feel sorry"—for him, for her, for them—also implies the same sense of superiority. If this hero really represents the nonconformist rebellion of the Fifties, he is a rebel without a past, apparently, and without a cause.

[11] *The Catcher in the Rye* protests, to be sure, against both the academic and social conformity of its period. But what does it argue *for?* When Holden mopes about the New York museum which is almost the true home of his discredited childhood, he remembers the Indian war-canoes "about as long as three goddam Cadillacs in a row." He refuses any longer to participate in the wealthy private boys' schools where "you have to keep making believe you give a damn if the football team loses, and all you do is talk about girls and liquor and sex all day, and everybody sticks together in these dirty little goddam cliques." Fair enough; while he also rejects the notion of a conventional future in which he would work in an office, make a lot of dough, ride in cabs, play bridge, or go to the movies. But in his own private vision of a better life,

this little catcher in the rye sees only those "thousands of little children" all playing near the dangerous cliff, "and nobody's around—nobody big, I mean—except me" to rescue them from their morbid fate.

[12] This is surely the differential revolt of the lonesome rich child, the conspicuous display of leisure-class emotions, the wounded affections, never quite faced, of the upper-class orphan. This is the *New Yorker* school of ambiguous finality at its best. But Holden Caulfield's real trouble, as he is told by the equally precocious Phoebe is that he doesn't like *any*thing that is happening. "You don't like any schools. You don't like a million things. You *don't*." This is also the peak of well-to-do and neurotic anarchism—the one world of cultivated negation in which all those thousands of innocent, pure little children are surely as doomed as their would-be and somewhat paranoid savior. "I have a feeling that you're riding for some kind of a terrible, terrible fall," says the last and best teacher in Holden's tormented academic career. But even this prophetic insight is vitiated by the fact that Mr. Antolini, too, is one of those flits and perverty guys from whom the adolescent hero escapes in shame and fear.

[13] He is still, and forever, the innocent child in the evil and hostile universe, the child who can never grow up. And no wonder that he hears, in the final pages of the narrative, only a chorus of obscene sexual epithets which seem to surround the little moment of lyric happiness with his childlike sister. The real achievement of *The Catcher in the Rye* is that it manages so gracefully to evade just those central questions which it raises, and to preserve both its verbal brilliance and the charm of its emotions within the scope of its own dubious literary form. It is still Salinger's best work, if a highly artificial one, and the caesuras, the absences, the ambiguities at the base of this writer's work became more obvious in his subsequent books.

. . . .

Questions

1. Explain the phrase "Ivy League Rebellion" (paragraph 2). What implications does Geismar expect you to draw from this phrase?
2. Geismar says that Salinger is probably the "*ultimate* artist" in "the *New Yorker* school of writing." What does he mean? What does the tone of this paragraph reveal about Geismar's attitude toward both Salinger and *The New Yorker*?
3. "The action of the novel is in fact centered about the athlete Stradlater" (paragraph 6). If you have read the novel, do you agree with this statement?
4. What basic structural defect does Geismar find in the novel? If you have read the novel, do you agree with his view?

5. Note Geismar's description of the novel as "highly artificial" and his complaint about "ambiguous elements." Precisely what do you think he is objecting to?
6. In describing Holden as "the lonesome rich child" and "the upper-class orphan," what attitude is Geismar adopting? How else might Holden be described?
7. What "central questions" does Geismar think the novel evades? Do you agree that these are central questions?

JUVENILE CONTEMPT AND *NEW YORKER* SENTIMENTALISM*

John W. Aldridge

Mr. Salinger's *The Catcher in the Rye,* like *The Adventures of Huckleberry Finn,* is a study in the spiritual picaresque, the journey that for the young is all one way, from holy innocence to such knowledge as the world offers, from the reality which illusion demands and thinks it sees to the illusion which reality insists, at the point of madness, we settle for. But the great difference between the two novels is the measure not merely of the change in time and history of a cultural situation, but of the changed moral circumstances in which innocence typically finds itself in crisis and lends itself to drama. The innocence of *Huckleberry Finn* is a compound of frontier ignorance, juvenile delinquency, and penny-dreadful heroism. It begs for the challenge of thugs, thieves, swindlers, and feuds, and that is what it gets and delights in, takes such delight in, in fact, that even when the dangers become real and the escapes increasingly narrow, we know it is all in fun, that this is innocence living out its concocted daydream of glory in which no one really gets hurt, and even the corpses climb to their feet and dust themselves off at dinnertime. Still, in the suspension of our disbelief, in the planned illusion of the novel itself, the innocence and the world of violence appear to be seriously and effectively opposed. The innocence is the raft to which Huck and Jim, in flight from the dangers of the shore, make their narrow escapes. It is the river itself, time, faith, continuity, moving endlessly and dependably beside and between the temporary and futile altercations of men. And it is the raft and the river together which give the innocence of *Huckleberry Finn* its focus and breadth of implication, so that it exists at once on the level of naiveté at which it re-

* From John W. Aldridge, *In Search of Heresy: American Literature in an Age of Conformity.* Copyright © 1956 by John W. Aldridge. Published by McGraw-Hill Book Co., Inc. Reprinted by permission of the author.

sponds to adventure and on the level of maturity at which it lends itself to allegory.

The innocence of Mr. Salinger's Holden Caulfield, on the other hand, is a compound of urban intelligence, juvenile contempt, and *New Yorker* sentimentalism, and the only challenge it begs for, the only challenge it has left to beg for, is the challenge of the genuine, the truly human, in a world which has lost both the means of adventure and the means of love. But it is in the nature of Holden's dilemma, his spiritual confinement in this world, that he lacks a concrete basis, can find no concrete embodiment, for the ideal against which he judges, and finds wanting, the life around him. He has objects for his contempt but no objects other than his sister for his love—no raft, no river, no Jim, and no Tom. He is forced, consequently, simply to register his contempt, his developing disillusionment; and it is inevitable that he should seem after a time to be registering it in a vacuum, for just as he can find no concrete equivalent in life for the ideal which he wishes life to embody, so the persons on whom he registers his contempt seem inadequate to it and unjustly accused by it. The boorish prep school roommate, the hyprocritical teacher, the stupid women in the Lavender Room, the resentful prostitute, the conventional girl friend, the bewildered cab driver, the affected young man at the theater, the old friend who reveals that his interest in Holden is homosexual—these people are all truly objectionable and deserve the places Holden assigns them in his secret hierarchy of class with its categories of phonies, bores, deceivers, and perverts. But they are nonetheless human, albeit dehumanized, and constitute a fair average of what the culture affords.² They are part of the truth which Holden does not see and, as it turns out, is never able to see—that this is what one part of humanity *is*; the lies, the phoniness, the hypocrisy are the compromises which innocence is forced by the world to make.² This is the reality on which Holden's illusion is finally broken, but no recognition follows, and no conversion.³ He remains at the end what he was at the beginning—cynical, defiant, and blind.⁴ And as for ourselves, there is identification but no insight, a sense of pathos but not of tragedy.⁵ It may be Mr. Salinger made the most of his subject, but his subject was not adequate to his intention, just as Holden's world is not adequate to his contempt, and that is probably because it does not possess sufficient humanity to make the search for humanity dramatically feasible. . . .

Questions

1. Comment on the title of Aldridge's book, *In Search of Heresy: American Literature in an Age of Conformity*, from which this excerpt is drawn.

2. Why does Aldridge draw the extended parallel with *Huckleberry Finn*? Is it appropriate? Discuss.
3. What does Aldridge mean by each of these terms: "urban intelligence," "juvenile contempt," "*New Yorker* sentimentalism"? Do these terms accurately describe Holden Caulfield? Explain.
4. Aldridge says that Holden "remains at the end what he was at the beginning—cynical, defiant, and blind." If you have read the novel, do you accept this interpretation?
5. Salinger's "subject was not adequate to his intention," Aldridge says. What basic critical assumption is made here? How relevant is it to assessing the novel?
6. What does Aldridge think is the basic cause of the failure of the novel?

THE LANGUAGE OF *THE CATCHER IN THE RYE**

A study of the language of J. D. Salinger's *The Catcher in the Rye* can be justified not only on the basis of literary interest, but also on the basis of linguistic significance. Today we study *The Adventures of Huckleberry Finn* (with which many critics have compared *The Catcher in the Rye*) not only as a great work of literary art, but as a valuable study in 1884 dialect. In coming decades, *The Catcher in the Rye* will be studied, I feel, not only as a literary work, but also as an example of teenage vernacular in the 1950s. As such, the book will be a significant historical linguistic record of a type of speech rarely made available in permanent form. Its linguistic importance will increase as the American speech it records becomes less current.

Most critics who looked at *The Catcher in the Rye* at the time of its publication thought that its language was a true and authentic rendering of teenage colloquial speech. Reviewers in the Chicago *Sunday Tribune*, the London *Times Literary Supplement*, the *New Republic*, the New York *Herald Tribune Book Review*, the New York *Times*, the *New Yorker*, and the *Saturday Review of Literature* all specifically mentioned the authenticity of the book's language. Various aspects of its language were also discussed in the reviews published in *America*, the *Atlantic*, the *Catholic World*, the *Christian Science Monitor*, the *Library Journal*, the Manchester *Guardian*, the *Nation*, the *New Statesman and Nation*, the New York *Times Book Review*, *Newsweek*, the

* From *American Speech*, Vol. XXXIV, October, 1959. Copyright © 1959 by Columbia University Press. Reprinted by permission.

Spectator, and *Time.*[1] Of these many reviews, only the writers for the *Catholic World* and the *Christian Science Monitor* denied the authenticity of the book's language, but both of these are religious journals which refuse to believe that the "obscenity" was realistic. An examination of the reviews of *The Catcher in the Rye* proves that the language of Holden Caulfield, the book's sixteen-year-old narrator, struck the ear of the contemporary reader as an accurate rendering of the informal speech of an intelligent, educated, Northeastern American adolescent.[2]

In addition to commenting on its authenticity, critics have often remarked—uneasily—the "daring," "obscene," "blasphemous" feature of Holden's language. Another commonly noted feature of the book's language has been its comic effect. And yet there has never been an extensive investigation of the language itself. That is what this paper proposes to do.

Even though Holden's language is authentic teenage speech, recording it was certainly not the major intention of Salinger. He was faced with the artistic task of creating an individual character, not with the linguistic task of reproducing the exact speech of teenagers in general. Yet Holden had to speak a recognizable teenage language, and at the same time had to be identifiable as an individual. This difficult task

---

[1] See reviews in *America,* LXXV (August 11, 1951), 463, 464; *Atlantic,* CLXXXVIII (1951), 82; *Catholic World,* CLXXIV (1951), 154; Chicago *Sunday Tribune,* July 15, 1951, Part 4, p. 3; *Christian Science Monitor,* July 19, 1951, p. 9; *Library Journal,* LXXVI (1951), 1125; *Times* [London] *Literary Supplement,* September 7, 1951, p. 561; Manchester *Guardian,* August 10, 1951, p. 4; *Nation,* CLXXIII (September 1, 1951), 176; *New Republic,* CXXV (July 16, 1951), 20, 21; *New Statesman and Nation,* XLII (August 18, 1951), 185; New York *Herald Tribune Book Review,* July 15, 1951, p. 3; New York *Times Book Review,* July 15, 1951, p. 5; New York *Times,* July 16, 1951, p. 19; *New Yorker,* XXVII (August 11, 1951), 71–76; *Newsweek,* XXXVIII (July 16, 1951), 89, 90; *Saturday Review of Literature,* XXXIV (July 14, 1951), 12, 13; *Spectator,* CLXXXVII (August 17, 1951), 224; *Time,* LVIII (July 16, 1951), 96, 97.

[2] If additional evidence of the authenticity of the book's language is required, one need only look at the phenomenal regard with which *The Catcher in the Rye* is held by today's college students, who were about Holden's age at the time the book was written. In its March, 1957, issue, the *Nation* published a symposium which attempted to discover the major influences upon the college students of today. Many teachers pointed out the impact of Salinger. Carlos Baker, of Princeton, stated: "There is still, as there has been for years, a cult of Thomas Wolfe. They have all read J. D. Salinger, Wolfe's closest competitor." Stanley Kunitz, of Queens College, wrote: "The only novelist I have heard praised vociferously is J. D. Salinger." Harvey Curtis Webster, of the University of Louisville, listed Salinger as one of the "stimulators." R. J. Kaufman, of the University of Rochester, called *The Catcher in the Rye* "a book which has completely aroused nearly all of them." See "The Careful Young Men," *Nation,* CLXXXIV (March 9, 1957), 199–214. I have never heard any Salinger partisan among college students doubt the authenticity of the language of their compatriot, Holden.

Salinger achieved by giving Holden an extremely trite and typical teen-age speech, overlaid with strong personal idiosyncrasies. There are two major speech habits which are Holden's own, which are endlessly re-peated throughout the book, and which are, nevertheless, typical enough of teenage speech so that Holden can be both typical and indi-vidual in his use of them. It is certainly common for teenagers to end thoughts with a loosely dangling "and all," just as it is common for them to add an insistent "I really did," "It really was." But Holden uses these phrases to such an overpowering degree that they become a clear part of the flavor of the book; they become, more, a part of Holden himself, and actually help to characterize him.

Holden's "and all" and its twins, "or something," "or anything," serve no real, consistent linguistic function. They simply give a sense of loose-ness of expression and looseness of thought. Often they signify that Holden knows there is more that could be said about the issue at hand, but he is not going to bother going into it:

> . . . how my parents were occupied and all before they had me (5.)[3]
> . . . they're *nice* and all (5.)
> I'm not going to tell you my whole goddam autobiography or anything (5.)
> . . . splendid and clear-thinking and all (6.)

But just as often the use of such expressions is purely arbitrary, with no discernible meaning:

> . . . he's my *brother* and all (5.)
> . . . was in the Revolutionary War and all (6.)
> It was December and all (7.)
> . . . no gloves or anything (7.)
> . . . right in the pocket and all (7.)

Donald Barr, writing in the *Commonweal,* finds this habit indicative of Holden's tendency to generalize, to find the all in the one:

> Salinger has an ear not only for idiosyncrasies of diction and syntax, but for mental processes. Holden Caulfield's phrase is "and all"—"She looked so damn *nice,* the way she kept going around and around in her blue coat and all"—as if each experience wore a halo. His fallacy is *ab uno disce omnes;* he ab-stracts and generalizes wildly.[4]

Heiserman and Miller, in the *Western Humanities Review,* comment specifically upon Holden's second most obvious idiosyncrasy: "In a phony world Holden feels compelled to reenforce his sincerity and

[3] Whenever *The Catcher in the Rye* is substantially quoted in this paper, a page number will be included in the text immediately after the quotation. The edition to which the page numbers refer is the Signet paperback reprint.

[4] Donald Barr, "Saints, Pilgrims, and Artists," *Commonweal,* LXVII (October 25, 1957), 90.

truthfulness constantly with, 'It really is' or 'It really did.' "⁵ S. N. Behrman, in the *New Yorker*, finds a double function of these "perpetual insistences of Holden's." Behrman thinks they "reveal his age, even when he is thinking much older," and, more important, "he is so aware of the danger of slipping into phoniness himself that he has to repeat over and over 'I really mean it,' 'It really does.' "⁶ Holden uses this idiosyncrasy of insistence almost every time that he makes an affirmation.

Allied to Holden's habit of insistence is his "if you want to know the truth." Heiserman and Miller are able to find characterization in this habit too:

The skepticism inherent in that casual phrase, "if you want to know the truth," suggesting that as a matter of fact in the world of Holden Caulfield very few people do, characterizes this sixteen-year-old "crazy mixed up kid" more sharply and vividly than pages of character "analysis" possibly could.⁷

Holden uses this phrase only after affirmations, just as he uses "It really does," but usually after the personal ones, where he is consciously being frank:

I have no wind, if you want to know the truth. (8.)
I don't even think that bastard had a handkerchief, if you want to know the truth. (34.)
I'm a pacifist, if you want to know the truth. (44.)
She had quite a lot of sex appeal, too, if you really want to know. (53.)
I was damn near bawling, I felt so damn happy, if you want to know the truth. (191.)

These personal idiosyncrasies of Holden's speech are in keeping with general teenage language. Yet they are so much a part of Holden and of the flavor of the book that they are much of what makes Holden to be Holden. They are the most memorable feature of the book's language. Although always in character, the rest of Holden's speech is more typical than individual. The special quality of this language comes from its triteness, its lack of distinctive qualities.

Holden's informal, schoolboy vernacular is particularly typical in its "vulgarity" and "obscenity." No one familiar with prep-school speech could seriously contend that Salinger overplayed his hand in this respect. On the contrary, Holden's restraints help to characterize him as a sensitive youth who avoids the most strongly forbidden terms, and who never uses vulgarity in a self-conscious or phony way to help him be "one of the boys." [F——], for example, is never used as a part of Hol-

---

⁵ Arthur Heiserman and James E. Miller, Jr., "J. D. Salinger: Some Crazy Cliff," *Western Humanities Review*, X (1956), 136.

⁶ S. N. Behrman, "The Vision of the Innocent," *New Yorker*, XXVII (August 11, 1951), 72.

⁷ Heiserman and Miller, *op. cit.*, p. 135.

den's speech. The word appears in the novel four times, but only when Holden disapprovingly discusses its wide appearance on walls. The Divine name is used habitually by Holden only in the comparatively weak *for God's sake, God,* and *goddam.* The stronger and usually more offensive *for Chrissake* or *Jesus* or *Jesus Christ* are used habitually by Ackley and Stradlater; but Holden uses them only when he feels the need for a strong expression. He almost never uses *for Chrissake* in an unemotional situation. *Goddam* is Holden's favorite adjective. This word is used with no relationship to its original meaning, or to Holden's attitude toward the word to which it is attached. It simply expresses an emotional feeling toward the object: either favorable, as in "goddam hunting cap"; or unfavorable, as in "ya goddam moron"; or indifferent, as in "coming in the goddam windows." *Damn* is used interchangeably with *goddam;* no differentiation in its meaning is detectable.

Other crude words are also often used in Holden's vocabulary. *Ass* keeps a fairly restricted meaning as a part of the human anatomy, but it is used in a variety of ways. It can refer simply to that specific part of the body ("I moved my ass a little"), or be a part of a trite expression ("freezing my ass off"; "in a half-assed way"), or be an expletive ("Game, my ass."). *Hell* is perhaps the most versatile word in Holden's entire vocabulary; it serves most of the meanings and constructions which Mencken lists in his *American Speech* article on "American Profanity."[8] So far is Holden's use of *hell* from its original meaning that he can use the sentence "We had a helluva time" to mean that he and Phoebe had a decidedly pleasant time downtown shopping for shoes. The most common function of *hell* is as the second part of a simile, in which a thing can be either "hot as hell" or, strangely, "cold as hell"; "sad as hell" or "playful as hell"; "old as hell" or "pretty as hell." Like all of these words, *hell* has no close relationship to its original meaning.

Both *bastard* and *sonuvabitch* have also drastically changed in meaning. They no longer, of course, in Holden's vocabulary, have any connection with the accidents of birth. Unless used in a trite simile, *bastard* is a strong word, reserved for things and people Holden particularly dislikes, especially "phonies." *Sonuvabitch* has an even stronger meaning to Holden; he uses it only in the deepest anger. When, for example, Holden is furious with Stradlater over his treatment of Jane Gallagher, Holden repeats again and again that he "kept calling him a moron sonuvabitch" (43).

The use of crude language in *The Catcher in the Rye* increases, as we should expect, when Holden is reporting schoolboy dialogue. When he is directly addressing the reader, Holden's use of such language drops

[8] See H. L. Mencken, "American Profanity," *American Speech,* XIX (1944), 242.

off almost entirely. There is also an increase in this language when any of the characters are excited or angry. Thus, when Holden is apprehensive over Stradlater's treatment of Jane, his *goddams* increase suddenly to seven on a single page (p. 39).

\3 Holden's speech is also typical in his use of slang. I have catalogued over a hundred slang terms used by Holden, and every one of these is in widespread use. Although Holden's slang is rich and colorful, it, of course, being slang, often fails at precise communication. Thus, Holden's *crap* is used in seven different ways. It can mean foolishness, as "all that David Copperfield kind of crap," or messy matter, as "I spilled some crap all over my gray flannel," or merely miscellaneous matter, as "I was putting on my galoshes and crap." It can also carry its basic meaning, animal excreta, as "there didn't look like there was anything in the park except dog crap," and it can be used as an adjective meaning anything generally unfavorable, as "The show was on the crappy side." Holden uses the phrases *to be a lot of crap* and *to shoot the crap* and *to chuck the crap* all to mean "to be untrue," but he can also use *to shoot the crap* to mean simply "to chat," with no connotation of untruth, as in "I certainly wouldn't have minded shooting the crap with old Phoebe for a while."

Similarly Holden's slang use of *crazy* is both trite and imprecise. "That drives me crazy" means that he violently dislikes something; yet "to be crazy about" something means just the opposite. In the same way, to be "killed" by something can mean that he was emotionally affected either favorably ("That story just about killed me.") or unfavorably ("Then she turned her back on me again. It nearly killed me."). This use of *killed* is one of Holden's favorite slang expressions. Heiserman and Miller are, incidentally, certainly incorrect when they conclude: "Holden always lets us know when he has insight into the absurdity of the endlessly absurd situations which make up the life of a sixteen-year-old by exclaiming, 'It killed me.' "[9] Holden often uses this expression with no connection to the absurd; he even uses it for his beloved Phoebe. The expression simply indicates a high degree of emotion—any kind. It is hazardous to conclude that any of Holden's slang has a precise and consistent meaning or function. These same critics fall into the same error when they conclude that Holden's use of the adjective *old* serves as "a term of endearment."[10] Holden appends this word to almost every character, real or fictional, mentioned in the novel, from the hated "old Maurice" to "old Peter Lorre," to "old Phoebe," and even "old Jesus." The only pattern that can be discovered in Hol-

[9] Heiserman and Miller, *op. cit.*, p. 136.
[10] *Ibid.*

den's use of this term is that he usually uses it only after he has previously mentioned the character; he then feels free to append the
familiar *old*. All we can conclude from Holden's slang is that it is typical
teenage slang: versatile yet narrow, expressive yet unimaginative, imprecise, often crude, and always trite.

Holden has many favorite slang expressions which he overuses. In
one place, he admits:

"Boy!" I said. I also say "Boy!" quite a lot. Partly because I have a lousy vocabulary and partly because I act quite young for my age sometimes. (12.)

But if Holden's slang shows the typically "lousy vocabulary" of even
the educated American teenager, this failing becomes even more obvious when we narrow our view to Holden's choice of adjectives and adverbs. The choice is indeed narrow, with a constant repetition of a few
favorite words: *lousy, pretty, crumby, terrific, quite, old, stupid*—all
used, as is the habit of teenage vernacular, with little regard to specific
meaning. Thus, most of the nouns which are called "stupid" could not
in any logical framework be called "ignorant," and, as we have seen,
old before a proper noun has nothing to do with age.

Another respect in which Holden was correct in accusing himself of
having a "lousy vocabulary" is discovered in the ease with which he
falls into trite figures of speech. We have already seen that Holden's
most common simile is the worn and meaningless "as hell"; but his
often-repeated "like a madman" and "like a bastard" are just about as
unrelated to a literal meaning and are easily as unimaginative. Even
Holden's nonhabitual figures of speech are usually trite: "sharp as a
tack"; "hot as a firecracker"; "laughed like a hyena"; "I know old Jane
like a book"; "drove off like a bat out of hell"; "I began to feel like a
horse's ass"; "blind as a bat"; "I know Central Park like the back of my
hand."

Repetitious and trite as Holden's vocabulary may be, it can, nevertheless, become highly effective. For example, when Holden piles one trite
adjective upon another, a strong power of invective is often the result:

He was a goddam stupid moron. (42.)
Get your dirty stinking moron knees off my chest. (43.)
You're a dirty stupid sonuvabitch of a moron. (43.)

And his limited vocabulary can also be used for good comic effect.
Holden's constant repetition of identical expressions in countless widely
different situations is often hilariously funny.

But all of the humor in Holden's vocabulary does not come from its
unimaginative quality. Quite the contrary, some of his figures of speech

are entirely original; and these are inspired, dramatically effective, and terribly funny. As always, Salinger's Holden is basically typical, with a strong overlay of the individual:

> He started handling my exam paper like it was a turd or something. (13.)
> He put my goddam paper down then and looked at me like he'd just beaten the hell out of me in ping-pong or something. (14.)
> That guy Morrow was about as sensitive as a goddam toilet seat. (52.)
> Old Marty was like dragging the Statue of Liberty around the floor. (69.)

Another aspect in which Holden's language is typical is that it shows the general American characteristic of adaptability—apparently strengthened by his teenage lack of restraint. It is very easy for Holden to turn nouns into adjectives, with the simple addition of a -y: "per-verty," "Christmasy," "vomity-looking," "whory-looking," "hoodlumy-looking," "show-offy," "flitty-looking," "dumpy-looking," "pimpy," "snobby," "fisty." Like all of English, Holden's language shows a versa-tile combining ability: "They gave Sally this little blue butt-twitcher of a dress to wear" (117) and "That magazine was some little cheerer upper" (176). Perhaps the most interesting aspect of the adaptability of Holden's language is his ability to use nouns as adverbs: "She sings it very Dixieland and whorehouse, and it doesn't sound at all mushy", (105).

As we have seen, Holden shares, in general, the trite repetitive vo-cabulary which is the typical lot of his age group. But as there are exceptions in his figures of speech, so are there exceptions in his vocabu-lary itself, in his word stock. An intelligent, well-read ("I'm quite illiter-ate, but I read a lot"), and educated boy, Holden possesses, and can use when he wants to, many words which are many a cut above Basic English, including "ostracized," "exhibitionist," "unscrupulous," "con-versationalist," "psychic," "bourgeois." Often Holden seems to choose his words consciously, in an effort to communicate to his adult reader clearly and properly, as in such terms as "lose my virginity," "relieve himself," "an alcoholic"; for upon occasion, he also uses the more vulgar terms "to give someone the time," "to take a leak," "booze hound." Much of the humor arises, in fact, from Holden's habit of writing on more than one level at the same time. Thus, we have such phrases as "They give guys the ax quite frequently at Pency" and "It has a very good academic rating, Pency" (7). [Salinger's spelling is *Pencey*.] Both sen-tences show a colloquial idiom with an overlay of consciously selected words.

Such a conscious choice of words seems to indicate that Salinger, in his attempt to create a realistic character in Holden, wanted to make him aware of his speech, as, indeed, a real teenager would be when communicating to the outside world. Another piece of evidence that Holden is conscious of his speech and, more, realizes a difficulty in communication, is found in his habit of direct repetition: "She likes me a lot. I mean she's quite fond of me." (141), and "She can be very snotty sometimes. She can be quite snotty." (150). Sometimes the repetition is exact: "He was a very nervous guy—I mean he was a very nervous guy." (165), and "I sort of missed them. I mean I sort of missed them." (169). Sometimes Holden stops specifically to interpret slang terms, as when he wants to communicate the fact that Allie liked Phoebe: "She killed Allie, too. I mean he liked her, too" (64).

There is still more direct evidence that Holden was conscious of his speech. Many of his comments to the reader are concerned with language. He was aware, for example, of the "phony" quality of many words and phrases, such as "grand," "prince," "traveling incognito," "little girls' room," "licorice stick," and "angels." Holden is also conscious, of course, of the existence of "taboo words." He makes a point of mentioning that the girl from Seattle repeatedly asked him to "watch your language, if you don't mind." (67), and that his mother told Phoebe not to say "lousy" (160). When the prostitute says "Like fun you are," Holden comments:

It was a funny thing to say. It sounded like a real kid. You'd think a prostitute and all would say "Like hell you are" or "Cut the crap" instead of "Like fun you are." (87.)

In grammar, too, as in vocabulary, Holden possesses a certain self-consciousness. (It is, of course, impossible to imagine a student getting through today's schools without a self-consciousness with regard to grammar rules.) Holden is, in fact, not only aware of the existence of "grammatical errors," but knows the social taboos that accompany them. He is disturbed by a schoolmate who is ashamed of his parents' grammar, and he reports that his former teacher, Mr. Antolini, warned him about picking up "just enough education to hate people who say, 'It's a secret between he and I'" (168).

Holden is a typical enough teenager to violate the grammar rules, even though he knows of their social importance. His most common rule violation is the misuse of *lie* and *lay*, but he also is careless about relative pronouns ("about a traffic cop that falls in love"), the double negative ("I hardly didn't even know I was doing it"), the perfect tenses ("I'd woke him up"), extra words ("like as if all you ever did at Pency was play polo all the time"), pronoun number ("it's pretty disgusting to watch somebody picking their nose"), and pronoun position ("I and this friend of mine, Mal Brossard"). More remarkable, however, than the instances of grammar rule violations is Holden's relative "correctness." Holden is always intelligible, and is even "correct" in many usually difficult constructions. Grammatically speaking, Holden's language seems to point up the fact that English was the only subject in which he was not failing. It is interesting to note how much more "correct" Holden's speech is than that of Huck Finn. But then Holden is educated, and since the time of Huck there had been sixty-seven years of authoritarian schoolmarms working on the likes of Holden. He has, in fact, been overtaught, so that he uses many "hyper" forms:

> I used to play tennis with he and Mrs. Antolini quite frequently. (163.)
> She'd give Allie or I a push. (64.)
> I and Allie used to take her to the park with us. (64.)
> I think I probably woke he and his wife up. (157.)

Now that we have examined several aspects of Holden's vocabulary and grammar, it would be well to look at a few examples of how he puts these elements together into sentences. The structure of Holden's sentences indicates that Salinger thinks of the book more in terms of spoken speech than written speech. Holden's faulty structure is quite common and typical in vocal expression; I doubt if a student who is "good in English" would ever create such sentence structure in writing. A student who showed the self-consciousness of Holden would not *write* so many fragments, such afterthoughts (e.g., "It has a very good academic rating, Pency" [7]), or such repetitions (e.g., "Where I lived at Pency, I lived in the Ossenburger Memorial Wing of the new dorms" [18]).

There are other indications that Holden's speech is vocal. In many places Salinger mildly imitates spoken speech. Sentences such as "You could tell old Spencer'd got a big bang out of buying it" (10) and "I'd've killed him" (42) are repeated throughout the book. Yet it is impossible to imagine Holden taking pen in hand and actually writing "Spencer'd" or "I'd've." Sometimes, too, emphasized words, or even parts of words, are italicized, as in "Now *shut up,* Holden. God damn it—I'm *warn*ing ya" (42). This is often done with good effect, imitating quite perfectly the rhythms of speech, as in the typical:

> I practically sat down on her *lap,* as a matter of fact. Then she *really* started to cry, and the next thing I knew, I was kissing her all over—*any*where—her eyes, her *nose,* her forehead, her eyebrows and all, her *ears*—her whole face except her mouth and all. (73.)

The language of *The Catcher in the Rye* is, as we have seen, an authentic artistic rendering of a type of informal, colloquial, teenage American spoken speech. It is strongly typical and trite, yet often somewhat individual; it is crude and slangy and imprecise, imitative yet occasionally imaginative, and affected toward standardization by the strong efforts of schools. But authentic and interesting as this language may be, it must be remembered that it exists, in *The Catcher in the Rye*, as only one part of an artistic achievement. The language was not written for itself, but as a part of a greater whole. Like the great Twain work with which it is often compared, a study of *The Catcher in the Rye* repays both the linguist and the literary critic; for as one critic has said, "In them, 1884 and 1951 speak to us in the idiom and accent of two youthful travelers who have earned their passports to literary immortality."[11]

Questions

1. What distinction does Costello draw in the first paragraph between "literary interest" and "linguistic significance"? Is the distinction valid?
2. Why is Costello at pains to establish the "authenticity" of Holden's language?
3. How does Costello regard Holden's idiosyncrasies in speech? Are these idiosyncrasies compatible with the statement that Holden's speech is that of "an intelligent, educated, Northeastern American adolescent"? What is the point to each of these qualifying words?
4. Comment on Costello's use of the term *crude words*. Can you suggest another term he might have used?
5. What is the function, according to Costello, of Holden's "trite" and "repetitive" vocabulary? Is this kind of vocabulary consistent with a work of literature?
6. Costello says that "Salinger thinks of the book more in terms of spoken speech than written speech." What is the difference?
7. What is Costello's attitude toward "obscenity" in the novel?
8. Comment on the style, organization, and documentation of this article. To what extent do you think these were influenced by the fact of publication in a scholarly journal?

RAISE HIGH THE BARRIERS, CENSORS*

Edward P. J. Corbett

About six years ago, at a Modern Language Association convention, a group of professors were discussing job openings, as is their wont at

11 Charles Kaplan, "Holden and Huck: the Odysseys of Youth," *College English*, XVIII (1956), 80.

* From *America*, January 7, 1961. Reprinted by permission of The America Press.

such gatherings. One of the teachers mentioned an offer he had had from a West Coast college. A pipe-smoker in the group blurted out: "For heaven's sake, stay away from *that* place. They recently fired a man for requiring his freshman students to read *The Catcher in the Rye*."

That firing may have been the earliest instance of a teacher getting into serious trouble over J. D. Salinger's book. Since that time, reports of irate protests from school boards, principals, librarians and parents have multiplied. The most publicized recent stir about the book was the reprimand that Mrs. Beatrice Levin received from her principal for introducing *The Catcher in the Rye* to her 16-year-old students at Edison High School in Tulsa, Okla. Scores of subsequent letters to the editor revealed other bans on the book in schools and libraries. Curiously enough, the same kind of censure was once visited upon the book to which *The Catcher in the Rye* has most often been compared—Mark Twain's *Huckleberry Finn*.

Adult attempts to keep *The Catcher in the Rye* out of the hands of young people will undoubtedly increase, for it is the one novel that young people of the postwar generation have been reading and discussing avidly. I had firsthand evidence of students' reactions when *The Catcher in the Rye* was one of the three novels (the other two were Huxley's *Brave New World* and Conrad's *Under Western Eyes*) eligible for review two years ago in the Jesuit English Contest, an annual event among ten Midwestern Jesuit colleges and universities. At least 90 per cent of our students elected to write on Salinger's book. In fact, I have never witnessed on our campus as much eager discussion about a book as there was about *The Catcher in the Rye*. There were a few repercussions from adults outside the university, but these subsided when the question was raised: "Would the Jesuit Educational Association assign a book that was going to corrupt young people?"

To the many people who have come to love the book and its hero, Holden Caulfield, all this controversy is puzzling and disturbing. They regard even the suggestion that the book needs defending as sacrilegious—almost as though they were being asked to vindicate the Constitution. Although their feelings of outrage are understandable, I feel that in view of the vast and continuing popularity of the book the objections should be confronted and appraised. My arguments in defense of *The Catcher in the Rye* are the common ones, quite familiar to those acquainted with other controversies about "forbidden" books.

The language of the book is crude, profane, obscene. This is the objection most frequently cited when the book has been banned. From one point of view, this objection is the easiest to answer; from another point of view, it is the hardest to answer.

Considered in isolation, the language *is* crude and profane. It would be difficult to argue, however, that such language is unfamiliar to our young people or that it is rougher than the language they are accustomed to hear in the streets among their acquaintances. But there is no question about it, a vulgar expression seen in print is much more shocking than one that is spoken. Lewd scribblings on sidewalks or on the walls of rest-rooms catch our attention and unsettle our sensibilities; and they become most shocking when they are seen in the sanctity of the printed page. Traditionally, novelists have been keenly aware of the shock value of printed profanities. Stephen Leacock has a delightful essay in which he reviews the many circumlocutions and typographical devices that novelists since the 18th century have employed to avoid the use of shocking expressions.

Granting the shock potential of such language, especially to youngsters, must we also grant it a corrupting influence? To deny that words can shape our attitudes and influence our actions would be to deny the rhetorical power of language. But to maintain that four-letter words of themselves are obscene and can corrupt is another matter. Interestingly enough, most reports about the banning of this novel have told that some principal or librarian or parent hastily paged through the book and spotted several four-letter words. That was evidence enough; the book must go. It is natural, although not always prudent, for adults to want to protect the young from shock. And this concern may be sufficient justification for adults wanting to keep the book out of the hands of grade-school children or the more immature high school students. But one of the unfortunate results of banning the book for this reason is that the very action of banning creates the impression that the book is nasty and highly corrosive of morals.

As has happened in many censorship actions in the past, parts are judged in isolation from the whole. The soundest defense that can be advanced for the language of this novel is a defense based on the art of the novel. Such a defense could be stated like this: Given the point of view from which the novel is told, and given the kind of character that figures as the hero, no other language was possible. The integrity of the novel demanded such language.

But even when readers have been willing to concede that the bold language is a necessary part of the novel, they have expressed doubts about the authenticity of Holden's language. Teen-age girls, I find, are especially skeptical about the authenticity of the language. "Prep-school boys just don't talk like that," they say. It is a tribute, perhaps, to the gentlemanliness of adolescent boys that when they are in the company of girls they temper their language. But, whatever the girls may think, prep-school boys do on occasion talk as Holden talks. As a matter of fact, Holden's patois is remarkably restrained in comparison with the blue-streak vernacular of his real-life counterparts. Holden's profanity becomes most pronounced in moments of emotional tension; at other times his language is notably tempered—slangy, ungrammatical, rambling, yes, but almost boyishly pure. Donald P. Costello, who made a study of the language of *The Catcher in the Rye* for the journal *American Speech* (October, 1959),[1] concluded that Salinger had given "an accurate rendering of the informal speech of an intelligent, educated, Northeastern American adolescent." "No one familiar with prep school speech," Costello goes on to say, "could seriously contend that Salinger overplayed his hand in this respect."

Holden's swearing is so habitual, so unintentional, so ritualistic that it takes on a quality of innocence. Holden is characterized by a desperate bravado; he is constantly seeking to appear older than he really is. Despite that trait, however, Holden's profanity does not stem from the same motivation that prompts other adolescents to swear—the urge to seem "one of the boys." His profanity is so much ingrained by habit into the fabric of his speech that he is wholly unaware of how rough his language is. Twice his little sister Phoebe reminds him to stop swearing so much. Holden doesn't even pause to apologize for his language; he doesn't even advert to the fact that his sister has reprimanded him. And it is not because he has become callous, for this is the same boy who flew into a rage when he saw the obscenity scribbed on a wall where it might be seen by little children.

Some of the episodes in the book are scandalous. The episode commonly cited as being unfit for adolescents to read is the one about the prostitute in the hotel room. A case could be made out for the view that young people should not be exposed to such descriptions. It would be much the same case that one makes out in support of the view that children of a certain age should not be allowed to play with matches. But a convincing case cannot be, and never has been, made out for the view that vice should never be portrayed in a novel.

One shouldn't have to remind readers of what Cardinal Newman once said, that we cannot have a sinless literature about a sinful people. That reminder, however, has to be made whenever a censorship controversy comes up. The proper distinction in this matter is that no novel

[1] Mr. Costello's article precedes this one [Eds.]

is immoral merely because vice is represented in it. Immorality creeps in as a result of the author's attitude toward the vice he is portraying and his manner of rendering the scene.

Let us consider the scene in question according to this norm in order to test the validity of the charge that it is scandalous. First of all, neither the novelist nor his character regards the assignation with the prostitute as proper or even as morally indifferent. The word *sin* is not part of Holden's vocabulary, but throughout the episode Holden is acutely aware that the situation in which he finds himself is producing an uncomfortable tension, a tormenting conflict, within him. And that vague awareness of disturbance, of something being "wrong," even if the character doesn't assign the label "sin" to it, is enough to preserve the moral tone of the scene in question.

Some readers seem to forget, too, that Holden didn't seek this encounter with the prostitute. He was trapped into it; he was a victim, again, of his own bravado. "It was against my principles and all," he says, "but I was feeling so depressed I didn't even *think*." Nor does he go through with the act. Embarrassment, nervousness, inexperience— all play a part in his rejection of the girl. But what influences his decision most, without his being aware of it, is his pity for the girl. That emotion is triggered by the sight of her green dress. It is that pity which introduces a moral note into Holden's choice. Nor does Salinger render this scene with the kind of explicit, erotic detail that satisfies the pruriency of readers who take a lickerish delight in pornography. All of the scenes about sexual matters are tastefully, even beautifully, treated. Is it any wonder that devotees of the novel are shocked by the suggestion that some of the scenes are scandalous?

Holden, constantly protesting against phoniness, is a phony himself. With this objection we move close to a charge against the novel that is damaging because it is based on sounder premises than the other two objections. No doubt about it, Salinger likes this boy, and he wants his readers to like the boy, too. If it could be shown that Salinger, despite his intentions, failed to create a sympathetic character, all the current fuss about the novel would be rendered superfluous, because the novel would eventually fall of its own dead weight.

Holden uses the word *phony* or some derivative of it at least 44 times. *Phoniness* is the generic term that Holden uses to cover all manifestations of cant, hypocrisy and speciosity. He is genuinely disturbed by such manifestations, so much so that, to use his own forthright term, he wants to "puke." The reason why he finds the nuns, his sister Phoebe and children in general so refreshing is that they are free of this phoniness.

But, as a number of people charge, Holden is himself a phony. He is an inveterate liar; he frequently masquerades as someone he is not; he fulminates against foibles of which he himself is guilty; he frequently vents his spleen about his friends, despite the fact that he seems to be advocating the need for charity. Maxwell Geismar puts this objection most pointedly when he says: "*The Catcher in the Rye* protests, to be sure, against both the academic and social conformity of its period. But what does it argue *for?*" Because of this inconsistency between what Holden wants other people to be and what he is himself, many readers find the boy a far from sympathetic character and declare that he is no model for our young people to emulate.

These readers have accurately described what Holden *does*, but they miss the point about what he *is*. Holden is the classic portrait of "the crazy, mixed-up kid," but with this significant difference: there is about him a solid substratum of goodness, genuineness and sensitivity. It is just this conflict between the surface and the substratum that makes the reading of the novel such a fascinating, pathetic and intensely moral experience. Because Holden is more intelligent and more sensitive than his confreres, he has arrived prematurely at the agonizing transition between adolescence and adulthood. He is precocious but badly seasoned. An affectionate boy, yearning for love and moorings, he has been cut off during most of his teen-age years from the haven of his family. Whatever religious training he has been exposed to has failed to touch him or served to confuse him. Accordingly, he is a young man adrift in an adult world that buffets and bewilders him.

The most salient mark of Holden's immaturity is his inability to discriminate. His values are sound enough, but he views everything out of proportion. Most of the manners and mores that Holden observes and scorns are not as monstrous as Holden makes them out to be. His very style of speech, with its extraordinary propensity for hyperbole, is evidence of this lack of a sense of proportion. Because he will not discriminate, he is moving dangerously close to that most tragic of all states, negation. His sister Phoebe tells him: "You don't like *any*thing that's happening." Holden's reaction to this charge gives the first glimmer of hope that he may seek the self-knowledge which can save him.

Holden must get to know himself. As Mr. Antolini, his former teacher, tells him: "You're going to have to find out where you want to go." But Holden needs most of all to develop a sense of humor. One of the most startling paradoxes about this book is that although it is immensely funny, there is not an ounce of humor in Holden himself. With the development of a sense of humor will come the maturity that can straighten him out. He will begin to see himself as others see him.

The lovely little scene near the end of the book in which Phoebe is going around and around on the carrousel can be regarded as an objective correlative of Holden's condition at the end of his ordeal by disillusionment. Up to this point, Holden has pursued his odyssey in a more or less straight line; but in the end, in his confusion and heartsickness, he is swirling around in a dizzying maelstrom. In the final chapter, however, it would appear that Holden has had his salutary epiphany. "I sort of *miss* everybody I told about," he says. Here is the beginning of wisdom. The reader is left with the feeling that Holden, because his values are fundamentally sound, will turn out all right.

I suspect that adults who object to Holden on the grounds of his apparent phoniness are betraying their own uneasiness. Holden is not like the adolescents in the magazine ads—the smiling, crew-cut, loafer-shod teenagers wrapped up in the cocoon of suburban togetherness. He makes the adults of my generation uncomfortable because he exposes so much of what is meretricious in our way of life.

In defending *The Catcher in the Rye,* one is liable to the danger of exaggerating J. D. Salinger's achievement and potential. As George Steiner has warned in the *Nation* (Nov. 14, 1959),[2] there is a vigorous "Salinger industry" under way now, which could put Salinger's work badly out of focus. Judged in the company of other postwar fiction, *The Catcher in the Rye* is an extraordinary novel. His earlier short stories, especially "For Esmé—with Love and Squalor," are truly distinguished. But the last two long, diffuse stories to appear in the *New Yorker,* "Zooey" and "Seymour," have been something of a disappointment. They are fascinating as experiments with the short-story form, but they strike me as being an accumulation of finger exercises rather than the finished symphony. If we admirers of Salinger can keep our heads about us, maybe we can make it possible for Salinger to build on the promise of his earlier work.

In the meantime, some concession must be made, I suppose, to the vigilantes who want to keep *The Catcher in the Rye* out of the hands of the very young. Future controversy will probably center on just what age an adolescent must be before he is ready for this book. That may prove to be a futile dispute. But I would hope that any decisions about the book would be influenced by the consideration, not that this is an immoral, corrupting book—for it is certainly not—but that it is a subtle, sophisticated novel that requires an experienced, mature reader. Above all, let the self-appointed censors *read* the novel before they raise the barriers.

2 Mr. Steiner's article follows this one [Eds.].

Questions

1. "My arguments in defense of *The Catcher in the Rye* are the common ones, quite familiar to those acquainted with other controversies about 'forbidden' books." What are the implications of this statement? Why do you suppose Corbett thought it necessary to say this?
2. Do you see any evidence that Corbett's article was specifically intended for such a journal as *America?* Explain.
3. How does Corbett dispose of the objections to the language of the novel? Is his argument convincing to you?
4. "One shouldn't have to remind readers of what Cardinal Newman once said, that we cannot have a sinless literature about a sinful people." Analyze this argument. Is it valid?
5. What is pornography? Why does Corbett believe that *The Catcher in the Rye* is not pornographic? Do you agree?
6. Corbett believes that the argument that "Holden is himself a phony" is potentially more damaging than other objections to the novel. What critical principles does he apply in discussing this argument?
7. What concession to the objectors does Corbett make in his final paragraph? What underlying moral principle does he apparently accept?
8. How would you define "an experienced, mature reader"? Under your definition, would you include yourself?

THE SALINGER INDUSTRY*

George Steiner

Writing in *The Nation* in March 1957, Mr. David L. Stevenson expressed surprise at the fact that Salinger is "rarely acknowledged by the official guardians of our literary virtue." He can now rest assured. The heavy guns are in action along the entire critical front. Salinger's unique role in contemporary letters has been accorded full recognition:

Salinger is probably the most avidly read author of any serious pretensions in his generation. (Arthur Mizener, *Harper's,* February, 1959)

There are, I am convinced, millions of young Americans who feel closer to Salinger than to any other writer. (Granville Hicks, *Saturday Review,* July 25, 1959)

The only Post-War fiction unanimously approved by contemporary literate American youth consists of about five hundred pages by Jerome David Salinger. (F. L. Gwynn and J. L. Blotner, *The Fiction of J. D. Salinger,* University of Pittsburgh Press, 1958)

Obviously, critics are interested to find out why this should be so. Salinger has caught with uncanny precision the speech and thought-

* From *The Nation,* November 14, 1959. Copyright © 1959 by the Nation Associates. Reprinted by permission.

rhythms of the young. "The talk of his characters is, so to speak, righter than right" (Hicks). He can make a kind of poetry of "the simplest occasion," giving the shapes of art to the swift, raw, undigested materials of urban and college life (Mizener). The crisis of a Salinger fable makes the reader aware of how we are "members all of the lonely crowd" (Stevenson). Salinger is the spokesman for the corner-of-the-mouth rebelliousness of the postwar generation; he expresses the "Ivy League Rebellion of the Fifties" (Maxwell Geismar). He speaks for the nonconformists who resist the old betrayals of rhetoric and illusion. As Ibsen would put it, he rejects the false "claims of the ideal" (William Wiegand, *Chicago Review,* II).

One might have thought that that was more than enough to account for the success of a good minor writer with an audience which is, by any traditional tokens, largely illiterate. But no. Where the Higher Criticism is at work more portentous issues are invoked. Writing in the *Western Humanities Review* (Spring, 1956), Professors Heiserman and Miller[1] tell us that *The Catcher in the Rye* belongs to an ancient narrative tradition, "perhaps the most profound in western fiction":

It is, of course, the tradition of the Quest. We use the medieval term because it signifies a seeking after what is tremendous, greater than the love of a woman. . . . Holden's Quest takes him outside society; yet the grail he seeks is the world and the grail is full of love. . . . Huck Finn had the Mississippi and at the end of the Mississippi he had the wild west beyond Arkansas. The hero of *The Waste Land* had Shantih, the peace which passes human understanding. Bloom had Molly and his own ignorance; Dedalus had Paris and Zurich. But for Holden, there is no place to go.

In the course of exegesis, Salinger's young lout is also compared with Alyosha Karamazov, Aeneas, Ulysses, Gatsby, Ishmael, Hans Castorp and Dostoevsky's Idiot, and always rather to his own advantage.

With Salinger firmly enthroned in the critical pantheon, the gates were open to the happy hunt for literary influences and analogues. In the *American Quarterly* (IX, 1957), Professor Edgar Branch rightly pointed out the extent to which *The Catcher* is related to *Huckleberry Finn.* "Holden is truly a kind of latter-day, urbanized Huck." Fair enough, and the comparison itself is high praise for any modern novel. But we plunge deeper: "Salinger's viewpoint also draws upon a mystical sense merely inchoate in Mark Twain's imagination" (poor fellow); it has an "awesome relevance to our collective civilized fate." A piece by Martin Green in the *Chicago Review* (Winter, 1958) starts out more modestly. Green shrewdly observes that there is between the heroes of

[1] The Heiserman and Miller article appears earlier in this section [Eds.].

Salinger and those of Kingsley Amis a suggestive similarity. Both, as Kenneth Tynan had seen earlier, reflect angry youth and an abdication from politics and idealism. But again, the summits beckon:

> Modern literature—the literature of Hemingway, Faulkner, Robert Penn Warren, Greene, Waugh, McCullers, Bowen, Buechner, etc.—I trust is now over. I trust that in these two new writers we see at last a positive, life-giving alternative. . . . Salinger also *creates* life.

In short: Salinger's tales are "comic masterpieces" (Charles Kaplan, *College English*, XVIII, 1956), and they may safely be compared with the classic in literature. The scholarly apparatus which such stature implies is also forthcoming. Professors Gwynn and Blotner provide a "Check-List of J. D. Salinger's Fiction" and a list of "Critical Studies of Salinger's Fiction." They devote a learned monograph to their man and come up with a pronouncement which caps the entire Salinger Industry:

> The problem he [Salinger] has set himself in this last period is no less than the utilization of transcendental mysticism in satiric fiction, something (as far as we know) never attempted before by an American writer, and by only a few in Western literature.

Roll of drums; exeunt Cervantes, Chekhov and other lesser souls.

In themselves, all these pomposities and exaggerations are of no great importance. But they do point to some of the things that are seriously wrong with contemporary American criticism.

First of all, they get Salinger's work badly out of focus and could do him a great deal of harm if he were so misguided as to read them (most probably he does not). Mr. Jerome David Salinger is neither Molière nor Chekhov. He is not yet Mark Twain (and by a long shot). Why should he be? He is a gifted and entertaining writer with one excellent short novel and a number of memorable stories to his credit. He has a marvelous ear for the semiliterate meanderings of the adolescent mind. He has caught and made articulate the nervous, quizzical, rough-edged spirit of the moment. He very obviously touches on major or traditional motifs: the failure of the bridges that are meant to link young and old, the mending power of a general, non-sexual love between human beings (something between friendship and compassion). "For Esmé—With Love and Squalor" is a wonderfully moving story, perhaps the best study to come out of the war of the way in which the greater facts of hatred play havoc in the private soul. "The Laughing Man" and "Down at the Dinghy" are fine sketches of the bruised, complicated world of children. But neither holds a candle to Joyce's *Araby* or to the studies of childhood in Dostoevsky. Of late, Salinger has begun parodying Salinger. His most recent chronicle of the Glass family is a piece of shapeless self-indulgence (*The New Yorker* is notoriously vulnerable to the delights of sheer length). The writer himself, moreover, is interesting. He has adopted a T. E. Lawrence technique of partial concealment. He does not sign books at Brentano's nor teach creative writing at Black Mountain. "I was with the Fourth Division during the war. I almost always write about very young people." That's about all he wants us to know.

Salinger's virtues account for part of his vast appeal. But only for part. The rest is less exalted. The young like to read about the young. Salinger writes *briefly* (no need to lug home a big book or something, Lord help us, not available in paperback). He demands of his readers nothing in the way of literacy or political interest (in my time, college bull-sessions raged over *Doctor Faustus;* but that meant having heard of Hitler or Nietzsche or being dimly aware of a past writer called Goethe). Salinger flatters the very ignorance and moral shallowness of his young readers. He suggests to them that formal ignorance, political apathy and a vague *tristesse* are positive virtues. They open the heart to mystic intimations of love. This is where his cunning and somewhat shoddy use of Zen comes in. Zen is in fashion. People who lack even the rudiments of knowledge needed to read Dante or the nerve required by Schopenhauer, snatch up the latest paperback on Zen. "Salinger's constant allusions to the Bhagavad Gita, Sri Ramakrishna, Chuang-tsu, and the rest are only efforts to find alternate ways of expressing what his stories are about," says Mizener. I wonder. They are more likely a shrewd insight into the kind of half-culture which the present college generation revels in. Twelfth-century madrigals are bound to come soon into the lives of Franny or Zooey or the late lamented Seymour.

These are the main facts. Why is literary criticism so determined to get them out of proportion?

First, there is a matter of language. Having added to the legacy of Germanic scholarship the jargon of the New Criticism, many American academic critics are no longer able to write with plainness or under-statement. They have a vested interest in the complex and the sublime. (Hence Messrs. Heiserman and Miller's capitalized Quest and their pious statement, "We use the medieval term." . . .) A new, probably rather minor achievement comes along, and at once critical language soars to sublimity. The result is a serious devalution of critical coin. If one writes about Salinger as do Gwynn and Blotner, just how is one to write about Cervantes or Turgenev? The entire sense of discrimination between values which should be implicit in a critic's language goes lost.

Secondly, there is a matter of economics. The young assistant or associate professor must publish in order to get advancement or to obtain one of those Fulbrights, Guggenheims or Fords which mark the ascent to Parnassus. Now suppose he is still faintly alive and does not care to write yet another paper on imagery in Pope or cancel-sheets in Melville. He wants to test his critical sense against a contemporary work. He does not know enough French or German to write about European masters. What is he to do? He turns to the American scene. The giants are no longer about. Faulkner is making tape recordings and Hemingway is adding further gore to *Death in the Afternoon* (surely one of the dullest books in our time). Along comes a small though clearly interesting fish like Salinger and out go the whaling fleets. The academic critic can do his piece with few footnotes, it will be accepted by critical reviews or little magazines, and it is another tally on the sheet of his career.

American literary criticism has become a vast machine in constant need of new raw material. There are too many critical journals, too many seminars, too many summer schools and fellowships for critics. One is reminded of the ambitions of Marcia, a character in the New York *Herald Tribune* comic strip, *Miss Peach*. Asked what she wished to become in life, the little brute answered, "A critic." And whom would she criticize? "Every man, woman, and child in the United States." There has never been, and cannot be, enough good literature produced at any given moment to supply a critical industry so massive and serious. The immediate past, moreover, has been a classic period for critics. With Eliot, Pound, Leavis, Edmund Wilson, Trilling, Blackmur, Tate and Yvor Winters in the field, just how much use is there in writing yet another essay on Dante or Shakespeare or Yeats? The quarry of greatness having been exhaustively mined, younger critics turn their big guns on to the smaller targets.

All this has serious consequences. There is, at the moment, a gross devaluation of standards (the Cozzens ecstasy of a few seasons back is a case in point). If criticism does not serve to distinguish what is great from what is competent, it is not carrying out its proper task. If it conspires to suggest that transcendent values are made articulate in anything quite as loose and glossy as the maunderings of Zooey, it is betraying its responsibilities. Of course, Salinger is a most skillful and original writer. Of course, he is worth discussing and praising. But not in terms appropriate to the master poets of the world, not with all the

pomp and circumstance of final estimation. By all means, let us have
Esmé, Daumier-Smith and all the Glasses. But let us not regard them
as the house of Atreus reborn.

Questions

1. What is the relationship between the three paragraphs at the beginning
   and the statement "With Salinger firmly enthroned in the critical pantheon . . ."?
2. Examine the first sentence of the third paragraph. What is the purpose of
   the phrase "good minor writer"? Who is the audience described as
   "largely illiterate"?
3. What qualities in Salinger's work does Steiner single out for praise? How
   does his discussion of these qualities differ from that of the critics he has
   been commenting upon?
4. What weaknesses does Steiner find in Salinger's fiction? Why does he
   think these weaknesses are a bad influence on Salinger's young readers?
5. Steiner mentions "the kind of half-culture which the present college generation revels in." Exactly what is he referring to? Do you think this is a
   valid statement?
6. "Having added to the legacy of Germanic scholarship the jargon of the
   New Criticism, many American academic critics are no longer able to
   write with plainness or understatement." Explain the allusions.
7. Why does Steiner use the term *critical industry* as well as *Salinger industry*? Why does he call it "a matter of economics"?
8. What sorts of statements does Steiner tuck away here and there in paren-
   theses? Are these statements relevant to the main lines of his discussion?
   Explain.
9. What does Steiner think is the "proper task" of criticism? What might
   other critics think proper tasks to be?

ASSIGNMENTS

1. Read (or reread) *The Catcher in the Rye*. Write a paper in which you
   indicate which of the preceding critical judgments you find most illuminating.
2. Write a paper of comparisons and contrasts between, for example, Geismar's essay and Wakefield's or between Steiner's and Heiserman and
   Miller's.
3. Is *The Catcher in the Rye* assigned reading in any courses in your college? Ask the instructors of such courses to tell you why they assign the
   novel. Prepare an oral or written report of your findings.
4. Do you know any high school pupil who has read *The Catcher in the
   Rye*? Ask him for his reactions to the novel, in some detail, and write a
   paper in which you report your findings and attempt to assess how much
   insight into the novel he reveals.

5. Prepare for a panel discussion in which the topic is drawn from Corbett's suggestion about just what age an adolescent should be before he is ready for *The Catcher in the Rye.*

6. After reading *The Catcher in the Rye,* write a paper in support or in refutation of Geismar's objections to the structure of the novel.

7. Look up Ernest Havemann's article "The Recluse in the Rye: The Search for the Mysterious J. D. Salinger," *Life* magazine, November 3, 1961. Write a critical analysis of the article.

8. Write a paper in which you attempt to classify the critical pieces included in this issue in terms of the categories suggested in the introductory essay. State the reasons for your assigning pieces to the various classifications.

9. Has there been a controversy about *The Catcher in the Rye* in your community? Locate newspaper accounts or other sources and prepare a report of your findings, including a statement of how or whether the controversy was settled.

10. Look up other critical essays on *The Catcher in the Rye* printed since 1961. Prepare a report in which you discuss one or two of the essays you have read and indicate the extent to which they agree or disagree with the essays included in this issue.

8. CRIMINOLOGY
Crime and Punishment

What is a crime? Sheldon Glueck, a Harvard criminologist, points out that a crime is "any act or failure to act that is prohibited by law and punishable by politically organized society in a formal judicial proceeding initiated in the name of the state."

From ancient times to the present, from the most primitive of societies to the most civilized, offenders against society's laws have been punished for serious crimes. Indeed, the Old Testament injunction still reverberates, "Eye for eye, tooth for tooth, hand for hand, foot for foot."

In our culture contrasting opinions are voiced with ever-increasing frequency. One maintains that imprisonment is vindictive and unsuccessful as either a reform measure or a deterrent to the commission of crime. Instead, sociologists and psychologists—among others—advocate the concept of rehabilitating the offender.

Charging "softness" and "coddling," equally insistent spokesmen have demanded increasing penalties and more severe punishments—thus discouraging not only criminals but those who would emulate them. Between the two extremes of "give 'em hell" and the elimination of prisons are a variety of proposals intended to rehabilitate the person convicted of wrongdoing. These include probation and parole systems, psychiatric centers, reformatories, and minimum-security institutions with an emphasis on vocational training. Claims and counterclaims about the efficacy of each of these solutions make the issue of society's treatment of offenders a complex one.

Further complicating the issue are statistics on recidivism, or the return to custody of previous offenders. Interpretations of the admittedly high rate of recidivism range from vehement demands for more effective punishment, meaning more prisons, extended sentences, and more stringent laws, to statements about the futility of prisons and harsh treatment as methods of reform.

Economic and sociological questions are closely linked to the problem of crime. Should increased expenditures go into maximum-security prisons? Would increased use of psychiatric counseling be more economical in the long run? Should more law enforcement officers be employed? Is slum clearance a solution? These questions lead inevitably to others. Do longer prison sentences reform? Can qualified psychiatrists be found? Are probation and parole the answers?

In the following pages the extent of the problem and proposed solutions are suggested. In "Meeting of Minds," a radio adaptation of an imaginary conversation among Aristotle, Montaigne, Freud, Dostoevski, Hegel, and Darrow, you are plunged into an overview of the problem of crime and its related social context. "Meeting of Minds" suggests both the timeliness and timelessness of the problem as well as attempting to give you the points of view of the participants.

J. Edgar Hoover, head of the Federal Bureau of Investigation, and Clarence Darrow, the most famous criminal lawyer of the century, take radically different positions on the causes of crime and the treatment of offenders. In "The Luxury of Punishment," a criminologist puts the basic issue of crime and punishment into the context of the relationships that bind this issue to others in our culture.

George Bernard Shaw challenges the logic of imprisonment. David Abrahamsen, a psychiatrist, offers his views in "Rehabilitation." George P. Vold, a sociologist, asks a key question, "Does the Prison Reform?" and attempts to interpret the statistics on recidivism. In "The Man and the Mask," a Los Angeles radio and TV newscaster denounces those whom he finds guilty of softness in treating criminals. A contrasting view is given by Dr. Karl Menninger, psychiatrist and founder of the Menninger Clinic. Two other selections include an excerpt from a speech by Chief Justice Earl Warren of the United States Supreme Court to parole officers and a statement by a contemporary sociologist, David Dressler.

A short excerpt from the book *The Operators* implies that problems of crime and criminal behavior must be viewed in the light of current morality. Mr. Gibney's excerpt takes on increased significance in the light of recent (1961) exposures of rigged pricing and collusion on bidding by executives of several giant corporations.

The concluding article, "The Climate of Justice," was written by Sheldon Glueck, a criminologist and sociologist at Harvard University. He not only recognizes the complexity of the tangled strands within the issue but also the complexities faced in assigning the causes of crime in the context of a rapidly changing society.

From THE MIKADO

W. S. Gilbert and
Sir Arthur Sullivan

A more humane Mikado never
    Did in Japan exist;
      To nobody second,
      I'm certainly reckoned
A true philanthropist.
It is my very humane endeavour
    To make, to some extent,
      Each evil liver
      A running river
Of harmless merriment.

My object all sublime
    I shall achieve in time—
To let the punishment fit the crime—
    The punishment fit the crime;
And make each prisoner pent
    Unwillingly represent
A source of innocent merriment—
    Of innocent merriment!

Questions

1. Gilbert and Sullivan have used the words *humane* and *philanthropist* in the opening stanza of the Mikado's song. Do these words suggest the literal attitude of Gilbert and Sullivan toward their Emperor of Japan? Does the emperor see himself in these terms? Explain.
2. Examine the rhymes of the first stanza and the refrain (the second stanza which is repeated throughout the song). How do the rhymed endings (feminine rhymes) affect the tone of the song?
3. In the refrain what natural assumption does the Mikado make about prisoners who have committed "crimes"?

MEETING OF MINDS*

Steve Allen

STEVE. Now, the topic for tonight's program is one on which you have all expressed considerably divergent opinions throughout the centuries. And I might add, it's a subject which is very much at issue in our time—it's Crime and Punishment.

HEGEL. Mr. Allen—

STEVE. Yes—Dr. Hegel.

HEGEL. Regarding Crime and Punishment—with all due respect to Mr. Dostoevski seated here on my left, I think that Crime and Punishment is a somewhat broad topic for the allotted time. May I suggest that Society and the Criminal might keep our discussion more precise.

STEVE. I have no objections to that, Dr. Hegel. Gentlemen . . . Very well, shall we begin by having you gentlemen introduce yourselves to our audience? We have seated you chronologically, as you can see. Will you start, sir?

ARISTOTLE. Aristotle is my name. I lived from 384 B.C. to 322 B.C.

MONTAIGNE. Michel de Montaigne. 1533–1592. (*An afterthought*) A.D.

HEGEL. George Hegel, Dr. of Philosophy. 1770–1831.

DOSTOEVSKI. I am Fyodor Dostoevski. 1821–1881.

FREUD. Sigmund Freud, M.D. Born 1856, died 1939.

DARROW. Clarence Darrow, 1857–1938.

STEVE. All right, gentlemen, let us begin.

(*Off mike ad-lib:* MONTAIGNE *asks for a glass of water. Pouring sounds follow.*)

STEVE (*cont'd*). I think a proper way to open the discussion would be to examine one of your own concepts about Society and the Criminal. In this case, the honorable Aristotle's recurring theme that *wickedness is voluntary*. Am I summarizing your view correctly, sir?

ARISTOTLE. You are.

* From "Meeting of Minds" by Steve Allen. Radio adaptation by Harve Fischman and Nat Hentoff. Broadcast June 26, 1960, on KPFK, Los Angeles. Reprinted by permission of the author and KPFK.

STEVE. Very well, would any of you other gentlemen care to take issue with that concept? Mr. Dostoevski.

DOSTOEVSKI. I believe that such a doctrine leads to a concept of responsibility only for one's *own* crimes. And it has always been my view that responsibility for crime belongs to us all. I believe that everyone of us is responsible for all men on earth, each one personally for all mankind and every individual man.

HEGEL (*wryly*). If I may say so, Mr. Dostoevski, that kind of policy can lead to some rather absurd ends. I wonder if you would agree, for example, with the social custom of the ancient Chinese. There, when anyone committed suicide, a strict investigation had to be made and all the enemies of the suicide were arrested and tortured. If the person who committed the *insult* that led to the suicide was found, he and his whole *family* were executed.

DOSTOEVSKI. No, no, no. I think your example distorts my meaning. By collective responsibility, I did not mean further punishment by the state.

HEGEL. *Who then?*

DOSTOEVSKI. Dr. Hegel, I admit the basic question! If we are responsible for our actions and for those of our fellow men—then who is to mete out punishment? But there is a *larger* question: can anyone judge a criminal until he recognizes that *he* is just such a criminal as the man standing before him!

DARROW. Can I just jump in here with some practical experience? I practiced quite a bit of law, and I say that the question you ask is meaningless because the judge you seek does not exist. *Everyone* judges his fellow man from his *own* standpoint and circumstances. The judge who may get 10,000 a year—or I suppose they're getting more than that now—for short hours and financial security, cannot equate his life with that of the common laborer pressed by debts.

STEVE. Are you suggesting that no one is fit to judge?

DARROW. Well now, just let me finish the point—

STEVE. Go ahead, sir—

DARROW. I am suggesting that in a society of human beings, there is no room for judgment, for condemnation, for punishment.

(*Ad-lib hubbub.*)

STEVE (*recognizing him*). Monsieur de Montaigne.

MONTAIGNE. Well I cannot agree with that, sir. I think there is a need for a form of judgment and punishment—but I believe it is the nature of that judgment and punishment that must be carefully considered. And this extends beyond the judge and the criminal. It applies to our very homes, to the way we judge and punish our children. For there is where it all begins. And yet there is where we are most apt to find cruel and violent punishments. Think of the effect of such violence in the education of a tender soul that is designed for honor and liberty! I have never observed other effects of whipping, for example, than to render boys more cowardly or more willfully obstinate. I condemn such violence—towards criminals, and more importantly, toward the child who can become the potential criminal.

DARROW. Now aren't you really agreeing with me? Aren't you pointing out that punishment as a concept does not work? That it only teaches the child to deceive or to conceal by lying to his accusers? If there is anything that the child needs in training, or the child turned criminal needs in *re-training* it is not punishment but *love* and *perfect confidence*. Only in such an atmosphere can a child develop its own ideas of right and wrong—the ideas that will determine the child's conduct. After all, what is wrong for the parent may *not* be wrong for the child. Right and wrong consist largely of intent.

HEGEL. Mr. Darrow—in your preoccupation with what seems to me a policy of *unrestricted* individual liberty, I think you lose sight of the value of *law*. Equitable law, designed for the common good, is the best bulwark for the common good. I recall that a father once asked a Greek philosopher how to best raise a son, and the answer was: "Make him a citizen of a state with good laws."

(*Warm laughter.*)

MONTAIGNE. If I may pick up the point again—

STEVE. Monsieur de Montaigne.

MONTAIGNE. I think we should examine the fallacy of the state with "good laws." For where is such an ideal state to be found? The laws are often made by fools, still more often by men who, out of hatred for equality, fail in equity—but always by *men*, vain and irresolute authors. I believe there is nothing so ordinarily faulty as the laws.

DOSTOEVSKI. Laws are not the paramount issue, sir. For laws bring punishment that is of little consequence when compared to the punishment the criminal heart brings upon itself. This is more complete than any earthly justice.

HEGEL (*caustically*). I can think of nothing more chaotic than a society in which the only law was the reliance upon the criminal heart to punish itself.

(*Ad-lib rumble.*)

STEVE. I believe that Dr. Freud has a comment.

FREUD. Yes—in relation to Dostoevski's point—the punishment the criminal brings upon himself. He is referring, of course, to the sense of guilt. And I think it is important to consider where this sense of guilt comes from.

DOSTOEVSKI. It is inborn, of course.

FREUD. I'm sorry. I cannot believe in the idea of an original—or natural —capacity in man for discriminating between good and evil. Evil, after all, is often not something that would *injure* our ego. On the contrary, evil may be something we *desire*, an act that will give *pleasure*. Therefore, there is an *extraneous* influence that . . .

MONTAIGNE (*Ad-libs interruption;* FREUD's *concept is foreign to him*).

FREUD (*strongly*). I haven't finished, sir. I say there *is* an *extraneous* influence that *first* leads man to choose between good and evil.

MONTAIGNE. No, it is not extraneous at *all*. It is our inner conscience . . . and so amazing is this power of conscience that it makes us betray, and fight *ourselves,* and if there is no outside witness, it brings us forward against ourselves. Punishment does not follow close *upon* sin; it is born at the *same instant* as the sin! Whoever *expects* punishment, *suffers* it.

FREUD. Monsieur Montaigne—what I am trying to point out is what motive it is that makes men *want* to be good or to fear punishment if they are *not* good. This motive exists even before the conscience starts to operate. This is an extraneous influence upon the young human mind which I characterize as the *dread of losing love.* It is born in the hours of man's helplessness and dependence upon others when loss of love is equated in the young mind with loss of food, sustenance and life itself. Then, however, this fear of losing the love of those in the outside world is followed by the development of the *inner authority*—which I have characterized as the *Superego* . . . (*Questioning hubbub*) It is here in the conscience that the *threatened* external unhappiness—the loss of love—becomes transformed into an actual and lasting inner unhappiness: The Sense of Guilt. We then have reason to punish ourselves not only for our actions, but for our wicked intentions as well. And all of this, this process of developing our superego, our conscience, is guided externally by the rules of conduct we absorb from our parents and the other authority figures about us. Now—if what I have said is valid, then the sense of guilt cannot be considered punishment or even a deterrent to crime—*for it is this very sense of guilt, this sought after state of unhappiness that is the reason for committing the so-called criminal act.*

(*Ad-lib mumbles; we hear the first words of* ARISTOTLE's *speech, off mike.*)

STEVE. Uh—one moment, sir—Aristotle, I know it is Dr. Freud to whom you are addressing your comment—but would you face into the microphone as you talk so that—

ARISTOTLE. Oh yes, yes. (*To* FREUD) Doctor Freud, first let me say that we are not as far apart as the centuries between us. (*Overtones of laughter, off mike*) I believe, for example, that if a man has suffered what you have called loss of love by doing something for which he is punished, he also feels there is nothing lovable any longer in him, and accordingly has no love for himself. This is the height of wretchedness, the *worst* of punishments. There is *no* escape from conscience in one form or another. Those who have done terrible deeds shrink from life and even destroy themselves. But if what you say is valid—and it is this self-punishment that leads to even further crimes, then it becomes all the more clear that self-punishment by the criminal offers no protection to the society. Therefore self-punishment is *not* enough—and punishment by the state is necessary.

DARROW. Necessary for what!

ARISTOTLE. For society.

DARROW. As an expression of man's *hatred for his fellow man!*

ARISTOTLE. Well, I would agree, Mr. Darrow, that we must distinguish between revenge and punishment. Punishment is inflicted for *the sake of the person* being punished while *revenge* primarily satisfied the feelings of the one *doing* the punishing.

DARROW. Horsefeathers! Now, I don't *see* the distinction between punishment and vengeance. Hatred is *hatred.* In punishment *every* effort is made to magnify the *ferocity* of the act and the delinquency of the condemned, so that the punishment will be fixed in hatred and carried out in the same spirit. This carefully created emotion is called "righteous indignation."

HEGEL. Not at all! Punishment takes the form of revenge only in a society that has neither judges nor laws. That is why the establishment of a government of laws is necessary. Under a well-organized state, the penalty a criminal receives under the law is necessary and just. By being punished, the criminal is honored as a rational being who knows what he is doing.

DARROW. What you're saying then is the state *must* punish to protect its citizens.

HEGEL. Certainly.

DARROW. Well, with all due respect to you, sir, I say that's baloney.

HEGEL. See here . . . the nature of any crime, no less than the will of the individual against whom the crime has been committed, requires that the injury caused by the criminal should be *annulled,* and the *method* is punishment suitable to the crime.

DARROW. More "baloney." I know of *no* evidence that punishing an individual in any manner aids society. If A is to be punished to make B safe, then even though it might help B, it is an unforgivable indignity and hurt to have made A endure pain for the sake of B. Assume that A knows that he will suffer pain for doing a certain act; what is the effect on A? This knowledge does not stifle the *desire* to do the act; if it has *any* effect, it simply makes him *cautious* in *accomplishing* the deed.

HEGEL. A criminal is punished because he has broken that basic sense of order that all men have and that causes men to live with each other under laws. In this sense, it is his *right* under the law to be punished.

DOSTOEVSKI. Herr Hegel, perhaps what Mr. Darrow is trying to say is this: Does punishment *ever* really *reform anyone?* All those sentences to exile with hard labor reform no one, and they deter hardly a single criminal; the number of crimes does not *diminish* but is considerably on the increase. Consequently the security of society is *not* preserved, because although the obnoxious member is sent far away another criminal always takes his place.

HEGEL (*heatedly*). No, Mr. Dostoevski, I think what Mr. Darrow is saying is—that there should be no punishment *at all!*

DARROW. That is correct, sir—and I'll say it again: There should be no punishment; no *trials,* no *lawyers,* no *judges* to pass upon moral guilt.

HEGEL. Preposterous! You can't . . .

DARROW (*overriding*). Those who cannot adjust themselves to rules should be examined by experts to find out why they cannot adjust. If need be, they should be kept under proper inspection. They should be helped in every way possible. Helped, do you understand? It is progress and growth I am after, not destruction and the perpetuation of crime.

FREUD. Hear, hear!

DARROW. Regardless of what a criminal has done he should be *released* when it seems *safe;* meanwhile he should be kept under supervision in *kindness* and *sympathy* instead of harshness.

HEGEL. Well, if you are talking of pardoning criminals after a suitable period of punishment—all right. *But* pardon is the remitting of a penalty which does not *suspend* the *law!* The law remains and the pardoned man is a criminal, as before.

DARROW. He most certainly is not!

HEGEL. But the pardon should not state that he has not committed a crime!

STEVE. Monsieur de Montaigne, yes sir . . .

MONTAIGNE. Well, I feel like I am stepping in as peacemaker . . . (*Relieved laughter off mike*) But, in a spirit of constructive discussion, gentlemen, I wonder if we might not all agree that there is no excuse for *inhuman excess* of punishment. I must say that the savages who roast and eat the bodies of the dead do not offend me so much as those who torment and persecute the *living!* The uttermost point that cruelty can attain—is, as Seneca wrote, "that man should kill man not in anger, not in fear, but only to watch the sight."

DARROW. Well, we must certainly agree on that. Perhaps the greatest offense against mankind is the zeal with which man punishes his fellow men. It has always been appalling to me that up to the nineteenth century in England, for example, there were over two hundred crimes punishable by death! Among them were picking pockets, stealing fish out of a pond and remaining in the country one month—

STEVE (*shocked*). What!

DARROW (*dryly*). —That applied to Gypsies only. The vigor with which my own countrymen hunted down blas-*feemers* and witches is known to you all. And, by the way, Warden Lewis Lawes of Sing Sing had a profound comment on that subject. He said: "When they stopped *killing* witches, witches ceased to exist."

ARISTOTLE. Yes, well put. But to cite these examples, Mr. Darrow, should not necessarily mean that all laws are cruel and all states unjust. In a good society the laws are tempered by equity. Equity guides us to be merciful to the weakness of human nature; to think less about the *laws* than about the men who *framed* them; and less about what he *said* than what he *meant;* not to consider the actions of the accused so much as his intentions; to ask not what a man is *now* but what he has *always* or *usually* been.

DOSTOEVSKI. I think that *more* is required than the *equity* of men. If anything preserves society and regenerates the criminal, it is only by his being able to recognize his wrongdoing as a son of the church. He must realize that his sin against society is actually a sin against the *church*. Who would become of the criminal if even the church were to reject him, as the civil law rejects him?

DARROW. But don't you see . . . civil law need *not* reject him! When men recover from the *obsession* that it is only *punishment* that keeps others from crime, they will be able to undertake the question of social order scientifically. They will accomplish *real* results without making a nightmare of life! There are more violations of law in America than in *any* European country. What is the remedy? Is it more and harder laws, or bigger and better *prisons,* or bigger and hotter frying pans on which to sizzle the victims of luck and chance?

MONTAIGNE. Certainly, harsher laws and punishments are not the answer. I rather sympathize with Artaxerxes who used to moderate the severity of the ancient laws of Persia by ordaining that when one of the nobility committed a crime, instead of being whipped, they were stripped and their clothing was whipped for them.

(*Ad-lib reaction.*)

DARROW. Those nobles got all the breaks, didn't they?

(*Laughter.*)

STEVE (*still chuckling*). Dr. Hegel.

HEGEL. Well, if I may be serious—getting back to the point. I do believe there have always been excesses in punishment. There have been times when the cruelty of man was ignited by suspicion and delusion. Beliefs about the devil, for example, occasioned an incalculable number of trials for witchcraft—not only in America, Mr. Darrow. It was impossible to prove the guilt of the accused; they were only *suspected.* In the sixteenth century this delusion raged like a pestilence. Torture was continued until a confession was extorted. If the accused *fainted* under the torture it was said that the *devil* was giving them *sleep*. If there were convulsions, it was said that the devil was laughing in them. If they held out steadfastly, the devil was supposed to be giving them power. But, and I think this is most important—*we may not cast aside law simply because it has been abused.*

STEVE. Dr. Freud.

FREUD. I suppose the time comes when every one of us has to abandon the illusory anticipations with which in our youth we regarded our fellow men and realize how much hardship and suffering we have been caused in life through their ill will. Civilization, therefore, expects to *prevent* the *worst* atrocities of brutal violence by taking upon *itself* the right to employ violence against criminals. Unfortunately, the law is *not able* to lay hands on the more *discreet* and *subtle* forms in which human aggressions are expressed. Men, let us be realistic, are *not* merely gentle, friendly creatures wishing for love, who simply defend themselves if attacked. A powerful measure of aggression has to be reckoned with as part of their *basic* instincts.

DOSTOEVSKI. Original sin.

FREUD. Whatever you choose to call it. The result is that their neighbor is to them not only a possible *helper* or sexual object, but also a *temptation* to them to gratify their aggressiveness on him, to *exploit* his capacity for work without pay, to seize his possessions, to cause him *pain*, to *kill* him. Anyone who calls to mind the invasion by the Huns or by the Mongols under Genghis Khan, or the sack of Jerusalem by the crusaders, even indeed the horrors of the World War, will have to bow his head humbly before the truth of this view of man.

ARISTOTLE. Is that not the more reason, Dr. Freud, for needing laws, and punishment *under* those laws? The law is valuable, in short, because it has a *compulsive* power, and when it ordains what is good, it's *not* burdensome.

HEGEL. Yes, including, if need be, capital punishment! I do not consider this excessive if justified.

(*Buzz.*)

DARROW. Well now, I simply cannot accept any justification for capital punishment. Are men kept from killing their fellows because they are afraid to kill? Everyone who kills, except those who kill in the heat of *passion*, prepares a way of *escape*. The killer *never* intends

to be caught, and often he is *not*. If the full *details* of execution.
could be vividly told—all normal human beings would be so
shocked as to get rid of the barbarism that inspires the desire to
have some unfortunate killed by the State.

DOSTOEVSKI. I still think the basic point about punishment from a State
of any kind, gentlemen, up to and including *capital* punishment
is that it is mechanical and in most cases, only *embitters* the criminal.

(*Buzz.*)

DARROW. Embitters him, hell. It kills him.

DOSTOEVSKI. Death is not the ultimate punishment, Mr. Darrow. The
recognition of sin by conscience. That is more painful.

(*Hubbub.*)

STEVE. Gentlemen—I'm afraid I have to step in here to tell you that—
although your time may not be up—ours is. We have just a few
moments left—and not nearly enough to get into the specific issue
of capital punishment. In the time we do have—do any of you have
any closing remarks—preferably *short* ones. (*Laughter*) Monsieur
Montaigne.

MONTAIGNE. Well, I would just like to quote Juvenal, who says, "The
main revenge is this: with himself as judge, no guilty man can
ever be absolved."

STEVE. Dr. Hegel.

HEGEL. Mr. Darrow to the contrary notwithstanding, I cannot retreat
from my basic position that there *is* such a thing as right conduct
that law is necessary and there can be no *effective* law without
punishment for those who *break* it.

STEVE. Mr. Darrow.

DARROW. I think the time has come to radically *reconsider* our ideas of
punishment. It is entirely possible, for example, that a person guilty
of homicide could safely be set free in a short time, and that a sneak
thief or a beggar could *never* be cured or released. To subject every
inmate of prisons to the same treatment is like giving every hospital patient the same surgical operation . . . and however absurd
this might seem to those who do not *think*, the time *will come* when
something like this will take the place of the archaic and pernicious
system that has long been outworn.

DOSTOEVSKI. *Not* without religion.

(*Hubbub*)

DARROW (*with a sigh*). Mr. Dostoevski, the defense rests.

(*Laughter.*)

STEVE. The Honorable Aristotle.

ARISTOTLE. What Mr. Darrow asks for is equity in the law, and that is always possible—and desirable—in a good society.

MONTAIGNE. But society, like life as a whole, is neither good nor evil in itself; it is the *scene* of good *and* evil according as you give them room. Therefore, I believe that all things are achievable by a man who in general is very imperfect and defective. For this reason, to judge a man really *properly*, we must chiefly examine his *ordinary* everyday actions.

FREUD. And know *ourselves* as we judge.

STEVE. Gentlemen, I'm afraid our time is up. To all of you, for the ideas presented here tonight—and those you've passed down to us from the centuries, we humbly thank you.

This has been a program called Meeting of Minds. The participants have been: Aristotle, Michel de Montaigne, George Hegel, Fyodor Dostoevski, Sigmund Freud and Clarence Darrow. . . .

Questions

1. What might be some of the reasons for presenting a radio symposium like this one? Who is the author of the script and what do you know about him?
2. What were the occupations of the participants in this discussion—Aristotle, Montaigne, Hegel, Dostoevski, Freud, and Darrow? What purpose is served by bringing them together for a discussion?
3. How do Aristotle and Dostoevski differ on the concept of responsibility for criminal behavior? Are their differences significant?
4. Does Montaigne's attitude toward crime and punishment place him closer to Hegel or Dostoevski? Explain.
5. How do the attitudes of Freud and Dostoevski seem similar? How are they different?
6. How do Aristotle and Freud conceive of punishment? Are there any fundamental differences in their points of view? Explain.
7. Darrow and Hegel quarrel about the terms *revenge, vengeance,* and *punishment.* What are the connotations of these words? Does Hegel accept Darrow's definitions? Are the differences between these two primarily a matter of words? Explain.
8. Both Darrow and Dostoevski object to punishment of the criminal by the state. In what ways do they disagree?

THE PERPETUATION OF OUR AMERICAN HERITAGE*

J. Edgar Hoover

[1] My pleasure in being with you today is marred by the realization that our Nation must still engage in a struggle to maintain the peace. Our military might must be maintained if America is to remain the land of the free and the home of the brave. And our home front must remain secure.

[2] Communist subversion and defiance of the law threaten the very foundations of our society. Perhaps to some this may be considered a "cold" war but, in reality, it is an exceedingly "hot" one. It is tragic that too many of our people are not taking the danger signals seriously. . . .

[3] We need to dedicate ourselves anew to the perpetuation of our American heritage, and to a nationwide recognition campaign to bring about a renewed appreciation of this heart-stirring heritage. It is disheartening that more young people appear to know the words of popular "soap-jingles" than the meaningful words of "The Star-Spangled Banner." It is time for all of us to reacquaint ourselves with our historical treasures and the moral values which inspired our forefathers to lead our country to the pinnacle of world leadership.

[4] Eleven years ago, when I last had the pleasure of attending a National Convention of your organization, our country had just emerged victorious from a devastating world conflict. As we then turned our attention to the problems confronting our Nation, we observed the rapidly growing, menacing two-headed monster of subversion and lawlessness. We recall that during the year 1946, 1,685,203 major crimes were reported by local, county and state law enforcement agencies in this country. In January, 1947, Communist Party membership in the United States was recorded as 74,000.

[5] Since 1946, we have made tremendous forward strides in many fields. Our technological achievements stagger the imagination. Let us, however, examine our progress with regard to other problems which confronted us in that period.

[6] Look at your watch as it ticks off 12 seconds. In that span a major crime has been committed somewhere in the United States.

[7] Last year a shocking total of 2,563,150 major crimes was reported by the Nation's police. The number is increasing this year. Actual Communist Party membership has declined. Thus, with an estimated popu-

* From *Vital Speeches of the Day*, October 1, 1957. Reprinted by permission.

lation increase during the past eleven years of some thirty million people, it would appear that we are losing the fight on crime and winning the battle against subversion. I assure you, nothing could be further from the truth. To give up in the war on crime or to ease up in the battle against subversion will bring national disaster.

.   .   .   .

[8] Daily, news reports remind us of the rampaging reign of lawlessness and, particularly, of the shameful juvenile crime picture expanding throughout the Nation. Not only has the number of juvenile offenders increased tremendously but so has the viciousness of their crimes. The harmless prank has given way to the premeditated act of violence. Disrespect for lawful authority has blossomed into complete disregard for the individual rights of others.

[9] Shockingly, arrests of persons under 18 years of age increased more than 17 per cent in cities during 1956, while the increase in population of this group was only about 3 per cent. Furthermore, almost 46 per cent of all arrests for major crimes in the United States were of youngsters under 18. This group, for example, accounted for more than 66 per cent of all auto theft arrests. They are no longer bad children; they are young criminals and must be dealt with accordingly.

[10] One cannot help but admire the overwhelming majority of our young people, particularly when the number and nature of the evil forces confronting them in their day-to-day living is considered. The wholesome majority of the youth of this country merit congratulations and encouragement. They, unfortunately must suffer the disgrace and shame brought down upon their age group by the relatively small percentage of youth who have become enmeshed in the tangled web of crime.

[11] The peddlers of obscene pictures and writings have so flooded the market with this toxic trash within the past few years that to find a news rack without samples of it is the rare exception.

.   .   .   .

[12] An aroused public is necessary—one that will not countenance the placing of this trash on public display. Parents and other guardians of the young must be aware of what is being read by those in their care. Guidance and concern for a child's mental and spiritual development are just as important as regard for its bodily needs. Stiffer legal penalties, particularly in local and state courts, are needed to replace the frequent wrist slap given those convicted of this vile trade. Not until longer sentences and heavier fines remove the financial advantages of this traffic will the producers, distributors and dealers of filth be driven out of this sickening business.

[13] There is today a vicious movement to undermine the traditional spiritual and moral principles of our Nation. Freedom, divorced from authority and discipline, is a frightening thing and is the first step toward total moral degeneration.

[14] The term "juvenile delinquency" is, of course, a misnomer. The large majority of cases involving juveniles have exhibited that the real delinquency originates in the home. Parental delinquency would certainly be a more descriptive term. To salvage our youth is the responsibility of adult America—it is inescapable, and we must turn our faces to it, not our backs.

[15] It is my firm conviction that only when the family returns to living as a unit will we be moving in the proper social direction. Millions of words have been written and spoken on this subject. The time for definite action is long overdue. Any lasting corrective steps will have to begin at the cornerstone of our society—the home. The child with a secure, happy, religious home rarely becomes delinquent. The youngsters whose parents care enough about them to be interested in their activities are not found in the juvenile courts and correctional institutions.

.   .   .   .

[16] We must pass on to our young people the greatness that is America's. We must remind all of our citizens of the wealth of our Nation's moral and spiritual treasures. By reflecting upon the glories of our past, we can advance together to even greater heights of achievement in the future. We can eradicate the blighting slums of juvenile crime and repel, by our own example of united strength, the threats of subversive destruction. In moral and spiritual issues, there can be no neutrality.

[17] An informed citizenry, alert to guard our heritage, will guarantee strengthened sinews and heightened resolve that our flag on high will never be replaced with the butcher-red emblem of barbarous, godless communist slavery. Ours must ever be the glorious red, white and blue symbol of American freedom and liberty. . . .

Questions

1. What is J. Edgar Hoover's purpose in using the following phrases: "if America is to remain the land of the free and the home of the brave," "to dedicate ourselves anew to the perpetuation of our American heritage," "to bring about a renewed appreciation of this heart-stirring heritage," and "to reacquaint ourselves with our historical treasures"?
2. In paragraphs 4, 6, and 7, Hoover gives us specific data. According to this data, what inferences might you draw about the growth of major crimes? Do the data prove that crime is increasing? Are other hypotheses possible?

3. While Hoover supplies Communist Party membership figures for 1947, he merely says that by 1957 the "Communist Party membership has declined," while population has increased by "some thirty million people." In the light of Hoover's judgment about the dangers of Communist subversion, why do you suppose no particular figures are supplied for 1957? Does the numerical decline support his judgment? Explain.

4. Hoover supplies statistics on juvenile crime and indicates that juveniles "are young criminals and must be dealt with accordingly." Why does he shift from the term *bad children* to the phrase *young criminals*?

5. What assumption does Hoover make about the results of "stiffer legal penalties"? Does he supply supporting evidence for this assumption?

6. One solution proposed by Hoover is the return of the family "to living as a unit." What assumption does he make? Is his judgment supported? What other judgments appear in the same paragraph (15)? Are they supported by evidence?

7. Analyze the emotional tone of the language in the last two paragraphs. How do you explain Hoover's use of this language?

THE LUXURY OF PUNISHMENT*

Gresham M. Sykes

. . . Recent events suggest a resurgence of the urge to get tough, to crack down on delinquency and crime. In Delaware, the only state in which public flogging is permissible as a penalty for crime, the legislature has tried to pass a bill making it not only permissible but mandatory. J. Edgar Hoover has just warned us that we must stop pampering juvenile delinquents; a number of officials have declared that killing the dope peddler is the only safe course; the U.S. Attorney General has expressed his desire for another Alcatraz. The "give 'em hell" school of penology, in short, seems due once again for a burst of popularity.

This recurrent cry for a crackdown is, of course, not confined to our handling of the criminal. There are periodic attacks on the frightful extravagance of government bureaucrats, the shocking rise in the divorce rate, the bad manners of modern youth—and, perhaps most notably, the alleged failure of our educational system. The solution for our social problems, we are told, is to find the individual villains in the piece and force them to return to the proven verities.

Why do these demands for a crackdown come and go? It may be that something really is rotten and since a consistently high level of indignation is hard to maintain, we get it in cycles. And it may be that the campaign for a crackdown is a pretty safe bandwagon; nobody is likely

* From *The Nation*, July 18, 1959. Copyright © 1959 by The Nation Associates, Inc. Reprinted by permission.

to get into trouble asking why Johnny can't read or lambasting the sins of bureaucracy. But in the case of crime and delinquency something more seems to be at work. There is a harshly punitive attitude toward the offender which has never vanished from our thinking and which periodically flares out under the stimulus of a particularly savage crime, a dramatic violation of parole, or a rebellion of prisoners. It is this readiness to respond with an emotional outburst which led Professor Robert Park to say a number of years ago, "We are always passing laws in America. We might as well get up and dance. The laws are largely to relieve emotions, and the legislatures are quite aware of that fact."

The trouble with these cyclical get-tough campaigns is that they represent a denial of experience, an escape from rationality—like kicking the cat in a moment of anger. However emotionally satisfying they may be, they obscure the real problem, namely the reduction of crime and delinquency; and the public is blinded to the advances we have made in techniques for handling the criminal.

We have come a long way from the early tradition of extreme harshness toward the offender—from, let us say, 1584, when it was decreed that the murderer of William of Orange should have his "right hand . . . burned off with a red-hot iron, that the flesh be torn from the bones in six different places with pincers, that he be quartered and disemboweled alive," and finally, "as a gesture of infinite mercy," he was to be killed. Mutilation, beating, branding, boiling, beheading—all have slowly been abandoned. If for nothing else, I suppose, we must admire our predecessors for their ingenuity in devising ways to inflict pain on their fellow men. But in any event, by the end of the seventeenth century the more sadistic and brutal forms of punishment had been largely replaced by imprisonment. . . .

There are many people who now believe that only under very limited conditions is punishment effective as a means of preventing crime. First, punishment must be commensurate with the crime, for otherwise it breeds a sense of martyrdom and resentment which encourages new illegal acts. Second, punishment must be both quick and certain, if it is to serve as a realistic deterrent. Third, punishment must stand as a symbol of the ethical condemnation of society and not as a personal gesture of retaliation. Fourth, punishment imposed by the legal system must be in accord with the values of society at large. And fifth, the psychology of the criminal act must be such that the theat of punishment has an opportunity to enter the individual's motivational structure.

We know, in reality, that these conditions are seldom met. Arbitrary sentencing procedures break down any neat equation between crime and punishment. Both the deliberate and unintentional inefficiences of our legal system create a situation in which punishment is neither quick nor certain; it has been estimated that for every one hundred major crimes committed in the United States each year, less than five persons are sent to prison. Public disparagement and suspicion of law-enforcement agencies undermines much of the ethical quality of punishment. Legal morality and popular morality are frequently in conflict. And the impulsive or unconscious motivation of much criminal behavior frequently renders punishment irrelevant.

Even if the necessary conditions for punishment's effectiveness were met, it is still doubtful if punishment is the best way to reduce crime and delinquency. Punishment, under ideal conditions, may deter some potential offenders. But we have come to realize that a society in which men conform to the law through fear is hardly preferable to a society in which the only answer to the deviant is revenge. The best objective —for practical reasons if for no other—is rehabilitation, the transformation of the offender to a point where he willingly follows the dictates of the law. Punishment, in short, may be a luxury that we can ill afford, for you seldom inculcate a love of virtue by hitting a man in the face. . . .

Questions

1. Sykes suggests that the "get tough" attitude in respect to crime also recurs in attacks on "extravagance" in government, the rise in divorce rates, and "the alleged failure of our educational system." Have you encountered articles on these subjects that seemed to suggest a related pattern? Explain.
2. Why does Sykes use the word *alleged* in the phrase given above?
3. Sykes says that in the case of crime, there is "a harshly punitive attitude toward the offender which has never vanished from our thinking." How does he explain this "punitive attitude"? Does he approve of it?
4. Sykes says that many people think that punishment is effective only under "very limited conditions," which he describes in detail. Does he identify these people? Why or why not? Why does he describe the "very limited conditions" in such detail?
5. He adds that these "limited conditions" are rarely met. Does he support this assertion?
6. What assumptions does Sykes make about his readers? Does his language suggest that he expects them to bring some knowledge to this essay?
7. What is the purpose of the reference to 1584 and the murderer of William of Orange? Is this section of the article effective? Explain.
8. Why does Sykes use the word *revenge* in his last paragraph?

From CRIME, ITS CAUSE AND TREATMENT*

Clarence Darrow

[1] The church has constantly taught from the first that God would punish the sinner with everlasting torment. It has taught that all are bad from birth and can be saved only by grace. The punishment to be suffered was as terrible as man's mind could conceive. It would continue infinitely beyond the time when it might be needed for correction or example. In spite of a few humane or over-sensitive ministers, the doctrine persists and is carefully preserved by the church. That the State likewise holds fast to the idea of vengeance, punishment for the sake of suffering, is just as evident. One needs only to note the force and degree of hatred of the good to the one accused of crime, and the zeal that is shown for a man hunt, to realize how deeply the feeling of vengeance is planted in the structure of man. The truth is that it was a part of life before religion and political institutions were evolved.

[2] Still, most people are now ashamed to admit that punishment is based on vengeance and, for that reason, various excuses and apologies have been offered for the cruelty that goes with it. Some of the more humane, or "squeamish," who still believe in punishment, contend that the object of this infliction is the reformation of the victim. This, of course, cannot be urged of the death penalty or even punishment for life, or for very long-term sentences. In these cases there is neither inducement to reform nor any object in the reformation. No matter how thorough the reform, the prisoner never goes back to society, or he returns after there is no longer a chance for him to be of use to the world or to enjoy life.

[3] Those who say that punishment is for the purpose of reforming the prisoner are not familiar with human psychology. The prison almost invariably tends to brutalize men and breeds bitterness and blank despair. The life of the ordinary prisoner is given over to criticism and resentment against existing things, especially to settled hatred of those who are responsible for his punishment. Only a few, and these are the weakest, ever blame themselves for their situation. Every man of intelligence can trace the various steps that led him to the prison door, and he can feel, if he does not understand, how inevitable each step was. The number of "repeaters" in prison shows the effect of this kind

* From Clarence Darrow, *Crime, Its Cause and Treatment.* Copyright 1922 by Thomas Y. Crowell Co. Reprinted by permission

of a living death upon the inmates. To be branded as a criminal and turned out in the world again leaves one weakened in the struggle of life and handicapped in a race that is hard enough for most men at the best. In prison and after leaving prison, the man lives in a world of his own; a world where all moral values are different from those professed by the jailer and society in general. The great influence that helps to keep many men from committing crime—the judgment of his fellows— no longer deters him in his conduct. In fact, every person who understands penal institutions—no matter how well such places are managed —knows that a thousand are injured or utterly destroyed by service in prison, where one is helped.

[4] Very few persons seriously believe that offenders are sent to prison out of kindness to the men. If there were any foundation for this idea, each prisoner would be carefully observed, and when he was fit would be returned to the world. Not even the parole laws, which provide various reasons and ways for shortening sentences, ever lay down the rule that one may be released when he has reformed.

[5] A much larger class of people offers the excuse that punishment deters from crime. In fact, this idea is so well rooted that few think of questioning it. The idea that punishment deters from crime does not mean that the individual prisoner is prevented from another criminal act. A convicted man is kept in jail for as long a time as in the judgment of the jury, the court, or the parole board, will make him atone, or at least suffer sufficiently for the offence. If the terms are not long enough, they can be made longer. The idea that punishment deters, means that unless A shall be punished for murder, then B will kill; therefore A must be punished, not for his own sake, but to keep B from crime. This is vicarious punishment which can hardly appeal to one who is either just or humane. But does punishing A keep B from the commission of crime? It certainly does not make a more social man of B. If it operates on him in any way it is to make him afraid to commit crime; but the direct result of scaring B is not to keep him from the commission of crime, but to make him use precautions that will keep him safe from discovery. How far the fear of detection and punishment prevents crime is, of course, purely theoretical and cannot be settled either by statistics or logic. One thing is sure, that if B is kept from crime, it is through fear, and of all the enemies of man, fear is the one which causes most misery and pain.

[6] There are many facts that show that the punishment of one does not deter others. Over and over again crimes are committed, by the young especially, that resemble in every detail a previous crime which

has received large publicity through the newspapers, often through the hanging of some culprit. Even the unthinking public, always clamoring for severe penalties, does not believe that the example of punishment deters. The public forbids the exhibition of pictures of hangings and of crimes. Somehow, vaguely and dimly as most men see everything, the public realizes that instead of punishments preventing crime, punishments suggest crime. In the olden days when men admitted that vengeance and punishment went together, they were at least more logical, for executions were in the open light of day so all might see and be deterred.

Questions

1. Darrow suggests that the concept of punishment is fostered by the church. Does he document his observation in this excerpt? Explain.
2. Darrow says that people would be "ashamed to admit that punishment is based on vengeance." If this is true, how do you explain it? Is the word *vengeance* likely to be used by those favoring punishment? Explain.
3. In his third paragraph Darrow uses a psychological series of reasons for indicting prisons. Does he support his judgments with concrete data?
4. Assess the merit of Darrow's logic in the A and B illustration in paragraph 5.
5. Darrow argues that punishment does not deter people from crimes. He cites the secrecy of executions as an example of his opponent's failure of logic: if punishment deters, why keep extreme punishments secret? Evaluate Darrow's argument.
6. Darrow suggests that the concept of punishment as a deterrent to crime is "so well rooted that few think of questioning it." Does his statement apply accurately to you? to others you know? Explain.

GIVING THEM HELL*

George Bernard Shaw

. . . When people are at last compelled to think about what they are doing to our unfortunate convicts, they think so unsuccessfully and confusedly that they only make matters worse. Take for example the official list of the results aimed at by the Prison Commissioners. First, imprisonment must be "retributory" (the word vindictive is not in official use). Second, it must be deterrent. Third, it must be reformative.

* From George Bernard Shaw, *The Crime of Imprisonment*. Copyright 1946 by The Philosophical Library, Inc. Reprinted by permission.

Now, if you are to punish a man retributively, you must injure him. If you are to reform him, you must improve him. And men are not improved by injuries. To propose to punish and reform people by the same operation is exactly as if you were to take a man suffering from pneumonia, and attempt to combine punitive and curative treatment. Arguing that a man with pneumonia is a danger to the community, and that he need not catch it if he takes proper care of his health, you resolve that he shall have a severe lesson, both to punish him for his negligence and pulmonary weakness and to deter others from following his example. You therefore strip him naked, and in that condition stand him all night in the snow. But as you admit the duty of restoring him to health if possible, and discharging him with sound lungs, you engage a doctor to superintend the punishment and administer cough lozenges, made as unpleasant to the taste as possible so as not to pamper the culprit. A Board of Commissioners ordering such treatment would prove thereby that either they were imbeciles or else they were hotly in earnest about punishing the patient and not in the least in earnest about curing him.

When our Prison Commissioners pretend to combine punishment with moral reformation they are in the same dilemma. We are told that the reformation of the criminal is kept constantly in view; yet the destruction of the prisoner's self-respect by systematic humiliation is deliberately ordered and practised; and we learn from a chaplain that he "does not think it is good to give opportunity for the exercise of Christian and social virtues one towards another" among prisoners. The only consolation for such contradictions is their demonstration that, as the tormentors instinctively feel that they must be liars and hypocrites on the subject, their consciences cannot be very easy about the torment. But the contradictions are obvious here only because I put them on the same page. The Prison Commissioners keep them a few pages apart; and the average reader's memory, it seems, is not long enough to span the gap when his personal interests are not at stake.

Questions

1. Why does Shaw use the parenthetical statement "the word vindictive is not in official use" in his opening paragraph?
2. How effective is Shaw's analogy in the second paragraph?
3. What does Shaw assume is the primary motive of the Prison Commissioners, retribution or reformation? Does he equate *retribution* and *punishment*? Are these words synonymous? What differences do they have in connotation?
4. Why does Shaw quote the chaplain in the last paragraph? Does the quotation effectively support Shaw's contentions? Explain.

5. Shaw indicates that he has telescoped—brought into close proximity—ideas which were separated in the Prison Commissioners' arguments. Why does he do so? Is this a legitimate technique? Do you accept his reasons? Explain.

REHABILITATION*

David Abrahamsen

[1] . . . statistics prove that in recent years fewer people are being sent to state and federal prisons than ever before in spite of the rise in population and the rise in crime, which obviously reflects a more enlightened view on the part of many of our judges. Still, in many cases when we don't know how to deal with an offender, we tend to put him in prison simply to get him out of the way.

[2] To be blunt, our prisons are failures. This is obvious when we take note of the large number of recidivists among offenders who have been imprisoned. According to Sellin's study for the American Law Institute, 50.5 percent of males committed to prisons in certain selected areas had been institutionalized before in penal institutions. Then too Glueck's study of 1,000 juvenile delinquents during the first five years after they were released from a penal institution indicated that 85.4 percent manifested recidivism. James V. Bennett, Director of the Federal Bureau of Prisons, made a statement in 1949 that approximately 60 percent of all the men released from prisons throughout the country returned again within a period of five years. Nathaniel Showstack stated that in 1955 84 percent of the men in California state prisons had been sentenced to prison or jail previously and that 70 percent of the men executed at San Quentin were recidivists.

[3] Of course, prison incarceration to some extent is a deterrent to crime in that it keeps the offender out of society for the time being. However, as conditions now are, this is probably its only virtue.

[4] The threat of punishment does not prevent a man from killing, robbing, raping, or committing any other crime. When a person commits a crime, he does not think of the consequences. The offender commits a crime because criminality is his particular outlet, just as the seriously mentally ill person's outlet is a psychosis. This is why the argument for the maintenance of capital punishment on the grounds

* From David Abrahamsen, *The Psychology of Crime*. Copyright © 1960 by David Abrahamsen. Published by Columbia University Press. Reprinted by permission of the author.

that fear of the death penalty will keep a potential murderer from committing his crime is invalid. . . .

[5] The principal considerations in dealing with an offender must be his particular personality make-up and the degree of danger he represents to himself and to society.

[6] . . . what actually happens is that all types of offenders—murderers, robbers, kleptomaniacs, embezzlers, exhibitionists, rapists, etc. —are indiscriminately thrown together in the same prison. This would not be so serious if they were given individualized treatment. But they are not. In fact, often no treatment at all is given. Only when the offender is obviously psychotic is he transferred to another institution to receive psychiatric help.

[7] . . . Although it strikes us as senseless and cruel to put a patient suffering from infantile paralysis in a hospital and then let him lie there without treatment, somehow it does not strike us as quite so illogical to do the same with a person who needs help just as desperately but on an emotional level.

[8] Psychiatric-psychological studies indicate that a large number of prisoners are emotionally or mentally disturbed. In fact, many of them commit crimes because of unconscious guilt feelings, which lead them to strive for punishment. Imprisonment without psychiatric treatment fulfills this very aim; thereby the law is unwittingly helping the offender obtain gratification for his unhealthy needs. It becomes a pattern, and when this type of offender is released, he does something wrong again, for which he has guilt feelings, so he commits another crime, back to prison and punishment—a vicious circle.

[9] Back in 1888, at the first meeting of the International Association of Criminal Law, it was maintained that punishment had to be adapted according to the type of offender. The aim of this new idea was to fight the principle of retaliation and to satisfy the demand for an effective prevention of crime. The Association also asserted that the protection of society from crime lay in determining how dangerous the offender was rather than the seriousness of his crime. It went further by saying that with this in mind, stronger penalties would be inflicted on habitual and dangerous offenders than on the great number of occasional and less dangerous ones. The more dangerous offenders would thereby be restricted from committing new crimes, while the less dangerous would be enabled to return to society and receive treatment outside of prison. The basis for classifying offenders according to the degree of their danger to society would rest on an evaluation of both their ingrained criminalistic tendencies and the social conditions under which their

offenses were committed. This revolutionary view of the criminal law, which embodied a new scientific concept of crime, had healthy repercussions in penal codes throughout Europe and later in America. Examination of the records of prisoners shows that only about 20 to 25 percent are dangerous and therefore in need of confinement in a maximum security prison. It seems a gross injustice to keep the large remaining number of nondangerous offenders there merely to retain these 25 percent within walls. If all prisoners were psychiatrically examined and classified, the remaining 75 percent might very well be placed in a rehabilitation center instead, where they would be treated and reeducated by individual and group therapy, according to their specific needs, until they could be returned to society.

[10] Logic would thus seem to tell us that our present system of definite sentences without treatment should be replaced by an indefinite term, with rehabilitation as the aim. As our system is today, an offender serves a certain length of time in prison without treatment and then is released and put into society, where he can commit more crimes, often of a worse nature. Many times he comes out a more hardened criminal than when he went in because he has an "ax to grind" at having been caught and incarcerated. More bitterness is therefore added to his other personality difficulties.

[11] The public in general turns its back upon men and women in prisons, and it only focuses its attention there when there are black headlines in the newspapers about a prison break or riot. But those of us who have spent time working with offenders in prisons are shocked by the waste of human material and human happiness. Not to speak of the mismanagement and neglect we see in many institutions here and abroad, how can one human being see another rotting in prison and, practically speaking, do nothing about it? So ingrained are the retaliatory principles that man not only demands that the offender be imprisoned, but also forgets about him once he is there. . . .

Questions

1. What connection does Abrahamsen see between recidivism and the use of prisons as a deterrent to crime?
2. Abrahamsen believes our prisons are failures. Does he support that belief with evidence? Is his evidence substantial? Explain.
3. Why does Abrahamsen use the "patient" analogy in paragraph 7? Is his illustration effective? Explain.
4. Abrahamsen indicates that "a large number of prisoners are emotionally or mentally disturbed" (paragraph 8). Does he support this assertion? Might a high rate of recidivism support this opinion? Are other hypotheses possible to explain recidivism? Explain.

5. Abrahamsen introduces the concept of maximum-security prisons. What does he think about such institutions? Why does he bring up this subject? Does he have any evidence for his beliefs?
6. What major assumption does Abrahamsen make about the purpose of sentencing? Does his concern with rehabilitation affect his attitudes toward prisons? Explain.
7. What psychological point does Abrahamsen imply in his last sentence?

DOES THE PRISON REFORM?[*]

George P. Vold

[1] The transition from the idea of imprisonment as a form of punishment to one of imprisonment as a device for the reformation of criminals constitutes a large chapter in the history of penology that need not be reviewed here. It should be noted, however, that always there has been the persisting problem of repeaters in crime. Undoubtedly the failure of the system of increasing severity of punishments, both corporal and institutional, to control recidivism had a considerable part in bringing about the so-called reformatory movement.

[2] It is a well-established fact that the savage punishments of earlier days were notoriously ineffective in keeping those punished from repeating their misconduct. . . .

[3] This present-day emphasis on the need for the rehabilitation of criminals makes the question of whether prisons do accomplish reformation one of crucial importance for modern penology. For the past several decades the prison—that historic institution that whatever else it sought to do must always guarantee the secure confinement of its inmates—has been the central unit or principal device for the implementation of whatever "treatment" our society has sought to carry out on its convicted offenders. As such it is the visible symbol of the entire penal system. If the prison fails to reform, then it follows as a necessary logical inference that the present penal system, as a whole, fails in any major accomplishment of its declared purpose and objective.

[4] Enthusiasm for the ideal of reformation as the objective of penal practice must not be permitted to color judgments about actual accomplishments in the realization of the ideal. If reformation is taking place, it should be apparent in terms of factual data about those involved in

* From *The Annals of the American Academy of Political and Social Science,* May, 1954. Copyright 1954 by The American Academy of Political and Social Science. Reprinted by permission.

crime and subjected to penal treatment. Information about the outcome of prison treatment must be examined with impersonal objectivity regardless of whether it gives comfort to or tends to discourage belief in the reformation ideal.

[5] Two general kinds of source materials are available that throw some light on the principal problem, namely, information about recidivism, that is, the failure to reform, and information about positive accomplishment, the story of those who have changed from criminality to noncriminality. The principal sources and indications, including some tending in both directions, will be summarized in the sections that follow. . . .

Table 1—Per Cent of All Arrests Reported to the FBI That Had Criminal Fingerprint Records Already on File

Year	Per Cent
1937	42.4
1938	44.0
1939	45.4
1940	50.0
1941	51.2
1942	49.1
1943	47.7
1944	49.3
1945	51.9
1946	54.2
1947	55.4
1948	58.0
1949	59.3
1950	60.2
1951	60.2
1952	60.6

Source: United States Department of Justice, *Uniform Crime Reports*, Washington, D.C., Annual Bulletins for the years indicated.

[6] It is still impossible to demonstrate statistically that reformation, when it occurs, is due to institutional treatment. Penology, in this sense, is in the same boat with medicine. When a sick patient recovers it is always somewhat problematical whether the recovery was brought about by the treatment prescribed, or whether the patient possessed recuperative powers and got well in spite of treatment. When the patient dies there is no question about failure of treatment, but when he recovers the situation is much less clear. Failure to achieve reformation

can be demonstrated—the inmate returns to crime and in due season comes back to the prison for postgraduate treatment. But for the one who does not come back—did he change his behavior because of prison training and treatment or in spite of it? No information now available can give any serious scientific answer to that problem.

[7] It is a basic fallacy of the sentimental approach to rehabilitation to assume that every inmate committed to prison constitutes an equally good prospect for rehabilitation. Actually, some are very poor risks while others are relatively much more promising prospects. Whether one views the apparent preponderance of recidivists in prison as an indication of failure to accomplish reformation or places the emphasis on the smaller segment successfully salvaged from further criminality seems to be largely a matter of temperament and point of view.

[8] The fact that from 20 to 40 per cent or more of offenders do not repeat their misconduct in such ways as to be returned to prison is of tremendous significance in view of the long chain of factors, involving all kinds of negative selection, that precede commitment to a penal institution. All recidivism studies show considerable proportions who did not recidivate. In the more careful follow-up studies this fact has been verified through elaborate individual case study.

[9] Thus the Glueck reformatory series revealed that a total of 140 cases out of an initial 417 achieved reformation in the sense of nondelinquency for fifteen years after release from the institution. This is approximately one-third of the whole group and should not be dismissed as insignificant.[1]

[10] All responsible prison administrators, parole agents, and others who have worked directly and intimately with the criminals in prison know, through personal knowledge of after-conduct, of numerous individual cases of whom it may truthfully be said that reformation has taken place—be it because of or in spite of prison experience.

[11] The conclusion is inescapable that some reformation or rehabilitation does take place in the course of present penal treatment procedures. Whether the proportion reformed represents all that possibly can be done is quite another matter. Presumably no type of treatment would rehabilitate 100 per cent of prison inmates. How increase the proportion who are reformed or rehabilitated? Suggestions for some more adequate answers to that question will have to come from other considerations than attention to recidivism per se.

[1] Sheldon and Eleanor T. Glueck, *Criminal Careers in Retrospect* (New York: The Commonwealth Fund, 1943), p. 121.

Questions

1. The May, 1954, issue of *The Annals of the American Academy of Political and Social Science*, from which this excerpt was taken, was devoted entirely to problems about crime and punishment and related areas. Since this is true, why does Vold write his first paragraph as he does? What basic assumptions has he made?
2. Evaluate the tone of paragraph 3. Does it sound like an impassioned appeal to emotion? How would you characterize it?
3. What is the purpose of Vold's fourth paragraph? Explain.
4. Vold uses statistical information about recidivism. What major conclusions does he draw from his statistical data?
5. Why does Vold use the sick patient analogy?
6. What is suggested about Vold's attitude toward rehabilitation in his opening sentence of paragraph 7?
7. Why does Vold make reference to "negative selection" in paragraph 8?
8. How would you assess paragraph 10? Is Vold ardent in championing prison effectiveness? Is he cautious about generalizing?
9. What does Vold imply in the last paragraph? Explain.

THE MAN AND THE MASK*

George Putnam

[1] . . . When crime and delinquency increase, it serves no good purpose to become indignant, or strike out at our kids. It's like breaking the mirror into which we're looking because we don't like the reflection we see. We're not going to instill in our children good concepts of sound citizenship by spasmodically preaching it. We're going to have to consistently practice it, for we see the future when we look into the faces of our children. We create it day by day right in our own homes. . . .

[2] Citizenship is not a *negative* something that can be forced into a person by fear—it is a *positive* something that must be built into the structure of each individual. . . .

[3] It seems to me that now more than ever before in our history, one is either *for* law enforcement—or he's *against* it. He's either *for* mob rule—or he's *for* the law. He either *loves* a cop—or he *hates* him.

[4] Who's opposed to law enforcement? A simple answer—the obvious answer—a coalition of racketeers, the Mafia, and the Communists. This is the *underworld*. But they could not exist for a fleeting moment

---

* Speech delivered by George Putnam before the California Peace Officers' Fortieth Annual Convention, Santa Monica, California, May 18, 1960. Reprinted by permission.

were they not sustained by what I choose to call the *overworld*—the shadow government—the so-called nice people who condone, or secretly deal with, these rotten elements. . . .

[5] We are surrounded by people who have lost faith in accepted principles—a group of political and economic evangelists, preaching collectivism and atheistic materialism. They are bent on the destruction of our Constitution, our Bill of Rights, our heritage. They are debunkers of what they call the "myths" of our great national heroes. They endeavor to drag the heroes of our past down to their *own* level of mediocrity, in order to feel at least equal, if not superior, to them. They condone *any* and *all* behavior. They battle for what they choose to call "freedom"—a catch-all label to cover self-indulgence!

[6] We witness a fantastic concentration on the rights of the individual; be he rapist, murderer, dope peddler, kidnaper—to the almost complete disregard of the rights of the vast majority of law abiding citizens. When will we learn that for every freedom and right enjoyed by us, there is a corresponding ratio of responsibility—responsibility to ourselves, our fellow man, and to our nation. Freedom is not a *sometime* thing. Freedom is to be *lived,* to be *fought* for, and if need be, to *die* for.

[7] But can there be liberty where there is no law? Can there be liberty where there is no respect for human rights, where justice cannot be invoked both for the *security* of society and the *punishment* of its criminals? Can freedom and liberty exist where there is no conscience in the individual, or in the community? If this republic could not endure half slave and half free, can it then endure half law-abiding and half lawless?

[8] There is a growing lack of respect for all law and social controls. It's time we search our souls to determine what we are doing in a positive way to eliminate these evils. It is time we place the responsibility of the individual *with* the individual!

[9] I swear to you, we are concentrating on shielding the criminal, on commiserating with the guilty! We are blaming their anti-social acts on environment, broken homes, a sub-economic condition. It's time we stop apologizing for the guilty, and begin protecting and shedding a few tears for the innocent victim.

[10] The exponents of commiseration and condonation have had a field day during this period since World War I. Let's begin to make parents criminally responsible for the criminal acts of their children, and let's amend our laws to reduce the age of responsibility to sixteen years—to deal not with juveniles, but young adult hoodlums—for that is what they are. . . .

[11] Let's take a look at our own state. Since 1956, law enforcement officers of the State of California, its counties, cities, and smallest hamlets, have been handcuffed by a series of decisions rendered in the courts, and kept in effect by those who appear hell bent on protecting the criminal. It has developed a revolving door policy in the treatment of our criminals. Short sentences, with judges handing out the minimum, rather than the maximum—probation, parole, and, superimposed on all this, the Adult Authority possessing powers greater than any court.

[12] In 1957, 369 first-degree robbers were paroled. The sentence for this offense is five years to life. Only ten served over 62 months, and most of them served exactly three years.

[13] In narcotics offenses, 523 males were paroled in 1957. The median time served was only two and a half years.

[14] It is my conclusion that prison terms in California are so short, they are not feared by criminals and do not serve as effective deterrents to crime.

[15] I question the Adult Authority in its handling of parole. They are being entirely too lenient. Statistics show that by the end of the third year after parole, 48.6 percent of the parolees have incurred suspension of their paroles because of violations. Most of these consist of new criminal conduct.

[16] Certainty of penalty is a deterrent to crime! I remain in favor of stiff sentences, including capital punishment. The latter, certainly, until we are better able to ascertain those who will be good rehabilitative risks, or until life imprisonment *without* parole means what it says. . . .

Questions

1. Why does Putnam link "crime" and "delinquency" in the opening sentence?
2. Putnam says in paragraph 2 that "Citizenship is not a *negative* something that can be forced into a person by fear." How does this statement compare with his statement in paragraph 14 about current prison terms not being "feared by criminals" and therefore not serving as effective deterrents?
3. Analyze the thought process used by Putnam in the third paragraph. What assumption is he making? Is the assumption justified? Explain.
4. Putnam has a simple solution to the question about who is responsible for crime. Does he support his opinion? Explain.
5. Who are the villains of our society according to paragraph 5? Are any of Putnam's judgments supported? Explain.
6. What is the tone of paragraphs 6 through 10?

7. What does Putnam think about current prison sentences? What would his attitude be toward increasing the number of prisons?
8. In his last paragraph, Putnam refers to punishment and to rehabilitation. Which of these does he regard as more basic? How do you know?

VERDICT GUILTY—NOW WHAT?*

Karl Menninger

Since ancient times criminal law and penology have been based upon what is called in psychology the pain-pleasure principle. There are many reasons for inflicting pain—to urge an animal to greater efforts, to retaliate for pain received, to frighten, or to indulge in idle amusement. Human beings, like all animals, tend to move away from pain and toward pleasure. Hence the way to control behavior is to reward what is "good" and punish what is "bad." This formula pervades our programs of childrearing, education, and the social control of behavior.

With this concept three out of four readers will no doubt concur.

"Why, of course," they will say. "Only common sense. Take me for example. I know the speed limit and the penalty. Usually I drive moderately because I don't want to get a ticket. One afternoon I was in a hurry; I had an appointment, I didn't heed the signs. I did what I knew was forbidden and I got caught and received the punishment I deserved. Fair enough. It taught me a lesson. Since then I drive more slowly in that area. And surely people are deterred from cheating on their income taxes, robbing banks, and committing rape by the fear of punishment. Why, if we didn't have these crime road blocks we'd have chaos!"

This sounds reasonable enough and describes what most people think —*part of the time*. But upon reflection we all know that punishments and the threat of punishments do *not* deter *some* people from doing forbidden things. Some of them take a chance on not being caught, and this chance is a very good one, too, better than five to one for most crimes. Not even the fear of possible death, self-inflicted, deters some speedsters. Exceeding the speed limit is not really regarded as criminal behavior by most people, no matter how dangerous and self-destructive. It is the kind of a "crime" which respectable members of society commit and condone. This is not the case with rape, bank-robbing, check-forging, vandalism, and the multitude of offenses for which the prison penalty system primarily exists. And from these offenses the average citizen, including the reader, is deterred by quite different restraints. For most of us it is our conscience, our self-respect, and our wish for the good opinion of our neighbors which are the determining factors in controlling our impulses toward misbehavior.

Today it is no secret that our official, prison-threat theory of crime control is an utter failure. Criminologists have known this for years. When pocket-picking was punishable by hanging, in England, the crowds that gathered about the gallows to enjoy the spectacle of an execution were particularly likely to have their pockets picked by skillful operators who, to say the least, were not deterred by the exhibition of "justice." We have long known that the perpetrators of most offenses are never detected; of those detected, only a fraction are found guilty and still fewer serve a "sentence." Furthermore, we are quite certain now that of those who do receive the official punishment of the law, many become firmly committed thereby to a continuing life of crime and a continuing feud with law enforcement officers. Finding themselves ostracized from society and blacklisted by industry they stick with the crowd they have been introduced to in jail and try to play the game of life according to this set of rules. In this way society skillfully converts individuals of borderline self-control into loyal members of the underground fraternity.

The science of human behavior has gone far beyond the common sense rubrics which dictated the early legal statutes. We know now that one cannot describe rape or bank-robbing or income-tax fraud simply as pleasure. Nor, on the other hand, can we describe imprisonment merely as pain. Slapping the hand of a beloved child as he reaches to do a forbidden act is utterly different from the institutionalized process of official punishment. The offenders who are chucked into our county and state and federal prisons are not anyone's beloved children; they are usually unloved children, grown-up physically but still hungry for human concern which they never got or never get in normal ways. So they pursue it in abnormal ways—abnormal, that is, from *our* standpoint. . . .

Most offenders whom we belabor are not very wise, not very smart, not even very "lucky." It is not the successful criminal upon whom we inflict our antiquated penal system. It is the unsuccessful criminal, the criminal who really doesn't know how to commit crimes, and who gets caught. Indeed, until he is caught and convicted a man is technically not even called a criminal. The clumsy, the desperate, the obscure, the friendless, the defective, the diseased—these men who commit crimes that do not come off—are bad actors, indeed. But they are not the professional criminals, many of whom occupy high places. In some instances the crime is the merest accident or incident or impulse, expressed under unbearable stress. More often the offender is a persistently perverse, lonely, and resentful individual who joins the only group to which he is eligible—the outcasts and the anti-social.

And what do we do with such offenders? After a solemn public ceremony we pronounce them enemies of the people, and consign them for arbitrary periods to institutional confinement on the basis of laws written many years ago. Here they languish until time has ground out so many weary months and years. Then with a planlessness and stupidity only surpassed by that of their original incarceration they are dumped back upon society, regardless of whether any change has taken place in them for the better and with every assurance that changes have taken place in them for the worse. Once more they enter the unequal tussle with society. Proscribed for employment by most concerns, they are expected to invent a new way to make a living and to survive without any further help from society.

Intelligent members of society are well aware that the present system is antiquated, expensive, and disappointing, and that we are wasting vast quantities of manpower through primitive methods of dealing with those who transgress the law. In 1917 the famous Wickersham report of the New York State Prison Survey Committee recommended the abolition of jails, the institution of diagnostic clearing houses or classification centers, the development of a diversified institutional system and treatment program, and the use of indeterminate sentences. *Forty-two years have passed.* How little progress we have made!

. . . With few exceptions offenders continue to be dealt with according to old-time instructions, written by men now dead who knew nothing about the present offender, his past life, the misunderstandings accumulated by him, or the provocation given to him.

The sensible, scientific question is: What kind of treatment could be instituted that would deter him or be most likely to deter him? Some of these methods are well known. For some offenders who have the money or the skillful legal counsel or the good luck to face a wise judge go a different route from the prescribed routine. Instead of jail and deterioration, they get the sort of re-education and re-direction associated with psychiatric institutions and the psychiatric profession. Relatively few wealthy offenders get their "treatment" in jail. This does not mean that justice is to be bought, or bought off. But it does mean that some offenders have relatives and friends who *care* and who try to find the best possible solution to the problem of persistent misbehavior, which is NOT the good old jail-and-penitentiary and make-'em-sorry treatment. It is a reflection on the democratic ideals of our country that these better ways are so often—indeed, *usually*—denied to the poor, the friendless, and the ignorant.

If we were to follow scientific methods, the convicted offender would be detained indefinitely pending a decision as to whether and how and when to reintroduce him successfully into society. All the skill and knowledge of modern behavioral science would be used to examine his personality assets, his liabilities and potentialities, the environment from which he came, its effect upon him, and his effects upon it.

Having arrived at some diagnostic grasp of the offender's personality, those in charge can decide whether there is a chance that he can be redirected into a mutually satisfactory adaptation to the world. . . .

The desirability of moving patients out of institutional control swiftly is something which we psychiatrists learned the hard way, and recently. Ten years ago, in the state hospital I know best, the average length of stay was five years; today it is three months. Ten years ago few patients were discharged under two years; today 90 per cent are discharged within the first year. Ten years ago the hospital was overcrowded; today it has eight times the turnover it used to have; there are empty beds and there is no waiting list.

But some patients do not respond to our efforts, and they have to remain in the hospital, or return to it promptly after a trial home visit. And if the *prisoner*, like some of the psychiatric patients, cannot be changed by genuine efforts to rehabilitate him, we must look *our* failure in the face, and provide for his indefinitely continued confinement, regardless of the technical reasons for it. This we owe society for its protection. . . .

Intelligent judges all over the country are increasingly surrendering the onerous responsibility of deciding in advance what a man's conduct will be in a prison and how rapidly his wicked impulses will evaporate there. With more use of the indeterminate sentence and the establishment of scientific diagnostic centers, we shall be in a position to make progress in the science of *treating* anti-social trends. Furthermore, we shall get away from the present legal smog that hangs over the prisons, which lets us detain with heartbreaking futility some prisoners fully rehabilitated while others, whom the prison officials know full well to be dangerous and unemployable, must be released, *against our judgment*, because a judge far away (who has by this time forgotten all about it) said that five years was enough. In my frequent visits to prisons I am always astonished at how rarely the judges who have prescribed the "treatment" come to see whether or not it is effective. What if doctors who sent their seriously ill patients to hospitals never called to see them! . . .

Let us return in conclusion to the initial question: "Verdict guilty—now what?" My answer is that now we, the designated representatives of the society which has failed to integrate this man, which has failed him in some way, hurt him and been hurt by him, should take over. It is *our* move. And our move must be a constructive one, an intelligent one, a purposeful one—not a primitive, retaliatory, offensive move. We, the agents of society, must move to end the game of tit-for-tat and blow-for-blow in which the offender has foolishly and futilely engaged himself and us. We are not driven, as he is, to wild and impulsive actions. With knowledge comes power, and with power there is no need for the frightened vengeance of the old penology. In its place should go a quiet, dignified, therapeutic program for the rehabilitation of the disorganized one, if possible, the protection of society during his treatment period, and his guided return to useful citizenship, as soon as this can be effected.

Questions

1. Dr. Menninger suggests that a majority of people would automatically think along the lines of rewarding the good and punishing the bad. Is his statement an accurate description of your "common sense" response?
2. What does Dr. Menninger think of punishment as a deterrent to crime?
3. Is the example of "speeders" an effective illustration? Explain.
4. Dr. Menninger speaks of criminologists' knowing that prison as a means of crime-control "is an utter failure." Is he qualified to speak for criminologists? How do you know?
5. What distinction does Menninger make between successful and unsuccessful committing of crime? Is this a useful distinction? Why? Why does Dr. Menninger make his distinction?
6. Why does Menninger make reference to the Wickersham Report?
7. What statistics does Menninger supply on the subject of average length of stay in state hospitals? Why does he furnish these statistics? What important inferences does he draw from them?
8. In the next to last paragraph, Menninger observes that he rarely sees judges when he visits prisons. What two important points is he making simultaneously? Are his points effective? How effective is the closing sentence of the paragraph, the analogy with "ill patients"?

THE PRINCIPLE OF PAROLE*

Earl Warren

[1] It has been my opportunity in life to see much of parole from different vantage points—first, of course, as a citizen; second, as a prosecutor; third, as the legal advisor of a parole system; fourth, as governor of my state charged with the administration of a parole system; and recently from the bench. I say to you frankly that it presents a different picture from each of these vantage points because from each of them our outlook is circumscribed. But each of these experiences has strengthened my belief in the importance of the work and my expectation for its accelerated progress in the future. . . .

[2] In so many quarters the principle of parole is little understood and reluctantly accepted. In so many others an appraisal of work done is made on the basis of the failures of a few parolees instead of on the basis of the rehabilitation of the vast majority. I consider the progress to have been made the hard way because so many people believe a parole system represents the coddling of prisoners, and because so many close their eyes and their minds to the fact that no one is ever committed to the supervision of a parole system until society has acknowledged its frustration; until our social institutions including the home, the school, and the church, have admitted their inability to successfully guide or rehabilitate the offender; and until a court has found that he is incorrigible and that the state has no other means of curbing his lawlessness except commitment to prison.

[3] Both reason and fairness should dictate that in these circumstances we have no right either to demand or expect a perfect rehabilitation record from any parole system, and that it is only where a fair opportunity is given that we can expect much progress in rehabilitation to be made. . . .

[4] It would be a very wholesome thing if out of this conference could come a public awareness of the fact that the parole of a prisoner is not an act of coddling but on the contrary it is an extension of the state's supervision while he is trying to re-establish himself in society. So many people do not realize that even for a good man the regimentation of prison life over a term of years would weaken his ability to com-

* From the Keynote Address to the National Probation and Parole Association, 1956. Copyright © 1956 by the National Council on Crime and Delinquency (formerly the National Probation and Parole Association). Reprinted by permission.

pete in society as much as a cast on his leg for a like period would weaken him for running. It would also be a wholesome result of this conference if many people could be made to realize that the vast majority of prisoners must be released eventually to become our neighbors and fellow workers in all walks of life. This holds true for more than nine out of every ten prisoners.

[5] There are in the nation at the present time approximately 200 state and federal prisons, reformatories and camps. They have a normal capacity of about 175,000. Last year there were approximately 90,000 new commitments. If it were not for the fact that 80,000 were released each year, the number of prisoners would soon engulf us. Should we release them outright or should we subject them to the supervision of parole? The average sentence pronounced by the court for all state prisoners is approximately eight years. If we had no adjusting release of prisoners, it would be but a few years until we would need many times the number of prisons with many times the capacity of those we have today. I am sure the future of penology is not to be found in any such solution.

[6] The maximum security prison has its place in our corrective systems, but we have every reason to hope that it will play a smaller part as time goes on. Different types of institutions, different degrees of restraint, varied opportunities for education and work—all looking toward the parole of the individual and his rehabilitation in society—are the objectives toward which we must work. The sooner the public, legislators, administrators and tax-conscious groups realize that the best security and the cheapest security we can have for our homes against the depredations of people who have once been committed to a penitentiary for serious crime is not only an enlightened prison system but also an understanding parole system, the sooner we can turn the tide of crime in favor of the law-abiding community. The sooner we can bring about team play by juvenile authorities, police, prosecutors, judges, probation officers, the staffs of correctional institutions, and parole officers the sooner we can make progress on the grand scale.

[7] All states and the federal government have some form of parole procedure. In some, however, parole is little more than a name. In some jurisdictions a probation officer will have more than 500 to supervise. In very few do they have less than 100. In none that I am aware of do they have as few as 40 to 50, which is considered an ideal work load. Who on earth could supervise 500 broken men with the limited skills and opportunities of the average ex-convict? All the large cities have thousands of policemen to guard against the commission of crime, but how many

parole officers do those same cities have to guide and rehabilitate those who are in the potential criminal class? The value of any parole system lies in the personal supervision given to the individual by trained and understanding people. To the extent that we fall short in supplying such supervision, we are missing our opportunity to make life and property more secure in America.

Questions

1. Why does Chief Justice Earl Warren begin his speech the way he does?
2. In paragraphs 2 and 4, Warren uses the word *coddling*. How does he use it each time and why?
3. Warren refers to the "failure of a few parolees" and the "rehabilitation of the vast majority." Does he support these assertions? Why does he make them?
4. Why does Warren present statistics on the number of prisons and the number of new commitments annually? Are his statistics pertinent to his major conclusions? Are they persuasive? Explain.
5. What major point does Warren make in his final paragraph? Do you find his data effective?
6. How would you assume his audience would respond to this speech? Why?

RESULTS IN PROBATION AND PAROLE*

David Dressler

[1] Do probation and parole "work"? We do not really know. There have been many inquiries on the subject but, because of methodological or other shortcomings, few valid answers.

[2] An excellent methodology, at least, was demonstrated by the Gluecks in their epochal *500 Criminal Careers*.[1] The Harvard research team painstakingly followed the careers of 510 men released from the Massachusetts Reformatory. Many of them had been on probation; all were exposed to institutional treatment, followed by parole. What had happened to them five to fifteen years after expiration of parole? Investigators interviewed the study group, checked personal statements against official records where possible. The stunning finding was that 80 percent of the men showed an unsuccessful outcome on parole, if the criterion of success be nonrecidivism.

* From David Dressler, *Practice and Theory of Probation and Parole*. Copyright 1951, © 1959 by Columbia University Press. Reprinted by permission.
[1] Sheldon Glueck and Eleanor T. Glueck, *500 Criminal Careers* (New York: Alfred A. Knopf, 1930).

[3] The procedures of the Glueck study were better than any undertaken before or since. But the findings have limited significance for several reasons. The volume was published in 1930, but the former parolees had not been exposed to the sort of treatment just coming into use. They left the reformatory between 1911 and 1922. Their parole periods ran through the 1920s. Massachusetts did not employ professional caseworkers or other highly trained counselors in this period. In other words, the study measured some kind of probation and parole work but not the sort just beginning to be practiced.

[4] Similarly, the Gluecks' *Five Hundred Delinquent Women*[2] studied treatment of an earlier era in correctional care. The women involved were committed to a reformatory sometime before 1915 and up to 1923. *One Thousand Juvenile Delinquents*[3] followed up cases referred by the Boston Juvenile Court to the Judge Baker Foundation for clinical examination between 1917 and 1922.

[5] The Gluecks' trail-blazing attracted few followers willing to be as meticulous in methodology. However, using somewhat similar techniques, Beard studied 500 cases of children placed on probation in 1924 by the Boston Juvenile Court. She followed their histories five to seven years after the probation period.[4] Speaking of treatment in the country at large, she writes: "Probation in its best sense has not even been tried."[5] For what they are worth, then, here are her findings: some 80 percent of her cases fell in the "successful" category at termination of probation. By the time of the follow-up, however, only some 50 percent of the total group continued without a record of delinquency.

[6] In 1939 the United States Attorney General reported on an analysis of 19,256 cases of probationers whose supervision had terminated within a three-year study period.[6] No field checks were made. Reliance was placed upon records from 25 probation units in 16 states and the District of Columbia. Some 61 percent of the cases had no recorded violation during the probation period. Revocation of probation had been ordered in 19 percent of the cases.

[7] The study leaves a great deal to be desired. It investigated behavior during the probation period only. There was no follow-up be-

---

[2] Sheldon Glueck and Eleanor T. Glueck, *Five Hundred Delinquent Women* (New York: Alfred A. Knopf, 1934).

[3] Sheldon Glueck and Eleanor T. Glueck, *One Thousand Juvenile Delinquents* (Cambridge, Mass.: Harvard University Press, 1934).

[4] Belle Boone Beard, *Juvenile Probation* (New York: American Book Co., 1934).

[5] *Ibid.*, p. 147.

[6] *Attorney General's Survey of Release Procedures* (Washington, D.C.: Department of Justice, 1939), II, 335, 342.

yond that. The relation between treatment and outcome was not indicated. Yet, obviously, caliber of staff and treatment methods must have run the gamut from poor to good among the many jurisdictions involved.

[8] Coming closer to modern practice chronologically was the study of adult probationers of the Erie County Probation Department, Buffalo, New York, in 1942. Two hundred cases indicted for felony were followed up five to seven years after discharge, partly by field interviews. Seventy-two percent had no known subsequent record. Twenty-eight percent had been convicted of 107 criminal charges.[7] But the 200 cases were selected on the basis of not having violated probation while under supervision. They had been "discharged with improvement." They therefore represented a highly selective sampling. The individuals would be expected to do better than an undifferentiated group.

[9] One of the more careful and comprehensive inquiries of recent date, by Rumney and Murphy, was published in 1952. It has the merit of recency and of emanating from one of the better probation departments (Essex County, New Jersey). An advantage over previous studies is that it uses criteria additional to conviction and probation violation as measures of success and failure.[8]

[10] The study group consisted of 1,000 offenders placed on probation in 1937. Information concerning the probationers was secured by search of records running through 1948, eleven years after supervision began and in most cases eight years after it terminated. Additionally, many former probationers were interviewed personally. It was found that 73 percent were discharged from probation "with improvement." Of the 764 probationers still alive and on whose after-probation history data were obtainable, 26 percent showed "marked improvement" and 33 percent some improvement. Fifty percent had not been arrested again, while 19 percent had been arrested once and 31 percent more than once since placement on probation.

[11] As indicated, subsequent arrest or conviction was not the sole criterion of success and failure. This has a definite logic, for social readjustment cannot be measured in those terms alone. However, the method of determining improvement or lack of it was far from precise. As to treatment involved, no one orientation or standard existed. The authors frankly recognize that personnel was not ideal and caseloads

[7] Reported in Charles Lionel Chute and Marjorie Bell, *Crime, Courts and Probation* (New York: Macmillan, 1956), pp. 135–36.

[8] Jay Rumney and Joseph P. Murphy, *Probation and Social Adjustment* (New Brunswick, N.J.: Rutgers University Press, 1952).

were prohibitive, so that even relatively well-trained workers could not do their best. In the adult male division, for instance, loads averaged 233 per officer.

[12] Many other studies have been undertaken, but they are less conclusive than the few we have mentioned. None unequivocally answers the question: What treatment resulted in what outcome?

[13] In fact, we still must answer another question: Does treatment, of whatever caliber or orientation, affect outcome? We think it does, we say it does, but we have no evidence to back us up. This is shocking, and the impact is not lessened by the realization that the casework field as a whole has done very little to study what it accomplishes. . . .

Questions

1. How does the tone of this article compare with the tone of the speech by Chief Justice Earl Warren, "The Principle of Parole"? Are the conclusions the same? Explain.
2. Dressler supplies considerable statistical data. What inferences does he draw from the data? Would you agree with his inferences? Explain.
3. What criticisms does Dressler make in paragraph 7? What are the implications of his criticisms?
4. Whom do you think Dressler means by *we* in the last paragraph? What inferences can you draw from your observations?

WHAT'S AN OPERATOR?*

Frank Gibney

[1] The morning of another good business day dawned bright and clear. The reputable executive had two Alka-Seltzer tablets and a cheerful breakfast and sent his children off to school with fatherly counsel. His wife was slightly troubled about the maid's Social Security payments, which were long past due; he suggested that she forget about them, since the maid was leaving soon anyway. Then he climbed into his Thunderbird and drove downtown.

[2] Traffic was heavy and he was forced to leave the car in a No Parking zone across from the office. He locked it carefully and on his way down the street ran into the veteran cop on the beat, who thanked him for a recent Christmas gift, the usual four bottles of good blended

* From Frank Gibney, *The Operators*. Copyright © 1960 by Frank Gibney. Reprinted by permission of Harper & Row, Publishers.

whiskey. Once in the office, he took care of the mail and some routine desk chores and settled at least one small but irritating personnel problem: when one of his middle-rank salesmen asked for a raise, he turned him down, but suggested with the broadest of winks that the man had carte blanche to go heavy on his expense account until the matter of raises came up formally late in the fall. Then he took an hour out with his personal income-tax consultant, who had just found a happy device for altering repair and depreciation costs on some rental property, for a handsome tax "profit." Before their conference was quite over, he handled an urgent long-distance call from his lawyer and unofficial investment counselor, who had found a good insolvent manufacturing company which was ripe for a nice tax-loss merger.

[3] A few minutes before one, the reputable businessman walked over to his club, where he habitually lunched and played squash on the company expense account. There he entertained two visiting college classmates at a lavish meal; he insisted on signing the check. Back in the office, he had time to detail one of his assistants to "take care of" the building inspector with jurisdiction over their new plant site, thus getting as much red tape as possible out of the way. In the meantime his secretary had drafted several routine letters for him to sign. Among them was a note to an executive of a smaller firm with whom he had just signed a contract, thanking him for the gift of a new-model TV set.

[4] At a brief conference later in the afternoon he congratulated his firm's controller on a bookkeeping device that was handily padding a few of the firm's more controversial accounts. Then he went into a half-hour huddle with the account executive from the ad agency about some trouble they had lately run into with the Federal Trade Commission on the subject of misleading commercials. (He advised the advertising man to keep up the same pitch until after the fall sales drive, FTC or no FTC.) In a crucial twenty-minute session, he won the consent of the firm's board chairman to the week's Big Deal, a sleight-of-hand exchange of shares with another company which ultimately promised a really large tax saving and some big stock profits, after several platoons of lawyers had worked out the corporate footwork. This done, he felt free to leave for home. Before he turned out the light in his office, he had his secretary wrap up one of the new company desk sets, which seemed just the thing for his study.

[5] The reputable executive, as anyone could gather from this selective but by no means improbable account of his daily rounds, is what most of his society—viewing his actions dispassionately—would call an "Operator." He is also, by legal definition, a criminal. His business day,

if he were successfully prosecuted, could conceivably result in a total of $31,500 in fines and no less than 33 years' imprisonment. Specific offenses would include:

> Penalty for willful nonpayment of employer's Social Security contributions: $10,000 fine and/or five years in jail.
>
> Penalty for attempting to influence a police officer with a gift: $5,000 fine and/or 10 years in jail.
>
> Penalty for filing a fraudulent income-tax return: $10,000 fine and/or five years in jail.
>
> Penalty for misusing an expense account, under Section 665 of the N. Y. State Penal Law: $500 fine and/or one year in jail.
>
> Penalty for bribing a public officer: $5,000 fine and/or 10 years in jail.
>
> Penalty for secretly accepting a gift in return for corporate loans: $500 fine and/or one year in jail.
>
> Penalty for appropriating company property to one's personal use: $500 fine and/or one year in jail.

[6] Yet no one would be more surprised than the businessman to be told this. About the criminal shading of some of his activities he would be blissfully ignorant. But even where his chicanery was done knowingly, his first reaction—if he were a typical Operator—would be one of surprised indignation that he, of all people, should be singled out for "persecution." After all, the reputable-looking Operator would protest, "Isn't everybody doing it?" . . .

Questions

1. Why does Gibney use the term *reputable executive* in his second sentence?
2. Why does he make the reference to the "maid's Social Security payments"? Is this reference consistent with the other details?
3. What is the significance of the veteran cop's receiving his usual "Christmas gift"? What do you notice about the context of this detail?
4. Is the phrase *corporate footwork* a good choice of language in paragraph 4? Explain.
5. Why does Gibney begin paragraph 5 with a statement about the "selective but by no means improbable account" of the reputable executive's daily routine? Can you draw any inferences about Gibney on the basis of this particular statement? Explain.
6. Why does Gibney define the executive as a "criminal"? Do you find his strategy effective? Explain.
7. What is the author's purpose in listing (a) the possible fines totaling $31,500, (b) the 33 years' imprisonment, and (c) the list of specific offenses? Does Gibney's specificity add to the effectiveness of his strategy?
8. What is the moral implication of Gibney's closing paragraph?

THE CLIMATE OF JUSTICE*

Sheldon Glueck

Mankind is essentially violent; and every society has had its crime. The content of the term has varied in different civilizations, but the concept itself has existed as long as men have lived together in organized society. From a legal point of view, a crime is any act or failure to act that is prohibited by law and punishable by politically organized society in a formal judicial proceeding initiated in the name of the state. But when we say that the act is prohibited by law, we should bear in mind that this is only the law of a particular time and place. Crime is a relative concept—relative to the society and culture within which the act is prohibited and to the time when it is prohibited. Acts which in some civilized countries are crimes by its laws may not be such in other places; acts which at some periods in any particular country are designated criminal may not be so at other periods. Infanticide and patricide have not been regarded as criminal among some primitive peoples; the prohibition of the manufacture, sale or transportation of liquor rendered certain acts criminal in our own country at one time and not so at another; gold hoarding was lawful but a short time ago; today it is punishable as a crime.

This relativity of crime to place and time makes it difficult to generalize about it. Nevertheless, there are certain acts which have been quite generally condemned and punished in all developed societies. Treason, a very uncommon offense, is one of these; murder, a much more frequent crime, is another. In most civilized communities, also, certain takings of property without the consent of the owner and acts of sexual aggression have long been stigmatized as criminal.

Now while such acts have been punished as crimes in civilized communities of varying degree of development, and by different methods, it is doubtful whether ever before conditions have existed, in the United States particularly, which make it so difficult to cope with them.

In the first place, our ideas of the aims of the state in dealing with criminals are today more complex than they were when the goal was simply to counteract private vengeance and self-help by vindictive punishment in the name of the state; or when punishment was regarded simply as the wages of sin. The introduction of humanitarian

* From Sheldon Glueck, *Crime and Justice*. Copyright 1936 by Sheldon Glueck. Published by Harvard University Press. Reprinted by permission of the publisher.

ideals of reform, together with the increasing call for the participation of the biologic and social sciences in the administration of justice, and the resultant internal conflict of the criminal law, have rendered its problems much more complex than they were in the past. Men are beginning to wonder whether vengeance, however camouflaged and rationalized in laws and judicial decisions, should have any place in a civilized society well on the way to the second half of the twentieth century. Their misgivings spring partly from increasing evidence of the biologic and social roots of crime, and partly from the accumulating evidence that traditional punitive methods are not bringing the expected results.

In a ruder civilization crime was attributed wholly to a perverse "will" and criminal responsibility was therefore easily determined. The tasks of criminal justice were simple: to fix guilt by some roughly appropriate procedure and to administer a dose of punishment prescribed in advance by parliament or legislature. The punishment was assumed to prevent both the repetition of criminality and its perpetration by others, while at the same time satisfying a natural impulse toward vengeance and restoring the disturbed "jural order." Finding that even reformatories fail in the great majority of cases to reform those entrusted to their care, thoughtful persons are more and more asking whether our methods of coping with offenders do not need to be radically transformed, and whether psychology, psychiatry, sociology and kindred sciences, though far from perfect, should not have a greater place in the administration of justice.

More and more are these inquiring minds recognizing that both humanitarian and scientific considerations should play a prominent role in the coping with acts that involve social derelictions as well as human weaknesses. A social instrument may be nicely scientific, but if it conflicts overmuch with man's hard-won humanitarian impulses, it will sooner or later land in the limbo of unwanted things. Two of the most scientific punitive instruments in existence are the guillotine and the electric chair; but if the next hundred years witness even half the development of humanitarianism that came about in the latter part of the eighteenth and early nineteenth centuries, they will be beaten into more useful medical and social instruments. But unbridled sentimentalism is also bad. Deep though our pity be, we cannot indulge in futile sentimentality while dangerous persons stalk the land. We must discipline our humane impulses with science and good sense. A head without a heart may lead to tyranny; a heart without a head may mean annihilation. These two principles, then, the ethical and the scientific,

must both be reckoned with; and their involvement in the current processes of Justice makes her task more difficult than it was in the past.

2

The second reason for the peculiar complexity of the tasks of Justice
in the modern scene arises from certain characteristics of our industrialized, dynamic civilization, the changes in human attitude and
mores that it has brought about, and the impairment of traditional
sources of authority. These phenomena need to be borne in mind if
we would understand the pathology and the problems of American
criminal law and procedure. For Justice does not live apart on Olym-
pus, but in the affairs of men. Judges and the judged, guards and prisoners, alike are subject to a pervasive culture which in large measure,
though in varying degree, determines their attitudes and behavior.
Failure to take into account sufficiently the culture medium of criminals
and of those who pursue and punish them may explain to some extent
at least the miscarriage of contemporary piecemeal and superficial
"reforms."

Analysis of the culture medium of modern crime and justice has extensive ramifications. Some of the roots of the phenomena to be described strike deep into the historic soil; others are more recent; but all
appear to have become particularly marked during the past few decades. Mechanization and urbanization, the dramatic history of big
business and the excesses of a largely unrestrained private profit motive,
changes in psychology and mores, the weakening of home, state, church
and other traditional sources of social control accompanied by the over-
burdening of the law—these and like phenomena are pertinent. A few
examples will suffice to illustrate the puzzling complexity of the tasks
of Justice in a machine age.

It is well known that the mechanical inventions of the twentieth
century have wrought a revolution in American customs and mores
no less marked than that induced during the English Industrial Revolution by the steam engine and machines derived from it. The automobile,
the radio, the cinema, the long-distance transmission of electric power,
and mass production in general have conspired to wrench behavior
and attitudes from their accustomed grooves, and with breath-taking
speed. In fact a chief characteristic of the industrial revolution is its
amazing tempo. Human institutions and human psychology can hardly
adapt themselves to such fundamental changes with like speed. Governmental agencies lag limpingly behind. What the potent and restless in-
ventive giant has done to individual habits and attitudes and social cus-

toms before man has had time to adjust himself planfully to the new conditions, causes growing concern. As will be seen from many points of view, the dynamic transformations of our epoch have distinct repercussions on crime and its control.

One of the profoundest accompaniments of the modern industrial revolution has of course been increasing urbanization. In 1900, 40 per cent of the population lived in cities; in 1930 the proportion had risen to over 56 per cent. The most characteristic patterning has been the clustering of "smaller cities within the orbits of the metropolitan centers," these lesser units having experienced the most rapid growth. Nearly half the population of the United States is located in but ninety-six such regions, whose rates of growth have been much higher than those of other regions. There are pulls toward a new decentralization dictated by economic disillusionments. But it cannot be expected that for a long time to come the stamp of the city matrix on the psychology, customs and mores of the people will be substantially altered. The deeper forces of our dynamic mass-production epoch will continue to do their work for weal or woe. The rapid means of communication which make possible suburban life also facilitate the continued moulding of the people's habits and attitudes by the newspaper, magazine, radio and cinema. Living in suburbs, people are drawn to the city for work and play, read its newspapers, partake of its amusements, and thus remain in spirit denizens of the city. Attitudes toward life, the estimation of values, and habits of conduct are still determined *en masse* by the large centers, and they spread with magical rapidity to suburban satellites and thence into the remotest rural regions. "The concentration of wealth, political influence, cultural advancement, in a population whose young people are as a rule pressing toward the city, combine to make the mores of the city prevail over the more stable mores of the rural dwellers."

The rush to the cities has had profound effects, some of which need but be mentioned to indicate their significance for both crime and the administration of justice. The demands of our industrial civilization have attracted to our cities peoples from various quarters of the earth, presenting wide differences in ethnic, religious, linguistic and cultural backgrounds. Difficulties of adjustment are enhanced by the crowding of these diverse elements into narrow, squalid homes and neighborhoods. Some of the resultant strains are reflected in both delinquency and law enforcement.

As concerns delinquency, modern city life intensifies opportunities for friction and crime. It multiplies the need for regulatory laws and the opportunities for their evasion. Not only do these influences make for increased lawlessness, but the irritation they cause also tends to reduce that "respect for law" which many still attribute to some mysterious ethical organ in the soul of man, but which is in fact the result of complex conditioning factors. City life tends to sharpen and dramatize economic inequalities; side by side with the luxurious displays of shop windows are the miseries of slums; crowded dwellings make wholesome life exceedingly hard to maintain; children seek the streets; recreational outlets tend to be harmful; gang life is stimulated. The rewards of urban criminality are higher than they were in the past. The anonymity of life in the city makes wrongdoing less subject to the criticism and control of neighbors. The surprising mobility of city-dwellers is illustrated by the fact that some two-thirds of the names in the Boston City Directory change addresses every year; this restless movement has a marked effect in preventing the rooting of individuals in definite communities and the building up of a sense of responsibility to one's neighbors.

Law enforcement is also seriously impeded. It is relatively easy to hide away in a large, crowded city, or to escape by automobile. Criminal investigation is much more complicated than in the days when the techniques of crime were simple and when officers, prosecutors and judges knew personally many of those who came into conflict with the law. Policing the city of today is a highly technical task, and the obtaining of well qualified jurors becomes ever more difficult. The tremendous amount of business transacted by urban police officers, prosecutors, judges and correctional administrators makes inefficiency and corruption easier than they were in a closely knit, predominantly rural community where the work of officials was open to direct scrutiny. The diversity in the traditions of the ethnic groups that compose a large part of the population of our cities makes it hard to obtain sufficient agreement on public policies and reform measures.

Whether in city or country, the mechanical inventions and patterns of enterprise of our age have transformed the very nature of crime. The sensational robberies and quick getaways with which we are daily regaled were largely unknown in the horse and buggy era. State lines and the cumbersome, over-technical methods of extradition have been rendered obsolete by the interstate activities of criminals. Such relatively recent correctional devices as probation and parole, of which supervision of offenders outside prisons is the essence, have been greatly weakened by the mobility of those under surveillance. Well organized and widely ramified rackets, employing huge capital, large staffs, branch agencies and standing counsel, are a phenomenon that only the age of "big business" could have given birth to.

Increasing mechanization of industry and the attendant reduction in hours of labor have brought about a marked increase in leisure time, and with this have come wider opportunities not alone for healthful recreational activities but for anti-social conduct as well. "Business, with its advertising and high pressure salesmanship, can exert powerful stimuli on the responding human organism. How can the appeals made by churches, libraries, concerts, museums and adult education for a goodly share in our growing leisure be made to compete effectively with the appeals of commercialized recreation?" This vital question must be answered if growing leisure is to be turned into wholesome channels.

But aside from the influence of increased leisure on delinquency, the exploitation of modern recreational methods complicates the problems of law enforcement. The dramatic devices of the stage and talking picture have been rapidly taken up by the radio, to a point where even courtrooms are invaded and court sessions dramatized. Attorneys in sensational affairs try their cases in the press, the "talkie," over the radio. The sensational sheet pays a high price for the life stories of defendants and jurymen; they and their relatives are painted as colorful figures. Reporters and "ghost writers" churn the most intimate human experiences into the scandal, sex and crime that are fed to a sensation-hungry public. The trials and public hangings of old were known to relatively few persons—those resident in the vicinity; the doings of the underworld and police of today are treated as spicy news, which is disseminated wholesale.

An increasing apprehension of economic insecurity is another significant psychologic phenomenon. The anxiety of the underprivileged has always been extreme; but in more stable times, whether under feudalism, Victorianism or the largely rural economy of our own past, there was a greater sense of security, of "belonging," than in an epoch in which social change is rapid, economic upheavals are vast and mystifying, and unemployment for long periods is the lot of millions. The highly efficient impersonality of the large corporation has doubtless contributed to this feeling. In the past it was much easier for the manufacturer and merchant to be in more or less direct and friendly contact with the problems of their employees as well as those of investors. But corporations have tended to separate ownership from management, to eliminate personal relations and to dehumanize industry. By providing substantial reserves for the protection of ownership while largely overlooking the protection of the workman, they have seriously weakened the security and contentment of the individual. In such a psychologic setting the efforts of even the best intentioned administrators of justice are likely to prove abortive in many instances, if not a sign of hypocrisy in the eyes of offenders.

The effect of the overstimulating machine age on mental health is difficult to gauge. Authoritative sources throw some light on the matter: there are more than 400,000 patients in the mental hospitals of the land, supported at an annual cost of more than $200,000,000, and their population is said to be increasing at the rate of 14,000 a year. About 75,000 cases are newly admitted to mental institutions every year. According to a recent study of mental disease expectancy, "in New York state approximately one person out of every twenty-two of the population becomes a patient in a mental hospital at some time during his lifetime." Whether these figures represent a really substantial growth in mental disorders is uncertain. Improvements in diagnostic technique and commitment laws and enlarged facilities for earlier recognition of mental illness, as well as for hospitalization, complicate the question; perhaps a substantial proportion of the reported increase is due to these factors. It is also authoritatively estimated that "approximately 1,000,000 of the boys and girls now in our public schools will break down mentally at some time in their lives, if the present rate of breakdown continues." The relationship of mental disorder to delinquency and criminality is not yet clearly established; but that it plays a significant role in the etiologic complex has been suggested by several important researches. The wider recognition of this relationship complicates the problems of criminal justice, all the way from arrest and trial to punishment or correction.

3

Another serious phenomenon is the growing disrespect for traditional symbols and agencies of authority, together with failure to substitute others. This is less directly related to the operations of our industrial era and is probably also due to other causes; but it is just as significant and pertinent a sign of the times as those already noted. Family, neighborhood, church, government, law, business—all these erstwhile sources of authority and hence of social control have been gradually loosening their hold on the people.

Consider, for example, family life and parental authority. The progressive disintegration of the family, particularly in urban regions, is evidenced by a number of grave symptoms. In the first place, there has been a persistent increase in divorce. While the trend toward a high rate was already apparent in the 1880's, the increase in more recent years has been such as to cause serious concern. In 1887 the rate of divorce per 1,000 of the total population was .47; in 1916 it had increased to 1.13; by 1929 it had risen to 1.66 per 1,000, although it dropped back in 1931 to 1.48, and in 1932 to 1.28. Judging by the long-time trend, it is questionable if further declines over a substantial period can be expected. Comparison of the chief countries concerning which information is at hand shows the highest incidence of divorce in the 1920's (though not the highest percentage of increase since 1900) to have been in the United States. . . .

. . . From another angle, in 1929 there was in the United States one divorce for every 6.1 marriages contracted; in 1931 one for every 5.8; in 1932 one for every 6.1. The high American rates do not include annulments, of which there were 4,408 in 1929 (one to every 280 marriages), nor desertions (the "poor man's divorce"), which are estimated at 50,000 a year. Moreover, the stability of the family is being destroyed earlier in the marital venture. Recently, the most usual period has been the fourth year; in the span from 1867 to 1886 it was the seventh.

Thus, owing to the heightened speed, intensity and complexity of modern life, as well as to more subtle influences, the marriage tie has been "increasingly regarded as a convenience rather than a sacred obligation." That serious effects on the next generation are to be expected may be inferred from the fact that in 1929, 37.2 per cent of the divorces occurred in families with children.

The instability of the family can also be seen from another angle. Recent researches indicate that pre-marital and extra-marital sex experiences are far more common than many had supposed. This is true not only of delinquent and criminal families and those of low economic status, but also of the so-called normal ones. A mass of books and articles in recent years have been devoted to the effects of the machine age and urban civilization upon the love folkways and mores. . . .

Not all the causes can be laid at the door of the modern industrial revolution, nor is the conflict between the individual and the group in respect to so fundamental an expression as the sexual impulse something new. Darwinism and the scientific attitude it engendered, the popularization in distorted form of the writings of psychoanalysts, a mounting reaction to the long-enduring religious policy of investing sexual matters with a cloak of uncleanliness, the general greater freedom of the sexes since the World War, are probably all involved. But economic emancipation of youth, the easy anonymity of the individual in the city, the large-scale exploitation of sex-stimulating entertainment and like influences seem to have played conspicuous roles.

In these various ways, by tending to disintegrate the family the forces of industrialism and the other influences noted have contributed to lessen the authority of parents. The old home of rural or small-town America is no more the typical one; no longer is it the center of industry and of social life, no longer the chief school of habit-formation and the inculcation of moral ideals. Its members spend most of their daytime hours outside the home in factory and shop, and many nighttime hours at the movies or in dance halls and night clubs. With emancipation of youth from family domination have come numerous influences which have subtle but potent relationships to both crime and law enforcement.

Questions

1. Who is Sheldon Glueck? When was his book *Crime and Justice* written? How pertinent is its content today? What inferences can you draw from the answers to the preceding questions?
2. Glueck notes the relativity of criminal acts. Does he support this concept of relativity?
3. Which of the ideas in the fourth paragraph have you encountered in more recent articles and speeches on crime and punishment? Be specific.
4. What assumptions does Glueck make about the "mechanical inventions of the twentieth century" in their relation to crime? Do you agree? Explain.
5. How does the shift from rural to urban culture affect the problems of crime, according to Glueck? Does he support his contentions?
6. Glueck refers to the influence of the "talkie" and the radio as well as the "sensational sheet." If he were to write this article today, what might he add? Is his indictment of the mass media still a current point of view? Explain.
7. What does Glueck have to say about "traditional symbols and agencies of authority"? Does he support his references to the "disintegration of the family"?
8. Does Glueck suggest any other major factors that may be related to the problem of increased crime?

ASSIGNMENTS

1. "Meeting of Minds" presents an imaginary conversation among people who actually interested themselves in the problem of crime and punishment. By careful reading or making inquiries of your professors, assess the accuracy of the attitudes toward crime and punishment ascribed to Dostoevski and Hegel as they appear in the radio dramatization. Prepare a report describing your findings.

2. Prepare a list of the important judgments made by J. Edgar Hoover in his speech "The Perpetuation of Our American Heritage." Then, characterize each judgment as well documented, fairly well documented, barely supported, or unsupported. In an oral report, describe your findings and the inferences you would draw from your evidence.

3. Look up Gresham M. Sykes and his book on crime. Prepare a report on his major judgments and the quality of his supporting data.

4. Clarence Darrow and George Bernard Shaw both oppose punishment as a means of curbing crime. Write a paper comparing the arguments, the language, and the evidence each man uses.

5. How do Vold's conclusions—drawn from the *Uniform Crime Reports* data—compare with the conclusions Hoover or Abrahamsen might draw from the same evidence? Prepare a written report as you think each of these men would write it, using the tabular data for your source of information.

6. Locate examples of simple dualistic thinking in Putnam's talk and list them. Prepare a list of inferences that you might also draw from your findings.

7. Prepare for a panel discussion on "The Role of Punishment in the Elimination of Crime." Be prepared to project yourself into the roles of Menninger, Dressler, Vold, or Putnam.

8. Warren's speech mentions the release of 80,000 prisoners. He then asks, "Should we release them outright or should we subject them to the supervision of parole?" Write a paper in which you analyze his thought processes, including any unstated assumptions, the emotional content of his words, and the logic of his sentence.

9. Make a list of Gibney's "executive's" practices. Ask several members of your community for their attitudes toward these practices. In your investigation, ask people whether they approve of the executive's *shrewdness;* ask a second group whether they approve of his *operation;* ask a third group for their responses to his *knowledgeable* handling of business details. (All the people you interview are responding to your original list —but called by different names.) Prepare a report on your findings; indicate whether the language of the questions had any bearing on the results.

10. Reread "The Climate of Justice" by Sheldon Glueck. Prepare a list of the major judgments in the chapter. Interview sociology and anthropology professors on their attitudes toward these judgments. Write a paper describing your findings and the inferences you would draw from them.

9. ECONOMICS
The Control of Inflation

"We live, it is said, in an age of inflation. Over the past two decades, prices in the United States have roughly doubled. That is, the buying power of one dollar over a market basket of typical cost-of-living items is only half of what it was in 1937." So observes George L. Bach, professor of Economics, in his book *Inflation*. Bach calls the present era an "age of inflation," not because inflation has suddenly become a problem, but because it is so pervasive and apparently uncontrollable. Every modern nation has experienced some inflation since the end of World War II. In a few instances the results have been devastating (Bolivia's dollar ratio has increased 11,067 times in ten years), but in most large industrial nations the results have been less spectacular and the situation is more often described as "creeping inflation."

Inflation, as a matter of fact, is not a new or unusual economic phenomenon. As long ago as 1776, Adam Smith in his classic *The Wealth of Nations* described a long-continued rise in prices throughout Europe after the discovery of the Western Hemisphere. To Smith the cause was simple: it was the increased flow of gold from the New World. Its cure was equally obvious: always maintain a strict balance between production, the supply of money, and consumption. Few of today's economic experts accept an explanation as simple as Adam Smith's. While most economists agree that runaway inflation is bad, and even that moderate inflation without economic checks is harmful, they take divergent views about the effects of a creeping inflation and what should be done about it. Some hold that inflation must be expected and planned for in any growing industrial economy, while others despair with each new index that reveals another rise in the cost of living. Still another group, the followers of Lord Keynes, the famous British economist and author of *The General Theory of Income*, advocates government spending through public works programs to reduce unemployment and stimulate commerce so that inflation can be checked by a "full" economy. Although the layman seems to have little knowledge of, or interest in, economic laws and theories, the consequences of a nation's economic policies and their impact on every citizen are too important to warrant an attitude of "leave it to the experts."

To provide a basis for understanding the economics of inflation, this issue begins with two preliminary statements. One, a short excerpt from a scholarly work by George L. Bach of Brown University, sets the problem in perspective. The second, part of a pamphlet prepared and distributed by the United States Chamber of Commerce, explains the mechanics of inflation in layman's language. Following are three pieces offering divergent accounts of who is responsible for our inflated economy. First, a speech by Arthur Summerfield, delivered to the Advertising Federation of America when he was Postmaster General of the United States, places the blame for inflation at the feet of labor union dictators. Second, an essay by Leon Keyserling, former Chairman of President Eisenhower's Council of Economic Advisers, finds fault with an administration that is stifling economic growth. Third, a magazine article by a conservative economist, Henry Hazlitt, attributes our inflation to excessive wage increases and a lack of government responsibility.

A less ominous view of the recent status of the American economy is presented through a series of five reports taken from the weekly *U.S. News & World Report*. Printed over a four-month period, these reports, when read separately, offer a mixed picture of the American economy, revealing both the dangers of inflation and the signs of economic growth. But when these reports are juxtaposed and read as a single report, the cumulative effect portrays an economy that is in general a healthy one.

A composite view of a different type is found in the next piece, "Defense Against Inflation." This report comes from a Committee on Economic Development made up of some of the nation's leading industrialists, bank presidents, financiers, and economists. Although the majority of the committee apparently agreed on the measures needed to combat inflation, it is significant that some minority reports are included, and these express strong arguments against the views of the majority.

Distinctly in contrast with some of the prevailing views is the next piece, "Argument for 'Creeping' Inflation," by the late Harvard professor and Presidential adviser, Sumner Slichter. Professor Slichter takes the position that many of the fears expressed about inflation are unjustified and that some degree of continuing inflation can be accepted in a properly balanced and rapidly expanding economy.

The concluding piece comes from the final chapter of the book *Can Inflation Be Controlled?* by Harold Moulton, President-Emeritus of

the Brookings Institution, a national foundation for the study of economic development. In confronting the difficult problem of the control
of inflation, Moulton points out the weaknesses and pitfalls in most
of the popular plans, and, at the same time, attempts to establish alternative economic guidelines for a free, industrial society.

AN AGE OF INFLATION[*]

George L. Bach

[1] We live, it is said, in an age of inflation. Over the past two decades, prices in the United States have roughly doubled. That is, the
buying power of one dollar over a market basket of typical cost-of-
living items is only half of what it was in 1937. In no major nation of
the world have prices risen by less than about this amount. In many,
prices have risen far more. In the United Kingdom, for example, the
cost of living has risen about 150 percent over the period. One British
pound will buy about 40 percent of what it would command in 1937. In
Brazil, the cost of living is now approximately fifteen times as high as in
1937. One cruzeiro will buy only about 7 percent as much as twenty
years ago. . . .

[2] Indeed, if we look at the broad sweep of world history, the
amazing thing is that man has not long since come to expect inflation
as the normal event, and a continuing stable value of his monetary
unit the exception. Inflation has vexed nations and their rulers since
the earliest days of recorded history. And no nation of the modern world
has avoided a major drop in the real purchasing power of its monetary
unit. In many cases, the drop has practically wiped out the buying
power of the nation's monetary unit.

[3] Not that prices have risen steadily. They have not. There have
been long valleys between the steep peaks of inflation in many nations,
and there is a striking coincidence between major wars and major in-
flations. But in every country, the net result over the decades has been
a persistent uptrend of prices.

[4] Most major American groups appear to be against inflation.
President Eisenhower and ex-President Truman; the CIO-AFL and the
National Association of Manufacturers; the Committee for Economic

[*] From George L. Bach, *Inflation: A Study in Economics, Ethics, and Politics*
(Colver Lectures in Brown University, 1957). Copyright © 1958 by Brown University Press. Reprinted by permission.

Development and the Farm Bureau—all have stressed the importance of preserving the purchasing power of the American dollar. Yet the reasons why these diverse groups oppose inflation are many, and often muddled, if we are to judge from the statements of their leaders.

[5] Inflation bleeds the little fellow and the working man. It increases profits at the expense of wages—or it transfers profits to the wage earner. It lowers the national standard of living. It leads inevitably to boom, bust and depression. It transfers income and wealth from the poor to the rich—or from the rich to the poor. It wipes out the value of savings and induces waste and dissolution. These are only a few of the claims gleaned from a casual reading of the daily papers and a sampling of the history books and campaign speeches of recent years. Nor is there any clear consensus among professional economists as to just who gains and who loses how much from inflation.

[6] Indeed, over the past few years the voice of the infidel has been heard in the temple of sound money. Maybe a little inflation now and then is a good thing—to stimulate economic progress and to prod the rentier class to do some work, rather than living comfortably off the rest of us through no greater exertion than clipping bond coupons. And this suggestion comes not as a course whisper from some unwashed radical, nor as a strident shout from ardent inflationists like the Greenbackers and the Populists of the 19th century. Indeed, it has come from the very pinnacle of respectability—Professor Sumner Slichter, perhaps the best known member of the Harvard Business School and Economics Department faculties and the most influential "business man's economist" of our day.

[7] Nor is Professor Slichter the only doubter. Several other influential economists, primarily of Keynesian and "guaranteed full employment" persuasion, have hinted at the Slichter position—though they seldom espouse inflation outright. Professor Earl Hamilton of the University of Chicago has argued learnedly in a series of important historical articles that the standard of living of the western world has risen fastest when gentle inflation has prevailed. And scratch many a businessman, farmer, or working man, and you will find not far under his surface pronouncements against inflation a willingness to have a quick sip of the forbidden drink—so long as he doesn't have to admit it publicly.

[8] It will be one of my main theses that inflation is likely to be a major social phenomenon of the half century ahead. If this is correct, it is important to analyze carefully and objectively just what the economic effects of inflation have been. . . .

Questions

1. What is Bach's attitude toward inflation? Explain.
2. What is the purpose of paragraph 5?
3. Examine the language in paragraph 6. What is Bach implying by statements like "the voice of the infidel has been heard in the temple of sound money" and "not as a course whisper from some unwashed radical"?
4. What is the point being made in the last sentence of paragraph 7?

THE MECHANICS OF INFLATION*

The Chamber of Commerce of the United States

[1] When prices and costs creep steadily upward during peacetime, the individual citizen has good reason to be concerned, to ask questions and to demand that appropriate steps be taken to hold inflation in check.

[2] When prices and costs continue to rise in the face of general monetary-credit restraints and balanced government budgets, alarm and vexation are created in the field of public policy. Congressional investigations, political oratory and public debate produce a greatly expanded supply of new diagnoses and prescriptions which often confuse more than enlighten.

[3] Inflation is rightly a cause of serious public concern, but it is also a subject about which there are many misapprehensions. There is an urgent need for greater public understanding of the mechanics of inflation—how it is generated, how it works and what can be done about it in a system of free enterprise. This report attempts to help meet that need.

[4] It analyzes and describes the process of inflation—the role of demand, costs and incomes. It discusses frankly market relationships, collective bargaining and other features of our modern economic system which make possible the generation and propagation of the "wage-price" spiral. Finally, it develops some long-run implications for public policy relating to the problem of maintaining high employment and economic growth without inflation.

[5] There is no search for "scapegoats" in this report. Nor does it pretend to reach final solutions. Its sole purpose is to help clarify the

---

* From *The Mechanics of Inflation: A Report of the Committee on Economic Policy of the Chamber of Commerce of the United States, 1958.*

issues, to stimulate objective thought and discussion and to promote economic understanding. . . .

Toward Greater Understanding

[6] Inflation is one of the most pervasive and persistent economic problems of our times—one which we may have to live with for a long time to come. It is an old problem which has plagued mankind since money was invented. At the same time it is also a new problem because it can never be solved once and for all.

[7] From the historical record, long experience and economic analysis, we have come to understand inflation rather well. Fundamentally, its causes are simple and its disturbing effects easy to recognize. Yet, in spite of our knowledge and experience, we do not seem to be able to reach agreement on how best to control its recurring attacks on our economic system and social framework.

[8] There are a number of fundamental reasons why inflation is so persistent and difficult to hold in check. First, inflation is the result of a combination of causes which vary in importance from one situation to another. History does not repeat itself in precise details. We live in a changing world: population grows; institutions change; new techniques of production, new tastes, new laws modify or replace the old; property and wealth are redistributed. As a result, inflationary processes and pressures always reappear in new guises creating new conflicts and interests which must be reconciled or resolved in the context of changed social and economic circumstances.

[9] Second, inflationary pressures are regenerated by man's conscious or unconscious revolt against the limitations of his environment. Economics is a "dismal science" because man does not like to be told that he cannot have his pie and eat it too. He wants more and bigger automobiles, highways, houses, gadgets, more comfort, leisure, governmental services, better schools, job opportunities and greater economic security. Collectively, he wants these things both now and tomorrow; and individually, he naturally wants a larger proportionate share, however rapidly or slowly the total economic pie grows in size. It is one of the tasks of social and economic organization to keep the sum total of all individual demands on the economic system within the bounds of the system's capacity to produce. In our imperfect world, it seems likely that man will always have natural inclination to overload the economy with excessive demands unless restrained by the discipline of the market and appropriate monetary and fiscal policies. Inflation is, in a sense, evidence of a lack of social discipline.

[10] Third, recognizing the problem and facing it squarely are two vastly different things. Facing the problem raises all sorts of uncomfortable issues of public policy on which disagreement is inevitable. In the arena of public policy, not only are there legitimate differences of opinion and judgment in correctly interpreting economic events, but many disagreements arise because of differences in explicit or implicit value judgments as to the many goals of public policy, the role of the individual and government and the kind of economic system we should try to maintain. Added to these difficulties are the pressures of vocal special pleaders who want the problem solved in a manner which will provide them with special economic advantage—naturally, they all identify their particular interests with the general welfare. It is, therefore, sometimes exceedingly difficult to distinguish between right policies advocated for wrong reasons and wrong policies proposed for right reasons, to say nothing of those which are right or wrong on two counts. Unfortunately, political expediency rather than rational choice often dictates the solution—or no solution.

[11] How shall we face the problem? We agree that the issues are important. We recognize the pernicious effects inflation has on our lives, the operation of the economic system and our social structure. But we do not seem to agree on what should be done, when and by whom. Amid the welter of inconsistent proposals, the clamor for special treatment, the scramble for economic or political advantage, we must somehow work out solutions to maintain reasonable stability of the value of our money, which also promote relatively full employment and orderly economic growth. At the same time, these solutions must be equitable and compatible with our free market institutions.

[12] What is badly needed is greater public understanding of how inflation works in our modern complex economic system, where and how inflationary forces are generated, how those forces operate and manifest themselves and how they can best be controlled in a free society.

[13] This study addresses itself to these questions. Its purpose is to look closely at the inflationary problem as it appears in modern dress, to analyze the mechanics of inflation as it occurs today and to discuss some of the problems of public policy. It is hoped that this pamphlet will throw some light on how we can best face an age-old, but acutely modern, problem.

The Setting of the Problem

[14] Rising prices are a symptom, rather than a cause, of inflation. The housewife, the wage earner or the businessman, however, generally

thinks that rising prices *are* inflation. Certainly, it is the rise in the general level of prices—of consumer goods, producers goods and the intermediate materials and services going into production—which destroys the purchasing power of the dollar and creates the real problems of inflation.

[15] There are many different definitions of inflation and different measures of its effects. To some analysts, inflation is an increase in the supply of money; to others it is an increase in the supply of money accompanied by a general rise in prices; to still others it is a general rise in money incomes proportionately greater than an increase in the real resources of the country. Actually, all these definitions have their uses, but they also inject semantic difficulties into any discussion. In what follows we shall try to avoid technical definitions and discuss inflation in general terms as a *process*—a process by which the general level of money prices, including the prices of productive services (incomes), are increased and the purchasing power of the dollar in all *major* uses is reduced.

[16] In simple terms, the process can be described as follows. Prices and incomes generally rise (become inflated) because the total volume of money spending increases faster than the physical supply of the goods and services on which the money is spent. The total volume of money spending, in turn, depends on (a) the supply or stock of money, and (b) how fast the stock of money is spent (i.e. its rate of turnover or velocity). Clearly, when the total volume of money expenditures increases more rapidly than the supply of goods and services bought and sold, the average dollar value—the average price or price level—must go up. Rising money prices of output must, at the same time, involve rising money incomes, since every price is divisible into wages, rent, interest and profit—neglecting taxes as a cost element for simplicity. Inflation of prices and incomes occurs when total money demand outruns the total supply of output, blowing up both the prices of output and the prices of resources.

[17] But why does total spending increase faster than supply? Where are the inflationary forces generated? How are they spread through our complex system of inter-related markets? How are costs and income related to the process?

[18] To answer these questions, we must first look at the structure of the economic system and identify those features of our economic organization which bear directly or indirectly on the problem—features which are too often overlooked in analysis and policy discussions. Then we will turn to an analysis of the inflationary process itself.

Economic Growth

[19] Since World War II, we have experienced tremendous expansion and growth—in population, the supply of capital and output. We all want growth and economic progress with ever-rising living standards. But rapid growth also produces growing pains and inflationary pressures which are more severe and somewhat different from those in a more stable economic environment. High levels of investment require a diversion of resources away from the production of goods for current consumption to the production of capital facilities. In other words, the nation in a very real sense must "save" an enlarged part of physical output in the form of capital goods—plant, machinery and equipment.

[20] During periods of economic expansion, when the economy is operating at high employment, the demands of consumers, business and government compete vigorously for limited output and limited resources. Total demand strains against physical capacity. Unless the total volume of money demand is kept within bounds, prices of goods, labor and materials will be bid up. Furthermore, voluntary money savings, the main source of funds for financing capital expansion, may become insufficient to meet heavy demands for funds. Powerful pressures build up for new creation of more credit and enlargement of the money supply. Money and credit may become "tight" under boom conditions without any direct monetary policy to tighten the money market. If bank credit is, however, substituted for money savings to feed an investment boom, inflation is inevitable.

[21] High pressure growth financed by inflation is extremely dangerous because it is chaotic growth which chokes itself off and plunges the system into disorder. Inflation is an uneven process. Some prices rise rapidly, others are "sticky" and lag behind, while others may actually fall. Investment plans and ordinary business calculations, difficult enough at best, cannot be made on a rational basis. Speculative excesses based on prospects of inflationary profits disturb the normal flow of economic life. The whole structure of production and markets becomes distorted, creating maladjustments which must be painfully corrected later through the catharsis of recession or depression.

The Role of Government

[22] Another important feature of modern economic life which must be taken into account is the enlarged role of government. Wars and rumors of war require continuous heavy commitments for national defense. In addition, the past 25 years have seen a tremendous expansion

of nondefense governmental activities. The government now produces all sorts of "goods and services" formerly not produced at all or produced privately. In 1957, federal, state and local governments absorbed directly approximately $87 billion worth of a gross output for the whole economy of $440 billion—roughly 20%. In addition, the governments transferred income of nearly $20 billion from one group to another under various benefit and welfare programs. These transfers plus the interest on the federal debt amounted to more than 7% of total personal income.

[23] No matter what restraints are imposed on the private sector of the economy, by the market or monetary controls, what the government does with respect to spending, taxing and debt management will loom very large in determining an inflationary or deflationary course of events. We have big government; but we simply cannot afford to have irresponsible big government, or the problem of controlling inflation will be insoluble. Perhaps the first line of defense against inflation is to control the politicians—to discipline them sharply for making promises that cannot be fulfilled, for overloading the economy and for avoiding uncomfortable political decisions imposed by the stern facts of life.

Full Employment Guarantees

[24] In addition to being a large buyer, producer, borrower and lender, government has, since the depression of the 1930's, been injected into the economic life in another way which has a direct and most important bearing on the problem of inflation. Under the Employment Act of 1946, the Federal Government is charged with the responsibility for maintaining conditions of "maximum employment and purchasing power." Although this injunction is vague and there is considerable disagreement as to how and when government should act to discharge its responsibility, the political climate is such that no administration dare risk anything beyond mild and temporary unemployment. For this reason, one may expect government policies to err on the inflationary side.

[25] But more important, "full employment guarantees" weaken the discipline of the market. When "maximum employment" is interpreted as "outlawing" all unemployment at all times, except for a frictional minimum, labor leaders and businessmen may raise wages and prices with little fear that they may face the normal penalties of unsold goods and unemployment. . . .

[26] Economists generally agree that reconciling full employment with price level stability within a free enterprise framework is one of

the major unsolved problems of our times. Unless some degree of flexibility, some "elbow room," in the form of selective price-wage adjustments and transitional unemployment, is left in the market, and unless the government is also held strictly responsible for maintaining stable monetary values, the problem will remain unsolved.

Market Structures: Price and Wage Rigidities

[27] A further major consideration is the structure of industry and markets, including the market for labor services. Modern technology, the organizational revolution of the 20th century and public policy (and apathy) have produced large-scale business enterprises and large, powerful labor unions. While we owe a great deal to the efficiency and productivity of large-scale industry, and although there is growing concern over the economic impact of labor organizations, the fact remains that in important sectors of the economy we do not have prices and wages that respond quickly to changing market conditions. In many cases, to varying degrees, both prices and wages are rigid or "sticky," and some are set by economic units having considerable market control or latitude in pricing and wage policies.

[28] This is not the place to consider the problems of industrial concentration, labor monopoly or the competitive limitations of the market. The important point here is simply that both prices and wages are flexible upward but inflexible downward. To maintain a stable general price level, some prices must fall as others rise, but under inflationary pressures rigid prices and wages constitute blocks under the price level which prevent normal market adjustments. In other words, inflexible prices and negotiated wages become "benchmarks" around which other prices and costs must adjust. They create an important upward bias in the price structure. At the same time, as mentioned above, wage demands and price increases can be pushed aggressively under boom conditions, and all the more so when the government weakens the market by writing a full-employment "blank check." . . .

Questions

1. In the introduction it is stated that the committee did not seek "scapegoats." Can you locate any scapegoats for inflation in this report? Explain.
2. In paragraph 5 examine the sentence, "Its sole purpose is to help clarify the issues, to stimulate objective thought and discussion and to promote economic understanding." Do you agree that this is the sole purpose of the report? Explain.
3. In paragraph 9 the authors refer to "man" and his inclinations. What definition of man do you think is intended here? Do you believe their argument here is universally valid? Why or why not?

4. In paragraph 9 what assumption is being made about the relationship of "man" to "social and economic organization"?

5. Examine the section Economic Growth. What kind of growth are we experiencing according to this section? What conclusions do the authors offer here? Do you consider the evidence and reasoning valid? Explain.

6. What is the point or idea in the section The Role of the Government? What evidence is offered in support? Do you consider it adequate? Why or why not?

7. In the section Full Employment Guarantees, what is their attitude toward unemployment?

8. Examine the language of the section Market Structures: Price and Wage Rigidities. What kind of words are used in connection with business and industry? What kind of words are used in connection with labor unions?

HOW DEEPLY DO YOU BELIEVE IN AMERICA?*

Arthur E. Summerfield

Today, if I may, I should like to lay before you some thoughts on our national security, and our philosophy of government. They are, of course, entirely interrelated.

We must begin with the premise that we are today engaged in a great economic struggle with the Soviet Union. . . .

Why? Because they are now concentrating on *all-out economic war,* and they believe they can defeat us in such a war without risking their own destruction. . . .

Ironically, they are counting on *us* to help. While they are pushing the Soviet economy faster, they expect the American economy to falter on at least two rocks of huge and disastrous proportions:

1. runaway inflation; and
2. political unwillingness to hold to the basic principles that have made our country so powerful and so great.

I believe their hope will be in vain. I believe we shall continue to build the strongest, finest, freest way of life the world will know.

But, my friends, *this* I also believe:

To do so, *America must maintain a sound economic philosophy, and sound policies firmly based on such philosophy.*

* From *Vital Speeches of The Day,* April 15, 1959. Reprinted by permission.

This is why I am selling, with all the energy and devotion I possess, the *sound growth of our country under a philosophy of government that can provide the greatest opportunity for all our people.*

What is this philosophy?

I think it can be simply stated:

It is a government that discharges every legitimate obligation to its citizens, but does so within the framework of a responsible fiscal policy.

It is a government that recognizes our free enterprise system—our industry and agriculture—as the very wellspring of prosperity and opportunity for all our people. It is a government, therefore, that promotes the sound growth of this system and its service to the people.

It is a government determined to place the best interest of *all* its citizens above special interests of any selfish group.

Such a government is essential to deal with the problems of these times. It is vital in fighting inflation and in grappling with our tremendous problems of taxation.

For, make no mistake, we *are* at grips with deadly inflationary forces. We *are* under the gun of onerous taxation—taxation that can effectively prevent the accumulation of private capital and the incentive for productive expansion.

In our battle against inflation, two facts today stand out very clearly:

The first is, that if public spending soars far beyond the revenues of Government, inflation will infuse itself more deeply and dangerously throughout economy.

Unrestrained spending can only result in deficit financing, higher taxes and cheaper dollars. And in such event, who must bear these burdens? You. You and your family—and every other citizen of our country!

Inflation feeds on the income and the savings of *every individual, every enterprise*, in America.

It eats away the savings we cherish for our family's security. It robs us of the real value of the dollars we earn. A quick glance at the family food basket can make that point painfully clear.

In 1939, a dollar would fill the basket with potatoes, bread, coffee, cabbage, milk and eggs. Today's dollar will buy only the cabbage, milk and eggs.

Twenty years ago, you could buy a pound of round steak, a pound of bacon, a pound of pork chops, and a pound of sugar for what it costs you today to buy just the pound of steak alone!

And so it goes with every thing we buy.

Every American, therefore, has compelling reason to be concerned over the gigantic spending schemes that already have been voted by one House or the other of the present Congress. Together, just to date, these schemes represent several billion dollars of needless, unjustifiable spending! And more of the same are in the offing.

All are the creations of political pressures of special groups.

But if they become law, it will be every American whose dollar is cheapened—every American whose paycheck must yield steeper taxes, —and every American whose children must bear the future debt.

The second fact in the inflation battle is the vast monopoly power of a handful of union dictators. This is the very core of our inflationary struggle.

Eighty per cent or more of the cost of what we buy is for labor. Obviously, industrial wage costs have a very direct bearing on everyone's cost of living.

Wage increases have been fundamental to the rising living standards of our people, and the vitality of our economy. They should continue to be. And they will be, so long as they are related to increased productive efficiency.

But when union dictators force wage costs far outrunning productivity gains, inflation is inevitable. With each round of wage and price increases, our dollar drops another notch in purchasing power. The wage earner who gets the increase soon finds that his new dollars, too, are siphoned off by a higher cost of living. And union members everywhere are hurt as badly as everyone else.

In the past ten years, a 28 per cent gain in industrial productivity has been overwhelmed by a 67 per cent rise in wage rates. The difference between these figures is wage-push inflation. Inevitably, this has priced more and more American products out of export markets, and reduced our ability to meet foreign competition in our own domestic markets.

The nation has been shocked by the colossal labor racketeering and corruption revealed in the hearings of the McClellan Committee. Our people—including the great body of union members—want these terrible abuses stopped, *now*.

But let us recognize that these abuses are but *symptoms of a much greater problem*.

Why are union racketeers contemptuous of public opinion? Because they operate within the framework of a tremendous concentration of power which aims to control the laws, the law-makers of our land, and eventually the White House itself. Thousands of our businessmen and

workers have been partially "brain-washed" into believing these influences cannot be successfully challenged, thereby weakening their will
to resist, to stand up and fight for what is right!

.   .   .   .

This is a grave moral and economic problem to which our Congress
should address itself with all earnestness. Many alarmed members of
ently are more concerned with the wrath of the union dictators than
their duty to the American people.
the Congress are doing so. But, quite obviously, too many others pres-

.   .   .   .

A hard and fateful struggle is being waged. Your voice and efforts are
more than important—they are *vital*.

They are vital on specific current issues. They are vital on long-range
issues. They are needed at campaign time, and between campaigns.

Sound political leadership must have the active support of those who
want sound government.

Some State governments today face virtual financial collapse.

Why?

Because those believing in sound political leadership have stood
aside as spendthrift politicians have joined forces with labor bosses in
an orgy of reckless spending and more and more taxation.

And what permanent solutions are being suggested by those in control?

The only suggestions so far have been the worn-out, old-fashioned
"soak the rich" ideas; specifically, a call for a corporation's profit tax,
and an income tax on so narrow a base that only a small per cent of the
citizens would have to pay the bills!

Nothing is being done to reduce expenditures. No studies are under
way to see where the tax dollars of these States have gone and are going. Nothing is being done through long-range state tax reforms to
make these States attractive once again to business and industry, and
to help provide more jobs.

My friends, the citizens of these States are learning the hard way that
more huge spending programs mean that the Government has to collect *more* in taxes to pay for them.

The more American business has to pay in taxes, the *less* it has left
to invest in new products and new plants.

And certainly, the less business is able to invest in new production,
the less it is able to create new jobs.

It is that simple.

Peaceful co-existence may have its virtues in some fields. But the welfare state and virile free enterprise can not exist side by side within the same economy. And I don't believe for one minute that the union members of our country, any more than the rest of us, want to surrender their freedom to a welfare state.

Instead of increasing the tax burden, we need to carry out an essential revision in our Federal tax structure.

This task, we know, will be tremendously difficult. But it is part and parcel of the basic solution for stopping inflation and spurring our economic growth. It must be done.

And this kind of program will be achieved only if we avoid the pitfalls of grandiose spending for non-essentials, and other inflationary pressures which swell the costs of government.

In summary, let me leave these thoughts with you:

We must maintain our initiative in military and world political strength.

We must be equally vigilant against the Soviet determination to defeat us politically with economic strength. This may well be the ultimate battleground the Kremlin has chosen.

To succeed, we must promote the sound growth of our whole economy—we must maintain a philosophy of government that provides the greatest opportunity for all our people.

We must keep the cost of living in check, while our standards of living go up, with a stable dollar. This means a balanced budget, and control of pressure on prices resulting from the irresponsible demands of a few union dictators.

.   .   .   .

There is nothing more important you can do than to devote some of your sales genius and best techniques to fighting this battle. Nothing is more essential to your company and its future!

Thousands of corporate mailings are made to stockholders every day. Why not employ these mailings to enlist their active support? Pressure-group government and labor monopoly power are definitely contrary to *their* interests.

I would dare to suggest that your companies, in these communications, tell your stockholders clearly how this struggle affects them, both as citizens and as owners of business. There are also many hard-hitting articles, speeches and other materials that could be included. Mailed regularly to the nation's 10 million stockholders, they could be of ever-expanding influence throughout the country.

The same can be said of communications with employees. They, too, can see this great competition in progress, and they need to know *from you* exactly what is at stake and they should be told the truth.

What do you want for America? How deep is your belief in America? It *is* very deep, I am certain. But it can be effective only as you let it be known.

I urge you to take your place among those who will speak, and work, and fight for sound government and a stronger America in the years ahead!

My friends, the greatest era in history—the Golden Era of unlimited opportunity, lies ahead.

We can make it mankind's most fruitful period if we but solve the problems we face and move forward, as we can, united for the well-being of America.

We will do so if we but realize that the all-out economic war with the Communists calls for just as much unity of purpose, just as much devotion to country, just as much selfless effort, yes just as much old-fashioned patriotism on the part of every American, as any military war ever did. . . .

Questions

1. How would you characterize the language of this speech? Use examples from the speech to support your analysis.
2. Summerfield states, "In our battle against inflation, two facts stand out very clearly." What are these two "facts"? Do you consider them to be facts? Explain.
3. What, according to Summerfield, are the two causes of inflation? Assess the reasoning and evidence he presents in support of his argument about causes.
4. Why do you suppose Summerfield uses the term *union dictators* instead of *union officials?*
5. What action does Summerfield want his listeners to take? If you were in the audience, what questions would you want answered before you would be willing to follow his advice?
6. What does Summerfield say is now being done about inflation? Do you agree with these statements? Explain.
7. In the eighth paragraph from the end, beginning "Thousands of corporate mailings . . .," do you find any inconsistency? Explain.
8. Why do you think the speaker makes references to the Soviet Union and the Communists at the beginning and end of his speech?
9. Examine the evidence presented in this speech. Do you consider it adequate? Do you think his audience considered it adequate? Explain.
10. What are the main emotional appeals that you find in this speech? How effective do you think they were?

NO SANTA CLAUS*

Warner & Swasey Machinery Company

No Santa Claus

FOR years workmen got higher and higher wages without enough more production to pay for them. Many got the idea it was all a gift from their labor leaders.

But of course the higher wages made costs higher; higher costs cannot help but mean higher prices.

And about a year ago the consumer (who decides everything in time) decided he had played Santa Claus long enough; he was through with paying more dollars for no more merchandise nor value. So—he stopped buying.

That, and only that, is what put millions out of work. They'll go back to work when their labor leaders let them do what honest workmen want—make their product worth the price.

In the meantime everyone loses including—especially including—the workmen.

When more efficient production brings down costs and prices, everyone benefits—everyone has more

When are we going to wake up to the fact that you can't bludgeon arithmetic with an unsound wage contract?

Sliding gear shaft being machined on a saddle type Warner & Swasey turret lathe.

WARNER & SWASEY
Cleveland
PRECISION MACHINERY SINCE 1880

YOU CAN PRODUCE IT BETTER, FASTER, FOR LESS WITH WARNER & SWASEY MACHINE TOOLS, TEXTILE MACHINERY, CONSTRUCTION EQUIPMENT

Questions

1. What is the significance of the Santa Claus metaphor?
2. Why do you suppose a large manufacturing company would pay to put an advertisement like this one in a weekly news magazine? What do you think they hope to achieve by this?
3. What does this advertisement tell you about the owners or managers of this

* Reprinted by permission of The Warner & Swasey Machinery Company.

company? What assumptions are they making about the readers of this magazine?

4. Is it always true that higher wages means higher costs? Explain.

5. Examine the cause and effect reasoning in the fifth and sixth paragraphs. Notice in the third paragraph the reference "about a year ago." What would have had to happen between 1960 and 1961 for the conclusions presented to be true? Read the selection from *U.S. News & World Report* entitled "Inflation and the U.S. Economy." Do the data presented support the conclusions in the advertisement? Why or why not?

6. What are the implications of the statement "you can't bludgeon arithmetic with an unsound wage contract"?

IS INFLATION THE PROBLEM?*

Leon Keyserling

. . . Precisely how to get growth without inflation is our supreme economic problem. But our economic thinking is not yet readjusted to this purpose.

If we are to think straight on this problem, which has become increasingly urgent since the first Sputnik, we must begin by determining the fundamental purposes of the modern US economy. While a stable price level is highly desirable, a static society may have a stable price level and go down to defeat on many or all fronts. Moreover, a stable price level without more, as during 1922–1929, can lead up to a depression. The great aims of our economy in these times are not to achieve any particular price trend as a be-all and end-all in itself. Instead, our fundamental economic purposes are these:

1. We must call forth the full use of our productive capabilities, including manpower and brains, technology and science, and natural resources. In the current state of our technology, this requires an annual over-all growth rate of about 5 percent after we take up fully the current economic slack. Until then, we need to grow much faster. The faster a nation increases total production, the stronger it becomes in an economic sense, and the better able to do what it needs to do, unless it is burning itself out by going so fast that it depletes its resources. We are in no danger of following the latter course.

2. We must apportion our total national production wisely, in accord with relative priorities of needs, so that we do not get what we need least at the expense of what we need most: for example, more gim-

* From *The New Republic*, February 9, 1959. Copyright © 1959 Harrison-Blaine, Inc. Reprinted by permission.

crack gadgets and less defense, international economic cooperation, schools.

3. We must combine economic progress and efficient use of resources with economic justice. To illustrate, the first two great purposes might be attained, even while the farm population lived by eating the income crumbs.

Broadly speaking, the significance of price and wage and farm income and profit trends in the private economy, and of public finance and monetary policy in the public area, is whether they facilitate or impede these three fundamental purposes. *They are means, not ends. And if the machinery is tooled to produce these ends, we get less inflation to boot.*

In order to put the President's[1] entire program in perspective, let us look for a moment at how far we have fallen short of our three fundamental purposes since the Korean War.

First, we have failed to use America's full productive powers. The figures which follow are all based upon uniform 1957 dollars, to make the comparisons exact. During the six-year period 1953–1958 inclusive, with recessions more than half of the time and with an inadequate growth rate the rest of the time, the US average annual over-all growth rate was only about 1.3 percent. However, an annual growth rate of about 4.5 percent was needed during that period to absorb our increasing capabilities to produce, in view of a growing labor force and an advancing technology. In consequence, *we lost more than $150 billion in potential national production, and furnished about 10 million manyears less of employment opportunity than we should have.*

Second, pressing national needs have been grossly neglected. Over the six-year period, tax revenues at all levels derived from a repressed economy were $30 billion to $40 billion lower than they would have been in a fully productive economy. Thus, we "could not afford" what we most need.

Third, these trends worked against economic justice. They bore down disproportionately upon all vulnerable groups: the unemployed, the farmer, the low-income family generally, the small businessman. They hurt the old people, because we "could not afford" to provide them with enough social security. And these damaging effects of low economic growth were compounded, because *a price inflation which fed the fat and stripped the lean was taking place at the same time.* Any housewife who does the shopping can testify to that.

[1] President Eisenhower [Eds.]

Now let us look at the causes of this triple default in order to see what went wrong and learn what corrective measures to take. For the six-year period 1953–58 as a whole, the more than $150 billion deficiency in total production resulted from a deficiency of about $17.5 billion in public consumption through public programs, a deficiency of about $96 billion in private consumption through private spending, and a deficiency of less than $40 billion in private investment caused when the other two deficiencies made it futile to continue investment in the expansion of productive facilities.

Despite its seemingly small relative size, the deficiency in public programs of about $17.5 billion really accounted in addition for about $35 billion to $50 billion of the deficiency in private consumption and private investment, because public outlays evoke other outlays. And this default in public outlays was practically entirely on the part of the federal government, because the states and localities were expanding their outlays up to, or in excess of, their limited power to obtain revenues. This must be borne in mind constantly, as one reads the Administration's repeated pleas to turn public programs back to the states and localities.

The deficiency in private consumption did not come about because consumers as a whole spent too little of their incomes and saved too much. On the contrary, the $96 billion deficiency in private consumer spending during the period 1953–1958 resulted from a deficiency of more than $130 billion in consumer income before taxes. Out of this, more than $30 billion was a deficiency in net farm operators' income, and more than $100 billion was a deficiency in the consumer income before taxes of other groups, made up practically entirely of a deficiency in wages.

These deficiencies in private buying power resulted from both governmental and private actions. The inadequate outlays by the federal government for essential public services had an adverse effect upon the whole private economy. Regressive and inequitable tax and monetary policies had similar results. The deficiency in farm income has been attributable to falling farm prices in contrast with rising non-farm prices, due primarily to a national farm policy which has abandoned the farmer to the "free market," while other markets were not "free."

This analysis is essential to an understanding of the cause and cure of the kind of inflation with which we have been plagued in recent years. For it has not been an inflation like that of wartime: it has not happened because of intense pressure against our productive capabilities, or shortages, or a hectic rate of economic growth, or civilian purchasing power in excess of civilian supplies. *The "new inflation" of recent years has occurred "paradoxically" in the face of high economic slack.* And moreover, it has been a selective inflation, with some prices and incomes rising too rapidly, while others were falling too fast, or (in the case of incomes) not rising fast enough.

Now, what has caused this selective inflation—for we have had it— since excessive demand was not a factor? The President has more than implied that the inflation has occurred in large measure because wages have gone up faster than productivity thus increasing production costs per unit and requiring price increases—the "cost-push" theory. This theory misses the real point: the lag in productivity behind wage increase in some instances was not technological, but was due instead to the inefficiencies of operating far below full capacity. And low-capacity operation was certainly not due to "excessive" wages; if wages had gone up less, even relative to productivity, we would have had a still bigger recession. Therefore, the correct remedy for the alleged inflationary gap between productivity and wages would have been—and is—to *lift actual productivity to its technological potential by expanding the economy,* not to contract the economy further by holding down wages.

Moreover, in most cases price increases were not due to "cost-push," wages or otherwise, but to excessive price increases relative to costs. The compelling evidence of this is that the excessive advances of prices compared with wages yielded a level of profits feeding an investment boom in plant and equipment recurrently outrunning private and public buying combined. The extraordinarily high profits in 1957 of some of our major industries *which were operating far below full production,* and their exceedingly high profits again now while even further short of full production, are much in point. This applies not only to industrial prices but also to many consumer prices, because the former affect the latter, and because increasing portions of our consumer-service industries are now huge and administer their prices.

These excessive price increases have in part reflected management's over-excited appetite for capital investment funds in the form of profits. But this hunger was not entirely the fault of industry. In part, industry feared with good reason that the spasmodic periods of high-level production would not be sustained in the absence of a nationwide full employment policy, and that industry needed to store up reserves against trouble.

In short, just as an automobile burns more gas per mile when racing at 80 miles an hour *or when dawdling at 13 miles an hour* than when running smoothly at 50, so our economy costs more to operate per unit of production either at the racing 8-percent growth rate of wartime *or at the 1.3 percent average growth rate of recent years* rather than at a 5 percent growth rate. The higher costs of too great or *too little speed* are both inflationary.

Despite these terribly costly lessons, the Economic Report of the President again expresses a determination to check economic growth by the same budgetary and tax and tight-money policies which have done so much damage on all scores thus far. The spurious crusade against inflation remains a crusade, not in the public interest but against adequate outlays for defense, international cooperation and domestic well-being. What are the implications of a continuation of these policies?

While the President's Economic Report hails the speed of our economic recovery, we are "recovering" at a rate insufficient to take up the accumulated slack, or to make full use of the continuing growth in our labor force and in productivity. Thus, some of our bellwether industries, while expanding their production and sales, are not re-employing many people. Unemployment in 1959 may well be nearly as high as in 1958. Looking further ahead, we are likely to "recover" from the most recent recession only to average an annual over-all growth rate in real terms of perhaps 2 percent.

What would this mean, compared with what would happen if we take up the economic slack more rapidly and thereafter maintain a 5 percent annual growth rate? For the seven-year period from the beginning of 1958 through the end of 1964, it would mean a difference of about $400 billion in total national production, and a difference of about 16.5 million man-years in job opportunity. With respect to our national needs, the higher growth rate (in contrast with the lower growth rate) would yield at existing tax rates about $70 billion more, or an average of about $10 billion a year more, by way of public revenues at all levels for domestic and international purposes. *This is the road to a balanced federal budget, accompanied by high enough public outlays to do at home and abroad what needs to be done and to induce a balanced national economy. And for reasons already given, the low growth rate would be more inflationary than the high growth rate.*

An economy functioning satisfactorily, one that serves the three great fundamentals, is less inflationary than an economy responding to repressive and regressive policies which neglect these fundamentals.

Above all, if we now become prey to the notion that "inflation is a greater danger to us than Khrushchev," we shall continue to lose more and more ground in the current world struggle. For, in its essence, the Administration's crusade against inflation is a campaign against the positive things we need to do. It plays upon illegitimate fears instead of raising legitimate hopes. It tells us that we are weak instead of rallying our strength. It sets up economic Maginot Lines instead of developing new economic weapons. It fails to recognize that in our economic policies just as in our international policies, we cannot have safety or stability by standing still.

Questions

1. What assumptions are being made in the two opening sentences?
2. What is Keyserling's point about stable prices? Do you agree or disagree? Explain.
3. In item 2 of the second paragraph, what does he mean by "gimcrack gadgets" and why does he use the phrase?
4. In his argument for increased economic growth and production, what assumption is he making about consumption? Do you consider it valid? Explain.
5. What does Keyserling consider to be the causes of our inflation? Why does he call it the "new" inflation?
6. What is his point about profits? Do you think his point is well made? Why or why not?
7. Where does Keyserling place the blame for our present economic ills? What does he think should be done about it? Do you agree or not? Why?
8. What are the implications of the phrase "the spurious crusade" in the fifth paragraph from the end?
9. In the last paragraph what is meant by "economic Maginot Lines"? Evaluate this choice of metaphor.
10. Examine the statistics used in this essay. In what form are they presented? Why?

JOBS BY INFLATION?*

Henry Hazlitt

[1] We are in a recession. Unemployment is alarmingly high. We must *act*. "I hope we can get action as soon as possible."

[2] Thus the Kennedy Administration. And what is this action we must take so precipitously? It is more government spending in all directions—on unemployment compensation, crop price supports, housing, highways, depressed areas, veterans, social security, federal aid to education, and scores of other projects. It is lowering interest rates and increasing loans. It is, in a word, inflation.

[3] Behind this proposed remedy is the same theory that has dominated the economic policy of most Western governments, especially our

* From *Newsweek*, March 6, 1961. Copyright © 1961 Weekly Publications, Inc. Reprinted by permission.

own, for the last quarter century. It is the theory made popular by union propaganda and the late Lord Keynes.

[4] Keynes himself recognized that raising wage rates would only increase unemployment. He lefthandedly conceded that unemployment might exist because real wage rates were already too high in comparison with prices and demand, so that the outlook for profits was too bleak to encourage full employment. But he argued that a direct lowering of money wage rates would be so strongly resisted by the unions as to be impossible. Therefore the only way to lower wage rates to a workable level was to lower the value of money. The way to do this was to inflate, to print more money, and so to raise prices and monetary demand to a level at which full employment would be possible again.

[5] This is the process to which we have resorted again and again in the last 28 years. Economically, it has seemed to work. We have had continuous inflation, but we have also (at least since 1942) had fairly continuous employment. Politically, it has kept whatever Administration was in power from having to face up to the problem of how to halt constant union wage demands and increases that exceeded the gains in labor's marginal productivity at the existing level of prices. We have floated ourselves out by ever new doses of inflation.

[6] Well, why can't we do it again? Why can't we keep it up forever?

[7] One reason it is especially dangerous to try it again now is that we have done it so much in the past that we have undermined international confidence in the dollar. Our labor costs of production on some items have been raised to a point that is pricing them out of the world market. American capital is being invested in new plants abroad rather than at home. Our existing inflation has already caused a deficit in our balance of payments. We have been losing gold at a dangerous rate. Further inflation will only intensify the problem.

[8] And we can't keep inflating forever because the process inevitably becomes accelerative. With every dose of monetary inflation and increase of prices, the unions make demands for still further wage increases to keep up with or get ahead of the latest price increase. Each round of wage increases leads to another dose of inflation to pay the new wage level. There is a perpetual and increasingly desperate race between the printing press and the union demands.

[9] Yet the whole race is needless. What is necessary for full employment is the coordination of wages and prices, at whatever average level. If this coordination does not exist, if a new dose of inflation simply touches off a new round of wage hikes, then the inflation is futile, even as a short-term expedient.

[10] What labor is chiefly suffering from today is too many victories. It is no mere coincidence that unemployment now is highest in lines in which wage rates are highest. As compared with average wages of $2.30 an hour in all manufacturing industries, wages in automobile plants are $2.87 an hour, in steel mills $3.02, in bituminous coal mines, $3.27. But in the excited calls of the Kennedy Administration for "action," there is complete silence regarding wage rates. They are treated as irrelevant.

[11] Yet not quite. Among the proposed remedies for unemployment are higher and longer unemployment benefits and higher minimum wages to keep wage rates up or to force them still higher.

Questions

1. In the second paragraph with what does Hazlitt equate inflation? Why?
2. What does Hazlitt find to be the cause of our present inflation?
3. Hazlitt twice refers to printing more money. Who prints the money and why, according to him? Can you think of other explanations of why more money is printed? Explain.
4. What assumptions does Hazlitt make about all wage increases? Are they valid? Why or why not?
5. In paragraph 5 what is the significance of that precise reference to "the last 28 years"?
6. In paragraph 10 Hazlitt cites certain hourly wage rates. Why? Are there other wage rates omitted which might bear on this also? Explain.
7. Notice that Hazlitt omits any discussion of prices and profits. Why?
8. What would Hazlitt propose be done to stop inflation? What is your evaluation of his solutions?

INFLATION AND THE U.S. ECONOMY*

U.S. News & World Report

I. Another Round of Inflation on the Way? [June 12, 1961]

At a time of recovery in business an old worry is coming back. This is worry about the prospect of a revived wage-price spiral that once again might put the U.S. dollar into trouble.

Worry about a revival of inflation cropped up at a recent meeting of 30 top economists called by Douglas Dillon, Secretary of the Treasury. Even those known as "New Deal economists" or "Keynesian economists" showed concern about the troubles that inflation—if it comes back—could cause the U.S. dollar.

* Reprinted from U. S. News & World Report, published at Washington.

All of the economists, reflecting a wide range of viewpoints, agreed that the recession is over and recovery under way. Some even expressed the opinion that moves made by the Eisenhower Administration and by the Federal Reserve Board to counter the recession had been "just about right."

It was at this point that a note of concern was sounded by some of the group.

The feeling was expressed that a rapid rise in spending by Government over the year ahead might "overstimulate" business and might generate a boom atmosphere. With business booming, union leaders would demand large increases in wages. Businessmen, faced with higher wage costs, would be under pressure to increase prices in order to preserve margins of profit.

It is that type of situation that generates a wage-price spiral. And it is an upward spiraling of prices that would tend to raise a question about the future of the U.S. dollar. Confidence in the dollar, restored recently after reaching a low point, is not as firm as it once was. . . .

The prospect is that actual spending in the year to start July 1 will pass 86 billion dollars. That is more than 5 billion dollars higher than the January estimate.

The trend of Government spending, pointed sharply higher, is to go on rising over the years as new programs grow in cost and old programs, possibly, keep on rising, too.

Along with this trend toward higher and higher Government spending in a time of rising business activity is another trend—toward so-called "cheap" money. . . .

White House policy at this time calls for continued pressure by the Federal Reserve Board to make money more abundant and cheaper to borrow.

Where fears center. It is in this field of "cheap" money that economists differ most sharply. All of them would like to see business activity expand and unemployment shrink. Many of them believe that abundant credit and low interest rates would encourage this expansion. But most sense a danger in this trend. . . .

One fear is that low interest rates in the United States would prompt people abroad to transfer their dollar holdings into other assets and that some U.S. citizens also would shift dollars abroad. This actually happened last year when short-term interest rates fell in the U.S. and rose in other countries.

Another danger seen is that abundant and "cheap" money in the United States, coupled with rising business activity, probably would spark a rising trend in prices. That trend, too, would make it more lifficult to sell U.S. products on world markets. And it would weaken world confidence in the dollar.

In that event, other countries would sell dollars and demand gold.

The economists generally agreed that this "balance of payments" problem still is a serious one, even though the dollar recently has shown strength. . . .

These claims against the dollar are prompting many economists to urge a "cautious" approach by the Kennedy Administration to problems connected with economic growth, full employment, "cheap" money, and wages and prices. The opinion is spreading that, in the words of one economist, "you can't have everything right away."

II. Your Income vs. Inflation. [June 26, 1961]

[1] Once again, a rise in business is reviving worry about possible inflation. Many people are wondering how much they have been hurt —or helped—by the inflation of the past. . . .

[2] *The raises needed.* If your family had income of $8,000 before taxes in 1948, you now need $10,344 a year to have the same buying power and same standard of living you had then. To put it another way, the breadwinner in this income bracket has had to have pay raises totaling more than 29 per cent just to stay even in the race with inflation.

[3] Above the $8,000 level, even steeper increases in income have been necessary to avoid falling behind in living standards. This is a reflection of the fact that the Government's graduated tax system takes a bigger portion of any pay boost as your income goes up.

[4] The man who made $20,000 in 1948 is no better off today with an income of $26,552, or almost one third more than he received a dozen years ago.

[5] With $100,000 before taxes in 1948, a family now needs $162,890 a year—an increase of nearly two thirds—to avoid a drop in living standards due to higher prices and higher taxes.

[6] *The raises received.* Actually, the typical family has made some material progress despite inflation. Incomes have gone up faster than prices. The "real" income of the average family is up 21.2 per cent since 1948, after allowing for the rise in living costs and taxes.

[7] The average factory worker has done even better. His pay was $2,815 in 1948 and $4,727 in 1960. Assuming he is the sole jobholder in a family of four, a factory worker with an average wage needed a 29 per cent pay boost from 1948 to 1960 to maintain "real" income. He got a pay boost of 68 per cent.

[8] On the other hand, people on fixed incomes and many who work in less favored jobs find that inflation means a painful setback any time it comes.

III. What It Takes Now To Be "Well Off." [July 24, 1961]

There was a time, not so many years ago, when a family was considered well off if it had an income of $5,000 or more a year. Today, half of all families in the United States enjoy incomes not only of $5,000 a year, but of $5,600 or more.

The average of all family incomes has now risen to $6,900, according to the latest study by the U.S. Department of Commerce.

Today a well-to-do family is likely to be thought of as having an income of at least $10,000, instead of $5,000 a year. One of every six families in the U.S. now falls in this category.

More are well off. Nearly 3.5 million families receive at least $15,000 annually and 6.3 million receive from $10,000 to $15,000. All told, this is an increase of nearly 8 million families at these income levels since 1947, the start of the prosperous postwar era.

There has also been a sharp increase in the number of families that stand just a notch lower on the income scale—those getting from $8,000 to $10,000 annually.

Out of these families that have more than enough for the necessities of life comes most of the demand for such things as a second car, a European trip or a boat. The auto companies, boat-builders, resorts and travel agents, in particular, count heavily on further increases in these upper-income groups to expand their markets in the future. Today, much of the spending at this level seems to be going for better clothing, recreation and education.

Fewer poor. Along with the increase in relatively well-to-do families has come a sharp decrease in the number living on low incomes.

Back in 1947, the average income of American families was $4,100. Nearly two thirds of all families made less than $4,000 a year. Today, only one family in three makes this little.

Many people are wondering whether this trend toward higher incomes is a product of inflation and whether people now are really any better off. The answer is this:

Some of the rise in incomes has been due to inflation and has been offset by the rise in living costs. That accounts for only part of the upward shift in incomes, however. The average American household has enjoyed a substantial improvement in living standards, and that im provement is continuing at present, in spite of the lingering effects of the recent recession.

Average family income this year will be a little higher than it was in 1960, even after allowing for changes in living costs. The recession has not cut into the income or living standards of the average family the way previous postwar recessions did.

World's highest. In short, more and more families in this country are achieving levels of income undreamed of by most people in the past and unequaled anywhere else in the world.

IV. Will It Be a Record Boom? *[August 7, 1961]*

The American people during the next 18 months, barring war, are going to enjoy better times than ever before.

This will be true of almost all groups of people. It will likewise be true of most lines of business.

Incomes will be at record highs and rising. Living standards will be in a strong rise. Prices for the most part will be relatively stable. Profits are going to break all records of the past.

The turn from recession to recovery already is strongly under way.

Total spending—known as the gross national product—is at a new high and headed up. Personal income, in total, exceeds that of any past period. Output of goods has recovered almost all of the ground lost in the latest recession.

With this trend set, Government now is to step in with a new program of spending on arms. Increase in buying of conventional weapons alone will be near 2 billions a year.

This arms program is put on top of an expanded highway program, a big program of exploration in space and a huge expansion of credits being made available for many forms of housing—public and private.

All of this adds up to the assurance of a record boom ahead. . . .

The new boom is developing against a background of surplus capacity in almost all fields. Industry, over all, now is using no more than 80 per cent of its facilities for production. At the same time more than 5 million persons who are listed as seeking work now lack jobs.

This means that expansion in business can go far before placing a strain either on the country's industrial plant or upon its supply of labor.

Inflation, as a result, probably can be held in check without use of direct controls by Government over wages and prices, or over credit.

President Kennedy said on July 25, however, that he would not hesitate to ask Congress for power to impose controls if there is a real revival of inflation. Pressures for voluntary action to avoid a new wage-price spiral will be strong.

The business upturn now under way, if inflation can be checked and if excesses can be avoided in security markets, probably will be prolonged.

A record boom will rest upon three factors:

1. Spending by Government will be in a sharp rise. Cash spending by the Federal Government in calendar year 1960 was less than 95 billion dollars. In 1961 it will be almost 105 billion. Next year, in calendar 1962, cash spending will approach 114 billion. This rise in spending by Government will be a powerful stimulus to business activity.
2. Individuals, with record incomes, will add their weight to the boom by spending more. Personal income in 1960 was just above 402 billions. It is rising in 1961 to more than 416 billions. Next year the rise will carry to around 444 billions. Out of these added billions of income will come a broad increase in demand for almost all kinds of goods and services.
3. Business, at the same time, will be stepping up its spending. Inventories have been drawn down to a low level in many fields. Investment in new plant and equipment was reduced when recession developed. With Government and individuals each to spend more, business will be forced to increase its investment both in inventories and in new facilities for production.

All of the elements are present for the sharpest rise in business activity since 1951, during the Korean War. . . .

Outlook: gain in jobs. Employment, as a result of the boom, will rise to new highs. Gains in employment have been moderate so far this year in spite of the increase in production. That is the usual pattern. In the early stages of recovery, production increases through greater efficiency and lengthened hours of work. But as recovery goes on, jobs open up more and more frequently.

A year from now, about 70.6 million people are expected to be holding jobs, against 68.8 million at present.

Because of the increase in the labor force, however, unemployment will not fall as much as total employment will rise. However, a year hence, the total number of jobless is expected to fall below 4 million, with the rate of unemployment around 5.4 per cent, against a recent rate of 6.8 per cent.

Profits of corporations will reflect the boom that is coming in business activity. Corporate profits, before taxes, hit a record in 1959 at 46.8

billion dollars. In the recession, they slipped to 45 billion in 1960. Now profits are rising again and this year probably will be well above 45 billion. Next year a profit record of close to 60 billion is likely.

Prices to hold steady? With all this rise in activity, prices are likely to be relatively steady. Wholesale prices have changed little from last year, despite recovery. Over the year ahead, a moderate increase in the wholesale-price level is to be expected but probably not more than 2 per cent.

Reason for price stability is the abundant supply of materials and the absence of inventory speculation.

Retail prices probably will continue to inch upward over the year ahead. But the rise in living costs also is expected to be held within a moderate range.

The outlook, in fact, suggests a record boom in output, income, sales and profits, but with only a mild dose of inflation.

V. A New Move To "Control" Prices. [September 4, 1961]

. . . Does the Government have any legal power to prevent prices from being raised? Is the Administration getting ready to seek such power from Congress? Are all price increases to be called into question? Just what is the official policy on wages as well as prices?

What's up, really, is an effort to control prices by threat and persuasion. The Government has no legal authority to forbid a price increase. It can act only when it can be shown that the markup results from a "conspiracy" or "monopoly" situation.

In such cases, companies can be prosecuted under the antitrust laws.

This is part of the threat now being held over the heads of the companies moving to raise prices. It is the position of some Administration officials that a uniform rise in steel prices would be evidence of "conspiracy" or "monopoly." Senator Gore even talked of breaking up the large steel companies under orders of the federal courts.

At the same time, you hear talk of reviving direct controls over wages and prices. The Administration has no such plans now, but officials do not rule out the possibility of asking such powers later if an inflationary spiral should develop.

The broad policy, as now disclosed, is to induce business to offset wage increases through savings from more efficient operations and new equipment. Federal economists argue that business should rely on expanding markets, rather than higher prices, to maintain and increase profits. They add that, if business takes this approach, the unions will have less reason to enforce excessive wage demands.

The first tests of this policy are coming in the steel and baking industries.

What figures show. The Senate was told that steel prices have risen too far already, and that any further rise will be inflationary here at home and make it more difficult for U.S. industry to meet the competition from abroad.

Government figures were cited in the debate to show that steel prices have gone up by more than 100 per cent since 1947, while industrial prices generally have risen only 35 per cent.

If allowance is made for increases in efficiency and output per man-hour, the cost of union labor in the steel mills has risen less than prices, according to the estimates of some congressional economists.

On that basis, the Senators argued, the companies, not the unions, have been to blame for inflation.

Senator Gore drew on information from the Council of Economic Advisers to show that increasing efficiency, due to higher output, will cover just about all of the cost of the October 1 wage boost and that the industry's profits will be at "normal" levels without a price boost. . . .

Questions

1. How do these reports differ from those you find in the daily newspaper? Who writes these reports? What is the source of the information?
2. Analyze the style of writing found in these five excerpts. Is it mostly reportative or mostly opinion? Explain.
3. In the first report ("Another Round of Inflation on the Way?") what are the causes for concern?
4. In the first report what is meant by the terms *wage-price spiral, confidence in the dollar,* and *cheap money?* What are the connotations of such terms in this article?
5. In the second report ("Your Income vs. Inflation") what attitude toward inflation is suggested by the first five paragraphs? Explain.
6. In paragraph 6 of "Your Income vs. Inflation," what is meant by " 'real' " income?
7. What does the evidence in paragraphs 6 and 7 of "Your Income vs. Inflation" tend to prove about whether the average American family has been helped or hurt during the past period of inflation?
8. What is the main purpose of the report "What It Takes Now to Be 'Well Off' "? Do you consider this title to be misleading? Why or why not?
9. In the report "Will It Be a Record Boom?" what are the factors that will contribute to the boom? How do these compare with the factors that are "causes for concern" in the first report ("Another Round of Inflation on the Way?")?
10. Why is only a mild dose of inflation expected? Do you agree or not? Why?

11. In the report "A New Move To 'Control' Prices," what is the tone of the first six paragraphs?
12. Compare the causes of the wage-price spiral and the failure to meet foreign competition in the first and last reports. How do you account for the differences?
13. Do you think these reports would have a different effect on a person who read them over a period of four months rather than at one time? Explain.

DEFENSE AGAINST INFLATION*

Research and Policy Committee[1] of the Committee for Economic Development

[1] We subscribe without reserve to the belief that the national goal should be to have a steadily rising living standard *for everyone*. It is because we are as an organization dedicated to this goal that we have undertaken to assess the nature, the causes and the results of inflation, and to propose public and private policies that will maintain price stability in an economy of growth and abundance.

[2] Our concern is with long-range inflation. By this we mean inflation resulting from economic forces of more than temporary nature; inflation, that is, as a built-in trend, the kind of inflation that settles in as a way of life.

[3] There is some tendency to believe that the acceptance of inflation is necessary to maintain high employment. But there is no evidence to support this belief. There have been periods in this country's history when the economy grew at a rapid rate while prices were rising, but there were other periods of rapid growth when prices were stable or falling. Even during the periods of rising prices, there was no general expectation that inflation would continue. It is this expectation that differentiates the present situation from the past. If we learn to accept inflation, the forces making for economic growth will certainly not be strengthened—the likelihood is that they will be weakened.

[4] While we have behind us a long experience of inflation, only in the last few years has the possibility of inflation as a permanent way of

---

* From *Defense Against Inflation: The Report of the Research and Policy Committee of the Committee for Economic Development, 1958.*

[1] The Research and Policy Committee is composed of 43 Trustees from among the 150 businessmen and educators who comprise the Committee for Economic Development. It is aided by a Research Advisory Board of leading economists, a small permanent Research Staff, and by advisers chosen for their competence in the field being considered.

life in America been generally recognized as real. During most of the
period that began in 1940, there were certain powerful and temporary
inflationary forces at work—World War II, its aftermath of pent-up
demand, and the Korean War. One could believe, even though one
could not be certain, that when these temporary forces disappeared
so would the inflation.

[5] But the inflation of 1955–57, although much smaller than the
surges of 1940–48 and 1950–51, was more troubling. We were not at
war. Our productive capacity had increased greatly. Employment was
high. The Federal Budget was in balance and the money supply was
growing only slowly. The causes of this inflation were difficult to distinguish. They might be similar in character to the causes of the war
and postwar inflation, although less powerful and different in origin.
Or they might be new forces—forces that did not exist or did not operate or were concealed by more powerful influences in the earlier period.
Whatever the causes, since the inflation occurred in conditions expected
to be characteristic of America for a long time to come, we are left
with no reason for thinking such inflation would not recur.

[6] This experience has brought to the fore a number of questions:

> Why do prices rise under such conditions?
> Does the rise mean that inflation is inevitable?
> Even if not strictly inevitable, is inflation a necessary price we must pay
> to achieve higher living standards?
> How can we maintain a satisfactory rate of growth of employment and
> production without inflation?

[7] This policy statement considers and attempts to answer these
questions.

[8] Although recent experience has focused American public attention on these questions, they are not new. In essentially their present
form they have concerned students of the American economy since the
nation committed itself, as reflected in the Employment Act of 1946,
to maintenance of high employment and high and rising standards of
living. And they continue to be important questions through all phases
of economic activity.

[9] The problem with which we are concerned is not whether prices
will be higher in 1958 than in 1957 but whether prices will be much
higher in 1967 and much higher still in 1977. We are concerned, and we
believe the nation is concerned, about the effects of long-run inflation
on the welfare of important groups in our population and on the growth
of the economy.

[10] The questions we have just asked are difficult; we cannot answer them quickly or dogmatically. But just because the considerations to which these questions lead us are complex, we feel it desirable to put down here in summary form the conclusions to which we come:[2]

1. We do not accept the idea that creeping inflation is desirable, or even acceptable, because there are forces that could convert a creep to a gallop and because even a creeping inflation erodes the value of long-run fixed-money obligations, which are important in our economy, and crucifies the weaker groups in our society.

2. A rising price level is not essential to real growth and sustained, productive employment. In fact, by distorting the normal incentives for efficiency in business and increased productivity of labor, it may well endanger the sustainability of growth.

3. There is danger of long-term inflation in this country, but inflation is not inevitable. The nation can have both stable prices and high employment—if it is willing to adopt the policies required to make them consistent.

4. We do not have to sacrifice high production to avoid inflation. The only thing we need to give up is an illusion: the illusion that we can get more out of the economy than we put into it, that we can consume more than we produce.

5. The responsibility for preventing inflation is a joint responsibility of government, business, labor and agriculture.

6. The government's chief responsibility is, through the exercise of its monetary and fiscal policies, to keep demand from rising faster than the nation's ability to produce. To clarify the responsibilities of government in this regard, the Employment Act of 1946 should be amended to include stable prices as a specific objective of policy along with "maximum production, employment and purchasing power."

7. There is danger that, even if government succeeds through monetary restraint and tax policy in keeping demand within bounds, prices may still rise because production costs rise, or for other reasons. We must rely on the forces of competition and on the voluntary exercise of restraint in price and wage policies by business and labor to prevent this from happening.[3] We reject government controls of prices and wages, in peacetime, to restrain inflation. Such controls would seriously impair the freedom and efficiency of the economy and, in any case, they could not restrain inflation for very long. But

[2] *Footnote by Ellott V. Bell, in which William Benton has asked to be associated:* "I do not believe that this policy statement comes to grips with the real difficulties of the inflation situation. There is no real effort to say why the policies of recent years have so signally failed to defend us against inflation. If we cannot even agree on where we failed, I do not think we can get very far in prescribing a recipe for success."

[3] *Footnote by William Benton:* "My experience leads me to reject wholly the hope of voluntary exercise of restraint in price and wage policies by business and labor."

we do believe that government has the responsibility to enact and enforce legislation to preserve competition in business and labor markets.

8. Business or labor should not force excessive increases in wages. By excessive, we mean: (a) Average wage rates (including fringe benefits as well as cash wages) should rise as fast—but not faster—than the rise of output per man-hour for the economy as a whole, which has averaged just over 2 per cent a year since 1900 and close to 3 per cent a year since World War II. Larger increases of wage rates would be justified if productivity *for the economy as a whole* could be raised more rapidly. We emphasize that wages should not rise in line with productivity in particular industries or firms. Moreover, labor and capital should both share the benefits of increased productivity, that is, wages should rise in *proportion* to the average gain in productivity, but should not absorb the whole gain. (b) Average profits per unit of output would be roughly constant if wages behaved in this way and if prices were stable on the average. The main justification for departure from this average behavior in particular cases is a surplus or shortage of particular categories of labor or product.

9. If the existing degree of competition in product and labor markets should prove to be inadequate, and the exercise of business and labor power insufficiently responsible, to preserve general price stability, we shall have to seek measures to strengthen competition. The laws to maintain competition in business need to be more vigorously enforced and constantly reviewed to assure their effectiveness. But the main problem is in the field of labor, where there is no law and not even a public philosophy or policy for the limitation of economic power. There is urgent need for objective consideration of the proper extent, character and uses of union power in our society. Existing laws should be reviewed to see whether they give or leave a degree of power to labor organizations that is not in the public interest.[4,5]

[4] *Footnote by Allan Sproul, in which William C. Foster and Philip D. Reed have asked to be associated:* "The principles set forth in paragraph numbered 8 picture the kind of a balanced economic situation we would like to achieve; they do not provide a practical guide to economic action. Nor can I place much confidence in the voluntary exercise of restraint (paragraph numbered 7) where arbitrary power exists. I believe we must concentrate, now, on trying to promote a better balance of power in product and labor markets, through measures which strengthen competition (paragraph numbered 9) in these markets. . . ."

[5] *Footnote by William Benton:* "Regretfully I disassociate myself from point nine above and from the body of the important statement which follows; regretfully, because I agree so completely with the preceding pages which brilliantly state the problem and the objectives of price stability in a growing economy.

I cannot agree with the emphasis throughout the body of this statement which so largely equates rising prices with rising wages. Wages, of course, can be a measurable factor in rising prices, but many distinguished economists feel the business community is today putting excessive emphasis on so-called labor monopoly as the whipping boy for inflation. Example: Many economists attribute the rising prices of recent years in large part to the rise of investments; plant and equipment expenditures rose 26% from 1955 to 1957. This is not even discussed in this statement. A

Questions

1. Why are the authors of this report concerned with inflation as "a way of life"?
2. Examine the four questions for investigation posed by this committee. What is there about the fourth question that would suggest there might be some preconceived answers to the first three questions?
3. In paragraph 8, what is the significance of singling out the Employment Act of 1946 and maintenance of high employment as a point of reference in the history of inflation?
4. Examine conclusion 8. What is the import of the statement that "increases of wage rates would be justified if productivity *for the economy as a whole* could be raised more rapidly" but that "wages should not rise in line with productivity in particular industries or firms"? Would a committee of union officials concur in this conclusion? Why or why not?
5. Examine conclusions 7 and 9. Do you find any inconsistencies? Explain.
6. Would this committee have any objections to governmental control over labor unions? How would this differ from control over industries?
7. Assess the argument of William Benton in the final footnote. Do you agree with his position? Explain.
8. What reasons can you think of for the inclusion of those footnotes which raised objections to the report? Do these tend to clarify the report or make it more confusing? Explain.

---

further deficiency of this document, it seems to me, is that in its discussion of inflation it lumps together the inflation developing over a long period of years without separating for analysis the war years, the reconversion years, and the most recent years.

I favor business competition and deplore the fact that the CED in its 16 year history has not devoted itself to the implementation of the Sherman and Clayton Acts. Point nine above glosses over the problem of competition throughout our business economy.

Finally, I regret that this statement does not sufficiently stress the urgent need for a high level of U. S. productivity, and the present need for national policies to implement the objectives of the Employment Act of 1946. I fear that the statement read by itself seems to elevate stability of prices over the national objectives of high employment and rapid economic growth. Some may feel that it is a rationalization for a position widely held in the business community—that we must have occasional unemployment and recession, including a receding or non-existent rate of economic progress, because it is necessary for stability of prices.

This seems to me a dangerous position, with the U.S.S.R. industries forging ahead 11% in the first quarter of this year while we were going backward with unemployment of 5½ million and part-time employment of 4 million.

Of highest urgency are national policies which will help to create annual increases in productivity of at least 4%, in contrast to our fifty-year average of 3%. Last month the Rockefeller Brothers report urged as essential a goal of 5%. This problem seems to me not only central to our national security but to an examination of the problem of inflation and other questions discussed herein."

THE ARGUMENT FOR "CREEPING" INFLATION[*]

Sumner Slichter

[1] The principal economic issue dividing the American people to-day is the issue of growth of the economy vs. stability of the price level. . . .

[2] Is it true . . . that there is no conflict between vigorous economic growth and a stable price level? Or must permanent inflation be accepted as a necessary condition to maximum growth? And if maximum growth entails creeping inflation, what will be the consequences for the economy? Will the United States price itself out of world markets? Will confidence in the dollar be undermined and will there be a disastrous flight from the dollar with creeping inflation developing into a gallop? Will creeping inflation produce great suffering among recipients of fixed incomes? Or are the consequences of creeping inflation greatly exaggerated?

[3] The recent inflation in the United States has been caused by a mixture of strong demand for goods and a strong upward push of costs, but the principal reason the price level has increased and slow inflation must be expected to continue more or less indefinitely is the strong tendency for labor costs to rise faster than output per man-hour. During the past ten years, for example, hourly compensation of employees in private industry outside agriculture has risen more than twice as fast as output per man-hour.

[4] The unions explain this by asserting that wages were simply chasing prices up, but the facts refute the claims of the union spokesmen. In *every one* of the past ten years the percentage rise in the hourly compensation of workers exceeded the percentage rise in the consumer price index. Furthermore, in nine out of the past ten years, the rise in hourly compensation of workers exceeded the rise in the wholesale prices of finished goods. Wages were not chasing prices up; on the contrary, prices were chasing wages, and were falling behind each year.

[5] The tendency for wages to outrun output per man-hour is bound to occur in an economy of private enterprise and powerful trade unions whenever the demand for goods is strong—that is, whenever the conditions are favorable for rapid growth. Wages could be prevented from outrunning output per man-hour if the bargaining power of unions

[*] From *The New York Times Magazine*, March 5, 1961. Reprinted by permission of The New York Times Co. and the Slichter estate.

were weakened and the bargaining power of employers strengthened by the maintenance of a fairly high rate of unemployment. . . .

[6] Fostering unemployment in order to keep wages from outrunning productivity, however, would mean retarding the growth of the economy. Hence the conflict between maximum growth and stable prices is real—the community must decide which it prefers. There is little doubt which way the decision will go because the loss to the community from a retarded rate of growth would increase at a compound rate and would soon become intolerably burdensome. Suppose that the economy, which is capable of increasing its productive capacity at the rate of 4 per cent a year, were held to a growth of only 2 per cent a year in order to keep the price level steady. At the end of ten years the economy would have a productive capacity more than 26 percentage points less than it would have had at the greater rate of growth.

[7] What about the long run effects of creeping inflation? Would not creeping inflation bring frequent recessions, so that in the long run more real growth would be achieved under a stable price level? There is no doubt that rapid growth entails the risk of recession, but the occasional recessions that accompany a high rate of growth need not be severe. Much progress has been made in building up resistance of the economy to contraction. The recession of 1958 illustrates this progress. The drop in business investment and the liquidation of inventories were moderately severe, but personal income and retail sales remained remarkably steady. As a result, the recession was both mild and short. In view of the growing capacity of the economy to resist contraction, one must reject the view that a stable price level is a necessary condition to the maximum rate of growth.

[8] Are not changes possible in our institutions, policies or business practices that would enable us to avoid creeping inflation and at the same time realize our maximum growth potential? There are many changes that would diminish the tendency for prices to rise, but none of them would assure that unions would not push up wages faster than industry could raise output per man-hour in the strong sellers' markets that would characterize a rapidly growing economy.

[9] The possibility of price and wage controls may be dismissed, partly because the people would not tolerate controls in time of peace and partly because controls are easily evaded by changing the quality of goods and by introducing substitute goods. Strong public hostility to excessive union wage claims will have some effect on wages, but not much. Union members expect their officers to get all that they can for the members and would displace officers whom they suspect of failing

to represent them faithfully. Union members, however, are not immune to public opinion, and strong public hostility to excessive demands will tend to weaken by a small amount the upward pressure of unions on wages.

[10] What about the possibility of curbing the power of the trade unions by organization on the part of employers, by depriving unions of some of their present privileges and immunities, or by imposing new restrictions on unions? . . .

[11] Depriving unions of some of their present extraordinary privileges, such as the use of coercive picketing to force people to join or the conscription of neutrals in labor disputes, would remove some glaring injustices, but would have little effect upon the bargaining power of most unions. Breaking up some of the large unions, as has been suggested by George Romney and others, would have consequences that are hard to predict. Unions would lose some of their present ability to support strikes by some members while other members work and pay special assessments into a strike fund. Nevertheless, the new unions might drive hard bargains. There would be rivalries among them and each would have a strong desire to make a good showing. . . .

[12] But whatever the possible results of the breaking up of unions, that step is not going to be taken. The American workers want their unions, and any effort to destroy or seriously weaken organized labor would cause the workers to rally to the support of the unions and make them stronger and more aggressive than ever.

[13] The most promising methods of checking the tendency of rising labor costs to push up prices are new methods of management that enlist the ingenuity and imagination of the men at the machines and benches in reducing the ratio of labor costs to income from sales. Experience in more than a score of plants shows that amazing things begin to happen when workers share in a plant-wide bonus, based upon their success in narrowing the ratio of labor costs to income from sales, and are given good opportunities to discuss their ideas regularly with management. The common interest that everyone in the plant has in reducing labor costs produces an almost startling degree of teamwork and cooperation. . . .

[14] The new methods of management may or may not be adequate to prevent wages from outrunning productivity, but they hold more promise for checking rising labor costs than any device that has yet been developed. . . .

[15] What will happen in the meantime? Fears that the United States will be priced out of world markets are far-fetched. Prices in

most other important industrial countries have been rising in recent years even faster than in the United States. Between 1950 and 1957, for example, the increase in the index of wholesale prices in Britain was more than twice as large as in the United States. In Sweden and Norway it was more than three times as large, in France almost three times as large, in West Germany almost twice as large, in Austria four times as large. . . .

[16] Also ill-founded are fears that creeping inflation will precipitate a flight from the dollar and that creeping inflation will sooner or later become a gallop. Every country in Europe has had creeping inflation during the past ten years. The idea has become pretty well accepted that a continued drop in the purchasing power of money is to be expected. And yet in virtually all countries the rise in prices between 1953 and 1957 was considerably less than in the period 1948 to 1953.

[17] As for a general flight from the dollar, the practical question arises: "Where is the money to go?" Other currencies have limited attractiveness because almost any country one might name has economic and political problems as formidable as those confronting the United States. Flight into commodities is not satisfactory because the future price of each commodity depends upon specific market conditions (supply, demand, competition of substitution) far more than on what happens to the general price level. Some shifting of investment is bound to occur and already has occurred, but the process tends to limit itself.

[18] For example, if the price level is expected to rise 2 per cent a year, a good bond yielding nominally 5 per cent has a true yield of 3 per cent. Such a bond may be as attractive as a stock that has been bid up so that it yields only 2.5 per cent.

[19] Our conclusion is that there is no immediate prospect that conflict can be avoided in advanced industrial countries between the desire for the maximum possible economic growth on the one hand and a stable price level on the other hand. This conflict is created by the rise of the relatively new institution of collective bargaining which is too well established and produces too many important benefits to be disturbed simply because it produces creeping inflation.

[20] But the prospect that we shall be living under creeping inflation does call for various common sense adaptations and adjustments. Efforts should be made to speed the adoption of the new methods of management that automatically reward workers for helping reduce the ratio of labor costs to sales income. Pension plans, including the Federal old-age and survivors insurance plan, should be adapted to creeping inflation. This means that they should either be fitted with

escalator clauses or revised every now and then to compensate for the rise in the price level.

[21] People should review their investment policies and should not hold long-term bonds or other long-term fixed-income investments unless the yield is sufficient to compensate them for the probable annual loss in purchasing power. Long-term wage contracts should contain escalator clauses. But in general, people should realize that living under creeping inflation in the future will not be essentially different from living under creeping inflation in the past—in fact, prices will probably rise considerably less in the next ten years than in the past ten. Most important of all people should realize that the alternative to creeping inflation is a fairly substantial amount of chronic unemployment. The problems of creeping inflation are a small price to pay for avoiding the much greater problems of unemployment and a rate of growth that falls far short of our potential.

Questions

1. Notice that in the second paragraph all the sentences are in question form. What purpose does this serve? Is there anything about the way the questions are worded that suggests Slichter's position? Explain.
2. What is the organizational pattern of this essay? Discuss its significance in relationship to the author's purpose.
3. How does Slichter account for the present inflation?
4. Examine paragraph 6. What does Slichter consider the basic conflict to be? What is his argument about maximum growth and stable prices? Do you agree or disagree? Why?
5. What is the author's attitude toward labor unions? Explain.
6. What is Slichter's basic position regarding inflation and its effect on our economy?
7. What solutions to our economic problems does Slichter present? Are they valid? Why or why not?

THE PROBLEM OF CONTROL*

Harold G. Moulton

In this final chapter we relate the findings of our analysis as a whole to the age-old problem of controlling inflation. Do we possess the means of preventing a progressively upward trend of prices over the years ahead? It will be necessary to consider separately the situation as it exists in war periods and under ordinary peacetime conditions.

* From Harold G. Moulton, *Can Inflation Be Controlled?* Copyright © 1958 Anderson Kramer Associates, Inc. Reprinted by permission.

It should be recalled that inflation has traditionally been ascribed to monetary causes. The several types of monetary factors involved include:

1. Debasing the standard money in which prices are expressed—by reducing the weight or content of the official dollar.
2. Increasing gold production, with a consequent fall in the value of the dollar unit.
3. Issuing irredeemable government Treasury notes.
4. Increasing the supply of credit currency by excessive bank loans.
5. Increasing the supply of money in circulation by means of Treasury deficits.
6. Financing long-term capital expansion by means of credit operations instead of solely out of savings.

Implicit in most of these interpretations is an underlying assumption, namely, that the level of commodity prices is the direct result of an increase in the over-all supply of money as compared with the over-all supply of goods. An increase in the Treasury deficit is called inflationary; while a decrease is said to be deflationary. An expansion of bank credit is called inflationary; a contraction deflationary. An increase in the supply of bank reserve money is regarded as inflationary; a decrease is deflationary. Expressions such as these permeate current financial literature—both as it relates to the causes of, and the remedies for, inflation. A somewhat similar conception is involved when the increase in money supply is attributed to higher wages—though in this case the increase in buying power admittedly does not originate in monetary policies.

The analysis in foregoing chapters has shown that the traditional assumption that the supply of money and the supply of goods are independent of one another is invalid. Rather both originate in, grow out of, productive operations in a pecuniary economy. The money income generated in the process of production—and accruing to individuals in the form of wages, interest, rents, and profits—is the money supply available for expenditure by the people. The magnitude of this supply of spendable money is governed by rates of remuneration for services rendered and, as we have seen, these normally depend upon quite other factors than the supply of gold or bank reserves or fiscal and monetary policies. Treasury and Federal Reserve policies have always been ineffective precisely because they cannot directly reach the factors responsible for the flow of money income. They may indirectly affect the situation but only by positive restrictions of credit which impede productive operations.

I. Under War-Time Conditions

It *is* possible to maintain a comparatively stable price level in time of war. American experience in both World War I and World War II shows that the price control system, while belatedly established, ultimately became reasonably effective. Had the control machinery been instituted earlier—before the pressure of the cost-price spiral had become intense—the regulations would have been much easier to enforce. The facts show that the upward spiral begins almost immediately in the realm of raw materials and special types of finished products. Hence it is perhaps too much to hope that an initial price rise of this type could be prevented at the outbreak of war—for such a rise commonly begins well before the declaration of war or the outbreak of hostilities.

War-time experience, both in the United States and in other countries, has conclusively shown that to be effective the price control authorities must have the power to control both the prices of labor and of agricultural produce and other raw materials. Not until costs of production were brought under control was it possible to control prices. Moreover, once costs were controlled, the price level was stabilized despite the continuance of deficit financing on a vast scale.

II. Under Conditions of Peace

The problem of price control under normal peace-time conditions is much more difficult than in time of war. That is to say, the sharp advances that have been characteristic of war periods can be prevented, while the gradual advances in peace-time periods of prosperity cannot. The numerous types of preventive remedies outlined in Chapter I will here be briefly summarized and analyzed.

1. Restoration of the gold standard. Advocates of the gold standard, it will be recalled, hold that anchoring the money supply to a gold base would serve as an automatic brake on the actions of banks and government, thereby stabilizing both economic and financial conditions. While minor readjustments would from time to time be required, long-term price movements would be gradual in character, being governed by changes in the value of gold as a standard commodity.

The factual record shows, however, . . . that long-term price movements were almost if not quite as marked before the departure from the gold standard as they have been since. The reason why the gold standard cannot prevent inflation is simply that the gold supply as such is in no way connected with the level of wages and other costs of production.

2. Balance the budget and reduce the debt. Our study has shown that there never has been any correlation between fiscal deficits or surpluses and the movements of commodity prices. Indeed, there has often been a sort of inverse correlation—for a simple reason: When business is expanding and prices rising, the demands upon government for relief are reduced appreciably; and at the same time tax collections are relatively high; thus there is likely to be a budget surplus. Conversely, when business is sluggish, the demands for federal expenditure increase and tax collections decline; hence deficits expand while prices remain stable or even recede.

Treasury financial operations cannot control the level of prices because the Treasury has no control over the wage and other contracts which govern costs of production. An increase in income taxes in order to reduce consumer purchasing power will not prevent rising prices if wage and other costs are rising. Indeed, a series of annual budget surpluses, sufficient to bring about a very substantial reduction in the public debt, would not affect the level of monetary costs, and hence, the level of prices. To cite a single example, the cash surpluses of the fiscal years 1947 and 1948, aggregating 26.7 billion dollars, were accompanied by sharply rising prices.

3. Raise the rate of interest at the Federal Reserve. This method of restraining inflation has long been extolled as an easily administered, almost automatic, control device. Primary reliance is placed on the deterrent effect of a higher cost of borrowed money—which would restrain borrowing, stabilize the money supply, and check the rise in prices. This method has been repeatedly tried and found wanting. In earlier crises it was contended that the remedy was applied belatedly; but such a charge cannot be made with respect to the crisis of the middle 1950's. Our analysis has shown that under modern conditions the rate of interest is an *inconsequential* element of cost—of virtually no moment in business calculations.

4. Restrict the over-all supply of credit. This method, recognizing the ineffectiveness of interest rate control, would rely upon an outright, positive restriction of credit. In short the central bank authorities would allow credit to increase only in exact proportion to the increase in the volume of goods. The reasoning is that the maintenance of equilibrium between goods and money would automatically stabilize prices.

This suggestion fails to understand that the volume of funds required for the operation of business depends not only upon the volume of goods produced but also upon the money cost per unit of output— which is governed by the rates of pay for work performed. So long as more money is paid out for a given volume of output, the ratio of money in circulation to goods in circulation increases.

Both the fiscal and the monetary methods of control proceed upon the assumption that one or another (or both) of these agencies of government is in a position to restrict the money supply as compared with the supply of goods. Our analysis has shown that an increase in money supply as compared with goods originates in contracts calling for higher rates of pay for the same output. Since the monetary and fiscal authorities have no voice in wage contracts they cannot affect the ratio of either money costs or money income of prices.

5. *Maintain equality between money savings and capital investment.* One school of thought holds that the primary cause of postwar inflation has been the use of credit for capital expansion and that the remedy lies in bringing about an equilibrium between current money savings and current new investment. Such an equilibrium would require either increasing savings or limiting investments to the existing volume of savings.

This proposed remedy fails to appreciate that in the capital goods industries, as well as in the consumer goods industries, prices are based primarily on costs of production; and that wage rates here also are of decisive importance. In any case no means has been suggested whereby investment might be limited to available money savings without affecting the rate of capital expansion.

There is thus no simple control device by which a long-term rise in the general level of prices may be prevented. So long as the amount of money disbursed into the channels of circulation is governed by rates of remuneration for services rendered, the only effective point of control would be at the wage bargaining counter. Concretely, in the United States today a 10 per cent increase of wage rates would involve additional disbursements through wage envelopes of more than 20 billion dollars annually. Such an increase in disbursements would at one and the same time constitute higher costs of production and increased money incomes available for the purchase of goods at the higher prices which would prevail. Unless the ratio of wage rates to productive output is held stable, prices will inevitably rise.

We thus come to the question whether in a private enterprise system inflation can be prevented or circumscribed by the development of a spirit of reasonableness or by enlightened self-interest in connection with wage negotiations. The forces which we are here discussing are an inherent part of the private enterprise system. Involved are elementary *rights*, including the right to engage in business to make profits, to organize and bargain collectively, and to seek the aid of government in protecting or furthering group interests. Involved also are compelling *human interests;* such as the desire of labor groups to obtain higher wages for themselves—which, it is commonly assumed, affluent corporations can readily pay; and the desire of farmers to protect themselves through federal aid from the economic adversities from which they have long suffered. In the light of these rights and interests, it may well be doubted whether occasional preachments by government officials or professional economists urging upon businessmen, labor unions, and farm organizations a policy of voluntary restraint to safeguard general financial stability would have any appreciable effect. Moral suasion is not an effective instrument of control.

While one may thus hold out little hope for stable prices over the years ahead, the essential requirements for continued prosperity and price stability may be succinctly stated. As Brookings Institution studies of *Income and Economic Progress* have shown, the gains accruing from technological advances should be divided three ways: (1) a portion should go to labor in the form of wage increases—as reward and as incentive; (2) a portion should go to business managers and stockholders—as reward and to provide funds for further expansion; and (3) a portion should, by means of lower prices, accrue to the general public—which includes farmers and those engaged in service and professional activities as well as the labor population as a whole.

Only as all groups in the body politic share in the gains of technological progress will maximum market possibilities be realized. The best long-term interests of labor will be served by demanding something less than the total gains from technological improvements. The best long-term interests of management will be furthered by passing along to the consuming public, whenever possible, some of the benefits of progress, through the medium of lower-priced products. Such a gradual but progressive reduction in industrial prices would not constitute a depressing factor. Rather, by sustaining and increasing mass purchasing power and relieving the pressure on agriculture, it would be a continuing stimulant to further expansion.

Questions

1. What is Moulton's main thesis about the control of inflation?
2. Examine the language of Moulton's chapter. How would you characterize its tone and style?

3. Which "side" of the argument about inflation does Moulton take?
4. Examine the overall organization of this piece. What pattern or format do you find? What is its significance?
5. Why does Moulton distinguish between wartime and peacetime inflation? What methods of control were used in wartime? Why aren't these methods used in peacetime?
6. In the third paragraph from the end, why does Moulton say "Moral suasion is not an effective instrument of control"? Do you agree or disagree? Why?
7. What are the implications of the first sentence in the next to last paragraph? What function does it have at this point in the chapter?
8. Examine Moulton's suggested solutions in the last paragraph. Do you think they will work? Why or why not?

ASSIGNMENTS

1. Go to the library and look up the statistics on unemployment in the United States in the past fifteen years. Prepare a report on the relationship between the amount of unemployment and rising prices in this period of time.
2. Arrange interviews with an economics instructor, a business or marketing instructor, and a political science instructor. Ask each one of them what his attitude toward inflation is, what he thinks the causes are, and what he thinks should be done about it. Be prepared to present an oral report comparing and contrasting the views that you came across.
3. Be prepared to participate in a classroom debate on the topic: *Resolved,* That the federal government should institute a program of direct price controls in order to eliminate inflation.
4. Prepare a research paper on the subject of industrial profits vs. union wage raises as the contributing factor in inflation. Make sure that you have adequate data and careful documentation to support inferences.
5. Compare the conclusions reached by Slichter, the Committee for Economic Development, Keyserling, and Moulton. Prepare a speech in which you argue for proposals you think most workable. You will need, also, to find additional data to support your position.
6. Prepare a follow-up study to the *U.S. News & World Report* series. Select a recent six-month period and study the articles in the magazine that deal with inflation and its problems. How do these articles compare with those printed on pages 369–376 of this book?
7. Review Benton's footnotes to the Committee for Economic Development report. Write a paper in which you suggest what Benton's attitude might be toward the articles by (*a*) Keyserling, (*b*) Slichter, or (*c*) Moulton.

10. FREEDOM OF EXPRESSION
Censorship

Almost no one in the United States professes a belief in censorship. That is, hardly anyone advocates the establishment of a governmental agency to determine what can and cannot be published. The closest approach to governmental control is found in those existing statutes permitting the government to impound the mails or to seize publications, art objects, and motion pictures upon entry into the United States. Many individuals or groups, however, who are outright opponents of governmental censorship, do not take the position that there is no need for some kind of "controls." Legislators, police authorities, and racial, religious, civic, professional, and business groups are outspoken and insistent in their demands for some kind of control over what the public should be permitted to read or view. Some demand that what they term "lurid publications" and "sensational" comics be kept off the newsstands or out of the hands of the young. Others insist on "labeling" or segregating in public libraries the writings of persons with alleged subversive affiliations. Still others require that motion pictures and television shows be checked for objectionable material prior to public viewing.

On the other hand, many writers, editors, and publishers hold that all forms of control and pressure that deny people freedom of access to information are indeed censorship and thus violate the constitutional guarantees of the First Amendment. And groups like the American Civil Liberties Union feel that they must be eternally vigilant in guarding against extra-legal methods of control or censorship lest our liberties be eroded away by those who advocate "just a little censorship" for the moral and political preservation of our society. For the most part, the opponents of censorship see the loss of political freedom as a more immediate and greater danger than the presumed moral corruption of our nation.

To others, the question here is not one of freedom but one of license. These persons often cite Justice Oliver Wendell Holmes' famous statement: "The most stringent protection of free speech would not protect a man in falsely shouting fire in a theater and causing a panic." They would not give so-called smut peddlers freedom or license to violate common decency and good taste. And, at this point, most spokesmen seem to agree that such violations should be prohibited by law. But, as you will see in several of the essays that follow, it is not easy, even in a court of law, to define what is pornographic or in violation of good taste.

In this issue, although we have not tried to be comprehensive or exhaustive—both because of the magnitude of the problem and the vastness of the literature—we have aimed at being representative of most of the currently held viewpoints and their consequences.

This issue begins with excerpts from *The Freedom to Read*, a study made by the National Book Committee and the Fund for the Republic. In the first chapter the authors set forth the arguments for and against censorship and to some degree point out how it operates in the United States. This is followed with a familiar passage from Plato, probably the most famous of all advocates of censorship.

An Oklahoma newspaper columnist reacts strongly to what he considers an obsession with sex and obscenity in our culture and foresees a moral breakdown in our nation. An equally strong statement from an opposing position is voiced in an article in *Playboy Magazine* by Henry Miller, author of *Tropic of Cancer* and other novels. In a lighter vein, John Lardner, in a column from *Newsweek* magazine's book section, describes the censorship activities of the Detroit Police Department. These three selections from mass media give some clues to the strength of the feelings involved in this controversy.

Another aspect of the problem that has produced heated controversy for the past three decades—the role of religious groups in censorship— is examined in the next four pieces. The right of—indeed, the necessity for—such groups to censor, ban, or list objectionable books and motion pictures is set forth by Father Harold Gardiner, S.J., in the first chapter of his book *Catholic Viewpoint on Censorship*. That this right can be extended to include the use of boycotts and threats, however, is challenged by the American Civil Liberties Union's statement on censorship activities of private groups. These two viewpoints and other aspects of the problem are discussed in the text of a CBS television program in which Edward R. Murrow invites Monsignor John J. McClafferty, former Executive Secretary of the Legion of Decency, movie producer Otto Preminger, and movie actress Deborah Kerr to talk about movies and censorship. In "Obscenity and Protestant Ethics," Harvey Cox, director of religious education at Oberlin College, calls upon Protestants to re-examine their attitudes and beliefs concerning Christian ethics and censorship in light of the tremendous growth of the mass media.

What can happen to our mass media when many different groups all begin to exert pressures growing out of their own private concepts of what is objectionable is pointed out by Fred B. Millett in a speech to the annual meeting of the American Association of University Professors. What can happen when some of these controversial materials are brought into courts of law is illustrated in the next selection, the now famous Judge Woolsey decision about the novel *Ulysses*. What often happens to many so-called objectionable or controversial books is described by Marjorie Fiske in a study of the practices of public and private librarians in the State of California.

The next to last essay in this issue presents the thinking of one of the least inhibited novelists of modern times: D. H. Lawrence. In this selection from his book, *Pornography and Obscenity*, Lawrence upsets conventional notions about the meanings of these terms. The last selection, written by Walter Gellhorn, a political scientist, examines restraints on reading as they relate to the larger issues of freedom and control in a governmental system that is pledged to both the freedom of the individual and the welfare of the society.

CENSORSHIP AND THE FREEDOM TO READ*

*Richard McKeon, Robert Merton, and
Walter Gellhorn*

Arguments concerning censorship and freedom have shown a remarkable continuity from antiquity to the present, but they have been profoundly altered in scope and incidence, as in manner and effectiveness of application, by changes in political institutions, social structures, economic processes, development of media of communication, extension of education, and increase of cultural contacts. These changes of context and application are sometimes taken to indicate a weakness of arguments and to afford grounds for suspicion of reason itself. The continued use of the same arguments, however, is no less impressive than their changing applications, and indicates the need to re-examine them. Three sets of interrelated arguments are used in the discussion of cen-

* From Richard McKeon, Robert Merton, and Walter Gellhorn, *The Freedom to Read*. Copyright © 1957 by R. R. Bowker Co. Reprinted by permission.

sorship today: (1) basic philosophic arguments. These proceed from principles found in the nature of man and freedom; they provide the grounds and the frame for (2) political arguments. These proceed from principles found in the nature and responsibilities of state and society; they establish the political and social mechanisms for (3) moral and legal arguments. These are applied to secure specific ends. . . .

Positions for or against censorship do not follow deductively from opposed philosophic views of freedom. People may share the same conception of freedom and yet may differ concerning the advisability of censoring expression or impeding communication. The discussion of censorship, however, does not occur in a vacuum of theoretic abstraction. It arises and runs its course in a context of political communities and institutions, and of moral consequences and assumptions. The contemporary political and moral contexts of the discussion of censorship in the United States, however, have the curious effect of making attitudes toward censorship appear to be simple logical consequences of fundamentally different ideas of freedom. Arguments for censorship in the American community today are for the most part based on the conception of freedom as doing as one ought; arguments against censorship, conversely, are for the most part based on the conception of freedom as doing as one pleases. Fundamental attitudes toward censorship are in these circumstances determined by choice between the two conceptions of freedom: censorship is proposed as a means by which to prevent the degradation of the individual virtues, the cultural values, and the common security of democracy; censorship is opposed as a danger to the freedom on which democratic values, security, and action are based.

If truth and virtue are known and valued, the general argument *for* censorship runs, whatever contravenes or endangers them should be controlled. The expressed purpose of censorship is to protect the individual and the community—the individual from the formative influences which might lead him into immorality or error and inspire actions harmful to himself and to others; the community from corruptive influences that might undermine its security, lessen respect for its institutions and confidence in its government, or pervert its values and traditions. The general proposition underlying censorship is some form of the conviction that those who are competent to recognize dangerous evil and error should have the responsibility and power to prevent or curtail their operation in the community, at least on the young, the inexperienced, or the uneducated.

If knowledge and virtue are grounded and grow in freedom, the general argument *against* censorship runs, the contents of knowledge, the precepts of virtue, the canons of taste, and the judgments of prudence cannot be set down authoritatively in advance. They are tested in free competition, and the individual is formed by the active exercise of freedom. Passive acceptance and conformity lead to the degradation of values and the enslavement of man. Freedom is an end pursued by men, but it is also the means by which individual men are formed to virtue and self-realization, and by which the common good is secured. The general proposition inspiring the long history of man's struggle for the acquisition of freedom of choice and decision is some form of the conviction that each man, in fact and by right, judges his own interests; and that he can learn to judge and choose well—and therefore to act wisely for himself and in association with others—only if he is free.

. . . The *purpose* of censorship is practical: to control and prevent effects deleterious to the individual and dangerous to the community. The causes of those effects are sought in communication and expression, where they are recognized not by their effects but by an immediate intuition and abhorrence assumed to be universal among right-minded men—they are taken to be statements which by their very nature mislead and pervert, misrepresent and subvert. The *pressures* for censorship arise from the practical problems characteristic of periods of crisis and change; but the arguments for censorship normally turn, not on inquiry into those problems and into means of solving them, but on the interrelated dangers of immorality, treason, irreligion, and error. It is tacitly assumed that none of these dangers needs to be defined independently, since each implicates the others, just as it is assumed that it is unnecessary to specify the characteristics of statements by which these dangers are advanced, for they are recognized readily and admitted by all. Finally, it is assumed that no evidence is required to prove that suppressing the statement removes a cause of the condition.

The interrelations of immorality, treason, irreligion, and error have permitted one or another of them to assume a fundamental place in arguments for censorship. The definitions of all four have therefore changed, but without felt need to depart beyond the familiar circle of arguments, to investigate the consequences of censorship, or to compare the actual consequences with the professed purposes. . . .

. . . With respect to philosophic arguments, we are convinced that the problem of censorship does not arise out of opposed conceptions of freedom, if those conceptions are properly understood. Advocacy of censorship, at present, is nevertheless based on a form of the conception of freedom as doing as one should; this conception conceals the use of vague definitions, loose interpretations of facts, and ungrounded assumptions concerning social and behavioral influences in judging and listing works to be censored. We are convinced that a better and more widespread understanding of the nature and operation of freedom, and of the implications of the various conceptions of freedom, would help solve the problems which occasion agitation for censorship. However, we have concentrated our attention, not on differences of fundamental principles, which we believe can coexist in a democracy, but on common assumptions which endanger those principles, including the principles of freedom.

The arguments for censorship seem to involve four reasons for suppressing statements and communications: because they contribute to immorality, irreligion, subversion, or error. The arguments do not operate independently; they are joined in a single circle of mutually confirmatory arguments. Two of these concepts—irreligion and error—have not been prominent in arguments for censorship in the United States, because arguments for repression on these grounds run counter to assumptions written into the Constitution and its judicial interpretation: that truth will triumph over error in free discussion of all problems, including religious differences, and that the free expression of heretical views contributes in discussion to truth and lessens the danger that heretical views will be imposed by authority. The concepts of irreligion and error have nevertheless reappeared in the development of the two remaining arguments—danger of immorality and danger to the state—which have been employed in recent efforts to extend censorship.

In the larger applications of the arguments, "immorality" may be extended to include effects on action, character, basic convictions, and treatment as member of a race or religion. "Danger to the state" may include subverting its common security, corrupting its common values, undermining its accepted doctrines, religious, social, or political, and misrepresenting its common life. In recent times, several of these applications have been stressed in propaganda for censorship, and in statutes and ordinances which feature phrases like "tending to corrupt the morals of the young," "inciting to crime and violence," and "seeking to overthrow the government by force or violence." These phrases depend for definition and effect on the familiar circle of arguments, which supplies the connection between felt abhorrence and alleged effect. Thus the Gathings Committee—the Select Committee of the House of Representatives on Current Pornographic Materials—laid down the judgment, in place of basic analysis, that the recent proliferation of obscene literature constitutes "a serious menace to the social structure of the Nation"; it recommended, in place of legal devices, the extension of the censor-

ship activities of the Post Office; increased activity by private groups
to demand the removal, under threat of boycott or legal and political
action, of books and magazines which they believed to be morally objectionable; and elimination by publishers of "objectionable" output.

. . . These general considerations reappear as the basic distinctions
which are relevant to political and legal applications of arguments. Since
strict or preventive censorship of the press is unconstitutional, the censorship of books has assumed the broad form of post-publication control
of distribution under the postal law, the customs law, state laws, and local
ordinances. It has been influenced by military censorship during wars,
the exercise of police powers, the activities of governmental agencies
which purchase books, and the voluntary self-censorship under strict
codes set up for motion pictures (for which preventive censorships also
exist in four states), radio, and television. The problems of censorship
of books therefore fall between the precedents established in a long
struggle to maintain the freedom of the press and the new practices of
the mass media.

. . . Moral and social uses of arguments to influence people are at
the center of the problems of censorship and of the freedom to read
books. They are influenced only indirectly by philosophic considerations of the validity of statement or inference, or by legal considerations
of constitutional principles or judicial procedures. Yet the arguments
are fundamentally the same; they escape the bonds of logic and precedent because the problem is said to be so urgent and the remedy so
obvious as to require neither technical information and niceties of inference nor legal formalities. The Gathings Committee justified its
recommendation on the grounds that the present calls for drastic action.
In general, the "drastic action" is intended to increase the scope and
application of censorship, as well as its celerity and efficacy. The means
available include boycott; pressure on booksellers, librarians, and public agencies which purchase books; bans, legal actions, and threats of
vice societies; the action of police, postal and customs officials; and,
finally, self-censorship induced by caution or fear.

The basic arguments for censorship are particularized when they are
applied to various problems by the various groups stirred to action by
those problems. (1) *Immorality* has become identified largely with
obscenity and the possible effects of obscenity on sexual behavior. The
concept of immorality is extended to include (2) *vulgarity and bad
taste,* which are evidenced by the use of tabued four-letter words and
by references to tabu subjects, such as homosexuality, narcotic addiction, suicide, miscegenation. "Immorality" also includes departure from

pre-determined attitudes: crime never pays, divorce is never justified, the clergy are never bad, adultery is never unpunished. It is not unrelated to (3) the representation of *crime and violence*, and the possible effect of such presentations in promoting juvenile delinquency.

Irreligion and impiety reappear (4) in efforts to prohibit "sacrilege" and "blasphemy." (5) Misrepresentations and *defamations* of racial, religious, or national groups are dangers that may be considered threats to the social order or to religion, or as libels prejudicial to the interests and reputations of groups. (6) Political, social, and economic doctrines may be held to be *subversive.* (7) Doctrines may be attacked, finally, not only for their effects on religion or political institutions, but also for the scientific *errors,* as in the successful campaign of scientists to induce the original publisher of Velikovsky's *Worlds in Collision* to cease publication. If the effort to prevent publication or to limit distribution fails, agitation may turn to labelling the books under attack.

These activities are dangerous because a small energetic group is able to impose the consequences of its judgments and prejudices on a community, frequently without the majority of the community becoming aware of what has happened. When the issues are discussed openly, an argument which justifies suppression as a defense of morality and the social order is not easily rebutted, even by a better-documented, and therefore more complex, demonstration that morality and order are not endangered in a particular case or that, in general, suppression does not in fact advance morality and patriotic purposes but does undermine the bases of morality and of constitutional rights. The real issues are usually not met directly; and when instead the issue posed is whether one is for or against obscenity, violence, and subversion, or whether one wants one's children to be exposed to them or not, it is usually too late to direct public attention to the definition or the causes of obscenity, violence, or subversion, or to induce consideration of the extraordinary extension those terms can have when applied without definition or control. Moreover, existing and responsible organizations are seldom prepared to undertake the emergency action required to counteract the effects of pressure groups dedicated to any of these programs of suppression.

Questions

1. What is the authors' attitude toward censorship? Cite examples from the essay to support your conclusions.
2. How would you describe the style and tone of this selection?
3. What relationships between censorship and concepts of freedom do the authors see?

4. What are the reasons for the existence of censorship according to this essay? Do you agree with these reasons or not? Explain.
5. The authors state the arguments for and against censorship. Do you find any slanting or distortion in these statements? Explain.
6. Examine the last paragraph. What point are the authors trying to make? Do you accept or reject their arguments? Discuss.

CENSORSHIP OF THE ARTS*

Plato

"And shall we just carelessly allow children to hear any casual tales which may be devised by casual persons, and to receive into their minds ideas for the most part the very opposite of those which we should wish them to have when they are grown up?"

"We cannot."

"Then the first thing will be to establish a censorship of the writers of fiction, and let the censors receive any tale of fiction which is good, and reject the bad; and we will desire mothers and nurses to tell their children the authorized ones only. Let them fashion the mind with such tales, even more fondly than they mold the body with their hands; but most of those which are now in use must be discarded."

.   .   .   .

"But shall our superintendence go no further, and are the poets only to be required by us to express the image of the good in their works, on pain, if they do anything else, of expulsion from our State? Or is the same control to be extended to other artists, and are they also to be prohibited from exhibiting the opposite forms of vice and intemperance and meanness and indecency in sculpture and building and the other creative arts; and is he who cannot conform to this rule of ours to be prevented from practicing his art in our State, lest the taste of our citizens be corrupted by him? We would not have our guardians grow up amid images of moral deformity, as in some noxious pasture, and there browse and feed upon many a baneful herb and flower day by day, little by little, until they silently gather a festering mass of corruption in their own soul. Let our artists rather be those who are gifted to discern the true nature of the beautiful and graceful; then will our youth dwell in a land of health, amid fair sights and sounds, and receive the good in everything; and beauty, the effluence of fair works, shall

* From Plato, *The Republic*, translated by Benjamin Jowett.

flow into the eye and ear, like a health-giving breeze from a purer region, and insensibly draw the soul from earliest years into likeness and sympathy with the beauty of reason."

"There can be no nobler training than that," he replied. . . .

Questions

1. Why would Plato establish a censorship in his republic?
2. What kinds of things does Plato believe should be censored?
3. What kind of people do you think Plato would choose as censors?
4. What cause-effect relationship does Plato assume exists between the arts and society? Comment on the validity of the assumption.

ALMOST ANYTHING GOES*

Jenkin Lloyd Jones

Movies are dirtier than ever.

Books are dirtier than ever.

The magazine stands are reeking.

We have come half-circle from the Victorianism of the past to the libertinism of the present. It's a little hard to see how we can get much lower.

Today you walk past the magazine stands of large drugstores and watch the furtive 15-year-olds thumbing through racks of stuff they wouldn't dare take home. So-called men's magazines are jammed with bedroom cartoons and full-color photos of naked chippies. Popular priced "sex magazines" maintain a scientific pose with nothing-left-to-the-imagination diagrams.

Even homosexuals seem to have their house publications. Have you seen the naked young man wearing gold bracelets in some of the so-called body-building magazines?

And well-established publications of generally serious content seem to feel that they have to have at least one lurid piece each month on prostitution, illegitimacy, sex-psychopathology, or physical incompatibility. These are the articles that get the cover blurbs.

The stands for pocket-sized books give the impression that all heroines are about to fall out of transparent negligees. The four-letter-word writers are having a field day. The fact that such old-time eyebrow-

* From *The Tulsa Tribune*, August 22, 1959. Reprinted by permission.

raisers as "Ulysses" and "Lady Chatterley's Lover" are now legally purchased in the United States hasn't made a ripple because there is worse and dirtier slush right around the corner.

Chief tragedy is the degradation of good literature. Even fine books are now displayed with covers hinting at wantonness and riot, apparently on the theory that Americans read only for biological kicks. War books, including those of real merit, are so full of profanity you can't let your children have them. An aspiring young Tulsa author has recently produced a novel containing a 40-page seduction. Most people, who have bought the book to look at the hot chapter, have read that and no other part of it. In balance, it isn't a bad novel, but the theory is that dirt "sells."

The mystery story has fallen on evil days. The whodunit has become a who doesn't, with the arts of crime detection lost somewhere between the sheets. So-called modern "historical novels" are usually nothing more than dreary recitals of rapes, bacchanalians and sadism, and whether the protagonists are Egyptians, Etruscans, Cavaliers or keelboatmen makes little difference. The bodies are the same; only the costumes are changed.

The movies moguls still produce a few fine, sensitive, artistic pictures. But where most B-grade movies used to be merely banal, today they are either shocking, brutal, smutty or all three. On too many nights the prospective moviegoer has a choice between being eaten by gigantic worms, participating in a gang rumble, or following hotrod girls into the bushes. In their desperate effort to lure people away from TV shows the movie exhibitors are alternately worshipping Minsky and Madame Tussaud.

Human beings are part angel, part animal. Neither the professional moralists nor the panderers to our brutish instincts seem to understand this. So human society gyrates between the two extremes.

The licentiousness of the court of Charles I of England was followed by the dour Commonwealth under Cromwell. During the first four Georges the British grew steadily more raucous until they were ready for a crepe-hanging reaction under Victoria. After Victoria the hell raising started again.

A few years ago American bluenoses were passing ordinances against one-piece bathing suits, burning innocuous books in Boston, and ordering pants riveted on the bronze cherubs in the capitol fountain at Jefferson City, Mo. This was the last gasp of the Anthony Comstock, Carry Nation and Bishop Cannon era. Good riddance to it.

But in the reaction we went haywire. Because people were anxious to get rid of silly guilt complexes we developed a cockeyed school of psychology that pretended guilt didn't exist at all. Everyone was a slave to his heredity or environment. If a man lusted or stole or murdered it was either his parents' fault or society's. You didn't discipline children in school because it broke their spirits. You didn't grade them down if they did poor work because maybe they were suffering from mental blocks of some kind. From these theories we have reaped the largest harvest of stumbling readers and juvenile delinquents in history.

The new sociology even got us into the business of subsidizing vice. Last month a New York social worker threw up her hands in horror at the suggestion that women who repeatedly have illegitimate children in order to cash in on the aid checks should be jailed or at least deprived of their children's custody.

"These poor people need more help, not less," the social worker exclaimed. Thus the taxpayers are kept at the business of making the production of miserable children under the lowest and most depraved circumstances a profitable thing.

All this is much more than just a moral issue. What is at stake is not only the survival of American culture, but the American state, itself.

Hanson W. Baldwin, the angry military expert of the New York Times, in an article in the August 8 issue of the Saturday Evening Post asserts that our fighting men have gone soft. He points to the fact that one-third of the American soldiers captured by the Reds in Korea were guilty of "collaborationism" in some degree. Indiscipline and immorality in our armed services is on the rise. He writes:

> From all this emerges a picture—not of an American who can lick any two or three enemies, but of a slow-witted, vacuous adolescent with an intellectual interest keyed to comic books, and a motivation conspicuous by its absence. This, of course, is a caricature and it cannot be applied across the board. But the fact remains that 40 percent of American youth are unqualified, mentally or physically or morally, for any kind of military service.

Great nations are rarely toppled until moral rot has weakened them. It was not until after painted boys began thronging the Agora that the tough, puritanical Spartans were able to crush the Athenian state.

The ruin of Rome was born in the orgies at Pompeii and Trasimene. When the decay had proceeded far enough the Huns came over the walls.

France, long famous for wine, women and truffles, folded up like a parasol in a tornado when the panzer divisions struck.

When I visited Russia last year I was as impressed by the spirit of discipline and hard work among Russian students as I was repelled by the Russian system of government. Let's not forget that Russia's present leaders have dedicated Russia's youth to our destruction. These tough, vigorous children of Eurasia are not going to be stopped easily by spoiled, lazy, and flabby American youngsters who wait for the school bus even where the ride is almost too short to permit them to slash the seat cushions.

A reaction to a nation's folly, of course, is always possible. There is always a chance for a people to catch themselves short of disaster.

Under De Gaulle an interesting change is taking place in France. There is a new Puritanism, a Francewide drive against excessive wine bibbing, a reawakened interest in Christian values. It is hard to believe, but today a filthy book "Lolita," which can be purchased in the United States, is banned in France. Brigitte Bardot is less popular with French audiences than with ours.

Arnold Gingrich, the American publisher, in a recent speech to the Institute Francais de Press at the University of Paris, asserts that the French had reached the vomit point. They had become nauseated with the licentiousness, the self-indulgence, the moral dishonesty that had brought them to their knees as a nation.

We may be getting close to the vomit point in America. Let's hope we can rededicate ourselves to some measure of decency and integrity before we have to fight for our lives.

Questions

1. What are the implications of the title of this piece?
2. How would you characterize Jones's language and tone? Cite examples to support your position.
3. What picture of American culture and morality does Jones present? What reasons does he advance for these conditions? How well are these supported?
4. What is Jones's concept of human nature? What in his article tells you his concept?
5. What explanation does Jones offer for the fall of the Athenian State, the ruin of Rome, and the fall of France? Do you agree or not? Explain.
6. What is the purpose of the reference to Russia and Russian students?
7. Why do you suppose the author chose France as an example rather than some other country?
8. What form of argument or method of proof predominates in this piece? Explain.
9. Do you think Jones would be in favor of censorship? Explain.

I DEFY YOU*

Henry Miller

For 27 years, Henry Miller's famed "Tropic of Cancer," an autobiographical ramble through the purlieus of la vie bohème of Paris in the Twenties, was legally unobtainable in the United States, although it enjoyed a large clandestine circulation here as well as abroad. First published in 1934 by the Obelisk Press in Paris, the allegedly obscene book finally achieved U.S. publication last June after the Department of Justice, the Post Office and—somewhat tardily—the U.S. Customs reluctantly withdrew all complaints. When the American edition appeared, that backbone of book-banning, Boston, quickly picked up the challenge and prohibited the sale of the Grove Press unexpurgated edition in Massachusetts. All summer long, against a background of nationwide sniping by police and other culturally discerning local culture groups, the publisher and the Commonwealth of Massachusetts maneuvered their forces for the major engagement in court last September. At the height of the battle, the issue much in doubt, author Miller shouted his defiance in this manifesto. [This note prefaced Miller's article in *Playboy*.]

It does not come as a great surprise to me to learn that, upon the recommendation of the Massachusetts Obscene Literature Control Commission—what a title!—the State of Massachusetts has instituted proceedings against the sale and distribution, even the lending, of my book. I write these lines in the village of Dragör, Denmark, where any of the so-called obscene books I have written may be freely bought and read—in Danish as well as English, French or any other language. To my knowledge nobody in this country has been corrupted or has committed any sexual crimes as a result of reading my books. Nor are the authorities of this country perturbed about the possible consequences of such reading upon the youth of the land. That the Danes are a peaceful, orderly, cultured people no one will deny. The freedom which they enjoy, and which they interpret literally, does not seem to have undermined them.

The ironical thing about the situation in America is that, having fought a disastrous war to insure "the four freedoms," we have today less freedom than we had before. The laws of the land, varying with each state, not only conflict with one another but are often absurd, outmoded and subversive to the public interests. Even more ironical is the fact that a state renowned for the part it played in the Revolution is known the world over for its reactionary views. It was in this same state that Sacco and Vanzetti were murdered in the name of justice.

To get to the point: This book which is labeled "obscene, indecent and impure," this book which has won the critical favor of Europe and other parts of the world, to say nothing of America, this book which is now virtually a "classic" by reason of its world-wide circulation throughout the last 27 years, this book which may be found on the shelves of many colleges and universities in America and is often pre-scribed as recommended reading by our professors of literature, this book which is already known to a large number of Massachusetts citi-zens and will eagerly be sought after by many more should it be sup-pressed, this book is now being pilloried like some common criminal. And by whom? By the general public? The public is not given a chance to voice its opinion. Or are we to believe that the voice of the people will find true and proper expression through the verdict of this body known as the Massachusetts Obscene Literature Control Commission? (What a title!) Is this the meaning of freedom? I strongly doubt that a man like Henry David Thoreau, a man like Walt Whitman, or a man like Thomas Jefferson would have interpreted freedom thus.

In the ultimate, I suppose we should be grateful to such organiza-tions as the Massachusetts Obscene Literature Control Commission for speaking up. Not only do they help to make the book better known throughout the land, give it a publicity which the publisher himself could not afford, not only do they increase the public's desire to have a taste of forbidden literature, but they unwittingly aid and abet their own citizens to break the law, for once a book is suppressed, nothing will stop people from laying hands on it. As for tracking down the "lenders" of the book, this is a pursuit better left to the ingenious minds of the servitors of dictators and tyrants. Or are we preparing to emulate these "enemies of freedom"? Are we too, getting ready to burn books? Even in the Dark Ages, let us not forget, the monks of old preciously safeguarded books and manuscripts which in this supposed age of en-lightenment are labeled "obscene, indecent and impure."

At this point I feel obliged to repeat a few self-evident facts. One, that no valid definition of "obscenity" has ever been established; two, that no man, no group, no court of law has the right to tell us what we may or may not read; three, that no proof has ever been offered that the reading of so-called obscene books has demoralized its [sic] readers; four, that by supposedly protecting the youth of the land through re-stricting the freedom of adults to read what they please, we are burning down the house to roast the pig.

And last but not least, what is wrong with obscenity, however it be defined? Do we live in a world so pure, so fragile, so delicate that a little obscenity can wreck it? Does its use, whether in literature or action, endanger our lives? (I could cite many things which have the approval of our governments, our courts, our schools, even our religious bodies, which constitute a grave menace to us all and make mock of the word civilized.)

What we are here dealing with, in my opinion, are archaic laws, Stone Age mentalities, sadists disguised as benefactors, impotents invested with authority, kill-joys, hypocrites, perverts. I am not defending myself—I accuse. Prove to me that you are worthy of judging this book and I may turn a respectful ear. Show me your clean hands, your clean heart, your clean conscience. I defy you.

Questions

1. In the prefatory note by the editors of *Playboy Magazine,* what indications can you find of their attitude toward censorship of Miller's novel?
2. Twice, in referring to the Massachusetts Obscene Literature Control Commission, Miller uses the exclamation "What a title!" Why?
3. In the first paragraph Miller says "nobody in this country has been corrupted or has committed any sexual crimes as a result of reading my books." What is his argument here? What do you think Miller would say if someone had committed a crime after reading one of his books?
4. What is the purpose of the second paragraph? Why does he refer to Sacco and Vanzetti?
5. Examine Miller's "self-evident" facts in the third to last paragraph. Are these facts? Explain.
6. What is Miller's attitude toward obscenity? Is it defensible? Explain.
7. Whom do you think Miller would consider worthy of judging his book?
8. Examine the overall organization of this piece. How would you describe it?

THE SMUT DETECTIVE*

John Lardner

Inspector Herbert W. Case, of the Detroit police license and censor bureau, the country's leading handicapper of literature, or smut sleuth, has often said that he will be glad to send his Detroit Line (of pocket-size books to be banned) to any town where the local censor asks for it.

He and his team of twelve censors think of themselves as "big brothers," the inspector said one time, to smaller communities who don't have

* From *Newsweek*, March 21, 1955. Copyright 1955 by Weekly Publications, Inc. Reprinted by permission.

the time and money to find out for themselves that Andersen's fairy tales are obscene. Or that Havelock Ellis is a dirty writer. Case's clockers are willing to shoulder the load of the work, if they have to—even when it means reading pornographers like Dos Passos and Hemingway so late into the night that these honest cops see verbs before their eyes as they stagger to bed.

"Inspector," a congressman asked Case a couple of years ago, "your men do not resent having to go through the stuff?"

The inspector replied that they were all dead game.

"We are in the middle of the stream, and swimming," he said, "and we want to keep on for a while."

But that doesn't mean that they like it. The question that burns in Case's mind, he has said, is, why do the publishers force the trouble and expense of saving the country on him? In other words, why do they go on publishing books?

It is not as though the licence and censor bureau—Case's handicapping service—has nothing else to do. In the year 1951 alone, the bureau inspected 241 juke boxes, cleaned up 69 burlesque scripts, and passed out seven warning tickets to saloons for improper lighting. This was in addition to 721 man-hours of "home reading" of filthy-minded novelists, and the banning of 39 books.

It was in 1951 that Case began "skimming off the filth, so to speak, at the top"; that is, keeping books off the stands to begin with, instead of letting them go on sale and knocking them down one by one. Between that time and the beginning of this year, 265 different books have been banned in Detroit. That does not include several hundred titles on the "objectionable," or I-wouldn't-sell-this-if-I-was-you, list. It's not illegal to display the books on the second list. It's just that no dealer in Detroit ever has.

Books banned by the Detroit Line—and recommended for banning to out-of-town censors who play the Line—include Ellis's "Psychology of Sex," Dos Passos's "1919," Salinger's "The Catcher in the Rye," Hemingway's "Across the River and Into the Trees," O'Hara's "The Farmer's Hotel," Willingham's "End as a Man," Andersen's "Fairy Tales," Norman Mailer's "Barbary Shore," Russell Thacher's "The Captain," Lillian Smith's "Strange Fruit," Jones's "From Here to Eternity," Uris's "Battle Cry," and Farrell's "A World I Never Made"— all in the pocket size designed to be read by the evil-minded nonrich.

The thought of Case's cops turning tiny page after tiny page in search of four-letter words, when they might be out fingerprinting stripteasers, is saddening—as Case says, "I think it definitely is the publisher's responsibility" to delouse literature in advance.

But there is relief, and a better day, in sight. Already, Case says, at least one paperback publisher has begun to play ball with society by sending his manuscripts to Case's copy desk for editing before publication. This does not mean, as yet, less work for the cops. They still have to read, in order to advise the publisher what to do. The chances are, however, that under their firm but kindly discipline, the publisher—and other publishers, as they, too, begin to avail themselves of Case's literary tips—will cut down their output considerably, and eventually cure themselves of publishing altogether. Like smoking or drinking, it's just a habit.

A Congressional investigator once asked Case if a publisher, having put out a special, clean Detroit edition of the book, could afford to print up the original, dirty version for other towns? Or would the Detroit model be national?

MR. CASE: It probably would.

He said a mouthful.

Questions

1. What is the tone of Lardner's article? Explain.
2. What is Lardner's purpose in using terms like "handicapper" and "handicapping service"?
3. Why does Lardner refer to the police (a) passing out warning tickets to saloons for improper lighting and (b) fingerprinting strip-teasers?
4. What thesis is Lardner upholding? What form of argument does he use to support his thesis?
5. Why does Lardner itemize the range of titles from Havelock Ellis' *Psychology of Sex* to Farrell's *A World I Never Made?*
6. How many of the books banned by the "Detroit Line" are hard-cover books in your own college library? What inferences can you draw from your discoveries?
7. Why the reference to 721 man-hours of "home reading"?
8. What possible inference can you draw from the congressman's question in the third paragraph?

From THE CATHOLIC VIEWPOINT ON CENSORSHIP*

Harold C. Gardiner, S.J.

[1] "The question is commonly raised why the popular press, in spite of its gigantic circulation, has a negligible political influence. The answer is surely that the great questions of policy are of their nature

* From Harold C. Gardiner, "Introduction" from *The Catholic Viewpoint on Censorship.* Copyright © 1958, 1961 by Doubleday & Co., Inc. Reprinted by permission.

complicated, and if issues are oversimplified so as to make them palatable for mass-circulation, they are necessarily presented in a way that makes their presentation valueless to those who have the responsibilities of decision."

[2] This animadversion on the popularization of political issues certainly applies to the subject matter of this book: censorship. The very word has been so bandied about that it means today anything or nothing. And when it is coupled with some other words—"democratic" or "American" or "constitutional," confusion gets worse confounded.

[3] In an effort to delimit the boundaries of our concern, let us make some distinctions. A censor is primarily one who not only disagrees with something (or someone) but who is able to enforce that disagreement through some channel of authority. I may disagree with your freedom to vote the Radical-Social-Demopublican ticket, but I will not be censoring that freedom until I can do something to prevent your so voting. Until the time I can take practical steps toward prevention, I am criticizing, carping, perhaps, or "crabbing," but not censoring—unless one wants to understand criticism as *being* a form of censorship.

[4] The power to disagree and then enforce that disagreement through some channel of authority—in short, the exercise of control—is, then, the sense in which the word "censorship" will be employed in all that follows. It would truly make for clarity of argument if all—the National Legion of Decency, the National Office for Decent Literature, the American Civil Liberties Union, the American Book Publishers Council, and all agencies concerned in the discussion—would resolve to discard the word "censorship" and adopt the word "control." "Censorship," strictly so called, can be exercised in our American constitutional framework only through legal channels; but control is exercised, and will and must be exercised, through channels that are "extra-legal," though never anti-legal. In other words, the state, through judges and courts, can alone bring censorship to bear on the problem of "indecent" literature and films; but society can and does bring "control" to bear long before the judges and courts can or ought to be called into the dispute.

[5] This is indeed, as we see it and as we shall treat later, one of the weaknesses of the stand of the American Civil Liberties Union, the American Book Publishers Council, and other agencies which are set stoutly against all forms of censorship. They are all too ready to make legal procedure the first court of appeal, when perhaps (please note the "perhaps") judges and courts ought to be the last source of decision. In this connection, let me again quote an anonymous opinion from the

London *Times Literary Supplement.* In a roundup of many books on
the problem of freedom and security in our modern world (among the
books were Alger Hiss's *In the Court of Public Opinion* and Samuel
Eliot Morison's *Freedom in Contemporary Society*), the reviewer remarks (June 28, 1957, pp. 390–91):

> Inasmuch as a citizen feels he cannot exert any influence on circumstances
> shaping his life . . . he will effectively die toward his society. The citizenry
> . . . will suffer a kind of schizophrenia: on the one hand their social instincts
> will still be urgent, but unsatisfiable; on the other hand, as a human-natural
> defense-mechanism, they will decry and debunk any form of social activity,
> for it would identify them with the powers-that-be and imply acquiescence
> in the various forms of deployment of those powers. . . . Thus . . . arises
> a vast number of non-citizens, citizens of nothing, attaching no positive value
> whatever to their society . . . having no emotive affection for it, living as
> atoms in it, fulfilling the barest minimum of obligations to 'get by,' and gener-
> ally betraying an 'I couldn't care less' mood. . . . Our Anglo-Saxon fore-
> fathers . . . would have called such persons Nithings.
>
> It is not the least of Clio's ironies that, in the measure of the State's arrogat-
> ing to itself more responsibility of each citizen's life, so have the citizens'
> loyalties ebbed away and the whole society has lost coherence.

[6] Social controls are being exercised every day in our society. The
advertising copywriter is perhaps one of the most potent controllers of
social life in modern times; "pressure groups" exist—and their influence
is not always an evil or a suspect one. In one sense it is precisely the
interplay of such social forces that gives vitality to a democratic society.
If the day ever comes when no group in the United States is passionately interested in a cause dear to its heart—and some of the causes may
be foolish and some of the hearts fatuous—then shall we be really
threatened with the "conformity" all those opposed to any form of censorship prophesy will come the moment the "censors" take over. As a
matter of fact, this anticipation of conformity under censorship is
largely a bugaboo with which to frighten the unthinking. In ages when
censorship did operate more stringently than at present, there was little
conformity to be discerned.

[7] Even in the period following the Council of Trent, "when the
Church became a mighty patron of the arts, strictly controlling them
as a means toward edification and devotion, the range of personal expression among artists was remarkable; so that painters such as Anni-
bale Carracci and Caravaggio could flourish at the same time. The same
holds true even among the portrait painters. Working amidst the rigid
ceremonial of the Spanish Court, Velasquez and Goya could produce
portraits conforming to every regulation for official work, but make

them devastating revelations of the individuals concerned. The examples quoted have all been taken from painting; but the same holds good for sculpture, music and literature."

[8] As in the past, so in the present. The censorship (control) activities under Catholic auspices which we shall examine in the second part of this book embody small threat indeed of imposing on the artist (the writer or the film producer) a dead uniformity that would spring from a timidity to experiment lest he would find himself running afoul of the "censors." As a matter of historical fact, it was immediately after the inauguration of the Legion of Decency, and as a direct result of the Legion's demand for moral improvement, that the motion-picture industry rose to new heights of artistic film-making. There is significance in the fact, too, that since the Legion began screening films in 1936, not a single picture that has won an Oscar has been a C (condemned) film; only seven have been rated B (morally objectionable in part for all). In other words, since 1936, fourteen of the twenty-one Oscar-winning films have been either A-1 or A-2. It is indeed hard to see how the Legion's activities have laid a dead hand of cultural conformity on the imagination of Hollywood.

[9] In all seriousness, the conformity we have to fear in our American society is the trend toward "letting the government do it." And an approach to such an attitude is in the making when groups like the American Civil Liberties Union try to control (censor) the efforts of other groups like the Legion and the National Office for Decent Literature (NODL) to control (censor). This statement gets us, of course, exactly nowhere; it results in the boring round-and-round-the-mulberry-bush routine of repeating, "You have no right to censor my right to censor." But I submit that if the Legion and the NODL ever get put out of business—as seems the goal the anti-censorship bodies have in mind—then the American cultural scene will be the poorer, because two vigorously protesting voices will have been stilled, and art has always flourished when it has had to meet the challenge of protest against some of its vagaries.

[10] A puzzle immediately faces one when trying to find out just what the opponents of censorship mean. Statement after statement, as will become evident in the body of this work, claims that *any* censorship is useless, because impractical; and dangerous, because in violation of our democratic traditions and practices. Censorship, one would accordingly conclude, is a bad thing, and the sooner we sweep away all forms of it the better. But at the same time, the anti-censorship groups proclaim as a prelude to their arguments that they, too, are strongly op-

posed to pornography, obscenity in literature and the arts. If so (and we take them at their word), then they are *ipso facto* in favor of at least the minimum censorship necessary to keep such stuff to a minimum availability. In other words, the anti-censors know what anyone realizes who gives the subject a moment's thought; namely, that in any civilized society *some* forms of censorship are simply inherent in the fact that people live together. But their manifestoes soft-pedal such a realization, and one cannot help feeling that, despite their stated distaste for obscenity, theirs is a laissez-faire philosophy which would allow *anything* in literature and the arts absolutely free circulation, with society helpless to do a thing except through strictly legal means.

[11] But law is not the only means at hand for society to use for the protection of the common good. Social forces such as custom and tradition are at work constantly, shaping and forming our democratic life—traditions and customs that may be somewhat opposed to one another, but which, existing in an atmosphere of free debate, enrich our cultural lives. The law may, indeed, have to be called upon or step in of its own accord to settle this or that dispute. The law may be and frequently is the final arbiter, but it is not always the first court of appeal.

[12] This leads to the second puzzle about the anti-censorship forces. Believing that strictly legal process is the only proper source for the control (censorship?) of books and films, they are driven to the point of practically accusing any extra-legal operations of being *anti*-legal. This is evident in the way in which they employ such words as "pressure," "boycott," "picketing." To be sure, statements of the ACLU (to take this very active organization as an example) do admit, if one reads them carefully, that boycott, for instance, is not necessarily illegal. But in press releases and in the general furor that is stirred up by a particular instance of censorship, "boycott" and "economic pressure" are bandied about in such fashion that the cursory reader is bound to get the impression that such methods of operation fly in the face of the law. This, as I shall try to develop later, is a "scare" tactic that proves more divisive, in my opinion, than the activities of the various "censorship" groups.

[13] A further demarcation of the subject matter of this book seems necessary. We are here dealing only with censorship in cultural matters; we shall have nothing to say about political censorship. Whether or not the FBI files should be kept secret or opened to defense counsels does not concern us here. And, to be still more specific, we shall treat censorship only in the matter of printed material (books, pocket-size books, magazines, comics, etc.) and motion pictures. These are the two fields that are currently most embroiled in the problem of cultural cen-

sorship, and to make the treatment concrete, we shall confine ourselves to the activities of the National Legion of Decency and the National Office for Decent Literature, the most prominent and active organs of "Catholic censorship."

[14] In this framework, then, the question to be treated is this: Is there anything like an official stand of the Catholic Church on the matter of censorship? Yes, there is. This position springs from some fundamental philosophy and from some positive ecclesiastical law. It can be found in the Code of Canon Law and in the authoritative commentaries on the Code. It is a position, needless to say, that directly affects Catholics only, for whom the law is made. It is, further, a position that does not rest merely on a statement of general principles; it descends to fairly detailed practice. This is *the* Catholic viewpoint.

[15] When we leave this fairly restricted field and examine the *operations* of censorship as engaged in by some Catholic agencies, we can no longer state that we are expounding *the* Catholic viewpoint. The principles on which the Legion and the NODL are based are certainly Catholic principles which are stated in Canon Law. But on the actual operation of these two bodies there is not unanimous Catholic consensus. Not every Catholic, loyal to the Legion principles though he may be, agrees on the B rating, let us say, given to a particular film. Not every Catholic thinks that the NODL is alert enough, to take another example, in disowning some types of use to which its list of disapproved books is put.

[16] *The* Catholic viewpoint about particular operations of Catholic censorship outside of that envisioned in the Code of Canon Law is that *there are several possible and legitimate viewpoints*. If this fact alone comes to the appreciation of those who so vigorously oppose the Legion and the NODL, this book will have been of some small service, for it will have revealed that the Church is not quite so monolithic, so "regimented" as many souls think.

[17] One final word. This book is not, in its author's mind, a debater's handbook. I hope that there is no note of simple attack and rebuttal in it. To be sure, charges leveled against the Legion and the NODL will have to be handled, but the purpose of it all is not to reduce opponents to silence. If the ACLU, the American Book Publishers Council, the Authors League, and others disagree with the Legion and the NODL, by all means let them continue to say so. But perhaps if they realize somewhat more clearly the spirit of *the* Catholic viewpoint on censorship, they may more temperately assess the goals and operations of Catholic agencies at work in our pluralistic society.

[18] That is the only hope I have in this book: not that discussion

will be stilled, but that further discussion may proceed with more reasonableness and intelligent responsibility on both sides—those who are against all censorship in both principle and practice, and those who are for it in principle and trying to work it out in practice in full accord with our American principles of freedom.

Questions

1. What purpose does the opening quotation serve?
2. Why does Gardiner distinguish between censorship and control? Do you agree or not that argument and discussion on this issue would be clarified if we discarded the word *censorship* and substituted the word *control?* Explain.
3. What argument or explanation about censorship and society is Gardiner advancing by use of the quotation from the *Times Literary Supplement?*
4. In paragraph 6 Gardiner states that: "In ages when censorship did operate more stringently than at present, there was little conformity to be discerned." Can you think of nations at present that operate under stringent censorship? Does there appear to be more or less conformity in those nations? Explain.
5. Examine the argument advanced in paragraph 8 about the motion picture industry and the Legion of Decency. Do you consider it valid? Why or why not?
6. What position does Gardiner take concerning legal processes in connection with censorship? What position does he take concerning boycott and economic pressure in connection with censorship or control? Do you agree with these positions? Explain.
7. In the final paragraph what two groups does he recognize as being involved in the censorship issue? Are there other possible groups or stands that one could hold with in this controversy? Explain.

STATEMENT ON CENSORSHIP ACTIVITY BY
PRIVATE ORGANIZATIONS AND THE NATIONAL
ORGANIZATION FOR DECENT LITERATURE*

American Civil Liberties Union

Throughout the United States, private organizations concerned with the morality of literature are increasingly going beyond their legitimate function of offering to their members, and calling to public attention, opinion or instruction about books, and are in effect imposing censor-

---

* Published by American Civil Liberties Union, 1957. Reprinted by permission of the ACLU with the added note: "Since publication of this report, the American Civil Liberties Union has noted much less reliance on 'seals of compliance' and other forms of economic pressure exerted by the NODL."

ship upon the general public. And since any kind of censorship infringes the principle of that constitutionally guaranteed freedom of the press which protects the free exchange of ideas in our country, it is imperative that the American people be warned of the danger in which their freedom stands. In discussing this kind of censorship, we make a clear distinction between the right of all organizations to express their opinion, which we defend, and acting in such a manner as to deny those who do not agree with their opinion an opportunity to read the literature themselves.

Background of the Problem

1. *The constitutional guarantee.* The First and Fourteenth Amendments to the United States Constitution, and the constitutions of the several states, prohibit governmental abridgment of freedom of the press. If one may read, one must be able to buy; if one may buy, others must be able to print and sell.

2. *Legal basis for limiting freedom of the press.* If curbs are to be placed on freedom of the press, and these curbs must be based on a clear and present danger of a substantive evil from the publication, they can be imposed only by our courts, through full legal process. And the courts, not private literature-reviewing organizations, are the proper tribunals for determining the existence of such danger.

3. *Existing pressures for further limitation of freedom of the press.* It is an historical fact that the travail and tension of our time has adversely affected our society and raised particular problems of juvenile delinquency. We share with other Americans deep concern about this problem, which has been a problem in other ages as well, but we do not believe that it is desirable to try to cure the evil by unwise or unlawful abridgment of our civil liberties.

4. *The form now assumed by further, improper limitation of freedom of the press.* First, some state legislatures, after vigorous demands by religious and other private organizations, have passed laws so sweeping as to permit censorship of any publication which administrators of the law may disapprove of. Rhode Island and New York now prohibit the display, sale or circulation to any person under 18 of any book dealing with "illicit sex or sexual immorality." This ban could affect the *Odyssey,* half of Shakespeare, the *Divine Comedy; The Scarlet Letter* and parts of the Bible; Henry James' *The Turn of the Screw* was cited by the Rhode Island commission as an example of a book thought harmful to minors. In South Carolina, the legislature passed a resolution directing the removal from public libraries of "books that are inimical to the traditions of South Carolina."

Second, less formal governmental censorship is illustrated by the fact that the Detroit Police Department has made such representations to the only two wholesalers of paperbound books and magazines in Detroit that they have agreed not to offer any magazine or paperbound book for sale in that city until it has been submitted to the police and cleared by them or in doubtful cases by the prosecuting attorney. The list of books disapproved by the prosecuting attorney for that jurisdiction has been frequently sent to the police in other cities and used as a quasi-official "banned" list. This situation displays the particularly abhorrent practice of pre-publication censorship, because, although the books have been printed, publication is not completed if there is a barrier to distribution.

Such formal and informal censorship actions by official authority violates the First Amendment. In nearly every instance where it has been possible to test the constitutional issue in a court, censorship has been defeated.

Third, a number of private groups, particularly church-related organizations, have prepared blacklists, threatened and imposed general boycotts, and awarded unofficial certificates of compliance. The most active of these groups is the National Organization for Decent Literature, a group within the Roman Catholic Church established in 1938 by the Catholic bishops of the United States. In 1955, the bishops set up a National Office for Decent Literature in Chicago, in order to coordinate the work nationally. There are other religious organizations, as well as racial, labor, parent-teachers and women's groups, who also engage in censorship activity, but our attention in this statement is focused on the NODL because of the prominence it has achieved and the great influence it has wielded in removing books from circulation.

The National Organization for Decent Literature

The NODL is a nationwide organization whose membership is largely made up of Roman Catholic laymen; it has active units in several towns and cities. The national and local membership receives guidance from officers and priests of the Roman Catholic church. The purpose of the NODL, as enunciated by the Bishops' Episcopal Committee, was "to organize and set in motion the moral forces of the entire country . . . against the lascivious type of literature which threatens moral, social, and national life;" it has emphasized its efforts to protect youth. The NODL Code, in addition to the negative pledge of removal of "objectionable" literature, also contains the positive pledge to "encourage publishing and distribution of good literature" and "to promote plans to develop worthwhile reading habits during the formative years." To evaluate the literature of our day in terms of its suitability for youth, the NODL, at last report, uses a reading committee of mothers of the Roman Catholic faith in the Chicago area. The NODL's focus has been on magazines, comic books, and paperbound books. It should be noted that the founders of the NODL sought from the beginning to enroll non-Catholics in their efforts. The NODL, says the Bishops' Committee, "appealed to all moral forces to combat the plague of indecent literature. The NODL office was, and is, merely a service organization to coordinate activities and supply information to all interested groups regardless of race, color or creed." The NODL's instruction manual, while listing procedures for individual committees to conduct Parish Decency Crusades, invites the cooperation of non-Catholic groups in the organization of local Decent Literature Committees to carry on the NODL work; such cooperation has not thus far been widespread.

It should be emphasized beyond the possibility of misunderstanding that the ACLU does not presume to object to the NODL's advising communicants of the Roman Catholic Church about any publication. Nor does the Union see any element of censorship in the NODL's informing the general public of its opinion that certain writings are immoral. Such criticism is a right of private freedom, and must immediately be protected when threatened.

From many towns and cities, come reports of extended NODL action which constitutes nothing less than censorship of what the American people as such may read. For example:

1. Roman Catholic parish groups, armed with the NODL list, call upon booksellers (bookstores, drug stores, tobacconists, etc.) and ask that the condemned titles not be offered for sale.

2. The NODL group informs a non-complying bookseller that they will refuse to buy any goods from him, in flagrant contradiction of its own assertion that its list is "merely an expression of a publication's nonconformity with the NODL Code, and that the list is not being used for purposes of boycott or coercion."

3. Newsdealers, druggists, and others who agree in advance not to sell anything to which the NODL objects are given monthly certificates of compliance.

4. Lists of complying, and often of non-complying, dealers are widely publicized and parishioners are strongly urged to confine their purchases of all commodities to complying dealers. Checkups are sug-

gested at fortnightly intervals, i.e., a private morals-police force is encouraged to come into being.

5. In many cases police, prosecuting attorneys, and military commanders on Army posts have issued instructions or orders that no books or magazines on the NODL list shall be sold within their jurisdiction, thus putting the authority of the state in the service of a private sectarian group. However, in a recent newspaper article, the Very Reverend Monsignor Thomas J. Fitzgerald, who directs the NODL work, stated, "We request government officials not to use the list . . . It is up to the courts to decide if a book is obscene."

If these were the acts of government officials, they would at once be challenged in court. That they are the acts of a non-official group makes them more difficult to attack, but they are nonetheless seriously violative of the principle of freedom.

A fundamental objection to these extended activities of the NODL is that the judgment of a particular group is being imposed upon the freedom of choice of the whole community. The novel which may be thought by a committee of Catholic mothers to be unsuitable for a Roman Catholic adolescent is thus made unavailable to the non-Catholic. It is plainly necessary to challenge the NODL as keeper, by self-election, of the conscience of the whole country.

The NODL Book List

The argument against censorship applies to all lawfully published books, but it is important to note that many of the authors and titles on the NODL list are considered among the most distinguished in literature.

Books by recipients of the Nobel Prize, the Pulitzer Prize, and the National Book Award have been made markedly less available to the reading public by the censorship of a private and anonymous jury acting under its own standards of morality and taste. And these are books which have been the object of responsible literary criticism and studied in hundreds of literature courses throughout the country.

The ACLU is gratified to record that Roman Catholic opinion is by no means unanimous in support of the activities of the NODL. Father John Courtney Murray, S.J. in recent public statements admirably setting the tone for national discussion of the problem, observes that: ". . . in a pluralist society no minority group has the right to impose its own religious or moral views on other groups, through the methods of force, coercion or violence." (The ACLU emphasizes that this prescription applies as well to majority groups.) Father Murray adds:

"Society has an interest in the artist's freedom of expression which is not necessarily shared by the family. If adult standards of literature would be dangerous for children, a child's standard of literature is rather appalling to an adult." He questions, as we do, the use to which the NODL list is put, particularly by public authorities and local zealots who substitute "coercion for cooperation."

The American Civil Liberties Union, which has prepared this statement and solicited signatures in support, is opposed to censorship, official or private, by police authority or by the NODL or any other group. It is our conviction that the people of this country should enjoy to the fullest extent the freedom embodied in the principle of the First Amendment. Specifically, the Union intends to expose in every way it can the use of lists of books as tools of general boycott, and to intervene on behalf of writers, publishers, vendors and purchasers who have the will to explore legal avenues for the maintenance of their freedom. We reiterate, meanwhile, that we will at all times defend the right of such an organization as the NODL to express its view.

This statement is signed by the officers of the American Civil Liberties Union who thereby indicate the intention of the Union to thwart censorship. Other persons who will not necessarily take part in the action of the ACLU have appended their signatures, because of their concern with the freedom of the press and literature and their general agreement with the principles herein set forth.

Questions

1. What kind of organization is the American Civil Liberties Union? Why would it be concerned with the problem of censorship?
2. Examine item 3 under Background of the Problem. What assumptions are being made here?
3. In item 4 why does the ACLU consider the South Carolina resolution removing books that are inimical to the traditions of South Carolina an improper limitation of freedom of the press?
4. Examine the list of five examples which the ACLU considers "nothing less than censorship." Do you consider all these examples as constituting acts of censorship? Why or why not?
5. Why does the ACLU point out that some of the authors of the books on the NODL list have been recipients of Nobel and Pulitzer Prizes?
6. What factual information would you want before you would accept or reject the ACLU charges against the NODL? Explain.
7. What are the implications of the quotation from Father Murray? Why do you think the ACLU uses this quotation?

MOVIES AND CENSORSHIP: CBS "SMALL WORLD" TELECAST[*]

Columbia Broadcasting System

ANNOUNCER. *Small World* is a four way trans-oceanic conversation filmed and edited by Murrow and Friendly.

DEBORAH KERR. This is Deborah Kerr, speaking from Klosters in Switzerland.

OTTO PREMINGER. This is Otto Preminger in Rome.

JOHN J. MC CLAFFERTY. This is Father McClafferty at the Catholic University of America, Washington, D.C.

EDWARD R. MURROW. This is *Small World*, and this is Ed Murrow in Hong Kong.

(*Commercial*)

MURROW. Good evening. Today on *Small World:* "Movies and Censorship"—or perhaps I should say "classification." From Washington, Monsignor John J. McClafferty, of the Catholic University of America, former head of the Legion of Decency. Monsignor, may I present that very fine actress, Miss Deborah Kerr. We all remember her in *Tea and Sympathy* and *From Here to Eternity*—two movies that are perhaps bench marks in the continuing controversy as to what the general audience should and should not see. Miss Kerr is in Klosters, Switzerland, tonight. Deborah, how's the snow?

KERR. Lovely, thank you. I understand from the skiers, it's great.

MC CLAFFERTY. How do you do, Miss Kerr.

KERR. How do you do, Monsignor.

MURROW. Our third guest ought really to be in Israel tonight, because he is filming *Exodus* there, but he's flown to Rome because the circuits from there are a little more reliable. Otto Preminger, produced *Anatomy of a Murder* and *The Moon Is Blue*. Both of these pictures brought him into very considerable controversy with the Legion of Decency and other organizations. Mr. Preminger, I'm delighted that three people of such differing views have agreed

[*] Reprinted by permission of the CBS Television Network, Miss Deborah Kerr, Otto Preminger, and the Rt. Rev. Msgr. John J. McClafferty.

to appear on *Small World* and disagree agreeably about the subject of censorship and movies.

PREMINGER. I am happy to be here and I can add to the conversation
about the weather. The weather in Haifa, Tel Aviv, and in Rome,
today, is delightful and very warm.

MURROW. Well, since we are going to talk about censorship or classification, I suggest we begin by trying to define it.

PREMINGER. I think that censorship is an evil institution, where the
State or other authorities try to impose their will on people who
otherwise should enjoy the free expression of a medium of communication. I think that censorship is the first step in totalitarian
government, regardless of whether the government is from the
right or from the left, and therefore, I call it evil. When we speak
about censorship today, we speak mainly about pre-censorship.
It is a submission of some work or expression that we want to put
into communication (like books, newspapers, or a speech on radio
or a motion picture)—to submit it before we show it to the public,
for permission to be shown.

MC CLAFFERTY. Yes. I gather, then, that Mr. Preminger, you make a
distinction between censorship in respect to prior restraint and
censorship in respect to post restraint.

PREMINGER. Naturally, I think that the laws of the United States give
the police, in every State, the right, if somebody shows something
obscene—whether it is in a magazine, in a book, or on the screen
—to confiscate it, and to start criminal procedure.

KERR. It's not done enough then—is it?

PREMINGER. Huh?

KERR. That's not done enough. I'm always astounded at how many
obscene magazines there are.

PREMINGER. Well, I am there with you as far as magazines are concerned, because I have suffered, personally, probably as much as
you, Deborah, but I must say that the freedom of the press is probably worthwhile taking a little abuse, personally.

KERR. Yes, I agree with you there, but it's so difficult this whole business of censorship. Isn't it? I feel like the Libran that I am, on the
scales between you, Otto, and you, Monsignor, in that I always see
both sides of the question, and . . .

PREMINGER. Well, I don't think it's really so difficult, because, at least
in the United States, the Supreme Court has very often, in almost

all cases, expressed, as far as the movies go, the opinion that pre-
censorship is illegal, and whenever the Supreme Court was asked,
it has declared censorship unconstitutional.

MC CLAFFERTY. I think I would differ with you with regard to that,
because as far as I know, the Supreme Court has not definitively
determined, up to the present time, with regard to the constitution-
ality, per se . . .

PREMINGER. That is true—because the Supreme Court . . .

MC CLAFFERTY. . . . of censorship.

PREMINGER. . . . tries to avoid making laws. But you must admit, Monsignor, that in no case has a Censorship Board won in front of the
United States Supreme Court, at least not since 1923, since the
Supreme Court has made it clear that motion pictures are a means
of communication.

MC CLAFFERTY. In a ruling of the Supreme Court, fairly recently, in
Kingsley vs. Brown, that Court held that prior restraint should be
considered in the case of the particular analysis of each film, and in
the case of *Roth* and in the case of *Alberts,* the Supreme Court has
undertaken to define rather precisely what obscene is, in terms of
a regulation or a control with regard to the exhibition of films.

PREMINGER. There is, of course, in the United States, another unofficial
censorship. There are private groups which I may call pressure
groups, which have never been very successful with books, magazines or newspapers, but have been very successful with the motion pictures during the last thirty years, telling them what they
may and may not show on the screen. I don't want to seem or
sound like a crusader, and I would like to keep the perspective of
good humor in this, but I made a small comedy called *The Moon
Is Blue,* and both the Code Administration in Hollywood and the
Legion of Decency declared that this cannot be shown on the
screens of the United States. In the United States there was a great,
great, tremendous publicity campaign against the picture, and I
was told by many people the picture would never be shown.

MC CLAFFERTY. May I make . . .

PREMINGER. So I played the picture anyway, and the picture was a
very big success all over the world, and particularly in the United
States, in spite of being banned by both the Motion Picture Code
Administration in Hollywood and the Legion of Decency, and I
really don't think that anybody's character has been corrupted by
seeing this rather harmless little comedy.

MC CLAFFERTY. We have to enter at this point a discussion of fundamental moral values, and also make a consideration of the nature
of the film as a medium of entertainment in terms of theme and
thesis, but before entering into that . . .

PREMINGER. But films are not a medium of entertainment. They are
mediums of communication.

MC CLAFFERTY. That it is.

PREMINGER. In fact, the theatre is the same medium or a very similar
medium, and why did nobody object to people seeing the same
comedy in the theatre, and why should it be sinful to see it in the
movies?

KERR. Isn't it because there are so many more people involved?

MC CLAFFERTY. Yes, definitely.

PREMINGER. Why shouldn't the people—this is a, a very—I am surprised,
Deborah, this is a rather, a rather snobbish and rather reactionary
point of view.

KERR. No, No.

PREMINGER. Why shouldn't many people see the same thing as a few?

KERR. Well, I don't mean many people. I think there are more children
involved.

MC CLAFFERTY. Yes, and adolescents.

KERR. And I am with you entirely, Otto. I have suffered myself, from
a very lovely play—it was *Tea and Sympathy*—being censored as
far as the movie is concerned, and consequently being ruined as a
movie, and yet its message that it carried was one of great, great
compassion and tenderness, and really a message for the world,
put through perhaps rather startling means. So, I am with you on
that, but I have to say that I do see both sides of the question. I
can see that in a mass medium, which television is, and movies are,
I think you have got to have some form of control. Should I say
control rather than censorship?

PREMINGER. But, darling, who should control it?

MC CLAFFERTY. Now, a State, and this is true, historically, has the right
of self-protection and self-preservation. It must exercise certain
kinds of responsible controls, whether it be in the field of public
safety; whether it be in the field of public morals. But in the United
States, with our cherished tradition, and thanks be to God for this
tradition, the tradition of freedom, the central issue is the right
balance between freedom and restraint.

PREMINGER. Well, there is no . . .

MC CLAFFERTY. Now, this freedom must be a responsibly exercised freedom with due cognizance taken of the social and moral welfare of the community; with due cognizance taken of the impressionable young people who view films, whose [life] habits and attitudes are being formed and shaped. For their own welfare and for society's well-being, these considerations should counsel us to be socially and morally responsible in this exercise of one of the most precious freedoms that we have.

PREMINGER. Monsignor, your speech would have converted me if it had been necessary. I agree with you in everything you said, but it does not touch the real, practical problem that we are trying to discuss here.

KERR. No, I don't think so either.

PREMINGER. Censorship becomes in almost all cases—or I would say in all cases—a political question and a political football, and that is the danger. Now, I must say that I, personally, think that no grown-up man or woman should be told what they can see. There is another question that Deborah has brought up before about children. Now, strangely enough, as much as I am against any kind of censorship, particularly private censorship by pressure groups, I am very much for self-classification of pictures, and wherever I can, I classify my own pictures and ask the exhibitors to, in their publicity, have a warning to parents . . .

KERR. Yes, well . . .

PREMINGER. . . . because I feel that parents should have a right to bring up their children in their own way, and if they don't want them to see pictures of some kind, they shouldn't see them.

KERR. But think about—think—there are too many parents that don't seem to have enough control over their children to stop them going to these pictures.

PREMINGER. But this cannot be helped by motion picture producers.

KERR. This is—this is the—this is the trouble, isn't it?

PREMINGER. I mean, there must be somebody else helping these parents. You cannot blame everything on—on motion pictures. If parents cannot control their children, then the motion picture censorship certainly won't help it, because there are many, many other areas where these children probably will be sinning and doing very bad things, regardless of motion pictures.

KERR. Yes, I agree. After all, we can—we can censor ourselves. We don't have to buy a newspaper if we find its policy offensive to us.

PREMINGER. That's right.

KERR. And we could just as well, you know, not go into the cinema if we don't like the subject.

MURROW. Excuse me. I am afraid I must censor all of us for one moment while we hear from Olin Mathieson.

(*Commercial*)

ANNOUNCER. *Small World* continues with Deborah Kerr, Otto Preminger, Monsignor John J. McClafferty, and Ed Murrow.

MC CLAFFERTY. I like very much, Miss Kerr, what you say about the individual having a responsibility to choose well and to not choose that which he may deem to be morally harmful to himself. I think that you can conceive of these ways of control in a series of expanding concentric circles. The first control, of course, is the control by the individual, according to the light of his conscience, and according to the information which he has at hand about the particular film in question. Then, of course, there is the area of parental control and the area of the counsel of voluntary associations. I don't term such counsel "censorship" or "pressure."

PREMINGER. No. I agree with you, as long as the Legion of Decency would tell only their members what to see and what not to see, I would never object to it.

MC CLAFFERTY. The Legion of De . . .

PREMINGER. But when the Legion of Decency threatens the theatres with boycott if they play certain pictures, then I think they go beyond what should be permissible.

MC CLAFFERTY. Yes. The Legion of Decency counsels its own members and, exercising its right of free association and free expression and free communication, makes known to its followers what its moral estimate of a given film is, but again, may I backtrack in the discussion, to something—or rather two things that you said, Mr. Preminger? First of all, you indicated that you felt you had a right to produce and exhibit whatever you wished. I do not think that that is an absolute right. I think that that is a right that must be exercised in a morally and socially responsible way in the light of the commonweal.

PREMINGER. That's right, but I must be the sole judge of what is morally responsible.

MC CLAFFERTY. Yes. And secondly, you said that each adult has the right to see what he wishes. Again, I do not think that that is an absolute right. I think that that is a right which must be exercised intelligently, prudently and wisely by the individual.

PREMINGER. But Monsignor, why should the censor's character not be corrupted when he sees these things, in order to tell people not to see them? And why should any other adult be corrupted when he sees them?

MC CLAFFERTY. Well, I . . .

PREMINGER. What makes the censor so special?

MC CLAFFERTY. I do not wish to be put into any position of advocating or sustaining, necessarily, official censorship. My own personal opinion is this (and I want to make it clear that I am not speaking for any group of any organization when I say it)—my own personal opinion would be against federal censorship of motion pictures. I would like to . . .

PREMINGER. I am all for that.

KERR. Otto, I am dying to ask you something.

PREMINGER. Yes?

KERR. About—you know, one has often thought, "Right, abolish censorship!" What happens if you abolish censorship?

PREMINGER. But we don't have censorship in the United States, Deborah.

KERR. No. What I was going to say, Otto, what I really wanted to ask you about was this, which has always bothered me. Were—it's all to do with censorship. If you have no censorship, or even if you have it in a very strict form, how can you—how can we . . . You are a sincere person. When you make your films, you do it with sincerity and you do it with taste, and I think taste is probably the keynote of this whole thing. I mean, anything, any message, can be given and point made if it's done with taste, but we are so wide open in our medium, and certainly in television, it seems to me, or perhaps less at the moment, I don't know, to the unscrupulous, half-talented person who sees in the making of a movie a great deal of money.

PREMINGER. Deborah, may I say that I personally believe in the good taste of the great masses? I have never heard of anybody becoming rich because he sold dirty books or dirty postcards, and I don't think anybody has ever become rich by making really dirty or obscene motion pictures.

KERR. Well, not rich—shall we say done rather well.

MURROW. Monsignor McClafferty, is it admissible that any group should attempt to control or influence what those who are not members to that group should see or hear?

MC CLAFFERTY. Well, it would be my thought that the voluntary group, exercising its right of free comment and moral evaluation, ought to communicate that moral evaluation to those who follow it, and communicate it likewise to the media of communication, so that that opinion may be communicated to the public at large.

PREMINGER. I must say that I would not object to it at all.

MC CLAFFERTY. I just wanted to make this point: I do not think that voluntary groups would wish to exercise coercive methods, but rather that they would wish to exercise persuasive methods.

PREMINGER. May I repeat my question which you did not answer, Monsignor, before? Then why does then the Legion of Decency, when it condemns a picture, also threaten the theatres that play it with boycott for their next pictures? Do you think this is right?

MC CLAFFERTY. First of all, I am not here as the spokesman of the Legion.

PREMINGER. No, but—but you are familiar with the practices of the Legion.

MC CLAFFERTY. I want to clarify the position in which I express myself. I express myself as an individual.

PREMINGER. I realize this, but I still, for information, would like to ask you this question—what your personal opinion about it is.

MC CLAFFERTY. The Legion does not go, according to my recollection of its operation, to a motion picture company and make demands that this or that be done, or that this or that not be done.

PREMINGER. But it's my own picture, *The Moon Is Blue*. Here both—both Archbishops of New York and Philadelphia published letters in the newspapers, threatening theatres which played the picture to be boycotted by the members of the Legion of Decency—also for future exhibitions which by themselves were not condemned.

MC CLAFFERTY. The action of the Legion, under the leadership of such spiritual leaders that you mention, was in furtherance of the pastoral Ministry of the Church, namely, the spiritual well-being of those who are members of the Church, and those and others who follow the Legion classifications. I do not know of any central policy of the national office of the Legion which imposes any boycott or abstention for a period of time. There may be efforts on the local level for such supplementary action, but that is within the discretion and within the freedom of those subsidiary local efforts, because the national office of the . . .

PREMINGER. Do you, personally, approve of such actions?

MC CLAFFERTY. . . . Legion would give to those local efforts the freedom which all of us would like to see observed in all of the sectors of society, namely, a responsibly used freedom.

PREMINGER. Do you, personally, Monsignor, approve of such actions?

MC CLAFFERTY. Well, I don't explicitly understand what you mean by "such actions." You mean boycott?

PREMINGER. Yes.

MC CLAFFERTY. I, personally, would prefer that such voluntary associations utilize persuasive and interpretative methods rather than coercive methods, but it may be that the judgment of prudent men on the . . .

PREMINGER. I am very glad to hear that.

MC CLAFFERTY. . . . on the local level—that they have high responsibilities and the highest within a given territory, to see to it that their people are protected morally and spiritually, and that the people not be roadblocked in their progress towards spiritual perfection—roadblocked by any such thing as a film that might be immoral or obscene.

PREMINGER. You agree, though, that this should only be done to members, by members, of a certain group, and should not extend to people who do not belong to the same creed, the same Legion, or the same group of people?

MC CLAFFERTY. Well, we must remember this—that just as the Code is based upon generally accepted moral standards, so too, the work of the Legion, generally, is based upon the fundamental Ten Commandments which should guide our relations to our neighbor in terms of rights and duties, and our relation to God in terms of our rights and duties. I believe, Mr. Preminger, that a great majority of the pictures which have been deemed worthy of receiving a so-called Oscar, have been rated in the "A" category by the Legion of Decency. I think this is a tribute not only to the good judgment of the Legion, but also to the good judgment of the audience, in having such a coincidence of opinion with respect to films that are judged to be worthwhile and outstanding.

PREMINGER. I want to state here, that neither Greta Garbo nor Ernest

Lubitsch, nor Chaplin ever received an Oscar, and these certainly are three geniuses of the motion picture business.

KERR. Hear! Hear!

PREMINGER. Does anyone disagree?

KERR. No—not me!

PREMINGER. I think a producer has a right to make social comments, and it still can be very entertaining. As, for instance, recently, a picture *On the Beach* has proved—which made considerable social comments and still seems to be doing very, very well at the box office—and I do feel that pictures can be controversial and attack certain principles that might be very dear to certain segments of the population, without really insulting those segments of the population, if they are done in good taste and with the right feeling for drama.

MC CLAFFERTY. There is also the hazard, I believe, that when certain subject materials are shown on the screen, certain impressionable and perhaps unstable audience members may be tempted toward an experimental adoption of such a way of life . . .

KERR. Yes.

MC CLAFFERTY. . . . or toward an experimental use of such a way of life.

PREMINGER. But that is always true. We live in a very hazardous world.

KERR. That's why I would do away with horror films. I think they are much worse . . .

MC CLAFFERTY. Yes.

KERR. . . . all the dreadful tortures they practice and horrible things they do to people—ugh!

MC CLAFFERTY. When the Senate was investigating juvenile delinquency, a number of clinical experts testified, and in their opinion, there was a likely connection, a presumed connection between the amount and character of violence and horror on the screen, and the rising tide of juvenile delinquency, and I believe that this rising tide of juvenile delinquency is one of the reasons why there has been some resurgence of opinion and pressure within the population for some forms of control on the mass media of communication.

KERR. Yes.

MURROW. I'm sorry. Monsignor McClafferty, Miss Deborah Kerr, Mr.

Otto Preminger, thank you all very much, indeed. Next week's guests in just a moment.

Questions

1. What kind of audience do you suppose such a television program is designed for?
2. Why does Murrow make two references to censorship as "classification"?
3. Murrow suggests that the discussion begin by defining *censorship*. What definitions are presented by the various participants?
4. Miss Kerr states that she always sees both sides of the question. What do you think she means by this? Do the rest of her statements tend to support her assertion? Explain.
5. Why does Preminger insist that movies are a medium of communication rather than entertainment? Would you agree with him? Explain.
6. What is the attitude of each of the four participants toward censorship? Cite examples to support your statements.
7. According to Monsignor McClafferty, does the Legion of Decency speak just for Catholics? Explain.
8. What is Preminger's main argument against censorship? Do you consider it valid? Why or why not?

OBSCENITY AND PROTESTANT ETHICS*

Harvey G. Cox, Jr.

[1] The great success of Vladimir Nabokov's novel *Lolita* has raised an old problem for Protestants: the use and misuse of sex in literature and the arts. And behind that problem swarms a plethora of related problems of increasing importance about which Protestantism remains divided and uncertain: book-banning, TV and movie censorship, and the whole relationship of Christian ethics to mass communications.

[2] *Lolita* has been called "obscene." If we take the adjective in the strict dictionary sense ("offensive to modesty") its aptness can hardly be denied (except perhaps by those endowed with a near-cosmic sophistication). The novel's relentless exposure of the slickness of American roadside culture is by way of what one critic has called a theme of "brazen depravity." For many readers this closes the issue. "Obscenity" describes a breed of cats in which distinctions and gradations seem not only inappropriate but somehow ethically questionable. The "obscene book" deserves no more critical appraisal than that. Its writer finds himself classed with public lavatory artists and Peeping Toms,

* From *The Christian Century*, April 8, 1959. Copyright © 1959 Christian Century Foundation. Reprinted by permission.

although, let it be said, he may still reap a handsome stipend from a society whose treasure is not always where it says its heart is.

[3] But *does* this close the case? The assertion that it does is certainly debatable. At least one critic has maintained that *Lolita* is the story, not of "the debauchery and debauching of one little twelve-year-old, but of an entire society." Is it possible that a book can be "offensive to modesty" and still worth reading, possibly even worth defending? This is a hard question for Protestants to face. It calls to mind the frequent quandary of the Protestant voter, faced with a decision at the polls between a gin-guzzling rowdy with a good voting record, and a teetotaling reactionary. Neither situation, however, calls for a suspension of the ethical sense. Both require a fresh realization that truth breaks into human life in ways which are often offensive to all concerned. What is needed, in short, is a "doctrine of obscenity," a theologically grounded understanding of the sexual which defers to neither name-calling nor nihilism. We cannot afford to drown literature of lasting significance, or the social criticism we need for our soul's health, in the same tub with pornographic trivialities.

[4] Just what is "obscenity"? It is clearly one of the few things our culture is still self-consciously and unequivocally against. Labeling something "obscene" is an astonishingly effective tactic in a country in which a similar word, "subversive," has lost some of the fetish value it had a few years back. The two words do have a certain strange kinship. Both have had the magical power at various times to conjure up faceless phantoms, to obscure the actual points of contention, and to prejudge those against whom the incantation was directed. The Protestant conscience soon saw through the danger of unexamined labels in political life, but it has not shown as much discernment in the literary area. "Obscenity" still has a ritual efficacy. It raises our moral hackles even when we don't know what it is. The problem reaches far beyond the case of *Lolita*. It becomes especially grievous in the mass media where the Protestant voice, when it is not simply inept, is divided or downright questionable.

[5] The Protestant record in the matter of book-banning, for example, is at best a mixed one. The quasi-official committees emerging in many small towns, charged with the sober responsibility of watching over the "moral level" of the Bijou's films and Rexall's book racks, usually include well intentioned church people and even ministers. Sometimes denominational leaders and National Council of Churches officials, to their embarrassment, are consulted by these committees for help as to which books and movies should be "advised" and which

"discouraged." Such vigorous sentinels of public morality, needless to say, exert a powerful influence on theater owners and drugstore operators, especially in our close-knit small towns. Their activities amount to *de facto* censorship and are of questionable legality in some states. They make Protestant criticisms of the Roman Catholic *Index* of prohibited books sound hollow.

[6] Film censorship especially is an issue over which Protestants can summon much heat but little agreement. Let me recount what happened in Ohio. Noticing that a film censorship bill had been introduced into the legislature in 1957, the churches of Ohio leaped into a flurry of activity—on both sides! Some Protestant churches remembered that the previous censorship law, which had been voided by our Supreme Court, had become an undisguised political bludgeon. The old law, likewise phrased in clauses about "obscenity" and "indecency," had been used to bar from Ohio screens several films the censors had found objectionable on quite different grounds. For example, *Spain in Flames* (a pro-loyalist Spanish civil war film) and a short subject taking the labor side of the 1926 coal strike had been excluded; also a U.N.-produced film depicting the tragic impact of war on young children, although this was shown in forty-seven other states.

[7] However, in 1957 the word "obscenity" again exercised its magical potency. Many church organizations vigorously supported the bill. The sponsor of the legislation, an ambitious young Cleveland Democrat, found himself suddenly popular among women's groups in firmly Republican sections of the state. They pledged him their support in his crusade to "rid Ohio of commercial filth." Numerous church social action committees, wearied with controversy and looking for an issue on which everyone could agree, joined his cause. After all, who could be *for* filth?

[8] The Protestant attitude toward the bill reached a climax of contradictory passion when the hearings on it began. Two ministers met by chance in the capitol and shook hands warmly when they discovered they had both come to testify on the bill—until they found they were on opposite sides.

[9] Fortunately the fate of this film-censorship bill was not left entirely to the churches. It was finally defeated because of the work of many independent groups and the determined good sense of the chairman of the education committee, to which the bill was referred. A small-town newspaper editor, he recognized a camel's nose when he saw one.

[10] Protestant disagreement over matters of sex and censorship arises from different aspects of the same religious tradition. The Puritan

distaste for bawdiness and lechery is often at loggerheads with the sectarian Protestant insistence on freedom of expression. Yet the Puritan attitude itself is curiously ambivalent about sex, a mixture of fascination and chill suspicion. This ambivalence is the theme of the crowning work of the Puritan literary tradition, Hawthorne's *The Scarlet Letter*. The secularized deposit of this attitude allows the modern American to read a novel about sexual deviation provided he can protect himself from the artistic power of the book by assuming a moral superiority toward it. Could Nabokov's sad picture of a tiring sexual gourmet have anything to say to hedonistic America? Of course not! The book is *obscene*. It can be read to be clucked over, to be loudly defended in proof of one's moral emancipation, or for what little secret titillation it offers. But that is all. "It's obscene" not only annihilates something we to be against for other reasons; it also protects us from the pain of self-examination.

[11] But even an honest and biblically sound Protestant consensus on sex and obscenity would not solve the problem. What effect could such a consensus have on American mass communications? The pyramid empires of the communications and entertainment industries are not as directly approachable as other power centers in our society. M.G.M. does not hold hearings before its writers begin work on a script. The editors of *Time* and *Life* do not turn to the people for re-election every four years, though their decisions often influence us as much as the decisions of the people we elect. Our responsibility to the mass media demands that we know how the industry is organized, how it looks to those "inside," and where the decisions are really made. Some observers believe that Protestantism's responsibility to the mass media will require a degree of flexibility to which we have been unaccustomed, and may eventually demand modifications in the historic forms of Protestant polity. The alternative may be simply to relinquish any voice in what the mass media do. Deadlines fall with inexorable regularity and cannot always wait for all the "ayes" to be counted. The show must go on.

[12] A further question remains. How much influence *should* Protestants have in national media? The fact that everyone is against obscenity makes it more, not less, difficult to achieve a public consensus. What responsibility do Protestants have, in this particular trackless waste, to those who see things differently? There will always be those who differ about the value of Nabokov and Spillane—and *Martin Luther*. Assuming for the moment that Protestants could agree among themselves as to whether a book or movie or TV sequence deserves public attention—to what degree can we impose our judgments on "the

others"? Our stake in the open society reaches too deeply back into our biblical faith to allow for any tinkering with it, even to our advantage. That our Roman Catholic fellow Americans have not always been punctilious in observing the ground rules of democratic procedure should serve as a caution to us, rather than as a stimulus to equal sectarian zeal. The well publicized incidents surrounding *The Miracle* and *The Game of Love*, though disquieting in themselves, draw attention away from the hand of Roman Catholic moral theology in Hollywood's production code. The Protestant's view of man and history (when he takes it seriously) will simply not allow him to impose his ethical-aesthetic tastes in this manner, even if he could.

[13] Can we find a way to formulate a Protestant ethic for the mass media which will at the same time secure the rights of the minority, though that minority's tastes offend our moral sensibilities? The accepted presence of *Ulysses* and *Madame Bovary* on the bookshelf of the mousiest college sophomore should remind us that books of timeless worth have often suffered the interdict of obscenity. In morality, as in theology, last week's heretic is next week's saint.

[14] But support of the beleaguered minority can never be the whole basis of a Protestant tactic, either in politics or in the mass media. In a society on the road from production to consumption values, a society in which the mass media play a central and formative role, we must candidly face the truth that Protestants stand theologically unequipped to know what charges of "obscenity," "indecency" and "sacrilege" mean. We can neither dismiss such labels with a superior, post-Kinseyan shrug, nor overlook the fact that they have often been used as empty smear words to advance the interests of this or that bloc. The battle for influence in the media of mass communication is a sharp one. But if we merely retreat in confusion from the crossfire, there are others with hardier spirits, and perhaps less disinterested objectives, who will be more than willing to fashion the images which shape the values of a nation.

[15] We need a vigorous and authentically biblical ethic of sexuality and obscenity, one that sees through the veneer and can distinguish art from tinsel, that can test the spirits to see of whom and of what they witness. The need is urgent. The tubes are flickering and the presses are rolling, and the moment is now.

Questions

1. What is the purpose of this article?
2. What is Cox's attitude toward his reader? What assumptions is he making about his audience?

3. What reasons does Cox advance for the inability of Protestants to agree on obscenity and censorship? Do you consider them valid? Explain.

4. In paragraph 5 why does Cox say it is sometimes "to their embarrassment" when National Council of Churches officials are consulted by small town committees?

5. What point does Cox make throughout the article about the use of labeling in the censorship controversy?

6. Cox states that "Protestants stand theologically unequipped to know what charges of 'obscenity,' 'indecency' and 'sacrilege' mean." What does he mean by this? Do you agree with him or not? Why?

7. What assumptions does Cox make about Protestantism and democracy? Do you consider these assumptions valid? Why or why not?

THE VIGILANTES*

Fred B. Millett

On the evening of December 21, 1953, in the course of a C.B.S. television program, "This is Show Business," the well-known American playwright, Mr. George S. Kaufman, made the *ad lib.* remark, "Let's make this *one* program on which no one sings 'Silent Night.'" Before the show had ended, the switchboard of the Columbia Broadcasting System began receiving calls objecting to Mr. Kaufman's remark on the grounds that it was "anti-religious." During the next few days, between 200 and 500 letters protesting the remark were received by either the Columbia Broadcasting System or the show's sponsor, The American Tobacco Company. As a result, Mr. Kaufman was dropped from the show until calmer counsels prevailed and he was permitted to rejoin it. In the preceding May, an amateur production of *Mr. Roberts* closed after one performance at the Mitchell Air Force Base, Long Island, because several unidentified persons objected to Air Force personnel's being allowed to hear the salty language which had been tolerated by all and sundry members of its audience during the play's three-year run on Broadway. Last November, the Motion Picture Production Code Administration denied the appeal of Paramount Pictures to be permitted to retain in the dialogue of a picture depicting actual battle conditions in Korea three uses of the word "hell" and one use of the word "damn." A month or so ago, a most distinguished audience assembled for the private showing of a double-bill of moving pictures. The audience consisted of the Justices of the Supreme Court of the United States. The pictures were an old German movie entitled "M," and a

---

* From *AAUP Bulletin,* Spring 1954. Reprinted by permission.

French movie, entitled "La Ronde," which had played for two years in the most exclusive cinema in London's West End. In assembling to view these pictures, the Justices were not moved by a common interest in either abnormal psychology or licentious behavior. They were assembled to decide whether or not the sovereign state of Ohio had acted legally in banning "M," and whether the New York State Board of Censors had acted legally in banning "La Ronde" on the grounds that it "would tend to corrupt public morals." In that stronghold of public morality, Jersey City, the police recently advised booksellers to remove from prominent display all copies of James Jones's novel, *From Here to Eternity.* In Detroit, booksellers were discouraged from offering for sale pocket-sized editions of certain of the works of Hemingway, although they were permitted to sell the books in hard covers. In Cleveland, a dealer was told that he could sell a portfolio of reproductions of Renoir's paintings but that he should not display it. . . . These instances involving censorship are only a few of many examples that might be cited of the wave of suppression that has swept over this free land of ours during the past two or three years. . . .

Censorship, generally, falls into two significantly distinct classes, hidden and public. Of the two classes, the first is, of course, the more insidious because it is uncontrollable. Such hidden censorship is part and parcel of the system in accordance with which motion pictures are produced in the United States. All pictures that are to receive the approval of the Motion Picture Producers Code Administration must secure the approval *before* the pictures can be released. There is plenty of evidence that many of the specific stipulations of the Code are hopelessly outmoded. A specific ruling of the Code bans "pointed profanity and every other profane or vulgar expression, however used." It was this specific ruling that brought about the enforced elimination of three "hell's" and one "damn" from the picture showing actual battle conditions in Korea. Public censorship is that exercised by a legally constituted body such as the New York State Board of Regents, which may refuse to permit the showing of a picture anywhere within the limits of the sovereign state of New York. A more dangerous form of public censorship, however, occurs when private individuals or pressure-groups exert their influence to prevent the public sale of books or the public showing of moving pictures.

Three recent instances of attempted censorship deserve somewhat more detailed comment. "La Ronde," a French moving picture, based on Arthur Schnitzler's classic dialogues, *Reigen,* directed by Max Ophuls, and acted by a distinguished French cast, had been shown legally not only in fifteen of the states but also in the District of Columbia. The Motion Picture Division of the New York State Board of Regents, however, refused, as I have said, to permit the showing of the picture within the state, and the ruling of the Board was sustained by the Court of Appeals by a three-to-two decision. The case was carried to the Supreme Court of the United States, and recently that court ruled that the New York State Board of Regents had no legal right to prevent the showing of the picture and that, in its judgment, the showing of it would not "tend to corrupt public morals." Thus, at long last, the innocent denizens of New York City were allowed to witness, if they so chose, a public showing of this famous film. Of "La Ronde," Mr. Bosley Crowther, the *New York Times* moving-picture critic, wrote, it "is a philosophical exploration of the delusions of illicit love. Some of it is obvious, some of it subtle and vague. . . . It is hard to imagine anyone without a good bit of sophistication understanding very well what's going on. It is ridiculous to think of this picture having been banned for being 'immoral.' Yet the only reason we're seeing it in this state is because the Supreme Court found the term 'immoral' inadequate as a standard for condemning a film."

The case of the motion picture, "The Moon Is Blue," is even more preposterous. As a play, F. Hugh Herbert's little comedy had played for months in a New York theatre without arousing any great enthusiasm or attracting adverse comment. Then, a film, made from the play, failed to receive the approval of the Motion Picture Producers Code Administration but was passed by the New York Board of Censors. As the time came for the showing of the film, protests against it appeared in various places. In Chicago, the police allowed the film to be shown but only to adult audiences. In Kansas City, Missouri, the police censors asked for five elisions. The Motion Picture Censorship Board of the State of Kansas demanded sixty-six elisions. In New York, the picture was attacked as containing serious violations of morality and decency. A showing of the picture in Jersey City was raided by the police, led by the Director of Public Safety, and the theatre manager was haled into court. The description of the cause of all this to-do may be entrusted to the judicious Mr. Crowther. The movie, he wrote, is "a skimpy little story of a girl who is frank about sex but wonderously deft in deflecting the passes of predatory wolves." What apparently upset the guardians of the Motion Picture Production Code was not only the frequent use in dialogue of such tabooed words as "virgin," "mistress," and "pregnant," but also a dissipated father's indifference to his daughter's sexual behavior. But, Mr. Crowther concludes, "the theme of this confection is as moral as a Sunday school book. . . . It is virtue that triumphs. The good little girl gets the man."

Certainly the most momentous attempt to prevent the exhibition of a moving picture involved the film called "The Miracle." Directed by Roberto Rossellini, the picture tells the story of a half-witted Italian peasant girl who is seduced by a stranger whom she believes to be a vision of St. Joseph. Proud of what seems to her a miraculous pregnancy, she is tormented by the villagers, who stage a mock-procession in her honor. In the end, she crawls away to bear her child in the shadow of an empty church. The New York Film Critics voted "Three Ways of Love," of which "The Miracle" was a part, the "best foreign movie of the year," but, under pressure, they made their award in the Rainbow Room of the R.C.A. Building at Rockefeller Center, and not in a public theatre. The attack on this picture was violent and inflammatory; it was accused of being both blasphemous and sacrilegious. Angry picket-lines marched and counter-marched before the theatre; there were threats that the theatre would be bombed. Although its showing had been licensed by the Motion Picture Division of the New York State Board of Regents, the License Commissioner of New York City immediately imposed a temporary ban on the showing of the film, and when he was enjoined from imposing this ban, the Board of Regents, after its special sub-committee had voted unanimously that the picture was sacrilegious, reversed the decision of its Motion Picture Division and banned the film. Legal recourse to the New York Court of Appeals resulted in a unanimous decision to sustain the Regents' ban. But Joseph Burstyn, the distributor of the picture, carried the case to the Supreme Court of the United States, and, finally, the Justices rendered a unanimous decision that the State of New York's banning of the film was unconstitutional. "New York requires," Mr. Justice Clark wrote, "that permission to communicate ideas be obtained in advance from state officials who judge the works and pictures sought to be communicated. . . . Such a previous restraint is a form of infringement upon freedom of expression to be especially condemned." On the issue of sacrilege, he wrote, "In seeking to apply the definition of 'sacrilegious,' the censor is set adrift upon a boundless sea amid myriad currents of religious views, with no charts but those provided by the most vocal and powerful orthodoxies. . . . Under such a standard the most careful and tolerant censor would find it virtually impossible to avoid favoring one religion over another." . . .

I should like to conclude by commenting on three propositions concerning censorship which it seems to me follow logically from the evi-

dence I have submitted and mountains of evidence that have accumulated through the centuries: (1) Censorship in the field of literature
and the other arts is usually stupid, and always unintelligent. (2) The
censorship of literature is almost invariably self-defeating. (3) The
censorship of literature is anti-democratic; in other words, it is fundamentally opposed to the philosophy of democracy.

(1) Censorship in the field of literature and the other arts is usually
stupid and always unintelligent, because the critical assumptions that
underlie censorship are aesthetically indefensible. The censor of literature does not condemn a literary work because it is a bad literary work;
by his very nature, he is usually incapable of distinguishing between
a good and a bad literary work, even if he thought it important to make
such a judgment. The censor condemns a literary work and would prevent its circulation because it contains or implies ideas or attitudes that
he regards as erotically, ethically, politically, religiously, or philosophically reprehensible, ideas and attitudes that he thinks would do damage, not to himself, mind you, but to other persons who might be exposed to them. Now, a literary work is not a good work because it contains ideas, of whatever sort, of which the censor would approve, nor
is it a bad work because it contains ideas, of whatever sort, of which the
censor would disapprove. If this were the case, a hymn embodying the
soundest theology in the most banal style would be a good hymn, and
a hymn expressing heretical ideas in a superb poetic style would be a
bad hymn. Persons who are interested in rooting out heresies might
condemn the second hymn as heretical; critics could hardly condemn
it as being a bad hymn.

The relationship between the idea and the form of a literary work,
and the relative significance of these elements in the evaluation of
literary works are not, I admit, elementary problems. . . . The excellence of a poem does not depend on the validity of the doctrine it expresses. The excellence of a poem depends finally on what is said, the
manner in which it is said and, I should add, the relationship between
the matter and the manner. If an artist is serious, he attempts in a work
of art to express something that he regards as true and something that
he considers it important to say. He also endeavors to give the most
appropriate and appealing form possible to what he is trying to say. On
both reader and critic, it is the form that makes the most immediate
impression, but, if he is a good reader and a good critic, he will be able
to grasp accurately not only the idea embodied in the form but the
author's attitude toward that idea, his feeling about it. He is then, as
either reader or critic, quite free to indicate that what the artist thought

it important to say does not seem to him to be important or illuminating or weighty. But, so long as he is acting as a literary critic, he cannot condemn the work *merely* because its content seems dubious or dangerous. In the last analysis, the excellence of a literary work depends on a very subtle analysis and weighing of the content, the form, and the relationship between the content and the form.

(2) That the censorship of literature is usually self-defeating is so obvious as hardly to need explication. The very fact that a censor openly designates a work as dubious or dangerous is enough to draw the attention of at least a considerable segment of the public to a work that might otherwise have gone unnoticed. When the official custodians of the public morals of Boston were more active, it used to be said that some publishers looked forward eagerly to having their books banned there so that a considerable sale would be assured elsewhere. . . . The unintentional effect of censorship may also be suggested by the fact that the touring company of *The Moon Is Blue* now uses as advertising slogans, "SEE what the film couldn't show! *Hear* what the movie couldn't say!" . . .

(3) Finally, the censorship of literature is in basic opposition to the principle of freedom of thought and expression that is one of the basic tenets of a philosophy of democracy. Since I am not a political philosopher, I may perhaps be permitted to use as my authority a distinguished member of the Council of the Association, Professor Ralph Barton Perry. In his essay, "What Does It Mean to be Free?" he writes, "Freedom means *effective choice*. Man is free, in other words, in proportion as *he does or thinks what he chooses*. . . . It is choice that imposes on human life what is perhaps its greatest burden: for it is very hard to choose. It is because he has the capacity for choice that man is a moral being." Later, he says, "It is surprising how many who consider themselves good Americans, after three centuries during which this creed has been proclaimed, embodied in our state and federal constitutions, and consecrated in our tradition, still do not understand what the principle means. They still tend to lapse into the primitive view that it means freedom to think and communicate *true* or *safe* opinions."

The relevance of these principles to the problem of the censorship of literature requires no demonstration. An essential condition of freedom of thought and expression is the freedom of the artist to say what he believes to be true and important and the freedom of the reader to choose whatever expressions arouse his interest, satisfy his curiosity, or add to his understanding of the human plight. As Professor Perry says, "Whoever determines what alternatives shall be made known to man controls what that man shall choose *from*. He is deprived of freedom in proportion as he is denied access to *any* ideas, or is confined to any range of ideas short of the totality of relevant possibilities."

The urge to censor literature has countless and tangled roots. But one of the major roots is a view of human nature that is in basic opposition to that implied in the philosophy of democracy. The view of human nature that is held by most censors is that expressed with terrifying eloquence by Dostoievski's Grand Inquisitor in the apologue Ivan recites in *The Brothers Karamazov*. The Grand Inquisitor, the anti-Christ of Dostoievski's apologue, holds the view that man is "weak, vicious, worthless, and rebellious." Man "is tormented by no greater anxiety than to find some one quickly to whom he can hand over that gift of freedom with which the ill-fated creature is born." Opposed to this view is the Christian view, the view of Christ, whose view of man's capacity to choose, the Grand Inquisitor denounces. "Instead of taking men's freedom from them, Thou didst make it greater than ever! Didst Thou forget that man prefers peace, and even death, to freedom of choice in the knowledge of good and evil? . . . Instead of giving a firm foundation for setting the conscience of man at rest forever, Thou didst choose what was utterly beyond the strength of men. . . . In place of the rigid ancient law, man must hereafter with free heart decide for himself what is good and what is evil."

The burden of choice is heavy, but, within the framework of democracy—I should even go so far as to say within the Christian framework —the burden is inescapable. In these contexts, not only must man be entrusted with the responsibility of choosing between what is good and what is evil, but he must have access to all kinds and varieties of literature in order that his choices may be as meaningful as possible. Within the increasingly complicated structure of the modern state, in the face of the confusing chaos of creeds, doctrines, and dogmas, man may, to be sure, shift the responsibility of choice to whatever official or unofficial shoulders he may select, but in so far as he abnegates his own responsibility for choice, he becomes less than a mature and responsible moral or aesthetic being.

Questions

1. Why does Millett use "The Vigilantes" as the title of his speech? How might his audience respond to this title? Why?
2. To whom is Millett speaking? What methods of appeal does he use that are particularly suited to his audience?
3. Notice the structure of the first paragraph. What is its function in this speech?

4. What method of argument does Millett use in the first half of the speech? What method does he use in the second half?
5. What distinctions does Millett make between a literary critic and a censor? What is his purpose in making these distinctions?
6. Restate in your own words Millett's basic concept about the relationship between idea and form in a literary work. Why does Millett make this point?
7. How does the illustration from *The Brothers Karamazov* support one of Millett's basic principles?
8. How would Millett have the censoring done in our society and by whom? Explain.

THE UNITED STATES V. *ULYSSES*

John M. Woolsey

United States District Court

SOUTHERN DISTRICT OF NEW YORK

United States of America, *Libelant* v. One Book called "Ulysses," Random House, Inc., *Claimant*	OPINION A. 110–59

[1] The motion for a decree dismissing the libel herein is granted, and, consequently, of course, the government's motion for a decree of forfeiture and destruction is denied.

[2] . . . I have read "Ulysses" once in its entirety and I have read those passages of which the government particularly complains several times. In fact, for many weeks, my spare time has been devoted to the consideration of the decision which my duty would require me to make in this matter.

[3] "Ulysses" is not an easy book to read or to understand. But there has been much written about it, and in order properly to approach the consideration of it it is advisable to read a number of other books which have now become its satellites. The study of "Ulysses" is, therefore, a heavy task.

[4] The reputation of "Ulysses" in the literary world, however, warranted my taking such time as was necessary to enable me to satisfy myself as to the intent with which the book was written, for, of course, in any case where a book is claimed to be obscene it must first be deter-

mined, whether the intent with which it was written was what is called, according to the usual phrase, pornographic, that is, written for the purpose of exploiting obscenity.

[5] If the conclusion is that the book is pornographic, that is the end of the inquiry and forfeiture must follow.

[6] But in "Ulysses," in spite of its unusual frankness, I do not detect anywhere the leer of the sensualist. I hold, therefore, that it is not pornographic.

[7] In writing "Ulysses," Joyce sought to make a serious experiment in a new, if not wholly novel, literary genre. He takes persons of the lower middle class living in Dublin in 1904 and seeks, not only to describe what they did on a certain day early in June of that year as they went about the city bent on their usual occupations, but also to tell what many of them thought about the while.

[8] Joyce has attempted—it seems to me, with astonishing success— to show how the screen of consciousness with its ever-shifting kaleidoscopic impressions carries, as it were on a plastic palimpsest, not only what is in the focus of each man's observation of the actual things about him, but also in a penumbral zone residua of past impressions, some recent and some drawn up by association from the domain of the subconscious. He shows how each of these impressions affects the life and behavior of the character which he is describing.

[9] What he seeks to get is not unlike the result of a double or, if that is possible, a multiple exposure on a cinema film, which would give a clear foreground with a background visible but somewhat blurred and out of focus in varying degrees.

[10] To convey by words an effect which obviously lends itself more appropriately to a graphic technique, accounts, it seems to me, for much of the obscurity which meets a reader of "Ulysses." And it also explains another aspect of the book, which I have further to consider, namely, Joyce's sincerity and his honest effort to show exactly how the minds of his characters operate.

[11] If Joyce did not attempt to be honest in developing the technique which he has adopted in "Ulysses," the result would be psychologically misleading and thus unfaithful to his chosen technique. Such an attitude would be artistically inexcusable.

[12] It is because Joyce has been loyal to his technique and has not funked its necessary implications, but has honestly attempted to tell fully what his characters think about, that he has been the subject of so many attacks and that his purpose has been so often misunderstood and misrepresented. For his attempt sincerely and honestly to realize his

objective has required him incidentally to use certain words which are generally considered dirty words and has led at times to what many think is a too poignant preoccupation with sex in the thoughts of his characters.

[13] The words which are criticized as dirty are old Saxon words known to almost all men and, I venture, to many women, and are such words as would be naturally and habitually used, I believe, by the types of folk whose life, physical and mental, Joyce is seeking to describe. In respect of the recurrent emergence of the theme of sex in the minds of his characters, it must always be remembered that his locale was Celtic and his season spring.

[14] Whether or not one enjoys such a technique as Joyce uses is a matter of taste on which disagreement or argument is futile, but to subject that technique to the standards of some other technique seems to me to be little short of absurd.

[15] Accordingly, I hold that "Ulysses" is a sincere and honest book, and I think that the criticisms of it are entirely disposed of by its rationale.

[16] Furthermore, "Ulysses" is an amazing tour de force when one considers the success which has been in the main achieved with such a difficult objective as Joyce set for himself. As I have stated, "Ulysses" is not an easy book to read. It is brilliant and dull, intelligible and obscure, by turns. In many places it seems to me to be disgusting, but although it contains, as I have mentioned above, many words usually considered dirty, I have not found anything that I consider to be dirt for dirt's sake. Each word of the book contributes like a bit of mosaic to the detail of the picture which Joyce is seeking to construct for his readers.

[17] If one does not wish to associate with such folk as Joyce describes, that is one's own choice. In order to avoid indirect contact with them one may not wish to read "Ulysses"; that is quite understandable. But when such a great artist in words, as Joyce undoubtedly is, seeks to draw a true picture of the lower middle class in a European city, ought it to be impossible for the American public legally to see that picture?

[18] To answer this question it is not sufficient merely to find, as I have found above, that Joyce did not write "Ulysses" with what is commonly called pornographic intent, I must endeavor to apply a more objective standard to his book in order to determine its effect in the result, irrespective of the intent with which it was written.

[19] The statute under which the libel is filed only denounces, in so far as we are here concerned, the importation into the United States from any foreign country of "any obscene book." Section 305 of the

Tariff Act of 1930, title 19 United States Code, § 1305 (19 USCA § 1305). It does not marshal against books the spectrum of condemna-tory adjectives found, commonly, in laws dealing with matters of this kind. I am, therefore, only required to determine whether "Ulysses" is obscene within the legal definition of that word.

[20] The meaning of the word "obscene" as legally defined by the courts is: Tending to stir the sex impulses or to lead to sexually impure and lustful thoughts. . . .

[21] Whether a particular book would tend to excite such impulses and thoughts must be tested by the court's opinion as to its effect on a person with average sex instincts—what the French would call *l'homme moyen sensuel*—who plays, in this branch of legal inquiry, the same role of hypothetical reagent as does the "reasonable man" in the law of torts and "the man learned in the art" on questions of invention in patent law.

[22] The risk involved in the use of such a reagent arises from the inherent tendency of the trier of facts, however fair he may intend to be, to make his reagent too much subservient to his own idosyncrasies. Here, I have attempted to avoid this, if possible, and to make my re-agent herein more objective than he might otherwise be, by adopting the following course:

[23] After I had made my decision in regard to the aspect of "Ulys-ses," now under consideration, I checked my impressions with two friends of mine who in my opinion answered to the above-stated re-quirement for my reagent.

[24] These literary assessors—as I might properly describe them—were called on separately, and neither knew that I was consulting the other. They are men whose opinion on literature and on life I value most highly. They had both read "Ulysses," and, of course, were wholly unconnected with this cause.

[25] Without letting either of my assessors know what my decision was, I gave to each of them the legal definition of obscene and asked each whether in his opinion "Ulysses" was obscene within that defini-tion.

[26] I was interested to find that they both agreed with my opinion: That reading "Ulysses" in its entirety, as a book must be read on such a test as this, did not tend to excite sexual impulses or lustful thoughts, but that its net effect on them was only that of a somewhat tragic and very powerful commentary on the inner lives of men and women.

[27] It is only with the normal person that the law is concerned. Such a test as I have described, therefore, is the only proper test of ob-scenity in the case of a book like "Ulysses" which is a sincere and seri-

ous attempt to devise a new literary method for the observation and description of mankind.

[28] I am quite aware that owing to some of its scenes "Ulysses" is a rather strong draught to ask some sensitive, though normal, person to take. But my considered opinion, after long reflection, is that, whilst in many places the effect of "Ulysses" on the reader undoubtedly is somewhat emetic, nowhere does it tend to be an aphrodisiac.

[29] "Ulysses" may, therefore, be admitted into the United States.

JOHN M. WOOLSEY
United States District Judge

December 6, 1933

Questions

1. For what audience is a judge's case decision intended? Why do such decisions sometimes run to several thousand words in length?
2. What is the purpose of paragraphs 2, 3, and 4?
3. Woolsey sets forth three main criteria for determining whether or not a book is pornographic. Locate and state these three criteria.
4. What is Woolsey's attitude toward the use of "dirty" words in a book?
5. What is the significance of Woolsey's statement that the legal definition of obscenity, "tending to stir the sex impulses . . .," must be tested as to its effect on the average person—*l'homme moyen sensuel?*
6. What is meant by the statement in the next to last paragraph: "the effect of 'Ulysses' on the reader undoubtedly is somewhat emetic, nowhere does it tend to be an aphrodisiac"?

AN ATMOSPHERE OF CAUTION*

Marjorie Fiske

It was not at all unusual, once the librarian had been briefed about the study, for him to jump at once into a discussion of his awareness of caution (his own or other people's) as though he had been waiting for an opportunity to unburden himself. Several felt that the study itself was a rather "courageous" enterprise (a few called it "dangerous") and asked whether there was not a possibility that "someone will clamp down." Some respondents, mainly persons on the staff level in large and highly bureaucratized school or public library systems, recalled that they had felt uneasy when they read about the study in their professional journal and hoped they would not be interviewed. In

* From Marjorie Fiske, *Book Selection and Censorship.* Copyright © 1959 by Regents of the University of California. Reprinted by permission.

speculating about the reasons for their feelings of caution, a remark about "this day and age" was not at all infrequent, and some mention of Senator Joseph McCarthy occasionally followed, qualified by a hasty, "I know he has been discredited nationally, but around here . . ." The area "around here" was usually not clearly defined. An alternative explanation was "California has a lot of crackpots, you know." But the respondent's own community was invariably "a literate and broadminded town." There is acute awareness of the climate of opinion, but it is often sensed as something "out there," in some other part of the state.

. . . .

The twenty-six communities in which this study was conducted are as diverse in their social as in their geographical characteristics. There are conservative segments of "old" communities which have become more conservative in the struggle to preserve tradition against the influx of new populations. There are sizable cities—mere villages twenty years ago—with little tradition at all. There are towns long characterized by a constrictive triumvirate of press, politics and voluntary groups; and there are communities traditionally conspicuous for courageous newspapers, far-seeing public officials, and an enlightened citizenry.

. . . .

As we have seen, neither librarians nor school administrators explained their feelings of caution by pointing to an increase of direct pressures on their institutions. What strikes them, as they look about in their communities, is not attacks on ideas but the avoidance of them. One librarian noticed that her own young son could find no answer, either in school or in the children's section of the public library, to his question, "What *is* Communism anyway?" Another believes that people feel intimidated by ideas and are, therefore, increasingly fearful of libraries. Events such as the recent last-minute change of a high school radio forum from "Communism and Capitalism in America" to "To Go Steady or Not To Go Steady," because some parents did not wish to have their children discuss the first topic in public, can be reported by nearly every observer of a local scene.

. . . .

The hush which has fallen over ideological discussion is not restricted to any one political arena or subject field. In talking about books or authors that have been restricted or removed from their collections, librarians had as much difficulty in remembering names and titles objected to from the right as from the left, and sometimes even references to *Little Black Sambo* and *Huckleberry Finn* were whispered. In extreme cases, librarians may live a nightmare that has strong paranoid undertones:

I have avoided buying [books about Communism] because I do not trust my own judgment. I have traveled a lot . . . I might seem dangerous to some people. They might object to what I bought . . . The public thinks they own their schools and should choose the books.

Today nondemocratic ideologies evoke anxiety. There is worry about the fact that they exist, but no very concrete idea of what in particular makes them dangerous. Anything which seems potentially troublesome is simply dumped into the witches' brew labeled "controversial" or "un-American." A book or an author complained about by any person for any reason may, quite legitimately, be called controversial. The fact that this term can be applied to a work is often taken to mean that it is "bad." The pros and cons of controversy are forgotten in the stress on the *con* in controversial.

.   .   .   .

It is not only the word "controversial" which is laden with emotional affect. "To censor," in all of its variations, and the word "pressure" are disliked or avoided by many of our respondents. "Why," asked a county library department head, "do you keep referring to pressure groups? To the public librarian, all groups are pressure groups." Words deriving from "to censor" were avoided not only in connection with a given librarian's own practice of book selection (sometimes clearly censorial) but in more abstract discussions of library philosophy. Librarians "screen," "select," and "guide." As a librarian in a large municipal library put it, "We haven't been censoring but we have been 'conservative.' After all, this is a conservative community, and that is how parents here want it to be." But, ruminated a few, when we take actual or potential controversiality into account in the screening, selecting and guiding, are we not indeed censoring? Others do not ask; the word is avoided. Selection which by-passes the controversial is justified by use of the same terms of opprobrium used by would-be censors. In speaking of contemporary works of fiction, one municipal librarian reported her views as follows: "If they are out-and-out obscene they should not be in the library at all . . . [but] 'touchy' books . . . have a legitimate place in the public library. . . . [However] since some people do find them objectionable, they are kept on reserve." Or, as another public librarian said: "You have to screen the organizations that want to put on exhibits because you don't want any 'neo-Communists' in the library. You also have to make sure there is nothing in the exhibits that might be considered controversial."

Such remarks, which were by no means infrequent in the interviews, were often followed by some such observation as "this means that we now have a good deal of freedom, you see." What these librarians seem to mean is that institutions having "conservative" policies are not as likely to attract public attention. Public attention sometimes results in community controversy and community controversy sometimes results in restrictive measures. Then you *really* have restrictions. This is the same line of reasoning that led some of our respondents to accuse those who have been involved in public episodes of using the wrong language. If, say these critics, the administrator or the school librarian had said, "We've called those books in for review," rather than, "We've withdrawn them," the segment of the public which is opposed to restrictive practices would not have become aroused, the restrictors would have been pacified, and no episode would have developed.

Some librarians have adopted an even more positivistic semantic philosophy, much of which is formally sanctioned in library policy and training. There is little talk of avoiding the controversial, or even of being conservative; rather, library materials must be in "good taste," they must be "suitable" or they must be "appropriate." In school libraries or library systems, the equivalent is likely to be the irreproachable statement, "Our materials must supplement the curriculum." The less sanguine school librarian adds "and everyone knows that the curriculum, after all the commotion about textbooks, is pure!"

Questions

1. How would you characterize the language of this piece? Explain.
2. What point is Miss Fiske trying to make about librarians and censorship?
3. According to Miss Fiske, what are the characteristics and attitudes of most librarians? Do your experiences tend to confirm or deny her conclusions? Explain.
4. What connections does Miss Fiske see between the term *controversial* and censorship?
5. Why were words deriving from *to censor* avoided by some librarians?
6. What does Miss Fiske mean when she states: "Some librarians have adopted an even more positivistic semantic philosophy"?

From PORNOGRAPHY AND OBSCENITY*

D. H. Lawrence

[1] What they are depends, as usual, entirely on the individual. What is pornography to one man is the laughter of genius to another.

[2] The word itself, we are told, means "pertaining to harlots"—the graph of the harlot. But nowadays, what is a harlot? If she was a woman who took money from a man in return for going to bed with him—really, most wives sold themselves, in the past, and plenty of harlots gave themselves, when they felt like it, for nothing. If a woman hasn't got a tiny streak of a harlot in her, she's a dry stick as a rule. And probably most harlots had somewhere a streak of womanly generosity. Why be so cut and dried? The law is a dreary thing, and its judgments have nothing to do with life.

[3] The same with the word *obscene:* nobody knows what it means. Suppose it were derived from *obscena:* that which might not be represented on the stage; how much further are you? None! What is obscene to Tom is not obscene to Lucy or Joe, and really, the meaning of a word has to wait for majorities to decide it. If a play shocks ten people in an audience, and doesn't shock the remaining five hundred, then it is obscene to ten and innocuous to five hundred; hence, the play is not obscene, by majority. But *Hamlet* shocked all the Cromwellian Puritans, and shocks nobody to-day, and some of Aristophanes shocks everybody to-day, and didn't galvanise the later Greeks at all, apparently. Man is a changeable beast, and words change their meanings with him, and things are not what they seemed, and what's what becomes what isn't, and if we think we know where we are it's only because we are so rapidly being translated to somewhere else. . . .

[4] . . . The reaction to any word may be, in any individual, either a mob-reaction or an individual reaction. It is up to the individual to ask himself: Is my reaction individual, or am I merely reacting from my mob-self?

[5] When it comes to the so-called obscene words, I should say that hardly one person in a million escapes mob-reaction. The first reaction is almost sure to be mob-reaction, mob-indignation, mob-condemnation. And the mob gets no further. But the real individual has second thoughts and says: Am I really shocked? Do I *really* feel outraged and

* Reprinted from *Pornography and Obscenity* by D. H. Lawrence, by permission of Alfred A. Knopf, Inc. Copyright 1930 by Alfred A. Knopf, Inc.

indignant? And the answer of any individual is bound to be: No, I am not shocked, not outraged, nor indignant. I know the word, and take it for what it is, and I am not going to be jockeyed into making a mountain out of a mole-hill, not for all the law in the world.

[6] Now if the use of a few so-called obscene words will startle man or woman out of a mob-habit into an individual state, well and good. And word prudery is so universal a mob-habit that it is time we were startled out of it.

[7] But still we have only tackled obscenity, and the problem of pornography goes even deeper. When a man is startled into his individual self, he still may not be able to know, inside himself, whether Rabelais is or is not pornographic: and over Aretino or even Boccaccio he may perhaps puzzle in vain, torn between different emotions.

[8] One essay on pornography, I remember, comes to the conclusion that pornography in art is that which is calculated to arouse sexual desire, or sexual excitement. And stress is laid on the fact, whether the author or artist *intended* to arouse sexual feelings. It is the old vexed question of intention, become so dull to-day, when we know how strong and influential our unconscious intentions are. And why a man should be held guilty of his conscious intentions, and innocent of his unconscious intentions, I don't know, since every man is more made up of unconscious intentions than of conscious ones. I am what I am, not merely what I think I am.

[9] However! We take it, I assume, that *pornography* is something base, something unpleasant. In short, we don't like it. And why don't we like it? Because it arouses sexual feelings?

[10] I think not. No matter how hard we may pretend otherwise, most of us rather like a moderate rousing of our sex. It warms us, stimulates us like sunshine on a grey day. After a century or two of Puritanism, this is still true of most people. Only the mob-habit of condemning any form of sex is too strong to let us admit it naturally. And there are, of course, many people who are genuinely repelled by the simplest and most natural stirrings of sexual feeling. But these people are perverts who have fallen into hatred of their fellow-men: thwarted, disappointed, unfulfilled people, of whom, alas, our civilisation contains so many. And they nearly always enjoy some unsimple and unnatural form of sex excitement, secretly.

[11] Even quite advanced art critics would try to make us believe that any picture or book which has "sex appeal" was *ipso facto* a bad book or picture. This is just canting hypocrisy. Half the great poems, pictures, music, stories of the whole world are great by virtue of the

beauty of their sex appeal. Titian or Renoir, the Song of Solomon or *Jane Eyre*, Mozart or "Annie Laurie," the loveliness is all interwoven with sex appeal, sex stimulus, call it what you will. Even Michelangelo, who rather hated sex, can't help filling the Cornucopia with phallic acorns. Sex is a very powerful, beneficial and necessary stimulus in human life, and we are all grateful when we feel its warm, natural flow through us, like a form of sunshine.

[12] So we can dismiss the idea that sex appeal in art is pornography. It may be so to the grey Puritan, but the grey Puritan is a sick man, soul and body sick, so why should we bother about his hallucinations? Sex appeal, of course, varies enormously. There are endless different kinds, and endless degrees of each kind. Perhaps it may be argued that a mild degree of sex appeal is not pornographical, whereas a high degree is. But this is a fallacy. Boccaccio at his hottest seems to me less pornographical than *Pamela* or *Clarissa Harlowe* or even *Jane Eyre*, or a host of modern books or films which pass uncensored. At the same time Wagner's *Tristan and Isolde* seems to me very near to pornography, and so, even, do some quite popular Christian hymns.

[13] What is it, then? It isn't a question of sex appeal, merely: nor even a question of deliberate intention on the part of the author or artist to arouse sexual excitement. Rabelais sometimes had a deliberate intention, so in a different way, did Boccaccio. And I'm sure poor Charlotte Brontë or the authoress of *The Sheik*, did not have any deliberate intention to stimulate sex feelings in the reader. Yet I find *Jane Eyre* verging towards pornography and Boccaccio seems to me always fresh and wholesome.

[14] The late British Home Secretary, who prides himself on being a very sincere Puritan, grey, grey in every fibre, said with indignant sorrow in one of his outbursts on improper books: "—and these two young people, who had been perfectly pure up till that time, after reading this book went and had sexual intercourse together!!!" *One up to them!* is all we can answer. But the grey Guardian of British Morals seemed to think that if they had murdered one another, or worn each other to rags of nervous prostration, it would have been much better. The grey disease!

[15] Then what is pornography, after all this? It isn't sex appeal or sex stimulus in art. It isn't even a deliberate intention on the part of the artist to arouse or excite sexual feelings. There's nothing wrong with sexual feelings in themselves, so long as they are straightforward and not sneaking or sly. The right sort of sex stimulus is invaluable to human daily life. Without it the world grows grey. I would give every-

body the gay Renaissance stories to read, they would help to shake off a lot of grey self-importance, which is our modern civilised disease.

[16] But even I would censor genuine pornography, rigorously. It would not be very difficult. In the first place, genuine pornography is almost always underworld, it doesn't come into the open. In the second, you can recognize it by the insult it offers, invariably, to sex, and to the human spirit.

[17] Pornography is the attempt to insult sex, to do dirt on it. This is unpardonable. Take the very lowest instance, the picture postcard sold underhand, by the underworld, in most cities. What I have seen of them have been of an ugliness to make you cry. The insult to the human body, the insult to a vital human relationship! Ugly and cheap they make the human nudity, ugly and degraded they make the sexual act, trivial and cheap and nasty.

[18] It is the same with the books they sell in the underworld. They are either so ugly they make you ill, or so fatuous you can't imagine anybody but a cretin or a moron reading them, or writing them.

[19] It is the same with the dirty limericks that people tell after dinner, or the dirty stories one hears commercial travellers telling each other in a smoke-room. Occasionally there is a really funny one, that redeems a great deal. But usually they are just ugly and repellent, and the so-called "humour" is just a trick of doing dirt on sex.

[20] Now the human nudity of a great many modern people is just ugly and degraded, and the sexual act between modern people is just the same, merely ugly and degrading. But this is nothing to be proud of. It is the catastrophe of our civilisation. I am sure no other civilisation, not even the Roman, has showed such a vast proportion of ignominious and degraded nudity, and ugly, squalid dirty sex. Because no other civilisation has driven sex into the underworld, and nudity to the w.c.

[21] The intelligent young, thank heaven, seem determined to alter in these two respects. They are rescuing their young nudity from the stuffy pornographical hole-and-corner underworld of their elders, and they refuse to sneak about the sexual relation. This is a change the elderly grey ones of course deplore, but it is in fact a very great change for the better, and a real revolution. . . .

Questions

1. What is the tone of the second paragraph? What is its purpose in this piece?
2. In the last sentence of the third paragraph, what does Lawrence mean

when he says, "and if we think we know where we are it's only because
we are so rapidly being translated to somewhere else"?
3. What is Lawrence's attitude toward obscenity? How does he define it?
4. Why does Lawrence frequently make references to the "grey Puritan"?
Who is the "grey Puritan"?
5. What is Lawrence's attitude toward literature and art that arouse sexual
desires? What arguments does he advance in favor of "sex appeal"? Do
you accept these as valid? Why or why not?
6. What does Lawrence mean when he says that "genuine pornography is
almost always underworld"? What assumption is he making about "genuine pornography" and the arousal of sexual desires?
7. Do you agree or not with Lawrence when he says it would not be very
difficult to censor genuine pornography? Explain.
8. Why, according to Lawrence, does genuine pornography exist? Do you
agree? Why or why not?

RESTRAINTS ON BOOK READING*

Walter Gellhorn

[1] Books are not big business in the United States. The gross annual
receipts of all American publishers from the sales of all manner of
books—including the *Bible, First-Grade Arithmetic, Aunt Emma's
Cookbook*, and *How to Build Your Own Spaceship*—aggregated in 1955
only a bit more than half the net profits, after taxes, of the General
Motors Corporation. If the term "bookstore" be given an extremely
loose definition, there are perhaps 1,500 bookstores in the United States
—as against 18,000 blacksmith shops. To be sure, there are other means
of book distribution, including "book clubs" and public libraries. But
Americans are not assiduous bookworms. Sweden, in relation to population, enjoys ten times as many public libraries as does the United States;
Denmark has seven bookstores to our one; a recent series of interviews
showed that while only one out of every five Americans shyly admitted
that he was reading a book (or, at least, reading at a book) during the
survey period, more than half the people questioned in Britain were
so engaged at that time.

[2] If quantitative measurements like these were to be given overriding significance, restraints on book reading might perhaps be un-
ruffling. Books, however, have a special importance for the nation's
health. Paradoxically, their significance derives in part from the economically "small time" character of the publishing business. The book
trade is old-fashioned. It still resembles the nineteenth century more

* From Walter Gellhorn, *Individual Freedom and Governmental Restraints.*
Copyright © 1956 by Louisiana State University Press. Reprinted by permission.

than it does the twentieth. Many small, personally operated firms compete actively with one another. Publishers of books unlike publishers of newspapers need not be press owners; so entry into business does not require a vast initial capital expenditure. The resulting entrepreneurial variety encourages the publication of books that might never appear if choice were entirely in the hands of a few industrial giants. Moreover, while best sellers are undoubtedly welcomed by even the most altruistic publisher, a small edition of a hard-cover book is economically feasible; an unsuccessful book is not a major catastrophe. In this respect book publishers are released from the pressure apparently felt by those who cater exclusively to a mass market that, they fear, might vanish if any part of it were antagonized or offended. Hence new ideas, which almost always antagonize or offend, are not so severely limited in books as elsewhere in our increasingly integrated society. And, apart from introducing ideas that may require extensive textual development, books remain the chief hope that diversity, and even elevation, of taste may survive the standardizing, leveling down influences of mass communications.

[3] These considerations warrant particular attention to censorship of books, though all forms of censorship have certain common features and rest on similar hypotheses.

[4] Censorship is a loosely used word. Strictly, it means prohibiting expression or communication. When legally enforcible, this connotes official action to prevent the writing or, if too late to prevent the writing, to prevent the publication or other circulation of what the censors deem objectionable. Today the term has been extended to wholly unofficial action as well. It embraces group activity aimed at eliminating particular works or kinds of works, or limiting their availability, after their publication. Official censorship, based on law or administrative regulation, usually observes the forms of legal procedures, though its permissible content has sometimes been defined so vaguely that the attendant procedures have given little real protection. Unofficial censorship derives its force not from legal mechanisms, but, at its best, from persuasion and, at its worst, from implacable economic or political pressure abetted by misuse of police authority.

[5] Both kinds of censorship have long been applied to books. They generate problems that can be considered only in relation to the supposed needs that arouse demands for prohibitory controls and in the light of the dangers that the controls create.

[6] Among the wise and good men of the world there have almost always been some who have felt that censorship advances rather than limits man's freedom. Plato, Augustine, and Spinoza among many

others asserted that no man is free who acts erroneously because influenced by passion or mistaken ideas. When what is true and good is known, anything that would subvert it should be controlled—not to narrow man's freedom, but to save him from the unfreedom of immorality or harmful doctrine that might damage him or the community. In this view censorship rests in one or another degree upon the belief that those who are qualified to identify evil and mistake should be empowered to prevent their dissemination.

[7] There is another appraisal, however, that leads to a different conclusion. Aristotle—and, in more recent times and in our own country, Dewey and Holmes among others—maintained that a man is free only so long as he may make his own choices. If choice is foreclosed by another's judgment about what is virtuous or wise, freedom is lost. More importantly, in this philosophic approach, the chances of discovering what really is virtuous or wise diminish when experimentalism and disagreement are impossible. Holmes' insistence that "the best test of truth is the power of the thought to get itself accepted in the competition of the market" is a reflection of Aristotle's democratic faith in the value of the individual's own search for virtue and his free action in association with others to secure the common good.

[8] Censorship, in one view, aims at preserving freedom through reinforcing what its proponents regard as the true values and beliefs. Opposition to censorship, in the other view, does not derive from hostility to the virtues the procensors prize, but reflects, rather, a conviction that in the end the values of a free society will be attained through freedom rather than repression. The advocates of censorship, in other words, regard it as a means by which to prevent debasement of the individual virtues, the cultural standards, and the common security of democracy. Its opponents regard it, by contrast, as a danger to the freedom which fosters those virtues and standards, and without which democracy cannot survive. These two quite different conceptions must be kept in mind, because their adherents sometimes too readily believe that the other side is unconcerned with values or is uninterested in freedom. In fact, both seek the same general ends. The question remains whether censorship will advance or retard their attainment.

.   .   .   .

[9] Those who urge increased repression of allegedly obscene books are of course convinced that "obscenity" can be identified. In reality, however, the word does not refer to a thing so much as to a mood. It is a variable. Its dimensions are fixed in part by the eye of the individual

beholder and in part by a generalized opinion that shifts with time and place.

[10] Partly, too, the concept of obscenity is itself a product of censorship and concealment. Our grandfathers, we moderns hear incredulously, strained hotly for a peek of a prettily turned ankle; their voyeurism was stimulated by clothing styles reflecting a moral conviction that the existence of female legs should be kept a secret. The Japanese, conditioned by their training to regard kissing as an entirely private exercise, are said to find American movies filled with obscenity because they unabashedly portray heterosexual osculation; and as a consequence films that do not bring a blush to the most demure Americans must be drastically edited before they are deemed appropriate for general exhibition in Japan. A hundred years ago Nathaniel Hawthorne's *Scarlet Letter* was thought unfit for modest maidens, a fact that probably led to its being read so eagerly and widely as to assure its becoming an American classic, now very grudgingly studied in high school courses from coast to coast. Nobody today cringes at mention of venereal disease, but not long ago it was one of the "dirty little secrets" that D. H. Lawrence insisted became dirty (and slyly cherished) only because of futile attempts to suppress mention of them—just as, in linguistics, words derive their deliciously vile connotations from restraints rather than from use. The late Harry Reichenbach, press agent extraordinary, put Lawrence's theory to practical commercial uses. He managed, by calling attention to a row of strategically placed asterisks, to persuade the Post Office Department to deny the mails to Elinor Glyn's *Three Weeks*. When the ban was lifted, as of course it eventually was, the demand for the shoddy novel moved it triumphantly to the best seller lists. According to one account, he made a "masterpiece" of an inferior painting called "September Morn," an innocuous representation of a nude woman standing up to her knees in sea water. Her arms were carefully intertwined to provide a reasonably chaste covering of her front, but only goose pimples covered her exposed flanks. Reichenbach bribed some boys to stand in front of a Brooklyn art dealer's window display, pointing and grimacing at this not very exciting spectacle. An anonymous telephone call brought the "vice crusader" Anthony Comstock storming to the scene, and, after him, the police. All this led to vast popularity for a picture that might otherwise have hung inconspicuously in the home of some Brooklyn burgher. Seven million copies were ultimately distributed, bringing the picture within the vision of almost every American male who patronized a barber shop; the original was sold for some $10,000.

[11] But let us put aside for the moment the possibility that repression creates rather than stifles the evil of obscenity. The difficulty of definition remains. The Reverend Dr. James Wesberry says that "determining what is or is not obscene would not be difficult for me to do personally"—but he then quickly acknowledges with some puzzlement that what is obnoxious to him "would probably not get a guilty verdict in the courts." His perplexity is not unique. An international conference at Geneva on Suppression of the Circulation and Traffic in Obscene Publications accomplished much less than had been hoped, because the delegates could not agree upon what obscenity is. One prominent censor reportedly said a year or two ago: "I don't discriminate between nude women, whether or not they are art. It's all lustful to me." The remark shows, as Eric Larrabee has observed, that one man's sex may be another's psychoneurosis; it casts much more light on the censor than it does on obscenity.

[12] It is easy to make fun of the untutored; but even the highly cultivated and literate person runs into real trouble when he seeks to define the undefinable. A very able and highly respected priest, for example, falls back upon "custom" and "common estimation" rather than upon precise definition to help in applying the principle that "if this object rouses to genital commotion, it is obscene"; but, recognizing that "it is not a matter of absolute certainty that this particular object will so arouse even the normal man," he urges acceptance of the idea that "even if it is not certain that such and such an object will arouse to sexual passion, nevertheless, if the probability swings in that direction, then the object is, for practical purposes, obscene." No doubt these words were not intended to be read literally, for a net cast so widely would bring in an unsuspected catch. Many persons profess, for example, to see a phallic symbol in the radiator ornamentation of motor cars; shall the ornamentation, which may thus arouse a "genital commotion" in one sensitive to symbols, be banned? In a carefully conducted survey 85 per cent of a group of boys between the ages of 12 and 16 (the tender years of adolescence about which censorial groups are particularly concerned) reported "genital commotions" resulting from such varied and seemingly non-erotic stimuli as carnival rides, playing a musical solo, fast car-driving, and seeing a column of marching soldiers. Perhaps we could tolerate doing away with such "obscenities"; but what would we do about the similarly "obscene" stimuli of taking school tests, receiving grade cards, and listening to the national anthem? Questioning of a large number of American college women disclosed that dancing, music, and, to some extent, reading had been

among the sources of their sexual stimulation; but far and away the largest number very simply and directly stated that the chief stimulus was MAN—an obscene object susceptible of only a limited censorship. In truth, if the suggested test of obscenity were to be taken very seriously, it would lead to a fruitless effort to fetter life itself—and would certainly necessitate the censoring of brassiere advertisements, rock and roll music, and "sacrosanct institutions like the pin-up picture or the drive-in theater, which have done more to keep sex going in America than Steinbeck has." Unless the human race is to vanish entirely, we can scarcely afford to regard the arousing of normal sexual desires as a social danger to be curbed at all costs.

[13] Federal Judge Ernest Tolin, faced with the perplexing question of what constitutes obscenity, decided to consult the settled authority of judicial utterances. His researches were more baffling than enlightening, for in 1954 he discovered fourteen different judicial definitions of the term. "No one seems to know what obscenity is. Many writers have discussed the obscene, but few can agree upon even its essential nature," complained Professors Lockhart and McClure after completing one of the most exhaustive studies yet made in this field.

[14] The view that reading is readily translated into behavior is shared by many reputable persons. Mr. J. Edgar Hoover, as an example, has been quoted as contending that "the increase in the number of sex crimes is due precisely to sex literature madly presented in certain magazines. Filthy literature is the great moral wrecker. It is creating criminals faster than jails can be built." And Dr. Frederic Wertham, a psychiatrist of high standing, has waged a virtual crusade against comic books because his clinical observation has convinced him that the comics have sexually stimulated and emotionally brutalized many children.

[15] With all respect to those who accept these assertions as self-evident truths, I doubt that the available evidence supports them. I think that they overstate the significance of words and pictures and understate the other elements of life that shape human behavior.

[16] Admittedly, the premises underlying censorship have not as yet been fully tested by empirical research. Hence one cannot demonstrate unequivocally that books do not promote juvenile delinquency, sexual perversion, sadism, and the other evils the censors fear will flow from reading. Such objective evidence as does exist, does not sustain the fear.

[17] We start with the proposition than an interest in pornography is seemingly not the molder of a man's personality but the reflection of it. Indeed, certain psychological experiments suggest that one who finds pornographic elements in allegedly obscene books is very likely to discover them also in apparently innocuous books, through a process of self-selection and emphasis that the reader himself brings to the words. This same process of self-selection—this tendency to read and see what accords with pre-existing interests—probably controls the effects of reading as well as the determination of what will be read. The fact that "sex maniacs" may read pornography does not mean that they became what they are because of their reading, but that their reading became what it is because of them. Their personality, according to modern scientific findings that confirm a proposition stated long ago by the Jesuit fathers, was probably basically formed before they ever learned to read.

[18] So far as disclosed by the most exhaustive study of juvenile delinquency yet made in America, reading seems to be of small moment in shaping antisocial tendencies. Sheldon and Eleanor Glueck searchingly inquired into numerous cases to identify the influences that produced delinquency. Reading (if it was influential at all) was of such slight significance that it was altogether omitted from their statement of "factors with probable causal significance." Judge George W. Smyth, just retired after being for many years acclaimed as one of the nation's outstanding children's court judges, has described to the New York State Temporary Commission on Youth and Delinquency the causes that had seemingly contributed to delinquency in cases recently adjudged by him. Reading *difficulty* was mentioned as among the 878 causative factors that had had effect upon the troubled children before him; *reading,* no matter of what, found not a single place in his list.

[19] Judge Smyth's observation is confirmed by other workers in the field of undesirable juvenile behavior. The Bureau of Mental Health Services of the Domestic Relations Court of New York has found a marked reading retardation among the children whose conduct has brought them before the court. Far from discovering that delinquency grew out of reading, the clinicians have discovered that among New Yorkers it is more likely to grow out of inability to read. This is no transitory condition, but, as a succession of studies has shown, has been true for decades. The importance of the "common sense" or "hunch" or "experience" that seeks to ascribe delinquent behavior to undesirable reading, should not be minimized. But heavily laying the finger of blame upon reading matter, even upon the despised comic books with all their crudities and offensiveness, is likely to divert attention from

much more serious problems. Censorship is a nostrum rather than a remedy. Reliance on it will simply delay therapeutic and preventive steps that must be taken if youthful antisocial conduct is to be lessened.

[20] Dr. Marie Jahoda and the staff of New York University's Research Center for Human Relations recently surveyed the available studies bearing on the impact of reading on human conduct, good and bad. Every indication points to a primary conclusion: "Direct experiences have a much greater directive power on human behavior than do vicarious experiences."

[21] To say that one's personality is formed before he acquires reading habits is, of course, not the equivalent of saying that reading cannot conceivably affect behavior. Reading, like other environmental factors, may modify an individual's personality predispositions, though unlikely in itself to make a "bad" man out of a previously "good" one. The question remains, however, whether fiction will frequently provide what Dr. Wertham calls the "added impetus" to antisocial impulses, serving as a trigger mechanism to set off an explosion that otherwise might not have occurred.

[22] Nobody is in a position, on the basis of what is now known about human beings, to deny this possibility. But there is at least one other possibility to be offset against it and, more importantly, a probability that diminishes its significance as an argument in support of censorship. The offsetting *possibility* derives from the Aristotelian concept of emotional catharsis, shared now by many psychiatrists who believe that aggressions and frustrations that might otherwise flare into overt conduct are not fanned to flame but, instead, are more often dissipated, or at least made temporarily quiescent, by reading. The *probability* is that fictional reading (even comic book reading) about sexual conduct or about violence and brutality has small behavioral consequence as compared with the more realistic impressions derived from reading newspapers—or even from seeing motion pictures or television that purport to mirror reality. Years ago, in commenting upon some of the classics that might be deemed obscene, Lord Macaulay said: "We find it difficult to believe that in a world so full of temptations as this, any gentleman whose life would have been virtuous if he had not read Aristophanes and Juvenal will be made vicious by reading them." Change Macaulay's illustrations and his point holds good today.

.   .   .   .

[23] The modern varieties of book censorship are not nearly so deeply rooted as most people suppose. Suppression in one guise or another is age-old. But the English obscenity law dates only from 1857,

in the Victorian era, and the United States statutory framework began to be built only in 1873, when Congress was overcome by Anthony Comstock.

[24] Before there were statutes in the Anglo-American system there was common sense—and common law. The heart of the common law approach, it seems to me, is this: No person should be deemed free to obtrude upon another an unwilling exposure to offensiveness—or, if you will, to obscenity.

[25] The law of obscenity began, according to most legal scholars, with the case of young and bon vivant Sir Charles Sedley (or Sydlye, according to taste) in 1663. Sir Charles, still drunk after a spree of several days' duration, appeared nude on a balcony overlooking London's Covent Garden, from which vantage point he flung down upon a gaping crowd not only a torrent of profane and indelicate words, but also some bottles filled with what the judges described as an "offensive liquor." No matter what one may think of the later development of obscenity law, one can muster up no sympathy for young Sedley, who was duly found guilty of a criminal offense despite the absence of any statutory definition or direct judicial precedent.

[26] The words Sedley used were probably not wholly unfamiliar to those who heard them. I doubt that they corrupted anyone's morals or coarsened any previously delicate taste. His offensiveness lay in his imposing his words upon auditors who, being about their lawful business in the neighborhood, had no choice but to listen. Few persons over the age of ten are likely to be baffled by four-letter words, but this does not mean that every foul-mouthed ruffian is at liberty to bellow them in the town square. The courts have long held, wholly independently of statutes, that utterances of obscene language in public places, near a dwelling, or in the presence of ladies could be punished. A decent regard for the sensibilities of others is all that makes communal life possible. Existence is difficult enough without the intrusions of wrongheaded nastiness upon a captive audience.

.   .   .   .

[27] Not long ago the city of Pascagoula, Mississippi (population, 4,000) was outraged by a local humorist who adorned his ancient motor car with a prominently lettered sign: "All you ladies that smoke cigarettes throw your butts in here." The automobile, strategically parked in front of the local post office, drew the townspeople's eyes and, seemingly, stirred their indignation, for the owner was soon indicted for "showing and having in his possession an obscene writing." However

deplorable may be the seeming mirthlessness of Pascagoula, is there not a good deal to be said for upholding local tastes in matters of this sort? A civilized being must refrain in public places from sexual or scatological behavior repugnant to the citizenry, just as he refrains in his neighbor's parlor.

[28] Despite a strong personal preference for a society in which the idiosyncratic is accepted calmly, I think that courts should within rather generous limits sustain community attacks upon "public indecency." There is always, of course, a degree of danger that what purports to be the prevailing community sentiment may in fact itself be an idiosyncrasy—as seems to be the case when, as occasionally happens, some sex-mad constable charges that a pantalooned woman is indecently exposed. In the main, however, the community is entitled to demand external respect for its mores, allowing nonconformists the right to appeal for change in prevailing attitudes but not to flout them openly meanwhile.

[29] Trouble arises when this permissible pressure for conformity spills over into censorship, where it has no justification at all. It is one thing to say that nobody should force upon everybody's unwilling eyes or ears a communication they deem outrageous. It is quite another to say that everybody must first approve the content of the communication before it may be transmitted to anybody who is willing to receive it. Books are voluntarily read. They are not obtruded upon the passer-by, regardless of his choice. To be let alone, as Justice Brandeis said, is the most precious of all human rights. In the one case it dictates that none should be compelled to read or listen to what he abhors. In the other it dictates that none should be precluded from writing or reading as his own rather than another's taste may determine. . . .

Questions

1. What is the purpose of the first two paragraphs?
2. What does Gellhorn consider to be the case for censorship and the case against censorship? What does he consider to be the fundamental issue or controversy?
3. Gellhorn states that "Partly, too, the concept of obscenity is itself a product of censorship and concealment." What does he mean by this? How does he support this statement?
4. Examine paragraph 12. What point is Gellhorn trying to make? Do you agree with him? Explain.
5. What position does Gellhorn take concerning definitions and determinations of what is obscene?
6. What arguments does Gellhorn advance concerning the relationship between reading and behavior? Do you consider them valid? Explain.

7. Does Gellhorn reject all forms of censorship or does he accept some censorship? Explain.
8. How would you characterize the language in this piece? Give examples in support of your conclusion.

ASSIGNMENTS

1. Without consulting a dictionary or other sources, write your own definition of obscenity. Compare it with others in class and check for any common agreements.
2. Read one of the controversial books referred to in this issue such as *Lolita, Ulysses, Lady Chatterley's Lover, etc*. Write a paper in which you present your decision as to the alleged obscenity or immorality of the book and whether or not you would want to prevent others from reading it.
3. Go to a local bookstore or magazine stand and ask the operator if he has ever been supplied with a list of forbidden or objectionable books, and if so, what he did about it. Also, inquire about whether or not he has ever refused to stock or display certain books or magazines, and what he would do if someone objected to his selling an "objectionable" book or magazine. Report your findings to the class.
4. Interview a school librarian and a public librarian about their library's policy concerning controversial or objectionable books. Make a report of your findings.
5. Make a study of a recent censorship controversy (in literature, movies, or television) and write a documented report of your findings.
6. In a number of foreign countries—Great Britain, for example—motion pictures are classified as suitable for various age groups or as suitable for unrestricted audiences. Find an account of such a classification system. Write a paper in which you describe the system and then indicate whether or not you think a comparable system should be applied in the United States.
7. Prepare for participation in a panel discussion in which several members of the class examine the issue: "Censorship—of what, by whom, for whom?"
8. Look up an account of a censorship case in v   the issue is not alleged immorality or obscenity, but some other grou   as in the cases in recent years involving *Huckleberry Finn, The Me   iant of Venice*, or *Robin Hood*. Write a report of your findings   explanation of your own position on the affair.
9. Examine Preminger's statements in th   transcript. Write a paper indicating how Jones, Gardiner, and Millett would probably respond to his remarks.

11. SOCIAL PHILOSOPHY
Conformity vs. Individualism

Ours has been called an age of conformity. In most contexts the phrase is probably intended to be derogatory. Today, conformity suggests—at one extreme—an undeviating pattern of uncritical acceptance of the dominant social, political, religious, economic, moral, and philosophical mores. In more favorable contexts conformity is equated with a sense of order and propriety, with the sensible and effective adjustment of the individual to his world.

While this project focuses primarily on the issue of conformity vs. individualism in contemporary America, you should realize that the roots of this issue go far back in time. Moreover, the attitudes taken by different cultures—in different places and at different times—toward conformity and individualism have varied greatly, depending upon the value systems of the cultures themselves. Even the words *conformity* and *individualism* have been so elastic in meaning as to be virtually indefinable without a cultural context. Finally, as the opening paragraph has already intimated, the particular meanings of conformity and individualism assumed by any culture have depended upon which of the concepts the culture tended to approve.

In this project the controversy between conformity (in its varied senses) and individualism (in its different senses) is represented by a considerable range of views. A poem by W. H. Auden depicts a society that has lost its individuality. Robert Lindner, a psychologist, moves in the same direction with a denunciation of conformity, especially under the more palatable—and therefore insidious—name of "adjustment." Earl Russell, eminent philosopher-mathematician, provides some historical perspectives of the issue and then details the contributions of non-conformists to the progress of society in several key areas. Paul Tillich, renowned theologian and philosopher, in a commencement address urges graduates to avoid conformity despite social and psychological pressures encouraging it. However, novelist Joyce Cary, writing from the context of his experiences with a primitive tribe in Africa, challenges the assumption that ours is a conforming society.

Erich Fromm, the psychoanalyst, asserts that ours is an excessively conformist society; he attributes this defect to the fact that our social patterns with their stress on conformity originate in early childhood when we first learn to inhibit our feelings. A rebellion against both inhibitions and mass pressures to conform is advocated by the "Beat Generation," whose philosophy is described in an article by John Clellon Holmes. Dean Robert Elliot Fitch, a theologian, attacks the "irresponsible" character of the beatniks and even assails such American literary stalwarts—who are spokesmen for individualism—as Ralph Waldo Emerson and Walt Whitman in his denunciation of what Fitch calls the "self-centered self."

Emerson—represented here with excerpts from "Self-Reliance"—and Henry David Thoreau—with excerpts from *Walden*—were nineteenth century Americans who may well be the most famous proponents in literature of American individualism. Indeed, Thoreau's advice on resisting pressures to conform served in our century as a guide to Mahatma Gandhi's effective passive resistance against the British in the fight for Indian independence. Former President Herbert Hoover calls for American individualism, particularly a rugged economic individualism.

In *Confessions of a Conformist*, Morris Freedman, a professor of English, attacks proponents of non-conformity, suggesting that ritual non-conformity is more dangerous today than conformity itself. David Riesman, a well-known sociologist, indicates that all societies inculcate some conformity quite naturally in their members and, in the book *The Lonely Crowd*, coins the widely used terms *tradition-directed, inner-directed*, and *other-directed* to show how different kinds of societies foster conformity. In the concluding essay of this project, Ruth Benedict, an anthropologist, declares "[There] is no proper antagonism between the rôle of society and that of the individual," challenging the assumption that these are, in reality, in irreconcilable conflict.

You will probably be amused by Jules Feiffer's cartoon. You might note, however, that it provides a relevant comment—in visual form—on the issue of conformity vs. individualism. The cartoon further indicates that materials pertinent to this issue may be found in diverse forms.

Here, then, is the concluding project of this part of the book. It is longer and more complex, with more ramifications, than the preceding projects. It not only deals with abstract concepts of social philosophy but also bears on the value systems expressed or implied in the selections in earlier issues. Moreover, in confronting the issues in conformity vs. individualism, greater demands are made upon you. Out of your experience with identifying fundamental assumptions, logical or illogical thought processes, and strategies of advocacy, you should be prepared to put your critical insights and understandings to valuable use. What are the basic positions taken by the writers represented in this project? Why are they taken? What are their further implications? Finally, this issue may well be central to your own evolving philosophy: How do I perceive myself as an individual? What insights can I utilize in defining my role in society?

THE UNKNOWN CITIZEN*

W. H. Auden

(*To JS/07/M/378*
This Marble Monument
Is Erected by the State)

He was found by the Bureau of Statistics to be
One against whom there was no official complaint,
And all the reports on his conduct agree
That, in the modern sense of an old-fashioned word, he was a saint,
For in everything he did he served the Greater Community.
Except for the War till the day he retired
He worked in a factory and never got fired,
But satisfied his employers, Fudge Motors Inc.
Yet he wasn't a scab or odd in his views,
For his Union reports that he paid his dues,   10
(Our report on his Union shows it was sound)
And our Social Psychology workers found
That he was popular with his mates and liked a drink.
The Press are convinced that he bought a paper every day
And that his reactions to advertisements were normal in every way.
Policies taken out in his name prove that he was fully insured,
And his Health-card shows he was once in hospital but left it cured.
Both Producers Research and High-Grade Living declare
He was fully sensible to the advantages of the Instalment Plan
And had everything necessary to the Modern Man,   20
A phonograph, a radio, a car and a frigidaire.

Our researchers into Public Opinion are content
That he held the proper opinions for the time of year;
When there was peace, he was for peace; when there was war, he went.
He was married and added five children to the population,
Which our Eugenist says was the right number for a parent of his gen-
        eration,
And our teachers report that he never interfered with their education.
Was he free? Was he happy? The question is absurd:
Had anything been wrong, we should certainly have heard.

Questions

1. What is the tone of this poem? How do you know?
2. What is the purpose of lines 4 and 5? What basic assumption is being
   underlined? Why?
3. Why does Auden use negative statements, such as the following: line 2,
   "no official complaint"; line 7, "never got fired"; and line 9, "wasn't a scab
   or odd"?
4. What is Auden's purpose in referring to "Social Psychology workers"?
5. What effect is produced by the line beginning "When there was peace
   . . ."? How is the effect produced?
6. What inference can you draw from the reference to the "Eugenist"?
7. What values of Auden's are implied in the closing lines?
8. What significance do you find in the title given to this poem?

From MUST YOU CONFORM?*

Robert Lindner

And now . . . *must* you conform, *must* we conform? This is the
question that confronts every man today, the question that must be answered before silence descends and the voice of humanity fades to a
whimper. It is a question only a few fortunate ones can still ask, a question that cannot even be raised behind the barbed wire where half of
humanity lives.

Must we conform? Must we fit ourselves into the pattern that molds
Mass Man? Must we bend, submit, adjust, give in? Must we, finally,
cease to be men?

The forces of Society tell us that we must. Aligned already with the
emergent dominant class, they and the institutions they represent have
put individuality and liberty on the sacrificial altar. For a brief moment

of respite, and in the vain hope that they will in this way themselves escape a destiny just over the horizon, they have become its heralds. In chorus, these forces proclaim the myth that smooths the way of the conqueror and robs their fellows of the will to resist tyranny.

Abroad in the world today is a monstrous falsehood, a consummate fabrication, to which all social agencies have loaned themselves and into which most men, women and children have been seduced. In previous writings, I have called this forgery "the Eleventh Commandment"; for such, indeed, has become the injunction: You Must Adjust!

Adjustment, that synonym for conformity that comes more easily to the modern tongue, is the theme of our swan song, the piper's tune to which we dance on the brink of the abyss, the siren's melody that destroys our senses and paralyzes our wills. But this is something known only to the few who have penetrated its disguises and glimpsed the death's head beneath: for the many, adjustment is the only way of life they know, the only way of life permitted to them by the powers that govern their existences from cradle to grave.

You must adjust . . . This is the motto inscribed on the walls of every nursery, and the processes that break the spirit are initiated there. In birth begins conformity. Slowly and subtly, the infant is shaped to the prevailing pattern, his needs for love and care turned against him as weapons to enforce submission. Uniqueness, individuality, difference —these are viewed with horror, even shame; at the very least, they are treated like diseases, and a regiment of specialists are available today to "cure" the child who will not or cannot conform. Does he violate the time-table of Gesell?—Call the pediatrician, quickly! Does he contradict Spock?—Get the telephone number of the nearest child analyst! Is he unhappy? maladjusted? lonely? too noisy? too quiet? too slow? too fast? —Let us be thankful for the special schools, the nurseries and, above all, for the magazines on the rack at the corner drugstore!

You must adjust . . . This is the legend imprinted in every schoolbook, the invisible message on every blackboard. Our schools have become vast factories for the manufacture of robots. We no longer send our young to them primarily to be taught and given the tools of thought, no longer primarily to be informed and acquire knowledge; but to be "socialized"—which in the current semantic means to be regimented and made to conform. The modern report card reflects with horrible precision the preoccupations of our teachers and the philosophy of our educators. Today, in the public schools, grades are given for the "ability" of a child to "adjust" to group activities, for whether he is "liked" by others, for whether he "enjoys" the subjects taught, for whether he "gets along" with his schoolmates. In the private schools, especially in those which designate themselves "progressive," the situation is more frightening, in some cases known to me actually revealing a cynical kind of anti-intellectualism. So the school takes up where the parent leaves off; and the children who emerge from it with a few shreds of individuality clinging to their blue jeans or bobby-socks are rare birds, indeed. But even if they manage to retain some uniqueness after passing through the mill of primary and secondary education, the young who go on to institutions of higher learning are exposed to pressures to conformity that must surely deprive them of the pitiful remnants of singularity and independence they still have.

In the colleges and universities it is not necessarily the teachers or the system of education that command adjustment, although currently, with academic freedom under attack and access to knowledge blocked, professors live in fear of saying or doing anything unorthodox. Here the Eleventh Commandment is more often enjoined by the young themselves upon themselves. By this time completely enslaved by the myth, they have acquired title to it, and now it comprises almost the whole of their philosophy and the basis of their code of conduct. This phenomenon, moreover, is a recent one, apparently dating from the last war. It has been brought to my attention by teachers in many colleges I have visited during the last few years. The collegian of today, they tell me, is hardly to be compared with the student of, say, twenty years ago. Today's undergraduate is almost a caricature of conformism. Like the new uniform he wears—the uniform of the junior executive that is *de rigueur* on Madison Avenue—his opinions, attitudes, tastes and behavior are ultra-conservative. In the world that is being born he will have little conflict about exchanging his charcoal grays for the deeper black of the élite guard.

You must adjust . . . This is the command etched above the door of every church, synagogue, cathedral, temple, and chapel. It constitutes a passport to salvation, an armor against sin: it sums the virtues and describes the vices. For there is no formal religion that does not insist, as its first requirement, on a confession of conformity. Nor is there, any longer, a religion that offers a path to Heaven other than the autobahn of submission. One and all, they have conspired, in the name of the Spirit, against the spirit of man: one and all, they have sold him into slavery. Under threat of damnation, hell-fire, purgatory, eternal non-being or even re-incarnation as some lower form of life, they have ordered him to renounce protest, to forego revolt, to be passive, to surrender. And while most of them were founded upon protest and by

rebellion, these are the very things they now uniformly hold in horror.)
With Caesar and poverty, with war and hate, with disease and violence,
with famine, crime and destruction, our priests, ministers, rabbis,
imams, yogin, hierophants and lamas have signed a treaty to guarantee
human tractability. All they have to sell us subverts the nature of man.
Conformity, humility, acceptance—with these coins we are to pay our
fares to paradise. Meanwhile, we must adjust, we must accept. And
among the things we are to accept, in our time, are the following: riot
guns, tear gas, trans-hydrogen explosives, character assassination, radioactive dust, tanks, nerve gases, guilt by association, atomic sub-
marines, concentration camps, gas masks, guided missiles, censorship
over thought and expression, rubber hoses, bacteriological warfare,
purges, slave labor, bomb shelters, liquidations, brain-washing, Roy
Cohn's opinions and Bishop Sheen's God . . .

You must adjust . . . This is the slogan emblazoned on the banners
of all political parties, the inscription at the heart of all systems that
contend for the loyalties of men. Our lives today, more than ever before, are governed by politics. Some observers, as a matter of fact, insist
that modern man be called *homo politicus;* for there is hardly an area
of existence that remains untouched by politics, hardly an act that in
some way does not involve the manner in which our social affairs are
regulated or the principles by which they are determined. Love, hate,
friendship, enmity—these and other emotions have come to have political significance and, to some extent, to involve political choices. But
there is no freedom even here, since conformity is of the essence of all
the organizations that rule over us. Paradoxically, the systems which
most loudly proclaim the right of human liberty and offer themselves as
the instruments of change are those systems that oppress most heavily.
On the way to power their sole condition is discipline, the severe regulation of mind and act so that the aim of the organization, the seizure
somehow of power, can be achieved. At this stage of struggle, the surrender of individuality is urged or forced, but those of whom conformity is exacted are the voluntary adherents, the dedicated, the
passionate few who believe truly in the slogans, in the high-sounding
words of deliverance from slavery, and give over their selves to the
Party. Once in power, however, what has been the dedication of a few
is elevated to the religion of the many. In the congealing amber of
politics the individual is pressed and imprisoned. The erstwhile revolutionary, no longer rebel but policeman and bureaucrat, becomes an
oppressor; and against the revolution he has wrought he now turns—or,
becoming a heretic, he dies. Meanwhile, for the masses, what has been

an act of faith is now an order to surrender. Simple discipline, obedience and passivity are not enough when the Party becomes the All, for only in the collective orgasm of conformity can power be affirmed. Now is the day of the Committee, the high noon of the Inquisitor, the time of the midnight awakening, the bright lights, the spittle in the face and the breaking of bones, the long corridor, the Confession, and the merciful bullet in the back of the head.

You must adjust . . . This is the creed of the sciences that have sold themselves to the status quo, the prescription against perplexity, the placebo for anxiety. For psychiatry, psychology and the medical or social arts that depend from them have become devil's advocates and sorcerers' apprentices of conformity. Joined in the criminal conspiracy against human nature, they have poisoned the last oasis for the relief of man. Of all betrayals, their treachery has been the greatest, for in them we have placed our remaining hope, and in them, sadly, hope has fled. Equating protest with madness and non-conformity with neurosis, in the clinics and hospitals, the consulting rooms and offices, they labor with art and skill to gut the flame that burns eternally at the core of being. Recklessly and with the abandon of some demented sower of noxious seeds, they fling abroad their soporifics, their sedatives, their palliative drugs and their opiate dopes, lulling the restlessness of man, besotting him so that he sleepwalks through his days and does not recognize the doom-writing on the wall. Or with the soft persuasion and counsel that apes wisdom, with pamphlets and tracts and books that flow over the mind and drown it in a rising flood of imbecilic recipes for contented existence, they prepare his ankles for chains, his back for the brand, and his head for a crown of thorns. But if these do not "cure" him into conformity, do not level him into the mass, there remain in the arsenals of adjustment the ultimate weapons: the little black box for shock "therapy" and the swift and silent knife for psychosurgery. From the skies the lightning and the thunder are stolen to be discharged into the brain, the seat of reason, the home of evolution and the treasury of manhood. In the convulsion that follows, resistance ebbs and another sheep is added to the flock. Or the scalpel, quiet and sterile, probes with unerring aim toward the target behind the eyes . . . up, down, to one side, then the other . . . and a walking zombie, the penultimate conformist, stands where a man once stood, "cured" of his humanity.

The question remains: must we conform? Or can we, somehow, resist the powers that conspire to domesticate us? Can we woo or win our liberty from an emergent dominant segment devoted to raw power? Can we, in short, recover Society for all humanity? And if so, with what arms are we to redeem our almost-lost manhood? How can we withstand the total onslaught I have hardly begun to describe? Where are we to find the weapons of resistance?

I believe that the question of conformity, in the long run, answers itself. I think that if there was a possibility, once, of a yes or no—if at one time humans could decide "we must conform" or "we must not"—that possibility has been lost in the long reaches of evolution, far back along the corridors of Time. The simple truth, stark and severe in its simplicity, is that *we cannot conform;* for it seems there is an ingredient in the composition of our cells, a chemistry in our blood, and a substance in our bones that will not suffer man to submit forever.

Built into man, the foundation of his consciousness, the source of his humanity and the vehicle of his evolution up from the muck of a steaming primeval swamp, is an instinct. I have chosen to call it the "instinct of rebellion," since it reveals itself as a drive or urge toward mastery over every obstacle, natural or man-made, that stands as a barrier between man and his distant, perhaps never-to-be-achieved but always-striven-after goals. It is this instinct that underwrites his survival, this instinct from which he derives his nature: a great and powerful dynamic that makes him what he is—restless, seeking, curious, forever unsatisfied, eternally struggling and eventually victorious. Because of the instinct of rebellion man has never been content with the limits of his body: it has led him to extend his senses almost infinitely, so that his fingers now probe space, his eyes magnify the nuclei of atoms, and his ears detect whispers from the bottoms of seas. Because of the instinct of rebellion man has never been content with the limits of his mind: it has led him to inquire its secrets of the universe, to gather and learn and manipulate the fabulous inventory of the cosmos, to seek the very mysteries of creation. Because of the instinct of rebellion, man has never been content, finally, with the limits of his life: it has caused him to deny death and to war with mortality.

Man is a rebel. He is committed by his biology *not* to conform, and herein lies the paramount reason for the awful tension he experiences today in relation to Society. Unlike other creatures of earth, man cannot submit, cannot surrender his birthright of protest, for rebellion is one of his essential dimensions. He cannot deny it and remain man. In order to live he must rebel. Only total annihilation of humanity as a species can eliminate this in-built necessity. Only with the death of the last man will the revolt that is the essence of his nature also die.

But this is cold comfort in the present when the forces of conformity have collected against the spirit of man. It offers us, in the modern world, faced as we are with these forces, little satisfaction to know that the destiny of man is to conquer and that the final victory will be his.

What about now? What about today?

I suggest that the answer to the all-important question in the here and now lies in the mobilization and implementation of the instinct of rebellion. We must, in short, become acquainted with our protestant nature and learn how to use it in our daily lives, how to express it ourselves, how to infuse it throughout all levels of our culture, and how to nourish it in our young.

Today, in the struggle between man and Society over the issue of conformity, Society is winning because man, the rebel, does not yet know how to rebel successfully—positively. His protest is expressed in negative forms, in ways which may discharge somewhat the energy of his rebellious instinct but which yield him little profit; indeed, in ways which are often actually harmful to himself and to the community. Non-conformity, as it is now conceived, is largely exhibited as psychosis, neurosis, crime, and psychosomatic illness; or it appears as pitifully hopeless and vain little defiances of convention and custom in dress, manner, opinion and taste. All of these ways are negative, unproductive, totally inadequate to meet the situation man faces.

The productive way toward non-conformity is the way of positive rebellion, of protest that at once affirms the rebellious nature of man *and* the fundamental human values. These values reside in the common treasury of humanity. They form the basic aspirations of all humans everywhere and are expressed most clearly in the great documents and contracts—such as our own Bill of Rights—which men have seen fit to declare from time to time. *Rebellion and protest in their name, and conducted in a fashion which does not in any way violate their spirit, is positive rebellion, authentic rebellion.*

Our instruction in the methods of positive rebellion, of affirmative protest, must come from two sources—one inner, one outer. The first of these, the inner source, is the slower and less dependable one. It requires that men themselves awaken to the knowledge, first, that rebellion is native in them and that there exist positive ways of protest which await discovery. The inspiration and example of the all-too-few positive rebels in our culture may assist this admittedly protracted and precarious self-awakening by contagion.

The outer source of instruction is more rapid and more sure. It consists of direct tuition in positive rebellion by those to whom we have always looked, and will always look, for edification: our psychologists, educators, and artists.

While it is true, as I have charged, that these guides in human affairs have always identified with—and in some cases sold themselves to—the emerging dominant segment; and while it is true that in the current crisis they have shamefully ranged themselves on the side of conformity, it is no less true that they have done so largely out of desperation and ignorance. They have not known about the instinct at the very navel of man's being, and in their unawareness have been forced into the position they now occupy. But if once they become informed, if once they learn about the existence of such an instinct and its cosmic possibilities, it is unavoidable that the motives which inspired them toward the vocation they practice will fuse with this knowledge and become animated by it. In this manner will the methods of positive rebellion, of life-affirming protest, be explored and spread about.

The answer to the question, "Must we conform?" is a resounding No! No . . . not only because, in the end, we are creatures who cannot conform and who are destined to triumph over the forces of conformity; but *no* because there is an alternate way of life available to us here and now. It is the way of positive rebellion, the path of creative protest, the road of productive revolt. This is the way natural to man, the way he must and will take to achieve the values he aspires to just because he is human. By taking it, man can find the future of which he dreams, the future in which he will achieve his far, high, and unforseeable goals. . . .

Questions

1. What observations might you make about the language of the first paragraph?
2. Lindner calls adjustment a "synonym for conformity." Do you agree?
3. Do the Gesell and Spock references support Lindner's contention?
4. Why does Lindner suggest that the undergraduate will "have little conflict about exchanging his charcoal grays for the deeper black of the élite guard"? Why does he select the particular words he uses?
5. Why does Lindner list "riot guns," "tear gas," etc., in such extended detail?
6. Lindner observes that "the systems which most loudly proclaim the right of human liberty . . . oppress most heavily." To what is he referring?
7. What basic assumptions does Lindner make about the nature of man?
8. Lindner says, "Non-conformity, as it is now conceived, is largely exhibited as psychosis, neurosis . . . and vain little defiances of convention and custom in dress, manner, opinion and taste." Assess the language and ideas in this statement.
9. Lindner urges "the methods of positive rebellion, of life-affirming protest." Do you agree? Explain your response.
10. Why does Lindner keep repeating "*You must adjust*"?

THE ROLE OF INDIVIDUALITY*

Bertrand Russell

In this lecture I propose to consider the importance, both for good and evil, of impulses and desires that belong to some members of a community but not to all. In a very primitive community such impulses and desires play very little part. Hunting and war are activities in which one man may be more successful than another, but in which all share a common purpose. So long as a man's spontaneous activities are such as all the tribe approves of and shares in, his initiative is very little curbed by others within the tribe, and even his most spontaneous actions conform to the recognized pattern of behavior. But as men grow more civilized there comes to be an increasing difference between one man's activities and another's, and a community needs, if it is to prosper, a certain number of individuals who do not wholly conform to the general type. Practically all progress, artistic, moral, and intellectual, has depended upon such individuals, who have been a decisive factor in the transition from barbarism to civilization. If a community is to make progress, it needs exceptional individuals whose activities, though useful, are not of a sort that ought to be general. There is always a tendency in highly organized society for the activities of such individuals to be unduly hampered, but on the other hand, if the community exercises no control, the same kind of individual initiative which may produce a valuable innovator may also produce a criminal. The problem, like all those with which we are concerned, is one of balance; too little liberty brings stagnation, and too much brings chaos.

There are many ways in which an individual may differ from most of the other members of his herd. He may be exceptionally anarchic or criminal; he may have rare artistic talent; he may have what comes in time to be recognized as a new wisdom in matters of religion and morals, and he may have exceptional intellectual powers. It would seem that from a very early period in human history there must have been some differentiation of function. The pictures in the caves in the Pyrenees which were made by Paleolithic men have a very high degree of artistic merit, and one can hardly suppose that all the men of that time were capable of such admirable work. It seems far more probable

---

* From Bertrand Russell, *Authority and the Individual*. Copyright 1949 by Bertrand Russell. Reprinted by permission of Simon & Schuster, Inc.

that those who were found to have artistic talent were sometimes allowed to stay at home making pictures while the rest of the tribe hunted. The chief and the priest must have begun from a very early time to be chosen for real or supposed peculiar excellences: medicine men could work magic, and the tribal spirit was in some sense incarnate in the chief. But from the earliest time there has been a tendency for every activity of this kind to become institutionalized. The chieftain became hereditary, the medicine men became a separate caste, and recognized bards became the prototypes of our Poets Laureate. It has always been difficult for communities to recognize what is necessary for individuals who are going to make the kind of exceptional contribution that I have in mind, namely, elements of wildness, of separateness from the herd, of domination by rare impulses of which the utility was not always obvious to everybody.

In this lecture I wish to consider both in history and in the present day the relation of the exceptional man to the community, and the conditions that make it easy for his unusual merits to be socially fruitful. I shall consider this problem first in art, then in religion and morals, and, finally, in science.

The artist in our day does not play nearly so vital a part in public life as he has done in many former ages. There is a tendency in our days to despise a court poet, and to think that a poet should be a solitary being proclaiming something that Philistines do not wish to hear. Historically the matter was far otherwise; Homer, Virgil, and Shakespeare were court poets, they sang the glories of their tribe and its noble traditions. (Of Shakespeare, I must confess, this is only partially true, but it certainly applies to his historical plays.) Welsh bards kept alive the glories of King Arthur, and these glories came to be celebrated by English and French writers; King Henry II encouraged them for imperialistic reasons. The glories of the Parthenon and of the medieval cathedrals were intimately bound up with public objects. Music, though it could play its part in courtship, existed primarily to promote courage in battle—a purpose to which, according to Plato, it ought to be confined by law. But of these ancient glories of the artist little remains in the modern world except the piper to a Highland regiment. We still honor the artist, but we isolate him; we think of art as something separate, not as an integral part of the life of the community. The architect alone, because his art serves a utilitarian purpose, retains something of the ancient status of the artist.

The decay of art in our time is not only due to the fact that the social function of the artist is not as important as in former days; it is due also to the fact that spontaneous delight is no longer felt as something which it is important to be able to enjoy. Among comparatively unsophisticated populations folk dances and popular music still flourish, and something of the poet exists in very many men. But as men grow more industrialized and regimented, the kind of delight that is common in children becomes impossible to adults, because they are always thinking of the next thing, and cannot let themselves be absorbed in the moment. This habit of thinking of the "next thing" is more fatal to any kind of aesthetic excellence than any other habit of mind that can be imagined, and if art, in any important sense, is to survive, it will not be by the foundation of solemn academies, but by recapturing the capacity for wholehearted joys and sorrows which prudence and foresight have all but destroyed.

The men conventionally recognized as the greatest of mankind have been innovators in religion and morals. In spite of the reverence given to them by subsequent ages, most of them during their lifetime were in a greater or less degree in conflict with their own comunities. Moral progress has consisted, in the main, of protest against cruel customs, and of attempts to enlarge the bounds of human sympathy. Human sacrifice among the Greeks died out at the beginning of the fully historical epoch. The Stoics taught that there should be sympathy not only for free Greeks but for barbarians and slaves, and, indeed, for all mankind. Buddhism and Christianity spread a similar doctrine far and wide. Religion, which had originally been part of the apparatus of tribal cohesion, promoting conflict without just as much as co-operation within, took on a more universal character, and endeavored to transcend the narrow limits which primitive morality had set. It is no wonder if the religious innovators were execrated in their own day, for they sought to rob men of the joy of battle and the fierce delights of revenge. Primitive ferocity, which had seemed a virtue, was now said to be a sin, and a deep duality was introduced between morality and the life of impulse—or rather between the morality taught by those in whom the impulse of humanity was strong, and the traditional morality that was preferred by those who had no sympathies outside their own herd.

Religious and moral innovators have had an immense effect upon human life, not always, it must be confessed, the effect that they intended, but nevertheless on the whole profoundly beneficial. It is true that in the present century we have seen in important parts of the world a loss of moral values which we had thought fairly secure, but we may hope that this retrogression will not last. We owe it to the moral innovators who first attempted to make morality a universal and not merely a tribal matter, that there has come to be a disapproval of slavery, a feeling of duty towards prisoners of war, a limitation of the powers of husbands and fathers, and a recognition, however imperfect, that subject races ought not to be merely exploited for the benefit of their conquerors. All these moral gains, it must be admitted, have been jeopardized by a recrudescence of ancient ferocity, but I do not think that in the end the moral advance which they have represented will be lost to mankind.

The prophets and sages who inaugurated this moral advance, although for the most part they were not honored in their own day, were, nevertheless, not prevented from doing their work. In a modern totalitarian state matters are worse than they were in the time of Socrates, or in the time of the Gospels. In a totalitarian state an innovator whose ideas are disliked by the government is not merely put to death, which is a matter to which a brave man may remain indifferent, but is totally prevented from causing his doctrine to be known. Innovations in such a community can come only from the government, and the government now, as in the past, is not likely to approve of anything contrary to its own immediate interests. In a totalitarian state such events as the rise of Buddhism or Christianity are scarcely possible, and not even by the greatest heroism can a moral reformer acquire any influence whatever. This is a new fact in human history, brought about by the much increased control over individuals which the modern technique of government has made possible. It is a very grave fact, and one which shows how fatal a totalitarian regime must be to every kind of moral progress.

In our own day an individual of exceptional powers can hardly hope to have so great a career or so great a social influence as in former times, if he devotes himself to art or to religious and moral reform. There are, however, still four careers which are open to him: he may become a great political leader, like Lenin; he may acquire vast industrial power, like Rockefeller; he may transform the world by scientific discoveries, as is being done by the atomic physicists; or, finally, if he has not the necessary capacities for any of these careers, or if opportunity is lacking, his energy in default of other outlet may drive him into a life of crime. Criminals, in the legal sense, seldom have much influence upon the course of history, and therefore a man of overweening ambition will choose some other career if it is open to him.

The rise of men of science to great eminence in the state is a modern phenomenon. Scientists, like other innovators, had to fight for recognition: some were banished; some were burnt; some were kept in dungeons; others merely had their books burnt. But gradually it came to be realized that they could put power into the hands of the state. The French revolutionaries, after mistakenly guillotining Lavoisier, employed his surviving colleagues in the manufacture of explosives. In modern war the scientists are recognized by all civilized governments as the most useful citizens, provided they can be tamed and induced to place their services at the disposal of a single government rather than of mankind.

Both for good and evil almost everything that distinguishes our age from its predecessors is due to science. In daily life we have electric light, and the radio, and the cinema. In industry we employ machinery and power which we owe to science. Because of the increased productivity of labor we are able to devote a far greater proportion of our energies to wars and preparations for wars than was formerly possible, and we are able to keep the young in school very much longer than we formerly could. Owing to science we are able to disseminate information and misinformation through the press and the radio to practically everybody. Owing to science we can make it enormously more difficult than it used to be for people whom the government dislikes to escape. The whole of our daily life and our social organization is what it is because of science. The whole of this vast development is supported nowadays by the state, but it grew up originally in opposition to the state, and where, as in Russia, the state has reverted to an earlier pattern, the old opposition would again appear if the state were not omnipotent to a degree undreamt of by the tyrants of former ages.

The opposition to science in the past was by no means surprising. Men of science affirmed things that were contrary to what everybody had believed; they upset preconceived ideas and were thought to be destitute of reverence. Anaxagoras taught that the sun was a red-hot stone and that the moon was made of earth. For this impiety he was banished from Athens, for was it not well known that the sun was a god and the moon a goddess? It was only the power over natural forces conferred by science that led bit by bit to a toleration of scientists, and even this was a very slow process, because their powers were at first attributed to magic.

It would not be surprising if, in the present day, a powerful antiscientific movement were to arise as a result of the dangers to human life that are resulting from atom bombs and may result from bacteriological warfare. But whatever people may feel about these horrors, they dare not turn against the men of science so long as war is at all probable, because if one side were equipped with scientists and the other not, the scientific side would almost certainly win.

Science, in so far as it consists of knowledge, must be regarded as having value, but in so far as it consists of technique the question whether it is to be praised or blamed depends upon the use that is made of the technique. In itself it is neutral, neither good nor bad, and any ultimate views that we may have about what gives value to this or that must come from some other source than science.

The men of science, in spite of their profound influence upon modern life, are in some ways less powerful than the politicians. Politicians in our day are far more influential than they were at any former period in human history. Their relation to the men of science is like that of a magician in the Arabian Nights to a djinn who obeys his orders. The djinn does astounding things which the magician, without his help, could not do, but he does them only because he is told to do them, not because of any impulse in himself. So it is with the atomic scientists in our day; some government captures them in their homes or on the high seas, and they are set to work, according to the luck of their capture, to slave for the one side or for the other. . . .

The great men who stand out in history have been partly benefactors of mankind and partly quite the reverse. Some, like the great religious and moral innovators, have done what lay in their power to make men less cruel towards each other, and less limited in their sympathies; some, like the men of science, have given us a knowledge and understanding of natural processes which, however it may be misused, must be regarded as in itself a splendid thing. Some, like the great poets and composers and painters, have put into the world beauties and splendors which, in moments of discouragement, do much to make the spectacle of human destiny endurable. But others, equally able, equally effective in their way, have done quite the opposite. I cannot think of anything that mankind has gained by the existence of Jenghiz Khan. I do not know what good came of Robespierre, and, for my part, I see no reason to be grateful to Lenin. But all these men, good and bad alike, had a quality which I should not wish to see disappear from the world—a quality of energy and personal initiative, of independence of mind, and of imaginative vision. A man who possesses these qualities is capable of doing much good, or of doing great harm, and if mankind is not to sink into dullness such exceptional men must find scope, though one could wish that the scope they find should be for the benefit of mankind. There may be less difference than is sometimes thought between the temperament of a great criminal and a great statesman. It may be that Captain Kidd and Alexander the Great, if a magician had interchanged them at birth, would have each fulfilled the career which, in fact, was fulfilled by the other. The same thing may be said of some artists; the memoirs of Benvenuto Cellini do not give a picture of a man with that respect for law which every right-minded citizen ought to have. In the modern world, and still more, so far as can be guessed, in the world of the near future, important achievement is and will be almost impossible to an individual if he cannot dominate some vast organization. If he can make himself head of a state like Lenin, or monopolist of a great industry like Rockefeller, or a controller of credit like the elder Pierpont Morgan, he can produce enormous effects in the world. And so he can if, being a man of science, he persuades some government that his work may be useful in war. But the man who works without the help of an organization, like a Hebrew prophet, a poet, or a solitary philosopher such as Spinoza, can no longer hope for the kind of importance which such men had in former days. The change applies to the scientist as well as to other men. The scientists of the past did their work very largely as individuals, but the scientist of our day needs enormously expensive equipment and a laboratory with many assistants. All this he can obtain through the favor of the government, or, in America, of very rich men. He is thus no longer an independent worker, but essentially part and parcel of some large organization. This change is very unfortunate, for the things which a great man could do in solitude were apt to be more beneficial than those which he can only do with the help of the powers that be. A man who wishes to influence human affairs finds it difficult to be successful, except as a slave or a tyrant: as a politician he may make himself the head of a state, or as a scientist he may sell his labor to the government, but in that case he must serve its purposes and not his own.

And this applies not only to men of rare and exceptional greatness, but to a wide range of talent. In the ages in which there were great poets, there were also large numbers of little poets, and when there were great painters there were large numbers of little painters. The great German composers arose in a milieu where music was valued, and where numbers of lesser men found opportunities. In those days poetry, painting, and music were a vital part of the daily life of ordinary men, as only sport is now. The great prophets were men who stood out from a host of minor prophets. The inferiority of our age in such respects is an inevitable result of the fact that society is centralized and organized to such a degree that individual initiative is reduced to a minimum. Where art has flourished in the past it has flourished as a rule amongst small communities which had rivals among their neighbors, such as the Greek city-states, the little principalities of the Italian Renaissance, and the petty courts of German eighteenth-century rulers. Each of these rulers had to have his musician, and once in a way he was Johann Sebastian Bach, but even if he was not he was still free to do his best. There is something about local rivalry that is essential in such matters. It played its part even in the building of the cathedrals, because each bishop wished to have a finer cathedral than the neighboring bishop. It would be a good thing if cities could develop an artistic pride leading them to mutual rivalry, and if each had its own school of music and painting, not without a vigorous contempt for the school of the next city. But such local patriotisms do not readily flourish in a world of empires and free mobility. A Manchester man does not readily feel towards a man from Sheffield as an Athenian felt towards a Corinthian, or a Florentine towards a Venetian. But in spite of the difficulties, I think that this problem of giving importance to localities will have to be tackled if human life is not to become increasingly drab and monotonous.

The savage, in spite of his membership of a small community, lived a life in which his initiative was not too much hampered by the community. The things that he wanted to do, usually hunting and war, were also the things that his neighbors wanted to do, and if he felt an inclination to become a medicine man he only had to ingratiate himself with some individual already eminent in that profession, and so, in due course, to succeed to his powers of magic. If he was a man of exceptional talent, he might invent some improvement in weapons, or a new skill in hunting. These would not put him into any opposition to the community, but, on the contrary, would be welcomed. The modern man lives a very different life. If he sings in the street he will be thought to be drunk, and if he dances a policeman will reprove him for impeding the traffic. His working day, unless he is exceptionally fortunate, is occupied in a completely monotonous manner in producing something which is valued, not, like the shield of Achilles, as a beautiful piece of work, but mainly for its utility. When his work is over, he cannot, like Milton's Shepherd, "tell his tale under the hawthorn in the dale," because there is often no dale anywhere near where he lives, or, if there is, it is full of tins. And always, in our highly regularized way of life, he is obsessed by thoughts of the morrow. Of all the precepts in the Gospels, the one that Christians have most neglected is the commandment to take no thought for the morrow. If he is prudent, thought for the morrow will lead him to save; if he is imprudent, it will make him apprehensive of being unable to pay his debts. In either case the moment loses its savor. Everything is organized, nothing is spontaneous.

The Nazis organized "Strength Through Joy," but joy prescribed by the government is likely to be not very joyful. In those who might otherwise have worthy ambitions, the effect of centralization is to bring them into competition with too large a number of rivals, and into subjection to an unduly uniform standard of taste. If you wish to be a painter you will not be content to pit yourself against the men with similar desires in your own town; you will go to some school of painting in a metropolis where you will probably conclude that you are mediocre, and having come to this conclusion you may be so discouraged that you are tempted to throw away your paint-brushes and take to money-making or to drink, for a certain degree of self-confidence is essential to achievement. In Renaissance Italy you might have hoped to be the best painter in Siena, and this position would have been quite sufficiently honorable. But you would not now be content to acquire all your training in one small town and pit yourself against your neighbors. We know too much and feel too little. At least we feel too little of those creative emotions from which a good life springs. In regard to what is important we are passive; where we are active it is over trivialities. If life is to be saved from boredom relieved only by disaster, means must be found of restoring individual initiative, not only in things that are trivial, but in things that really matter. I do not mean that we should destroy those parts of modern organization upon which the very existence of large populations depends, but I do mean that organization should be much more flexible, more relieved by local autonomy, and less oppressive to the human spirit through its impersonal vastness, than it has become through its unbearably rapid growth and centralization, with which our ways of thought and feeling have been unable to keep pace.

Questions

1. What distinction does Russell make between primitive and more civilized groups as far as conformity is concerned?
2. How does Russell explain the "decay of art in our time"? Is this related to the problem of conformity? Explain.
3. What assumption does Russell make in the sentence beginning "The decay of art in our time . . ."? Does he support his assumption? Do you agree with him? Explain.
4. Russell suggests that moral progress stemmed from "innovators [who] were execrated in their own day." Do you agree? Does he support this assertion?
5. Does Russell believe that the development of science has contributed to conformity in the present? Does he disapprove of science? Explain.
6. Russell believes that the able individual, unallied with a large organization, is less likely to be influential today than formerly. Why? Do you agree? What possible solution does he believe might prove useful?

7. Do Russell's assumptions reveal his attitude toward conformity? Explain.
8. Examine the last two paragraphs. How does Russell compare the art of the past with the art of today? Does he support his position? Do you agree with him? Explain.
9. Describe the tone of this lecture.

CONFORMITY*

Paul Tillich

Conformity is a word that does not necessarily have negative connotations. We all must conform to some given forms of life and thought. Education—even if it has a better ideal than adjustment—aims at giving us a form. And in doing so, it makes us conform to the sources and bearers of such form. There are cultures, highly advanced as well as primitive ones, that in this way produce conformity for long periods of history. It was in Great Britain that my unqualified rejection of conformity was shaken, for there I found a powerful conformity that does not destroy the creative potentialities in the individual. This is so, I realized, because Great Britain lives consciously out of the past. Her conformism has an historical dimension.

Conformity is a negative force if the individual form that gives uniqueness and dignity to a person is subdued by the collective form. If this happens—often in connection with the loss of the historical dimension—a structure appears for which it probably would be more adequate to use the word "patternization"—the process in which persons are modeled according to a definite pattern. Patternization is what determines our period, both in learning and in life. And the questions I want to ask now are: What are the patternizing powers in our present culture, and are we able to resist them? Are we still able to say "no" in matters of serious concern, in spite of the tremendous strength of the patternizing forces?

In recent years several scientific books have appeared which describe the contemporary processes of patternization and add criticism and warning. Such warning was anticipated in fiction, in Huxley's *Brave New World* and, in a more sinister way, in Orwell's *1984*. In both novels a kind of negative utopia is presented—a total reversal of the positive utopias that opened the modern period of Western history. The conquest of nature by reason, which in the utopias of the Renaissance was

* From *Social Research*, Autumn 1957. Copyright © 1957 by The New School for Social Research. Reprinted by permission.

considered the main liberating power, is now seen as a means for the enslavement of man by patterns of life and thought that deprive him of the possibility of freedom and individual self-affirmation. According to the negative utopias of the last decades, an age of total patternization is about to come upon us.

The series of scientific books to which I referred confirms this diagnosis. Sociological analyses as given in *The Lonely Crowd, The Organization Man, The Hidden Persuaders, Mass Culture,* and others—besides several significant magazine articles—show what one of these books, written in German, expresses in its title: *The Future Has Already Begun.* The material presented in all these writings is rather impressive. One can distinguish three main causes of the present process of patternization: our technical civilization as such; the intentional imposition of patterns on the masses by interested groups; and the striving for security in many people, especially in the youngest generation.

That technical civilization as such, in its objective structures, is conducive to patternization is in complete contrast to its origins. It was born out of the courage of people who asked the questions that soon undercut the security of mediaeval conformity. How then could it happen that the answers to these questions became the principles under which present-day patternizing conformism developed? It happened because in the new structure of society the subject who asked the critical questions, that is, man as man, was more and more pushed aside and almost removed. The human self that once had the courage to say "no" to a thousand years of sacred conformity could not find a place in the world created by it. Man was interpreted theoretically as a bundle of conditioned reflexes without a determining center; and in practice he was treated as a commodity, a cog in the big machine of production and consumption, an object among objects, to be tested, calculated, and managed. This refers to everyone within industrial mass society, even to the central wheels of the machine. Even those who determine are determined by the structure of the society they control. Therefore, as the communist revolutions have shown, the replacement of one ruling group by another does not change the patternizing structures of industrial mass society.

This is the objective situation. Like every human situation, it becomes reality through human action and reaction, and most conspicuous among those whose actions make for patternized conformity are the political manipulators of mass reactions. The manipulation of men is not, of course, a one-way road. It is successful only if the reaction of the manipulated is not negative. Even the totalitarian systems are established by revolutionary armies, not seriously resisted by the masses, and after their establishment their controlling groups cannot afford to neglect the reaction of the people in the long run; from time to time they observe signs of a silent resistance and change their methods of control. But political patternization, whether it has a more one-way or a more two-way character, works to eliminate the possibility of a nonconformist "no." Concentration camps and labor camps are not so much tools for the extermination of actual enemies as threatening symbols of the transformation of human beings into manageable objects.

In the democratic section of the world, political manipulation is much more a two-way road, but there too it drives millions toward a model-conformity. The schizophrenic split of mankind into East and West, and the secrecy connected with it, makes an independent political judgment almost impossible for most people. It prevents the rise of fresh political philosophies, since every nonconformist political thought is denounced as neutralist or worse. Courage is demanded for the expression of serious political disagreement even by a student, because it may later wreck his career. But if students and the generation they represent are silenced, where can we turn to hear the voice of nonconformity? Certainly not to the controlling powers in economy, to advertising, or to mass culture—those three powerful tools of patternization.

As to the first of these, I do not need to dwell on the screening and testing that precede an appointment to even the lowest executive position in big business and civil administration. It is well known that they delve into hidden trends of the unconscious, into all phases of private life, into marriage and the relation of the wife to the enterprise and her willingness to subject herself to its social requests. Sociologists believe that the image of the executive will become the pattern, vigorously imposed on all groups of society. And they even derive from this pattern the peculiar character of the present movement toward religion. They may be right!

The political as well as the economic manipulation of our society is supported and often controlled by the managers of advertising. This also is a two-way road. The advertiser can create needs only if he knows the hidden desires of the people. Out of this necessity the "depth approach" in advertising has developed. When I first read about this method I remembered that once I had given a sermon about the meaning of depth—and I shuddered. And I believe that Freud too would shudder at the use of his discoveries in advertising depth research. Certainly, there are hidden motives that determine the buying of a special brand of shaving cream or car, the attention to a special advertisement. But when the managers of advertising and their allies and customers in business and politics use this knowledge to direct our lives and thoughts, they actualize just those elements in us that do *not* constitute our real self but come from our childhood memories, our resentments, our daydreams, our contingent desires. All this does belong to us, but it is not we ourselves, in our deciding, responsible center—the point of our freedom and personal dignity. This center must be avoided by the manipulators, because out of it may arise the "no" that could destroy their attempts to condition our reactions. We would cease to be a calculable object, and this would be disastrous for all methods of manipulation. We would again become individual persons, and cease to be examples of one of the several types of reaction defined by the depth-approach of motivation research.

The problem of mass culture and its patternizing effect is an inexhaustible subject in itself. It too is ambiguous, not simply good and not simply bad. But in any case, it is one of the driving forces toward model-conformity. It is a matter of mass distribution, and for this very reason it cannot avoid the stereotype, standardization, and the lowest common denominator. Cultural creations of past and present become manipulated consumer goods. One can hardly avoid the impression that the means of mass communication through which these cultural commodities are distributed to everybody have the effect that children receive much too early the status of adults while adults remain children, never allowed to grow into maturity. Maturity, personal as well as cultural, presupposes a suffering under problems, a necessity to decide, a possibility of saying "no." Unfortunately, one gets the further impression that the methods used in some places for producing a religious revival are essentially of the same type as those we find in the marketing of mass culture. This is tragic, because religion is supposed to be the place where the ultimate source and power of nonconformism become manifest, the place where the prophetic "no" to all patterns, religious as well as non-religious, is heard and pronounced.

These are the conditioning forces in the process of patternization. But they would not be so powerful as they are if it were not for the third factor I mentioned: a state of mind, especially in the youngest generation, that is ready to subject itself to these forces. One can observe in many young people an intense desire for security, internal and external, a will to be accepted by the group at any price, an unwillingness to show individual traits, a conscious rejection of nonconformist attitudes in the older generation, an acceptance of a well circumscribed

happiness without serious risks. It is difficult for my generation to understand this attitude. Therefore we should restrain ourselves from
harsh judgment. But nobody can doubt that it confirms the assertion
that "the future has already begun."

This is the picture. How do we react to it? A few weeks ago I gave
a speech to a large group of architects and referred to the patternizing
effect of many suburban housing projects, not only through the monot-
ony of the buildings but also through the abolition of privacy and with
it of the possibility of the self to encounter itself in solitude. I was then
asked whether this does not agree with human nature, which makes
collectivism unavoidable. My answer is no, and must be, as is shown
even by the possibility of asking such a question. The totally patternized
man would have lost the capability of asking questions and deliberating
about answers. He would cease to be a man.

Today as always there are symptoms of resistance to patternization,
symptoms that reveal something about human nature. The first is what
the French call *ennui*, being bored with existence itself. This is an
important potentiality of man. It saves our children from being drowned
by comics and television. It forces the managers of mass culture to
change the fashion of music and dance and all their other products
from time to time. And to do this, they have to follow the guidance
of a less conformist minority.

Another symptom of resistance to the patternizing processes is the
awareness of these processes in science and art. We have become conscious of the threat of dehumanization. The literature to which I referred has abundantly exposed the dangerous forces. And as an old
religious symbol teaches us, an exposed demon has lost much of its
power. This is why the manipulators of conformity try, often unconsciously, to make the books of exposé just another in the line of goods
for mass consumption.

A third symptom of the presence of nonconformist forces in human
nature is the spirit of rebellion, which still exists in many places in the
Western world, even in the lonely-crowd attitude of the younger generation. It is a spirit which in its best manifestation is the courage to
say "yes" to one's birthright as a unique, free, and responsible individual, and consequently to say "no" to whatever would destroy the freedom and dignity of man—even at the price of taking socially unpleasant
and dangerous consequences upon oneself. Such courage is able to do
what is even more difficult than resisting external pressures: it is able
to resist internal compulsions, such as a socially conditioned, uneasy,
and anxious conscience. It is not in willfulness but in the courage to

take a moral risk that one has the right to say "no" even to the commands of an anxious conscience.

The courage that resists patternized conformity is ultimately rooted in a dimension of human experience that transcends fashions and patterns, anxieties and compulsions, generations and nations. It is the dimension that appears if somebody asks with radical seriousness the question of the ultimate meaning of his life. Whether or not one call this the religious question, it is one that is rooted in the true, unfathomable depth of every human being. Out of this depth arises the courage to resist paternization. In religious language one would call it the prophetic spirit. But this spirit is not restricted to historical religion, which often has betrayed it. It can and must appear in our daily life, in our professional work, in our social behavior, in our political conviction, in our cultural preferences, in our human relations, in our creative eros.

The future of our country would look brighter if at each commencement in every college and in every university at least a few students entered their vocational life with the decision to resist the seemingly irresistible powers of patternizing conformity. It is my wish and my hope that many in this outgoing class will remain determined to preserve their human integrity and their power to say "no," even under severe pressures by the patterns of life and thought prescribed by society. We hope for nonconformists among you, for your sake, for the sake of our nation, for the sake of humanity.

Questions

1. Do you agree with Tillich's opening sentence? Explain.
2. Does the rest of the first paragraph—a particular context—affect your attitude toward the opening sentence? Discuss.
3. How do you respond to Tillich's word *patternization*? Why?
4. Does he support the statement that "an age of total patternization is about to come upon us"?
5. Does Tillich see the communist state as patterning differently from the democracies? Explain.
6. Tillich observes, "Sociologists believe that the image of the executive will become the pattern . . ." Do your own observations confirm this diagnosis? Explain.
7. Tillich describes "intense desire for security" in young people. Do you agree? How do you feel about the tone that he takes in this section of his commencement address?
8. Tillich makes a distinction between "willfulness" and "the courage to take a moral risk." What is the significance of this distinction?
9. Would you describe this address as optimistic? Explain.

THE MASS MIND: OUR FAVORITE FOLLY[*]

Joyce Cary

[1] Every age, they say, has its special bit of nonsense. The eighteenth century had its noble savage, and the nineteenth, its automatic progress. Now we have this modern nonsense about the "mass man." We are all told constantly that people are becoming more and more standardized. That mass education, mass amusements, mass production, ready-made clothes, and a popular press are destroying all individuality —turning civilization into a nice, warmed, sterilized orphan asylum where all the little lost souls wear the same uniforms, eat the same meals, think the same thoughts, and play the same games.

[2] This belief is now so completely accepted that it underlies half the writing and thinking of the time, like chalk under the downs. You don't see it but it gives shape to what you do see. If you deny it you will get exactly the same response as Galileo when he said that the earth moved through the sky. You will be told, "Use your eyes. And don't talk nonsense. Look at the crowds in the street or at any football match. Go to the films, read the newspapers. Consider the disappearance of national dress all over the world—the immense development of laws restricting individual liberty, standardizing our lives. Go on a tour to famous sights—year by year there will be bigger crowds of morons gaping at them and listening to the spiel of some bored guide— a piece nicely designed to satisfy the mass mind."

[3] And you will be referred to history and old travel accounts to learn how various and delightful the world was, in dress and thought and individuality, one hundred or even fifty years ago.

[4] I was convinced of all this myself till I went to administer the affairs of a primitive tribe in Africa. There I found that the tribal mind was much more truly a mass mind than anything I had known in Europe. The nearest approximation to it was among illiterate peasantry in remote country districts. Tribesmen and primitive peasants are intensely narrow and conservative. Their very simple ideas and reactions guide them in a mysterious and dangerous world.

[5] I found that young chiefs with enterprise and ambition were keen to learn about the world outside the tribe. If they got away from

[*] From *Harper's Magazine,* March, 1952. Copyright 1952 by Harper & Row, Publishers. Reprinted by permission of the author's estate.

it, they tended to put on European dress. To them, European dress was not a mark of the mass mind, but of the free and independent mind.

[6] Likewise, when a European peasantry becomes educated and enterprising, it breaks away from the national dress which seems a badge of servitude and backwardness. To tourists, no doubt, this is a misfortune. As a keen tourist and sight-seer, I wish all Scotsmen would wear the kilt and all Turks the tarboosh. I'm delighted that some are beginning to do so again. But these are individualists, eccentrics, nationalists—national dress is not a tribal uniform to them, but a proclamation of difference, an assertion of self.

[7] Education, contact with other peoples, breaks up tribal uniformity of thought and custom, brings in new ideas. That is, it makes for difference. The celebrated eccentrics of former centuries were either lunatics—or educated men.

[8] New ideas also make for conflict. Old African chiefs hated roads and railways: they said they brought in strangers who corrupted the young people with new ideas and made them rebellious. They were quite right. It is far easier to rule a primitive tribe than a modern democracy where every individual is ready to criticize the government, where everyone has his own ideas about politics and religion, and where dozens of societies, unions, religious sects claim independence and support ambitious leaders who are ready to fight at any time for their "rights."

[9] The more education a man has the more likely he is to be independent in his views and obstinate in sticking to them. A committee of professors, I can assure you, is much harder to manage than a council of African chiefs.

[10] And this throws light on another argument brought forward to prove that individuality is vanishing from the world—the enormous increase of law and regulation, the growing power of the police. In my primitive African tribe, law enforcement was in the hands of village chiefs. There was very little theft. I could leave my bungalow wide open and unguarded for three weeks at a time and nothing was ever taken. We had crimes of passion and crimes of witchcraft, but no criminal class, no crooks as you know them in the big city, no cranks, no anarchists—so we did not require an elaborate structure of law.

[11] You do not need traffic police where there is no wheeled traffic. You do not need postal bylaws where no one knows how to write. But the modern state, simply because of the independence of its citizens, the complication of their demands, needs a huge machine of law and police. This is not a proof of the mass mind but the exact opposite—

of a growing number of people who think and act for themselves, and, rightly or wrongly, are ready to defy the old simple rules founded on custom.

[12] Thus, the modern state has lost its mass mind in getting education. But, you will say, this education destroys the primitive mass mind only to replace it with a number of mob minds: in the crowds which queue for the films or a match, read the same newspapers, and shout for the same spellbinders. Mass education is driving out the sound, traditional culture to bring in a lot of half-baked slogans. It produces the shallow brain seeking only to be distracted from serious reflection.

[13] But these "mobs" have no resemblance to those of the tribal world where every individual does the same thing at the same time—hunts, dances, drinks in the mass. Even if he had the will to do anything else, it would not be there to do. The modern individual has an immense choice of occupation and amusement. So that the "mass" of sight-seers at any show place today is actually composed of individuals who have freely chosen to join that crowd and will join a different one tomorrow. What looks like a proof of the mob mind is really evidence of spreading interest among the people and a variety of occupations. And if some of these interests are "popular," aimed at a crowd which is not very critical or reflective, they are a good deal more so than interests which were the only recourse of their ancestors—dog-fighting, bear-baiting, the fit-up melodrama or one-night stand, once a year, and booze.

[14] In the best educated countries, you find the biggest demand for something new in amusement as well as for instruction. Education enlarges all the interests of a man. Apart from what he learns, he acquires a general curiosity and a wider taste.

[15] Compare the press of today with that of a hundred or even fifty years ago. You will find a far greater variety of subjects appealing to a greater variety of tastes. You will find instructive articles on matters formerly dealt with only in the special magazines. Perhaps they don't aim at a learned audience, but they help the general reader to get some idea of what the experts are doing in atomic research or medicine or even astronomy. If you want to write a best seller, your best subject nowadays is probably cosmology.

[16] But if a hundred thousand people are ready to buy a book on the nature of the universe, you have a mass demand at the bookshops. The mass demand is not a proof of falling standards: it means that millions are being educated who would formerly have been left in the illiterate mass. There are "masses" reading learned works just as there

are other "masses" going to popular films. The number of people with
a good university education is many hundred times what it was fifty
years ago, and that explains the immense development of arts and
literature in experimental forms that would have had no chance of
appreciation before. And in the millions in the next category who have
just become literate in the last generation, whose reactions to education
have given rise to this illusion of an increasing "mass mind," what we
are seeing is not a collapse of standards, but a very rapid improvement.
The crowds at the cinemas and the bus loads on the sight-seeing tours
are on the way up. They have already left the mass; they are individuals
seeking ideas for themselves.

[17] The mass mind idea is not only a bit of nonsense. It leads to a
profound defeatism, to the secret and unacknowledged belief that the
dictators hold all the trumps.

[18] The reasoning, when you bring it to light, is something like this.
There are two kinds of education in the world: the free, which develops
the individual according to his nature, and the specialized, which turns
out doctors, scientists, mechanics—useful servants of the state or of
industry. In a democracy each individual has both types. In the Soviet
he gets only the specialized—the whole plan is to make him a state
slave.

[19] But it seems that free education merely debases the standards
of thought and life by producing mob minds without spiritual strength.
Meanwhile the Soviet acquires millions of workers, docile as serfs, yet
skillful as our own craftsmen. Aiming deliberately at the creation of a
mass mind it will easily defeat the free world, where opinions are shallow and divided.

[20] But this is based on bad psychology. The West is not producing
a mass mind, but a variety of strong minds with the richest sense of
adventure and will for discovery. The East is not succeeding in obtaining a mass mind either—it is going in the opposite direction. Merely
by process of education, it is producing every year people who can
at least think a little more freely than illiterate peasants, who are very
likely therefore to think critical thoughts, however much they may hide
them. That is why the task of the dictatorship becomes constantly more
difficult, why it is obliged to stiffen its grip, to hire more police, to bribe
more spies, and to purge its own party, every year or so, of "deviators."

[21] What I suggest is that no kind of education, however narrow,
can produce the mass mind. The reason is that minds are creative, that
thoughts wander by themselves and cannot be controlled by the clever-
est police. All education is free in this sense; it cannot be shut up within

walls. To teach people to think, if only to make them more useful as soldiers and mechanics, is to open all thoughts to them—a whole world of new ideas. And though the dictator may wish to think of them as a proletariat they have already begun to leave the proletariat.

[22] The "mass mind" is a delusion. How many dictators have been amazed when their rule, which seemed so strong, has collapsed in a few hours, without a friend?

Questions

1. What is Cary's strategy in the two opening sentences? Do they aid his thesis? Explain.
2. Are the illustrations in paragraph 2 effective? Have you encountered the kinds of statement Cary describes?
3. What is the tone of the short, third paragraph? What function does this paragraph serve?
4. Do the three opening sentences in paragraph 4 support the thesis effectively? What strategies has Cary used?
5. How does Cary explain "mass" sight-seers? What method does he use to support his rejection of the "mass mind"?
6. How does Cary view mass demand? Why does he use "a book on the nature of the universe" as an illustration?
7. What relationships does Cary see between education and individualism? Between education and the mass mind?
8. This article is obviously aimed at many people in our culture who fear the perils of conformity. Is Cary more prone to conformity than to individualism? Explain.
9. What is the thesis in this article? What are the chief arguments used to develop this thesis?

THE ILLUSION OF INDIVIDUALITY*

Erich Fromm

[1] But what about ourselves? Is our own democracy threatened only by Fascism beyond the Atlantic or by the "fifth column" in our own ranks? If that were the case, the situation would be serious but not critical. But although foreign and internal threats of Fascism must be taken seriously, there is no greater mistake and no graver danger than not to see that in our own society we are faced with the same phenomenon that is fertile soil for the rise of Fascism anywhere: the insignificance and powerlessness of the individual.

* From Erich Fromm, *Escape from Freedom.* Copyright 1941 by Erich Fromm. Reprinted by permission of Holt, Rinehart & Winston, Inc.

[2] This statement challenges the conventional belief that by freeing the individual from all external restraints modern democracy has achieved true individualism. We are proud that we are not subject to any external authority, that we are free to express our thoughts and feelings, and we take it for granted that this freedom almost automatically guarantees our individuality. *The right to express our thoughts,* however, *means something only if we are able to have thoughts of our own;* freedom from external authority is a lasting gain only if the inner psychological conditions are such that we are able to establish our own individuality. Have we achieved that aim, or are we at least approaching it? . . . In discussing the two aspects of freedom for modern man, we have pointed out the economic conditions that make for increasing isolation and powerlessness of the individual in our era; in discussing the psychological results we have shown that this powerlessness leads either to the kind of escape that we find in the authoritarian character, or else to a compulsive conforming in the process of which the isolated individual becomes an automaton, loses his self, and yet at the same time consciously conceives of himself as free and subject only to himself.

[3] It is important to consider how our culture fosters this tendency to conform, even though there is space for only a few outstanding examples. The suppression of spontaneous feelings, and thereby of the development of genuine individuality, starts very early, as a matter of fact with the earliest training of a child. This is not to say that training must inevitably lead to suppression of spontaneity if the real aim of education is to further the inner independence and individuality of the child, its growth and integrity. The restrictions which such a kind of education may have to impose upon the growing child are only transitory measures that really support the process of growth and expansion. In our culture, however, education too often results in the elimination of spontaneity and in the substitution of original psychic acts by superimposed feelings, thoughts, and wishes. (By original I do not mean, let me repeat, that an idea has not been thought before by someone else, but that it originates in the individual, that it is the result of his own activity and in this sense is *his* thought.) To choose one illustration somewhat arbitrarily, one of the earliest suppressions of *feelings* concerns hostility and dislike. To start with, most children have a certain measure of hostility and rebelliousness as a result of their conflicts with a surrounding world that tends to block their expansiveness and to which, as the weaker opponent, they usually have to yield. It is one of the essential aims of the educational process to eliminate this antag-

onistic reaction. The methods are different; they vary from threats and punishments, which frighten the child, to the subtler methods of bribery or "explanations," which confuse the child and make him give up his hostility. The child starts with giving up the expression of his feeling and eventually gives up the very feeling itself. Together with that, he is taught to suppress the awareness of hostility and insincerity in others; sometimes this is not entirely easy, since children have a capacity for noticing such negative qualities in others without being so easily deceived by words as adults usually are. They still dislike somebody "for no good reason"—except the very good one that they feel the hostility, or insincerity, radiating from that person. This reaction is soon discouraged; it does not take long for the child to reach the "maturity" of the average adult and to lose the sense of discrimination between a decent person and a scoundrel, as long as the latter has not committed some flagrant act.

[4] On the other hand, early in his education, the child is taught to have feelings that are not at all "his"; particularly is he taught to like people, to be uncritically friendly to them, and to smile. What education may not have accomplished is usually done by social pressure in later life. If you do not smile you are judged lacking in a "pleasing personality"—and you need to have a pleasing personality if you want to sell your services, whether as a waitress, a salesman, or a physician. Only those at the bottom of the social pyramid, who sell nothing but their physical labor, and those at the very top do not need to be particularly "pleasant." Friendliness, cheerfulness, and everything that a smile is supposed to express, become automatic responses which one turns on and off like an electric switch.[1]

[5] To be sure, in many instances the person is aware of merely making a gesture; in most cases, however, he loses that awareness and thereby the ability to discriminate between the pseudo feeling and spontaneous friendliness.

[6] It is not only hostility that is directly suppressed and friendliness that is killed by superimposing its counterfeit. A wide range of spon-

---

[1] As one telling illustration of the commercialization of friendliness I should like to cite *Fortune's* report on "The Howard Johnson Restaurants." (*Fortune*, September, 1940, p. 96.) Johnson employs a force of "shoppers" who go from restaurant to restaurant to watch for lapses. "Since everything is cooked on the premises according to standard recipes and measurements issued by the home office, the inspector knows how large a portion of steak he should receive and how the vegetable should taste. He also knows how long it should take for the dinner to be served and he knows the exact degree of friendliness that should be shown by the hostess and the waitress."

taneous emotions are suppressed and replaced by pseudo feelings. Freud has taken one such suppression and put it in the center of his whole system, namely the suppression of sex. Although I believe that the discouragement of sexual joy is not the only important suppression of spontaneous reactions but one of many, certainly its importance is not to be underrated. Its results are obvious in cases of sexual inhibitions and also in those where sex assumes a compulsive quality and is consumed like liquor or a drug, which has no particular taste but makes you forget yourself. Regardless of the one or the other effect, their suppression, because of the intensity of sexual desires, not only affects the sexual sphere but also weakens the person's courage for spontaneous expression in all other spheres.

[7] In our society emotions in general are discouraged. While there can be no doubt that any creative thinking—as well as any other creative activity—is inseparably linked with emotion, it has become an ideal to think and to live without emotions. To be "emotional" has become synonymous with being unsound or unbalanced. By the acceptance of this standard the individual has become greatly weakened; his thinking is impoverished and flattened. On the other hand, since emotions cannot be completely killed, they must have their existence totally apart from the intellectual side of the personality; the result is the cheap and insincere sentimentality with which movies and popular songs feed millions of emotion-starved customers.

[8] There is one tabooed emotion that I want to mention in particular, because its suppression touches deeply on the roots of personality: the sense of tragedy. As we saw in an earlier chapter, the awareness of death and of the tragic aspect of life, whether dim or clear, is one of the basic characteristics of man. Each culture has its own way of coping with the problem of death. For those societies in which the process of individuation has progressed but little, the end of individual existence is less of a problem since the experience of individual existence itself is less developed. Death is not yet conceived as being basically different from life. Cultures in which we find a higher development of individuation have treated death according to their social and psychological structure. The Greeks put all emphasis on life and pictured death as nothing but a shadowy and dreary continuation of life. The Egyptians based their hopes on a belief in the indestructibility of the human body, at least of those whose power during life was indestructible. The Jews admitted the fact of death realistically and were able to reconcile themselves with the idea of the destruction of individual life by the vision of a state of happiness and justice ultimately to be reached by mankind

in this world. Christianity has made death unreal and tried to comfort the unhappy individual by promises of a life after death. Our own era simply denies death and with it one fundamental aspect of life. Instead of allowing the awareness of death and suffering to become one of the strongest incentives for life, the basis for human solidarity, and an experience without which joy and enthusiasm lack intensity and depth, the individual is forced to repress it. But, as is always the case with repression, by being removed from sight the repressed elements do not cease to exist. Thus the fear of death lives an illegitimate existence among us. It remains alive in spite of the attempt to deny it, but being repressed it remains sterile. It is one source of the flatness of other experiences, of the restlessness pervading life, and it explains, I would venture to say, the exorbitant amount of money this nation pays for its funerals.

[9] In the process of tabooing emotions modern psychiatry plays an ambiguous role. On the one hand its greatest representative, Freud, has broken through the fiction of the rational, purposeful character of the human mind and opened a path which allows a view into the abyss of human passions. On the other hand psychiatry, enriched by these very achievements of Freud, has made itself an instrument of the general trends in the manipulation of personality. Many psychiatrists, including psychoanalysts, have painted the picture of a "normal" personality which is never too sad, too angry, or too excited. They use words like "infantile" or "neurotic" to denounce traits or types of personalities that do not conform with the conventional pattern of a "normal" individual. This kind of influence is in a way more dangerous than the older and franker forms of name-calling. Then the individual knew at least that there was some person or some doctrine which criticized him and he could fight back. But who can fight back at "science"?

[10] The same distortion happens to original *thinking* as happens to feelings and emotions. From the very start of education original thinking is discouraged and ready-made thoughts are put into people's heads. How this is done with young children is easy enough to see. They are filled with curiosity about the world, they want to grasp it physically as well as intellectually. They want to know the truth, since that is the safest way to orient themselves in a strange and powerful world. Instead, they are not taken seriously, and it does not matter whether this attitude takes the form of open disrespect or of the subtle condescension which is usual towards all who have no power (such as children, aged or sick people). Although this treatment by itself offers strong discouragement to independent thinking, there is a worse handi-

cap: the insincerity—often unintentional—which is typical of the average adult's behavior toward a child. This insincerity consists partly in the fictitious picture of the world which the child is given. It is about as useful as instructions concerning life in the Arctic would be to someone who has asked how to prepare for an expedition to the Sahara Desert. Besides this general misrepresentation of the world there are the many specific lies that tend to conceal facts which, for various personal reasons, adults do not want children to know. From a bad temper, which is rationalized as justified dissatisfaction with the child's behavior, to concealment of the parents' sexual activities and their quarrels, the child is "not supposed to know" and his inquiries meet with hostile or polite discouragement.

[11] The child thus prepared enters school and perhaps college. I want to mention briefly some of the educational methods used today which in effect further discourage original thinking. One is the emphasis on knowledge of facts, or I should rather say on information. The pathetic superstition prevails that by knowing more and more facts one arrives at knowledge of reality. Hundreds of scattered and unrelated facts are dumped into the heads of students; their time and energy are taken up by learning more and more facts so that there is little left for thinking. To be sure, thinking without a knowledge of facts remains empty and fictitious; but "information" alone can be just as much of an obstacle to thinking as the lack of it.

[12] Another closely related way of discouraging original thinking is to regard all truth as relative. Truth is made out to be a metaphysical concept, and if anyone speaks about wanting to discover the truth he is thought backward by the "progressive" thinkers of our age. Truth is declared to be an entirely subjective matter, almost a matter of taste. Scientific endeavor must be detached from subjective factors, and its aim is to look at the world without passion and interest. The scientist has to approach facts with sterilized hands as a surgeon approaches his patient. The result of this relativism, which often presents itself by the name of empiricism or positivism or which recommends itself by its concern for the correct usage of words, is that thinking loses its essential stimulus—the wishes and interests of the person who thinks; instead it becomes a machine to register "facts." Actually, just as thinking in general has developed out of the need for mastery of material life, so the quest for truth is rooted in the interests and needs of individuals and social groups. Without such interest the stimulus for seeking the truth would be lacking. There are always groups whose interest is furthered by truth, and their representatives have been the pioneers of human thought; there are other groups whose interests are furthered by con-

cealing truth. Only in the latter case does interest prove harmful to the cause of truth. The problem, therefore, is not that there is *an* interest at stake, but *which kind* of interest is at stake. I might say that inasmuch as there is some longing for the truth in every human being, it is because every human being has some need for it.

[13] This holds true in the first place with regard to a person's orientation in the outer world, and it holds especially true for the child. As a child, every human being passes through a state of powerlessness, and truth is one of the strongest weapons of those who have no power. But the truth is in the individual's interest not only with regard to his orientation in the outer world; his own strength depends to a great extent on his knowing the truth about himself. Illusions about oneself can become crutches useful to those who are not able to walk alone; but they increase a person's weakness. The individual's greatest strength is based on the maximum of integration of his personality, and that means also on the maximum of transparence to himself. "Know thyself" is one of the fundamental commands that aim at human strength and happiness.

[14] In addition to the factors just mentioned there are others which actively tend to confuse whatever is left of the capacity for original thinking in the average adult. With regard to all basic questions of individual and social life, with regard to psychological, economic, political, and moral problems, a great sector of our culture has just one function—to befog the issues. One kind of smokescreen is the assertion that the problems are too complicated for the average individual to grasp. On the contrary it would seem that many of the basic issues of individual and social life are very simple, so simple, in fact, that everyone should be expected to understand them. To let them appear to be so enormously complicated that only a "specialist" can understand them, and he only in his own limited field, actually—and often intentionally—tends to discourage people from trusting their own capacity to think about those problems that really matter. The individual feels helplessly caught in a chaotic mass of data and with pathetic patience waits until the specialists have found out what to do and where to go.

[15] The result of this kind of influence is a twofold one: one is a scepticism and cynicism towards everything which is said or printed, while the other is a childish belief in anything that a person is told with authority. This combination of cynicism and naïveté is very typical of the modern individual. Its essential result is to discourage him from doing his own thinking and deciding.

[16] Another way of paralyzing the ability to think critically is the destruction of any kind of structuralized picture of the world. Facts lose the specific quality which they can have only as parts of a structuralized

whole and retain merely an abstract, quantitative meaning; each fact is just *another* fact and all that matters is whether we know more or less. Radio, moving pictures, and newspapers have a devastating effect on this score. The announcement of the bombing of a city and the death of hundreds of people is shamelessly followed or interrupted by an advertisement for soap or wine. The same speaker with the same suggestive, ingratiating, and authoritative voice, which he has just used to impress you with the seriousness of the political situation, impresses now upon his audience the merits of the particular brand of soap which pays for the news broadcast. Newsreels let pictures of torpedoed ships by followed by those of a fashion show. Newspapers tell us the trite thoughts or breakfast habits of a debutante with the same space and seriousness they use for reporting events of scientific or artistic importance. Because of all this we cease to be genuinely related to what we hear. We cease to be excited, our emotions and our critical judgment become hampered, and eventually our attitude to what is going on in the world assumes a quality of flatness and indifference. In the name of "freedom" life loses all structure; it is composed of many little pieces, each separate from the other and lacking any sense as a whole. The individual is left alone with these pieces like a child with a puzzle; the difference, however, is that the child knows what a house is and therefore can recognize the parts of the house in the little pieces he is playing with, whereas the adult does not see the meaning of the "whole," the pieces of which come into his hands. He is bewildered and afraid and just goes on gazing at his little meaningless pieces.

[17] What has been said about the lack of "originality" in feeling and thinking holds true also of the act of *willing*. To recognize this is particularly difficult; modern man seems, if anything, to have too many wishes and his only problem seems to be that, although he knows what he wants, he cannot have it. All our energy is spent for the purpose of getting what we want, and most people never question the premise of this activity: that they know their true wants. They do not stop to think whether the aims they are pursuing are something they themselves want. In school they want to have good marks, as adults they want to be more and more successful, to make more money, to have more prestige, to buy a better car, to go places, and so on. Yet when they do stop to think in the midst of all this frantic activity, this question may come to their minds: "If I do get this new job, if I get this better car, if I can take this trip—what then? What is the use of it all? Is it really I who wants all this? Am I not running after some goal which is supposed to make me happy and which eludes me as soon as I have reached it?"

These questions, when they arise, are frightening, for they question the very basis on which man's whole activity is built, his knowledge of what he wants. People tend, therefore, to get rid as soon as possible of these disturbing thoughts. They feel that they have been bothered by these questions because they were tired or depressed—and they go on in the pursuit of the aims which they believe are their own.

[18] Yet all this bespeaks a dim realization of the truth—the truth that modern man lives under the illusion that he knows what he wants, while he actually wants what he is *supposed* to want. In order to accept this it is necessary to realize that to know what one really wants is not comparatively easy, as most people think, but one of the most difficult problems any human being has to solve. It is a task we frantically try to avoid by accepting ready-made goals as though they were our own. Modern man is ready to take great risks when he tries to achieve the aims which are supposed to be "his"; but he is deeply afraid of taking the risk and the responsibility of giving himself his own aims. Intense activity is often mistaken for evidence of self-determined action, although we know that it may well be no more spontaneous than the behavior of an actor or a person hypnotized. When the general plot of the play is handed out, each actor can act vigorously the role he is assigned and even make up his lines and certain details of the action by himself. Yet he is only playing a role that has been handed over to him.

[19] The particular difficulty in recognizing to what extent our wishes—and our thoughts and feelings as well—are not really our own but put into us from the outside, is closely linked up with the problem of authority and freedom. In the course of modern history the authority of the Church has been replaced by that of the State, that of the State by that of conscience, and in our era, the latter has been replaced by the anonymous authority of common sense and public opinion as instruments of conformity. Because we have freed ourselves of the older overt forms of authority, we do not see that we have become the prey of a new kind of authority. We have become automatons who live under the illusion of being self-willing individuals. This illusion helps the individual to remain unaware of his insecurity, but this is all the help such an illusion can give. Basically the self of the individual is weakened, so that he feels powerless and extremely insecure. He lives in a world to which he has lost genuine relatedness and in which everybody and everything has become instrumentalized, where he has become a part of the machine that his hands have built. He thinks, feels, and wills what he believes he is supposed to think, feel, and will; in this very

process he loses his self upon which all genuine security of a free individual must be built.

[20] The loss of the self has increased the necessity to conform, for it results in a profound doubt of one's own identity. If I am nothing but what I believe I am supposed to be—who am "I"? We have seen how the doubt about one's own self started with the breakdown of the medieval order in which the individual had had an unquestionable place in a fixed order. The identity of the individual has been a major problem of modern philosophy since Descartes. Today we take for granted that we are we. Yet the doubt about ourselves still exists, or has ever grown. In his plays Pirandello has given expression to this feeling of modern man. He starts with the question: Who am I? What proof have I for my own identity other than the continuation of my physical self? His answer is not like Descartes'—the affirmation of the individual self—but its denial: I have no identity, there is no self excepting the one which is the reflex of what others expect me to be: I am "as you desire me."

[21] This loss of identity then makes it still more imperative to conform; it means that one can be sure of oneself only if one lives up to the expectations of others. If we do not live up to this picture we not only risk disapproval and increased isolation, but we risk losing the identity of our personality, which means jeopardizing sanity.

[22] By conforming with the expectations of others, by not being different, these doubts about one's own identity are silenced and a certain security is gained. However, the price paid is high. Giving up spontaneity and individuality results in a thwarting of life. Psychologically the automaton, while being alive biologically, is dead emotionally and mentally. While he goes through the motions of living, his life runs through his hands like sand. Behind a front of satisfaction and optimism modern man is deeply unhappy; as a matter of fact, he is on the verge of desperation. He desperately clings to the notion of individuality; he wants to be "different," and he has no greater recommendation of anything than that "it is different." We are informed of the individual name of the railroad clerk we buy our ticket from; handbags, playing cards, and portable radios are "personalized," by having the initials of the owner put on them. All this indicates the hunger for "difference" and yet these are almost the last vestiges of individuality that are left. Modern man is starved for life. But since, being an automaton, he cannot experience life in the sense of spontaneous activity he takes as surrogate any kind of excitement and thrill: the thrill of drinking, of sports, of vicariously living the excitements of fictitious persons on the screen.

[23] What then is the meaning of freedom for modern man?

[24] He has become free from the external bonds that would prevent him from doing and thinking as he sees fit. He would be free to act according to his own will, if he knew what he wanted, thought, and felt. But he does not know. He conforms to anonymous authorities and adopts a self which is not his. The more he does this, the more powerless he feels, the more is he forced to conform. In spite of a veneer of optimism and initiative, modern man is overcome by a profound feeling of powerlessness which makes him gaze toward approaching catastrophes as though he were paralyzed.

[25] Looked at superficially, people appear to function well enough in economic and social life; yet it would be dangerous to overlook the deep-seated unhappiness behind that comforting veneer. If life loses its meaning because it is not lived, man becomes desperate. People do not die quietly from physical starvation; they do not die quietly from psychic starvation either. If we look only at the economic needs as far as the "normal" person is concerned, if we do not see the unconscious suffering of the average automatized person, then we fail to see the danger that threatens our culture from its human basis: the readiness to accept any ideology and any leader, if only he promises excitement and offers a political structure and symbols which allegedly give meaning and order to an individual's life. The despair of the human automaton is fertile soil for the political purposes of Fascism.

Questions

1. What does the opening paragraph reveal about Fromm's attitudes toward conformity?
2. According to Fromm, "our culture fosters this tendency to conform." How does this happen? Does he support this contention?
3. What connection does Fromm perceive between thinking and feeling?
4. How does Fromm respond to psychological terms like *infantile, neurotic,* and *normal* (paragraph 9)? Why does he respond as he does?
5. Compare Fromm's attitude toward "facts" with the attitude attributed to Professor Agassiz in the Scudder essay, "A Great Teacher's Method" (pp. 569–572).
6. Why does Fromm object to "relativism"? What assumption does he seem to make about the relationship between a "structuralized picture" and "relativism" (paragraphs 12–16)?
7. What is the significance of the word *supposed* in paragraph 18?
8. Fromm observes that modern man wants to be "different" and "desperately clings to the notion of individuality." Is this observation consistent with his earlier statement about our becoming automatons? Explain.
9. How has Fromm organized his material? Is there a basic pattern or structure? Explain.

IT STARTED WITH MY MOTHER*

Jules Feiffer

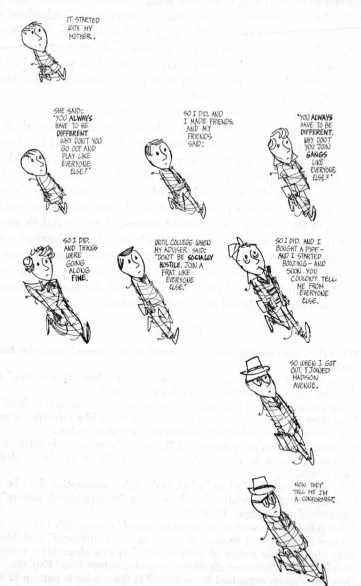

IT STARTED WITH MY MOTHER.

SHE SAID: "YOU **ALWAYS** HAVE TO BE **DIFFERENT**. WHY DON'T YOU GO OUT AND PLAY LIKE EVERYONE ELSE?"

SO I DID. AND I MADE FRIENDS. AND MY FRIENDS SAID:

"YOU **ALWAYS** HAVE TO BE **DIFFERENT**. WHY DON'T YOU JOIN **GANGS** LIKE EVERYONE ELSE?"

SO I DID. AND THINGS WERE GOING ALONG **FINE**.

UNTIL COLLEGE WHEN MY ADVISER SAID: "DON'T BE **SOCIALLY HOSTILE**. JOIN A FRAT LIKE EVERYONE ELSE."

SO I DID. AND I BOUGHT A PIPE—AND I STARTED. BOOZING — AND SOON YOU COULDN'T TELL ME FROM EVERYONE ELSE.

SO WHEN I GOT OUT, I JOINED MADISON AVENUE.

NOW THEY TELL ME I'M A CONFORMIST.

* With permission of McGraw-Hill Book Co., Inc. from *Sick, Sick, Sick* by Jules Feiffer. Copyright © 1958 by Jules Feiffer.

Questions

1. What basic point has Feiffer made in this cartoon?
2. What assumption has he made about the existence of conformity in our time?
3. Satire requires that the objects satirized be recognized as coming close to reality, a reality deplored by the satirist. Does this brief description of satire fit Feiffer's cartoon?
4. What common value system links the mother, the friends, and the college adviser?
5. Do you see a relationship between words and pictures in this cartoon? Explain.

THE PHILOSOPHY OF THE BEAT GENERATION*

John Clellon Holmes

[1] . . . Parents, civic leaders, law-enforcement officers, and even literary critcs most often have been amused, irritated or downright shocked by the behavior of this generation. They have noted more delinquency, more excess, more social irresponsibility in it than in any generation in recent years, and they have seen less interest in politics, community activity, and the orthodox religious creeds. They have been outraged by the adulation of the late James Dean, seeing in it signs of a dangerous morbidity, and they have been equally outraged by the adulation of Elvis Presley, seeing in it signs of a dangerous sensuality. They have read statistics on narcotics addiction, sexual promiscuity, and the consumption of alcohol among the young—and blanched. They have lamented the fact that "the most original (literary) work being done in this country has come to depend on the bizarre and the offbeat for its creative stimulus"; and they have expressed horror at the disquieting kind of juvenile crime—violent and without an object—which has erupted in most large cities.

[2] They see no signs of a search for spiritual values in a generation whose diverse tragic heroes have included jazzman Charlie Parker, actor Dean and poet Dylan Thomas; and whose interests have ranged all the way from bebop to rock and roll; from hipsterism to Zen Buddhism; from vision-inducing drugs to Method Acting. To be told that this is a generation whose almost exclusive concern is the discovery of something in which to believe seems to them to fly directly in the face of all the evidence.

[3] And yet, though everyone who reads the newspapers, looks at television or goes to the movies is probably well-acquainted with the behavior of the Beat Generation, very little attention has been given to the attitudes behind that behavior. And this despite the fact that it is what people think, and not only what they do, which gives us a glimpse of the way they are.

[4] Perhaps all generations feel that they have inherited "the worst of all possible worlds," but the Beat Generation probably has more claim to the feeling than any that have come before it. The historical climate which formed its attitudes was violent, and it did as much violence to ideas as it did to the men who believed in them. One does not have to be consciously aware of such destruction to feel it. Conventional notions of private and public morality have been steadily atrophied in the last ten or fifteen years by the exposure of treason in government, corruption in labor and business, and scandal among the mighty of Broadway and Hollywood. The political faiths which sometimes seem to justify slaughter have become steadily less appealing as slaughter has reached proportions that stagger even the mathematical mind. Orthodox religious conceptions of good and evil seem increasingly inadequate to explain a world of science-fiction turned fact, past-enemies turned bosom-friends, and honorable-diplomacy turned brink-of-war. Older generations may be distressed or cynical or apathetic about this world, or they may have somehow adjusted their conceptions to it. But the Beat Generation is specifically the *product* of this world, and it is the only world its members have ever known. . . .

[5] But instead of the cynicism and apathy which accompanies the end of ideals, and which gave the Lost Generation a certain poetic, autumnal quality, the Beat Generation is altogether too vigorous, too intent, too indefatigable, too curious to suit its elders. Nothing seems to satisfy or interest it but extremes, which, if they have included the criminality of narcotics, have also included the sanctity of monasteries. Everywhere the Beat Generation seems occupied with the feverish production of answers—some of them frightening, some of them foolish—to a single question: how are we to live? And if this is not immediately recognizable in leather-jacketed motorcyclists and hipsters "digging the street," it is because we assume that only answers which recognize man as a collective animal have any validity, and do not realize that this generation cannot conceive of the question in any but personal terms, and knows that the only answer it can accept will come out of the dark night of the individual soul. . . .

[6] A large proportion of this generation lived vicariously in the

short, tumultuous career of actor James Dean. He was their idol in much the same way that Valentino was the screen idol of the Twenties, and Clark Gable was the screen idol of the Thirties. But there was a difference, and it was *all* the difference. In Dean, they saw not a day-dream Lothario who was more attractive, mysterious and wealthy than they were, or a virile man of action with whom they could fancifully identify to make up for their own feelings of powerlessness, but a wist-ful, reticent youth, looking over the abyss separating him from older people with a level, saddened eye; living intensely in alternate explo-sions of tenderness and violence; eager for love and a sense of purpose, but able to accept them only on terms which acknowledged the facts of life as he knew them: in short, themselves.

[7] To many people, Dean's mumbling speech, attenuated silences, and rash gestures seemed the ultimate in empty mannerisms, but the young generation knew that it was not so much that he was inarticulate or affected as it was he was unable to believe in some of the things his scripts required him to say. He spoke to them right through all the expensive make-believe of million-dollar productions, saying with his sighs, and the prolonged shifting of his weight from foot to foot: "Well, I suppose there's no way out of this, but we know how it *really* is. . . ." They knew he was lonely, they knew he was flawed, they knew he was confused. But they also knew that he "dug," and so they delighted in his sloppy clothes and untrimmed hair and indifference to the proprie-ties of fame. He was not what they wanted to be; he was what they *were*. He lived hard and without complaint; and he died as he lived, going fast. Or as Kerouac's characters express it:

> We gotta go and never stop going till we get there.
> Where we going, man?
> I don't know, but we gotta go.

[8] Only the most myopic, it seems to me, can view this need for mobility (and it is one of the distinguishing characteristics of the Beat Generation) as a flight rather than a search. . . .

[9] . . . Even the crudest and most nihilistic member of the Beat Generation, the young slum hoodlum, is almost exclusively concerned with the problem of belief, albeit unconsciously. It seems incredible that no one has realized that the only way to make the shocking juvenile murders coherent at all is to understand that they are specifically moral crimes. The youth, who last summer stabbed another youth and was reported to have said to his victim, "Thanks a lot, I just wanted to know what it felt like," was neither insane nor perverted. There was no justi-

fication for his crime, either in the hope of gain or in the temporary hysteria of hate, or even in the egotism of a Loeb and Leopold, who killed only to prove they could get away with it. His was the sort of crime envisaged by the Marquis De Sade a hundred and fifty years ago —a crime which the cruel absence of God made obligatory if a man were to prove that he was a man and not a mere blot of matter. Such crimes, which are no longer rarities and which are all committed by people under twenty-five, cannot be understood if we go on mouthing the same old panaceas about broken homes and slum environments and bad company, for they are spiritual crimes, crimes against the identity of another human being, crimes which reveal with stark and terrifying clarity the lengths to which a desperate need for values can drive the young. For in actuality it is the longing for values which is expressed in such a crime, and not the hatred of them. It is the longing to do or feel something meaningful, and it provides a sobering glimpse of how completely the cataclysms of this century have obliterated the rational, humanistic view of Man on which modern society has been erected.

[10] The reaction to this on the part of young people, even those in a teen-age gang, is not a calculated immorality, however, but a return to an older, more personal, but no less rigorous code of ethics, which includes the inviolability of comradeship, the respect for confidences, and an almost mystical regard for courage—all of which are the ethics of the tribe, rather than the community; the code of a small compact group living in an indifferent or a hostile environment, which it seeks not to conquer or change, but only to elude.

[11] On a slightly older level, this almost primitive will to survive gives rise to the hipster, who moves through our cities like a member of some mysterious, nonviolent Underground, not plotting anything, but merely keeping alive an unpopular philosophy, much like the Christian of the first century. He finds in bop, the milder narcotics, his secretive language and the night itself, affirmation of an individuality (more and more besieged by the conformity of our national life), which can sometimes only be expressed by outright eccentricity. But his aim is to be asocial, not antisocial; his trancelike "digging" of jazz or sex or marijuana, is an effort to free himself, not exert power over others. In his most enlightened state, the hipster feels that argument, violence and concern for attachments are ultimately Square, and he says, "Yes, man, yes!" to the Buddhist principle that most human miseries arise from these emotions. . . .

[12] This conviction of the creative power of the unfettered individ-

ual soul stands behind everything in which the members of this generation interest themselves. If they are curious about drugs, for instance, their initial reason is as much the desire to tap the unknown world inside themselves as to escape from the unbearable world outside. "But, man, last night," they will say, "I got so high I knew *everything*. I mean, I knew *why*."

[13] In the arts, modern jazz is almost exclusively the music of the Beat Generation, as poetry (at least until Kerouac's novel) is its literature. If the members of this generation attend to a wailing sax in much the same way as men once used to attend the words and gestures of sages, it is because jazz is primarily the music of inner freedom, of improvisation, of the creative individual rather than the interpretive group. It is the music of a submerged people, who *feel* free, and this is precisely how young people feel today. For this reason, the short, violent life of alto-saxist Charlie Parker (together with those of Dean and Dylan Thomas) exerts a strong attraction on this generation, because all three went their own uncompromising way, listening to their inner voices, celebrating whatever they could find to celebrate, and then willingly paying the cost in self-destruction. But if young people idolize them, they have no illusions about them as martyrs, for they know (and almost stoically accept) that one of the risks of going so fast, and so far, is death. . . .

[14] In this world, the world of the Beat Generation, Kerouac unfailingly found tenderness, humility, joy and even reverence; and, though living in what many critics considered a nightmare-jungle of empty sensation, his characters nevertheless could say over and over:

> No one can tell us that there is no God. We've passed through all forms. . . . Everything is fine, God exists, we know time. . . . Furthermore we know America, we're at home. . . . We give and take and go in the incredibly complicated sweetness. . . .

[15] Whatever else they may be, these are not the words of a generation consumed by self-pity over the loss of their illusions; nor are they the words of a generation consumed by hatred for a world they never made. They seem rather to be the words of a generation groping toward faith out of an intellectual despair and moral chaos in which they refuse to lose themselves. . . .

[16] Everywhere young people are reacting to the growing collectivity of modern life, and the constant threat of collective death, with the same disturbing extremity of individualism. Everywhere they seem

to be saying to their elders: "We are different from you, and we can't believe in the things you believe in—if only because *this* is the world you have wrought." Everywhere, they are searching for their own answers.

[17] For many of them, the answer may well be jail or madness or death. They may never find the faith that Kerouac believes is at the end of their road. But on one thing they would all agree: the valueless abyss of modern life is unbearable. And if other generations have lamented the fact that theirs was "the worst of all possible worlds," young people today seem to know that it is the only one that they will ever have, and that it is *how* a man lives, not why, that makes all the difference. Their assumption—that the foundation of all systems, moral or social, is the indestructible unit of the single individual—may be nothing but a rebellion against a century in which this idea has fallen into disrepute. But their recognition that what sustains the individual is belief—and their growing conviction that only spiritual beliefs have any lasting validity in a world such as ours—should put their often frenzied behavior in a new light, and will certainly figure large in whatever future they may have.

Questions

1. Has Holmes assessed the attitudes of "parents, civic leaders, law-enforcement officers, and even literary critics" correctly when he suggests they are "amused, irritated or downright shocked by the behavior of this generation" (paragraph 1)? Explain.
2. What important point does Holmes make in paragraph 3? Why does he make this point?
3. Holmes refers to "the worst of all possible worlds" (paragraph 4). Do you recognize his allusion?
4. In paragraph 5 what assumption does Holmes identify as being unacceptable to the Beat Generation? What is his purpose here?
5. How does Holmes explain the Beat Generation's "need for mobility"? Do you agree? Explain.
6. What are Holmes' attitudes toward juvenile crimes? How do you respond to his statements? Why?
7. What prompts Holmes to refer to the hipster as being "much like the Christian of the first century" (paragraph 11)?
8. Why does Holmes quote Jack Kerouac in paragraph 14?
9. How much of this essay is factual? How much of it is opinion?

THE IRRESPONSIBLES*

Robert Elliot Fitch

"It's not my fault! it's not my fault! Nothing in this lousy world is my fault, don't you see that? I don't want it to be and it can't be and it won't be." This outcry comes from Kerouac's Sal Paradise, but it expresses the deep conviction of multitudes of irresponsibles in the age of self-pity. It is a curious paradox that, while the self is the center of all things, the self is never to blame for anything.

The fault is always the fault of someone or of something else. This is implicit in all the letters which are addressed to Abigail Van Buren. "Dear Abby: This is my problem . . . My husband . . ." "Dear Abby: Here is my problem . . . My wife . . ." Or it may be my son, my daughter, my mother-in-law, my neighbors. It is never Me.

Blame it on God, the girls, or the government, on heredity, or on environment, on the parents, on the siblings, on the cold war, on the pressures toward conformity, on being unloved and unwanted. But don't blame it on me, the very center around which the whole universe revolves. This me is like the innocent and apparently un-menacing Dennis, who stands before an accusing mother, in the middle of the parlor, with his body twisted about as he looks back on the carpet at some curious mud tracks which lead right up to his heels. Says Dennis, in bewilderment, "I don't know what that stuff is . . . it just keeps following me."

One torment from which we all suffer is the stress and strain of modern life. In this connection the California State Department of Public Health has made a careful and scientific inquiry into the factors which tend to produce alcoholics. These factors, as reported in the San Francisco *Chronicle*, all come under the heading of "high stress." This "high stress," we are told, can be created by obvious irritations "such as a nagging wife, a bothersome mother-in-law, or an unbalanced family budget, as well as the vexations of one-way streets, airplane noise and the accoutrements of the atomic age." We also learn that "plenty of 'high stress' can also be brewed in the unconscious mind. The victim is troubled but doesn't know what troubles him."

In other words, it is enough simply to be alive today to be a neurotic. Nobody is likely to be subject to all of these strains, but surely anybody has enough of some of them—the airplane noise, the mother-in-law, the unbalanced budget—to be able to make out a good case for his loss of self-control. Of course the report says that the bottle is not the only means of escape from the torment of modern life. Others may do it by "attempting suicide, gambling, chasing women, over-eating, and otherwise over-indulging." At any rate, a tax-supported public agency fulfills its duty to the prejudices of the day by solemnly providing a set of scientific alibis for irresponsibility that can be appropriated by just about anyone. . . .

However, the universal alibi of irresponsibility is centered in the family. The family can be regarded as a focal point for the forces both of heredity and of environment. Moreover, everybody has had, one way or another, a father and a mother. The father alone is a sufficient excuse for almost any irregularity of conduct—be he famous, or infamous, or mediocre, or non-functional. If the poor child has a famous father, then we know he must spend his life in a desperate effort to measure up to an impossible standard of excellence. If the poor child has an infamous father, then he must spend his life in a desperate effort to overcome the shameful heritage which is his own. If the poor child has an ordinary, average father, then he is bound to rebel against this example of mediocrity, and to strive for some kind of distinction whether by conventional or by unconventional means. If the poor child's father is out of the picture after the time of conception, then we have another set of complexes and fixations, all of which relate to the mother.

Ideally, no doubt, there would be a minimizing of risk if fathers could be eliminated altogether. This goal seems to be a little way off. But we take hope from the fact that the federal government, in collaboration with the University of Wisconsin's genetics department, has developed a revolutionary, fatherless potato. This potato has only half the chromosomes of the normal variety, and breeds truer to form. Unfortunately, it has poor survival value.

The nice thing about the parental alibi is that it can always be made to work in either of two opposite directions. If a young man is a poor student, he may complain that his parents were relative illiterates, and never taught him the love of good books and habits of steady reading. Or he may complain that his parents were excessive in their addiction to scholarship, that he was so much surrounded by learning from early childhood that he developed a revulsion against it and since then can't bear the sight of a book. If someone is always late to appointments, he may protest that he had strict, old-fashioned parents, who were so rigorous in their insistence on punctuality that he was compelled to adopt the principle of continual tardiness as an affirmation of the freedom of his personality. Or he may protest that his parents were singularly careless and indifferent concerning times and seasons, and that, having grown up in this atmosphere of delightful laxity, he is unable to bring himself around to more scrupulous behavior. In any case the blame rests on the parent, never on the offspring.

One can draw just as good alibis from his siblings, if he has some, or even if he has none. A careful study of Freud, Jung, Adler, and of modern psychologists makes it quite plain that brothers and sisters are among the very worst hazards in life. It is dangerous to be the oldest child; it is perilous to be the youngest; it is tough to be the one in the middle. It is upsetting to be the only boy with several sisters. It is disturbing to be the only girl with several brothers. It is ruinous to be one child among a dozen. It is dangerous to be an only child. It is dangerous to be a child. Perhaps the perfect arrangement would be to eliminate parents, to skip childhood, and to be incubated and hatched at an advanced age, all ready to wear the honorifics of our society as "free, mature adults." Unfortunately, that would deprive us of all the alibis for irresponsibility, which are occasionally useful even to the most "mature mind."

A more strictly contemporary complaint would have it that we live in a "cold and impersonal world," and that this has disastrous effects on personality. One can imagine the Pilgrim Fathers' resorting to some such excuse for their shortcomings. Certainly their world was cold enough in the winter. And it was impersonal enough, with savages, a wilderness, and famine haunting their very doorsteps. Somehow they seem never to have thought of this excellent alibi. One can also imagine a citizen of some collectivist society making such a protest. Nothing could be more cold and impersonal than collectivism—more lacking in warmth of feeling for the individual, more contemptuous of his rights as a person. Yet here, too, there seems to be no one with ingenuity enough to make the lament.

Where the complaint of a "cold and impersonal world" is warranted, the complaint is not made. Where the complaint of a "cold and impersonal world" is not warranted, it is made. The plain fact is that our world in the United States suffers, not from an excess of impersonality, but from an excess of the opposite. Our society is too self-centered in its concerns. It is at this moment one of the most egocentric societies in history. Once again we bestow the fee upon the foul disease. We insist upon having as a remedy a more generous application of that which is the source of our ailment—the emphasis on the individual person.

Questions

1. Do the "Dear Abby" letters support Fitch's major thesis?
2. Why does Fitch include "the pressures toward conformity" in his listing at the beginning of the third paragraph?
3. Fitch describes the family as "the universal alibi of irresponsibility." Do his illustrations sound familiar? Are they effective? Why?
4. What is the tone of the paragraph beginning "One can draw just as good alibis from his siblings . . ."?
5. Fitch refers to collectivism as "contemptuous" of the individual's rights. What basic assumption is he making?
6. In his attack on the excesses of individualism, do you assume Fitch would favor greater conformism? If so, conformism to what?

From WALDEN

Henry David Thoreau

[1] When I wrote the following pages, or rather the bulk of them, I lived alone, in the woods, a mile from any neighbor, in a house which I had built myself, on the shore of Walden Pond, in Concord, Massachusetts, and earned my living by the labor of my hands only. I lived there two years and two months. At present I am a sojourner in civilized life again.

[2] I should not obtrude my affairs so much on the notice of my readers if very particular inquiries had not been made by my townsmen concerning my mode of life, which some would call impertinent, though they do not appear to me at all impertinent, but, considering the circumstances, very natural and pertinent. Some have asked what I got to eat; if I did not feel lonesome; if I was not afraid; and the like. Others have been curious to learn what portion of my income I devoted to charitable purposes; and some, who have large families, how many poor children I maintained. I will therefore ask those of my readers who feel no particular interest in me to pardon me if I undertake to answer some of these questions in this book. In most books, the I, or first person, is omitted; in this it will be retained; that, in respect to egotism, is the main difference. We commonly do not remember that it is, after all, always the first person that is speaking. I should not talk so much about myself if there were anybody else whom I knew as well. Unfortunately, I am confined to this theme by the narrowness of my experience. Moreover, I, on my side, require of every writer, first or last, a simple and sincere account of his own life, and not merely what he has heard of other men's lives; some such account as he would

send to his kindred from a distant land; for if he has lived sincerely, it must have been in a distant land to me. Perhaps these pages are more particularly addressed to poor students. As for the rest of my readers, they will accept such portions as apply to them. I trust that none will stretch the seams in putting on the coat, for it may do good service to him whom it fits. . . .

[3] I see young men, my townsmen, whose misfortune it is to have inherited farms, houses, barns, cattle, and farming tools; for these are more easily acquired than got rid of. Better if they had been born in the open pasture and suckled by a wolf, that they might have seen with clearer eyes what field they were called to labor in. Who made them serfs of the soil? Why should they eat their sixty acres, when man is condemned to eat only his peck of dirt? Why should they begin digging their graves as soon as they are born? They have got to live a man's life, pushing all these things before them, and get on as well as they can. How many a poor immortal soul have I met well-nigh crushed and smothered under its load, creeping down the road of life, pushing before it a barn seventy-five feet by forty, its Augean stables never cleansed, and one hundred acres of land, tillage, mowing, pasture, and wood-lot! The portionless, who struggle with no such unnecessary inherited encumbrances, find it labor enough to subdue and cultivate a few cubic feet of flesh. . . .

[4] I sometimes wonder that we can be so frivolous, I may almost say, as to attend to the gross but somewhat foreign form of servitude called Negro Slavery, there are so many keen and subtle masters that enslave both North and South. It is hard to have a Southern overseer; it is worse to have a Northern one; but worst of all when you are the slave-driver of yourself. Talk of a divinity in man! Look at the teamster on the highway, wending to market by day or night; does any divinity stir within him? His highest duty to fodder and water his horses! What is his destiny to him compared with the shipping interests? Does not he drive for Squire Make-a-stir? How godlike, how immortal, is he? See how he cowers and sneaks, how vaguely all the day he fears, not being immortal nor divine, but the slave and prisoner of his own opinion of himself, a fame won by his own deeds. Public opinion is a weak tyrant compared with our own private opinion. What a man thinks of himself, that it is which determines, or rather indicates, his fate. . . .

[5] The mass of men lead lives of quiet desperation. What is called resignation is confirmed desperation. From the desperate city you go into the desperate country, and have to console yourself with the bravery of minks and muskrats. A stereotyped but unconscious despair is concealed even under what are called the games and amusements of

mankind. There is no play in them, for this comes after work. But it is a characteristic of wisdom not to do desperate things.

[6] When we consider what, to use the words of the catechism, is the chief end of man, and what are the true necessaries and means of life, it appears as if men had deliberately chosen the common mode of living because they preferred it to any other. Yet they honestly think there is no choice left. But alert and healthy natures remember that the sun rose clear. It is never too late to give up our prejudices. No way of thinking or doing, however ancient, can be trusted without proof. What everybody echoes or in silence passes by as true to-day may turn out to be falsehood to-morrow, mere smoke of opinion, which some had trusted for a cloud that would sprinkle fertilizing rain on their fields. What old people say you cannot do, you try and find that you can. Old deeds for old people, and new deeds for new. Old people did not know enough once, perchance, to fetch fresh fuel to keep the fire a-going; new people put a little dry wood under a pot, and are whirled round the globe with the speed of birds, in a way to kill old people, as the phrase is. Age is no better, hardly so well, qualified for an instructor as youth, for it has not profited so much as it has lost. One may almost doubt if the wisest man has learned anything of absolute value by living. Practically, the old have no very important advice to give the young, their own experience has been so partial, and their lives have been such miserable failures, for private reasons, as they must believe; and it may be that they have some faith left which belies that experience, and they are only less young than they were. I have lived some thirty years on this planet, and I have yet to hear the first syllable of valuable or even earnest advice from my seniors. They have told me nothing, and probably cannot tell me anything to the purpose. Here is life, an experiment to a great extent untried by me; but it does not avail me that they have tried it. If I have any experience which I think valuable, I am sure to reflect that this my Mentors said nothing about. . . .

[7] The whole round of human life seems to some to have been gone over by their predecessors, both the heights and the valleys, and all things to have been cared for. According to Evelyn, "the wise Solomon prescribed ordinances for the very distances of trees; and the Roman praetors have decided how often you may go into your neighbor's land to gather the acorns which fall on it without trespass, and what share belongs to that neighbor." Hippocrates has even left directions how we should cut our nails; that is, even with the ends of the fingers, neither shorter nor longer. Undoubtedly the very tedium and ennui which presume to have exhausted the variety and the joys of life are as old as

Adam. But man's capacities have never been measured; nor are we to judge of what he can do by any precedents, so little has been tried. . . .

[8] The greater part of what my neighbors call good I believe in my soul to be bad, and if I repent of anything, it is very likely to be my good behavior. What demon possessed me that I behaved so well? You may say the wisest thing you can, old man,—you who have lived seventy years, not without honor of a kind,—I hear an irresistible voice which invites me away from all that. One generation abandons the enterprises of another like stranded vessels.

[9] I think that we may safely trust a good deal more than we do. We may waive just so much care of ourselves as we honestly bestow elsewhere. Nature is as well adapted to our weakness as to our strength. The incessant anxiety and strain of some is a well-nigh incurable form of disease. We are made to exaggerate the importance of what work we do; and yet how much is not done by us! or, what if we had been taken sick? How vigilant we are! determined not to live by faith if we can avoid it; all the day long on the alert, at night we unwillingly say our prayers and commit ourselves to uncertainties. So thoroughly and sincerely are we compelled to live, reverencing our life, and denying the possibility of change. This is the only way, we say; but there are as many ways as there can be drawn radii from one centre. . . .

[10] None can be an impartial or wise observer of human life but from the vantage ground of what *we* should call voluntary poverty. Of a life of luxury the fruit is luxury, whether in agriculture, or commerce, or literature, or art. There are nowadays professors of philosophy, but not philosophers. Yet it is admirable to profess because it was once admirable to live. To be a philosopher is not merely to have subtle thoughts, nor even to found a school, but so to love wisdom as to live according to its dictates, a life of simplicity, independence, magnanimity, and trust. It is to solve some of the problems of life, not only theoretically, but practically. The success of great scholars and thinkers is commonly a courtier-like success, not kingly, not manly. They make shift to live merely by conformity, practically as their fathers did, and are in no sense the progenitors of a nobler race of men. . . .

[11] It is desirable that a man be clad so simply that he can lay his hands on himself in the dark, and that he live in all respects so compactly and preparedly that, if an enemy take the town, he can, like the old philosopher, walk out the gate emptyhanded without anxiety. While one thick garment is, for most purposes, as good as three thin ones, and cheap clothing can be obtained at prices really to suit customers; while a thick coat can be bought for five dollars, which will last as many years, thick pantaloons for two dollars, cowhide boots for a

dollar and a half a pair, a summer hat for a quarter of a dollar, and a winter cap for sixty-two and a half cents, or a better be made at home at a nominal cost, where is he so poor that, clad in such a suit, *of his own earning*, there will not be found wise men to do him reverence?

[12] When I ask for a garment of a particular form, my tailoress tells me gravely, "They do not make them so now," not emphasizing the "They" at all, as if she quoted an authority as impersonal as the Fates, and I find it difficult to get made what I want, simply because she cannot believe that I mean what I say, that I am so rash. When I hear this oracular sentence, I am for a moment absorbed in thought, emphasizing to myself each word separately that I may come at the meaning of it, that I may find out by what degree of consanguinity *They* are related to *me*, and what authority they may have in an affair which affects me so nearly; and, finally, I am inclined to answer her with equal mystery, and without any more emphasis of the "they",—"It is true, they did not make them so recently, but they do now." Of what use this measuring of me if she does not measure my character, but only the breadth of my shoulders, as it were a peg to hang the coat on? We worship not the Graces, nor the Parcae, but Fashion. She spins and weaves and cuts with full authority. The head monkey at Paris puts on a traveller's cap, and all the monkeys in America do the same. I sometimes despair of getting anything quite simple and honest done in this world by the help of men. They would have to be passed through a powerful press first, to squeeze their old notions out of them, so that they would not soon get upon their legs again; and then there would be some one in the company with a maggot in his head, hatched from an egg deposited there nobody knows when, for not even fire kills these things, and you would have lost your labor. . . .

[13] Who knows but if men constructed their dwellings with their own hands, and provided food for themselves and families simply and honestly enough, the poetic faculty would be universally developed, as birds universally sing when they are so engaged? But alas! we do like cowbirds and cuckoos, which lay their eggs in nests which other birds have built, and cheer no traveller with their chattering and unmusical notes. Shall we forever resign the pleasure of construction to the carpenter? What does architecture amount to in the experience of the mass of men? I never in all my walks came across a man engaged in so simple and natural an occupation as building his house. We belong to the community. It is not the tailor alone who is the ninth part of a man; it is as much the preacher, and the merchant, and the farmer. Where is this division of labor to end? and what object does it finally serve? No doubt another *may* also think for me; but it is not therefore

desirable that he should do so to the exclusion of my thinking for myself. . . .

[14] While my townsmen and women are devoted in so many ways to the good of their fellows, I trust that one at least may be spared to other and less humane pursuits. You must have a genius for charity as well as for anything else. As for Doing-good, that is one of the professions which are full. Moreover, I have tried it fairly, and, strange as it may seem, am satisfied that it does not agree with my constitution. Probably I should not consciously and deliberately forsake my particular calling to do the good which society demands of me, to save the universe from annihilation; and I believe that a like but infinitely greater steadfastness elsewhere is all that now preserves it. But I would not stand between any man and his genius; and to him who does this work, which I decline, with his whole heart and soul and life, I would say, Persevere, even if the whole world call it doing evil, as it is most likely they will. . . .

Questions

1. What reasons does Thoreau offer for the use of his first person narration? Do you agree with him? Explain.
2. How does Thoreau feel about the inheritance of property? To what extent do you agree or disagree with him? Why?
3. Thoreau says, "The mass of men lead lives of quiet desperation" (paragraph 5). What evidence does he offer for this observation? What do your observations prompt you to think on this subject? Explain.
4. Why does Thoreau use the word *prejudices* in paragraph 6?
5. How does Thoreau's attitude toward "old people" compare with your attitude? Explain.
6. Why does Thoreau refer to the directions by Hippocrates on "how we should cut our nails" (paragraph 7)?
7. According to Thoreau, what is the quality of the tailoress' thinking (paragraph 12)? Explain.
8. Examine Thoreau's analogy between humans and birds (paragraph 13). Why does he use this analogy? How valid is his argument? Explain.

From SELF-RELIANCE

Ralph Waldo Emerson

. . . Society everywhere is in conspiracy against the manhood of every one of its members. Society is a joint-stock company, in which the members agree, for the better securing of his bread to each shareholder, to surrender the liberty and culture of the eater. The virtue in most request is conformity. Self-reliance is its aversion. It loves not realities and creators, but names and customs.

Whoso would be a man, must be a nonconformist. He who would gather immortal palms must not be hindered by the name of goodness, but must explore if it be goodness. Nothing is at last sacred but the integrity of your own mind. Absolve you to yourself, and you shall have the suffrage of the world. I remember an answer which when quite young I was prompted to make to a valued adviser who was wont to importune me with the dear old doctrines of the church. On my saying, "What have I to do with the sacredness of traditions, if I live wholly from within?" my friend suggested,—"But these impulses may be from below, not from above." I replied, "They do not seem to me to be such; but if I am the Devil's child, I will live then from the Devil." No law can be sacred to me but that of my nature. Good and bad are but names very readily transferable to that or this; the only right is what is after my constitution; the only wrong what is against it. A man is to carry himself in the presence of all opposition as if every thing were titular and ephemeral but he. I am ashamed to think how easily we capitulate to badges and names, to large societies and dead institutions. Every decent and well-spoken individual affects and sways me more than is right. I ought to go upright and vital, and speak the rude truth in all ways. If malice and vanity wear the coat of philanthropy, shall that pass? If an angry bigot assumes this bountiful cause of Abolition, and comes to me with his last news from Barbadoes, why should I not say to him, "Go love thy infant; love thy wood-chopper; be good-natured and modest; have that grace; and never varnish your hard, uncharitable ambition with this incredible tenderness for black folk a thousand miles off. Thy love afar is spite at home." Rough and graceless would be such greeting, but truth is handsomer than the affectation of love. Your goodness must have some edge to it,—else it is none. The doctrine of hatred must be preached, as the counteraction of the doctrine of love, when that pules and wines. I shun father and mother and wife and brother when my genius calls me. I would write on the lintels of the door-post, *Whim.* I hope it is somewhat better than whim at last, but we cannot spend the day in explanation. Expect me not to show cause why I seek or why I exclude company. Then again, do not tell me, as a good man did to-day, of my obligation to put all poor men in good situations. Are they *my* poor? I tell thee thou foolish philanthropist that I grudge the dollar, the dime, the cent I give to such men as do not belong to me and to whom I do not belong. There is a class of persons to whom by all spiritual affinity I am bought and sold; for them I will go to prison if need be; but your miscellaneous popular charities; the education at college of fools; the building of meeting-houses to the vain end to which many now stand; alms to sots, and the thousandfold Relief Societies;—though I confess with shame I sometimes succumb and give the dollar, it is a wicked dollar, which by and by I shall have the manhood to withhold.

Virtues are, in the popular estimate, rather the exception than the rule. There is the man *and* his virtues. Men do what is called a good action, as some piece of courage or charity, much as they would pay a fine in expiation of daily non-appearance on parade. Their works are done as an apology or extenuation of their living in the world,—as invalids and the insane pay a high board. Their virtues are penances. I do not wish to expiate, but to live. My life is for itself and not for a spectacle. I much prefer that it should be of a lower strain, so it be genuine and equal, than that it should be glittering and unsteady. I wish it to be sound and sweet, and not to need diet and bleeding. I ask primary evidence that you are a man, and refuse this appeal from the man to his actions. I know that for myself it makes no difference whether I do or forbear those actions which are reckoned excellent. I cannot consent to pay for a privilege where I have intrinsic right. Few and mean as my gifts may be, I actually am, and do not need for my own assurance or the assurance of my fellows any secondary testimony.

What I must do is all that concerns me, not what the people think. This rule, equally arduous in actual and in intellectual life, may serve for the whole distinction between greatness and meanness. It is the harder because you will always find those who think they know what is your duty better than you know it. It is easy in the world to live after the world's opinion; it is easy in solitude to live after our own; but the great man is he who in the midst of the crowd keeps with perfect sweetness the independence of solitude.

The objection to conforming to usages that have become dead to you is that it scatters your force. It loses your time and blurs the impression of your character. If you maintain a dead church, contribute to a dead Bible-society, vote with a great party either for the government or against it, spread your table like base housekeepers, —under all these screens I have difficulty to detect the precise man you are: and of course so much force is withdrawn from your proper life. But do your work, and I shall know you. Do your work, and you shall reinforce yourself. A man must consider what a blindman's-buff is this game of conformity. If I know your sect I anticipate your argument. I hear a preacher announce for his text and topic the expediency of one of the institutions of his church. Do I not know beforehand that not possibly can he say a new and spontaneous word? Do I not know that with all this ostentation of examining the grounds of the institution he will do no such thing? Do I not know that he is pledged to himself not to look but at one side, the permitted side, not as a man, but as a parish minister? He is a retained attorney, and these airs of the bench are the emptiest affectation. Well, most men have bound their eyes with one or another handkerchief, and attached themselves to some one of these communities of opinion. This conformity makes them not false in a few particulars, authors of a few lies, but false in all particulars. Their every truth is not quite true. Their two is not the real two, their four not the real four; so that every word they say chagrins us and we know not where to begin to set them right. Meantime nature is not slow to equip us in the prison-uniform of the party to which we adhere. We come to wear one cut of face and figure, and acquire by degrees the gentlest asinine expression. There is a mortifying experience in particular, which does not fail to wreak itself also in the general history; I mean the "foolish face of praise," the forced smile which we put on in company where we do not feel at ease, in answer to conversation which does not interest us. The muscles, not spontaneously moved but moved by a low usurping wilfulness, grow tight about the outline of the face, with the most disagreeable sensation.

For nonconformity the world whips you with its displeasure. And therefore a man must know how to estimate a sour face. The bystanders look askance on him in the public street or in the friend's parlor. If this aversation had its origin in contempt and resistance like his own he might well go home with a sad countenance; but the sour faces of the multitude, like their sweet faces, have no deep cause, but are put on and off as the wind blows and a newspaper directs. Yet is the discontent of the multitude more formidable than that of the senate and the college. It is easy enough for a firm man who knows the world to brook the rage of the cultivated classes. Their rage is decorous and prudent, for they are timid, as being very vulnerable themselves. But when to their feminine rage the indignation of the people is added, when the ignorant and the poor are aroused, when the unintelligent brute force that lies at the bottom of society is made to growl and mow, it needs the habit of magnanimity and religion to treat it godlike as a trifle of no concernment.

The other terror that scares us from self-trust is our consistency; a reverence for our past act or word because the eyes of others have no other data for computing our orbit than our past acts, and we are loath to disappoint them.

But why should you keep your head over your shoulder? Why drag about this corpse of your memory, lest you contradict somewhat you have stated in this or that public place? Suppose you should contradict yourself; what then? It seems to be a rule of wisdom never to rely on your memory alone, scarcely even in acts of pure memory, but to bring the past for judgment into the thousand-eyed present, and live ever in a new day. In your metaphysics you have denied personality to the Deity, yet when the devout motions of the soul come, yield to them heart and life, though they should clothe God with shape and color. Leave your theory, as Joseph his coat in the hand of the harlot, and flee.

A foolish consistency is the hobgoblin of little minds, adored by little statesmen and philosophers and divines. With consistency a great soul has simply nothing to do. He may as well concern himself with his shadow on the wall. Speak what you think now in hard words and to-morrow speak what to-morrow thinks in hard words again, though it contradict every thing you said to-day.—"Ah, so you shall be sure to be misunderstood."—Is it so bad then to be misunderstood? Pythagoras was misunderstood, and Socrates, and Jesus, and Luther, and Copernicus, and Galileo, and Newton, and every pure and wise spirit that ever took flesh. To be great is to be misunderstood. . . .

Questions

1. Evaluate the opening paragraph. Comment on the "joint-stock company" metaphor.

2. What is Emerson's attitude toward the "dear old doctrines of the church"? How do you know?

3. Emerson says: "No law can be sacred to me but that of my nature. Good and bad are but names very readily transferable to that or this; the only right is what is after my constitution; the only wrong what is against it." What are the implications of these sentences? What consequences would follow general acceptance of these statements?

4. What is Emerson's attitude toward philanthropy? Why? Why does he contribute his dollar?

5. Emerson says that he must not concern himself with "what the people think." He describes this rule as arduous. Do you agree? Explain.

6. Emerson says that "For nonconformity, the world whips you with its displeasure." Do you agree? If you do, can you cite examples? If not, can you cite examples?

7. Emerson distinguishes between the rage of the "cultivated classes" and the "unintelligent brute force." Why does he make this distinction? Why does he use the word *feminine* in reference to the cultivated classes? Can you suggest current illustrations for Emerson's distinctions?

8. Why does Emerson attack "a foolish consistency"?
9. Which of the following terms best describes Emerson's style: ironic, abstract, aphoristic, phlegmatic, imaginative, colloquial? Explain your choice or choices.

THE FUTURE*

Herbert Hoover

[1] Individualism has been the primary force of American civilization for three centuries. It is our sort of individualism that has supplied the motivation of America's political, economic, and spiritual institutions in all these years. It has proved its ability to develop its institutions with the changing scene. Our very form of government is the product of the individualism of our people, the demand for an equal opportunity, for a fair chance.

[2] The American pioneer is the epic expression of that individualism, and the pioneer spirit is the response to the challenge of opportunity, to the challenge of nature, to the challenge of life, to the call of the frontier. That spirit need never die for lack of something for it to achieve. There will always be a frontier to conquer or to hold as long as men think, plan, and dare. Our American individualism has received much of its character from our contacts with the forces of nature on a new continent. It evolved government without official emissaries to. show the way; it plowed and sowed two score of great states; it built roads, bridges, railways, cities; it carried forward every attribute of high civilization over a continent. The days of the pioneer are not over. There are continents of human welfare of which we have penetrated only the coastal plain. The great continent of science is as yet explored only on its borders, and it is only the pioneer who will penetrate the frontier in the quest for new worlds to conquer. The very genius of our institutions has been given to them by the pioneer spirit. Our individualism is rooted in our very nature. It is based on conviction born of experience. Equal opportunity, the demand for a fair chance, became the formula of American individualism because it is the method of American achievement.

[3] After the absorption of the great plains of the West came the era of industrial development with the new complex of forces that it has brought us. Now haltingly, but with more surety and precision than

* From Herbert Hoover, *American Individualism*. Copyright 1922 and published by Doubleday, Page & Co. Reprinted by permission of the author.

ever before and with a more conscious understanding of our mission, we are finding solution of these problems arising from new conditions, for the forces of our social system can compass and comprise these.

[4] Our individualism is no middle ground between autocracy— whether of birth, economic or class origin—and socialism. Socialism of different varieties may have something to recommend it as an intellectual stop-look-and-listen sign, more especially for Old World societies. But it contains only destruction to the forces that make progress in our social system. Nor does salvation come by any device for concentration of power, whether political or economic, for both are equally reversions to Old World autocracy in new garments.

[5] Salvation will not come to us out of the wreckage of individualism. What we need today is steady devotion to a better, brighter, broader individualism—an individualism that carries increasing responsibility and service to our fellows. Our need is not for a way out but for a way forward. We found our way out three centuries ago when our forefathers left Europe for these shores, to set up here a commonwealth conceived in liberty and dedicated to the development of individuality.

[6] There are malign social forces other than our failures that would destroy our progress. There are the equal dangers both of reaction and radicalism. The perpetual howl of radicalism is that it is the sole voice of liberalism—that devotion to social progress is its field alone. These men would assume that all reform and human advance must come through government. They have forgotten that progress must come from the steady lift of the individual and that the measure of national idealism and progress is the quality of idealism in the individual. The most trying support of radicalism comes from the timid or dishonest minds that shrink from facing the result of radicalism itself but are devoted to defense of radicalism as proof of a liberal mind. Most theorists who denounce our individualism as a social basis seem to have a passion for ignorance of its constructive ideals.

[7] An even greater danger is the destructive criticism of minds too weak or too partisan to harbor constructive ideas. For such, criticism is based upon the distortion of perspective or cunning misrepresentation. There is never danger from the radical himself until the structure and confidence of society has been undermined by the enthronement of destructive criticism. Destructive criticism can certainly lead to revolution unless there are those willing to withstand the malice that flows in return from refutation. It has been well said that revolution is no summer thunderstorm clearing the atmosphere. In modern society it

is a tornado leaving in its path the destroyed homes of millions with their dead women and children.

[8] There are also those who insist that the future must be a repetition of the past; that ideas are dangerous, that ideals are freaks.

[9] To find that fine balance which links the future with the past, whose vision is of men and not of tools, that possesses the courage to construct rather than to criticize—this is our need. There is no oratory so easy, no writing so trenchant and vivid as the phrase-making of criticism and malice—there is none so difficult as inspiration to construction.

[10] We cannot ever afford to rest at ease in the comfortable assumption that right ideas always prevail by some virtue of their own. In the long run they do. But there can be and there have been periods of centuries when the world slumped back toward darkness merely because great masses of men became impregnated with wrong ideas and wrong social philosophies. The declines of civilization have been born of wrong ideas. Most of the wars of the world, including the recent one, have been fought by the advocates of contrasting ideas of social philosophy.

[11] The primary safeguard of American individualism is an under-standing of it; of faith that it is the most precious possession of American civilization, and a willingness courageously to test every process of national life upon the touchstone of this basic social premise. Development of the human institutions and of science and of industry have been long chains of trial and error. Our public relations to them and to other phases of our national life can be advanced in no other way than by a willingness to experiment in the remedy of our social faults. The failures and unsolved problems of economic and social life can be corrected; they can be solved within our social theme and under no other system. The solution is a matter of will to find solution; of a sense of duty as well as of a sense of right and citizenship. No one who buys "bootleg" whiskey can complain of gunmen and hoodlumism.

[12] Humanity has a long road to perfection, but we of America can make sure progress if we will preserve our individualism, if we will preserve and stimulate the initiative of our people, if we will build up our insistence and safeguards to equality of opportunity, if we will glorify service as a part of our national character. Progress will march if we hold an abiding faith in the intelligence, the initiative, the character, the courage, and the divine touch in the individual. We can safeguard these ends if we give to each individual that opportunity for which the spirit of America stands. We can make a social system as perfect as our

generation merits and one that will be received in gratitude by our children.

Questions

1. Why does Hoover refer to our "sort of individualism" and our "very form of government" (paragraph 1)?
2. What does Hoover mean when he says that individualism "evolved government without official emissaries to show the way" (paragraph 2)? Why does he say this? How accurate is this statement?
3. Hoover says, "Our individualism is rooted in our very nature. It is based on conviction born of experience" (paragraph 2). How would you assess the logic of these two sentences? Explain.
4. Hoover observes, ". . . the equal dangers both of reaction and radicalism" (paragraph 6). On which of these does he concentrate? Why? What inferences might you draw from his emphases?
5. Examine the language of paragraph 7. What are the connotations of the words used? Why is the "tornado" metaphor used?
6. What is Hoover's attitude toward "criticism and malice"? Why does he link these terms?
7. Hoover calls for "faith" in American individualism and urges "willingness courageously to test every process of national life upon the touchstone of this basic social premise" (paragraph 11). Is his thinking primarily inductive or deductive? Explain.
8. Does Hoover envision conformity as the direct opposite of individualism? If not, what does he perceive as the opposite to his "individualism"?
9. How would you describe the level of abstraction in this essay? How might the level of generality here relate to the effectiveness of this essay? Explain.

HOW FREE IS FREE?*

Morris Freedman

[1] The fundamental issue in the question of conformity is freedom. The nonconformist insists that only he is truly free. Only he resists the mass pressures of our contemporary society. Only he exercises individualism and independence. But, as I have tried to argue, it is in conformity that one finds the richest possibilities for varied, for authentic, for meaningful freedom. The freedom of nonconformity is an empty and idle freedom.

[2] My case is most obvious and easiest to prove, I suppose, against fashionable, conforming nonconformity. The exclusions, the taboos, the

enthusiasms, the stereotyped evaluations, the automatic responses—
these are as formalized for the professional nonconformist as the text
and movement of any church ritual. You can almost exactly predict the
behavior, the reactions, the very words and gestures of this ritualist
under all sorts of conditions and stimuli. Coffee houses, east coast and
west coast and in between, are crawling with identical types. It is not
that there is some kind of central organization, a nonconformist union,
laying down rules of speech and behavior, details of costume. It's
simply that the patterns of nonconformism are ready at hand for anyone
to adopt once you accept the basic premise that anything popular or
conventional or supported by a majority or catering to the people is in
and of itself bad: advertising, popular songs, movies, automobiles, ties,
ranch houses. The mechanical nonconformists betray their cause in the
very process of advocating it: as I have said, they are eager to ram
their values down everyone's throat. Nor is it necessary to adopt the
code of the nonconformist in every detail to practice occasional and
partial nonconformism with as much smug satisfaction as the fanatic.

[3] But I think I can make my point even if I exclude the mindless
robots. Nonconformism, if it remains true to itself, must ultimately become free-floating, asocial, abstract, unrelated to a context. The absolute nonconformist, of course, would be the man on a desert island. This
is extreme, obviously, but we often see close approximations to this
ideal.

[4] The desert-island nonconformist differs from the fashionable one
as much as he does from the conformist himself. The desert-island man
lives without a society around him. He knows little of the news, nothing
about popular things; he cannot carry on social conversations; he is
unaware of his dress; he does not vote or listen to the radio or watch
television; in short, he carries around him total insulation from the daily
world. He lives at the heart of an egocentric circle. If he is an expert in
a particular field, he is likely to be ignorant of contiguous or parallel
fields, let alone unrelated ones.

[5] What kind of freedom is this? Robinson Crusoe on his island had
this freedom. Anyone isolated from the rest of mankind—the lighthouse
keeper, the weather-station man in the Arctic, the savage in the jungle
—has this freedom. If we live in any society, we live, as Rousseau defined the matter, by a social contract. We live with a consciousness of
the presence and needs of other persons.

[6] The desert-island nonconformist may have the excuse for his
isolation that he is not willful; he is simply unaware. His behavior, his
alienation, is not a matter of ideology but of personality. It is instinctive, not chosen. Whatever his excuse or explanation, the fact remains

that he is at the extreme end of nonconformism. He is indeed an ideal for many conscious conformists. While in society, he is simultaneously outside it. He has his cake while he eats it.

[7] But is not such a type as trapped by his limitations as Crusoe was? Are not all sorts of experiences and possibilities closed to him? Consider the nonconformists who boast of not ever watching television or going to the movies or nightclubs or paying attention to advertisements. Nonconformism in such instances is not the free exercise of taste. It is not connected with the reasoned rejection of a particular object. It rejects everything in a class. This is not discrimination any more than the Russian rejection of anything capitalistic is a matter of choice. This is behavior of the most restricted, most imprisoned sort. Our professional nonconformists are as much prisoners of their reflexes as Pavlov's dogs.

[8] It is certainly nothing new to say that freedom can only exist within society. Society after all is responsible for creature comforts. Only society offers any real possibilities for minimizing poverty, for easing ill health. Poor and diseased, how free can we be? But society offers everything else in addition to basic comforts. Our freedom means something only insofar as we can think, talk, act, move about freely (within the usual limits that our freedom does not infringe on anyone else's). We can think only in the contexts of history, of knowledge, of acquaintance with writings and works of art. We can feel only in relation to ourselves and other persons. These are social things. It would mean nothing to say we could talk or move about freely if there were not the means to do either widely: freedom of speech in a public park or at the American exposition in Moscow (reported by some of the American aides of outspoken Russian visitors criticizing their governments) do not compare with such freedom in the press or on radio or television, all social media; the right to move about means little without the socially created devices of the train, the plane, the automobile. What does it mean to feel freely if we cannot express or suggest our feelings in some social way?

[9] The great complaint nonconformists make about society, of course, is that it restricts thought, speech, behavior; that it imposes values, judgments, tastes. Conformism to them is opposed to individualism, to uniqueness. But it must be clear to anyone of independent mind that conformism in the western world in the mid-twentieth century encourages and rewards handsomely all sorts of cranky, crotchety, highly individualistic responses. Some of the most popular books on the best-seller lists week after week are tracts against our times, against cars, against advertising, against movies, against schools, against big com-

panies, against politics. Indeed many of these conform so totally to a pattern of tone that they are anything but unique. These books are often nothing but a violation of the quite genuine freedom within our "conformist" society: they pretend to be daring and bold and iconoclastic; they are often nothing more than sophomoric, repetitive, and flatulent. If I were looking for evidence to *prove* that our society was actually a conforming one, I would cite just these shallow pretensions to independently critical thought.

.   .   .   .

[10] Over and over again we can cite from our personal experiences examples of conservatives and "conformists" who are far more tolerant, independent, original than the persons we know who insist on flaunting their identity as "liberals" and "nonconformists." An acquaintance of mine who parrots current nonconformist slogans as earnestly as any church dogma once described himself to me as "one hundred and ten per cent nonconformist." (At that he may have been right: exceeding one hundred per cent, he may have been turning back on himself.) Nonconformists are prone to label by stereotypes, to see the world and all its issues and all its peoples in monochromatic black or white.

[11] As one looks at the current social scene without blinders or distorting lenses, I think he will clearly see that our so-called conformists, our Babbitts and "conservatives," grant more freedom to dissenters than our self-styled non-conformists—beatniks, bohemians, and bums though they may be. Nonconformists are so insistent on easy, glib, all-inclusive labels because they are, after all, lonely and lost. They are air people, floating away from society in balloons; they want company on their lonely, vagrant journeys. And since they, like all persons, need a sense of society, they create a kind of anti-society, in which all the usual values of society are sternly turned topsy-turvy. Their freedom is like the freedom of persons under Communism; their love is the love of 1984; their final nonconformity is a thoroughly disciplined conformity.

[12] Freedom cannot exist in a vacuum. Freedom has meaning only in a context: free where? free when? free to do what? free from whom? In Shaw's play *Saint Joan*, Joan rejects the "freedom" to remain alive if she has to remain so for the rest of her days in prison. Shaw knew what freedom meant under all circumstances; it was never simply a gesture unrelated to a time and a place. Was not Socrates the object of attack of the "enlightened thinkers" of his society?

[13] Conformists recognize that freedom is rooted not only in a society but in an individual. We can be free only to the degree that this

means something in society and to the degree that it means something to us personally. How free is the person driven by unconscious forces? It is the nonconformist who is arrogant about his independence. He rejects the notion that he may be his own worst censor, his own worst tyrant. All of Freudian theory is rooted in a full, deep, circumstantial sense of society, past and present, in all of its dimensions. Freud was entirely a man of his milieu. Freudians recognize well that conformism need not be an escape or an evasion of true individuality, but may be an aid to it. We must recognize reality, know where we are, before we can leave it. The nonconformists in their bursts and fits of alienation are always making fairy-tale journeys. They are terrified by bogeymen and mirages. Only the conformists can make real departures, can arrive anywhere.

[14] The conformism I talk about, it must be clear, is not the empty minded, follow-the-leader kind of thing nonconformists are always so gleefully and cheaply attacking. But even follow-the-leader conformism is less invidious than doctrinaire nonconformism, because it makes no pretense of being anything but conformism; it simply does not know any better.

[15] The conformism I have in mind, the sort in which real liberty is rooted, is merely based on a recognition of reality, on an acceptance of the limitations of existence (both social and individual), and on an indifference to affectations and poses advertising some phony uniqueness. One mark of the genuinely free man is that he will not casually make a value judgment as to the comparative merit in and of themselves of an abstract conformism or nonconformism *out of context*. The truly free man does not find it necessary to prove his freedom either by asserting it blatantly for himself or denying its presence contemptuously in others. He is free to make the multitudes of decisions and responses it is necessary to make to live with the greatest self-realization and self-expression in our world; he is not bound by any party to predetermined stands. He can like or not like a particular wine. He can choose to buy or not to buy a particular automobile. He can choose to follow or ignore fashion—in furniture, clothes, politics, movies, music, writing, foods, homes. He can choose to vote or not to vote for the current great liberal. He can afford to exercise this kind of gross independence because he knows that only so can he be free, free of the petty nose-thumbing of rejection, free of the thoughtless embraces of acceptance.

[16] Perhaps what we need, here as in so many other places, is a new vocabulary. The barbarous phrase "conforming nonconformist" is ac-

curate enough, but it is clearly paradoxical. All I am criticizing, I hope it is clear, is conformism, blind acceptance of any dogma, however it masks itself, however much it pretends to be nonconformism. I do believe that in the present scene nonconformism has betrayed itself shabbily. It has been guilty of far more dishonesty and distortion and deception than the most narrow conformism has ever been. Nonconformism for intellectuals—for persons of any sophistication and character—seems to me bankrupt.

[17] I speak well of conformists, and I identify myself as one (to my astonishment), because I find in it much healthier possibilities than in contemporary nonconformism. Precisely because I do believe that "individuality" and "independence" are to be cherished, I argue against a nonconformist cant which insists on defining "individuality" and "independence" by mob logic and mob technique. I assert that creativity and originality never follow patterns; I believe that they must be related to a responsive and responsible sense of the total world; I suggest that they may come most meaningfully in our time from that sort of conformism which works within the more limited bounds of necessity and possibility rather than those extravagantly unlimited ones of an arrogant willfulness.

[18] Whenever I confess to conformism defiantly, I feel silly. One should not really take seriously the ominous strictures, the finger-pointing postures, of our nonconformist oracles. These prophetic discussions of our times are often about as profound as an exchange at the office water-cooler. In this respect, I suppose I am, without qualification or apology, a genuine enough conformist. The world's issues are more important than the problems that bother us daily, the ones concerned with chrome or coffee or calypso. There are the classical concerns of history and art, life and study, scholarship and science, philosophy and love. I am happy to confess that I am the sort of conformist who finds himself in the end bored by diatribes, frivolous or earnest, against fleeting phenomena. Even fashionable nonconformism, oppressive as it is, may, in the large perspective, be only a temporary aberration. At least, I hope we can make it so.

Questions

1. Why does Freedman use the word *ritualist* in paragraph 2?
2. Why is reference made to Rousseau and the "social contract" (paragraph 5)?
3. Analyze the logic of Freedman's arguments in paragraph 9.
4. What persuasive devices are employed in paragraph 10? Discuss their appropriateness.
5. Freedman says that "conservatives" are more likely to grant freedom than "nonconformists." Does he support this assertion?

6. What assumption does Freedman make in his reference to Socrates (paragraph 12)? Does he support his assumption?
7. Freedman equates "conformism" and the "genuinely free man." Why?
8. The closing paragraph says that the "world's issues are more important than the problems that bother us daily." Why is this statement made?
9. Freedman closes with a statement about being "bored by diatribes." What does he imply? Why? Do you find any evidence of "diatribes" in his chapter?

From THE LONELY CROWD*

David Riesman with Nathan Glazer and Reuel Denney

. . . The link between character and society—certainly not the only one, but one of the most significant, and the one I choose to emphasize in this discussion—is to be found in the way in which society ensures some degree of conformity from the individuals who make it up. In each society, such a mode of ensuring conformity is built into the child, and then either encouraged or frustrated in later adult experience. . . .

One of the categories I make use of is taken from demography, the science that deals with birth rates and death rates, with the absolute and relative numbers of people in a society, and their distribution by age, sex, and other variables, for I tentatively seek to link certain social and characterological developments, as cause and effect, with certain population shifts in Western society since the Middle Ages.

It seems reasonably well established, despite the absence of reliable figures for earlier centuries, that during this period the curve of population growth in the Western countries has shown an S-shape of a particular type (as other countries are drawn more closely into the net of Western civilization, their populations also show a tendency to develop along the lines of this S-shaped curve). The bottom horizontal line of the S represents a situation where the total population does not increase or does so very slowly, for the number of births equals roughly the number of deaths, and both are very high. In societies of this type, a high proportion of the population is young, life expectancy is low, and the turnover of generations is extremely rapid. Such societies are said to be in the phase of "high growth potential"; for should something happen to decrease the very high death rate (greater production of food, new sanitary measures, new knowledge of the causes of disease, and so on), a "population explosion" would result, and the population would increase very rapidly. This in effect is what happened in the West, starting with the seventeenth century. This spurt in population was most marked in Europe, and the countries settled by Europeans, in the nineteenth century. It is represented by the vertical bar of the S. Demographers call this the stage of "transitional growth," because the birth rate soon begins to follow the death rate in its decline. The rate of growth then slows down, and demographers begin to detect in the growing proportion of middle-aged and aged in the population the signs of a third stage, "incipient population decline." Societies in this stage are represented by the top horizontal bar of the S, again indicating, as in the first stage, that total population growth is small—but this time because births and deaths are low. . . .

. . . Each of these three different phases on the population curve appears to be occupied by a society that enforces conformity and molds social character in a definably different way.

The society of high growth potential develops in its typical members a social character whose conformity is insured by their tendency to follow tradition: these I shall term *tradition-directed* people and the society in which they live *a society dependent on tradition-direction.*

The society of transitional population growth develops in its typical members a social character whose conformity is insured by their tendency to acquire early in life an internalized set of goals. These I shall term *inner-directed* people and the society in which they live *a society dependent on inner-direction.*

Finally, the society of incipient population decline develops in its typical members a social character whose conformity is insured by their tendency to be sensitized to the expectations and preferences of others. These I shall term *other-directed* people and the society in which they live one *dependent on other-direction.* . . .

A definition of tradition-direction. Since the type of social order we have been discussing is relatively unchanging, the conformity of the individual tends to be dictated to a very large degree by power relations among the various age and sex groups, the clans, castes, professions, and so forth—relations which have endured for centuries and are modified but slightly, if at all, by successive generations. The culture controls behavior minutely, and, while the rules are not so complicated that the young cannot learn them during the period of intensive socialization, careful and rigid etiquette governs the fundamentally influential sphere of kin relationships. Moreover, the culture, in addition to its economic tasks, or as part of them, provides ritual, routine, and religion to occupy and to orient everyone. Little energy is directed toward finding new solutions of the age-old problems, let us say, of agricultural technique or "medicine," the problems to which people are acculturated.

It is not to be thought, however, that in these societies, where the activity of the individual member is determined by characterologically grounded obedience to traditions, the individual may not be highly prized and, in many instances, encouraged to develop his capabilities, his initiative, and even, within very narrow time limits, his aspirations. Indeed, the individual in some primitive societies is far more appreciated and respected than in some sectors of modern society. For the individual in a society dependent on tradition-direction has a well-defined functional relationship to other members of the group. If he is not killed off, he "belongs"—he is not "surplus," as the modern unemployed are surplus, nor is he expendable as the unskilled are expendable in modern society. . . .

In societies in which tradition-direction is the dominant mode of insuring conformity, relative stability is preserved in part by the infrequent but highly important process of fitting into institutionalized roles such deviants as there are. In such societies a person who might have become at a later historical stage an innovator or rebel, whose belonging, as such, is marginal and problematic, is drawn instead into roles like those of the shaman or sorcerer. That is, he is drawn into roles that make a socially acceptable contribution, while at the same time they provide the individual with a more or less approved niche. The medieval monastic orders may have served in a similar way to absorb many characterological mutations.

In some of these societies certain individuals are encouraged toward a degree of individuality from childhood, especially if they belong to families of high status. But, since the range of choice, even for high-status people, is minimal, the apparent social need for an individuated type of character is also minimal. It is probably accurate to say that character structure in these societies is very largely "adjusted," in the sense that for most people it appears to be in tune with social institutions. Even the few misfits "fit" to a degree; and only very rarely is one driven out of his social world.

This does not mean, of course, that the people are happy; the society to whose traditions they are adjusted may be a miserable one, ridden with anxiety, sadism, and disease. The point is rather that change, while never completely absent in human affairs, is slowed down. . . .

A definition of inner-direction. In western history the society that emerged with the Renaissance and Reformation and that is only now vanishing serves to illustrate the type of society in which inner-direction is the principal mode of securing conformity. Such a society is characterized by increased personal mobility, by a rapid accumulation of capital (teamed with devastating technological shifts), and by an almost constant *expansion:* intensive expansion in the production of goods and people, and extensive expansion in exploration, colonization, and imperialism. The greater choices this society gives—and the greater initiatives it demands in order to cope with its novel problems—are handled by character types who can manage to live socially without strict and self-evident tradition-direction. These are the inner-directed types. . . .

. . . *The source of direction for the individual is "inner" in the sense that it is implanted early in life by the elders and directed toward generalized but nonetheless inescapably destined goals.*

We can see what this means when we realize that, in societies in which tradition-direction is the dominant mode of insuring conformity, attention is focused on securing external *behavioral* conformity. While behavior is minutely prescribed, individuality of character need not be highly developed to meet prescriptions that are objectified in ritual and etiquette—though to be sure, a social character *capable* of such behavioral attention and obedience is requisite. By contrast, societies in which inner-direction becomes important, though they also are concerned with behavioral conformity, cannot be satisfied with behavioral conformity alone. Too many novel situations are presented, situations which a code cannot encompass in advance. . . .

. . . While any society dependent on inner-direction seems to present people with a wide choice of aims—such as money, possessions, power, knowledge, fame, goodness—these aims are ideologically interrelated, and the selection made by any one individual remains relatively unalterable throughout his life. Moreover, the means to those ends, though not fitted into as tight a social frame of reference as in the society dependent on tradition-direction, are nevertheless limited by the new voluntary associations—for instance, the Quakers, the Masons, the Mechanics' Associations—to which people tie themselves. Indeed, the term "tradition-direction" could be misleading if the reader were to conclude that the force of tradition has no weight for the inner-directed character. On the contrary, he is very considerably bound by traditions: they limit his ends and inhibit his choice of means. The point is rather that a splintering of tradition takes place, connected in part with the increasing division of labor and stratification of society. Even if the individual's choice of tradition is largely determined for him by his family, as it is in most cases, he cannot help becoming aware of the existence of competing traditions—hence of tradition as such. As a result he possesses a somewhat greater degree of flexibility in adapting himself to ever changing requirements and in return requires more from his environment. . . .

The tradition-directed person, as has been said, hardly thinks of himself as an individual. Still less does it occur to him that he might shape his own destiny in terms of personal, lifelong goals or that the destiny of his children might be separate from that of the family group. He is not sufficiently separated psychologically from himself (or, therefore, sufficiently close to himself), his family, or group to think in these terms. In the phase of transitional growth, however, people of inner-directed character do gain a feeling of control over their own lives and see their children also as individuals with careers to make. At the same time, with the shift out of agriculture and, later, with the end of child labor, children no longer become an unequivocal economic asset. And with the growth of habits of scientific thought, religious and magical views of human fertility—views that in an earlier phase of the population curve made sense for the culture if it was to reproduce itself—give way to "rational," individualistic attitudes. Indeed, just as the rapid accumulation of productive capital requires that people be imbued with the "Protestant ethic" (as Max Weber characterized one manifestation of what is here termed inner-direction), so also the decreased number of progeny requires a profound change in values—a change so deep that, in all probability, it has to be rooted in character structure.

As the birth rate begins to follow the death rate downward, societies move toward the epoch of incipient decline of population. Fewer and fewer people work on the land or in the extractive industries or even in manufacturing. Hours are short. People may have material abundance and leisure besides. They pay for these changes however—here, as always, the solution of old problems gives rise to new ones—by finding themselves in a centralized and bureaucratized society and a world shrunken and agitated by the contact—accelerated by industrialization —of races, nations, and cultures. . . .

A definition of other-direction. The type of character I shall describe as other-directed seems to be emerging in very recent years in the upper middle class of our larger cities: more prominently in New York than in Boston, in Los Angeles than in Spokane, in Cincinnati than in Chillicothe. . . . [He] is said to be shallower, freer with his money, friendlier, more uncertain of himself and his values, more demanding of approval. . . .

It is my impression that the middle-class American of today is decisively different from those Americans of Tocqueville's writings who nevertheless strike us as so contemporary, and much of this book will be

devoted to discussing these differences. It is also my impression that
the conditions I believe to be responsible for other-direction are affecting increasing numbers of people in the metropolitan centers of
the advanced industrial countries. My analysis of the other-directed
character is thus at once an analysis of the American and of contemporary man. Much of the time I find it hard or impossible to say where
one ends and the other begins. Tentatively, I am inclined to think that
the other-directed type does find itself most at home in America, due
to certain unique elements in American society, such as its recruit-
ment from Europe and its lack of any feudal past. As against this, I am
also inclined to put more weight on capitalism, industrialism, and urbanization—these being international tendencies—than on any charac-
ter-forming peculiarities of the American scene.

Bearing these qualifications in mind, it seems appropriate to treat
contemporary metropolitan America as our illustration of a society—so
far, perhaps, the only illustration—in which other-direction is the
dominant mode of insuring conformity. It would be premature, however, to say that it is already the dominant mode in America as a
whole. But since the other-directed types are to be found among the
young, in the larger cities, and among the upper income groups, we
may assume that, unless present trends are reversed, the hegemony of
other-direction lies not far off.

If we wanted to cast our social character types into social class molds,
we could say that inner-direction is the typical character of the "old"
middle class—the banker, the tradesman, the small entrepreneur, the
technically oriented engineer, etc.—while other-direction is becoming
the typical character of the "new" middle class—the bureaucrat, the
salaried employee in business, etc. . . .

. . . *What is common to all the other-directed people is that their
contemporaries are the source of direction for the individual—either
those known to him or those with whom he is indirectly acquainted,
through friends and through the mass media. This source is of course
"internalized" in the sense that dependence on it for guidance in life is
implanted early. The goals toward which the other-directed person
strives shift with that guidance: it is only the process of striving itself
and the process of paying close attention to the signals from others that
remain unaltered throughout life.* This mode of keeping in touch with
others permits a close behavioral conformity, not through drill in behavior itself, as in the tradition-directed character, but rather through
an exceptional sensitivity to the actions and wishes of others.

Of course, it matters very much who these "others" are: whether they
are the individual's immediate circle or a "higher" circle or the anony-

mous voices of the mass media; whether the individual fears the hostility of chance acquaintances or only of those who "count." But his
need for approval and direction from others—and contemporary others
rather than ancestors—goes beyond the reasons that lead most people
in any era to care very much what others think of them. While all
people want and need to be liked by some of the people some of the
time, it is only the modern other-directed types who make this their
chief source of direction and chief area of sensitivity. . . .

. . . The inner-directed person, though he often sought and sometimes achieved a relative independence of public opinion and of what
the neighbors thought of him, was in most cases very much concerned
with his good repute and, at least in America, with "keeping up with
the Joneses." These conformities, however, were primarily external, typified in such details as clothes, curtains, and bank credit. For, indeed,
the conformities were to a standard, evidence of which was provided
by the "best people" in one's milieu. In contrast with this pattern, the
other-directed person, though he has his eye very much on the Joneses,
aims to keep up with them not so much in external details as in the
quality of his inner experience. That is, his great sensitivity keeps him
in touch with others on many more levels than the externals of appearance and propriety. . . .

The three types compared. One way to see the structural differences
between the three types is to see the differences in the emotional sanction or control in each type.

The tradition-directed person feels the impact of his culture as a
unit, but it is nevertheless mediated through the specific, small number
of individuals with whom he is in daily contact. These expect of him
not so much that he be a certain type of person but that he behave in
the approved way. Consequently the sanction for behavior tends to be
the fear of being *shamed.*

The inner-directed person has early incorporated a psychic gyroscope
which is set going by his parents and can receive signals later on from
other authorities who resemble his parents. He goes through life less
independent than he seems, obeying this internal piloting. Getting off
course, whether in response to inner impulses or to the fluctuating
voices of contemporaries, may lead to the feeling of *guilt.*

Since the direction to be taken in life has been learned in the privacy
of the home from a small number of guides and since principles, rather
than details of behavior, are internalized, the inner-directed person is
capable of great stability. . . .

Contrasted with such a type as this, the other-directed person learns
to respond to signals from a far wider circle than is constituted by his

parents. The family is no longer a closely knit unit to which he belongs but merely part of a wider social environment to which he early becomes attentive. In these respects the other-directed person resembles the tradition-directed person: both live in a group milieu and lack the inner-directed person's capacity to go it alone. . . .

The tradition-directed person takes his signals from others, but they come in a cultural monotone; he needs no complex receiving equipment to pick them up. The other-directed person must be able to receive signals from far and near; the sources are many, the changes rapid. What can be internalized, then, is not a code of behavior but the elaborate equipment needed to attend to such messages and occasionally to participate in their circulation. As against guilt-and-shame controls, though of course these survive, one prime psychological lever of the other-directed person is a diffuse *anxiety*. This control equipment, instead of being like a gyroscope, is like a radar. . . .

. . . If a predominantly other-directed individual were placed in an environment without peers, he might fall back on other patterns of direction. Similarly, it is clear that no individual, and assuredly no society, ever exists without a heavy reliance on tradition, much as this may appear to be overlaid by swings of fashion.

It is important to emphasize these overlappings of the several types in part because of the value judgments that readers are likely to attach to each type in isolation. Since most of us value independence we are likely to prefer the inner-directed type and overlook two things. First, the gyroscopic mechanism allows the inner-directed person to appear far more independent than he really is: he is no less a conformist to others than the other-directed person, but the voices to which he listens are more distant, of an older generation, their cues internalized in his childhood. Second, as just indicated, this type of conformity is only one, though the predominant, mechanism of the inner-directed type: the latter is not characteristically insensitive to what his peers think of him, and may even be opportunistic in the highest degree. Thus, he need not always react to other people as if they were merely stand-ins for his parents. Rather, the point is that he is somewhat less concerned than the other-directed person with continuously obtaining from contemporaries (or their stand-ins: the mass media) a flow of guidance, expectation, and approbation. . . .

. . . Tradition-direction seems to be dominant in Latin America, agricultural southern Europe, in Asia and Africa. Inner-directed types seem to be dominant in rural and small-town United States and Canada, in northwestern Europe, and to a degree in Central Europe. One notices an energetic campaign to introduce the inner-directed pattern in eastern Europe, in Turkey, and in parts of Asia. And one notices the beginnings of dominance by other-directed types in the metropolitan centers of the United States and, more doubtfully, their emergence in the big cities of northwestern Europe. This last and newest type is spreading outward into areas where inner-direction still prevails, just as the latter is spreading into unconquered areas where tradition-directed types still hang on. . . .

Questions

1. What fundamental assumption do you find in the first paragraph?
2. State in your own words what is meant by "tradition-directed," "inner-directed," and "other-directed" people.
3. How do the authors think the three groups above are related to the population curve?
4. What observations do they make about "happiness" in relation to types of people?
5. What do they say about the force of tradition for the inner-directed person? Why do you suppose they make this point?
6. The other-directed person is described as emerging from New York rather than Boston, Los Angeles rather than Spokane, Cincinnati rather than Chillicothe. Why?
7. Why do the authors say that the inner-directed person is "less independent than he seems"?
8. What is the tone of these excerpts from *The Lonely Crowd*? How do you explain the tone?

THE INDIVIDUAL AND THE PATTERN OF CULTURE*

Ruth Benedict

[1] There is no proper antagonism between the rôle of society and that of the individual. One of the most misleading misconceptions due to this nineteenth-century dualism was the idea that what was subtracted from society was added to the individual and what was subtracted from the individual was added to society. Philosophies of freedom, political creeds of *laissez faire*, revolutions that have unseated dynasties, have been built on this dualism. The quarrel in anthropological theory between the importance of the culture pattern and of the in-

---

* The selection from Ruth Benedict, *Patterns of Culture*, copyright 1934, is reprinted by permission of and arrangement with Houghton Mifflin Company, the authorized publishers.

dividual is only a small ripple from this fundamental conception of the nature of society.

[2] In reality, society and the individual are not antagonists. His culture provides the raw material of which the individual makes his life. If it is meagre, the individual suffers; if it is rich, the individual has the chance to rise to his opportunity. Every private interest of every man and woman is served by the enrichment of the traditional stores of his civilization. The richest musical sensitivity can operate only within the equipment and standards of its tradition. It will add, perhaps importantly, to that tradition, but its achievement remains in proportion to the instruments and musical theory which the culture has provided. In the same fashion a talent for observation expends itself in some Melanesian tribe upon the negligible borders of the magico-religious field. For a realization of its potentialities it is dependent upon the development of scientific methodology, and it has no fruition unless the culture has elaborated the necessary concepts and tools.

[3] The man in the street still thinks in terms of a necessary antagonism between society and the individual. In large measure this is because in our civilization the regulative activities of society are singled out, and we tend to identify society with the restrictions the law imposes upon us. The law lays down the number of miles per hour that I may drive an automobile. If it takes this restriction away, I am by that much the freer. This basis for a fundamental antagonism between society and the individual is naïve indeed when it is extended as a basic philosophical and political notion. Society is only incidentally and in certain situations regulative, and law is not equivalent to the social order. In the simpler homogeneous cultures collective habit or custom may quite supersede the necessity for any development of formal legal authority. American Indians sometimes say: "In the old days, there were no fights about hunting grounds or fishing territories. There was no law then, so everybody did what was right." The phrasing makes it clear that in their old life they did not think of themselves as submitting to a social control imposed upon them from without. Even in our civilization the law is never more than a crude implement of society, and one it is often enough necessary to check in its arrogant career. It is never to be read off as if it were the equivalent of the social order.

[4] Society in its full sense . . . is never an entity separable from the individuals who compose it. No individual can arrive even at the threshold of his potentialities without a culture in which he participates. Conversely, no civilization has in it any element which in the last analysis is not the contribution of an individual. Where else could any

trait come from except from the behaviour of a man or a woman or a child?

[5] It is largely because of the traditional acceptance of a conflict between society and the individual, that emphasis upon cultural be- haviour is so often interpreted as a denial of the autonomy of the indi- vidual. The reading of Sumner's *Folkways* usually rouses a protest at the limitations such an interpretation places upon the scope and initia- tive of the individual. Anthropology is often believed to be a counsel of despair which makes untenable a beneficent human illusion. But no anthropologist with a background of experience of other cultures has ever believed that individuals were automatons, mechanically carrying out the decrees of their civilization. No culture yet observed has been able to eradicate the differences in the temperaments of the persons who compose it. It is always a give-and-take. The problem of the indi- vidual is not clarified by stressing the antagonism between culture and the individual, but by stressing their mutual reinforcement. This rap- port is so close that it is not possible to discuss patterns of culture with- out considering specifically their relation to individual psychology.

[6] We have seen that any society selects some segment of the arc of possible human behaviour, and insofar as it achieves integration its in- stitutions tend to further the expression of its selected segment and to inhibit opposite expressions. But these opposite expressions are the congenial responses, nevertheless, of a certain proportion of the carriers of the culture. We have already discussed the reasons for believing that this selection is primarily cultural and not biological. We cannot, there- fore, even on theoretical grounds imagine that all the congenial re- sponses of all its people will be equally served by the institutions of any culture. To understand the behaviour of the individual, it is not merely necessary to relate his personal life-history to his endowments, and to measure these against an arbitrarily selected normality. It is necessary also to relate his congenial responses to the behaviour that is singled out in the institutions of his culture.

[7] The vast proportion of all individuals who are born into any so- ciety always and whatever the idiosyncrasies of its institutions, assume . . . the behaviour dictated by that society. This fact is always inter- preted by the carriers of that culture as being due to the fact that their particular institutions reflect an ultimate and universal sanity. The actual reason is quite different. Most people are shaped to the form of their culture because of the enormous malleability of their original en- dowment. They are plastic to the moulding force of the society into which they are born. It does not matter whether it requires delusions of

self-reference, or with our own civilization the amassing of possessions. In any case the great mass of individuals take quite readily the form that is presented to them.

[8] They do not all, however, find it equally congenial, and those are favoured and fortunate whose potentialities most nearly coincide with the type of behaviour selected by their society. Those who, in a situation in which they are frustrated, naturally seek ways of putting the occasion out of sight as expeditiously as possible are well served in Pueblo culture. Southwest institutions . . . minimize the situations in which serious frustration can arise, and when it cannot be avoided, as in death, they provide means to put it behind them with all speed.

[9] On the other hand, those who react to frustration as to an insult and whose first thought is to get even are amply provided for on the Northwest Coast. They may extend their native reaction to situations in which their paddle breaks or their canoe overturns or to the loss of relatives by death. They rise from their first reaction of sulking to thrust back in return, to "fight" with property or with weapons. Those who can assuage despair by the act of bringing shame to others can register freely and without conflict in this society, because their proclivities are deeply channelled in their culture. In Dobu those whose first impulse is to select a victim and project their misery upon him in procedures of punishment are equally fortunate. . . .

[10] In any group of individuals we can recognize those to whom . . . different reactions to frustration and grief are congenial: ignoring it, indulging it by uninhibited expression, getting even, punishing a victim, and seeking restitution of the original situation. In the psychiatric records of our own society, some of these impulses are recognized as bad ways of dealing with the situation, some as good. The bad ones are said to lead to maladjustments and insanities, the good ones to adequate social functioning. It is clear, however, that the correlation does not lie between any one "bad" tendency and abnormality in any absolute sense. The desire to run away from grief, to leave it behind at all costs, does not foster psychotic behaviour where, as among the Pueblos, it is mapped out by institutions and supported by every attitude of the group. The Pueblos are not a neurotic people. Their culture gives the impression of fostering mental health. Similarly, the paranoid attitudes so violently expressed among the Kwakiutl are known in psychiatric theory derived from our own civilization as thoroughly "bad"; that is, they lead in various ways to the breakdown of personality. But it is just those individuals among the Kwakiutl who

find it congenial to give the freest expression to these attitudes who nevertheless are the leaders of Kwakiutl society and find greatest personal fulfilment in its culture.

[11] Obviously, adequate personal adjustment does not depend upon following certain motivations and eschewing others. The correlation is in a different direction. Just as those are favoured whose congenial responses are closest to that behaviour which characterizes their society, so those are disoriented whose congenial responses fall in that arc of behaviour which is not capitalized by their culture. These abnormals are those who are not supported by the institutions of their civilization. They are the exceptions who have not easily taken the traditional forms of their culture.

.   .   .   .

[12] Most ethnologists have had . . . experiences in recognizing that the persons who are put outside the pale of society with contempt are not those who would be placed there by another culture. Lowie found among the Crow Indians of the plains a man of exceptional knowledge of his cultural forms. He was interested in considering these objectively and in correlating different facets. He had an interest in genealogical facts and was invaluable on points of history. Altogether he was an ideal interpreter of Crow life. These traits, however, were not those which were the password to honour among the Crow. He had a definite shrinking from physical danger, and bravado was the tribal virtue. To make matters worse he had attempted to gain recognition by claiming a war honour which was fraudulent. He was proved not to have brought in, as he claimed, a picketed horse from the enemy's camp. To lay false claim to war honours was a paramount sin among the Crow, and by the general opinion, constantly reiterated, he was regarded as irresponsible and incompetent.

[13] Such situations can be paralleled with the attitude in our civilization toward a man who does not succeed in regarding personal posessions as supremely important. Our hobo population is constantly fed by those to whom the accumulation of property is not a sufficient motivation. In case these individuals ally themselves with the hoboes, public opinion regards them as potentially vicious, as indeed because of the asocial situation into which they are thrust they readily become. In case, however, these men compensate by emphasizing their artistic temperament and become members of expatriated groups of petty artists, opinion regards them not as vicious but as silly. In any case

they are unsupported by the forms of their society, and the effort to express themselves satisfactorily is ordinarily a greater task than they can achieve.

[14] The dilemma of such an individual is often most successfully solved by doing violence to his strongest natural impulses and accepting the rôle the culture honours. In case he is a person to whom social recognition is necessary, it is ordinarily his only possible course. One of the most striking individuals in Zuñi had accepted this necessity. In a society that thoroughly distrusts authority of any sort, he had a native personal magnetism that singled him out in any group. In a society that exalts moderation and the easiest way, he was turbulent and could act violently upon occasion. In a society that praises a pliant personality that "talks lots"—that is, that chatters in a friendly fashion—he was scornful and aloof. Zuñi's only reaction to such personalities is to brand them as witches. He was said to have been seen peering through a window from outside, and this is a sure mark of a witch. At any rate, he got drunk one day and boasted that they could not kill him. He was taken before the war priests who hung him by his thumbs from the rafters till he should confess to his witchcraft. This is the usual procedure in a charge of witchcraft. . . .

[15] The individuals we have so far discussed are not in any sense psychopathic. They illustrate the dilemma of the individual whose congenial drives are not provided for in the institutions of his culture. This dilemma becomes of psychiatric importance when the behaviour in question is regarded as categorically abnormal in a society. Western civilization tends to regard even a mild homosexual as an abnormal. The clinical picture of homosexuality stresses the neuroses and psychoses to which it gives rise, and emphasizes almost equally the inadequate functioning of the invert and his behaviour. We have only to turn to other cultures, however, to realize that homosexuals have by no means been uniformly inadequate to the social situation. They have not always failed to function. In some societies they have even been especially acclaimed. Plato's *Republic* is, of course, the most convincing statement of the honourable estate of homosexuality. It is presented as a major means to the good life, and Plato's high ethical evaluation of this response was upheld in the customary behaviour of Greece at that period.

[16] The American Indians do not make Plato's high moral claims for homosexuality, but homosexuals are often regarded as exceptionally able. In most of North America there exists the institution of the *berdache*, as the French called them. These men-women were men who at

puberty or thereafter took the dress and occupations of women. Sometimes they married other men and lived with them. Sometimes they
were men with no inversion, persons of weak sexual endowment who
chose this rôle to avoid the jeers of the women. The berdaches were
never regarded as of first-rate supernatural power, as similar men-
women were in Siberia, but rather as leaders in women's occupations,
good healers in certain diseases, or, among certain tribes, as the genial
organizers of social affairs. They were usually, in spite of the manner
in which they were accepted, regarded with a certain embarrassment.
It was thought slightly ridiculous to address as "she" a person who was
known to be a man and who, as in Zuñi, would be buried on the men's
side of the cemetery. But they were socially placed. The emphasis in
most tribes was upon the fact that men who took over women's occupations excelled by reason of their strength and initiative and were therefore leaders in women's techniques and in the accumulation of those
forms of property made by women. One of the best known of all the
Zuñis of a generation ago was the man-woman We-wha, who was, in
the words of his friend, Mrs. Stevenson, "certainly the strongest person
in Zuñi, both mentally and physically." His remarkable memory for
ritual made him a chief personage on ceremonial occasions, and his
strength and intelligence made him a leader in all kinds of crafts.

[17] The men-women of Zuñi are not all strong, self-reliant personages. Some of them take this refuge to protect themselves against their
inability to take part in men's activities. One is almost a simpleton, and
one, hardly more than a little boy, has delicate features like a girl's.
There are obviously several reasons why a person becomes a berdache
in Zuñi, but whatever the reason, men who have chosen openly to assume women's dress have the same chance as any other persons to
establish themselves as functioning members of the society. Their response is socially recognized. If they have native ability, they can give
it scope; if they are weak creatures, they fail in terms of their weakness
of character, not in terms of their inversion. . . .

[18] Trance is a similar abnormality in our society. Even a very mild
mystic is aberrant in Western civilization. In order to study trance or
catalepsy within our own social groups, we have to go to the case histories of the abnormal. Therefore the correlation between trance experience and the neurotic and psychotic seems perfect. As in the case
of the homosexual, however, it is a local correlation characteristic of our
century. Even in our own cultural background other eras give different
results. In the Middle Ages when Catholicism made the ecstatic experience the mark of sainthood, the trance experience was greatly valued,

and those to whom the response was congenial, instead of being over-whelmed by a catastrophe as in our century, were given confidence in the pursuit of their careers. It was a validation of ambitions, not a stigma of insanity. Individuals who were susceptible to trance, there-fore, succeeded or failed in terms of their native capacities, but since trance experience was highly valued, a great leader was very likely to be capable of it. . . .

[19] It is clear that culture may value and make socially available even highly unstable human types. If it chooses to treat their peculiari-ties as the most valued variants of human behaviour, the individuals in question will rise to the occasion and perform their social roles without reference to our usual ideas of the types who can make social adjust-ments and those who cannot. Those who function inadequately in any society are not those with certain fixed "abnormal" traits, but may well be those whose responses have received no support in the institutions of their culture. The weakness of these aberrants is in great measure illusory. It springs, not from the fact that they are lacking in necessary vigour, but that they are individuals whose native responses are not reaffirmed by society. They are, as Sapir phrases it, "alienated from an impossible world." . . . But our civilization must deal with cultural standards that go down under our eyes and new ones that arise from a shadow upon the horizon. We must be willing to take account of changing normalities even when the question is of the morality in which we were bred. Just as we are handicapped in dealing with ethi-cal problems so long as we hold to an absolute definition of morality, so we are handicapped in dealing with human society so long as we identify our local normalities with the inevitable necessities of exist-ence.

[20] No society has yet attempted a self-conscious direction of the process by which its new normalities are created in the next generation. Dewey has pointed out how possible and yet how drastic such social engineering would be. For some traditional arrangements it is obvious that very high prices are paid, reckoned in terms of human suffering and frustration. If these arrangements presented themselves to us merely as arrangements and not as categorical imperatives, our reasonable course would be to adapt them by whatever means to rationally selected goals. What we do instead is to ridicule our Don Quixotes, the ludicrous em-bodiments of an outmoded tradition, and continue to regard our own as final and prescribed in the nature of things.

[21] In the meantime the therapeutic problem of dealing with our psychopaths of this type is often misunderstood. Their alienation from the actual world can often be more intelligently handled than by insist-

ing that they adopt the modes that are alien to them. Two other courses are always possible. In the first place, the misfit individual may cultivate a greater objective interest in his own preferences and learn how to manage with greater equanimity his deviation from the type. If he learns to recognize the extent to which his suffering has been due to his lack of support in a traditional ethos, he may gradually educate himself to accept his degree of difference with less suffering. Both the exaggerated emotional disturbances of the manic-depressive and the seclusion of the schizophrenic add certain values to existence which are not open to those differently constituted. The unsupported individual who valiantly accepts his favourite and native virtues may attain a feasible course of behaviour that makes it unnecessary for him to take refuge in a private world he has fashioned for himself. He may gradually achieve a more independent and less tortured attitude toward his deviations and upon this attitude he may be able to build an adequately functioning existence.

[22] In the second place, an increased tolerance in society toward its less usual types must keep pace with the self-education of the patient. The possibilities in this direction are endless. Tradition is as neurotic as any patient; its overgrown fear of deviation from its fortuitous standards conforms to all the usual definitions of the psychopathic. This fear does not depend upon observation of the limits within which conformity is necessary to the social good. Much more deviation is allowed to the individual in some cultures than in others, and those in which much is allowed cannot be shown to suffer from their peculiarity. It is probable that social orders of the future will carry this tolerance and encouragement of individual difference much further than any cultures of which we have experience.

[23] The American tendency at the present time leans so far to the opposite extreme that it is not easy for us to picture the changes that such an attitude would bring about. Middletown is a typical example of our usual urban fear of seeming in however slight an act different from our neighbours. Eccentricity is more feared than parasitism. Every sacrifice of time and tranquility is made in order that no one in the family may have any taint of nonconformity attached to him. Children in school make their great tragedies out of not wearing a certain kind of stockings, not joining a certain dancing-class, not driving a certain car. The fear of being different is the dominating motivation recorded in Middletown.

[24] The psychopathic toll that such a motivation exacts is evident in every institution for mental diseases in our country. In a society in which it existed only as a minor motive among many others, the psy-

chiatric picture would be a very different one. At all events, there can be no reasonable doubt that one of the most effective ways in which to deal with the staggering burden of psychopathic tragedies in America at the present time is by means of an educational program which fosters tolerance in society and a kind of self-respect and independence that is foreign to Middletown and our urban traditions.

[25] Not all psychopaths, of course, are individuals whose native responses are at variance with those of their civilization. Another large group are those who are merely inadequate and who are strongly enough motivated so that their failure is more than they can bear. In a society in which the will-to-power is most highly rewarded, those who fail may not be those who are differently constituted, but simply those who are insufficiently endowed. The inferiority complex takes a great toll of suffering in our society. It is not necessary that sufferers of this type have a history of frustration in the sense that strong native bents have been inhibited; their frustration is often enough only the reflection of their inability to reach a certain goal. There is a cultural implication here, too, in that the traditional goal may be accessible to large numbers or to very few, and in proportion as success is obsessive and is limited to the few, a greater and greater number will be liable to the extreme penalties of maladjustment.

[26] To a certain extent, therefore, civilization in setting higher and possibly more worth-while goals may increase the number of its abnormals. But the point may very easily be overemphasized, for very small changes in social attitudes may far outweigh this correlation. On the whole, since the social possibilities of tolerance and recognition of individual difference are so little explored in practice, pessimism seems premature. Certainly other quite different social factors which we have just discussed are more directly responsible for the great proportion of our neurotics and psychotics, and with these other factors civilizations could, if they would, deal without necessary intrinsic loss.

[27] We have been considering individuals from the point of view of their ability to function adequately in their society. This adequate functioning is one of the ways in which normality is clinically defined. It is also defined in terms of fixed symptoms, and the tendency is to identify normality with the statistically average. In practice this average is one arrived at in the laboratory, and deviations from it are defined as abnormal.

[28] From the point of view of a single culture this procedure is very useful. It shows the clinical picture of the civilization and gives considerable information about its socially approved behaviour. To gener-

alize this as an absolute normal, however, is a different matter. As we have seen, the range of normality in different cultures does not coincide. . . . Any society, according to its major preoccupations, may increase and intensify even hysterical, epileptic, or paranoid symptoms, at the same time relying socially in a greater and greater degree upon the very individuals who display them.

[29] This fact is important in psychiatry because it makes clear another group of abnormals which probably exists in every culture: the abnormals who represent the extreme development of the local cultural type. This group is socially in the opposing situation from the group we have discussed, those whose responses are at variance with their cultural standards. Society, instead of exposing the former group at every point, supports them in their furthest aberrations. They have a license which they may almost endlessly exploit. For this reason these persons almost never fall within the scope of any contemporary psychiatry. They are unlikely to be described even in the most careful manuals of the generation that fosters them. Yet from the point of view of another generation or culture they are ordinarily the most bizarre of the psychopathic types of the period.

[30] The Puritan divines of New England in the eighteenth century were the last persons whom contemporary opinion in the colonies regarded as psychopathic. Few prestige groups in any culture have been allowed such complete intellectual and emotional dictatorship as they were. They were the voice of God. Yet to a modern observer it is they, not the confused and tormented women they put to death as witches, who were the psychoneurotics of Puritan New England. A sense of guilt as extreme as they portrayed and demanded both in their own conversion experiences and in those of their converts is found in a slightly saner civilization only in institutions for mental diseases. They admitted no salvation without a conviction of sin that prostrated the victim, sometimes for years, with remorse and terrible anguish. It was the duty of the minister to put the fear of hell into the heart of even the youngest child, and to exact of every convert emotional acceptance of his damnation if God saw fit to damn him. It does not matter where we turn among the records of New England Puritan churches of this period, whether to those dealing with witches or with unsaved children not yet in their teens or with such themes as damnation and predestination, we are faced with the fact that the group of people who carried out to the greatest extreme and in the fullest honour the cultural doctrine of the moment are by the slightly altered standards of our generation the victims of intolerable aberrations. From the point of view of a

comparative psychiatry they fall in the category of the abnormal.

[31] In our own generation extreme forms of ego-gratification are culturally supported in a similar fashion. Arrogant and unbridled egoists as family men, as officers of the law and in business, have been again and again portrayed by novelists and dramatists, and they are familiar in every community. Like the behaviour of Puritan divines, their courses of action are often more asocial than those of the inmates of penitentiaries. In terms of the suffering and frustration that they spread about them there is probably no comparison. There is very possibly at least as great a degree of mental warping. Yet they are entrusted with positions of great influence and importance and are as a rule fathers of families. Their impress both upon their own children and upon the structure of our society is indelible. They are not described in our manuals of psychiatry because they are supported by every tenet of our civilization. They are sure of themselves in real life in a way that is possible only to those who are oriented to the points of the compass laid down in their own culture. Nevertheless a future psychiatry may well ransack our novels and letters and public records for illumination upon a type of abnormality to which it would not otherwise give credence. In every society it is among this very group of the culturally encouraged and fortified that some of the most extreme types of human behaviour are fostered.

[32] Social thinking at the present time has no more important task before it than that of taking adequate account of cultural relativity. In the fields of both sociology and psychology the implications are fundamental, and modern thought about contacts of peoples and about our changing standards is greatly in need of sane and scientific direction. The sophisticated modern temper has made of social relativity, even in the small area which it has recognized, a doctrine of despair. It has pointed out its incongruity with the orthodox dreams of permanence and ideality and with the individual's illusions of autonomy. It has argued that if human experience must give up these, the nutshell of existence is empty. But to interpret our dilemma in these terms is to be guilty of an anachronism. It is only the inevitable cultural lag that makes us insist that the old must be discovered again in the new, that there is no solution but to find the old certainty and stability in the new plasticity. The recognition of cultural relativity carries with it its own values, which need not be those of the absolutist philosophies. It challenges customary opinions and causes those who have been bred to them acute discomfort. It rouses pessimism because it throws old formulæ into confusion, not because it contains anything intrinsically

difficult. As soon as the new opinion is embraced as customary belief, it will be another trusted bulwark of the good life. We shall arrive then at a more realistic social faith, accepting as grounds of hope and as new bases for tolerance the coexisting and equally valid patterns of life which mankind has created for itself from the raw materials of existence.

Questions

1. What basic assumption does Benedict question in the opening paragraph? What does she mean by "nineteenth century dualism"?
2. What basic ideas do you find in paragraph 5? Do these ideas come as a surprise to you? Explain.
3. Why does Benedict refer to ethnologists' experiences with "persons who are put outside the pale of society" (paragraph 12)? Does Benedict support her judgment? Explain.
4. Benedict refers to the "dilemma of the individual whose congenial drives are not provided for in the institutions of his culture" (paragraph 15). How effective are her illustrations and examples?
5. What key point does Benedict make in her reference to the experience of "trance" (paragraph 18)?
6. Why does the author refer to Middletown? Can you explain the reference?
7. Does the comment about the "Puritan divines of New England" (paragraph 30) have any relevance to our contemporary society? If so, how?
8. Benedict speaks of "cultural relativity" (paragraph 32). What does she mean? How does "cultural relativity" relate to "conformity"? Explain.

ASSIGNMENTS

1. Read Thoreau's "Essay on Civil Disobedience." Write an imaginative account of how your local newspaper might respond to Thoreau's statements if they were given in a public speech.
2. Emerson refers to Pythagoras, Jesus, Socrates, Luther, Copernicus, Galileo, and Newton as men who were misunderstood. Prepare an oral report in which you indicate who these men were and why they were eligible for Emerson's illustrative purposes.
3. Read at least four poems by Walt Whitman including "One's-Self I Sing." Prepare a paper describing the probable response to these poems by Robert Elliot Fitch and John Clellon Holmes. Support your judgments with appropriate illustrations.
4. Tillich says, "Conformity is a word that does not necessarily have negative connotations." Test this hypothesis by interviewing at least ten people. Prepare a report on your findings. (You might also ask them *why* they answer your questions as they do.)
5. Prepare a report describing how Lindner might respond to Riesman's essay. Or, if you prefer, prepare your report describing how Riesman would respond to Lindner's "Must You Conform?"

6. In *The New Republic* of July 3, 1961, Irving Howe reviews Morris Freedman's book *Confessions of a Conformist*. Write a paper evaluating Howe's review. (You will also want to read more of Freedman's book and Howe's exchange with Freedman in the July 24, 1961, issue of *The New Republic*.)

7. Find a speech or article by a spokesman—Senator Barry Goldwater, for example—for the conservative position on individualism. Assess the arguments; indicate how the author defines his terms.

8. Read a short story by Shirley Jackson called "The Lottery." Prepare for a panel discussion in which you indicate how Emerson, Fromm, Fitch, Hoover, Riesman, or Benedict might respond to the story.

9. There is a commonly held view that the present generation of college students is moving toward greater conformity. What evidence do you find on your own campus supporting or rejecting this view? Prepare a speech in which you present your findings and your conclusions.

10. Prepare to participate in a panel discussion in which you advance your own position on the problem of the individual and his relationship to the demands of society. Supplement your reading and experience by drawing on other sources such as religious, philosophical, inspirational, and educational materials.

PART II

READINGS IN LANGUAGE, THOUGHT, AND COMMUNICATION

INTRODUCTION

Since language largely reflects our experience and thinking—and our thinking affects our language—hopes for improving communication skills (reading, writing, listening, speaking) depend first on sharpening our critical thinking. Such thinking does not occur in a vacuum. Therefore, the materials in Part I of this book present conflicts in which you encounter ideas, language, varieties of thought processes, and an array of communication techniques. To guide you in coping with the complexities in the projects, the second part of the text has been provided. Here are essays designed to refine your understanding of the tangled threads woven through the issues. For example, take the topic of "Crime and Punishment." In this conflict, as in most, you will find people, some passionately partisan, attempting to influence your attitudes and thinking. Their statements and language, their arguments and strategies, their communication techniques—all are designed to become your experiences and eventually your thinking, feeling, and language. How will you respond to the appeals, to the arguments? Why will you respond as you do? Will you be sensitive to the complex communication processes occurring? Will you have the necessary critical skills for intelligent assessment? Will you be able to identify the issues, evaluate the merit of the appeals, recognize the language skills employed? Will you recognize the valid, detect the illogical, respond to evidence? And if you become involved yourself—as many of you will—how effective will you be in stating your own beliefs and your supporting evidence?

We believe that the essays in this section of the book will help you in working your way through the materials in the projects. For example, the Davis article will alert you to several common devices, logical and illogical, used in persuasion while the Thouless essay will clarify the role of emotional language in communication.

The major purpose of these sixteen pieces, then, is to increase your awareness of how language operates, how thought processes influence language and even experience, and how effective communication grows out of increased critical insight. As your communication skills of reading and listening develop, you should learn how to turn your increased awareness and perception to your communicating in writing and speaking—and thereby attain greater facility in your use of language.

The insights into language and thought processes in this section of the text come from a group of perceptive and articulate individuals —all concerned with specific aspects of communication. These articles have been written by scientists and psychologists, philosophers and logicians, professors of English and sociology. In style, time, and specific subject matter—as well as their preoccupations—they differ widely. But the writers are all sophisticated students of language, critical thinking, and communication processes.

As you read these essays, their inter-relationships will become increasingly apparent. To the extent that you learn to employ the analytical tools provided by these writers, you will find the conflicts in Part I less tangled and confusing.

As a convenience, we have grouped the following pieces into a four-part classification. Just as Mr. Jones might be classified as an American, a lawyer, a Democrat, a New Yorker, or a tennis enthusiast, so also may these articles be arranged into various categories. We have attempted, with each essay, to identify the writer's most vital intention—despite the fact that these articles have a breadth that makes categorization arbitrary. Indeed, the close relationships among the categories increases the arbitrary nature of too-neat pigeon-holing. Some essays permitted obvious classification, for example, Plato's "The Allegory of the Cave." But, classifying Beardsley's "Meaning and Context" depended on our own judgment of his essential purposes.

We begin with Reality and Observation—as a basic means of describing experience. In Plato's "The Allegory of the Cave," the age-old philosophical question of illusion vs. reality appears. The Scudder essay, taken from an autobiographical account of how Professor Agassiz trained his science students at Harvard, serves as a practical example of how we observe and suggests factors that may be involved in acute perceiving. Scientists and psychologists today are still carrying on experiments to learn more about the nature of man's sensory perception. "The Method of Scientific Investigation" by the nineteenth century scientist, Thomas Henry Huxley, is an excellent description of the inductive method applied to fairly simple problems. Modern science, coping with more complex problems—of organized and disorganized complexity—is described by Dr. Warren Weaver, coauthor of *The Mathematical Theory of Communication*.

Under the classification Thought Processes, you will find four articles. Francis Bacon's "Idols of the Mind" contrasts inductive and deductive thought processes. "Four Kinds of Thinking" by James Harvey Robinson not only examines processes of thinking but also describes rationalization and notes the relationships between people's opinions and their environments. "The Gonks and the Tiger" by Raymond Rogers describes symbol-making and observes how symbols affect attitudes and thinking. Inextricably linked to symbol-making is the tendency toward myth-making, a subject almost irresistible to today's psychologists. Completing this section is "Logical Fallacies," by a former professor from Harvard. It is a detailed examination of simple logic and typical examples of illogical argument.

The next classification, The Improvement of Communication Skills, includes essays which have the major purpose of improving student performance in actual communication. A chapter from Hayakawa's *Language in Thought and Action*—a book which became a best seller—emphasizes the distinctions between the language of opinion and the language of report. The Beardsley chapter, "Meaning and Context," assesses the importance of context in shaping meaning. Carl Rogers, a psychologist, and F. J. Roethlisberger discuss human factors acting as barriers to communication. Darrell Huff's article, "How to Lie with Statistics," is a popularization of basic statistical principles and also depicts many current examples of statistical manipulation and misrepresentation. Huff's emphases make his article useful to the student of propaganda analysis in those cases where irresponsible or deliberately deceptive use is made of numerical data. Finally, the Rapoport essay deals with problems of definition and clarity, two key ingredients in clear communication.

The last classification, Language and Thought and Feeling, includes a chapter by a linguistic scientist, Archibald A. Hill. He describes the basic assumptions and methods used by modern linguists in their fresh —and often stimulating—approach to the actual structures of the English language. In a chapter from *How to Think Straight*, Robert Thouless, a British psychologist, emphasizes the mutual relationships of language and thought and feeling. Thouless obviously agrees with the concluding piece in this section, "A Word in Your Ear," a sociologically oriented study of man and his linguistic behavior, which suggests that we often begin by speaking as we think and end by thinking as we speak. To language and thought the psychologist adds emotional feelings and personal observation (environment), producing the complex patterns of human communication.

To repeat, this section of the book should produce a clearer understanding of the materials appearing in Part I. As your understanding of language, thought, and communication processes makes your reading and listening more sensitive, inevitably these more acute perceptions will begin to affect the quality of your own thinking and lead to more critical appraisals of your experiences.

Ultimately, by repeated practice in writing and speaking, reinforced by your growing powers of critical self-assessment, you should become more competent in evaluating papers and talks—your own and those of others—more aware of techniques and their effects upon an audience, and more responsible in using your language.

1. REALITY AND OBSERVATION

THE ALLEGORY OF THE CAVE*

Plato

And now, I said, let me show in a figure how far nature is enlightened or unenlightened:—Behold! human beings living in an underground den, which has a mouth open towards the light and reaching all along the den; here they have been from their childhood, and have their legs and necks chained so that they cannot move, and can only see before them, being prevented by the chains from turning round their heads. Above and behind them a fire is blazing at a distance, and between the fire and the prisoners there is a raised way; and you will see, if you look, a low wall built along the way, like the screen which marionette players have in front of them, over which they show the puppets.

I see.

And do you see, I said, men passing along the wall carrying all sorts of vessels, and statues and figures of animals made of wood and stone and various materials, which appear over the wall? Some of them are talking, others silent.

You have shown me a strange image, and they are strange prisoners.

Like ourselves, I replied; and they see only their own shadows, or the shadows of one another, which the fire throws on the opposite wall of the cave?

True, he said; how could they see anything but the shadows if they were never allowed to move their heads?

And of the objects which are being carried in like manner they would only see the shadows?

Yes, he said.

And if they were able to converse with one another, would they not suppose that they were naming what was actually before them?

Very true.

And suppose further that the prison had an echo which came from the other side, would they not be sure to fancy when one of the passers-

* From Plato, *The Republic*, translated by Benjamin Jowett.

by spoke that the voice which they heard came from the passing shadows?

No question, he replied.

To them, I said, the truth would be literally nothing but the shadows of the images.

That is certain.

And now look again, and see what will naturally follow if the prisoners are released and disabused of their error. At first, when any of them is liberated and compelled suddenly to stand up and turn his neck round and walk and look towards the light, he will suffer sharp pains; the glare will distress him, and he will be unable to see the realities of which in his former state he had seen the shadows; and then conceive some one saying to him, that what he saw before was an illusion, but that now, when he is approaching nearer to being and his eye is turned towards more real existence, he has a clearer vision,—what will be his reply? And you may further imagine that his instructor is pointing to the objects as they pass and requiring him to name them,—will he not be perplexed? Will he not fancy that the shadows which he formerly saw are truer than the objects which are now shown to him?

Far truer.

And if he is compelled to look straight at the light, will he not have a pain in his eyes which will make him turn away to take refuge in the objects of vision which he can see, and which he will conceive to be in reality clearer than the things which are now being shown to him?

True, he said.

And suppose once more, that he is reluctantly dragged up a steep and rugged ascent, and held fast until he is forced into the presence of the sun himself, is he not likely to be pained and irritated? When he approaches the light his eyes will be dazzled, and he will not be able to see anything at all of what are now called realities.

Not all in a moment, he said.

He will require to grow accustomed to the sight of the upper world. And first he will see the shadows best, next the reflections of men and other objects in the water, and then the objects themselves; then he will gaze upon the light of the moon and the stars and the spangled heaven; and he will see the sky and the stars by night better than the sun or the light of the sun by day?

Certainly.

Last of all he will be able to see the sun, and not mere reflection of him in the water, but he will see him in his own proper place, and not in another; and he will contemplate him as he is.

Certainly.

He will then proceed to argue that this is he who gives the season and the years, and is the guardian of all that is in the visible world, and in a certain way the cause of all things which he and his fellows have been accustomed to behold?

Clearly, he said, he would first see the sun and then reason about him.

And when he remembered his old habitation, and the wisdom of the den and his fellow-prisoners, do you not suppose that he would felicitate himself on the change, and pity them?

Certainly, he would.

And if they were in the habit of conferring honours among themselves on those who were quickest to observe the passing shadows and to remark which of them went before, and which followed after, and which were together; and who were therefore best able to draw conclusions as to the future, do you think that he would care for such honours and glories, or envy the possessors of them? Would he not say with Homer,

> Better, to be the poor servant of a poor master,

and to endure anything, rather than think as they do and live after their manner?

Yes, he said, I think that he would rather suffer anything than entertain these false notions and live in this miserable manner.

Imagine once more, I said, such an one coming suddenly out of the sun to be replaced in his old situation; would he not be certain to have his eyes full of darkness?

To be sure, he said.

And if there were a contest, and he had to compete in measuring the shadows with the prisoners who had never moved out of the den, while his sight was still weak, and before his eyes had become steady (and the time which would be needed to acquire this new habit of sight might be very considerable) would he not be ridiculous? Men would say of him that up he went and down he came without his eyes; and that it was better not even to think of ascending; and if any one tried to loose another and lead him up to the light, let them only catch the offender, and they would put him to death.

No question, he said.

This entire allegory, I said, you may now append, dear Glaucon, to the previous argument; the prison-house is the world of sight, the light of the fire is the sun, and you will not misapprehend me if you interpret

the journey upwards to be the ascent of the soul into the intellectual
world according to my poor belief, which, at your desire, I have expressed—whether rightly or wrongly God knows. But, whether true or
false, my opinion is that in the world of knowledge the idea of good
appears last of all, and is seen only with an effort; and, when seen, is
also inferred to be the universal author of all things beautiful and right,
parent of light and of the lord of light in this visible world, and the
immediate source of reason and truth in the intellectual; and that this
is the power upon which he who would act rationally either in public
or private life must have his eye fixed.

I agree, he said, as far as I am able to understand you.

Moreover, I said, you must not wonder that those who attain to this
beatific vision are unwilling to descend to human affairs; for their souls
are ever hastening into the upper world where they desire to dwell;
which desire of theirs is very natural, if our allegory may be trusted.

Yes, very natural.

And is there anything surprising in one who passes from divine con-
templations to the evil state of man, misbehaving himself in a ridiculous
manner; if, while his eyes are blinking and before he has become accustomed to the surrounding darkness, he is compelled to fight in courts of
law, or in other places, about the images or the shadows of images of
justice, and is endeavouring to meet the conceptions of those who have
never yet seen absolute justice?

Anything but surprising, he replied.

Any one who has common sense will remember that the bewilder-
ments of the eyes are of two kinds, and arise from two causes, either
from coming out of the light or from going into the light, which is true
of the mind's eye, quite as much as of the bodily eye; and he who remembers this when he sees any one whose vision is perplexed and
weak, will not be too ready to laugh; he will first ask whether that soul
of man has come out of the brighter life, and is unable to see because
unaccustomed to the dark, or having turned from darkness to the day
is dazzled by excess of light. And he will count the one happy in his
condition and state of being, and he will pity the other; or, if he have a
mind to laugh at the soul which comes from below into the light, there
will be more reason in this than in the laugh which greets him who returns from above out of the light into the den.

That, he said, is a very just distinction.

But then, if I am right, certain professors of education must be wrong
when they say that they can put a knowledge into the soul which was
not there before, like sight into blind eyes.

They undoubtedly say this, he replied.

Whereas, our argument shows that the power and capacity of learning exists in the soul already; and that just as the eye was unable to turn from darkness to light without the whole body, so too the instrument of knowledge can only by the movement of the whole soul be turned from the world of becoming into that of being, and learn by degrees to endure the sight of being, and of the brightest and best of being, or in other words, of the good.

A GREAT TEACHER'S METHOD*

Samuel H. Scudder

It was more than fifteen years ago [about 1860] that I entered the laboratory of Professor Agassiz, and told him I had enrolled my name in the Scientific School as a student of natural history. He asked me a few questions about my object in coming, my antecedents generally, the mode in which I afterwards proposed to use the knowledge I might acquire, and, finally, whether I wished to study any special branch. To the latter I replied that, while I wished to be well grounded in all departments of zoology, I purposed to devote myself specially to insects.

"When do you wish to begin?" he asked.

"Now," I replied.

This seemed to please him, and with an energetic "Very well!" he reached from a shelf a huge jar of specimens in yellow alcohol.

"Take this fish," said he, "and look at it; we call it a haemulon; by and by I will ask what you have seen."

With that he left me, but in a moment returned with explicit instructions as to the care of the object entrusted to me.

"No man is fit to be a naturalist," said he, "who does not know how to take care of specimens."

I was to keep the fish before me in a tin tray, and occasionally moisten the surface with alcohol from the jar, always taking care to replace the stopper tightly. Those were not the days of ground-glass stoppers and elegantly shaped exhibition jars; all the old students will recall the huge neckless glass bottles with their leaky, wax-besmeared corks, half eaten by insects, and begrimed with cellar dust. Entomology was a cleaner science than ichthyology, but the example of the Professor, who had unhesitatingly plunged to the bottom of the jar to produce the fish,

* From *Every Saturday*, 1874.

was infectious; and though this alcohol had a "very ancient and fishlike smell," I really dared not show any aversion within these sacred precincts, and treated the alcohol as though it were pure water. Still I was conscious of a passing feeling of disappointment, for gazing at a fish did not commend itself to an ardent entomologist. My friends at home, too, were annoyed when they discovered that no amount of eau-de-Cologne would drown the perfume which haunted me like a shadow.

In ten minutes I had seen all that could be seen in that fish, and started in search of the Professor—who had, however, left the Museum; and when I returned, after lingering over some of the odd animals stored in the upper apartment, my specimen was dry all over. I dashed the fluid over the fish as if to resuscitate the beast from a fainting-fit, and looked with anxiety for a return of the normal sloppy appearance. This little excitement over, nothing was to be done but to return to a steadfast gaze at my mute companion. Half an hour passed —an hour—another hour; the fish began to look loathsome. I turned it over and around; looked it in the face—ghastly; from behind, beneath, above, sideways, at a three-quarters' view—just as ghastly. I was in despair; at an early hour I concluded that lunch was necessary; so, with infinite relief, the fish was carefully replaced in the jar, and for an hour I was free.

On my return, I learned that Professor Agassiz had been at the Museum, but had gone, and would not return for several hours. My fellow-students were too busy to be disturbed by continued conversation. Slowly I drew forth that hideous fish, and with a feeling of desperation again looked at it. I might not use a magnifying-glass; instruments of all kinds were interdicted. My two hands, my two eyes, and the fish: it seemed a most limited field. I pushed my finger down its throat to feel how sharp the teeth were. I began to count the scales in the different rows, until I was convinced that that was nonsense. At last a happy thought struck me—I would draw the fish; and now with surprise I began to discover new features in the creature. Just then the Professor returned.

"That is right," said he; "a pencil is one of the best of eyes. I am glad to notice, too, that you keep your specimen wet, and your bottle corked."

With these encouraging words, he added:

"Well, what is it like?"

He listened attentively to my brief rehearsal of the structure of parts whose names were still unknown to me: the fringed gill-arches and movable operculum; the pores of the head, fleshy lips and lidless eyes;

the lateral line, the spinous fins and forked tail; the compressed and arched body. When I had finished, he waited as if expecting more, and then, with an air of disappointment:

"You have not looked very carefully; why," he continued more earnestly, "you haven't even seen one of the most conspicuous features of the animal, which is as plainly before your eyes as the fish itself; look again, look again!" and he left me to my misery.

I was piqued; I was mortified. Still more of that wretched fish! But now I set myself to my task with a will, and discovered one new thing after another, until I saw how just the Professor's criticism had been. The afternoon passed quickly; and when, toward its close, the Professor inquired:

"Do you see it yet?"

"No," I replied, "I am certain I do not, but I see how little I saw before."

"That is next best," said he, earnestly, "but I won't hear you now; put away your fish and go home; perhaps you will be ready with a better answer in the morning. I will examine you before you look at the fish."

This was disconcerting. Not only must I think of my fish all night, studying, without the object before me, what this unknown but most visible feature might be; but also, without reviewing my discoveries, I must give an exact account of them the next day. I had a bad memory; so I walked home by Charles River in a distracted state, with my two perplexities.

The cordial greeting from the Professor the next morning was reassuring; here was a man who seemed to be quite as anxious as I that I should see for myself what he saw.

"Do you perhaps mean," I asked, "that the fish has symmetrical sides with paired organs?"

His thoroughly pleased "Of course! of course!" repaid the wakeful hours of the previous night. After he had discoursed most happily and enthusiastically—as he always did—upon the importance of this point, I ventured to ask what I should do next.

"Oh, look at your fish!" he said, and left me again to my own devices. In a little more than an hour he returned, and heard my new catalogue.

"That is good, that is good!" he repeated; "but that is not all; go on"; and so for three long days he placed that fish before my eyes, forbidding me to look at anything else, or to use any artificial aid. "Look, look, look," was his repeated injunction.

This was the best entomological lesson I ever had—a lesson whose influence has extended to the details of every subsequent study; a legacy

the Professor had left to me, as he has left it to many others, of inestimable value, which we could not buy, with which we cannot part.

A year afterward, some of us were amusing ourselves with chalking
outlandish beasts on the Museum blackboard. We drew prancing star-
fishes; frogs in mortal combat; hydra-headed worms; stately crawfishes,
standing on their tails, bearing aloft umbrellas; and grotesque fishes
with gaping mouths and staring eyes. The Professor came in shortly
after, and was as amused as any at our experiments. He looked at the
fishes.

"Haemulons, every one of them," he said; "Mr. ——— drew them."

True; and to this day, if I attempt a fish, I can draw nothing but
haemulons.

The fourth day, a second fish of the same group was placed beside
the first, and I was bidden to point out the resemblances and differences
between the two; another and another followed, until the entire family
lay before me, and a whole legion of jars covered the table and surrounding shelves; the odor had become a pleasant perfume; and even
now, the sight of an old, six-inch, worm-eaten cork brings fragrant
memories.

The whole group of haemulons was thus brought in review; and,
whether engaged upon the dissection of the internal organs, the prepa-
ration and examination of the bony framework, or the description of
the various parts, Agassiz's training in the method of observing facts
and their orderly arrangement was ever accompanied by the urgent
exhortation not to be content with them.

"Facts are stupid things," he would say, "until brought into connection with some general law."

At the end of eight months, it was almost with reluctance that I left
these friends and turned to insects; but what I had gained by this outside experience has been of greater value than years of later investigation in my favorite groups.

THE METHOD OF SCIENTIFIC INVESTIGATION[*]

Thomas Henry Huxley

The method of scientific investigation is nothing but the expression
of the necessary mode of working of the human mind. It is simply the
mode by which all phenomena are reasoned about, rendered precise

[*] From the third lecture in "On Our Knowledge of the Causes of the Phenomena
of Organic Nature" (1863), as reprinted in *Darwiniana*, 1896.

and exact. There is no more difference, but there is just the same kind of difference, between the mental operations of a man of science and those of an ordinary person, as there is between the operations and methods of a baker or of a butcher weighing out his goods in common scales, and the operations of a chemist in performing a difficult and complex analysis by means of his balance and finely graduated weights. It is not that the action of the scales in the one case, and the balance in the other, differ in the principles of their construction or manner of working; but the beam of one is set on an infinitely finer axis than the other, and of course turns by the addition of a much smaller weight.

You will understand this better, perhaps, if I give you some familiar example. You have all heard it repeated, I dare say, that men of science work by means of induction and deduction, and that by the help of these operations, they, in a sort of sense, wring from Nature certain other things, which are called natural laws, and causes, and that out of these, by some cunning skill of their own, they build up hypotheses and theories. And it is imagined by many, that the operations of the common mind can be by no means compared with these processes, and that they have to be acquired by a sort of special apprenticeship to the craft. To hear all these large words, you would think that the mind of a man of science must be constituted differently from that of his fellow men; but if you will not be frightened by terms, you will discover that you are quite wrong, and that all these terrible apparatuses are being used by yourselves every day and every hour of your lives.

There is a well-known incident in one of Molière's plays, where the author makes the hero express unbounded delight on being told that he had been talking prose during the whole of his life. In the same way, I trust that you will take comfort, and be delighted with yourselves, on the discovery that you have been acting on the principles of inductive and deductive philosophy during the same period. Probably there is not one here who has not in the course of the day had occasion to set in motion a complex train of reasoning, of the very same kind, though differing of course in degree, as that which a scientific man goes through in tracing the causes of natural phenomena.

A very trivial circumstance will serve to exemplify this. Suppose you go into a fruiterer's shop, wanting an apple—you take up one, and, on biting it, you find it sour; you look at it, and see that it is hard and green. You take up another one, and that too is hard, green, and sour. The shopman offers you a third; but, before biting it, you examine it, and find that it is hard and green, and you immediately say that you will not have it, as it must be sour, like those that you have already tried.

Nothing can be more simple than that, you think; but if you will take the trouble to analyse and trace out into its logical elements what has been done by the mind, you will be greatly surprised. In the first place you have performed the operation of induction. You found that, in two experiences, hardness and greenness in apples went together with sourness. It was so in the first case, and it was confirmed by the second. True, it is a very small basis, but still it is enough to make an induction from; you generalise the facts, and you expect to find sourness in apples where you get hardness and greenness. You found upon that a general law that all hard and green apples are sour; and that, so far as it goes, is a perfect induction. Well, having got your natural law in this way, when you are offered another apple which you find is hard and green, you say, "All hard and green apples are sour; this apple is hard and green; therefore this apple is sour." That train of reasoning is what logicians call a syllogism, and has all its various parts and terms—its major premise, its minor premise, and its conclusion. And, by the help of further reasoning, which, if drawn out, would have to be exhibited in two or three other syllogisms, you arrive at your final determination, "I will not have that apple." So that, you see, you have, in the first place, established a law by induction, and upon that you have founded a deduction, and reasoned out the special particular case. Well now, suppose, having got your law, that at some time afterwards you are discussing the qualities of apples with a friend: you will say to him, "It is a very curious thing—but I find that all hard and green apples are sour!" Your friend says to you, "But how do you know that?" You at once reply, "Oh, because I have tried them over and over again, and have always found them to be so." Well, if we were talking science instead of common sense, we should call that an experimental verification. And, if still opposed, you go further, and say, "I have heard from the people in Somersetshire and Devonshire, where a large number of apples are grown, that they have observed the same thing. It is also found to be the case in Normandy, and in North America. In short, I find it to be the universal experience of mankind wherever attention has been directed to the subject." Whereupon, your friend, unless he is a very unreasonable man, agrees with you, and is convinced that you are quite right in the conclusion you have drawn. He believes, although perhaps he does not know he believes it, that the more extensive verifications are—that the more frequently experiments have been made, and results of the same kind arrived at—that the more varied the conditions under which the same results are attained, the more certain is the ultimate conclusion, and he disputes the question no further. He sees that the experiment has been tried under all sorts of conditions, as to time, place, and people, with the same result; and he says with you, therefore, that the law you have laid down must be a good one, and he must believe it.

In science we do the same thing—the philosopher exercises precisely the same faculties, though in a much more delicate manner. In scientific inquiry it becomes a matter of duty to expose a supposed law to every possible kind of verification, and to take care, moreover, that this is done intentionally, and not left to a mere accident, as in the case of the apples. And in science, as in common life, our confidence in a law is in exact proportion to the absence of variation in the result of our experimental verifications. For instance, if you let go your grasp of an article you may have in your hand, it will immediately fall to the ground. That is a very common verification of one of the best established laws of nature—that of gravitation. The method by which men of science establish the existence of that law is exactly the same as that by which we have established the trivial proposition about the sourness of hard and green apples. But we believe it in such an extensive, thorough, and unhesitating manner because the universal experience of mankind verifies it, and we can verify it ourselves at any time; and that is the strongest possible foundation on which any natural law can rest.

So much, then, by way of proof that the method of establishing laws in science is exactly the same as that pursued in common life. Let us now turn to another matter (though really it is but another phase of the same question), and that is, the method by which, from the relations of certain phenomena, we prove that some stand in the position of causes towards the others.

I want to put the case clearly before you, and I will therefore show you what I mean by another familiar example. I will suppose that one of you, on coming down in the morning to the parlour of your house, finds that a tea-pot and some spoons which had been left in the room on the previous evening are gone—the window is open, and you observe the mark of a dirty hand on the windowframe, and perhaps, in addition to that, you notice the impress of a hob-nailed shoe on the gravel outside. All these phenomena have struck your attention instantly, and before two seconds have passed you say, "Oh, somebody has broken open the window, entered the room, and run off with the spoons and the tea-pot!" That speech is out of your mouth in a moment. And you will probably add, "I know there has; I am quite sure of it!" You mean to say exactly what you know; but in reality you are giving expression to what is, in all essential particulars, an hypothesis. You do not *know* it at all; it is nothing but an hypothesis rapidly framed in your own mind. And it is an hypothesis founded on a long train of inductions and deductions.

What are those inductions and deductions, and how have you got at this hypothesis? You have observed in the first place that the window is open; but by a train of reasoning involving many inductions and deductions, you have probably arrived long before at the general law—and a very good one it is—that windows do not open of themselves; and you therefore conclude that something has opened the window. A second general law that you have arrived at in the same way is, that tea-pots and spoons do not go out of a window spontaneously, and you are satisfied that, as they are not now where you left them, they have been removed. In the third place, you look at the marks on the window-sill, and the shoe-marks outside, and you say that in all previous experience the former kind of mark has never been produced by anything else but the hand of a human being; and the same experience shows that no other animal but man at present wears shoes with hob-nails in them such as would produce the marks in the gravel. I do not know, even if we could discover any of those "missing links" that are talked about, that they would help us to any other conclusion! At any rate the law which states our present experience is strong enough for my present purpose. You next reach the conclusion that, as these kinds of marks have not been left by any other animal than men, or are liable to be formed in any other way than by a man's hand and shoe, the marks in question have been formed by a man in that way. You have, further, a general law, founded on observation and experience—and that, too, is, I am sorry to say, a very universal and unimpeachable one—that some men are thieves; and you assume at once from all these premises—and that is what constitutes your hypothesis—that the man who made the marks outside and on the window-sill, opened the window, got into the room, and stole your tea-pot and spoons. You have now arrived at a *vera causa,* you have assumed a cause which, it is plain, is competent to produce all the phenomena you have observed. You can explain all these phenomena only by the hypothesis of a thief. But that is a hypothetical conclusion, of the justice of which you have no absolute proof at all; it is only rendered highly probable by a series of inductive and deductive reasonings.

I suppose your first action, asuming that you are a man of ordinary common sense, and that you have established this hypothesis to your own satisfaction, will very likely be to go off for the police, and set them on the track of the burglar, with the view to the recovery of your prop erty. But just as you are starting with this object, some person comes in, and on learning what you are about, says, "My good friend, you are going on a great deal too fast. How do you know that the man who really made the marks took the spoons? It might have been a monkey that took them, and the man may have merely looked in afterwards." You would probably reply, "Well, that is all very well, but you see it is contrary to all experience of the way tea-pots and spoons are abstracted; so that, at any rate, your hypothesis is less probable than mine." While you are talking the thing over in this way, another friend arrives, one of that good kind of people that I was talking of a little while ago. And he might say, "Oh, my dear sir, you are certainly going on a great deal too fast. You are most presumptuous. You admit that all these occurrences took place when you were fast asleep, at a time when you could not possibly have known anything about what was taking place. How do you know that the laws of Nature are not suspended during the night? It may be that there has been some kind of supernatural interference in this case." In point of fact, he declares that your hypothesis is one of which you cannot at all demonstrate the truth, and that you are by no means sure that the laws of Nature are the same when you are asleep as when you are awake.

Well, now, you cannot at the moment answer that kind of reasoning. You feel that your worthy friend has you somewhat at a disadvantage. You will feel perfectly convinced in your own mind, however, that you are quite right, and you say to him, "My good friend, I can only be guided by the natural probabilities of the case, and if you will be kind enough to stand aside and permit me to pass, I will go and fetch the police." Well, we will suppose that your journey is successful, and that by good luck you meet with a policeman; that eventually the burglar is found with your property on his person, and the marks correspond to his hand and to his boots. Probably any jury would consider those facts a very good experimental verification of your hypothesis, touching the cause of the abnormal phenomena observed in your parlour, and would act accordingly.

Now, in this supposititious case, I have taken phenomena of a very common kind, in order that you might see what are the different steps in an ordinary process of reasoning, if you will only take the trouble to analyse it carefully. All the operations I have described, you will see, are involved in the mind of any man of sense in leading him to a conclusion as to the course he should take in order to make good a robbery and punish the offender. I say that you are led, in that case, to your conclusion by exactly the same train of reasoning as that which a man of science pursues when he is endeavouring to discover the origin and laws of the most occult phenomena. The process is, and always must be, the same; and precisely the same mode of reasoning was employed by Newton and Laplace in their endeavours to discover and define the causes of the movements of the heavenly bodies, as you, with your own common sense, would employ to detect a burglar. The only difference is that, the nature of the inquiry being more abstruse, every step has to be most carefully watched, so that there may not be a single crack or flaw in your hypothesis. A flaw or crack in many of the hypotheses of daily life may be of little or no moment as affecting the general correctness of the conclusions at which we may arrive; but, in a scientific inquiry, a fallacy, great or small, is always of importance, and is sure to be in the long run constantly productive of mischievous if not fatal results.

Do not allow yourselves to be misled by the common notion that an hypothesis is untrustworthy simply because it is an hypothesis. It is often urged, in respect to some scientific conclusion, that, after all, it is only an hypothesis. But what more have we to guide us in nine-tenths of the most important affairs of daily life than hypotheses, and often very ill-based ones? So that in science, where the evidence of an hypothesis is subjected to the most rigid examination, we may rightly pursue the same course. You may have hypotheses, and hypotheses. A man may say, if he likes, that the moon is made of green cheese: that is an hypothesis. But another man, who has devoted a great deal of time and attention to the subject, and availed himself of the most powerful telescopes and the results of the observations of others, declares that in his opinion it is probably composed of materials very similar to those of which our own earth is made up: and that is also only an hypothesis. But I need not tell you that there is an enormous difference in the value of the two hypotheses. That one which is based on sound scientific knowledge is sure to have a corresponding value; and that which is a mere, hasty, random guess is likely to have but little value. Every great step in our progress in discovering causes has been made in exactly the same way as that which I have detailed to you. A person observing the occurrence of certain facts and phenomena asks, naturally enough, what process, what kind of operation known to occur in Nature, applied to the particular case, will unravel and explain the mystery? Hence you have the scientific hypothesis; and its value will be proportionate to the care and completeness with which its basis had been tested and verified. It is in these matters as in the commonest affairs of practical life: the guess of the fool will be folly, while the guess of the wise man will contain wisdom. In all cases, you see that the value of the result depends on the patience and faithfulness with which the investigator applies to his hypothesis every possible kind of verification.

SCIENCE AND COMPLEXITY*

Warren Weaver

. . . How can we get a view of the role that science should play in the developing future of man? How can we appreciate what science really is, and—equally important—what it is not? . . .

Speaking roughly, one may say that the seventeenth, eighteenth, and nineteenth centuries formed the period in which physical science learned how to analyze two-variable problems. Thus during that three hundred years, science developed the experimental and analytical techniques for handling problems in which one quantity—say, a gas pressure—depends primarily upon a second quantity—say, the volume of the gas. The essential character of these problems rests in the fact that, at least under a significant range of circumstances, the first quantity depends wholly upon the second quantity, and not upon a large number of other factors. Or in any event, and to be somewhat more precise, the behavior of the first quantity can be described with a useful degree of accuracy by taking into account only its dependence upon the second quantity, and by neglecting the minor influence of other factors.

These two-variable problems are essentially simple in structure, and precisely for the reason that the theories or the experiments related to them need deal with only two quantities, changes in one of which cause changes in the other. The restriction to two variables meant simplicity in theory, and simplicity in experiment: and simplicity was a necessary condition for progress at that stage of development of science. It turned out, moreover, that vast progress could be made in the physical sciences by theories and experiments of this essentially simple character. The great scientists of this period could analyze how the intensity of light varies with the distance from the source; how the strength of a beam depends upon its dimensions or upon the physical properties of its material; how electric current is related to voltage; how gravitational attraction depends upon distance; how steam pres-

* From *The Scientists Speak*. Edited by Warren Weaver. Copyright 1947 by Boni & Gaer, Inc. Reprinted by permission.

sure is related to steam temperature; and hundreds of other such things. The resulting knowledge made possible great advance in our understanding and control of nature, great practical advances in technology. It was this kind of two-variable science which laid, over the period up to 1900, the foundations for our theories of light, of sound, of heat, and of electricity. It was this kind of two-variable science—or minor extensions of it to handle three or four variables—which brought us the telephone and the radio, the automobile and the airplane, the phonograph and the moving pictures, the turbine and the Diesel engine and the modern hydroelectric power plant. . . .

To sum up, physical science before 1900 was largely concerned with two-variable *problems of simplicity;* while the life sciences, in which these problems of simplicity are not so often significant, had not yet become highly quantitative or analytical in character.

Subsequent to 1900—and actually earlier, if we remember heroic pioneers such as Josiah Willard Gibbs—the physical sciences developed an attack on nature of an essentially and dramatically new kind. Rather than study problems which involved two variables or at most three or four, some imaginative minds went to the other extreme, and said: "Let us develop analytical methods which can deal with two billion variables." That is to say, the physical scientists (with the mathematicians often in the vanguard) developed powerful techniques of probability theory and of statistical mechanics which can deal with what we may call problems of *disorganized complexity.* . . .

. . . It [a problem of disorganized complexity] is a problem in which the number of variables is very large, and one in which each of the many variables has a behavior which is individually erratic, or perhaps totally unknown. But in spite of this helter-skelter or unknown behavior of all the individual variables, the system as a whole possesses certain orderly and analyzable average properties.

A wide range of experience comes under this label of disorganized complexity. The method applies with increasing precision when the number of variables increases. It applies with entirely useful precision to the experience of a large telephone exchange, predicting the average frequency of calls, the probability of overlapping calls of the same number, etc. It makes possible the financial stability of a life insurance company. Although the company can have no knowledge whatsoever concerning the approaching death of any one individual, it has dependable knowledge of the average frequency with which deaths will occur. . . .

The whole structure of modern physics, our present concept of the nature of the physical universe and of the accessible experimental facts concerning it, rests on these statistical concepts. Indeed, the whole question of evidence, and the way in which knowledge can be inferred from evidence, is now recognized to depend on these same statistical ideas; so that probability notions are essential to any theory of knowledge itself.

And yet this new method of dealing with disorganized complexity, so powerful an advance over the earlier two-variable methods, leaves a great field untouched. One is tempted to oversimplify, and say that scientific methodology went from one extreme to the other—from two variables to an astronomical number—and left untouched a great middle region. The importance of this middle region, moreover, does not depend primarily on the fact that the number of variables is moderate—large compared to two, but small compared to the number of atoms in a pinch of salt. The problems in this middle region, in fact, will often involve a considerable number of variables. The really important characteristic of the problems of this middle region which science has as yet little explored or conquered lies in the fact that these problems, as contrasted with the disorganized situations with which statistics can cope, show the essential feature of *organization*. In fact, we will refer to this group of problems as those of *organized complexity*. . . .

These new problems—and the future of the world depends on many of them—require science to make a third great advance, an advance which must be even greater than the nineteen-century conquest of problems of simplicity or the twentieth-century victory over problems of disorganized complexity. Science must, over the next fifty years, learn to deal with these problems of organized complexity.

Is there any promise on the horizon that this new advance can really be accomplished? There is much general evidence, and there are two recent instances of specially promising evidence. . . .

The first piece of evidence is the wartime development of new types of electronic computing devices. These devices are, in flexibility and capacity, more like a human brain than like the traditional mechanical computing device of the past. They have "memories" in which can be stored vast amounts of information. They can be "told" to carry out computations of very intricate complexity, and can be left unattended while they go forward automatically with their task. The astounding speed with which they proceed is illustrated by the fact that one small part of such a machine, if set to multiplying two ten-digit numbers, can perform such multiplications some forty thousand times faster than a human operator can say "Jack Robinson."

This combination of flexibility, capacity, and speed makes it seem likely that such devices will have a tremendous impact on science. They will make it possible to deal with problems which previously were simply too complicated. And, more importantly, they will justify and inspire the development of new methods of analysis which are applicable to these new problems of organized complexity.

The second of the wartime advances is the "mixed-team" approach. . . . Although mathematicians, physicists, and engineers were essential, the best of the groups also contained physiologists, biochemists, psychologists, and a variety of representatives of other fields of the biochemical and social sciences. Among the outstanding members of English mixed teams, for example, were an endocrinologist and an X-ray crystallographer. Under the pressure of war, these mixed teams pooled their resources and focused all their different insights on the common problems. They found, in spite of the modern tendencies toward intense scientific specialization, that such diverse groups could work together and could form a whole which was much greater than the mere sum of its parts. They found that they could tackle certain problems of organized complexity, and get useful answers. . . .

Let us return now to our original question. What is science? What is it not? What may we hope from it?

Science clearly is a way of solving problems—not all problems, but a large class of important and practical ones. The problems with which it can deal are those in which the predominant factors are subject to the basic laws of logic, and are for the most part measurable. Science is a way of organizing reproducible knowledge about such problems, of focusing and disciplining imagination, of weighing evidence, of deciding what is relevant and what is not; of impartially testing hypotheses, of ruthlessly discarding what proves to be inaccurate or inadequate, of finding, interpreting, and facing facts, and of making the facts of nature the servants of man.

The essence of science, just like anything else, is not to be found in its outward appearance, in its physical manifestations: it is to be found in its inner spirit. That austere but exciting technique of inquiry known as the scientific method is what is important about science. This scientific method requires of its practitioners high standards of personal honesty, open-mindedness, focused vision, and love of the truth. These are solid virtues, but science has no exclusive lien on them. The poet has these virtues also, and often turns them to higher uses. . . .

There are even broader claims which can be made for science and the scientific method. As an essential part of his characteristic procedure, the scientist insists on precise definition of terms and clear characterization of his problem. It is easier, of course, to define terms accurately in scientific fields than in many other areas. It remains true, however, that science is an almost overwhelming illustration of the effectiveness of a well-defined and accepted language, a common set of ideas, a common tradition. The way in which this universality has succeeded in cutting across barriers of time and space, across political and cultural boundaries, is significant indeed. Perhaps better than in any other intellectual enterprise of man, science has solved the problem of communicating ideas, and has demonstrated that world-wide co-operation and communion of interest which then inevitably results.

2. THOUGHT PROCESSES

IDOLS OF THE MIND *

Francis Bacon

XIX

There are and can be only two ways of searching into and discovering truth. The one flies from the senses and particulars to the most general axioms, and from these principles, the truth of which it takes for settled and immovable, proceeds to judgment and to the discovery of middle axioms. And this way is now in fashion. The other derives axioms from the senses and particulars, rising by a gradual and unbroken ascent, so that it arrives at the most general axioms last of all. This is the true way, but as yet untried.

XX

The understanding left to itself takes the same course (namely, the former) which it takes in accordance with logical order. For the mind longs to spring up to positions of higher generality, that it may find rest there; and so after a little while wearies of experiment. But this evil is increased by logic, because of the order and solemnity of its disputations.

XXI

The understanding left to itself, in a sober, patient, and grave mind, especially if it be not hindered by received doctrines, tries a little that other way, which is the right one, but with little progress; since the understanding, unless directed and assisted, is a thing unequal, and quite unfit to contend with the obscurity of things.

XXII

Both ways set out from the senses and particulars, and rest in the highest generalities; but the difference between them is infinite. For

* Francis Bacon, *Novum Organum*, 1620.

the one just glances at experiment and particulars in passing, the other dwells duly and orderly among them. The one, again, begins at once by establishing certain abstract and useless generalities, the other rises by gradual steps to that which is prior and better known in the order of nature.

XXIII

There is a great difference between the *Idols* of the human mind and the *Ideas* of the divine. That is to say, between certain empty dogmas, and the true signatures and marks set upon the works of creation as they are found in nature.

XXXIX

There are four classes of idols which beset men's minds. To these for distinction's sake I have assigned names,—calling the first class *Idols of the Tribe;* the second, *Idols of the Cave;* the third, *Idols of the Market-place;* the fourth, *Idols of the Theater.*

XL

The formation of ideas and axioms by true induction is no doubt the proper remedy to be applied for the keeping off and clearing away of idols. To point them out, however, is of great use, for the doctrine of idols is to the interpretation of nature what the doctrine of the refutation of sophisms is to common logic.

XLI

The Idols of the Tribe have their foundation in human nature itself, and in the tribe or race of men. For it is a false assertion that the sense of man is the measure of things. On the contrary, all perceptions, as well of the sense as of the mind, are according to the measure of the individual and not according to the measure of the universe. And the human understanding is like a false mirror, which, receiving rays irregularly, distorts and discolors the nature of things by mingling its own nature with it.

XLII

The Idols of the Cave are the idols of the individual man. For everyone (besides the errors common to human nature in general) has a cave or den of his own, which refracts and discolors the light of nature; owing either to his own proper and peculiar nature or to his education and conversation with others; or to the reading of books, and the authority of those whom he esteems and admires; or to the differences of impressions, accordingly as they take place in a mind preoccupied and predisposed or in a mind indifferent and settled; or the like. So that the spirit of man (according as it is meted out to different individuals) is in fact a thing variable and full of perturbation, and governed as it were by chance. Whence it was well observed by Heraclitus that men look for sciences in their own lesser worlds, and not in the greater or common world.

XLIII

There are also idols formed by the intercourse and association of men with each other, which I call Idols of the Market-place, on account of the commerce and consort of men there. For it is by discourse that men associate; and words are imposed according to the apprehension of the vulgar. And therefore the ill and unfit choice of words wonderfully obstructs the understanding. Nor do the definitions or explanations wherewith in some things learned men are wont to guard and defend themselves, by any means set the matter right. But words plainly force and overrule the understanding, and throw all into confusion, and lead men away into numberless empty controversies and idle fancies.

XLIV

Lastly, there are idols which have immigrated into men's minds from the various dogmas of philosophies, and also from wrong laws of demonstration. These I call Idols of the Theater; because in my judgment all the received systems are but so many stage-plays, representing worlds of their own creation after an unreal and scenic fashion. Nor is it only of the systems now in vogue, or only of the ancient sects and philosophies, that I speak: for many more plays of the same kind may yet be composed and in like artificial manner set forth; seeing that errors the most widely different have nevertheless causes for the most part alike. Neither again do I mean this only of entire systems, but also of many principles and axioms in science, which by tradition, credulity, and negligence have come to be received. . . .

FOUR KINDS OF THINKING*

James Harvey Robinson

We do not think enough about thinking, and much of our confusion is the result of current illusions in regard to it. Let us forget for the moment any impressions we may have derived from the philosophers, and see what seems to happen in ourselves. The first thing that we notice is that our thought moves with such incredible rapidity that it is almost impossible to arrest any specimen of it long enough to have a look at it. When we are offered a penny for our thoughts we always find that we have recently had so many things in mind that we can easily make a selection which will not compromise us too nakedly. On inspection we shall find that even if we are not downright ashamed of a great part of our spontaneous thinking it is far too intimate, personal, ignoble or trivial to permit us to reveal more than a small part of it. I believe this must be true of everyone. We do not, of course, know what goes on in other people's heads. They tell us very little and we tell them very little. The spigot of speech, rarely fully opened, could never emit more than driblets of the ever renewed hogshead of thought—*noch grösser wie's Heidelberger Fass.* We find it hard to believe that other people's thoughts are as silly as our own, but they probably are.

We all appear to ourselves to be thinking all the time during our waking hours, and most of us are aware that we go on thinking while we are asleep, even more foolishly than when awake. When uninterrupted by some practical issue we are engaged in what is now known as a *reverie.* This is our spontaneous and favorite kind of thinking. We allow our ideas to take their own course and this course is determined by our hopes and fears, our spontaneous desires, their fulfillment or frustration; by our likes and dislikes, our loves and hates and resentments. There is nothing else anything like so interesting to ourselves as ourselves. All thought that is not more or less laboriously controlled and directed will inevitably circle about the beloved Ego. It is amusing and pathetic to observe this tendency in ourselves and in others. We learn politely and generously to overlook this truth, but if we dare to think of it, it blazes forth like the noontide sun.

The reverie of "free association of ideas" has of late become the subject of scientific research. While investigators are not yet agreed on the results, or at least on the proper interpretation to be given to them, there can be no doubt that our reveries form the chief index to our fundamental character. They are a reflection of our nature as modified by often hidden and forgotten experiences. We need not go into the matter further here, for it is only necessary to observe that the reverie is at all times a potent and in many cases an omnipotent rival to every other kind of thinking. It doubtless influences all our speculations in its persistent tendency to self-magnification and self-justification, which are its chief preoccupations, but it is the last thing to make directly or indirectly for honest increase of knowledge. Philosophers usually talk as if such thinking did not exist or were in some way negligible. This is what makes their speculations so unreal and often worthless.

The reverie, as any of us can see for himself, is frequently broken and interrupted by the necessity of a second kind of thinking. We have to make practical decisions. Shall we write a letter or no? Shall we take the subway or a bus? Shall we have dinner at seven or half-past? Shall we buy U. S. Rubber or a Liberty Bond? Decisions are easily distinguishable from the free flow of the reverie. Sometimes they demand a good deal of careful pondering and the recollection of pertinent facts; often, however, they are made impulsively. They are a more difficult and laborious thing than the reverie, and we resent having to "make up our mind" when we are tired, or absorbed in a congenial reverie. Weighing a decision, it should be noted, does not necessarily add anything to our knowledge, although we may, of course, seek further information before making it.

A third kind of thinking is stimulated when any one questions our belief and opinions. We sometimes find ourselves changing our minds without any resistance or heavy emotion, but if we are told that we are wrong we resent the imputation and harden our hearts. We are incredibly heedless in the formation of our beliefs, but find ourselves filled with an illicit passion for them when anyone proposes to rob us of their companionship. It is obviously not the ideas themselves that are dear to us, but our self-esteem, which is threatened. We are by nature stubbornly pledged to defend our own from attack, whether it be our person, our family, our property, or our opinion. A United States Senator once remarked to a friend of mine that God Almighty could not make him change his mind on our Latin-American policy. We may surrender, but rarely confess ourselves vanquished. In the intellectual world at least peace is without victory.

Few of us take the pains to study the origin of our cherished convictions; indeed, we have a natural repugnance to so doing. We like to continue to believe what we have been accustomed to accept as true, and the resentment aroused when doubt is cast upon any of our assumptions leads us to seek every manner of excuse for clinging to them. *The result is that most of our so-called reasoning consists in finding arguments for going on believing as we already do.*

I remember years ago attending a public dinner to which the Governor of the state was bidden. The chairman explained that His Excellency could not be present for certain "good" reasons; what the "real" reasons were the presiding officer said he would leave us to conjecture. This distinction between "good" and "real" reasons is one of the most clarifying and essential in the whole realm of thought. We can readily give what seem to us "good" reasons for being a Catholic or a Mason, a Republican or a Democrat, an adherent or opponent of the League of Nations. But the "real" reasons are usually on a quite different plane. Of course the importance of this distinction is popularly, if somewhat obscurely, recognized. The Baptist missionary is ready enough to see that the Buddhist is not such because his doctrines would bear careful inspection, but because he happened to be born in a Buddhist family in Tokyo. But it would be treason to his faith to acknowledge that his own partiality for certain doctrines is due to the fact that his mother was a member of the First Baptist church of Oak Ridge. A savage can give all sorts of reasons for his belief that it is dangerous to step on a man's shadow, and a newspaper editor can advance plenty of arguments against the Bolsheviki. But neither of them may realize why he happens to be defending his particular opinion.

The "real" reasons for our beliefs are concealed from ourselves as well as from others. As we grow up we simply adopt the ideas presented to us in regard to such matters as religion, family relations, property, business, our country, and the state. We unconsciously absorb them from our environment. They are persistently whispered in our ear by the group in which we happen to live. Moreover, as Mr. Trotter has pointed out, these judgments, being the product of suggestion and not of reasoning, have the quality of perfect obviousness, so that to question them

. . . is to the believer to carry skepticism to an insane degree, and will be met by contempt, disapproval, or condemnation, according to the nature of the belief in question. When, therefore, we find ourselves entertaining an opinion about the basis of which there is a quality of feeling which tells us that to inquire into it would be absurd, obviously unnecessary, unprofitable, undesirable, bad form, or wicked, we may know that that opinion is a non-rational one, and probably, therefore, founded upon inadequate evidence.[1]

[1] *Instincts of the Herd*, p. 44.

Opinions, on the other hand, which are the result of experience or of honest reasoning do not have this quality of "primary certitude." I remember when as a youth I heard a group of business men discussing the question of the immortality of the soul, I was outraged by the sentiment of doubt expressed by one of the party. As I look back now I see that I had at the time no interest in the matter, and certainly no least argument to urge in favor of the belief in which I had been reared. But neither my personal indifference to the issue, nor the fact that I had previously given it no attention, served to prevent an angry resentment when I heard *my* ideas questioned.

This spontaneous and loyal support of our preconceptions—this process of finding "good" reasons to justify our routine beliefs—is known to modern psychologists as "rationalizing"—clearly only a new name for a very ancient thing. Our "good" reasons ordinarily have no value in promoting honest enlightenment, because, no matter how solemnly they may be marshaled, they are at bottom the result of personal preference or prejudice, and not of an honest desire to seek or accept new knowledge.

In our reveries we are frequently engaged in self-justification, for we cannot bear to think ourselves wrong, and yet have constant illustrations of our weaknesses and mistakes. So we spend much time finding fault with circumstances and the conduct of others, and shifting on to them with great ingenuity the onus of our own failures and disappointments. *Rationalizing is the self-exculpation which occurs when we feel ourselves, or our group, accused of misapprehension or error.*

The little word *my* is the most important one in all human affairs, and properly to reckon with it is the beginning of wisdom. It has the same force whether it is *my* dinner, *my* dog, and *my* house, or *my* faith, *my* country, and *my* God. We not only resent the imputation that our watch is wrong, or our car shabby, but that our conception of the canals of Mars, of the pronunciation of "Epictetus," of the medicinal value of salicine, or the date of Sargon I, is subject to revision.

Philosophers, scholars, and men of science exhibit a common sensitiveness in all decisions in which their *amour propre* is involved. Thousands of argumentative works have been written to vent a grudge. However stately their reasoning, it may be nothing but rationalizing, stimulated by the most commonplace of all motives. A history of philosophy and theology could be written in terms of grouches, wounded pride, and aversions, and it would be far more instructive than the usual treatments of these themes. Sometimes, under Providence, the lowly impulse of resentment leads to great achievements. Milton wrote his treatise on divorce as a result of his troubles with his seventeen-year-old wife, and when he was accused of being the leading spirit in a new sect, the Divorcers, he wrote his noble *Areopagitica* to prove his right to say what he thought fit, and incidentally to establish the advantage of a free press in the promotion of Truth.

All mankind, high and low, thinks in all the ways which have been described. The reverie goes on all the time not only in the mind of the mill hand and the Broadway flapper, but equally in weighty judges and godly bishops. It has gone on in all the philosophers, scientists, poets, and theologians that have ever lived. Aristotle's most abstruse speculations were doubtless tempered by highly irrelevant reflections. He is reported to have had very thin legs and small eyes, for which he doubtless had to find excuses, and he was wont to indulge in very conspicuous dress and rings and was accustomed to arrange his hair carefully. Diogenes the Cynic exhibited the impudence of a touchy soul. His tub was his distinction. Tennyson in beginning his "Maud" could not forget his chagrin over losing his patrimony years before as the result of an unhappy investment in the Patent Decorative Carving Company. These facts are not recalled here as a gratuitous disparagement of the truly great, but to insure a full realization of the tremendous competition which all really exacting thought has to face, even in the minds of the most highly endowed mortals.

And now the astonishing and perturbing suspicion emerges that perhaps almost all that had passed for social science, political economy, politics, and ethics in the past may be brushed aside by future generations as mainly rationalizing. John Dewey has already reached this conclusion in regard to philosophy. Veblen and other writers have revealed the various unperceived presuppositions of the traditional political economy, and now comes an Italian sociologist, Vilfredo Pareto, who, in his huge treatise on general sociology, devotes hundreds of pages to substantiating a similar thesis affecting all the social sciences. This conclusion may be ranked by students of a hundred years hence as one of the several great discoveries of our age. It is by no means fully worked out, and it is so opposed to nature that it will be very slowly accepted by the great mass of those who consider themselves thoughtful. As a historical student I am personally fully reconciled to this newer view. Indeed, it seems to me inevitable that just as the various sciences of nature were, before the opening of the seventeenth century, largely masses of rationalizations to suit the religious sentiments of the period, so the social sciences have continued even to our own day to be rationalizations of uncritically accepted beliefs and customs.

It will become apparent as we proceed that the fact that an idea is ancient and that it has been widely received is no argument in its favor, but should immediately suggest the necessity of carefully testing it as a probable instance of rationalization.

This brings us to another kind of thought which can fairly easily be distinguished from the three kinds described above. It has not the usual qualities of the reverie, for it does not hover about our personal complacencies and humiliations. It is not made up of the homely decisions forced upon us by everyday needs, when we review our little stock of existing information, consult our conventional preferences and obligations, and make a choice of action. It is not the defense of our own cherished beliefs and prejudices just because they are our own—mere plausible excuses for remaining of the same mind. On the contrary, it is that peculiar species of thought which leads us to *change* our mind.

It is this kind of thought that has raised man from his pristine, subsavage ignorance and squalor to the degree of knowledge and comfort which he now possesses. On his capacity to continue and greatly extend this kind of thinking depends his chance of groping his way out of the plight in which the most civilized peoples of the world now find themselves. In the past this type of thinking has been called Reason. But so many misapprehensions have grown up around the world that some of us have become suspicious of it. I suggest, therefore, that we substitute a recent name and speak of "creative thought" rather than of Reason. *For this kind of meditation begets knowledge, and knowledge is really creative inasmuch as it makes things look different from what they seemed before and may indeed work for their reconstruction.*

In certain moods some of us realize that we are observing things or making reflections with a seeming disregard of our personal preoccupations. We are not preening or defending ourselves; we are not faced by the necessity of any practical decision, nor are we apologizing for believing this or that. We are just wondering and looking and mayhap seeing what we never perceived before.

Curiosity is as clear and definite as any of our urges. We wonder what is in a sealed telegram or in a letter in which some one else is absorbed, or what is being said in the telephone booth or in low conversation. This inquisitiveness is vastly stimulated by jealousy, suspicion, or any hint that we ourselves are directly or indirectly involved. But there appears to be a fair amount of personal interest in other people's affairs even when they do not concern us except as a mystery to be unraveled or a tale to be told. The reports of a divorce suit will have "news value" for many weeks. They constitute a story, like a novel or play or moving picture. This is not an example of pure curiosity, however, since we readily identify ourselves with others, and their joys and despair then become our own.

We also take note of, or "observe," as Sherlock Holmes says, things which have nothing to do with our personal interests and make no personal appeal either direct or by way of sympathy. This is what Veblen so well calls "idle curiosity." And it is usually idle enough. Some of us when we face the line of people opposite us in a subway train impulsively consider them in detail and engage in rapid inferences and form theories in regard to them. On entering a room there are those who will perceive at a glance the degree of preciousness of the rugs, the character of the pictures, and the personality revealed by the books. But there are many, it would seem, who are so absorbed in their personal reverie or in some definite purpose that they have no bright-eyed energy for idle curiosity. The tendency to miscellaneous observation we come by honestly enough, for we note it in many of our animal relatives.

Veblen, however, uses the term "idle curiosity" somewhat ironically, as is his wont. It is idle only to those who fail to realize that it may be a very rare and indispensable thing from which almost all distinguished human achievement proceeds, since it may lead to systematic examination and seeking for things hitherto undiscovered. For research is but diligent search which enjoys the high flavor of primitive hunting. Occasionally and fitfully idle curiosity thus leads to creative thought, which alters and broadens our own views and aspirations and may in turn, under highly favorable circumstances, affect the views and lives of others, even for generations to follow. An example or two will make this unique human process clear.

Galileo was a thoughtful youth and doubtless carried on a rich and varied reverie. He had artistic ability and might have turned out to be a musician or painter. When he had dwelt among the monks at Valambrosa he had been tempted to lead the life of a religious. As a boy he busied himself with toy machines and he inherited a fondness for mathematics. All these facts are of record. We may safely assume also that, along with many other subjects of contemplation, the Pisan maidens found a vivid place in his thoughts.

One day when seventeen years old he wandered into the cathedral of his native town. In the midst of his reverie he looked up at the lamps hanging by long chains from the high ceiling of the church. Then something very difficult to explain occurred. He found himself no longer thinking of the building, worshippers, or the services; of his artistic or religious interest; of his reluctance to become a physician as his father wished. He forgot the question of a career and even the *graziosissime donne*. As he watched the swinging lamps he was suddenly wondering if mayhap their oscillations, whether long or short, did not occupy the same time. Then he tested this hypothesis by counting his pulse, for that was the only timepiece he had with him.

This observation, however remarkable in itself, was not enough to produce a really creative thought. Others may have noticed the same thing and yet nothing came of it. Most of our observations have no assignable results. Galileo may have seen the warts on a peasant's face formed a perfect isosceles triangle, or he may have noticed with boyish glee that just as the officiating priest was uttering the solemn words, *ecce agnus Dei*, a fly lit on the end of his nose. To be really creative, ideas have to be worked up and then "put over," so that they become a part of man's social heritage. The highly accurate pendulum clock was one of the later results of Galileo's discovery. He himself was led to reconsider and successfully to refute the old notions of falling bodies. It remained for Newton to prove that the moon was falling, and presumably all the heavenly bodies. This quite upset all the consecrated views of the heavens as managed by angelic engineers. The universality of the laws of gravitation stimulated the attempt to seek other and equally important natural laws and cast grave doubts on the miracles in which mankind had hitherto believed. In short, those who dared to include in their thought the discoveries of Galileo and his successors found themselves in a new earth surrounded by new heavens.

On the 28th of October, 1831, two hundred and fifty years after Galileo had noticed the isochronous vibrations of the lamps, creative thought and its currency had so far increased that Faraday was wondering what would happen if he mounted a disk of copper between the poles of a horseshoe magnet. As the disk revolved, an electric current was produced. This would doubtless have seemed the idlest kind of experiment to the staunch business men of the time who, it happened, were just then denouncing the child-labor bills in their anxiety to avail themselves to the full of the results of earlier idle curiosity. But should the dynamos and motors which have come into being as the outcome of Faraday's experiment be stopped this evening, the business man of today, agitated over labor troubles, might, as he trudged home past lines of "dead" cars, through dark streets to an unlighted house, engage in a little creative thought of his own and perceive that he and his laborers would have no modern factories and mines to quarrel about if it had not been for the strange, practical effects of the idle curiosity of scientists, inventors, and engineers.

The examples of creative intelligence given above belong to the realm of modern scientific achievement, which furnishes the most striking instances of the effects of scrupulous, objective thinking. But there are, of course, other great realms in which the recording and embodiment of acute observation and insight have wrought themselves into the higher life of man. The great poets and dramatists and our modern story-tellers have found themselves engaged in productive reveries, noting and artistically presenting their discoveries for the delight and instruction of those who have the ability to appreciate them.

The process by which a fresh and original poem or drama comes into being is doubtless analogous to that which originates and elaborates so-called scientific discoveries; but there is clearly a temperamental difference. The genesis and advance of painting, sculpture, and music offer still other problems. We really as yet know shockingly little about these matters, and indeed very few people have the least curiosity about them. Nevertheless, creative intelligence in its various forms and activities is what makes man. Were it not for its slow, painful, and constantly discouraged operations through the ages man would be no more than a species of primate living on seeds, fruit, roots, and uncooked flesh, and wandering naked through the woods and over the plains like a chimpanzee.

The origin and progress and future promotion of civilization are ill understood and misconceived. These should be made the chief theme of education, but much hard work is necessary before we can reconstruct our ideas of man and his capacities and free ourselves from innumerable persistent misapprehensions. There have been obstructionists in all times, not merely the lethargic masses, but the moralists, the rationalizing theologians, and most of the philosophers, all busily if unconsciously engaged in ratifying existing ignorance and mistakes and discouraging creative thought. Naturally, those who reassure us seem worthy of honor and respect. Equally naturally, those who puzzle us with disturbing criticisms and invite us to change our ways are objects of suspicion and readily discredited. Our personal discontent does not ordinarily extend to any critical questioning of the general situation in which we find ourselves. In every age the prevailing conditions of civilization have appeared quite natural and inevitable to those who grew up in them. The cow asks no questions as to how it happens to have a dry stall and a supply of hay. The kitten laps its warm milk from a china saucer, without knowing anything about porcelain; the dog nestles in the corner of a divan with no sense of obligation to the inventors of upholstery and the manufacturers of down pillows. So we humans accept our breakfasts, our trains and telephones and orchestras and movies, our national Constitution, our moral code and standards of manners, with the simplicity and innocence of a pet rabbit. We have absolutely inexhaustible capacities for appropriating what others do for us with no thought of a "thank you." We do not feel called upon to make any least contribution to the merry game ourselves. Indeed, we are usually quite unaware that a game is being played at all.

We have now examined the various classes of thinking which we can readily observe in ourselves and which we have plenty of reasons to believe go on, and always have been going on, in our fellow-men. We can sometimes get quite pure and sparkling examples of all four kinds, but commonly they are so confused and intermingled in our reverie as not to be readily distinguishable. The reverie is a reflection of our longings, exultations, and complacencies, our fears, suspicions, and disappointments. We are chiefly engaged in struggling to maintain our self-respect and in asserting that supremacy which we all crave and which seems to us our natural prerogative. It is not strange, but rather quite inevitable, that our beliefs about what is true and false, good and bad, right and wrong, should be mixed up with the reverie and be influenced by the same considerations which determine its character and course. We resent criticisms of our views exactly as we do of anything else connected with ourselves. Our notions of life and its ideals seem to us to be *our own* and as such necessarily true and right, to be defended at all costs.

We very rarely consider, however, the process by which we gained our convictions. If we did so, we could hardly fail to see that there was ~~lly little ground for our confidence in them. Here and there, in this department of knowledge or that, some one of us might make a fair claim to have taken some trouble to get correct ideas of, let us say, the situation in Russia, the sources of our food supply, the origin of the Constitution, the revision of the tariff, the policy of the Holy Roman Apostolic Church, modern business organization, trade unions, birth control, socialism, the League of Nations, the excess-profits tax, preparedness, advertising in its social bearings; but only a very exceptional person would be entitled to opinions of all of even these few matters. And yet most of us have opinions on all these, and on many other questions of equal importance, of which we may know even less. We feel compelled, as self-respecting persons, to take sides when they come up for discussion. We even surprise ourselves by our omniscience. Without taking thought we see in a flash that it is most righteous and expedient to discourage birth control by legislative enactment, or that one who decries intervention in Mexico is clearly wrong, or that big advertising is essential to big business and that big business is the pride of the lands. As godlike beings, why should we not rejoice in our omniscience?

It is clear, in any case, that our convictions on important matters are not the result of knowledge or critical thought, nor, it may be added, are they often dictated by supposed self-interest. Most of them are *pure prejudices* in the proper sense of that word. We do not form them ourselves. They are the whispering of "the voice of the herd." We have in the last analysis no responsibility for them and need assume none. They are not really our own ideas, but those of others no more well informed or inspired than ourselves, who have got them in the same careless and humiliating manner as we. It should be our pride to revise our ideas and not to adhere to what passes for respectable opinion, for such opinion can frequently be shown to be not respectable at all. We should, in view of the considerations that have been mentioned, resent our supine credulity. As an English writer has remarked:

If we feared the entertaining of an unverifiable opinion with the warmth with which we fear using the wrong implement at the dinner table, if the thought of holding a prejudice disgusted us as does a foul disease, then the dangers of man's suggestibility would be turned into advantages.[2]

The purpose of this essay is to set forth briefly the way in which the notions of the herd have been accumulated. This seems to me the best, easiest, and least invidious educational device for cultivating a proper distrust for the older notions on which we still continue to rely.

The "real" reasons, which explain how it is we happen to hold a particular belief, are chiefly historical. Our most important opinions—those, for example, having to do with traditional, religious, and moral convictions, property rights, patriotism, national honor, the state, and indeed all the assumed foundations of society—are, as I have already suggested, rarely the result of reasoned consideration, but of unthinking absorption from the social environment in which we live. Consequently, they have about them a quality of "elemental certitude," and we especially resent doubt or criticism cast upon them. So long, however, as we revere the whisperings of the herd, we are obviously unable to examine them dispassionately and to consider to what extent they are suited to the novel conditions and social exigencies in which we find ourselves to-day.

The "real" reasons for our beliefs, by making clear their origins and history, can do much to dissipate this emotional blockade and rid us of our prejudices and preconceptions. Once this is done and we come critically to examine our traditional beliefs, we may well find some of

2 *Ibid.*, p. 45.

them sustained by experience and honest reasoning, while others must be revised to meet new conditions and our more extended knowledge. But only after we have undertaken such a critical examination in the light of experience and modern knowledge, freed from any feeling of "primary certitude," can we claim that the "good" are also the "real" reasons for our opinions.

I do not flatter myself that this general show-up of man's thought through the ages will cure myself or others of carelessness in adopting ideas, or of unseemly heat in defending them just because we have adopted them. But if the considerations which I propose to recall are really incorporated into our thinking and are permitted to establish our general outlook on human affairs, they will do much to relieve the imaginary obligation we feel in regard to traditional sentiments and ideals. Few of us are capable of engaging in creative thought, but some of us can at least come to distinguish it from other and inferior kinds of thought and accord to it the esteem that it merits as the greatest treasure of the past and the only hope of the future.

THE GONKS AND THE TIGER*

Raymond Rogers

About a million years or so ago there lived an ancestor of the modern Gonks named Zero Gonk. He was a muscular, stoop-shouldered, hairy-faced banana-eater called Zero because, in any emergency, his reaction time was zero point zero zero. In his time, living was largely a matter of meeting emergencies of the most elemental sort. There was always the danger of being torn limb from limb. Zero was admirably equipped to live that kind of life.

A fundamental part of his equipment was a large, mental picture in color. Whereas the modern Gonks have a great many pictures cluttering up their minds, their ancestor had only one: The Tiger. It was unusually clear and vivid.

Fundamental to Zero's method of dealing with tigers was a constant attempt to detect their approach as long as possible before they arrived. To this end, he tried to make as many abstractions as he could—sights, sounds, odors—while The Tiger was still far away. The way Zero interpreted his abstractions is of particular interest. In response to a large number of the abstractions he made—scents and sights and

* From *ETC.*, Winter 1950. Copyright 1950 by International Society for General Semantics. Reprinted by permission.

sounds—he behaved as though there could be one meaning and only one: The Tiger. This interpretation he always made so quickly that it merits a special name: "flash-association." A scent on the breeze was flash-associated with this vivid mental picture of The Tiger so instantaneously that Zero had the feeling of having seen it, touched it, been clawed by it.

Instantly, after the flash-association had occurred, everything became a blur to Zero and he was dimly conscious of wind whistling past his ears. The next thing he clearly knew, he was in the top of a tree, while the tiger (it *was* a tiger) bellowed and clawed the trunk below. Zero didn't have to stop and decide that he would climb to the top of the nearest tree, and he didn't have to figure out how he would get there. He had an automatic control system, entirely separate from his thinking apparatus which, set in motion by the flash-association, took him to the nearest treetop in the *least* possible time. There was no deliberation about it. The whole thing was like pushing buttons and throwing switches to turn on lights and start electric motors. The symbol had but one possible meaning.

It is obvious, of course, that one reason for the automatic hook-ups and for the dominance of the automatic system over the thinking system was the stark necessity for speed. But the main reason was that, for Zero, mechanical reaction was the safest kind of reaction. Suppose he interpreted a sound as meaning The Tiger when it actually meant something else, and made a needless trip to the closest treetop. He lost nothing by such an erroneous interpretation, whereas he would have lost everything by an error in the other direction. Though it is impossible to avoid errors, Zero's nervous makeup was so designed that he would always err in a manner safest to him. And there really was, for him, no consideration other than safety. He didn't have to worry about what his neighbors might think. If he interpreted a sign wrongly, and there proved to be no tiger approaching they would not remain on the ground laughing at him. They, too, would be sitting in nearby treetops.

And so a fixed, standard interpretation for all of a large group of symbols, together with a fixed, standard response to them, worked very well indeed for Zero Gonk. His nervous system became specialized for mechanical reaction, and he passed this specialization along to the next Gonk.

From Reaction to Interpretation

For a very long time after the time of Zero Gonk, during the lives of a great many later generations of Gonks, The Tiger remained their most dangerous enemy, and avoiding tigers remained the outstanding problem of living. Day in and day out, day and night, from one moment to the next, all Gonks had to be prepared to ascend the nearest tree at any instant. The mental picture of The Tiger, the flash-association of a great many sensory abstractions with this picture, and the resulting mechanical reaction became thoroughly incorporated into Gonk behavior.

If it hadn't been for the tigers, the Gonks would have had no trouble at all. They never went hungry because plenty of bananas grew on the trees, and they needed no shelter because the climate was warm and dry. Most of their other needs were fulfilled either automatically or without much effort on their part. Thus, they became highly specialized tiger-avoiders with no other particular abilities because no others were needed. All children were trained and endlessly drilled in the technique of tiger-avoiding, and a vast culture gradually developed and accumulated around this all-important activity. The Gonk heroes and heroines were people who could detect the approach of tigers before their fellows did on the basis of more subtle sensory abstractions, and the ones who reacted most quickly when the sign of a tiger was perceived. The stories that were told and preserved in Gonk tradition were stories of hairbreadth escapes from the raking claw, and people with scars upon their glutei were regarded with the greatest awe and admiration. All in all, the Gonks were happy creatures during this phase of their history. They often looked back upon this period with nostalgia and thought of it as the time of "the good old days" when, as we have mentioned, life was simple.

After a few eons had passed, however, a change began to occur in the climate—it gradually grew colder. This change had far-reaching effects upon the Gonks' tiger-infested tropical paradise, and these effects in turn reacted very unfavorably upon the Gonks' long-established behavior pattern. As it grew colder, the bananas and tigers both became less and less abundant. The Gonks readily noted the decrease in the number of bananas; it became harder and harder to find enough of them to make a square meal.

It was not so easy, however, to mark the disappearance of the tigers. For so many ages the Gonks had reacted to every possible sign of The Tiger—every rustling of the underbrush, every unusual scent on the breeze, every flash of color in the distance—as though it meant, beyond any doubt, the actual presence of a tiger, that they had an overpowering tendency to overestimate the actual number of tigers around them. For this reason, the decrease in the number of tigers was for a number of generations hardly noted at all. For many years after actual tigers had become a rarity, the Gonks still continued to scramble up trees at the slightest unusual sight, scent, or sound.

Even as the advancing cold deprived the Gonks of their traditional food supply and of the natural enemy to which they had become so well accustomed, it brought them a new and very satisfactory source of food. The temperature became suitable for rabbits. Although rabbit meat proved at first to be somewhat distasteful to them, the Gonks found that they could learn to like it, and that rabbits could be chased down and clubbed to death easily enough: a people whose chief occupation was escaping from tigers had no trouble at all in running down the swiftest of rabbits.

But the need for subsisting on rabbits introduced a seriously complicating factor into the lives of the Gonks. Bananas grow on trees and can be plucked at leisure; rabbits do not. Rabbits hide in bushes and make every effort to keep from being seen. In moving about through the bushes rabbits make rustling noises, and in running from bush to bush they allow only very slight glimpses of themselves—usually they are registered by the eyesight only as tawny flashes.

It doesn't take much imagination to see what the Gonks were up against after the disappearance of the bananas and the arrival of the rabbits. Put yourself in the place of one of them: you hear a rustling in the bushes and glimpse a tawny streak. Conditioned by long ages of training, your automatic control system instantly goes into action, you are dimly conscious of the rustling of air past your ears, and you find yourself swaying in the top of a tree. You look downward, expecting to see a bellowing tiger clawing at the tree trunk, but there is no tiger. Instead, you see a big jackrabbit disappearing over the brow of a hill an eighth of a mile away—too far away, even though you can run like the wind. Your dinner is gone.

And so, after the appearance of the rabbits, living became very complex for the Gonks. There were always rustlings going on in the bushes —there was one tawny flash after another from bush to bush. The question was, did the rustlings and flashes symbolize tigers or rabbits? There were two possible meanings for these signs, instead of just one meaning as there had been in the good old days, and this made life much more than two times as complicated as it had been. The automatic reaction which had served the Gonks so well for such a long time was no longer the safest possible reaction—it was no longer foolproof. It still gave them the maximum protection against tigers, to be sure, but this was no longer the only protection they needed. Death under the tiger's claw is not the only death there is. One can starve to death too. As soon as it became apparent that the rustlings could have *two* possible meanings, each of which called for a different reaction, interpretation became of primary importance.

In their long later development as users of signs and symbols the Gonks passed through a number of critical stages, but this particular stage was the most critical of all: the era when *interpreting* signs became more important than reacting quickly to them.

How to Interpret a Symbol

Looking back from the vantage point of accumulated human experience upon this early crisis of the Gonks', we feel a strong temptation to editorialize, to kibitz, to say how we would have met the problem if we had been in their places. It seems easy enough, so many eons later, to figure out how the thing *should* have been handled.

In the first place, it would seem that anyone faced with the problem of interpreting a doubtful rustling in the bushes would have to stop reacting automatically as though all rustlings meant "tiger." Certainly it seems to us that no progress in interpretation could be made until the flash-association and the mechanical reaction were brought under control.

Second—but what is the use of going on with this sort of second-guessing? The Gonks never did achieve this first step, and so of course they never went beyond it. They never did stop their flash-associating and their mechanical reacting, and they never did make the sort of approach to symbol interpretation that we might have made. However, this is not to say that they failed to develop a method of interpretation. They *did* develop a method—they had to do it in order to survive. Furthermore, their method is not to be considered unworthy just because it is illogical; it is in fact one of the major intellectual achievements of human history. It worked roughly as follows:

All the Gonks got hungry, of course, as soon as the bananas disappeared, but the biggest and strongest men of the group got hungriest the quickest. These big strong men were first and most profoundly affected by the appearance of the rabbits. It was extremely unnerving to them to see a rabbit disappearing over the hill after they had scrambled to the top of a tree to escape what they thought was a tiger. As they got hungrier and hungrier, and more and more unnerved, they began to think more and more often about rabbits and less and less often about The Tiger. The thing that finally happened was that their mental picture of The Tiger was displaced by a new mental picture of The Rabbit.

This was a major change, of course, and for a time it caused a great deal of confusion in the nervous systems of these big strong hungry Gonks. When a rustling in the bushes was flash-associated with their mental picture of The Rabbit, their automatic control systems *still* wanted to react as they always had and caused them to scramble up a tree. After a period of inner turmoil and nervous chaos, however, a very neat readjustment worked itself out. When a flash-association occurred, these big strong Gonks *still* felt a whistling of wind past their ears, the same as ever, but instead of taking them *away* from the rustling as before, their control mechanisms took them *toward* the rustling, and when the whole thing was over they found a dead rabbit in their hands, sometimes with a few bites already missing from his carcass.

As you can readily see, this was a very efficient solution to the food problem, as far as the big strong men were concerned. By the time this reversal of reaction occurred, there were no more tigers left, and so the big strong men were in no danger at all no matter how many bushes they charged. Rabbits were fully as plentiful as bananas had formerly been, and so it didn't take them long to satisfy their appetites. After they became satiated, however, they still continued to charge bushes and catch rabbits because the rustlings continued to come from the bushes and of course the subsequent flash-association and mechanical reaction was set off by each rustling. This means that the food problem was solved for all the rest of the Gonks—the smaller and weaker males, the elderly, the females, and the young—whose automatic control mechanisms had not undergone the great reversal and who therefore continued to respond to each rustling by scrambling up a tree. Those who had undergone the reversal brought in enough rabbits not only for themselves but for everyone else as well.

It should be possible at this point for the reader to feel some appreciation of the ingenuity of the Gonks' solution. There they were with a sign which had two possible meanings. Some of them reacted as though one of the meanings was correct, and the rest reacted as though the other meaning was correct. Thus, all possible interpretations were covered by the group without fundamentally changing their basic method of reacting. And, along with being able to stick by their traditional behavior and avoid learning anything new, they were able to survive!

The Higher Reality

After a time, it was noticed by the rabbit-chasing members of the group that a great deal of time had passed since anyone had seen a tiger. This, of course, was not noticed by the other Gonks because they continued to react to all rustlings as though they had been made by tigers. But it was noticed by rabbit-chasers, and they began to wonder about it. As they said to each other from time to time, it seemed quite remarkable that not a single one of them had met a tiger in any of the bushes he had charged.

Ultimately, they began to suspect in a very small way that the tigers were gone. As more and more time went by, the suspicion grew, and finally it came to be discussed quite openly among them—that is, among the rabbit-chasers. At first, by an unspoken agreement among themselves, the rabbit-chasers kept their suspicions from the rest of the Gonks. Later, after the suspicion had grown to become almost a certainty, they explicitly agreed among themselves to keep the whole thing a secret in order to protect their group prestige. It was nice to have the rest of the population believing that they ran great risks and exhibited great courage every day in the course of doing their work. Thus, the disappearance of the tigers came to be a sort of trade secret among the rabbit-chasers. It was passed down from father to son and jealously guarded for generations.

Of course, a secret shared by so many people could hardly be kept forever. There was a good deal of fraternization between the rabbit-chasers and the tiger-avoiders, and somebody at some time or other apparently talked indiscreetly. At any rate, the tiger-avoiders finally caught on and came to share the suspicion that there were no tigers, and that their scrambling up trees was unnecessary. With them, too, the suspicion grew and finally achieved the status of a certainty.

Here again one is tempted to editorialize and kibitz and become logical, to give a reasonable account of the way the Gonks *should* have reacted to this important bit of information. One might suppose that the tiger-avoiders would have relaxed and gradually overcome their age-old mechanical reactions to rustlings in the bushes—that they would have eventually stopped scrambling up trees. It is easy to imagine that the tiger-avoiders and the rabbit-chasers might have come to talk openly about the disappearance of the tigers, and possibly to laugh together at the thought of the long period during which both groups had behaved so foolishly—one group keeping the secret for no very good reason, while the other continued to scramble up trees.

But these things did not happen.

When the tiger-avoiders began to suspect, and later to feel certain, that there were no more tigers, they did not relax and gradually stop scrambling up trees. They didn't even feel happy about the new information—in fact, they actually didn't accept it as new knowledge at all. It conflicted with their previous knowledge; it didn't fit in comfortably with their mental picture of The Tiger, charging and bellowing in pursuit of them.

Mental pictures which have been serviceable for a long time come to be accepted as being correct and true. We come to depend upon them just as completely as we depend upon the solid ground under us, and anything abstracted from the outside world which casts doubt upon them is just as profoundly disturbing as an earthquake which shakes the ground we stand on.

Naturally, a return of the tigers would have stabilized the whole thing for the tiger-avoiders; it would have relieved them of the threat of having to change their mental pictures and their matching behavior patterns. But there was nothing they could do to bring the tigers back. What does one do when he finds that his mental picture does not conform to outside reality, and that the outside world cannot be changed? Is there anything that can be done to avoid the awful ordeal of changing the mental picture?

There was one way out, and the Gonks found it. They developed a simple yet powerful method of preserving their mental picture. It consisted of withdrawing from the outside world, of taking the threatened mental picture out of contact with destructive new abstractions, of turning attention determinedly upon the mental picture and refusing to allow anything to disturb it.

Who Says There Are No Tigers?

It must be acknowledged that the method of mental picture preservation that the Gonks worked out can be effective only if the facts that are being dodged are the sort of external facts that *can* be dodged. Some facts, of course, cannot. But the absence of tigers, after all, was a negative perception. Nobody had seen one for several hundred years, but that was clearly no proof that one might not someday be seen. There was no way to demonstrate, beyond any question of doubt, that they were gone, and this is the thing that made the method possible.

The first step was to make the mental picture of The Tiger even more abstract than it had been before. This was done by increasing the number of natural happenings that could symbolize The Tiger. Instead of just recognizing the rustlings in the bushes and tawny streaks between bushes as representing The Tiger, a great number of other things came to be accepted as Tiger symbols. The sound of thunder was The Tiger bellowing at the foot of some tree somewhere—a tree in which a Gonk had found safety. Lightning was the tawny streak of The Tiger's charge through the forest, and wind was caused by the terrifying speed of the charge. With these and many other symbols of The Tiger's existence there was soon much less reason for doubting His reality.

The technique of mental picture preservation is essentially an extension of the fundamental processes of abstraction, symbolization, and manipulation of symbols. You search around for some new symbols to represent the thing depicted in your mental picture, and if you can find enough of them, you have no trouble in overcoming the perceptions that threaten your picture. This technique seems simple, but it actually calls for a great deal of ingenuity, cleverness, and pure artistry.

A tremendous amount of work went into the creation of Tiger symbols among the Gonks. The whole load of belief could not be borne by the naturally occurring symbols like those mentioned above. They were somewhat too abstract for some people—not all Gonks had the intelligence and imagination to appreciate them. There had to be other, more obvious ones, which could be used to give the feeling of The Tiger's presence to everyone, and which could be understood by anyone, no matter how limited his intelligence.

Of course, the basic behavior pattern of scrambling up trees was, of itself, highly symbolic, and served to keep the illusion alive until other symbols could be developed. These others each went through a long period of evolutionary development, but each of them finally emerged as an individual behavior pattern of its own, carried out repetitively, over and over in the same way, a system of habits, a small play-acting routine heavily freighted with meaning for those who participated.

The rabbit-chasers were the center of one of these routines. A little play was acted out in which a rabbit-chaser charged upon a bush after a rabbit, only to run into The Tiger—that is, a medicine man wearing a mask to resemble The Tiger's head. Feeling ran so strong during this play-acting sequence, however, that all the Gonks *felt* that it was actually The Tiger and not just a facsimile. The rabbit-chaser would grapple with The Tiger and strangle Him with his bare hands. In this and other sequences the rabbit-chasers were recognized as men of superdaring, and they came to be looked upon as the elite of Gonk society. A number of minor subsymbols were used to emphasize their status—special rabbit-skin clothing, a special headdress, a special mark branded upon their foreheads with red-hot embers, etc.

Some brilliant member of the group reasoned that if The Tiger were well fed, He would be less likely to catch and devour any of the Gonks, and this gave rise to another little play-acting routine. Some of the rabbits that were caught were "fed" to The Tiger by burning them in a fire, and it became standard practice to feed every seventh rabbit to The Tiger in this way. After a sufficient number of repetitions of this symbolic act, almost any Gonk was able to identify the fire quite literally with The Tiger. When one of the Gonks died, it was said that The Tiger had finally caught him, and his body was burned formally before the whole group to symbolize what had happened.

A Great Split

As time went on, the ceremonies of the Gonks became more and more refined and effective, so that there was no longer any possibility that the mental picture of The Tiger would be destroyed even if no one ever saw another tiger in the flesh. As ceremonial technique developed, it assumed more and more of the burden of protecting the cherished mental picture, and it became less and less necessary to pretend in everyday living that the existence of The Tiger was real. Thus, two apparently paradoxical developments took place side by side: on ceremonial occasions, the Gonks behaved in a more and more unrealistic and fantastic manner, whereas in everyday living they became more and more realistic and down-to-earth. And although the paradox is evident to any objective onlooker, it isn't and it never has been apparent to the Gonks.

As the ages marched along, they gradually stopped flash-associating rustlings in the bushes with their well-preserved mental picture of The Tiger. They stopped scrambling up trees. They took to walking quite unconcernedly through the forest, no matter how many rustlings they heard. Everybody began to catch rabbits, and the rabbit-catchers were no longer a truly distinct occupational group, although their distinction was maintained very strictly in the traditional ceremonies. Even the ceremonial distinction came in time to mean less, since everybody wanted to be inducted into the Rabbit-Catchers Brotherhood as soon as it came to be openly accepted in everyday life that there were no more tigers.

And so the Gonks finally came to live on two different levels—part of the time on one and part of the time on the other. In everyday living, they proceeded as though there were no tigers—which there weren't. On ceremonial occasions, they proceeded as though The Tiger were the most profound reality in their lives.

This split in their way of living—this remarkable schizoid feature of their existence—is the culmination of their intellectual development and the most noteworthy single feature of it. If we miss or ignore this feature we fail to understand the significance of the Gonk's whole symbolic evolution. They finally reached the point where they could, in effect, say "Tigers do not exist," and at the same time "The Tiger *does* exist." Furthermore, they could say these things without being aware of any contradiction at all.

Of course, they did not make these statements in the form of simple verbal declarations. So stated, the contradiction would have been obvious. These things were each said indirectly, by means of extremely varied and complex symbols, in such a way that the contradiction between them was far more easily missed than marked. It was an achievement of no small subtlety and sophistication in the field of symbolization. It earned for the Gonks the reputation of being the founders of Civilization.

LOGICAL FALLACIES*

Robert Gorham Davis

Undefined Terms

The first requirement for logical discourse is knowing what the words you use actually mean. Words are not like paper money or counters in a game. Except for technical terms in some of the sciences, they do not have a fixed face value. Their meanings are fluid and changing, influenced by many considerations of context and reference, circumstance and association. This is just as true of common words such as *fast* as it is of literary terms such as *romantic*. Moreover, if there is to be communication, words must have approximately the same meaning for the reader that they have for the writer. A speech in an unknown language means nothing to the hearer. When an adult speaks to a small child or an expert to a layman, communication may be seriously limited by lack of a mature vocabulary or ignorance of technical terms. Many arguments are meaningless because the speakers are using important words in quite different senses.

Because we learn most words—or guess at them—from the contexts in which we first encounter them, our sense of them is often incomplete

* From *Handbook for English A*, Harvard University. Copyright 1940, 1941, 1944, 1947 by The President and Fellows of Harvard University. Reprinted by permission of Robert Gorham Davis and the President and Fellows of Harvard University.

or wrong. Readers sometimes visualize the Assyrian who comes down like the wolf on the fold as an enormous man dressed in cohorts (some kind of fancy armor, possibly) gleaming in purple and gold. "A rift in the lute" suggests vaguely a cracked mandolin. Failure to ascertain the literal meaning of figurative language is a frequent reason for mixed metaphors. We are surprised to find that the "devil" in "the devil to pay" and "the devil and the deep blue sea" is not Old Nick, but part of a ship. Unless terms mean the same thing to both writer and reader, proper understanding is impossible.

Abstractions

The most serious logical difficulties occur with abstract terms. An abstraction is a word which stands for a quality found in a number of different objects or events from which it has been "abstracted" or taken away. We may, for instance, talk of the "whiteness" of paper or cotton or snow without considering qualities of cold or inflammability or usefulness which these materials happen also to possess. Usually, however, our minds carry over other qualities by association. See, for instance, the chapter called "The Whiteness of the Whale" in *Moby Dick*.

In much theoretic discussion the process of abstraction is carried so far that although vague associations and connotations persist, the original objects or events from which the qualities have been abstracted are lost sight of completely. Instead of thinking of words like *sincerity* and *Americanism* as symbols standing for qualities that have to be abstracted with great care from examples and test cases, we come to think of them as real things in themselves. We assume that Americanism is Americanism just as bicycle is a bicycle, and that everyone knows what it means. We forget that before the question, "Is Arthur Godfrey sincere?" can mean anything, we have to agree on the criteria of sincerity.

When we try to define such words and find examples, we discover that almost no one agrees on their meaning. The word *church* may refer to anything from a building on the corner of Spring Street to the whole tradition of institutionalized Christianity. *Germany* may mean a geographical section of Europe, a people, a governing group, a cultural tradition, or a military power. Abstractions such as *freedom, courage, race, beauty, truth, justice, nature, honor, humanism, democracy,* should never be used in a theme unless their meaning is defined or indicated clearly by the context. Freedom for whom? To do what? Under what circumstances? Abstract terms have merely emotional value unless they are strictly defined by asking questions of this kind. The study of a word such as *nature* in a good unabridged dictionary will show that even the dictionary, indispensable though it is, cannot determine for us the sense in which a word is being used in any given instance. Once the student understands the importance of definition, he will no longer be betrayed into fruitless arguments over such questions as whether free verse is "poetry" or whether you can change "human nature."

Name-Calling

It is a common unfairness in controversy to place what the writer dislikes or opposes in a generally odious category. The humanist dismisses what he dislikes by calling it *romantic;* the liberal, by calling it *fascist;* the conservative, by calling it *communistic.* These terms tell the reader nothing. What is *piety* to some will be *bigotry* to others. *Non-Catholics* would rather be called *Protestants* than *heretics.* What is *right-thinking* except a designation for those who agree with the writer? Social security measures become *creeping socialism;* industrial organizations, *forces of reaction;* investigation into Communism *witch hunts;* prison reform, *coddling;* progressive education, *fads and frills.* Such terms are intended to block thought by an appeal to prejudice and associative habits. Three steps are necessary before such epithets have real meaning. First, they must be defined; second, it must be shown that the object to which they are applied actually possesses these qualities; third, it must be shown that the possession of such qualities in this particular situation is necessarily undesirable. Unless a person is alert and critical both in choosing and in interpreting words, he may be alienated from ideas with which he would be in sympathy if he had not been frightened by a mere name.

Generalization

Similar to the abuse of abstract terms and epithets is the habit of presenting personal opinions in the guise of universal laws. The student often seems to feel that the broader the terms in which he states an opinion, the more effective he will be. Ordinarily the reverse is true. An enthusiasm for Thomas Wolfe should lead to a specific critical analysis of Wolfe's novels that will enable the writer to explain his enthusiasm to others; it should not be turned into the argument that Wolfe is "the greatest American novelist," particularly if the writer's knowledge of American novelists is somewhat limited. The same questions of *who* and *when* and *why* and under what *circumstances* which are used to check abstract terms should be applied to generalizations. Consider how contradictory proverbial wisdom is when detached from particular circumstances. "Look before you leap," but "he who hesitates is lost."

Superlatives and the words *right* and *wrong, true* and *untrue, never* and *always* must be used with caution in matters of opinion. When a student says flatly that X is true, he often is really saying that he or his family or the author of a book he has just been reading, persons of certain tastes and background and experience, *think* that X is true. If his statement is based not on logic and examination of evidence, but merely reproduces other people's opinions, it can have little value or relevance unless these people are identified and their reasons for thinking so explained. Because many freshmen are taking survey courses in which they read a single work by an author or see an historical event through the eyes of a single historian whose bias they may not be able to measure, they must guard against this error.

Sampling

Assertions of a general nature are frequently open to question because they are based on insufficient evidence. Some persons are quite ready, after meeting one Armenian or reading one medieval romance, to generalize about Armenians and medieval romances. One ought, of course, to examine objectively as many examples as possible before making a generalization, but the number is far less important than the representativeness of the examples chosen. The Literary Digest Presidential Poll, sent to hundreds of thousands of people selected from telephone directories, was far less accurate than the Gallup Poll which questioned far fewer voters, but selected them carefully and proportionately from all different social groups. The "typical" college student, as portrayed by moving pictures and cartoons, is very different from the "average" college student as determined statistically. We cannot let uncontrolled experience do our sampling for us; instances and examples which impress themselves upon our minds do so usually because they are exceptional. In propaganda and arguments extreme cases are customarily treated as if they were characteristic.

If one is permitted abitrarily to select some examples and ignore others, it is possible to find convincing evidence for almost any theory, no matter how fantastic. The fact that the mind tends naturally to remember those instances which confirm its opinions imposes a duty upon the writer, unless he wishes to encourage prejudice and superstition, to look carefully for exceptions to all generalizations which he is tempted to make. We forget the premonitions which are not followed by disaster and the times when our hunches failed to select the winner in a race. Patent medicine advertisements print the letters of those who survived their cure, and not of those who died during it. All Americans did not gamble on the stock exchange in the twenties or become Marxists in the thirties, and all Vermonters are not thin-lipped and shrewd. Of course the search for negative examples can be carried too far. Outside of mathematics or the laboratory, few generalizations can be made airtight, and most are not intended to be. But quibbling is so easy that resort to it is very common, and the knowledge that people can and will quibble over generalizations is another reason for making assertions as limited and explicitly conditional as possible.

False Analogy *Most persuasive*

Illustration, comparison, analogy are most valuable in making an essay clear and interesting. It must not be supposed, however, that they prove anything or have much argumentative weight. The rule that what is true of one thing in one set of circumstances is not necessarily true of another thing in another set of circumstances seems almost too obvious to need stating. Yet constantly nations and businesses are discussed as if they were human beings with human habits and feelings; human bodies are discussed as if they were machines; the universe, as if it were a clock. It is assumed that what held true for seventeenth century New England or the thirteen Atlantic colonies also holds true for an industrial nation of 160,000,000 people. Carlyle dismissed the arguments for representative democracy by saying that if a captain had to take a vote among his crew every time he wanted to do something, he would never get around Cape Horn. This analogy calmly ignores the distinction between the lawmaking and the executive branches of constitutional democracies. Moreover, voters may be considered much more like the stockholders of a merchant line than its hired sailors. Such arguments introduce assumptions in a metaphorical guise in which they are not readily detected or easily criticized. In place of analysis they attempt to identify their position with some familiar symbol which will evoke a predictable, emotional response in the reader. The revival during the 1932 presidential campaign of Lincoln's remark, "Don't swap horses in the middle of the stream," was not merely a picturesque way of saying keep Hoover in the White House. It made a number of assumptions about the nature of depressions and the function of government. This propagandist technique can be seen most clearly in political cartoons.

Degree

Often differences in degree are more important than differences in kind. By legal and social standards there is more difference between an habitual drunkard and a man who drinks temperately, than between a temperate drinker and a total abstainer. In fact differences of degree produce what are regarded as differences of kind. At known temperatures ice turns to water and water boils. At an indeterminate point affection becomes love and a man who needs a shave becomes a man with a beard. The fact that no men or systems are perfect makes rejoinders and counter-accusations very easy if differences in degree are ignored. Newspapers in totalitarian states, answering American accusations of brutality and suppression, refer to lynchings and gangsterism here. Before a disinterested judge could evaluate these mutual accusations, he would have to settle the question of the degree to which violent suppression and lynching are respectively prevalent in the countries under consideration. On the other hand, differences in degree may be merely apparent. Lincoln Steffens pointed out that newspapers can create a "crime wave" any time they wish, simply by emphasizing all the minor assaults and thefts commonly ignored or given an inch or two on a back page. The great reported increases in insanity may be due to the fact that in a more urban and institution-alized society cases of insanity more frequently come to the attention of authorities and hence are recorded in statistics.

Causation

The most common way of deciding that one thing causes another thing is the simple principle: *post hoc, ergo propter hoc,* "After this, therefore because of this." Rome fell after the introduction of Christianity; therefore Christianity was responsible for the fall of Rome. Such reasoning illustrates another kind of faulty generalization. But even if one could find ten cases in which a nation "fell" after the intro-duction of Christianity, it still would not be at all certain that Christi-anity caused the fall. Day, it has frequently been pointed out, follows night in every observable instance, and yet night cannot be called the cause of day. Usually a combination of causes produces a result. Sitting in a draught may cause a cold, but only given a certain physical condition in the person sitting there. In such instances one may dis-tinguish between necessary and sufficient conditions. Air is a necessary condition for the maintenance of plant life, but air alone is not suf-ficient to produce plant life. And often different causes at different times may produce the same result. This relation is known as plurality of causes. If, after sitting in a stuffy theatre on Monday, and then again after eating in a stuffy restaurant on Thursday, a man suffered from headaches, he might say, generalizing, that bad air gave him headaches. But actually the headache on Monday may have been caused by eye-strain and on Thursday by indigestion. To isolate the causative factor it is necessary that all other conditions be precisely the same. Such isolation is possible, except in very simple instances, only in the laboratory or with scientific methods. If a picture falls from the wall every time a truck passes, we can quite certainly say that the truck's passing is the proximate or immediate cause. But with anything as complex and conditional as a nation's economy or human character, the determination of cause is not easy or certain. A psychiatrist often sees a patient for an hour daily for a year or more before he feels that he understands his neurosis.

Ordinarily when we speak of cause we mean the proximate or immediate cause. The plants were killed by frost; we had indigestion from eating lobster salad. But any single cause is one in an unbroken series. When a man is murdered, is his death caused by the loss of blood from the wound, or by the firing of the pistol, or by the malice aforethought of the murderer? Was the World War "caused" by the assassination at Sarajevo? Were the Navigation Acts or the ideas of John Locke more important in "causing" the American Revolution? A complete statement of cause would comprise the sum total of the conditions which preceded an event, conditions stretching back indefinitely into the past. Historical events are so interrelated that the isolation of a causative sequence is dependent chiefly on the particular preoccupations of the historian. An economic determinist can "explain" history entirely in terms of economic development; an idealist, entirely in terms of the development of ideas.

Syllogistic Reasoning

The formal syllogism of the type,

> All men are mortal
> John is a man
> Therefore John is mortal,

is not so highly regarded today as in some earlier periods. It merely fixes an individual as a member of a class, and then assumes that the individual has the given characteristics of the class. Once we have decided who John is, and what "man" and "mortal" mean, and have canvassed all men, including John, to make sure that they are mortal, the conclusion naturally follows. It can be seen that the chief difficulties arise in trying to establish acceptable premises. Faults in the premises are known as "material" fallacies, and are usually more serious than the "formal" fallacies, which are logical defects in drawing a conclusion from the premises. But although directly syllogistic reasoning is not much practiced, buried syllogism can be found in all argument, and it is often a useful clarification to outline your own or another writer's essay in syllogistic form. The two most frequent defects in the syllogism itself are the undistributed and the ambiguous middle. The middle term is the one that appears in each of the premises and not in the conclusion. In the syllogism.

> All good citizens vote
> John votes
> Therefore John is a good citizen,

the middle term is not "good citizens," but "votes." Even though it were true that all good citizens vote, nothing prevents bad citizens from voting also, and John may be one of the bad citizens. To distribute the middle term "votes" one might say (but only if that is what one meant),

> All voters are good citizens
> John is a voter
> Therefore John is a good citizen.

The ambiguous middle term is even more common. It represents a problem in definition, while the undistributed middle is a problem in generalization. All acts which benefit others are virtuous, losing money at poker benefits others, therefore losing at poker is a virtuous act. Here the middle term "act which benefits others" is obviously used very loosely and ambiguously.

Non-Sequitur

This phrase, meaning "it does not follow," is used to characterize the kind of humor found in pictures in which the Marx Brothers used to perform. It is an amusing illogicality because it usually expresses, beneath its apparent incongruity, an imaginative, associative, or personal truth. "My ancestors came over on the Mayflower; therefore I am naturally opposed to labor unions." It is not logically necessary that those whose ancestors came over on the Mayflower should be opposed to unions; but it may happen to be true as a personal fact in a given case. It is usually a strong personal conviction which keeps people from realizing that their arguments are non-sequiturs, that they do not follow the given premises with logical necessity. Contemporary psychologists have effectively shown us that there is often such a wide difference between the true and the purported reasons for an attitude that, in rationalizing our behavior, we are often quite unconscious of the motives that actually influence us. A fanatical antivivisectionist, for instance, may have temperamental impulses toward cruelty which he is suppressing and compensating for by a reasoned opposition to any kind of permitted suffering. We may expect, then, to come upon many conclusions which are psychologically interesting in themselves, but have nothing to do with the given premises.

Ignoratio Elenchi

This means, in idiomatic English, "arguing off the point," or ignoring the question at issue. A man trying to show that monarchy is the best form of government for the British Empire may devote most of his attention to the charm of Elizabeth II and the affection her people felt for her. In ordinary conversational argument it is almost impossible for disputants to keep to the point. Constantly turning up are tempting side-issues through which one can discomfit an opponent or force him to irrelevant admissions that seem to weaken his case.

Begging the Question; Arguing in a Circle

The first of these terms means to assume in the premises what you are pretending to prove in the course of your argument. The function of logic is to demonstrate that because one thing or group of things is true, another must be true as a consequence. But in begging the question you simply say in varying language that what is assumed to be true is assumed to be true. An argument which asserts that we shall enjoy immortality because we have souls which are immaterial and indestructible establishes nothing, because the idea of immortality is already contained in the assumption about the soul. It is the premise which needs to be demonstrated, not the conclusion. Arguing in a circle is another form of this fallacy. It proves the premise by the conclusion and the conclusion by the premise. The conscience forbids an act because it is wrong; the act is wrong because the conscience forbids it.

Arguments ad Hominem and ad Populum

It is very difficult for men to be persuaded by reason when their interest or prestige is at stake. If one wishes to preach the significance of physiognomy, it is well to choose a hearer with a high forehead and a determined jaw. The arguments in favor of repealing the protective tariff on corn or wheat in England were more readily entertained by manufacturers than by landowners. The cotton manufacturers in New England who were doing a profitable trade with the South were the last to be moved by descriptions of the evils of slavery. Because interest and desire are so deeply seated in human nature, arguments are frequently mingled with attempts to appeal to emotion, arouse fear, play upon pride, attack the characters of proponents of an opposite view, show that their practice is inconsistent with their principles; all matters which have, strictly speaking, nothing to do with the truth or falsity, the general desirability or undesirability, of some particular measure. If men are desperate enough they will listen to arguments proper only to an insane asylum but which seem to promise them relief.

After reading these suggestions, which are largely negative, the student may feel that any original assertion he can make will probably contain one or several logical faults. This assumption is not true. Even if it were, we know from reading newspapers and magazines that worldly fame is not dimmed by the constant and, one suspects, conscious practice of illogicality. But generalizations are not made only by charlatans and sophists. Intelligent and scrupulous writers also have a great many fresh and provocative observations and conclusions to express and are expressing them influentially. What is intelligence but the ability to see the connection between things, to discern causes, to relate the particular to the general, to define and discriminate and compare? Any man who thinks and feels and observes closely will not want for something to express.

And in his expression a proponent will find that a due regard for logic does not limit but rather increases the force of his argument. When statements are not trite, they are usually controversial. Men arrive at truth dialectically; error is weeded out in the course of discussion, argument, attack, and counterattack. Not only can a writer who understands logic show the weaknesses of arguments he disagrees with, but also, by anticipating the kind of attack likely to be made on his own ideas, he can so arrange them, properly modified with qualifications and exceptions, that the anticipated attack is made much less effective. Thus, fortunately, we do not have to depend on the spirit of fairness and love of truth to lead men to logic; it has the strong support of argumentative necessity and of the universal desire to make ideas prevail.

3. THE IMPROVEMENT OF COMMUNICATION SKILLS

THE LANGUAGE OF REPORTS*

S. I. Hayakawa

For the purposes of the interchange of information, the basic symbolic act is the *report* of what we have seen, heard, or felt: "There is a ditch on each side of the road." "You can get those at Smith's hardware store for $2.75." "There aren't any fish on that side of the lake, but there are on this side." Then there are reports of reports: "The longest waterfall in the world is Victoria Falls in Rhodesia." "The Battle of Hastings took place in 1066." "The papers say that there was a big smash-up on Highway 41 near Evansville." Reports adhere to the following rules: first, they are *capable of verification;* second, they *exclude,* as far as possible, *inferences* and *judgments.* (These terms will be defined later.)

Verifiability

Reports are verifiable. We may not always be able to verify them ourselves, since we connot track down the evidence for every piece of history we know, nor can we all go to Evansville to see the remains of the smash-up before they are cleared away. But if we are roughly agreed on the names of things, on what constitutes a "foot," "yard," "bushel," and so on, and on how to measure time, there is relatively little danger of our misunderstanding each other. Even in a world such as we have today, in which everybody seems to be quarreling with everybody else, *we still to a surprising degree trust each other's reports.* We ask directions of total strangers when we are traveling. We follow directions on road signs without being suspicious of the people who put them up. We read books of information about science, mathematics, automotive engineering, travel, geography, the history of costume, and other such factual matters, and we usually assume that the author

---

* From S. I. Hayakawa, *Language in Thought and Action.* Copyright 1941, 1949 by Harcourt, Brace & World, Inc. Reprinted by permission.

is doing his best to tell us as truly as he can what he knows. And we are safe in so assuming most of the time. With the emphasis that is being given today to the discussion of biased newspapers, propagandists, and the general untrustworthiness of many of the communications we receive, we are likely to forget that we still have an enormous amount of reliable information available and that deliberate misinformation, except in warfare, still is more the exception than the rule. The desire for self-preservation that compelled men to evolve means for the exchange of information also compels them to regard the giving of false information as profoundly reprehensible.

At its highest development, the language of reports is the language of science. By "highest development" we mean greatest general usefulness. Presbyterian and Catholic, workingman and capitalist, German and Englishman, *agree* on the meanings of such symbols as $2 \times 2 = 4$, *100°C., HNO₃, 3:35 A.M., 1940 A.D., 5000 r.p.m., 1000 kilowatts, pulex irritans,* and so on. But how, it may be asked, can there be agreement about even this much among people who are at each other's throats about practically everything else: political philosophies, ethical ideals, religious beliefs, and the survival of my business *versus* the survival of yours? The answer is that circumstances *compel men to agree,* whether they wish to or not. If, for example, there were a dozen different religious sects in the United States, each insisting on its own way of naming the time of the day and the days of the year, the mere necessity of having a dozen different calendars, a dozen different kinds of watches, and a dozen sets of schedules for business hours, trains, and radio programs, to say nothing of the effort that would be required for translating terms from one nomenclature to another, would make life as we know it impossible.

The language of reports, then, including the more accurate reports of science, is "map" language, and because it gives us reasonably accurate representations of the "territory," it enables us to get work done. Such language may often be what is commonly termed "dull" or "uninteresting" reading: one does not usually read logarithmic tables or telephone directories for entertainment. But we could not get along without it. There are numberless occasions in the talking and writing we do in everyday life that *require that we state things in such a way that everybody will agree with our formulation.*

Inferences

The reader will find that practice in writing reports is a quick means of increasing his linguistic awareness. It is an exercise which will constantly provide him with his own examples of the principles of language and interpretation under discussion. The reports should be about first-hand experience—scenes the reader has witnessed himself, meetings and social events he has taken part in, people he knows well. They should be of such a nature that they can be verified and agreed upon. For the purpose of this exercise, inferences will be excluded.

Not that inferences are not important—we rely in everyday life and in science as much on *inferences* as on reports—in some areas of thought, for example, geology, paleontology, and nuclear physics, reports are the foundations, but inferences (and inferences upon inferences) are the main body of the science. An inference, as we shall use the term, is *a statement about the unknown made on the basis of the known.* We may *infer* from the handsomeness of a woman's clothes her wealth or social position; we may *infer* from the character of the ruins the origin of the fire that destroyed the building; we may *infer* from a man's calloused hands the nature of his occupation; we may *infer* from a senator's vote on an armaments bill his attitude toward Russia; we may *infer* from the structure of the land the path of a prehistoric glacier; we may *infer* from a halo on an unexposed photographic plate that it has been in the vicinity of radioactive materials; we may *infer* from the noise an engine makes the condition of its connecting rods. Inferences may be carelessly or carefully made. They may be made on the basis of a great background of previous experience with the subject matter, or no experience at all. For example, the inferences a good mechanic can make about the internal condition of a motor by listening to it are often startlingly accurate, while the inferences made by an amateur (if he tries to make any) may be entirely wrong. But the common characteristic of inferences is that they are statements about matters which are not directly known, made on the basis of what has been observed.

The avoidance of inferences in our suggested practice in report writing requires that we make no guesses as to what is going on in other people's minds. When we say, "He was angry," we are not reporting; we are making an inference from such observable facts as the following: "He pounded his fist on the table; he swore; he threw the telephone directory at his stenographer." In this particular example, the inference appears to be fairly safe; nevertheless, it is important to remember, especially for the purposes of training oneself, that it is an inference. Such expressions as "He thought a lot of himself," "He was scared of girls," "He has an inferiority complex," made on the basis of casual social observation, and "What Russia really wants to do is to establish a world communist dictatorship," made on the basis of casual newspaper reading, are highly inferential. One should keep in mind their inferential character and, in our suggested exercises, should substitute for them such statements as "He rarely spoke to subordinates in the plant," "I saw him at a party, and he never danced except when one of the girls asked him to," "He wouldn't apply for the scholarship although I believe he could have won it easily," and "The Russian delegation to the United Nations has asked for A, B, and C. Last year they voted against M and N, and voted for X and Y. On the basis of facts such as these, the newspaper I read makes the inference that what Russia really wants is to establish a world communist dictatorship. I tend to agree."

Judgments

In our suggested writing exercise, judgments are also to be excluded. By judgments, we shall mean *all expressions of the writer's approval or disapproval of the occurrences, persons, or objects he is describing.* For example, a report cannot say, "It was a wonderful car," but must say something like this: "It has been driven 50,000 miles and has never required any repairs." Again statements like "Jack lied to us" must be suppressed in favor of the more verifiable statement, "Jack told us he didn't have the keys to his car with him. However, when he pulled a handkerchief out of his pocket a few minutes later, a bunch of car keys fell out." Also a report may not say, "The senator was stubborn, defiant, and uncooperative," or "The senator courageously stood by his principles"; it must say instead, "The senator's vote was the only one against the bill."

Many people regard statements like the following as statements of "fact": "Jack *lied* to us," "Jerry is a *thief*," "Tommy is *clever*." As ordinarily employed, however, the word *"lied"* involves first an inference (that Jack knew otherwise and deliberately misstated the facts) and secondly a judgment (that the speaker disapproves of what he has inferred that Jack did). In the other two instances, we may substitute such expressions as, "Jerry was convicted of theft and served two years at Waupun," and "Tommy plays the violin, leads his class in school, and is captain of the debating team." After all, to say of a man that he is a "thief" is to say in effect, "He has stolen *and will steal again*"— which is more of a prediction than a report. Even to say, "He has stolen," is to make an inference (and simultaneously to pass a judgment) on an act about which there may be difference of opinion among those who have examined the evidence upon which the conviction was obtained. But to say that he was "convicted of theft" is to make a statement capable of being agreed upon through verification in court and prison records.

Scientific verifiability rests upon the external observation of facts, not upon the heaping up of judgments. If one person says, "Peter is a deadbeat," and another says, "I think so too," the statement has not been verified. In court cases, considerable trouble is sometimes caused by witnesses who cannot distinguish their judgments from the facts upon which those judgments are based. Cross-examinations under these circumstances go something like this:

WITNESS. That dirty double-crosser Jacobs ratted on me.
DEFENSE ATTORNEY. Your honor, I object.
JUDGE. Objection sustained. (Witness's remark is stricken from the record.) Now, try to tell the court exactly what happened.
WITNESS. He double-crossed me, the dirty, lying rat!
DEFENSE ATTORNEY. Your honor, I object!
JUDGE. Objection sustained. (Witness's remark is again stricken from the record.) Will the witness try to stick to the facts?
WITNESS. But I'm telling you the facts, your honor. He did double-cross me.

This can continue indefinitely unless the cross-examiner exercises some ingenuity in order to get at the facts behind the judgment. To the witness it is a "fact" that he was "double-crossed." Often hours of patient questioning are required before the factual bases of the judgment are revealed.

Many words, of course, simultaneously convey a report and a judgment on the fact reported. . . . For the purposes of a report as here defined, these should be avoided. Instead of "sneaked in," one might say "entered quietly"; instead of "politicians," "congressmen," or "aldermen," or "candidates for office"; instead of "bureaucrat," "public official"; instead of "tramp," "homeless unemployed"; instead of "dictatorial set-up," "centralized authority"; instead of "crackpots," "holders of uncommon views." A newspaper reporter, for example, is not permitted to write, "A crowd of suckers came to listen to Senator Smith last evening in that rickety firetrap and ex-dive that disfigures the south edge of town." Instead he says, "Between seventy-five and a hundred people heard an address last evening by Senator Smith at the Evergreen Gardens near the South Side city limits."

Snarl-Words and Purr-Words

. . . it is important to remember that we are considering language not as an isolated phenomenon, but language in action—language in the full context of the nonlinguistic events which are its setting. The making of noises with the vocal organs is a muscular activity, and like other muscular activities, often involuntary. Our responses to powerful stimuli, such as to something that makes us very angry, are a complex of muscular and physiological events: the contracting of fighting muscles, the increase of blood pressure, change in body chemistry, clutching one's hair, and so on, *and* the making of noises, such as growls and snarls. We are a little too dignified, perhaps, to growl like dogs, but we do the next best thing and substitute series of words, such as "You dirty double-crosser!" "The filthy scum!" Similarly, if we are pleasurably agitated, we may, instead of purring or wagging the tail, say things like "She's the sweetest girl in all the world!"

Speeches such as these are, as direct expressions of approval or disapproval, judgments in their simplest form. They may be said to be human equivalents of snarling and purring. "She's the sweetest girl in all the world" is not a statement about the girl; it is a purr. This seems to be a fairly obvious fact; nevertheless, it is surprising how often, when such statement is made, both the speaker and the hearer feel that something has been said about the girl. This error is especially common in the interpretation of utterances of orators and editorialists in some of their more excited denunciations of "Reds," "greedy monopolists," "Wall Street," "radicals," "foreign ideologies," and in their more fulsome dithyrambs about "our way of life." Constantly, because of the impressive sound of the words, the elaborate structure of the sentences, and the appearance of intellectual progression, we get the feeling that something is being said about something. On closer examination, however, we discover that these utterances merely say, "What I hate ('Reds,' 'Wall Street,' or whatever) I hate very, very much," and "What I like ('our way of life') I like very, very much." We may call such utterances "snarl-words" and "purr-words." They are not reports describing conditions in the extensional world in any way.

To call these judgments "snarl-words" and "purr-words" does not mean that we should simply shrug them off. It means that we should be careful to *allocate the meaning correctly*—placing such a statement as "She's the sweetest girl in the world" as a revelation of the speaker's state of mind, and not as a revelation of facts about the girl. If the "snarl-words" about "Reds" or "greedy monopolists" are accompanied by verifiable reports (which would also mean that we have previously agreed as to who, specifically, is meant by the term "Reds" or "greedy monopolists"), we might find reason to be just as disturbed as the speaker. If the "purr-words" about the sweetest girl in the world are accompanied by verifiable reports about her appearance, manners, skill in cooking, and so on, we might find reason to admire her too. But "snarl-words" and "purr-words" as such, unaccompanied by reports, offer nothing further to discuss, except possibly the question, "Why do you feel as you do?"

It is usually fruitless to debate such questions as "Was President Roosevelt a great statesman or merely a skillful politician?" "Is the music of Wagner the greatest music of all time or is it merely hysterical screeching?" "Which is the finer sport, tennis or baseball?" "Could Joe Louis in his prime have licked Bob Fitzsimmons in his prime?" To take sides on such issues of conflicting judgments is to reduce oneself to the same level of stubborn imbecility as one's opponents. But to ask questions of the form, "Why do you like (or dislike) Roosevelt (or Wagner, or tennis, or Joe Louis)?" is to learn something about one's friends and neighbors. After listening to their opinions and their reasons for them, we may leave the discussion slightly wiser, slightly better informed, and perhaps slightly less one-sided than we were before the discussion began.

How Judgments Stop Thought

A judgment ("He is a fine boy," "It was a beautiful service," "Baseball is a healthful sport," "She is an awful bore") is a conclusion, summing up a large number of previously observed facts. The reader is probably familiar with the fact that students almost always have difficulty in writing themes of the required length because their ideas give out after a paragraph or two. The reason for this is that those early paragraphs contain so many judgments that there is little left to be said. When the conclusions are carefully excluded, however, and observed facts are given instead, there is never any trouble about the length of papers; in fact, they tend to become too long, since inexperienced writers, when told to give facts, often give far more than are necessary, because they lack discrimination between the important and the trivial.

Still another consequence of judgments early in the course of a written exercise—and this applies also to hasty judgments in everyday thought—is the temporary blindness they induce. When, for example, an essay starts with the words, "He was a real Wall Street executive," or "She was a typical cute little co-ed," if we continue writing at all, we must make all our later statements consistent with those judgments. The result is that all the individual characteristics of this particular "executive" or this particular "co-ed" are lost sight of entirely; and the rest of the essay is likely to deal not with observed facts, but with the writer's private notion (based on previously read stories, movies, pictures, and so forth) of what "Wall Street executives" or "typical co-eds" look like. The premature judgment, that is, often prevents us from seeing what is directly in front of us. Even if the writer feels sure at the beginning of a written exercise that the man he is describing is a "loafer" or that the scene he is describing is a "beautiful residential suburb," he will conscientiously keep such notions out of his head, lest his vision be obstructed.

Slanting

In the course of writing reports of personal experiences, it will be found that in spite of all endeavors to keep judgments out, some will creep in. An account of a man, for example, may go like this: "He had apparently not shaved for several days, and his face and hands were covered with grime. His shoes were torn, and his coat, which was several sizes too small for him, was spotted with dried clay." Now, in spite of the fact that no judgment has been stated, a very obvious one is implied. Let us contrast this with another description of the same man. "Although his face was bearded and neglected, his eyes were clear, and he looked straight ahead as he walked rapidly down the road. He looked very tall; perhaps the fact that his coat was too small for him emphasized that impression. He was carrying a book under his left arm, and a small terrier ran at his heels." In this example, the impression about the same man is considerably changed, simply by the inclusion of new details and the subordination of unfavorable ones. Even if explicit judgments are kept out of one's writing, implied judgments will get in.

How, then, can we ever give an impartial report? The answer is, of course, that we cannot attain complete impartiality while we use the language of everyday life. Even with the very impersonal language of science, the task is sometimes difficult. Nevertheless, we can, by being aware of the favorable or unfavorable feelings that certain words and facts can arouse, attain enough impartiality for practical purposes. Such awareness enables us to balance the implied favorable and unfavorable judgments against each other. To learn to do this, it is a good idea to write two essays at a time on the same subject, both strict reports, to be read side by side: the first to contain facts and details likely to prejudice the reader in favor of the subject, the second to contain those likely to prejudice the reader against it. For example:

For	*Against*
He had white teeth.	His teeth were uneven.
His eyes were blue, his hair blond and abundant.	He rarely looked people straight in the eye.
He had on a clean blue shirt.	His shirt was frayed at the cuffs.
He often helped his wife with the dishes.	He rarely got through drying dishes without breaking a few.
His pastor spoke very highly of him.	His grocer said he was always slow about paying his bills.

Slanting Both Ways at Once

This process of selecting details favorable or unfavorable to the subject being described may be termed slanting. Slanting gives no explicit judgments, but it differs from reporting in that it deliberately makes certain judgments inescapable. The writer striving for impartiality will, therefore, take care to slant both for and against his subject, trying as conscientiously as he can to keep the balance even. The next stage of the exercise, then, should be to rewrite the parallel essays into a single coherent essay in which details on both sides are included.

His teeth were white, but uneven; his eyes were blue, his hair blond and abundant. He did not often look people straight in the eye. His shirt was slightly frayed at the cuffs, but it was clean. He frequently helped his wife with the dishes, but he broke many of them. Opinion about him in the community was divided. His grocer said he was slow about paying his bills, but his pastor spoke very highly of him.

This example is, of course, oversimplified and admittedly not very graceful. But practice in writing such essays will first of all help to prevent one from slipping unconsciously from observable facts to judgments; that is, from "He was a member of the Ku Klux Klan" to "the dirty scoundrel!" Next, it will reveal how little we really want to be impartial anyway, especially about our best friends, our parents, our alma mater, our own children, our country, the company we work for, the product we sell, our competitor's product, or anything else in which our interests are deeply involved. Finally, we will discover that, even if we have no wish to be impartial, we write more clearly, more forcefully, and more convincingly by this process of sticking as close as possible to observable facts. There will be, as someone once remarked, more horsepower and less exhaust.

A few weeks of practice in writing reports, slanted reports, and reports slanted both ways will improve powers of observation, as well as ability to recognize soundness of observation in the writings of others.

A sharpened sense for the distinction between facts and judgments, facts and inferences, will reduce susceptibility to the flurries of frenzied public opinion which certain people find it to their interest to arouse. Alarming judgments and inferences can be made to appear inevitable by means of skillfully slanted reports. A reader who is aware of the technique of slanting, however, is relatively difficult to stampede by such methods. He knows too well that there may be other relevant facts which have been left out. . . .

The importance of trying to "slant both ways" lies not in the hope of achieving a godlike impartiality in one's thinking and writing—which is manifestly an impossible goal. It lies in discovering what poor reporters most of us really are—in other words, how little we see of the world since we of necessity see it from our own point of view. To discover one's own biases is the beginning of wisdom.

MEANING AND CONTEXT*

Monroe C. Beardsley

One of the fundamental facts about words is that the most useful ones in our language have many meanings. That is partly why they are so useful: they work overtime (but, as we shall see, not for nothing). Think of all the various things we mean by the word "foot" on different occasions: one of the lower extremities of the human body, a measure of verse, the ground about a tree, twelve inches, the floor in front of the stairs. The same is true of nearly every common noun or verb. The editors of *The American College Dictionary*, in their preliminary investigation of words most frequently used, found 55 distinct senses of the word "point" in 1,100 occurrences of the word, and they distinguished 109 different senses of the word "run."

Considering the number of ways of taking a particular word, the task of speaking clearly and being understood would seem pretty hopeless if it were not for another very important fact about language. Though a word may have many senses, these senses can be controlled, up to a point, by the *context* in which the word is used. When we find the word in a particular verbal setting—that is, take it with the words that come before and after it in a discourse—we can usually decide

* From Monroe C. Beardsley, *Thinking Straight: Principles of Reasoning for Readers and Writers.* © 1956, 2nd Ed. Prentice-Hall, Inc., Englewood Cliffs, N. J. Reprinted by permission.

quite definitely which of the many senses of the word is relevant. If a poet says his verse has three feet, it doesn't occur to you that he could mean it's a yard long or is three-legged (unless perhaps you are a critic planning to puncture the poet with a pun about his "limping verse"). The context rules out these maverick senses quite decisively.

We might be puzzled if we read in a newspaper that "in the suicide's pocket the police found a large envelope full of bills." In this sentence, as it stands, the word "bills" can easily be taken in two very different senses. But if the context were expanded so as to read, "The police were surprised to find in the suicide's pocket a large envelope full of bills of various denominations," we should understand that "bills" meant *paper money*, and we might wonder whether it was indeed suicide or accident. Or if the context were expanded differently, so as to read, "The police were surprised to find in the suicide's pocket a large envelope full of unpaid bills," we should understand that "bills" meant *requests for payment of a debt*, and we might wonder whether that explains the suicide.

This is a rather simple illustration of the way in which the context of a word helps to pick out one of its senses and fix that sense. But of course "context" is used broadly here: it may be the rest of a sentence (the *immediate* context), a page, a whole book, or a newspaper file. A "shady street" is one thing; a "shady neighborhood" is something else. The word "strike" means one action on the front page of a paper and another action on the sports page; the words "liberal" and "patriotic" mean certain attitudes in *The New York Times* and mostly different ones in *The Chicago Tribune*. When some time ago a British physicist announced with pleasure that the hydrogen bomb is "safe," his statement caused gasps of surprise; in the technical talk of atomic scientists, "safe" apparently means that it couldn't set off a chain reaction that might destroy the earth itself. This is not the way the man in the street uses the word.

Many common words like "line," "pipe," "base," "stock," and "head," have acquired many serviceable meanings in different occupational contexts—say, in the shoptalk of plumbers, pitchers, or plastic engineers. Think of what the word "wing" means to a birdwatcher, an airman, a stagehand, a general, or an architect. But just because these meanings are so completely distinct—no one can confuse the wing of an airplane with the wing of a house—it is easy to control them by very light contextual pressure. A word or two makes it clear that it is the airman's wing rather than the architect's that is referred to. But when the differences between the senses of a word are slighter and subtler (they may be even more important, however), the most careful management of the context may be required to get and keep one sense in focus. The exact meaning of a word like "middle class" or "evolution" or "justice" may depend upon the whole book in which it appears.

That is why it is often easy to misrepresent what someone has said by quoting some of his remarks out of their context. The words may not, strictly speaking, be *mis*quoted, but their meaning has been changed. The political candidate's promise to obtain peace or balance the budget is echoed and attacked by his opponent—who is careful to leave out the conditions and qualifications that originally surrounded it. Even if a writer is scrupulous enough to put in dots to indicate that something has been left out, he may not be *quite* scrupulous enough to stick to the original meaning. You have seen advertisements of a new play, with a few words from a review. The phrase ". . . emotional subtlety . . . (Bridgeport *Post*)" may be from a sentence that goes: "It has all the emotional subtlety of a barroom brawl." The phrase ". . . great drama . . . (New Haven *Register*)" may be from a sentence that goes: "No doubt it was considered a great drama when it first appeared in 1927, but . . ." And this is nothing to what a professional wiretapper can do if he records a telephone conversation and picks out words to rerecord on a new tape.

Representative Wayne L. Hays, a member of the Special House Committee set up by the 83rd Congress to investigate tax-exempt foundations, frequently argued during the committee's hearings that the "research directors" of the committee were willing to make judgments on passages torn out of contexts that might change their meaning considerably. He finally made a dramatic demonstration of this by producing three paragraphs which the associate research director testified were "closely comparable" with, and parallel to, Communist literature that he had read. They were excerpts from two papal encyclicals.

A loose and sloppy writer lays himself open particularly to accidental misquotation, but any writer would find it very hard to write a paragraph that is proof against a deliberate and skillful excerpt-lifter. Dean Sturges of the Yale Law School perhaps came as close as anyone can when, in 1949, the Harvard Law School *Record* asked him for an appropriate comment on the Harvard Law School's decision to admit women students for the first time. Dean Sturges is reported to have sent the following telegram:

YALE LAW FACULTY AND STUDENT BODY DEEPLY MOVED. FEEL IT QUITE POS-
SIBLE HARVARD MAY MAKE CONTRIBUTION TO WOMANHOOD. DOUBT MANY AD-
VERSE CONSEQUENCES HARVARD FACULTY OR STUDENT BODY. WE HAVE ALWAYS

FOLLOWED WITH GENUINE INTEREST LONG STRUGGLE HARVARD LIBERALS IN THIS MATTER. OUR MANY GENERATIONS OF WOMEN GRADUATES ARE OF COURSE A PRIDE AND JOY. BEST WISHES.

Try digging a quotable compliment out of that.

The importance of context in the interpretation of meaning varies from one discourse to another. In a technical article on mathematics or physics, most sentences can stand pretty much on their own feet and be well understood apart from their context. Scientific terms are designed to resist the influence of context so that they can pass from one context to another without changing their meaning. But sentences in ordinary discourse that contain pronouns often lean on other sentences that contain the antecedents of those pronouns. Moreover, some words in our language—and they are among the most useful, but the trickiest, ones—are so adaptable to their context, like chameleons, that they take most of their character from it, and when they are considered apart from any context, they have only the most indefinite meaning. Words like "efficient," "dangerous," "internal," "successful," "free," tell us very little unless we are told, for example, the *purpose* for which it is efficient, or the *standards* in terms of which the success is judged. Contexts like "freehanded," "free lunch," "free love," "free will," "freeborn," "free association," help to limit the word "free" to a somewhat more definite range of meaning, but even in such cases we often feel that we don't know exactly what the word "free" means unless the context provides answers to the questions: "Free *from* what?" "Free *for* what?" "Free *to do* what?"

Another thing that shows the importance of context is the fact that when people use the wrong word we sometimes know what word should have been used. When Mrs. Malaprop says, "I would by no means wish a daughter of mine to be a progeny of learning . . . I would have her instructed in geometry, that she might know something of the contagious countries," we understand what she thought she was saying because the context so clearly tells us what words are called for if the sentences are to make sense. A malapropism is a word that is wrongly used in a sentence in place of another word that sounds somewhat like it. And if we couldn't tell from the context what the appropriate word would be, we could never recognize a malapropism.

But of course it would be a mistake to overemphasize contextual influence and say that a word *never* has the same meaning in two different contexts. If this were true, language would be even more difficult to manage than it is now. A person who says, "I believe in the dictionary" and later "I believe in the Bible" is presumably using the word "believe" in the same sense in both contexts. Perhaps sometimes when we say that a word is used twice in the same sense we ignore slight differences that could be important for one purpose or another. It is a good idea to keep in mind that a change in context *may* make a change in the sense, but it doesn't seem that it *must*. In the present paragraph the word "context" has, up to this point, been used three times, in three slightly different (immediate) contexts; but it has about the same meaning each time.

It is only when the context is considerably different that the meaning is likely to change. A person who says, "I believe in the dictionary," and, later, "I don't believe in ghosts," is using the word "believe" in two very different senses. But in each of these contexts it can have only one possible meaning, and when the whole context is taken into account there *may* be no question what that meaning is. "I believe in a federal world government" means about the same as "I believe *there should be a federal world government.*" "I believe in extrasensory perception" means about the same as "I believe *there is such a thing as* extrasensory perception." "I believe in woman's intuition" means about the same as "I believe *that some of the things that* women intuit *are true.*"

When a word can have different meanings in different kinds of context, we can say that it has **variable meaning.** Its meaning *varies,* and it therefore has a variety of senses when it appears in the dictionary. Some words are more variable than others. But the variable meaning of words doesn't ordinarily give us any trouble so long as there is enough contextual control. The trouble arises when the context is not complete enough to rule out all but one possible meaning. If I say, "Henry rents the house," there is no way for you to tell from the sentence itself whether Henry rents the house *from* someone or *to* someone. When a word can have one (but not both) of two (or more) meanings in a certain context, we shall say that the word is ambiguous *in that context.*

The ambiguity of a word is always relative to a context: no word is ambiguous *in itself.* Some words like "freedom," "religion," "democracy," are ambiguous in quite a few contexts, and that is why you have to be careful in interpreting and in using them. Sometimes such words are said to be "meaningless," but the trouble with them is just the opposite: they have so many subtly different meanings that it takes a good deal of skill—more than most writers command—to keep their meanings well under control. And when the writer fails in this task, it is up to the reader. Other words, such as the common nouns, are variable in meaning but are hardly ever ambiguous. It takes a good deal of ingenuity to write a medium-sized sentence in which the word "foot" is ambiguous.

A case of ambiguity, as we have defined it, is a case where there is some *doubt* about the way a discourse is to be interpreted, and you have to choose between alternative readings. Unfortunately, this is not the way the word "ambiguity" is always used. When A. E. Housman, in his poem "To an Athlete Dying Young," writes,

> Home they brought him, shoulder high,
> Townsman of a stiller town,

the word "town" has at least two meanings: the young man's village is quieter for the funeral than it was on the day everyone cheered his victory, and also he is now among the noiseless dead. But "town" is not ambiguous here. It has *both* meanings at once, and there is no uncertainty about them at all.

This sort of double meaning, or **multiple meaning** as it may be called, is also characteristic of one type of pun. There is the old pun, for example, about the two women leaning out of their windows across an alley and shouting at each other angrily: they can never come to an agreement because they are arguing from different premises. Another type of pun is built on *homonyms,* that is, words that have the same sound but different senses ("boy," "buoy"; "recede," "reseed"; "bier," "beer"; "air," "heir"). If you want to call homonyms the same word because they have the same sound, you would then have to say that such words have an even more variable meaning than we supposed. On the whole, we may as well call them different words if they are spelt differently, and then we shall not need to say any more about homonyms, except to note that they can give rise to the sort of pun made by Macbeth when he says he will plant circumstantial evidence on the grooms:

> If he do bleed,
> I'll *gild* the faces of the grooms withal,
> For it must seem their *guilt.*

This sort of double entendre, whether in pun or poem, is sometimes called "ambiguity," but it is a very different thing from ambiguity in the sense in which we are using the term. . . . The important thing at the moment is to note that there is a difference. The high-pressure context of a poem can squeeze many senses, all at once, out of some of its words; this is the multiple meaning of poetic discourse. But we have ambiguity, in the strict sense, when the context is too loose and flabby to hold the words steadily to *any* definite sense. The poet has managed to say several things at once; the ambiguous writer has not quite succeeded in saying anything.

BARRIERS AND GATEWAYS TO COMMUNICATION*

Carl R. Rogers and
F. J. Roethlisberger

It may seem curious that a person like myself, whose whole professional effort is devoted to psychotherapy, should be interested in problems of communication. What relationship is there between obstacles to communication and providing therapeutic help to individuals with emotional maladjustments?

Actually the relationship is very close indeed. The whole task of psychotherapy is the task of dealing with a failure in communication. The emotionally maladjusted person, the "neurotic," is in difficulty, first, because communication within himself has broken down and, secondly, because as a result of this his communication with others has been damaged. To put it another way, in the "neurotic" individual parts of himself which have been termed unconscious, or repressed, or denied to awareness, become blocked off so that they no longer communicate themselves to the conscious or managing part of himself; as long as this is true, there are distortions in the way he communicates himself to others, and so he suffers both within himself and in his interpersonal relations.

The task of psychotherapy is to help the person achieve, through a special relationship with a therapist, good communication within himself. Once this is achieved, he can communicate more freely and more effectively with others. We may say then that psychotherapy is good communication, within and between men. We may also turn that statement around and it will still be true. Good communication, free communication within or between men, is always therapeutic.

It is, then, from a background of experience with communication in counseling and psychotherapy that I want to present two ideas: (1) I wish to state what I believe is one of the major factors in blocking or impeding communication, and then (2) I wish to present what in our

* From *Harvard Business Review*, July–August, 1952. Copyright 1952 by the President and Fellows of Harvard College. Reprinted by permission.

experience has proved to be a very important way of improving or facilitating communication.

Barrier: The Tendency to Evaluate

I should like to propose, as a hypothesis for consideration, that the major barrier to mutual interpersonal communication is our very natural tendency to judge, to evaluate, to approve (or disapprove) the statement of the other person or the other group. Let me illustrate my meaning with some very simple examples. Suppose someone, commenting on this discussion, makes the statement, "I didn't like what that man said." What will you respond? Almost invariably your reply will be either approval or disapproval of the attitude expressed. Either you respond, "I didn't either; I thought it was terrible," or else you tend to reply, "Oh, I thought it was really good." In other words, your primary reaction is to evaluate it from *your* point of view, your own frame of reference.

Or take another example. Suppose I say with some feeling, "I think the Republicans are behaving in ways that show a lot of good sound sense these days." What is the response that arises in your mind? The overwhelming likelihood is that it will be evaluative. In other words, you will find yourself agreeing, or disagreeing, or making some judgment about me such as "He must be a conservative," or "He seems solid in his thinking." Or let us take an illustration from the international scene. Russia says vehemently, "The treaty with Japan is a war plot on the part of the United States." We rise as one person to say, "That's a lie!"

This last illustration brings in another element connected with my hypothesis. Although the tendency to make evaluations is common in almost all interchange of language, it is very much heightened in those situations where feelings and emotions are deeply involved. So the stronger our feelings, the more likely it is that there will be no mutual element in the communication. There will be just two ideas, two feelings, two judgments, missing each other in psychological space.

I am sure you recognize this from your own experience. When you have not been emotionally involved yourself and have listened to a heated discussion, you often go away thinking, "Well, they actually weren't talking about the same thing." And they were not. Each was making a judgment, an evaluation, from his own frame of reference. There was really nothing which could be called communication in any genuine sense. This tendency to react to any emotionally meaningful statement by forming an evaluation of it from our own point of view is, I repeat, the major barrier to interpersonal communication.

Gateway: Listening with Understanding

Is there any way of solving this problem, of avoiding this barrier? I feel that we are making exciting progress toward this goal, and I should like to present it as simply as I can. Real communication occurs, and this evaluative tendency is avoided, when we listen with understanding. What does that mean? It means to see the expressed idea and attitude from the other person's point of view, to sense how it feels to him, to achieve his frame of reference in regard to the thing he is talking about.

Stated so briefly, this may sound absurdly simple, but it is not. It is an approach which we have found extremely potent in the field of psychotherapy. It is the most effective agent we know for altering the basic personality structure of an individual and for improving his relationships and his communications with others. If I can listen to what he can tell me, if I can understand how it seems to him, if I can see its personal meaning for him, if I can sense the emotional flavor which it has for him, then I will be releasing potent forces of change in him.

Again, if I can really understand how he hates his father, or hates the company, or hates Communists—if I can catch the flavor of his fear of insanity, or his fear of atom bombs, or of Russia—it will be of the greatest help to him in altering those hatreds and fears and in establishing realistic and harmonious relationships with the very people and situations toward which he has felt hatred and fear. We know from our research that such empathic understanding—understanding *with* a person, not *about* him—is such an effective approach that it can bring about major changes in personality.

Some of you may be feeling that you listen well to people and yet you have never seen such results. The chances are great indeed that your listening has not been of the type I have described. Fortunately, I can suggest a little laboratory experiment which you can try to test the quality of your understanding. The next time you get into an argument with your wife, or your friend, or with a small group of friends, just stop the discussion for a moment and, for an experiment, institute this rule: "Each person can speak up for himself only *after* he has first restated the ideas and feelings of the previous speaker accurately and to that speaker's satisfaction."

You see what this would mean. It would simply mean that before presenting your own point of view, it would be necessary for you to achieve the other speaker's frame of reference—to understand his thoughts and feelings so well that you could summarize them for him. Sounds simple, doesn't it? But if you try it, you will discover that it is one of the most difficult things you have ever tried to do. However, once you have been able to see the other's point of view, your own comments will have to be drastically revised. You will also find the emotion going out of the discussion, the differences being reduced, and those differences which remain being of a rational and understandable sort.

Can you imagine what this kind of an approach would mean if it were projected into larger areas? What would happen to a labor-management dispute if it were conducted in such a way that labor, without necessarily agreeing, could accurately state management's point of view in a way that management could accept; and management, without approving labor's stand, could state labor's case in a way that labor agreed was accurate? It would mean that real communication was established, and one could practically guarantee that some reasonable solution would be reached.

If, then, this way of approach is an effective avenue to good communication and good relationships, as I am quite sure you will agree if you try the experiment I have mentioned, why is it not more widely tried and used? I will try to list the difficulties which keep it from being utilized.

Need for Courage. In the first place it takes courage, a quality which is not too widespread. I am indebted to Dr. S. I. Hayakawa, the semanticist, for pointing out that to carry on psychotherapy in this fashion is to take a very real risk, and that courage is required. If you really understand another person in this way, if you are willing to enter his private world and see the way life appears to him, without any attempt to make evaluative judgments, you run the risk of being changed yourself. You might see it his way; you might find yourself influenced in your attitudes or your personality.

This risk of being changed is one of the most frightening prospects many of us can face. If I enter, as fully as I am able, into the private world of a neurotic or psychotic individual, isn't there a risk that I might become lost in that world? Most of us are afraid to take that risk. Or if we were listening to a Russian Communist, or Senator Joe McCarthy, how many of us would dare to try to see the world from each of their points of view? The great majority of us could not *listen;* we would find ourselves compelled to *evaluate,* because listening would seem too dangerous. So the first requirement is courage, and we do not always have it.

Heightened Emotions. But there is a second obstacle. It is just when emotions are strongest that it is most difficult to achieve the frame of reference of the other person or group. Yet it is then that the attitude is most needed if communication is to be established. We have not found this to be an insuperable obstacle in our experience in psychotherapy. A third party, who is able to lay aside his own feelings and evaluations, can assist greatly by listening with understanding to each person or group and clarifying the views and attitudes each holds.

We have found this effective in small groups in which contradictory or antagonistic attitudes exist. When the parties to a dispute realize that they are being understood, that someone sees how the situation seems to them, the statements grow less exaggerated and less defensive, and it is no longer necessary to maintain the attitude, "I am 100% right and you are 100% wrong." The influence of such an understanding catalyst in the group permits the members to come closer and closer to the objective truth involved in the relationship. In this way mutual communication is established, and some type of agreement becomes much more possible.

So we may say that though heightened emotions make it much more difficult to understand *with* an opponent, our experience makes it clear that a neutral, understanding catalyst type of leader or therapist can overcome this obstacle in a small group.

Size of Group. That last phrase, however, suggests another obstacle to utilizing the approach I have described. Thus far all our experience has been with small face-to-face groups—groups exhibiting industrial tensions, religious tensions, racial tensions, and therapy groups in which many personal tensions are present. In these small groups our experience, confirmed by a limited amount of research, shows that this basic approach leads to improved communication, to greater acceptance of others and by others, and to attitudes which are more positive and more problem-solving in nature. There is a decrease in defensiveness, in exaggerated statements, in evaluative and critical behavior.

But these findings are from small groups. What about trying to achieve understanding between larger groups that are geographically remote, or between face-to-face groups that are not speaking for themselves but simply as representatives of others? Frankly, we do not know the answers to these questions. I believe the situation might be put this way: As social scientists we have a tentative test-tube solution of the problem of breakdown in communication. But to confirm the validity of this test-tube solution and to adapt it to the enormous problems of communication breakdown between classes, groups, and nations would involve additional funds, much more research, and creative thinking of a high order.

Yet with our present limited knowledge we can see some steps which might be taken even in large groups to increase the amount of listening *with* and decrease the amount of evelation *about*. To be imaginative for a moment, let us suppose that a therapeutically oriented international group went to the Russian leaders and said, "We want to achieve a genuine understanding of your views and, even more important, of your attitudes and feelings toward the United States. We will summarize and resummarize these views and feelings if necessary, until you agree that our description represents the situation as it seems to you."

Then suppose they did the same thing with the leaders in our own country. If they then gave the widest possible distribution to these two views, with the feelings clearly described but not expressed in name-calling, might not the effect be very great? It would not guarantee the type of understanding I have been describing, but it would make it much more possible. We can understand the feelings of a person who hates us much more readily when his attitudes are accurately described to us by a neutral third party than we can when he is shaking his fist at us.

Faith in Social Sciences. But even to describe such a first step is to suggest another obstacle to this approach of understanding. Our civilization does not yet have enough faith in the social sciences to utilize their findings. The opposite is true of the physical sciences. During the war when a test-tube solution was found to the problem of synthetic rubber, millions of dollars and an army of talent were turned loose on the problem of using that finding. If synthetic rubber could be made in milligrams, it could and would be made in the thousands of tons. And it was. But in the social science realm, if a way is found of facilitating communication and mutual understanding in small groups, there is no guarantee that the finding will be utilized. It may be a generation or more before the money and the brains will be turned loose to exploit that finding.

Summary

In closing, I should like to summarize this small-scale solution to the problem of barriers in communication, and to point out certain of its characteristics.

I have said that our research and experience to date would make it appear that breakdowns in communication, and the evaluative tendency which is the major barrier to communication, can be avoided. The solution is provided by creating a situation in which each of the different parties comes to understand the other from the *other's* point of view. This has been achieved, in practice, even when feelings run high, by the influence of a person who is willing to understand each point of view empathically, and who thus acts as a catalyst to precipitate further understanding.

This procedure has important characteristics. It can be initiated by one party, without waiting for the other to be ready. It can even be initiated by a neutral third person, provided he can gain a minimum of cooperation from one of the parties.

This procedure can deal with the insincerities, the defensive exaggerations, the lies, the "false fronts" which characterize almost every failure in communication. These defensive distortions drop away with astonishing speed as people find that the only intent is to understand, not to judge.

This approach leads steadily and rapidly toward the discovery of the truth, toward a realistic appraisal of the objective barriers to communication. The dropping of some defensiveness by one party leads to further dropping of defensiveness by the other party, and truth is thus approached.

This procedure gradually achieves mutual communication. Mutual communication tends to be pointed toward solving a problem rather than toward attacking a person or group. It leads to a situation in which I see how the problem appears to you as well as to me, and you see how it appears to me as well as to you. Thus accurately and realistically defined, the problem is almost certain to yield to intelligent attack, or if it is in part insoluble, it will be comfortably accepted as such.

This then appears to be a test-tube solution to the breakdown of communication as it occurs in small groups. Can we take this small-scale answer, investigate it further, refine it, develop it, and apply it to the tragic and well-nigh fatal failures of communication which threaten the very existence of our modern world? It seems to me that this is a possibility and a challenge which we should explore.

From HOW TO LIE WITH STATISTICS*

Darrell Huff

"The average Yaleman, Class of '24," *Time* magazine reported last year after reading something in the New York *Sun,* a newspaper published in those days, "makes $25,111 a year."

Well, good for him!

But, come to think of it, what does this improbably precise and salubrious figure mean? Is it, as it appears to be, evidence that if you send your boy to Yale you won't have to work in your old age and neither will he? Is this average a mean or is it a median? What kind of sample is it based on? You could lump one Texas oilman with two hundred hungry free-lance writers and report *their* average income as $25,000-odd a year. The arithmetic is impeccable, the figure is convincingly precise, and the amount of meaning there is in it you could put in your eye.

In just such ways is the secret language of statistics, so appealing in a fact-minded culture, being used to sensationalize, inflate, confuse, and over-simplify. Statistical terms are necessary in reporting the mass data of social and economic trends, business conditions, "opinion" polls, this year's census. But without writers who use the words with honesty and understanding and readers who know what they mean, the result can only be semantic nonsense.

In popular writing on scientific research, the abused statistic is almost crowding out the picture of the white-jacketed hero laboring overtime without time-and-a-half in an ill-lit laboratory. Like the "little dash of powder, little pot of paint," statistics are making many an important fact "look like what she ain't." Here are some of the ways it is done.

The sample with the built-in bias. Our Yale men—or Yalemen, as they say in the Time-Life building—belong to this flourishing group. The exaggerated estimate of their income is not based on all members of the class nor on a random or representative sample of them. At least two interesting categories of 1924-model Yale men have been excluded.

First there are those whose present addresses are unknown to their classmates. Wouldn't you bet that these lost sheep are earning less than

* Reprinted from *How to Lie with Statistics* by Darrell Huff. Pictures by Irving Geis. By permission of W. W. Norton & Co., Inc. Copyright 1954 by Darrell Huff and Irving Geis.

the boys from prominent families and the others who can be handily reached from a Wall Street office?

There are those who chucked the questionnaire into the nearest wastebasket. Maybe they didn't answer because they were not making enough money to brag about. Like the fellow who found a note clipped to his first pay check suggesting that he consider the amount of his salary confidential: "Don't worry," he told the boss. "I'm just as ashamed of it as you are."

Omitted from our sample then are just the two groups most likely to depress the average. The $25,111 figure is beginning to account for itself. It may indeed be a true figure for those of the Class of '24 whose addresses are known and who are willing to stand up and tell how much they earn. But even that requires a possibly dangerous assumption that the gentlemen are telling the truth.

To be dependable to any useful degree at all, a sampling study must use a representative sample (which can lead to trouble too) or a truly random one. If *all* the Class of '24 is included, that's all right. If every tenth name on a complete list is used, that is all right too, and so is drawing an adequate number of names out of a hat. The test is this: Does every name in the group have an equal chance to be in the sample?

You'll recall that ignoring this requirement was what produced the *Literary Digest*'s famed fiasco. When names for polling were taken only from telephone books and subscription lists, people who did not have telephones or *Literary Digest* subscriptions had no chance to be in the sample. They possibly did not mind this underprivilege a bit, but their absence was in the end very hard on the magazine that relied on the figures.

This leads to a moral: You can prove about anything you want to by letting your sample bias itself. As a consumer of statistical data—a reader, for example, of a news magazine—remember that no statistical conclusion can rise above the quality of the sample it is based upon. In the absence of information about the procedures behind it, you are not warranted in giving any credence at all to the result.

The truncated, or gee-whiz, graph. If you want to show some statistical information quickly and clearly, draw a picture of it. Graphic presentation is the thing today. If you don't mind misleading the hasty looker, or if you quite clearly *want* to deceive him, you can save some space by chopping the bottom off many kinds of graphs.

Suppose you are showing the upward trend of national income month by month for a year. The total rise, as in one recent year, is 7 per cent. It looks like this:

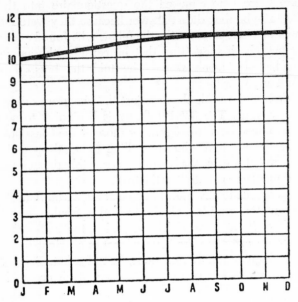

That is clear enough. Anybody can see that the trend is slightly upward. You are showing a 7 per cent increase and that is exactly what it looks like.

But it lacks schmaltz. So you chop off the bottom, this way:

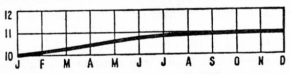

The figures are the same. It is the same graph and nothing has been falsified—except the impression that it gives. Anyone looking at it can just feel prosperity throbbing in the arteries of the country. It is a subtler equivalent of editing "National income rose 7 per cent" into ". . . climbed a whopping 7 per cent."

It is vastly more effective, however, because of that illusion of objectivity.

The souped-up graph. Sometimes truncating is not enough. The trifling rise in something or other still looks almost as insignificant as it is. You can make that 7 per cent look livelier than 100 per cent ordinarily does. Simply change the proportion between the ordinate and the abscissa. There's no rule against it, and it does give your graph a prettier shape.

But it exaggerates, to say the least, something awful:

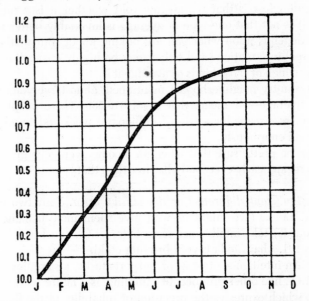

The well-chosen average. I live near a country neighborhood for which I can report an average income of $15,000. I could also report it as $3,500.

If I should want to sell real estate hereabouts to people having a high snobbery content, the first figure would be handy. The second figure, however, is the one to use in an argument against raising taxes, or the local bus fare.

Both are legitimate averages, legally arrived at. Yet it is obvious that at least one of them must be as misleading as an out-and-out lie. The $15,000-figure is a mean, the arithmetic average of the incomes of all the families in the community. The smaller figure is a median; it might be called the income of the average family in the group. It indicates that half the families have less than $3,500 a year and half have more.

Here is where some of the confusion about averages comes from. Many human characteristics have the grace to fall into what is called the "normal" distribution. If you draw a picture of it, you get a curve that is shaped like a bell. Mean and median fall at about the same point, so it doesn't make very much difference which you use.

But some things refuse to follow this neat curve. Income is one of them. Incomes for most large areas will range from under $1,000 a year to upward of $50,000. Almost everybody will be under $10,000, way over on the left-hand side of that curve.

One of the things that made the income figure for the "average Yale-man" meaningless is that we are not told whether it is a mean or a median. It is not that one type of average is invariably better than the other; it depends upon what you are talking about. But neither gives you any real information—and either may be highly misleading—unless you know which of those kinds of average it is.

In the country neighborhood I mentioned, almost everyone has less than the average—the mean, that is—of $10,500. These people are all small farmers, except for a trio of millionaire week-enders who bring up the mean enormously.

You can be pretty sure that when an income average is given in the form of a mean nearly everybody has less than that.

The insignificant difference or the elusive error. Your two children Peter and Linda (we might as well give them modish names while we're about it) take intelligence tests. Peter's I.Q., you learn, is 98 and Linda's is 101. Aha! Linda is your brighter child.

Is she? An intelligence test is, or purports to be, a sampling of intellect. An I.Q., like other products of sampling, is a figure with a statistical error, which expresses the precision or reliability of the figure. The size of this probable error can be calculated. For their tests the makers of the much-used Revised Stanford-Binet have found it to be about 3 per cent. So Peter's indicated I.Q. of 98 really means only that there is an even chance that it falls between 95 and 101. There is an equal probability that it falls somewhere else—below 95 or above 101. Similarly, Linda's has no better than a fifty-fifty chance of being within the fairly sizeable range of 98 to 104.

You can work out some comparisons from that. One is that there is rather better than one chance in four that Peter, with his lower I.Q. rating, is really at least three points smarter than Linda. A statistician doesn't like to consider a difference significant unless you can hand him odds a lot longer than that.

Ignoring the error in a sampling study leads to all kinds of silly conclusions. There are magazine editors to whom readership surveys are gospel; with a 40 per cent readership reported for one article and a 35 per cent for another, they demand more like the first. I've seen even smaller differences given tremendous weight, because statistics are a mystery and numbers are impressive. The same thing goes for market surveys and so-called public-opinion polls. The rule is that you cannot make a valid comparison between two such figures unless you know the deviations. And unless the difference between the figures is many times greater than the probable error of each, you have only a guess that the one appearing greater really is.

Otherwise you are like the man choosing a camp site from a report of mean temperature alone. One place in California with a mean annual temperature of 61 is San Nicolas Island on the south coast, where it always stays in the comfortable range between 47 and 87. Another with a mean of 61 is in the inland desert, where the thermometer hops around from 15 to 104. The deviation from the mean marks the difference, and you can freeze or roast if you ignore it.

The one-dimensional picture. Suppose you have just two or three figures to compare—say the average weekly wage of carpenters in the United States and another country. The sums might be $60 and $30. An ordinary bar chart makes the difference graphic. [See following.] That

is an honest picture. It looks good for American carpenters, but perhaps it does not have quite the oomph you are after. Can't you make that difference appear overwhelming and at the same time give it what I am afraid is known as eye-appeal? Of course you can. Following tradition, you represent these sums by pictures of money bags. If the $30 bag is one inch high, you draw the $60 bag two inches high. That's in proportion, isn't it?

The catch is, of course, that the American's money bag, being twice as tall as that of the $30 man, covers an area on your page four times as great. And since your two-dimensional picture represents an object that would in fact have three dimensions, the money bags actually would differ much more than that. The volumes of any two similar solids vary as the cubes of their heights. If the unfortunate foreigner's bag holds $30 worth of dimes, the American's would hold not $60 but a neat $240.

You didn't say that, though, did you? And you can't be blamed, you're only doing it the way practically everybody else does.

The ever-impressive decimal. For a spurious air of precision that will lend all kinds of weight to the most disreputable statistics, consider the decimal.

Ask a hundred citizens how many hours they slept last night. Come out with a total of, say, 7.813. Your data are far from precise to begin with. Most people will miss their guess by fifteen minutes or more and some will recall five sleepless minutes as half a night of tossing insomnia.

But go ahead, do your arithmetic, announce that people sleep an average of 7.813 hours a night. You will sound as if you knew precisely what you are talking about. If you were foolish enough to say 7.8 (or "almost 8") hours it would sound like what it was—an approximation.

The semi-attached figure. If you can't prove what you want to prove, demonstrate something else and pretend that they are the same thing.

In the daze that follows the collision of statistics with the human mind, hardly anybody will notice the difference. The semi-attached figure is a durable device guaranteed to stand you in good stead. It always has.

If you can't prove that your nostrum cures colds, publish a sworn laboratory report that the stuff killed 31,108 germs in a test tube in eleven seconds. There may be no connection at all between assorted germs in a test tube and the whatever-it-is that produces colds, but people aren't going to reason that sharply, especially while sniffling.

Maybe that one is too obvious and people are beginning to catch on. Here is a trickier version.

Let us say that in a period when race prejudice is growing it is to your advantage to "prove" otherwise. You will not find it a difficult assignment.

Ask that usual cross section of the population if they think Negroes have as good a chance as white people to get jobs. Ask again a few months later. As Princeton's Office of Public Opinion Research has found out, people who are most unsympathetic to Negroes are the ones most likely to answer yes to this question.

As prejudice increases in a country, the percentage of affirmative answers you will get to this question will become larger. What looks on the face of it like growing opportunity for Negroes actually is mounting prejudice and nothing else. You have achieved something rather remarkable: the worse things get, the better your survey makes them look.

The unwarranted assumption, or post hoc *rides again.* The interrelation of cause and effect, so often obscure anyway, can be most neatly hidden in statistical data.

Somebody once went to a good deal of trouble to find out if cigarette smokers make lower college grades than nonsmokers. They did. This naturally pleased many people, and they made much of it.

The unwarranted assumption, of course, was that smoking had produced dull minds. It seemed vaguely reasonable on the face of it, so it was quite widely accepted. But it really proved nothing of the sort, any more than it proved that poor grades drive students to the solace of tobacco. Maybe the relationship worked in one direction, maybe in the other. And maybe all this is only an indication that the sociable sort of fellow who is likely to take his books less than seriously is also likely to sit around and smoke many cigarettes.

Permitting statistical treatment to befog causal relationships is little better than superstition. It is like the conviction among the people of the Hebrides that body lice produce good health. Observation over the centuries had taught them that people in good health had lice and sick people often did not. *Ergo,* lice made a man healthy. Everybody should have them.

Scantier evidence, treated statistically at the expense of common sense, has made many a medical fortune and many a medical article in magazines, including professional ones. More sophisticated observers finally got things straightened out in the Hebrides. As it turned out, almost everybody in those circles had lice most of the time. But when a man took a fever (quite possibly carried to him by those same lice) and his body became hot, the lice left.

Here you have cause and effect not only reversed but intermingled.

There you have a primer in some ways to use statistics to deceive. A well-wrapped statistic is better than Hitler's "big lie": it misleads, yet it can't be pinned onto you.

Is this little list altogether too much like a manual for swindlers? Perhaps I can justify it in the manner of the retired burglar whose published reminiscences amounted to a graduate course in how to pick a lock and muffle a football: The crooks already know these tricks. Honest men must learn them in self-defense.

WHAT DO YOU MEAN?*

Anatol Rapoport

> *Student:* Yet in the word must some idea be.
> *Mephistopheles:* Of course! But only shun too oversharp a tension.
> For just where fails the comprehension,
> A word steps promptly in as deputy.
>
> GOETHE, *Faust*

For thousands of years philosophers have inquired into the "real" meanings of words, with no agreement to show for their efforts. From the semantic point of view, to inquire into the *real* meaning of any word, whether democracy or tyranny, friendship or virtue, taxation or education, is senseless.

Take the word "rot." To a German it means "red," to a Russian "mouth," and to us you know what. How good a philosopher do you have to be to discover the "real" meaning of "rot"?

---

* From Anatol Rapoport, *Science and the Goals of Man.* Copyright 1950 by Harper & Row, Publishers. Reprinted by permission.

One may object to this example, since there is nothing remarkable in the fact that a similar sound may have different meanings in different languages.

Take, then, the word "rod," and consider what it means to a land surveyor and what it means to a gangster, both presumably speaking English. Words do have a variety of sometimes unrelated meanings, and these are not inherent in the words themselves but in their *usage*. Usage depends on the experiences associated with the *use* of words. The various meanings of a word may overlap in spots. But it is no less important to know that other areas of their meanings may be far apart.

There is a mistaken belief that the etymology (ancestry) of a word is somehow a key to its "real" meaning.

Some time ago the Ukrainian delegate to the United Nations charged the government of Greece with "antidemocratic" motives in wanting to demilitarize the Bulgarian border. The Greek undersecretary of foreign affairs replied:

"Democracy is a Greek word, and Greece knows better than anyone else how to interpret it."

Sigmund Freud once pointed out in a lecture on hysteria that men as well as women were often subject to its symptoms. A distinguished Viennese professor upon hearing this walked angrily out of the hall.

"Never have I heard such nonsense," he fussed. "Men subject to hysteria! Why, the very word 'hysteria' is derived from the Greek word for *womb!*"

Both the Greek diplomat and the Viennese professor were making the same common mistake: they were confusing words with the things to which words are supposed to refer.

Words are invented by human beings, and their meanings are attributed to them by persons. These meanings arise out of experience. Different sets of experiences may map on the same word.

Definitions of Definitions

How, then, can the meaning of a word be made clear? Obviously by indicating the experiences associated with it. But how do we communicate experiences? By words. Are we in a vicious circle? It looks serious, but there may be a way out.

The question "What do you mean?" asks for the meaning of some words or expressions you are using. Meaning is associated with experience. So actually the question "What do you mean?" is a request to share the experiences associated with the words you are using. In answer to such a request, a definition is usually made.

We shall examine several types of definitions and gauge their usefulness from the standpoint of sharing experience.

1. *Defining a word by giving a synonym.*

Pocket dictionaries are full of such definitions. Asked to define "man" a pocket dictionary will often tell you that a "man" is a "human being."

2. *Making a definition by classification.*

Such definitions haunt the classroom. Pupils who can rattle off "Autocracy is a form of government in which power is concentrated in the hands of one man" and "Capitalism is an economic system based on competition and free enterprise" are most likely to get an A in civics. In the days of Aristotle (about 350 B.C.), "man" was often defined as a "rational animal," also a definition by classification. Such definitions tell first what sort of thing the word you are defining refers to (capitalism is a sort of economic system; man is a sort of animal); then it tells how to distinguish the *special* thing the word refers to (not *any* kind of economic system, but one based on competition and free enterprise; not *any* kind of animal, but a rational animal).

3. *Defining a word by enumerating words to which it refers collectively* (definition by enumeration).

Spices are cinnamon, cloves, paprika, ginger, and such.

The kings of the house of Stuart were James I, Charles I, Charles II, and James II.

4. *Defining by exhibiting an example.*

That is the way Robinson Crusoe taught English to Friday. He would point to a hairy animal and say "goat," to the strange object he carried and say "umbrella," etc. Friday learned fast. Children also learn to speak this way.

5. *The operational definition.*

Such definitions are commonly used in modern science. A physicist asked to define, say, the "Joule-Thompson effect" will *usually describe the experiments,* in which this effect can be *observed.* A more homely example of an operational definition can be found in the *recipe.*

An operational definition tells *what to do* in order to experience or to recognize the thing to which the word defined refers.

Now let us see how the different kinds of definitions serve their purpose. We recall that a definition is used to answer the question "What do you mean?"—a request to *share experience.*

Definition by synonym is useful only if the synonym is closer to our experiences than the word defined. Sometimes this is the case. People for whom "abdomen" is just a noise, may know very well what "belly" stands for. But the opposite situation is rare.

If you have used pocket dictionaries a great deal, where words are defined by synonyms, you must have experienced the disappointment of finding a synonym that means no more to you than the word you have looked up. The disappointment may grow into a minor frustration if you look up a synonym only to find it defined by the original "sticker."

Definitions by classification are more often useful than definitions by synonym. Their usefulness depends on the familiarity of the person who asks for the definition with the *class* of things into which the word defined is placed. For instance, Jones can explain the grapefruit to Ivanov, who may never have seen one, by such a definition.

"A grapefruit is a [citrus] fruit, more sour than an orange and less sour than a lemon, larger than both, and canary yellow."

Ivanov has eaten both lemons and oranges. He can form at least some idea of what a grapefruit is like. The shortcoming of a definition by classification is that it does not *necessarily* bring the word defined closer to experience.

A Jabberwock can be defined by "classifying" it.

"A Jabberwock is an animal with 'jaws that bite and claws that snatch.'" But the definition does not bring us any closer to an actual experience with a Jabberwock.

Similarly, one can define anything one pleases by stringing words together in such a way as to make it appear that one is clarifying meaning. Here are a few examples. It is easy to invent them.

"An irresistible force is a causative agency, able to overcome all obstacles."

"The First Cause is that event which was preceded by no other."

"The Good is what all things aim at."

"The devil is a being who is responsible for the existence of evil."

"Love is the affection which, being compounded of animal desire, esteem, and benevolence, becomes the bond of attachment and union between individuals of the different sexes, and makes them enjoy in the society of each other a species of happiness which they experience nowhere else."

Definitions which by their sentence structure seem to be clarifying something, but actually are not, resemble useless patent medicines. The harm of patent medicines is often not in themselves but in that the addicts keep hoping they will be helped and delay seeking competent advice and effective measures. Similarly, the addicts of definitions by classification (Aristotelian definitions) are often pedantic in "defining their terms" without realizing the futility of such definitions.

Definitions by enumeration are useful in defining classes of things if the names of the members of the class defined are closer to experience than the class itself. A person may not know to what the Pentateuch refers, but he may be familiar with Genesis, Exodus, Leviticus, Numbers, and Deuteronomy. He may have seen frogs, newts, and salamanders, but he may not know that biologists refer to all of them collectively as amphibia.

As a rule, definitions by enumeration do carry words closer to experience, because terms referring to collections of events are less directly connected with experience than the events themselves.

The weak spot in this sort of definition is that some words seem to refer not to classes, as, for example, the sun, and some classes are too large to enumerate. If I wanted to define "man" by enumeration, I would have to put down some two billion names, a fourth of them Chinese, a difficult and rather useless task. Fortunately, in some cases only a few examples are needed to make the meaning of the class clear. An "etc." placed at the end of such a partial list is a reminder that the class has not been exhausted.

A great advantage in making definitions by *exhibiting an example* is that one cannot define fictions that way. Just try to define Jabberwock or the First Cause by pointing to something and see how sticking to definition by exhibiting an example protects you from believing in ghosts. However, this advantage becomes a disadvantage when one wishes to define something which is not immediately at hand or something more abstract than objects to which one can point. Jonathan Swift made great fun of definition by example. He describes in his satire, *Gulliver's Travels,* how the academicians of Lagado decided to do away with spoken language altogether, arguing that

. . . since the words are only names for things, it would be convenient for all men to carry about them such things as were necessary to express the particular business they are to discourse on . . .

Accordingly, says Swift, the learned men of Lagado

adhere to the new scheme of expressing themselves by things, which hath only this inconvenience attending it, that if a man's business be very great, and of various kinds, he must be obliged in proportion to carry a greater bundle of things upon his back, unless he can afford one or two strong servants to attend him.

The great value of making a definition by exhibiting an example is that it does bridge the gap between words and experience. This, in fact, is the only purpose of definition. Definition by synonym and definition by classification may indirectly bridge this gap if the words used in the definition are closer to experience than the words defined. But this is not necessarily so. In the case of definition by example it is *necessarily* so, because what you exhibit is *not* a word. Still a difficulty remains, quite aside from Swift's objections, to this kind of definition. Many words refer to real things, and these may not be at hand to point to, or one may not point to them at all. Here are a few examples:

electric current	hydrogen
standard deviation	habeas corpus
the French language	mumps
acrophobia	sonata
chiaroscuro	taxes

The *operational definition* succeeds most effectively in connecting such *abstract* words with experience.

In discussing operational definitions of abstract physical concepts, Philipp Frank says:

These sentences [operational definitions] contain the abstract word of the physical principles like "current" . . . also the words of the everyday English language. Obviously, they contain words like "wire" and other words which describe the apparatus by which the intensity of a current is actually measured.

Note how the operational definition works. One cannot point to an ampere of electric current (the most one could point at would be the wire that carries it). But one does not dodge the issue by defining a word with other words without bothering to determine whether they are any closer to experience. One gives a set of *directions*, in words, to be sure, but words almost certainly closer to experience than the word defined (wire, magnet, etc.). If one follows these directions, one has the experience summarized by the words "one ampere of electric current."

Sometimes a definition that sounds like an Aristotelian one performs the job of an operational definition. If I say "Acrophobia is a mental disturbance characterized by a fear of high places" I seem to be making an Aristotelian definition. But it can easily be translated into an operational one: "Question a great many people on how they feel about high places, and you will find that a certain percentage of them will declare that they are 'afraid' of high places. Furthermore, if such a person happens to be on a roof or a mountain-top, he usually exhibits a quickening of heart beat and expresses a desire to get down. Such people are said to suffer from acrophobia."

Let us see what happens when we apply an operational definition to a fiction. A vampire, for example, can be defined by a good Aristotelian definition: "A vampire is a person who habitually sucks other people's blood." If we attempt to translate this definition into an operational one, we would have to say something like this: "Have a great many persons watched at night, and you will find that some go abroad and suck blood out of sleeping people, usually from a small lesion in the neck. Such people are called vampires." This operational definition is formally as good as the one of acrophobia except for one thing: you will probably not find any people with blood-sucking habits.

So it appears from the operations prescribed by the operational definition that if any "meaning" is to be attached to the word "vampire," it cannot refer to a person (since no such persons are observed). The operations have revealed that the Aristotelian definition of a "vampire," although formally flawless, is meaningless.

Practically all operational definitions say in fact "Do so-and-so, and you will find . . ." They *predict* an experience. They may also be called definitions by prediction.

In modern semantic literature, definitions by synonym and by classification are often called "intensional definitions," while those by enumeration, example, and operation are called "extensional definitions." From the standpoint of bridging the gap between words and experiences, extensional definitions are to be preferred. As a matter of fact, if that gap is bridged at all, somewhere a definition by example or an operational definition is involved.

The definition by example need not involve language at all. The syntactic structure of an operational definition involves an imperative form of a verb (do so-and-so) and a predictive assertion (you will find . . .). This structure is sometimes clumsy and may be discarded for the elegant structure of the Aristotelian definition (a so-and-so is a such-and-such which is characterized by a this-and-that); but a definition is to serve its purpose (sharing experience), an indication of experience must be involved.

"The stockyards are an area where animals are processed into meat" is a short, elegant definition of the stockyards. But the *reality* of the stockyards is implied in another, clumsier definition, which I would give to a visitor in Chicago if I wanted to bring the stockyards within the range of his experience.

"Take the Halsted Street car to 39th Street, etc. . . ."

"Hell is the place where the wicked go when they die" also looks like a definition. But when you try to translate it into operational terms you will immediately get into difficulties. You will be at a loss to indicate a proper procedure in order to experience hell.

Just as assertions about things must be traced to the experiences that gave rise to them, the meanings of words must also be traced in this way.

Words which fail to show an ancestry of experience may nevertheless be well "defined" by intensional definitions, that is, by other words. But they usually cannot be defined by extensional definitions, especially by exhibiting an example and by the operational definition, because these, by their very nature, imply connection with experience.

Extensional definitions, therefore, especially the operational ones, are more generally valuable for the purpose for which definitions are intended—to bridge the gap between words and experience.

An operational definition can do everything all the others can do and often more. In some cases only an operational definition can bridge the gap between words and experiences. Its drawback is that grammatically it is not very elegant. Therefore, if one is concerned with literary style, one might avoid the operational definition; but if one is concerned with communicating meaning, one should use it at the slightest indication that the meaning is otherwise not clear.

4. LANGUAGE AND
THOUGHT AND FEELING

WHAT IS LANGUAGE?*

Archibald A. Hill

1. Some Basic Assumptions

The subject of linguistics presents an initial difficulty because the word which designates it is unfamiliar. The word can easily be defined as the scientific analysis of language, but it is doubtful if such a definition is meaningful to anyone who lacks familiarity with this kind of analytic activity. It is far better to begin by defining language, since language is closer to the reader's experience. Yet even the definition of language presents unsuspected difficulties and needs preliminary discussion before it is attempted directly.

If a group of educated speakers are asked to define the language they are using, the reply will probably be "All the words and sentences used to express our thoughts." The definition is satisfactory in everyday situations, since long practice has made plain what is meant, and consequently most hearers know how to respond accurately. But for all that, the definition is not sufficiently accurate to be the basis for analysis. Terms like "words and sentences," which seem transparent to a speaker of a Western language, would be more misleading than enlightening if applied to some languages. Moreover, there are phenomena similar to language which this definition does not identify. Most important, the definition identifies language activity by thought. Language activity can be observed, and is therefore subject to verification. Thought can be observed only by subjective introspection, and so is not subject to verification. Language activity is therefore more knowable, thought less knowable. Obviously a definition must define the less knowable by the more knowable if it is to cast light. In what follows, such a

* From Archibald A. Hill, *Introduction to Linguistic Structures.* Copyright © 1958 by Harcourt, Brace & World, Inc. Reprinted by permission.

definition will be attempted. There must first be a warning, the need for which will be clearer as we advance. A definition is not a description. A definition gives only those characteristics which have diagnostic value for recognition. A description attempts to give all characteristics, preferably in the order of their importance. A definition necessarily leaves out much and may make use of relatively trivial characteristics, but it is not to be condemned for that reason.

Most professional students of language proceed from a few assumptions, one of which is that the fundamental forms of language activity are the sequences of sounds made by human lips, tongues, and vocal cords—the phenomena usually distinguished by the narrower name of "speech." Though this first assumption may seem like a truism, it is important, since many who accept it verbally still act as if they did not believe it. Some few even deny it. There are only two reasons for questioning the assumption. Writing has great permanence and great prestige. Further, the basis of our education is training in the manipulation of written symbols of ever-increasing complexity. Highly literate people, and those who would like to be literate, are therefore apt to think of writing as the real center of language and of speech as peripheral and derived—often badly—from the written forms.

There are a number of facts which should settle this question of priority. First, speech reaches back to the origins of human society; writing has a history of only about seven thousand years. Also, no contemporary community of men is without language, even though it is probably still true that most of the world's several thousand language communities remain in the preliterate stage, without benefit of alphabet or even picture symbol. Individual members of literate communities, furthermore, learn their language some years before they learn to read or write it; and adults, even adults who are professional writers, carry on a good deal more speech activity in daily living than activity involving writing. The final fact is that all writing systems are essentially representations of the forms of speech, rather than representations of ideas or objects in the nonlinguistic world. There are exceptions to this statement, like the Arabic numbers which work independently of the words for numbers in the Western languages. The exceptions, however, are in a minority disproportionate to the majority of symbols which always indicate the forms of language. The point can be driven home by a pair of simple examples. The symbol for *one* in Japanese writing is a single stroke, that for *two* two strokes, and so on. It might be thought that such a symbol has no relation to the Japanese word for *one* (*ichi*) but represents instead the nonlinguistic idea of "oneness." Actually the occurrence of the single stroke is correlated with the occurrence of the word. It occurs not only in the number but also in such forms as *ichiji, primary*. The Japanese symbol, therefore, has a quite different range from the letter sequence *one* of English, which is not used in the dissimilar word *primary*. The one-stroke symbol corresponds with the occurrence of the Japanese word *ichi,* proving that the one-stroke symbol is a representation of the word (though an understandably pictorial one), and not a direct representation of the idea of oneness.

Written symbols can be understood, furthermore, insofar as they fit into a linguistic structure, even when they refer to nothing in the nonlinguistic world. Thus, if an English text should have the sentence "He *sprashes* it," the second word could immediately be recognized as a verb in the third person singular and as a sequence of sounds quite in accord with English structural habits, though it represents nothing in the outside world at all. For the purposes of this book, therefore, the linguist's assumption that language is a set of sounds will be adopted. It is no contradiction of this assumption that the sounds can be secondarily translated into visual marks, grooves on a wax disk, electrical impulses, or finger movements.

Linguists assume that the description and analysis of language must begin with description of the sounds and their patterning and that description of meaning must be put off until the first task is done. Such an attitude is often misunderstood to be a denial of meaning, but this is not true. The linguist's desire to put off analysis of meaning is no more than an application of the principle of working from the more knowable to the less knowable, and though linguistics has not as yet had very striking results in semantic analysis, it can be hoped that the next few decades will see results of real value in semantics.

2. The Defining Characteristics of Language

Working with the assumptions given above, linguists can offer a set of five defining characteristics which serve to set off language from other forms of symbolic behavior and to establish language as a purely human activity. Often animal communication will have one or more of these five characteristics, but never all of them.

First, language, as has been said, is a set of sounds. This is perhaps the least important characteristic, since the communication of mammals and birds is also a set of sounds. On the other hand, the system of communication which is in some ways most strikingly like language, that of bees, is a set of body movements, not sounds. It would be easy, further, to imagine a language based on something else than sound, but no human language is so constructed. Even the manual language of the deaf is derived from the preexistent spoken language of the community.

Second, the connection between the sounds, or sequences of sounds, and objects of the outside world is arbitrary and unpredictable. That is to say, a visitor from Mars would be unable to predict that in London a given animal is connected with the sound sequence written *dog,* in Paris with the sequence *chien,* in Madrid with *perro.* The arbitrary quality of language symbols is not infrequently denied, for a number of reasons. Sometimes the denial is based on nothing more than the notion that the forms of one's native language are so inevitably right that they must be instinctive for all proper men. Sometimes the denial is more subtle. It is often maintained that all language, even though now largely arbitrary, must once have been a systematic imitation of objects by means of sound. It is true that there are some imitative words in all languages, but they are at best a limited part of the vocabulary. It is easy to imitate the noise of a barking dog, for instance, but difficult if not impossible to imitate a noiseless object, such as a rainbow. Though imitative words show similarity in many languages, absolute identity is rare. A dog goes "bow-wow" in English, but in related languages he often goes "wow-wow" or "bow-bow." The imitative words do not, after all, entirely escape from the general arbitrariness of language. The imitative origin of language appears, therefore, at worst unlikely and at best unprovable. The same injunction holds for theories of language origin which speculate that it is an imitation of facial or other gestures.

If it is assumed that language is arbitrary, what is meant by the statement? Just that the sounds of speech and their connection with entities of experience are passed on to all members of any community by older members of that community. Therefore, a human being cut off from contact with a speech community can never learn to talk as that community does, and cut off from all speech communities never learns to talk at all. In essence, to say that language is arbitrary is merely to say that it is social. This is perhaps the most important statement that can be made about language.

In contrast, much of animal communication is instinctive rather than social. That is to say, all cats mew and purr, and would do so even if they were cut off from all communication with other cats. On the other hand, some animal communication seems to share the social nature of human speech and is therefore learned activity. A striking example is the barking of dogs, which is characteristic only of the domesticated animal, not of dogs in the wild state. Similarly, the honey dances of bees may not be altogether without an arbitrary element. It is also likely that when more is known of the cries and chatterings of the great apes in the wild state, a considerable social element in their communication may be found. Nor should it be thought that all human communication is social. A part of our communication consists of instinctive reactions which accompany language, like the trembling of fear or the suffusion of blood which accompanies anger. Yet even in the nonlinguistic accompaniments of speech, the tones of voice and the gestures, it is now clear that there is more of arbitrary and socially learned behavior than had at one time been supposed.

Third, language is systematic. I cannot hope to make this statement completely clear at this point, since the whole of this book is devoted to an exposition of the system of language. However, some observations may now be made about the system of language. As in any system, language entities are arranged in recurrent designs, so that if a part of the design is seen, predictions can be made about the whole of it, as a triangle can be drawn if one side and two angles are given. Suppose there is an incomplete sentence like "John ——s Mary an ——." A good deal about what must fill the two blanks is obvious. The first must be a verb, the second a noun. Furthermore, not all verbs will go in the first blank, since it requires a verb whose third person singular is spelled with -s and which can take two objects (that is, not such a verb as *look* or *see*). Nor will all nouns fit in the second place, since an initial vowel is required, and the noun must be one which takes an article. There is no difficulty in deciding that the sentence could be either "John gives Mary an apple" or "John hands Mary an aspirin," but not "John *gaves* Mary an *book*."

Another observation that can be made about language systems is that every occurrence of language is a substitution frame. Any sentence is a series of entities, for each of which a whole group of other entities can be substituted without changing the frame. Thus the sentence "John gives Mary an apple" is such a substitution frame. For *John* there can be replacements like *he, Jack, William, the man, her husband,* or many others. For the verb, entities like *buys, takes, offers,* as well as the alternatives *hands* or *gives,* may be used. This characteristic of extensive substitutability for all parts of any language utterance is of some importance in that it enables us to say that parrots, no matter how startlingly human their utterances may be, are not carrying on language activity. A parakeet may produce the sentence "Birds can't talk!" with human pitch, voice tones, and nearly perfect sounds. But the bird never says "Dogs can't talk!" or "Birds can't write!" His utterance is a unit, not a multiple substitution frame.

Still another characteristic of language systems is that the entities of language are grouped into classes, always simpler, more predictable, and more sharply separated than the infinite variety of objects in the world. For instance, a whole series of objects is grouped under the single word *chair,* and *chair* is put into the large class of nouns. In dealing with objects in the outside world it may be difficult to decide whether something is a chair, a stool, or merely a rock. In language, we think of nouns and verbs as quite separate and are apt to say that the one class represents things, the other events. But in the outside world, as the physicists tell us, it is often hard to decide whether an object is best described as thing or as event.

To return once more to the defining characteristics of language, the fourth characteristic is that it is a set of symbols. That is to say, language has meaning. In this form the statement is a platitude and does not distinguish language from other activities which are also symbolic. The nature of language symbols turns out to be rather different from the symbols of other types of communication. The simplest nonlinguistic symbol can be defined as a substitute stimulus. Pavlov's famous dogs, fed at the sound of a bell, eventually began to drool at the sound of the bell even when no food was present. The dogs were responding to a substitute stimulus. Nonlinguistic symbols can also be substitute responses, and these can also be taught to animals. A dog who learns to "speak" at the sight of food has learned such a substitute response. In human speech, however, one of the most striking facts is that we can talk about things which are not present, and we can talk about things which ordinarily produce a strong physical reaction without experiencing that reaction. For instance, I can talk about apples even though there are none in the room, and I can talk about them without always making my mouth water, even when I am hungry. This type of language, which occurs without an immediately present stimulus or response, is called "displaced speech," and it is obviously of great importance. It is what enables man to know something of the past and of the world beyond the limited range of his vision and hearing at a given moment.

The crucial fact in producing this almost miraculous and purely human effect seems to be that a given language entity can be both substitute stimulus and substitute response, and can also be a stimulus for further language responses or a response to other language stimuli. I can talk about apples when they are absent because "something reminds me of them." That is, I can make language responses to what is before me, and these language responses can stimulate the further response *apple* without any direct physical stimulus to my vision, touch, or smell. *Apple* can call forth still further language entities, like *pear* or *banana*, in an endless chain; these entities are also both stimuli and responses. When human speakers do this, they are setting up what philosophers call a "universe of discourse." The ability to make connected discourse within the symbol system is what enables men to talk at length, and profitably, about things they have never seen. By means of language men make elaborate models of distant experience and eventually test their accuracy by acting upon them. All that is known of animal communication leads to the supposition that precisely what is absent from it is the kind of symbolic activity here described, symbolic activity connected not merely with experience but with all parts of the symbol system itself. We believe, in short, that animals are incapable of displaced speech.

The paragraphs above are rather general, so that a concrete example may be helpful. Let us suppose that two speakers of English are together in a room. One of them is cold. A direct response for him would be to close the window.

Instead of this he can use the substitute response, which is also substitute stimulus: "John, please close the window for me." John can either close the window or reply with a further substitute: "Just a minute. Wait until I finish this page." Such a reply may produce acceptance or may lead to a discussion of John's procrastinating character, of the fact that his parents did not discipline him properly in youth and that modern young people are generally rebellious and unmannerly. To all of this John may reply that modern times are marked by progress and the disappearance of old taboos. In the meantime the window may have been quietly closed, or completely forgotten in the warmth of discussion. What is important is that each speaker has begun reacting, not to the immediate situation, but to the other speaker's language and to his own. And in so doing, each has been building a model of general social conditions, of wide scope and ultimately of some value, even in a random and unchecked conversation of the sort described.

We are now ready to turn to the last defining characteristic of language, the fact that it is complete. By this is meant that whenever a human language has been accurately observed, it has been found to be so elaborated that its speakers can make a linguistic response to any experience they may undergo. This complex elaboration is such a regular characteristic of all languages, even those of the simplest societies, that linguists have long ago accepted it as a universal characteristic. Nevertheless, in early books about language, and in the descriptions by linguistically untrained travelers today, there are statements that tribe X has a language with only two or three hundred words in it, forcing the tribe to eke out its vocabulary by gesture. Linguists maintain that all such statements are the product of lack of knowledge, and are false. Skepticism about such statements is borne out by the fact that in all instances where it was possible to check on tribe X, its language proved to be complete as usual, whereupon the statement was transferred to tribe Y, whose language was as yet unknown. The statement that human language is complete once again serves to distinguish it from animal activity. In the communication of bees, for instance, the subjects of systematic discourse are severely limited. Bees cannot, apparently, make an utterance equivalent to "The beekeeper is coming."

The statement that human language is always complete should not be interpreted to mean that every language has a word for everything. Obviously the ancient Greeks had no words for automobiles or atom bombs, and probably the modern Yahgan of Tierra del Fuego lack them as well. The completeness of language lies rather in the fact that a speaker of ancient Greek would have been perfectly capable of describing an automobile had he seen one, and further that had automobiles become important in ancient Greece, the speakers of Greek would have been perfectly capable of coining a word for them. It is a characteristic of vocabulary that, except in languages which have gone out of use, it is always expansible, in spite of the fact that resistance to new forms may frequently appear. Since language enables the user to make appropriate responses to all things and since vocabulary is thus characteristically "open," differences in vocabulary between two languages are not an accurate measure of the difference in efficiency or excellence of the two tongues. The fact that Eskimo does not have as highly developed a vocabulary of philosophy as does German merely indicates that the Eskimos are less interested in philosophy; on the other hand, Eskimo has a highly developed vocabulary for various kinds of snow, indicating that snow is important in Eskimo society. The completeness of human language and the openness of vocabulary make a groundless chimera of the occasionally expressed fear that a language might so degenerate as to become useless.

We can now attempt a definition of language, though the definition will be cumbersome. Language is the primary and most highly elaborated form of human symbolic activity. Its symbols are made up of sounds produced by the vocal apparatus, and they are arranged in classes and patterns which make up a complex and symmetrical structure. The entities of language are symbols, that is, they have meaning, but the connection between symbol and thing is arbitrary and socially controlled. The symbols of language are simultaneously substitute stimuli and substitute responses and can call forth further stimuli and responses, so that discourse becomes independent of an immediate physical stimulus. The entities and structure of language are always so elaborated as to give the speaker the possibility of making a linguistic response to any experience. Most of the above can be paraphrased by saying that every language is a model of a culture and its adjustment to the world.

3. Language and the Study of Its Nature

Since language is something that we habitually take for granted, it may not be clear, even after this discussion, why language and, even more, the study of language are important. Primarily they are important because language is a solely human activity, which separates man from other living beings. But though this may be readily granted, it is not always realized how fundamentally language is a defining characteristic of man. Even among students of man it is probably more common to define him as "the tool-making animal" than as "the talking animal." But it is quite possible that tool making is less crucially human than talking is. For one thing, it is natural that an archaeologist's attention should turn toward tools, which can be dug up, rather than toward language, which cannot. For another, it is not always easy to recognize how fundamental language is, even in our own society. There are individuals who lead nearly normal lives in spite of being deprived of speech, so that it may be argued that speech—admittedly the fundamental form of language—is a dispensable form of activity. Yet such speechless individuals always develop some form of substitute language, and all such substitutes presuppose the individual's membership in a society fully provided with speech. There are many things, such as wearing neckties, making movies, or cooking, which only human beings do. But many of these are not universal among men, and all of them are secondary. As for tool making, this activity is universally human, but it is in some sense shared with the higher primates. When, however, it is argued that tool making involves more than the use of a convenient stick or stone and is the purposeful molding of an object for future use, it would seem that the tool maker is an individual capable of displaced speech and of shaping his activity in accord with a symbolic model. In other words, as soon as man is defined as a maker of tools whose use lies in the future, we presuppose the existence of language. Therefore linguists, and many anthropologists, believe that language is the phenomenon most basic in human society. Historical anthropologists assume that when humanoid remains are found in a situation indicating an organized community, they are necessarily remains of a group possessed of language. If, then, it is language more than anything else we can observe which makes us men, it is ultimately the study of language which is most likely to throw light on the essential humanness of human beings. I wish at this point, however, to make a specific disclaimer. There are characteristics inaccessible to science which also distinguish man; the science of language is not concerned with these and should under no circumstances be understood as denying them. On the other hand, the existence of spiritual qualities ought equally to be understood as not being a bar to the study of those things which can be investigated by science.

If scientific study of language can throw light on human qualities and activities, there is no direction in which there is greater likelihood of illumination than in the investigation of thought, whether that investigation be understood as a part of psychology or a part of logic. It was said earlier that linguists do not deny the existence or importance of mind. The American linguist insists that language entities cannot be profitably investigated in terms of the mental concepts or thoughts back of them, but this insistence ought always to be understood as carrying with it the corollary that mental concepts can be profitably investigated in terms of the language entities which are so largely instrumental in their formation. It has also been said that language is basic to society. It is therefore probable that increased knowledge of language will mean increased knowledge of society. The promise is already recognized and has already borne fruit, since anthropologists have made brilliant use of linguistic insights. Less broad than thought and society, another area in which linguistic knowledge is beginning to prove useful is in the study of literature, if for no other reason than that literature is an art constructed in language. Similarly, the practical activity of language instruction, whether that of a foreign or the native tongue, can profit by knowledge of the nature of the material which is to be imparted.

I have up to now spoken of the importance of language study from the broad aspect of human knowledge; for the individual student the impact of language study is different. The native language provides its speakers an ever-present and deeply habituated instrument by which

they measure and control experience. All adults have had a long indoctrination in the attitude that language is both a transparent glass
through which we see the world and a tool by which we mold it. Therefore the first stages of study of language for the sake of knowledge
rather than with a practical aim are apt to be disquieting, or even to
seem useless. A somewhat parallel case can be drawn from optics. We
think of our eyes as instruments which transmit the "real" appearance
of objects directly to our minds. It is often disturbing to realize that
our eyes necessarily influence the appearance of objects and that a
surface which appears flat to us can scarcely appear so to the nearly
spherical eye of a fly. Yet to say that language study is apt to be difficult or disquieting is not the same thing as to say that it is of no value
to the individual. An important aim of education is the adjustment of
the individual to the world in which he has to live, and linguistic knowledge is a help toward that end. The individual's understanding of reality is increased if he can learn to distinguish the ways in which the
structure of his language may influence his perception of reality. Study
of language is one of the best ways in which a narrow belief in the
rightness of one's own ways of doing things, and the wrongness of every
other way, can be broken down. It is instructive to find that some languages, even among the European group, are not felt to be inadequate
because they do not distinguish between fingers and toes by separate
vocabulary items. The knowledge that there are languages which have
no tenses at all and others which attach tenses to their nouns is a good
introduction to the myriad ways in which men channel the basic human
needs, experiences, and activities which indeed remain much the same
throughout the world. A student trained in language is aware, on the
practical level, of language pitfalls. A very little training may prepare
him for failure of communication when an Englishman and an American talk about *corn*. More sophistication is needed for dealing with the
situation reported by Bloomfield in which an Englishman misunderstood his American pronunciation of *Comedy Theatre* as a request for
a nonexistent *Carmody Theatre*. In all such instances, the student
trained in language will deal with the inevitable failure of understanding in realistic terms, without wasting time in denouncing one group
or the other for not knowing its own language. And similarly, he is prepared to deal with the difficulties of a foreign language on a more
realistic level than by supposing that there is a one-to-one correspondence between its forms and those of English.

By now, I hope that some meaning has been given to the definition
of linguistics as the scientific study of language. Linguistics has for its

goal the understanding of language, and it is secure in the belief that such understanding will increase human knowledge. It strives to present a picture of language as complete as possible, as consistent as possible, and as simple as possible, again secure in the belief that if these conditions are fulfilled it will be as truly and revealingly a science as is chemistry or astronomy. This book is an attempt to take the reader through some of the first steps in this young science. The means chosen have been an explanation of the techniques and entities of linguistics in an extended sketch of English, followed by shorter sketches of different language structures. It is not assumed that a sketch of Eskimo will make the reader more capable of finding his way about in Greenland; rather it is hoped that he may gradually come to accept a scientific attitude in a kind of activity where most people, even those thoroughly educated, have not tried to be scientific, and where some, indeed, have resisted the suggestion that they should be. The first stages of investigation and statement may seem to be disturbing and even to introduce confusion where none existed before, but as the design of language and its analysis unfold, clarity emerges, and with it the security of understanding.

EMOTIONAL MEANINGS*

Robert H. Thouless

When we use a word in speech and writing, its most obvious purpose is to point to some thing or relation or property. This is the word's "meaning." We see a small four-footed animal on the road and call it a "dog," indicating that it is a member of the class of four-footed animals we call dogs. The word "dog" as we have used it there has a plain, straightforward, "objective" meaning. We have in no way gone beyond the requirements of exact scientific description.

Let us suppose also that one grandparent of the dog was a collie, another was an Irish terrier, another a fox terrier, and the fourth a bulldog. We can express these facts equally scientifically and objectively by saying that he is a dog of mixed breed. Still we have in no way gone beyond the requirements of exact scientific description.

Suppose, however, that we had called that same animal a "mongrel." The matter is more complicated. We have used a word which objec-

* From Robert H. Thouless, *How to Think Straight.* Copyright 1932, 1939 by Simon & Schuster, Inc. Reprinted by permission.

tively means the same as "dog of mixed breed," but which also arouses in our hearers an emotional attitude of disapproval toward the particular dog. A word, therefore, can not only indicate an object, but can also suggest an emotional attitude toward it. Such suggestion of an emotional attitude does go beyond exact and scientific discussion because our approvals and disapprovals are individual—they belong to ourselves and not to the objects we approve or disapprove of. An animal which to the mind of its master is a faithful and noble dog of mixed ancestry may be a "mongrel" to his neighbor, whose chickens are chased by it.

Similarly, a Negro may be indicated objectively as a "colored man" or he may be indicated with strong emotional disapproval and contempt as a "nigger." The use of the latter word debases any discussion in which it is used below the level of impartial and objective argument.

Once we are on the lookout for this difference between "objective" and "emotional" meanings, we shall notice that words which carry more or less strong suggestions of emotional attitudes are very common and are ordinarily used in the discussion of such controversial questions as those of politics, morals, and religion. This is one reason why such controversies cannot yet be settled.

There is a well-known saying that the word "firm" can be declined as follows: I am *firm,* thou art *obstinate,* he is *pigheaded.* That is a simple illustration of what is meant. "Firm," "obstinate," and "pigheaded" all have the same objective meaning—that is, following one's own course of action and refusing to be influenced by other people's opinions. They have, however, different emotional meanings: "firm" has an emotional meaning of strong approval, "obstinate" of mild disapproval, "pigheaded" of strong disapproval. . . .

Such thinking in wartime may do much harm by leading humane people to condone cruelty. When the ordinarily liberal-minded Swinburne wrote a poem during the Boer War on the death of a British officer who had been blamed for the bad condition of the camps in which the Boer women and children were interned, he said:

> Nor heed we more than he what liars dare say
> Of mercy's holiest duties left undone
> Toward *whelps* and *dams* of *murderous* foes, whom none
> Save we had spared or feared to starve and slay.

Whelps and *dams* clearly mean in objective fact *children* and *wives,* with the added meaning of the emotional attitude adopted toward the females and young of wild beasts, while *murderous* means no more in objective fact than that our foes killed us when they could (as we also killed them), with the added emotional meaning of an attitude toward them which is our attitude to those who are guilty of murder.

The use of emotionally toned words is not, of course, always to be condemned. They are always harmful when we are trying to think clearly on a disputable point of fact. In poetry, on the other hand, they have a perfectly proper place, because in poetry (as in some kinds of prose) the arousing of suitable emotions is an important part of the purpose for which the words are used.

In "The Eve of St. Agnes," Keats has written:

> Full on this casement shone the wintry moon,
> And threw warm gules on Madeline's fair breast.

These are beautiful lines. Let us notice how much of their beauty follows from the proper choice of emotionally colored words and how completely it is lost if these words are replaced by neutral ones. The words with strikingly emotional meanings are *casement, gules, Madeline, fair,* and *breast. Casement* means simply a kind of window with emotional and romantic associations. *Gules* is the heraldic name for red, with the suggestion of romance which accompanies all heraldry. *Madeline* is simply a girl's name, but one calling out favorable emotions absent from a relatively plain and straightforward name. *Fair* simply means, in objective fact, that her skin was white or uncolored— a necessary condition for the colors of the window to show—but also *fair* implies warm emotional preference for an uncolored skin rather than one which is yellow, purple, black, or any of the other colors which skin might be. *Breast* has also similar emotional meanings, and the aim of scientific description might have been equally well attained if it had been replaced by such a neutral word as *chest.*

Let us now try the experiment of keeping these two lines in a metrical form, but replacing all the emotionally colored words by neutral ones, while making as few other changes as possible. We may write:

> *Full on this window shone the wintry moon,*
> *Making red marks on Jane's uncolored chest.*

No one will doubt that all of its poetic value has been knocked out of the passage by these changes. Yet the lines still mean the same in external fact; they still have the same objective meaning. It is only the emotional meaning which has been destroyed.

Now if Keats had been writing a scientific description for a textbook on physics instead of a poem, it would have been necessary for him to have used some such coldly objective terms as the ones into which we have just translated his lines. Such emotionally charged phrases as *warm gules* and *fair breast* would only have obscured the facts to which the scientist exactly but unbeautifully refers when he speaks of "the selective transmission of homogeneous light by pigmented glass."

The purpose of the present essay is to deal with the kind of problem in which cold and scientific thinking is required. Most of the practical problems of life are of this order. The fact that I shall abuse the use of emotional thinking in connection with such problems as tariffs, social ownership, revolution, and war does not mean that there is no place for emotional thinking. Poetry, romantic prose, and emotional oratory are all of inestimable value, but their place is not where responsible decisions must be made. The common (almost universal) use of emotional words in political thinking is as much out of place as would be a chemical or statistical formula in the middle of a poem. Real democracy will come only when the solution of national and international problems is carried out by scientific methods of thought, purged of all irrelevant emotion. Into the action which follows decision we can put all the emotion which we have refused to allow in our thinking. Let us think calmly and scientifically about war, and then actively oppose it with all the passion of which we are capable.

The growth of the exact thinking of modern science has been largely the result of its getting rid of all terms suggesting emotional attitudes and using only those which unemotionally indicate objective facts. It was not always so. The old alchemists called gold and silver "noble" metals, and thought that this emotionally colored word indicated something belonging to the metals themselves from which their properties could be deduced. Other metals were called "base." Although these terms have survived as convenient labels for the modern chemist, they carry none of their old emotional significance.

In popular biological discussions, on the other hand, such words are still used with their full emotional meaning, as when the "nobility" of man is contrasted with his alleged "base" origin. In this respect, popular biological discussion differs from that of the textbook and the laboratory, in which are used terms almost as devoid of emotional meaning as those of physics or chemistry.

Psychology is still younger in the ranks of the sciences, and the clearing away from it of emotional words has not gone very far. "Passion," "emotion," "sex" are all terms of our science which carry strong emotional meanings, so that it is difficult to discuss a controversial matter in psychology without using words which rouse strong emotions and confuse all issues. A beginning is being made. "Intelligence" was a subject on which it was difficult to think clearly because it carried so much emotional meaning. Now Professor Spearman has replaced it by what he calls "g" (or the "general factor"), which is a conception derived from the statistical analysis of a large collection of figures, and yet which is in its essence all that was really scientific in the old conception of intelligence. Some day a psychological genius will give us X or Z to replace the old emotional conception of sex, and we shall be able to discuss psychoanalysis as objectively as a mathematical physicist can discuss the quantum theory.

When we turn to politics and international questions, we are still further from straight scientific thinking. Such words as "Bolshevik," "Fascist," "reactionary," "revolutionary," "constitutional," "national honor," etc., are all words used in national and international political thinking which carry more of emotional than of any other meaning. So long as such words are the ordinary terms of rival politicians, how can we hope to think straight in national and international affairs? If a chemist doing an experiment depended on such thought processes as a nation uses in selecting its rulers or in deciding on peace or war with other nations, he would blow up his laboratory. This, however, would be a trivial disaster in comparison with what may result from emotional thinking in politics. Better have a hundred chemical laboratories blown up than the whole of civilization!

We must look forward to and try to help on the day when the thinking about political and international affairs will be as unemotional and as scientific as that about the properties of numbers or the atomic weights of elements. The spirit of impartial investigation of facts unswayed by irrelevant emotions has given us great advances in the sciences. Its triumphs will be even greater when it is applied to the most important affairs of life. We look forward to the day when we shall be able to discuss and settle such questions as Tariffs, Public *vs.* Private Ownership, and Disarmament Treaties as successfully as physicists have discussed and settled Einstein's theory of relativity.

Let us try to study a few more examples of the use of words with emotional meanings taken from various sources. Accounts of wars are rich sources of such material, so we are not surprised to find in a book on the French Commune the statement that large numbers of the regular troops were *assassinated* during the street fighting by the Communards, while a much larger number of the latter were *summarily executed* by the regulars. In order to reduce this to a statement of objective fact it is clear that the one word "killed" should be used in place both of *assassinated* and *summarily executed*. We have already noticed

how such a choice of words with the same objective but opposite emotional meaning can be used to make us feel sympathetic to one and
hostile to the other of two sides in warfare. During the Spanish Civil
War, the supporters of the Government referred to themselves as the
"Loyalists" and called Franco a "Rebel" or an "Insurgent." The supporters of Franco, on the other hand, called themselves "Nationalists"
and referred to their opponents as "Reds." During the conflicts between
Red and White forces in Russia and in China, our newspapers told us
of the *atrocities* of the Bolsheviks and the *wise severity* of the White
commanders. Examination of the details (often possible only long
afterwards) shows that the objective facts of an *atrocity* and of *wise
severity* are much the same, and that they are not the kind of objective
facts which will call out an emotion of approval in a humane person.

A similar choice of words will be noticed in political discussion. A
fluent and forcible speech delivered by one of our own party is *elo-
quent*, a similar speech by one of the opposite party is *fanatical;* again
two words with the same objective meaning but with the opposite emotional meanings of approval and strong disapproval. The practical proposals of the opposition, moreover, are *panaceas*—a highly emotional
word calling out the strongly disapproving emotions which we feel
for those quack patent medicines which make extravagant claims.
Those who show enthusiasm in support of proposals with which a
speaker disagrees are *crackpots;* while those showing similar enthusiasm on his own side are called *sound.* If a politician wishes to attack
some new proposal he has a battery of these and other words with emotional meanings at his disposal. He speaks of "this suggested *panacea*
supported only by *fanatical crackpots";* and the proposal is at once discredited in the minds of the majority of people, who like to think of
themselves as moderate, distrustful of panaceas, and uninfluenced by
windy eloquence. Also, we may notice that it has been discredited
without the expenditure of any real thought, for of real objective argument there is none—only the manipulation of words calling out emotion.

It is not, however, only in warfare and politics that such words are
used in order to influence opinion more easily than can be done by
words embodying real thought. Art criticism is also a good source for
this kind of material. Ruskin said of Whistler's Nocturnes: "I have
heard and seen much of *Cockney impudence* before now, but never expected to hear a *coxcomb* ask two hundred guineas for *flinging a pot of
paint in the public's face.*" As in earlier passages, I have italicized the
words or phrases with strongly emotional meanings. Stripped of these
and reduced to a statement of objective fact, the passage would have

to be paraphrased in some such way as follows: "I have heard and seen much of the behavior of Londoners before now, but never expected to hear a painter ask two hundred guineas for painting a picture which seemed to me to have no meaning." Plainly not much is left of Ruskin's criticism after this operation has been performed on it.

As a last example, we may take a part of an attack made by a newspaper on a novel. This runs: "Its *vicious* plea for the acknowledgment and *condonation* of *sexual perversity*, and the grounds on which it is based, loosen the very *sheet anchor of conduct*." This passage calls out such strong emotions of abhorrence that most readers will be content to condemn the novel without further inquiry. Yet the effect is gained entirely by the choice of words with emotional meanings. It happens to deal with a subject on which emotions are strong, so a dispassionate examination is all the more necessary. We note that a *plea* is simply an argument, plus a suggestion of a repugnance for the kind of argument used; that *condonation* is tolerance plus an emotional suggestion that such toleration is indefensible; that *sexual* means something in the life of love of which we disapprove, and that a *perversity* is an unusualness plus an emotional suggestion of abhorrence. The loosening of a *sheet anchor* is a metaphor implying change and suggesting to a landsman the emotion of fear, while *conduct* is simply behavior of which we approve.

So reduced to its bare bones of statement of objective fact (ignoring for a moment the special difficulties raised by the word *vicious*), the passage becomes: "Its argument for the acknowledgment and tolerance of unusualness in the life of love, and the grounds on which it is based, change the principles of behavior." This clearly is an important statement if it is true, but is not enough in itself to condemn the book, because undoubtedly our principles of behavior do need changing from time to time. We can only decide intelligently whether or not they need changing in the particular case under discussion, when we have made a dispassionate statement of what the proposed changes are and why they are defended. As in all other cases, discussion of the question with emotionally charged words obscures the problem and makes a sensible decision difficult or impossible.

The word *vicious* has some special difficulties of its own. It arouses emotions of disapproval, but there is no word with the same objective meaning which would not. If we call the book bad, corrupt, or evil, the same emotions would be aroused. So we cannot perform the simple operation of replacing *vicious* by an emotionally neutral word with the same objective meaning. Can we then leave it out altogether, on the ground that it has no objective meaning, but that it is used merely to arouse emotion?

Here we are up against a problem about which there has been much dispute. Some people consider that all such words as "good," "bad," "beautiful," "ugly," only indicate one's own emotional reactions toward actions or things and in no sense properties of the actions or things themselves. But when we see a man steal a penny from a child and we call his action "bad," we are in fact saying something meaningful about the action itself and not merely about our own feelings. As to what that something is we may leave the philosophers to dispute; it may only be that the man's action has subtracted from the total amount of human happiness. So to say a book is *vicious* is not the same kind of thing as contrasting the *slaughter* of regular troops by Communards with the *execution* of the Communards by regular soldiers. The statement that the book is *vicious* has a meaning which is not merely emotional, although, of course, the statement may not be true.

On the other hand, it is clearly not quite the same kind of meaning as a simple statement of outside fact such as "This is a book." Whether the book is good or bad is a real question, but it is a question peculiarly difficult to decide. Our own statement one way or the other is likely to be nothing but a reflection of our own personal prejudices and to have, therefore, no sort of scientific exactness. At the same time, such words certainly arouse strong emotions and should, therefore, be used sparingly in honest argument. The use of words implying moral judgments in the course of argument is very generally an attempt to distort the hearers' view of the truth by arousing emotions.

If we are trying to decide a simple question of fact, such words should be left out, because it is easier to settle one question at a time. If a man is accused of poisoning his wife, the prosecuting attorney should not say, "This *scoundrel* who hounded his wife to her grave." The question to be decided is whether the man did poison his wife. If he did, he is a "scoundrel" undoubtedly, but calling him a scoundrel does not help to decide the question of fact. On the contrary, it makes a correct decision more difficult by rousing emotions of hatred for the accused in the minds of the jury. Another obvious objection to the use of the word "scoundrel" before the man is convicted, which puts it in the ranks of "crooked thinking," is that it "begs the question" or assumes what is to be proved. The man is only a scoundrel if he is guilty, and yet the word has been used in the course of an argument to prove that he is guilty.

These two objections can be urged against the word "vicious" in the condemnation of a book quoted above. It calls up strong emotions making a just decision of the nature of the book difficult, and it assumes exactly what the article professes to prove—that the book is a bad one.

The aim of this essay has been to distinguish one kind of crooked thinking, in the hope that those who recognize how their opinions can be twisted away from the truth by the use of words with emotional meanings may be able to recognize this source of error and to guard themselves against it. Those of its readers who have found anything new to them in the ideas of this chapter should not, I suggest, be content simply to read the essay, but should try to do some practical work on its subject matter. If you were studying botany, you would not be content merely to read books on botany. If you were, that would not carry you far in botanical knowledge. Instead you would gather plants from the hedges and weeds from your garden, dissecting them, examining them with a microscope or magnifying glass, and drawing them in your notebook. Psychology too should be studied by practical methods. Emotional thinking (like most of the other kinds of crooked thinking we shall be studying) is as common as a weed. It is to be found in the leading articles of newspapers, in the words of people carrying on discussions on political, religious, or moral questions, and in the speeches made by public men when these deal with controversial matters. In order to understand it, we should collect specimens by putting them down on paper and then we should dissect them. Current political and social controversy in the United States abounds in such words and phrases as "crackpots," "economic royalists," "the abundant life," "bureaucracy"—or, on the street level—"scabs," "finks," "nigger-lovers." The New York *Herald Tribune* habitually referred to the child labor bill for New York State as the "youth control bill"; the Hearst press dubbed New Deal the "Raw Deal"; Communists use the words "Trotzkyite" and "Fascist" to cover a multitude of sinners; Secretary Ickes managed to get some powerful emotional undertones from Ferdinand Lundberg's phrase, "America's Sixty Families."

With these ideas and phrases in mind, it is not difficult to set forth on a practical search for truth. I suggest that readers should copy out controversial phrases from newspapers, books, or speeches which contain emotionally colored words. Then they should underline all the emotional words, afterwards rewriting the passages with the emotional words replaced by neutral ones. Examine the passage then in its new form in which it merely states objective facts without indicating the writer's emotional attitude toward them, and see whether it is still good evidence for the proposition it is trying to prove. If it is, the passage is a piece of straight thinking in which emotionally colored words have been introduced merely as an ornament. If not, it is crooked thinking, because the conclusion depends not on the objective meaning of the passage but on the emotions roused by the words.

When we condemn such a use of emotional words in writings and speeches, we must remember that this is a symptom of a more deep-seated evil—their prevalence in our own private, unexpressed thinking. Many of our highly colored political speakers whose speeches stir us as we are stirred by romantic poetry show themselves unable to think calmly and objectively on any subject. They have so accustomed themselves to think in emotionally toned words that they can no longer think in any other way. They should have been poets or professional orators, but certainly not statesmen.

It really does not matter much if we sometimes use emotional words. We all do when we are trying to produce conviction. What does matter is that we should not lose the power to think without them. So a more important exercise than any we can perform on written material is one we can perform on our own minds. When we catch ourselves thinking in emotional phraseology, let us form a habit of translating our thoughts into emotionally neutral words. So we can guard ourselves from ever being so enslaved by emotional words and phrases that they prevent us from thinking objectively when we need to do so—that is, whenever we have to come to a decision on any debatable matter.

A WORD IN YOUR EAR*

Lister Sinclair

Two narrators take us to scenes that show the relationship between language and culture. One of them is "HERE," who likes to point out things about our own language; the other is "THERE," who finds his examples in distant lands. The other characters are self-explanatory.

HERE. Watch your language! Remember whom you're speaking to! To the ladies, speak Italian; to the gentlemen, French; to the birds, English; to the dogs, German; and Spanish should be spoken only to God!

(*Music*)

HERE. All people have language with which to express their feelings.

* From *Ways of Mankind*, a series of fourteen radio dramatizations. Published by the Beacon Press. Reprinted by permission of The Fund for Adult Education.

THERE. But language is not the same as expressing your feelings. Some people think animals have language because they can often express their feelings; as when in the arctic wilderness, we hear the wolf. (*An arctic wolf howls in the distance.*)

HERE. But there is all the difference in the world between that wolf and this. (*A human "wolf-whistle" is heard.*)

THERE. The four-legged wolf howl expresses its feelings there and then, and so does the wolf-whistle. But the whistler can back up his expression with language.

HUMAN. How about taking in a show on Saturday night?

HERE. And that is a communication about another time and another place. It is true language, not just expression of feeling. And all human beings have language—from the Eskimo by the Arctic Ocean, warm in his kayak with his suit of furs, to the Patagonian by the Antarctic Ocean, shivering in his canoe with a fire in it, because he wears almost no clothes at all. From one extreme to the other, all people have language.

(*Music*)

THERE. What's more, all these languages are adequate. They all do the job—communication. Their variety, both of sound and structure, is incredible, but each stands relatively unchanging with its own traditions and flavor. For instance, the Persian speaks.

PERSIAN. In Paradise, the serpent spoke Arabic, the most persuasive of all languages; Adam and Eve spoke Persian, the most poetic of all languages; and the angel Gabriel spoke Turkish, the most threatening of all languages.

HERE. On the other hand, in the Highlands of Scotland, the tradition goes that Scots Gaelic was the language spoken by Adam and Eve in Paradise.

THERE. As for English, many other peoples think it sounds like the twittering of birds, rapid, shrill, and mysterious. To the Navaho, whose speech is precise in the exact intonation of every syllable, English is just a lot of slop. And to anyone who speaks a language rich in vowels, such as Italian or Japanese, English, with its clustering clots of consonant strengths, is enough to give a crocodile the lockjaw.

HERE. For we often think that whatever we speak ourselves is the proper thing—that what the other fellow speaks is scarcely more than a string of grunts.

WIFE. I see by the paper there are over fifteen hundred different languages spoken in the world today.

HUSBAND (*engrossed in the sports section*). Oh.

WIFE. And it says there are more families of languages among the American Indians than in the whole of the Old World.

HUSBAND. Uh.

WIFE. Well, everyone knows Indians don't talk properly. They just grunt.

HUSBAND. Uh-uh.

WIFE. You aren't listening. (*Pause.*) Are you?

HUSBAND (*now puts down his paper*). Hmmm?

WIFE. Are you listening?

HUSBAND (*with the false enthusiasm of one who hasn't been*). M-hm!

WIFE. I say Indians don't talk properly. They just grunt.

HUSBAND. Huh?

WIFE. *Grunt!*

HUSBAND. Uh!

WIFE. What do you think?

HUSBAND. U-u-u-u-u-u-u-uh—language is language, and grunts are grunts.

(*Music*)

HERE. One man's speech is another man's jargon, but all people have language, and these languages are highly diverse in form. But always we begin by speaking as we think, and end by thinking as we speak. Our language is an expression of our culture, shaped by the way we are brought up: and on the other hand, the way we are brought up is shaped by our language.

THERE. For, as we know from our own language, English, language reflects place, time, age, sex, and circumstance. And this is true of other languages.

HERE. Language reflects place.

THERE. As everybody knows, very often the most foreign thing about a foreign country is the foreign language.

HERE. And English-speakers can't visit one another's country without meeting the great Transatlantic Rift.

AMERICAN. Lookit, Jack, when you get off the streetcar, get off the pavement, get on the sidewalk, go two blocks, turn right, there's a drugstore on the corner, take the elevator down to the gar*age*. You can't miss it.

ENGLISH. All right, chum. You mean, when I get off the tram, get off the road, get *on* the pavement, take the second turning to the right, there's a chemist's shop on the corner, take the lift down to the gar*age*. What do you mean, I can't miss it?

THERE. Language then, is a function of place.

(*Music*)

HERE. And language is a function of time. Listen to the Lord's Prayer as it sounded nearly six hundred years ago.

WICLIF. Oure Fadir that art in heuenes, halwid be thi name; thi kyngdom cumme to; be thi wille don as in heuen and in erthe; gif to vs this day oure breed ouer other substaunce; and forgeve to vs oure dettis, as we forgeve to oure dettours; and leede vs nat in to temptacioun, but delyuere vs fro yuel. Amen.

THERE. Then, quite soon after the Norman Conquest, English had a tang of French to it. But let's jump back beyond 1066 and listen to English in its hard Teutonic infancy as Anglo-Saxon—the Lord's Prayer in the year 1000 A.D.

ANGLO-SAXON. Faeder ure thu the eart on heofonum; si thin name gehalgod. To-becume thin rice. Gewurthe thin wille on eorthan swa swa on heofonum. Urne gedaeghwamlican hlaf syle us to daeg. And forgyf us ure gyltas swa swa we forgyfath urum gyltendum. And we gelaed thu us on costnunge ac alys us of yfele. Sothlice.

HERE. Language then is a function of time. And even modern English still keeps the record of that Norman Conquest. The Saxons became the servants, and looked after the beasts while they were alive, and their names are still the Saxon ones.

SAXON. Ox. Calf. Sheep. Swine.

THERE. Compare the German: Ochs. Kalb. Schaf. Schwein.

HERE. But when they were killed, their meat was served up to the Norman master; and on the table those animals' names are still the Norman ones.

NORMAN. Beef. Veal. Mutton. Pork.

THERE. Compare the French: Bœuf. Veau. Mouton. Porc. Language reflects culture.

(*Music*)

HERE. Language is a function of age. We don't expect a child to talk like a college professor.

INFANT. Simple harmonic motion can therefore be represented graphically by a sine or cosine curve.

THERE. Nor do we expect a college professor to talk like a child.

PROFESSOR. What's the matter? said the doctor. What's the matter? said the nurse. What's the matter? said the lady with the alligator purse.

(*Music*)

THERE. Language is also a function of sex. Among the Carayahi Indians of Brazil, the women and the men speak different languages. For example, the word for girl is *yadokoma* in the women's language, but *yadoma* in the men's. The men and women speak a slightly different language.

HERE. And in English? Here's a traveler chewing his cigar in the smoking room of the Santa Fe Chief. But he's speaking the women's language.

SALESMAN. I don't want to be catty, but, my dear, it was simply too terrible. I really thought I should have died. I just wanted to sink right through the floor. My gracious me, I thought, if Bert and Charlie aren't wearing that same cunning Homburg hat.

HERE. Unfortunately, in our society the men's language is taboo to women—that is to say, they are supposed not to know it. So I'm afraid we daren't give you an example of a lady speaking the men's language. Sailors present.

(*Music*)

THERE. Language is a function of occasion. There is a time for one kind of speech, and a time for another. Sir James Frazer tells us that in Siam there is a special language to be used when discussing the Siamese King. The hairs of his head, the soles of his feet, the breath of his body, indeed every single detail of his person, both outward and inward, have particular names. When he eats or drinks or walks, a special word indicates that these acts are being performed by the sovereign, and such words cannot possibly be applied to the acts of any other person whatever.

HERE. We do not perhaps carry things quite as far as that, but nonetheless a fellow may be greeted casually when he comes into the office.

AMIABLE. Hi, Charlie boy, how's the kid? What've you got to say for yourself?

HERE. But a few minutes later, when the board meeting convenes, he is addressed more formally.

AMIABLE. And now, Charles, we trust you have overcome the hardships of your journey. Would you be so good as to present your report regarding market conditions in the west.

THERE. The Chinese are famous for their elaborate forms of greeting. But other languages are far more complicated. For example, the Nootka Indians of Vancouver Island not only distinguish, by their choice of words, the sex of a person speaking, the sex of the person spoken to, and whether the speaker is more or less important than the person spoken to; but also, on top of this, have a special way of talking to a man who is left-handed, and a special way of talking to a man who is circumcised.

HERE. English cannot go this far. But, even so, language must be suitable to the occasion. Queen Victoria certainly knew this when she expressed her dislike of Gladstone.

QUEEN VICTORIA. Mr. Gladstone always addresses me as if I were a Public Meeting.

HERE. And imagine a politician proposing in the language he uses on the platform.

POLITICIAN. Unaccustomed as I am to private proposals, I kneel before you today, unwilling—nay, reluctant—to assume the burdens of matrimonial office, but nonetheless prepared to bow to your opinion, and dedicate myself unselfishly if I receive an unmistakable draft.

(Music)
(The Wedding March)

THERE. Language, therefore, by reflecting place, time, age, sex, and circumstance, is a function of society. Language reflects culture.

HERE. The easiest way to see this is through vocabulary. The Eskimos have no word for coconut, and the Samoans have no word for snow.

ESKIMO. And neither do the Eskimos.

HERE. I beg your pardon?

ESKIMO. We Eskimos have no word for snow. Ask me the word for snow, and I ask you: What kind of snow? Snow is to us Eskimos too important to be dismissed with one word. We have many words telling us, for instance, when it fell, and describing its exact condition to us. For the knowledge is vital, and our lives may depend on it.

THERE. Since language reflects society, whatever is important in society has many words in the language. The Arabs have a thousand words for sword. And the Siberian Chuckchee, who live on the shores of the Arctic Ocean, have thirty or so words describing the skins of the caribou. Here is just one of them:

CHUCKCHEE. Cechenyaqilhm.

THERE. This Chuckchee word means that the underleg of the caribou skin is greyish, and that it is light grey on the groins, but that the prevailing body color is brown. And there are innumerable similar examples. The Yurok Indians of California place a high value on woodpecker scalps and obsidian blades. And besides the ordinary set of numerals (1, 2, 3, and so forth) they have two extra sets— one for counting woodpecker scalps, and another one for counting obsidian blades.

HERE. English is full of relics of vocabulary that remind us that other days thought other things important. There was a time when English-speaking men lived very much by hunting. They had special words for congregations of animals: a flock of sheep and a herd of cattle, but a pride of lions, a skulk of foxes, and a gaggle of geese.

They also had special words for the carving of each of the animals and birds of the chase when they arrived on the table ready to eat. Nowadays if we have a pile of game birds we want carved, the cook will say:

COOK. Hey, mac!

MAC. Yeah?

COOK. Cut up them birds, will you?

HERE. For nowadays one game bird is much like another—out of season.

THERE. But to the Elizabethans, game birds were the very meat of life, and their carving required a special and ornate vocabulary.

COOK. You, sirrah!

MAC. Anon?

COOK. Dismember that heron, unbrace that mallard, allay that pheasant, wing that partridge, display that quail, unjoint that bittern, thigh that woodcock, lift that swan, and rear that goose. As for that curlew—

MAC. Aye, sir?

COOK. Unlatch it!

(*Music*)
(*"Come to the Cookhouse Door"*)

HERE. A noble handful that has been replaced by other rich treasures of vocabulary as *our* language (like all other languages) has changed to reflect our culture.

ESKIMO. As we Eskimos found out when I was sent down to study your culture. Your language is like ours, very often. Our Eskimo language, like many other North American Indian languages, is polysynthetic.

HERE. How's that—polysynthetic?

ESKIMO. Not an Eskimo word but an English word—polysynthetic. One word means a whole phrase, one word has in it the compressed wreckage of a phrase. Thus suppose we wish to say in Eskimo: "When they were about to go out they would take the boot-stretcher using it to thrash the dogs because they usually stay in the entrance passage."

That is twenty-six words in English. In Eskimo it is six words: *Anilerunik:* ("when they were about to go out"). *Kammiut* ("the boot-stretcher"). *Tingussaat* ("they would take it"). *Anaatara-longo* ("using it to thrash with"). *Qimmit* ("the dogs"). *Torsoo-neetaommata* ("because they usually stay in the entrance passage").

HERE. But where does English contain words that are the compressed wreckage of a phrase, as you put it?

ESKIMO. In English, not exactly like Eskimo, but nearly like. The other day I saw a newspaper headline: "UNRRA DP'S LAUD UNESCO." Back to my dictionary I go. There I find the word *laud*—nothing else. The other words are missing. Then it is explained to me. These other words are not normal English; they are instead the compressed wreckage of phrases. Four words: "UNRRA DP's LAUD UNESCO," means: "United States Relief and Rehabilitation Agency Displaced Persons Laud the United Nations Educational, Scientific, and Cultural Organization."

ESKIMO. Seventeen words compressed into four. Well, that's about average for Eskimo!

(*Music*)

THERE. Again, language reflects culture. As modern life sets up more elaborate agencies and organizations, modern language adapts itself, and forms words and builds polysynthetic forms almost like the Eskimo. Other languages besides English have been doing this. German, for example. *Gestapo* stands for *Geheime Staats Polizei* ("secret state police"). *Flak* is the compressed wreckage of *Flugzeugsabwehrkanone* ("anti-aircraft cannon.")

HERE. As we think, so we speak; as we speak, so we think. As we are taught reading, writing, and arithmetic, as we are taught our manners and the way things are done in the world we live in, so we are taught our language. And as we learn our language from our mother's lips, we also learn the customs and attitudes of our society. For language reflects these customs and attitudes—that is, language reflects culture.

THERE. (*A child wails and misbehaves.*) Over here, for instance, is a child misbehaving; and here comes its mother. She's going to tell it to behave properly. But let us notice carefully what word she uses.

MOTHER. John, be *good!* (*The child subsides.*)

HERE. Be good. The English-speaking child that misbehaves is bad, or naughty, or wicked. So is the Italian-speaking child, or the Greek-speaking one.

HERE. But listen to what the French mother says to her child.

FRENCH MOTHER. Jean, sois sage!

THERE. Sois sage: be wise. The French-speaking child that misbehaves is not bad, it is foolish, it is imprudent, it is injudicious.

HERE. In the Scandinavian countries, things are different again.

SWEDISH MOTHER. Jan, var snell!

NORWEGIAN MOTHER. Jan, ble snil!

HERE. Both mean the same thing: be friendly, be kind. So the misbehaving Scandinavian child is unfriendly, unkind, uncooperative.

THERE. Things are very different in Germany.

GERMAN MOTHER. Hans, sei artig!

THERE. Be in line! The misbehaving German child is not conforming, it is out of step, out of line. A mother of the Hopi Indians of the southwest United States has the same idea, only in a more gentle spirit.

HOPI MOTHER. No, no, no, no—that is not the Hopi way.

THERE. Hopi is the right thing, the proper way to do things, the way the affairs of the tribe, and indeed of the Universe, are managed. The Hopi child that misbehaves is not bad, or imprudent or un-friendly, or, quite, out of line. He is not on the Hopi way; he is not marching in step with the Hopi view of destiny and of life.

HERE. So, even in the words a mother says to her misbehaving child, we can detect again how language reflects culture.

MOTHER. Johnny, be good!

FRENCH MOTHER. Jean, sois sage: be wise!

SWEDISH MOTHER. Jan, var snell: be friendly!

GERMAN MOTHER. Hans, sei artig: get back in line!

HOPI MOTHER. No, no, no, no: that is not the Hopi way!

(*Music: "Rock-a-bye Baby"*)

THERE. East of New Guinea, in the southern Pacific, lie the Trobriand Islands. The people who live there are great mariners, lively and active. But they take no interest in things changing. If a thing changes, then it becomes something else, and they call it something else.

HERE. Just as we do not introduce an old gentleman with a long white beard as the bouncing baby boy Jim Jones.

JIM (*a very old man*). Very pleased to make your acquaintance.

THERE (*confidentially to* HERE). Buster here isn't any more a bouncing baby boy than I am.

JIM. Ah, but you see, once upon a time I was, in the long, long ago.

HERE (*dismissing him briskly*). But he isn't now. In fact, we don't think of him as a kind of modified infant, but as something else—an old gentleman, a different kind of animal.

THERE. Now the Trobriand Islanders think like this all the time. They raise a yam crop, and a first-rate yam has a special name.

TROBRIAND ISLANDER. Taytu.

THERE. But an overripe yam is not overripe taytu; it's different. It is:

TROBRIAND ISLANDER. Yowana.

THERE. And a yowana with underground shoots isn't yowana any more, but . . .

TROBRIAND ISLANDER. Silisata.

THERE. Though with new tubers on the underground shoots, it isn't silisata of any kind, but now:

TROBRIAND ISLANDER. Gadena.

THERE. Among the Trobriand Islanders, in short, the name of a thing alone is all you need say about it.

HERE. How different with us. Consider the case of a fellow being shown a new baby. (*A baby starts to cry.*) It is red-faced, boiled-looking, dribbling, cross-eyed, and squalling. The fond parents are watching you like hawks. You have to say something. But what?

FELLOW. How intelligent-looking?

HERE. But it looks like a moron!

FELLOW. How beautiful?

HERE. Just look at the ugly little beast!

FELLOW. How small and tiny?

HERE. For that, they'll kill you. He's three thirty-seconds of an ounce overweight: he's a giant!

FELLOW. How exactly like his father?

HERE. Say that, and he'll punch you right on the nose. There's nothing you can say. All you can do is shuffle around from one foot to the other and look as foolish as the baby.

THERE. But in the Trobriand Islands, the whole thing's simple. Show a Trobriand Islander the same messy, bellowing brat, and he says:

TROBRIAND ISLANDER. How baby!

THERE. How baby—which nobody can deny, and everyone's happy.

HERE. Yet our language is like the Trobriand in some ways, just as our society is like theirs in some ways. They place a high value on yams, and have an elaborate yam vocabulary. We place a high value on other things, and have an even more complicated and exact vocabulary to describe the special objects of *our* interest. Just look here. (*The traffic noises of a busy street.*) Standing on a downtown street corner, we have a Trobriand Islander, who has come to study our society. He's talking to a guy and writing down the answers.

TROBRIAND ISLANDER. What is the name of that thing on wheels going by now—the green one?

GUY. That's a Plymouth.

TROBRIAND ISLANDER. Plymouth. There is another green one, also a Plymouth.

GUY. No, it's green, but it ain't a Plymouth. That's a Studebaker. Studie has a kind of turret in the middle.

TROBRIAND ISLANDER. Then here is a great big Studebaker.

GUY. No, the big one with the kind of turret, that's a Cadillac.

TROBRIAND ISLANDER. Here is another big one. This is a Cadillac?

GUY. No, no—look at the back! That's a Lincoln.

HERE. And so it goes on of course. That Trobriand Islander will be there for a week. And then we'll break it to him that there's a difference between one year's model and the next. A week! He'll be there for a year.

THERE. But when he goes home, he'll talk to his friends just as our travelers come home and talk to us.

TROBRIAND ISLANDER. They are a very peculiar people attaching fantastic importance to little differences among their automobiles, so that a certain kind of small automobile is called a Plymouth; but with a turret in the middle, it is not a Plymouth with a turret, but a Studebaker. Quite a different word. And a big thing like a sort of Studebaker with other differences here and there is not a big Studebaker, but a different word again, a Cadillac. And so it goes on. They are a very peculiar people.

(*Music*)

THERE. Now we come to the most striking and interesting example of language reflecting culture—the wonderful and varied language of the Navaho Indians.

(*Music*)
(*Navaho "Night Way"*)

THERE. The Navaho Indians live in the great red desert of the southwest United States, not very far from the Grand Canyon, in Arizona. Their nomadic life is filled with uncertainties, and they seek security and balance in ritual and ceremony, by which they find their place in the natural harmony of the universe, and health and a sense of belonging.

HERE. Now life on this vast, unconsidering mountain desert is very much influenced by forces the Navaho do not command—the long drought, the sudden torrential rain, the sweep of epidemic disease.

THERE. And the Navaho view of the Universe seems to be connected with what they have learned from the country that is their home.

HERE. We try to control nature.

NAVAHO. We seek to understand it, and our place within it.

HERE. To us, the world is made up of beings and things that act on other beings and things.

NAVAHO. To us Navaho, the world is one of actions and events associated with things, among which our own acts are only a few among many.

HERE. Our own outlook is centered on things. Our language is centered on nouns, which are the names of things. The first words our children learn might well be the names of things.

MOTHER. Man. Ball. Boat. Bird.

NAVAHO. Our Navaho outlook is focused on actions and events, our language on verbs. The first words our children learn may well be those expressive of actions.

NAVAHO MOTHER. Standing. Rolling. Sailing. Flying.

HERE. Navaho words, like those of Eskimo, are often polysynthetic, the compressed wreckage of phrases. Take a single word.

NAVAHO. *Ná sh'ááh.*

HERE. And it means: "I am causing a round object to turn over, to turn upside down."

THERE. Navaho has many words for what we speak of as moving—a word for a round object moving, a fabric moving, and many more. And pronouns and adverbs are only parts of the verb, for the verb is central in Navaho speech just as actions are central in Navaho thinking.

HERE. We have a few verbs that are perhaps similar. The word *shrug* must carry with it the idea of *shoulder;* you can't shrug your stomach.

THERE. In English we say, "John is dying," just as we say, "John is walking," or "John is working"—for we speak even of death as though it were an act performed. But the Navaho, translated, says something like:

NAVAHO. Dying is taking place with John.

HERE. We are active toward nature; we think of our world as full of objects doing things to other objects; our language is centered on nouns, the names of things.

NAVAHO. We Navaho see ourselves as part of nature, in harmony with it; our world is one of actions to which we, and other things, are linked. Our language centers on the verb, expressive of acting.

THERE. Finally, here is an editorial in a Navaho newspaper. The writer is angry. He wants to know why a school is not built at Kayenta, though other places have schools. But he expresses his indignation in the Navaho way.

NAVAHO. The school at Kayenta, in vain we are hoping for it. Many children here have no school to attend. To one who comes here to see, there are 300 or more children who are in this state, who have no school. Therefore let a school become a reality here at Kayenta. Long ago this matter was brought up. Why is this so, please?

(*Music*)

THERE. So the Navaho treats his events as if they merely occurred, where we would try to put the blame on somebody.

HERE. And this is so much a part of English language, just as it is of English thoughts, that even translating the Navaho puts back into the speech some of the nouns that the Navaho didn't use.

THERE. Language, then, reflects thought, and formulates our way of thinking.

INDEX

Authors and Titles